LPIC-2: Linux Professional Institute Certification Study Guide: Exams 201 and 202

Exam 201 Objectives

OBJECTIVE	CHAPTER
Topic 201: Linux Kernel	
201.1 Kernel components	2
201.2 Compiling a kernel	2
201.3 Patching a kernel	2
201.4 Customize, build, and install a custom kernel and kernel modules	2
201.5 Manage/Query kernel and kernel modules at runtime	2
Topic 202: System Startup	
202.1 Customizing system startup and boot processes	1
202.2 System recovery	1
Topic 203: Filesystem and Devices	
203.1 Operating the Linux filesystem	3
203.2 Maintaining a Linux filesystem	3
203.3 Creating and configuring filesystem options	3
203.4 udev device management	3
Topic 204: Advanced Storage Device Administration	
204.1 Configuring RAID	4
204.2 Adjusting storage device access	4
204.3 Logical volume manager	4
Topic 205: Networking Configuration	
205.1 Basic networking configuration	5
205.2 Advanced network configuration and troubleshooting	5
205.3 Troubleshooting network issues	5
205.4 Notify users on system-related issues	1
Topic 206:System Maintenance	
206.1 Make and install programs from source	1
206.2 Backup operations	4
Topic 207: Domain Name Server	
207.1 Basic DNS server configuration	6
207.2 Create and maintain DNS zones	6
207.3 Securing a DNS server	6

Sybex®
An Imprint of
WILEY

D1606634

Exam 202 Objectives

Exam objectives are subject to change at any time without prior notice and at LPI's sole discretion. Please visit LPI's Web site (http://www.lpi.org) for the most current listing of exam objectives.

Sybex®
An Imprint of
WILEY

LPIC-2
Linux Professional Institute Certification
Study Guide

Roderick W. Smith

Wiley Publishing, Inc.

Senior Acquisitions Editor: Jeff Kellum
Development Editor: Jennifer Leland
Technical Editors: Ross Brunson and Don Corbet
Production Editor: Liz Britten
Copy Editor: Kim Wimpsett
Editorial Manager: Pete Gaughan
Production Manager: Tim Tate
Vice President and Executive Group Publisher: Richard Swadley
Vice President and Publisher: Neil Edde
Media Project Manager 1: Laura Moss-Hollister
Media Associate Producer: Doug Kuhn
Media Quality Assurance: Marilyn Hummel
Book Designers: Judy Fung, Bill Gibson
Proofreader: WordOne, New York
Indexer: Ted Laux
Project Coordinator, Cover: Katie Crocker
Cover Designer: Ryan Sneed

Copyright © 2011 by Wiley Publishing, Inc., Indianapolis, Indiana

Published simultaneously in Canada

ISBN: 978-1-118-00015-1

No part of this publication may be reproduced, stored in a retrieval system or transmitted in any form or by any means, electronic, mechanical, photocopying, recording, scanning or otherwise, except as permitted under Sections 107 or 108 of the 1976 United States Copyright Act, without either the prior written permission of the Publisher, or authorization through payment of the appropriate per-copy fee to the Copyright Clearance Center, 222 Rosewood Drive, Danvers, MA 01923, (978) 750-8400, fax (978) 646-8600. Requests to the Publisher for permission should be addressed to the Permissions Department, John Wiley & Sons, Inc., 111 River Street, Hoboken, NJ 07030, (201) 748-6011, fax (201) 748-6008, or online at http://www.wiley.com/go/permissions.

Limit of Liability/Disclaimer of Warranty: The publisher and the author make no representations or warranties with respect to the accuracy or completeness of the contents of this work and specifically disclaim all warranties, including without limitation warranties of fitness for a particular purpose. No warranty may be created or extended by sales or promotional materials. The advice and strategies contained herein may not be suitable for every situation. This work is sold with the understanding that the publisher is not engaged in rendering legal, accounting, or other professional services. If professional assistance is required, the services of a competent professional person should be sought. Neither the publisher nor the author shall be liable for damages arising herefrom. The fact that an organization or Web site is referred to in this work as a citation and/or a potential source of further information does not mean that the author or the publisher endorses the information the organization or Web site may provide or recommendations it may make. Further, readers should be aware that Internet Web sites listed in this work may have changed or disappeared between when this work was written and when it is read.

For general information on our other products and services or to obtain technical support, please contact our Customer Care Department within the U.S. at (877) 762-2974, outside the U.S. at (317) 572-3993 or fax (317) 572-4002.

Wiley also publishes its books in a variety of electronic formats. Some content that appears in print may not be available in electronic books.

Library of Congress Cataloging-in-Publication Data.

Smith, Roderick W.

  LPIC-2 : Linux Professional Institute certification study guide (exams 201 and 202) / Roderick W. Smith.

     p. cm.

  ISBN-13: 978-1-118-00015-1 (pbk.)
  ISBN-10: 1-118-00015-3 (pbk.)
  ISBN: 978-1-118-00042-4 (ebk)
  ISBN: 978-1-118-00044-8 (ebk)
  ISBN: 978-1-118-00043-1 (ebk)

  1. Electronic data processing personnel—Certification. 2. Linux—Examinations—Study guides. I. Title.

  QA76.3.S4774 2011

  005.4'32—dc22

                                                            2011005893

TRADEMARKS: Wiley, the Wiley logo, and the Sybex logo are trademarks or registered trademarks of John Wiley & Sons, Inc. and/or its affiliates, in the United States and other countries, and may not be used without written permission. All other trademarks are the property of their respective owners. Wiley Publishing, Inc., is not associated with any product or vendor mentioned in this book.

10 9 8 7 6 5 4 3 2 1

Dear Reader,

Thank you for choosing *LPIC-2: Linux Professional Institute Certification Study Guide.* This book is part of a family of premium-quality Sybex books, all of which are written by outstanding authors who combine practical experience with a gift for teaching.

Sybex was founded in 1976. More than 30 years later, we're still committed to producing consistently exceptional books. With each of our titles, we're working hard to set a new standard for the industry. From the paper we print on, to the authors we work with, our goal is to bring you the best books available.

I hope you see all that reflected in these pages. I'd be very interested to hear your comments and get your feedback on how we're doing. Feel free to let me know what you think about this or any other Sybex book by sending me an email at `nedde@wiley.com`. If you think you've found a technical error in this book, please visit `http://sybex.custhelp.com`. Customer feedback is critical to our efforts at Sybex.

Best regards,

Neil Edde
Vice President and Publisher
Sybex, an Imprint of Wiley

Acknowledgments

Although this book bears my name as author, many other people contributed to its creation. Without their help, this book wouldn't exist, or at best would exist in a lesser form. Jeff Kellum was the acquisitions editor and so helped get the book started. Jennifer Leland, the development editor, and Liz Britten, the production editor, oversaw the book as it progressed through all its stages. Ralph Bonnell was the technical editor, who checked the text for technical errors and omissions—but any mistakes that remain are my own. Kim Wimpsett, the copy editor, helped keep the text grammatical and understandable. The proofreader, Jen Larsen, and technical proofreader, Don Corbet, checked the text for typos. I'd also like to thank Neil Salkind and others at Studio B, who helped connect me with Wiley to write this book.

About the Author

Roderick W. Smith, LPIC-2, LPIC-1, CompTIA Linux+, is a Linux consultant, author, and open source programmer. He is the author of over twenty books on Linux and other open source technologies, including *LPIC-1 Study Guide, 2nd Edition, Linux+ Complete Study Guide,* and *Linux Administrator Street Smarts,* all from Sybex.

Contents at a Glance

Contents

Table of Exercises

Introduction

Why should you learn about Linux? It's a fast-growing operating system, and it's inexpensive and flexible. Linux is also a major player in the small and mid-sized server field, and it's an increasingly viable platform for workstation and desktop use as well. By understanding Linux, you'll increase your standing in the job market. Even if you already know Windows or Mac OS and your employer uses these systems exclusively, understanding Linux will give you an edge when you're looking for a new job or when you're looking for a promotion. For instance, this knowledge will help you make an informed decision about if and when you should deploy Linux.

The Linux Professional Institute (LPI) has developed its LPI-2 certification as an intermediate certification for people who want to further their careers involving Linux. The exam is meant to certify that an individual has the skills necessary to install, operate, and troubleshoot a Linux system and is familiar with Linux-specific concepts and basic hardware.

The purpose of this book is to help you pass both of the LPI-2 exams (201 and 202). Because these exams cover the Linux kernel, system startup, filesystems, disk devices, network options, system maintenance, DNS servers, Web servers, file servers, email servers, network client management, security, and troubleshooting, those are the topics that are emphasized in this book. You'll learn enough to manage a Linux system and how to configure it for many common tasks. Even after you've taken and passed the LPI 201 and 202 exams, this book should remain a useful reference.

What Is Linux?

Linux is a clone of the Unix operating system (OS) that has been popular in academia and many business environments for years. Formerly used exclusively on large mainframes, Unix and Linux can now run on small computers—which are actually far more powerful than the mainframes of just a few years ago. Because of its mainframe heritage, Unix (and hence also Linux) scales well to perform today's demanding scientific, engineering, and network server tasks.

Linux consists of a kernel, which is the core control software, and many libraries and utilities that rely on the kernel to provide features with which users interact. The OS is available in many different distributions, which are collections of a specific kernel with specific support programs.

Why Become LPI Certified?

Several good reasons to get your LPI certification exist. The LPI Web site suggests four major benefits:

Relevance LPI's exams were designed with the needs of Linux professionals in mind. This was done by performing surveys of Linux administrators to learn what they actually need to know to do their jobs.

Quality   The LPI exams have been extensively tested and validated using psychometric standards. The result is an ability to discriminate between competent administrators and those who must still learn more material.

Neutrality   LPI is a nonprofit organization that doesn't itself market any Linux distribution. This fact removes the motivation to create an exam that's designed as a way to market a particular distribution.

Support   The LPI exams are supported by major players in the Linux world. LPI serves the Linux community.

How to Become LPI Certified

The LPI certification is available to anyone who passes the test. You don't have to work for a particular company. It's not a secret society.

To take an LPI exam, you must first register with LPI to obtain an ID number. You can do this online at `https://www.lpi.org/caf/Xamman/register`. Your ID number will be emailed to you. With the ID number in hand, you can register for the exams with either of the two firms that administer them: Thomson Prometric and Pearson VUE. The exams can be taken at any Thomson Prometric or Pearson VUE testing center. If you pass, you'll get a certificate in the mail saying that you've passed. To find the Thomson Prometric testing center nearest you, call (800) 294-3926. Contact (877) 619-2096 for Pearson VUE information. Alternatively, register online at `http://securereg3.prometric.com` for Thomson Prometric or `http://www.vue.com/lpi/` for Pearson VUE. However you do it, you'll be asked for your name, mailing address, phone number, employer, when and where you want to take the test (that is, which testing center), and your credit card number (arrangement for payment must be made at the time of registration).

Who Should Buy This Book

Anybody who wants to pass the LPIC-2 exams may benefit from this book. You should already be familiar with Linux and the material covered by the LPIC-1 exams. If you're not, you should start with my *LPIC-1 Study Guide* before tackling this book. This book picks up where my *LPIC-1 Study Guide* left off, providing the knowledge you need up to a proficiency level sufficient to pass the LPIC-2 201 and 202 exams. If you're already familiar with the Linux topics covered in this book, it can serve as a review and as a refresher course for information with which you may not be completely familiar. In either case, reading this book will help you pass the LPIC-2 exams.

Even if you don't plan to take the LPIC-2 exams, this book can be a useful tutorial and reference for intermediate Linux topics. Use it as you would any other computer book, ignoring the end-of-chapter material—or using it, if you like.

This book is written with the assumption that you know a moderate amount about Linux. You should be familiar with command-line use of the OS, including staple commands such as mv, cp, ls, cat, less, ps, free, and uptime, to name but a few. You should be comfortable with at least one Linux text editor, such as Vi, Emacs, or NEdit. You should be able to bring up a network interface and understand the principles of server configuration, even if the details for specific servers remain foggy.

As a practical matter, you'll need a Linux computer with which to practice and learn in a hands-on way. You can install any of the many personal Linux distributions, such as Fedora, Ubuntu, OpenSUSE, Mandriva, Debian, Slackware, or Gentoo. Consult http://distrowatch.com for information on and links to these and other distributions. Be aware that some of the LPIC-2 material describes configuration file locations that vary from one distribution to another. Picking a popular distribution, such as Fedora or Ubuntu, increases the odds that your system will be similar to what the LPIC-2 exam developers used.

How This Book Is Organized

This book consists of 12 chapters plus supplementary information: this introduction, the assessment test after the introduction, and a glossary. The chapters are as follows:

- Chapter 1, "System Startup and Advanced System Management," covers Linux's boot process, including interacting with boot loaders and configuring startup scripts. It continues with information on how to compile software from source code and providing information to your users.

- Chapter 2, "Linux Kernel Configuration," describes how to compile and install a Linux kernel from source code, as well as how to adjust kernel options once you've done so.

- Chapter 3, "Basic Filesystem Management," focuses on creating, using, and maintaining filesystems, including hard disk filesystems, optical disc filesystems, and the udev filesystem that manages access to hardware.

- Chapter 4, "Advanced Disk Management," covers advanced disk access methods, including RAID, LVM, disk hardware tuning, and backup software and procedures.

- Chapter 5, "Networking Configuration," describes tools used to bring up and manage a network, including wireless (Wi-Fi) tools, basic routing options, VPN configuration, and network diagnostics.

- Chapter 6, "DNS Server Configuration," describes how to set up and manage a DNS server, including caching-only configurations, managing zone files, running a slave server, and DNS security considerations.

- Chapter 7, "Advanced Network Configuration," describes miscellaneous network servers and tools, including DHCP server configuration, use of an LDAP server, NAT and firewall features, and SSH server setup.

- Chapter 8, "Configuring File Servers," focuses on the Samba and NFS servers for Linux, which are used to serve files primarily to Windows and Unix/Linux systems, respectively. This chapter also covers the cross-platform FTP server.

- Chapter 9, "Configuring Web and Email Servers," covers these two important types of servers, including the Apache Web server, Web proxy servers, the sendmail and Postfix SMTP servers, the Procmail utility, and the Courier and Dovecot POP/IMAP servers.

- Chapter 10, "Security," covers the PAM authentication system, TCP Wrappers, tools to protect ports and manage network packets, and security information resources.

- Chapter 11, "System Troubleshooting I: Boot and Kernel Problems," covers tools and techniques to resolve problems involving the boot loader, the kernel, and miscellaneous software problems.

- Chapter 12, "System Troubleshooting II: System Resources and the User Environment," covers problems late in the system startup process, difficulties with accounts and shells, tools for studying running processes, and the cron system for running programs in the future.

Chapters 1 through 6 cover the LPIC 201 exam, and Chapters 7 through 12 cover the LPIC 202 exam. These make up Part I and Part II of the book, respectively.

Each chapter begins with a list of the LPIC objectives that are covered in that chapter. The book doesn't cover the objectives in order. Thus, you shouldn't be alarmed at some of the odd ordering of the objectives within the book. At the end of each chapter, you'll find a couple of elements you can use to prepare for the exam:

Exam Essentials   This section summarizes important information that was covered in the chapter. You should be able to perform each of the tasks or convey the information requested.

Review Questions   Each chapter concludes with 20 review questions. You should answer these questions and check your answers against the ones provided after the questions. If you can't answer at least 80 percent of these questions correctly, go back and review the chapter, or at least those sections that seem to be giving you difficulty.

The review questions, assessment test, and other testing elements included in this book and on the accompanying CD-ROM are *not* derived from the LPI exam questions, so don't memorize the answers to these questions and assume that doing so will enable you to pass the exam. You should learn the underlying topic, as described in the text of the book. This will let you answer the questions provided with this book *and* pass the exam. Learning the underlying topic is also the approach that will serve you best in the workplace—the ultimate goal of a certification like LPI's.

To get the most out of this book, you should read each chapter from start to finish and then check your memory and understanding with the chapter-ending elements. Even if you're already familiar with a topic, you should skim the chapter; Linux is complex enough that there are often multiple ways to accomplish a task, so you may learn something even if you're already competent in an area.

Bonus CD-ROM Contents

This book comes with a CD-ROM that contains several additional elements. Items available on the CD-ROM include the following:

Sybex Test Engine   All the questions in this book appear on the CD-ROM—including the 30-question assessment test at the end of this introduction and the 240 questions that make up the 20-question review question sections for each chapter. In addition, there are two 50-question bonus practice exams, exclusive to the CD.

Electronic "Flashcards"   The CD-ROM includes 120 questions in "flashcard" format (a question followed by a single correct answer). You can use these to review your knowledge of the LPIC exam objectives.

Glossary as a PDF File   The book's glossary is available as a fully searchable PDF that runs on all Windows platforms as well as on Linux.

The CD-ROM is compatible with both Linux and Windows.

Conventions Used in This Book

This book uses certain typographic styles in order to help you quickly identify important information and to avoid confusion over the meaning of words such as on-screen prompts. In particular, look for the following styles:

- *Italicized text* indicates key terms that are described at length for the first time in a chapter. (Italics are also used for emphasis.)

- A `monospaced` font indicates the contents of configuration files, messages displayed at a text-mode Linux shell prompt, filenames, text-mode command names, and Internet URLs.

- *`Italicized monospaced text`* indicates a variable—information that differs from one system or command run to another, such as the name of a client computer or a process ID number.

- **`Bold monospaced text`** is information that you're to type into the computer, usually at a Linux shell prompt. This text can also be italicized to indicate that you should substitute an appropriate value for your system. (When isolated on their own lines, commands are preceded by non-bold monospaced $ or # command prompts, denoting regular user or system administrator use, respectively.)

In addition to these text conventions, which can apply to individual words or entire paragraphs, a few conventions highlight segments of text:

A note indicates information that's useful or interesting but that's somewhat peripheral to the main text. A note may be relevant to a small number of networks, for instance, or it may refer to an outdated feature.

A tip provides information that can save you time or frustration and that may not be entirely obvious. A tip may describe how to get around a limitation or how to use a feature to perform an unusual task.

Warnings describe potential pitfalls or dangers. If you fail to heed a warning, you may end up spending a lot of time recovering from a bug, or you may even end up restoring your entire system from scratch.

Sidebars

A sidebar is like a note but longer. The information in a sidebar is useful, but it doesn't fit into the main flow of the text.

 Real World Scenario

Real-World Scenarios

A real-world scenario is a type of sidebar that describes a task or example that's particularly grounded in the real world. This may be a situation I or somebody I know has encountered, or it may be advice on how to work around problems that are common in real, working Linux environments.

EXERCISES

An exercise is a procedure you should try on your own computer to help you learn about the material in the chapter. Don't limit yourself to the procedures described in the exercises, though! Try other commands and procedures to really learn about Linux.

The Exam Objectives

Behind every computer industry exam, you can be sure to find exam objectives—the broad topics in which exam developers want to ensure your competency. The official LPI objectives for the LPIC 201 and 202 exams are listed here. (They're also printed at the start of the chapters in which they're covered.)

 Exam objectives are subject to change at any time without prior notice and at LPI's sole discretion. Please visit the LPIC Certification page of LPI's Web site (`http://wiki.lpi.org/wiki/LPIC-2_Objectives`) for the most current listing of exam objectives.

The objectives list at the beginning of this book and at the beginning of each chapter includes only the basic objective titles. You should consult the complete LPI exam list to learn what commands, files, and procedures you should be familiar with before taking the exam.

The LPIC-201 Exam

Topic 201: Linux Kernel

201.1 Kernel components

201.2 Compiling a kernel

201.3 Patching a kernel

201.4 Customize, build, and install a custom kernel and kernel modules

201.5 Manage/query kernel and kernel modules at runtime

Topic 202: System Startup

202.1 Customizing system startup and boot processes

202.2 System recovery

Topic 203: Filesystem and Devices

203.1 Operating the Linux filesystem

203.2 Maintaining a Linux filesystem

203.3 Creating and configuring filesystem options

203.4 udev device management

Topic 204: Advanced Storage Device Administration

204.1 Configuring RAID

204.2 Adjusting storage device access

204.3 Logical Volume Manager

Assessment Test

1. You want to temporarily stop the `postfix` server while you make some changes to its configuration. Which of the following commands, when typed by `root`, will do this on at least some distributions? (Choose all that apply.)

   A. `stop postfix`

   B. `kill -9 postfix`

   C. `xinetd postfix stop`

   D. `/etc/rc.d/postfix stop`

2. How can you check for recent kernel messages related to the second Ethernet device (`eth1`) on a computer?

   A. Type `cat /proc/sys/eth1/km`.

   B. Type `ifconfig eth1 --messages`.

   C. Type `dmesg | grep eth1`.

   D. Type `ifconfig eth1 show`.

3. What is the purpose of the `initrd` line in a GRUB configuration?

   A. It tells the kernel that the disk uses the Initial Reduced Disk format, a type of compression common on Linux and some FreeBSD systems.

   B. It passes the name of the program the Linux kernel should launch as its first process (normally `init`) from GRUB to the kernel.

   C. It tells GRUB what initialization tools to use when writing its stage 0 boot loader to the hard disk, therefore affecting what types of disks it supports.

   D. It tells GRUB where to find the initial RAM disk, which holds kernel modules and configuration files used by the kernel before it has mounted its disk-based root filesystem.

4. Your computer's swap space is spread across two hard disks, one of which is significantly faster than the other. How can you adjust the `/etc/fstab` entries for the two swap partitions to optimize swap performance?

   A. Use the `pri=`*priority* option on each swap partition, giving a lower *priority* value to the disk with better performance.

   B. Use the `pri=`*priority* option on each swap partition, giving a higher *priority* value to the disk with better performance.

   C. List both devices together, as in `/dev/sda2,/dev/sdb4`, specifying the higher-performance disk first in the list.

   D. List both devices together, as in `/dev/sda2,/dev/sdb4`, specifying the higher-performance disk last in the list.

5. As part of a security check, you want to ensure that your Web server computer, www .pangaea.edu, runs only the Web server software (on TCP port 80) and a Secure Shell (SSH) login server (on TCP port 22). What command can you run from a remote computer to ensure that this is so? (Consider only TCP traffic.)

    A. tshark www.pangaea.edu

    B. nmap -sT www.pangaea.edu

    C. netstat -ap

    D. nc www.pangaea.edu 80

6. When configuring a source code package, you see the following error message:

    ```
    checking for Qt... configure: error: Qt (>= Qt 3.0) (headers and
    libraries) not found. Please check your installation!
    ```

    Which of the following actions is *most* likely to correct this problem?

    A. Locate and install an appropriate Qt binary library package.

    B. Locate and install an appropriate Qt development package.

    C. Type ./configure --ignore-qt to ignore the problem.

    D. Edit the Makefile by hand to eliminate the Qt dependence.

7. What uname parameter can you use to determine your currently running kernel's version number (such as 2.6.35.4)?

    A. -r or --kernel-release

    B. -v or --kernel-version

    C. -s or --kernel-name

    D. -o or --operating-system

8. An external disk with a single partition (/dev/sdb1) uses ReiserFS, and when it's automounted, it's given an ugly name based on the disk's UUID. You know that your automounter uses a disk's label when one is available, so you want to give the filesystem the label MyStuff. How can you do this *without* damaging existing data on the disk?

    A. mkreiserfs -l MyStuff /dev/sdb1

    B. tune2fs -L MyStuff /dev/sdb1

    C. reiserfstune -l MyStuff /dev/sdb1

    D. label -t reiserfs -n MyStuff /dev/sdb1

9. You're replacing an old PATA disk, /dev/hdb, with a new SATA disk, /dev/sdc. You use an LVM configuration with one physical volume, /dev/hdb2, on /dev/hdb. How can you transfer the data from /dev/hdb2 to its new home on /dev/sdc1, after adding /dev/sdc1 to the volume group?

    A. cp /dev/hdb2 /dev/sdc1

    B. vgconvert /dev/hdb2 /dev/sdc1

    C. vgextend /dev/sdc1

    D. pvmove /dev/hdb2 /dev/sdc1

10. What is the effect of the following command, assuming the device files have conventional meanings?

```
# dd if=/dev/sdb3 of=/dev/dvd
```

    A. It performs a raw copy of the filesystem on /dev/sdb3 to a blank optical disc.

    B. It creates a tarball containing the files on /dev/sdb3 and stores that tarball on a blank optical disc.

    C. It performs an incremental backup of the contents of /dev/sdb3 to a blank optical disc.

    D. Nothing; it's an invalid use of the dd command.

11. What type of record is found in reverse zone files but not in forward zone files?

    A. SOA

    B. NS

    C. A

    D. PTR

12. A DNS server is running on a computer with two network interfaces, eth0 (192.168.7.92) and eth1 (172.24.21.19). You want the server to be accessible only to the eth1 network. What /etc/named.conf configuration will help accomplish this goal?

    A. zone { 172.24.21.19; };

    B. allow-transfer { 172.24.21.19; };

    C. listen-on { 172.24.21.19; };

    D. forwarders { 172.24.21.19; };

13. You're preparing to compile a Linux kernel. Before proceeding, you want to ensure that you've removed all the old configuration and temporary files. What would you type to do so?

    A. make clean

    B. make modules

    C. make mrproper

    D. make bzImage

14. After assembling a RAID array on /dev/md0 from /dev/sda1, /dev/sdb1, and /dev/sdc1, you use fdisk to create four primary partitions on this device. What device filenames will they have?

    A. /dev/md1, /dev/md2, /dev/md3, and /dev/md4

    B. /dev/md0p1, /dev/md0p2, /dev/md0p3, and /dev/md0p4

    C. /dev/sdd1, /dev/sdd2, /dev/sdd3, and /dev/sdd4

    D. None of the above; you can't partition a RAID array

15. You want to connect a laptop computer to a public Wi-Fi network, but you don't know its name or other relevant data. What command can you type as `root` to find this information? (Assume that your wireless network interface is `wlan0`.)

   A. `iwlist wlan0 search`

   B. `iwlist wlan0 find`

   C. `iwlist wlan0 discover`

   D. `iwlist wlan0 scanning`

16. In which of the following situations does it make the *most* sense to use NAT?

   A. Computers on your network need to be able to run client programs and access the Internet, but you run no servers that should be accessible from the Internet.

   B. You have obtained a large block of IPv6 addresses, and you want to use them to host a large number of servers for several protocols.

   C. You run a small and highly secure private network with internal servers and no need for external Internet access except from one system that runs a Web server.

   D. None of the above; NAT is a dangerous and insecure protocol that should be avoided whenever possible.

17. What types of information can a DHCP server deliver to clients, in addition to their IP addresses? (Select all that apply.)

   A. A suggested default Web page for Web browsers

   B. A gateway computer's IP address

   C. The IP address of a Windows NetBIOS name server

   D. The client's Ethernet hardware address

18. Your outgoing mail server runs Postfix, and you find the following line in its configuration file. What is the effect of this line?

`myorigin = luna.edu`

   A. Postfix will accept mail addressed to users in the `luna.edu` domain and reject or forward mail addressed to other domains.

   B. If a mail client omits the hostname in the return address of an outgoing email message, `@luna.edu` will be appended to the username in the address.

   C. All return addresses in outgoing email messages are changed so that they appear to come from the specified user but in the `luna.edu` domain.

   D. Postfix checks the current computer's domain name and refuses to run if that domain name is not `luna.edu`.

19. You're configuring Dovecot for a site that uses the maildir format for incoming mail, storing email in the `Mail` folder in users' home directories. What option can you set in its configuration file to tell Dovecot to use this directory?

   A. `mail_location = maildir:~/Mail`

   B. `set_directory = ~/Mail`

   C. `mail_directory = ~/Mail;format=maildir`

   D. `inmail: ~/Mail=maildir`

20. You're taking over administration of a computer that runs Pure-FTPd and launches the server via a local startup script. You discover the `--chrooteveryone` option, among others, as an option to the Pure-FTPd binary in the local startup script. What is the effect of this option?

   A. The server locks itself into a `chroot` jail for all users *except* for `root`.

   B. The server locks itself into a `chroot` jail for all users *including* `root`.

   C. The server locks itself into a `chroot` jail for all users *except* for anonymous users.

   D. The server locks itself into a `chroot` jail for all users *except* for the account used to run the server.

21. What is the filename of the Xorg-X11 X server's log file?

   A. `/var/log/X11.log`

   B. `/var/log/Xorg.0.log`

   C. `/var/log/Xorg-X11.log`

   D. `/var/log/Xorg.X11.log`

22. What can you expect to find in the `/etc/profile.d` directory?

   A. Configuration options for the ProFile file manager software

   B. Extended information ("profiles") about users

   C. Scripts to supplement the main global login `bash` script

   D. Filesystem mount points and mount options

23. How is the login process handled on text-mode virtual terminals on a computer that uses the SysV initialization system?

   A. A master SysV startup script for all virtual terminals exists in `/etc/init.d`, with runlevel-specific directories holding links to this file.

   B. Each virtual terminal has its own SysV startup script in `/etc/init.d`, with runlevel-specific directories holding links to these files.

   C. Lines in `/etc/inittab` associate `getty` programs with each virtual terminal, and these `getty` processes launch the `login` program.

   D. The kernel controls each virtual terminal directly; boot loader options tell it how many virtual terminals to activate and what login program to use.

24. You're adding a Samba server to an existing Windows (NetBIOS) domain called PICTURE. What smb.conf line will you use to inform Samba of the name of the Windows domain?

    A. workgroup = PICTURE

    B. domain PICTURE.COM

    C. domain = PICTURE

    D. security = PICTURE

25. What is a consequence of the following configuration, found in /etc/exports, assuming that an NFS server is running on the computer?

```
/home helpman(no_root_squash,rw)
```

    A. The root user on the computer called helpman will be unable to mount the /home export from the server.

    B. The root user on the computer called helpman will be able to read and write every file in the server's /home directory tree.

    C. All users on the computer called helpman will be able to read and write every file in the server's /home directory tree.

    D. The computer called helpman may only mount the server's /home export directly on its own root (/) directory (that is, as /home).

26. An individual has an account, samuel, on the computer langhorne.example.com and another account, mark, on the computer tesla.luna.edu. Once logged into langhorne .example.com, how can this user log into his account on tesla.luna.edu using SSH, assuming an SSH server is running on the latter system?

    A. ssh tesla.luna.edu

    B. ssh mark@tesla.luna.edu

    C. ssh user=mark tesla.luna.edu

    D. ssh tesla.luna.edu --user mark

27. What type of computer is *least* likely to use an unmodified version of GRUB Legacy?

    A. A PC with an Intel $x86$ CPU, SATA hard disk, and BIOS

    B. A PC with an AMD $x86$-64 CPU, SATA hard disk, and BIOS

    C. A PC with an Intel $x86$-64 CPU, PATA hard disk, and BIOS

    D. A PC with an Intel $x86$-64 CPU, SATA hard disk, and EFI

28. What is the difference between the stop and graceful-stop options to apache2ctl?

    A. The stop option terminates Apache under all circumstances, whereas graceful-stop terminates the server only if all network devices are operational.

    B. The stop option terminates Apache without cleaning up log files, whereas graceful-stop writes extra shutdown data to log files.

    C. The stop option terminates Apache immediately, whereas the graceful-stop option permits in-progress transfers to complete.

    D. The stop option terminates all Apache subprocesses, whereas graceful-stop terminates only those subprocesses you specify.

29. You're creating a PAM `auth` stack for authenticating users using several different authentication methods (standard Unix logins, LDAP, and so on). You want each PAM module to use the password collected by the first module, without attempting to collect its own password under any circumstances. What option can you pass to all but the first module in the stack to accomplish this goal?

   A. `use_first_pass`

   B. `likeauth`

   C. `try_first_pass`

   D. `auth_like_first`

30. Which of the following is an advantage of `iptables` over TCP Wrappers as a security tool?

   A. You can write `iptables` rules that restrict access by username; TCP Wrappers doesn't support this feature.

   B. You can write `iptables` rules that shut down attackers' computers; TCP Wrappers can't do this.

   C. You can write `iptables` rules that restrict the activities of clients; TCP Wrappers affects only servers.

   D. You can write `iptables` rules that work on privileged ports; TCP Wrappers works only on unprivileged ports.

Answers to Assessment Test

1. **A, D.** Option A presents the syntax for stopping a service that is controlled via the Upstart system. If the `postfix` server is controlled in this way, option A should temporarily stop it. Option D will work on systems that use SysV startup scripts, with the main scripts stored in `/etc/rc.d`. (Some SysV systems put the main scripts elsewhere, but `/etc/rc.d` is used on some systems, making this option valid.) Option B is incorrect because the `kill` command takes a process ID (PID) number, not a process name. It's also generally preferable to use a SysV or Upstart script to shut down a service started via this system, rather than killing it directly. Option C is incorrect because, although `xinetd` is a super server that manages certain other servers, it's not invoked in this way to shut down one of the servers it manages. Also, `postfix` is normally run directly, not via a super server.

2. **C.** The kernel ring buffer, which can be viewed by typing `dmesg`, contains kernel messages, most of which relate to hardware, including network devices. Using `grep` to scan the output for messages related to `eth1`, as in option C, will do as the question asks. Option A presents a fictitious file in the real `/proc` filesystem, and so is incorrect. Options B and D both deploy `ifconfig` in incorrect ways; this tool cannot display kernel messages related to an Ethernet device.

3. **D.** Option D correctly describes the purpose of the `initrd` line. Options A, B, and C are all fictitious. In particular, there is no such thing as an Initial Reduced Disk format, and the GRUB configuration file doesn't affect the tools used to write the stage 0 boot loader. Option B, although incorrect in reference to the `initrd` line, describes the function of the `init=` kernel argument, as in `init=/bin/bash` to launch `bash` as the initial process—a useful trick in certain recovery situations.

4. **B.** The `pri=priority` option in `/etc/fstab` sets the priority for swap space, with higher-priority swap areas being used first. Thus, option B is correct. (The `-p` or `--priority` command-line option to `swapon` can achieve the same effect.) Option A is exactly backwards. Options C and D are both incorrect because `/etc/fstab` requires specifying *one* device filename (or other device specifier, such as a label or UUID value) per line; you can't list two devices on a single line.

5. **B.** The Nmap utility is used to scan another computer for the presence of open ports, which usually indicate servers. Option B presents the correct syntax for scanning www.pangaea.edu's TCP ports for servers, as the question specifies. If anything but ports 22 and 80 are open, they should be shut down. The `tshark` utility of option A is part of the Wireshark package, which is a packet sniffer. This utility doesn't perform a port scan, so it won't do as the question specifies. Option C's `netstat` utility could be used *on the target server computer* to scan for unwanted open ports, but the question specifies that you're using another computer to do the scanning, so option C is incorrect. The `nc` tool of option D is a general-purpose network connection utility. Although you could write a script using `nc` to do as the question asks, the specific command in option D is insufficient to the task.

6. B. In most cases, a message such as this one can be overcome only by installing an appropriate development package, as option B specifies. Such a package contains the headers needed to compile the software, and it usually includes -dev, -devel, or a similar string in its name. Installing a binary library package, as option A specifies, will probably do no good since such packages usually lack the header files that are missing. (You may need such a package to run the software once it's compiled, though.) Option C specifies a fictitious option to configure; however, it is sometimes possible to use a --without-*PACKAGE* option (as in --without-qt) to work around such problems. This will work only if the software uses the library optionally, however, so even --without-qt would be far from guaranteed to be supported or work. If a configure script exists, the Makefile is likely to be very difficult to edit by hand; and even if you managed the task, chances are the software would fail to compile because the source code relies on the library at a fairly fundamental level. Thus, option D is incorrect.

7. A. The -r or --kernel-release parameter to uname produces the kernel version number, as the question specifies, so option A is correct. Counterintuitively, the -v or --kernel-version parameter does not produce this information; instead, it produces some additional data, such as whether the kernel includes symmetric multi-processing (SMP) support and the date and time it was compiled. Thus, option B is incorrect. The -s or --kernel-name parameter to uname produces the output Linux for a Linux kernel, so option C is incorrect. The -o or --operating-system parameter to uname normally displays GNU/Linux on a Linux system, so option D is incorrect.

8. C. The reiserfstune program adjusts features of ReiserFS, including the filesystem label, and option C presents the correct syntax to do as the question describes. Option A will create a new filesystem on the partition with the label MyStuff; however, because this option creates a new filesystem, existing data will be destroyed, which the question forbids. Option B presents the correct syntax to do the requested job on a partition containing an ext2, ext3, or ext4 filesystem, but the question specifies that the disk uses ReiserFS. Option D's label command is fictitious.

9. D. Option D performs the specified task. Option A is inappropriate because the cp command operates on regular filesystem files; and even if it could copy the contents of /dev/hdb2 to /dev/sdc1, this would be a low-level copy that would corrupt the existing physical volume data on /dev/sdc1. The vgconvert command converts an old LVM version 1 volume group into the newer version 2 format. The syntax in option B is wrong, too. Option C presents the correct syntax to prepare volume group data on /dev/sdc1, but the question specified that this had already been done.

10. D. The dd command cannot write directly to an optical disc; to write to an optical disc, you need a tool such as cdrecord, growisofs, or the kernel's packet-writing support and UDF driver. Thus, option D is correct. The dd utility can't write directly to optical discs, so option A is incorrect. Furthermore, dd doesn't create tarballs by itself; you'd need to involve tar to do this, so option B is incorrect. The incremental backups mentioned in option C would require specific options to tar or some other backup tool, and dd is ill-equipped to perform incremental backups.

11. D. Pointer (PTR) records allow a DNS server to return a hostname when it's given an IP address, which is the function of reverse zone files. Thus, these records are found in reverse zone files but not in forward zone files, and option D is correct. Start of Authority (SOA) and name server (NS) records are required in both zone file types, so options A and B are both incorrect. Address (A) records are found in forward zone file but not in reverse zone files, so option C is incorrect.

12. C. The `listen-on` directive does as the question specifies, so option C is correct. (Of course, the server might remain accessible to the other network if a router connects the two networks. If so, `iptables` rules might be useful to further secure the server.) Option A misuses the `zone` directive, which normally identifies a zone for which the server is authoritative and points the server at the relevant zone file. Option B presents the correct syntax for the `allow-transfer` directive, which is used to enable transfers to slave servers; it makes little sense to allow transfers to the server's own IP address. Option D also makes no sense; this `forwarders` statement tells the server that it should forward DNS requests to itself!

13. C. The `mrproper` target to `make` in the Linux kernel cleans out old temporary files and removes the configuration file, as the question specifies, so option C is correct. The `clean` target removes old temporary files, as the question specifies, but it doesn't remove the old configuration files, as the question also specifies, so option A is incorrect. The `modules` target builds kernel modules but not the main kernel file, so option B is incorrect. The `bzImage` target builds the kernel in the common `bzImage` format but does not build kernel modules, so option D is incorrect.

14. B. Option B shows the form of device filenames used by partitions of a RAID array and so is correct. Option A shows the filenames that would traditionally be used by the second, third, fourth, and fifth RAID arrays, not partitions of the first RAID array. Option C specifies the device filenames for a fourth physical hard disk, if one is present. Contrary to option D's assertion, it is legal to partition a software RAID array.

15. D. The `iwlist` utility can scan for available Wi-Fi networks. To do so, you pass it the interface name and the sub-command name `scan` or `scanning`, as in option D. The remaining options present incorrect sub-commands; `search`, `find`, and `discover` are all invalid names.

16. A. Network Address Translation (NAT) is a way to connect multiple computers to a larger network using a single IPv4 address on the larger network. It prevents outside systems from being able to access servers on the protected network, except by special configuration, but it enables protected systems to access the wider network. This set of features makes it a good fit for the scenario described in option A. Because option B involves IPv6 addresses and servers running in that address block, it's a poor fit for use of NAT, so option B is incorrect. Because the highly secure network requires no incoming or outgoing network access except for one computer, it would be better served by having no Internet access at all except for the Web server computer; thus, option C is incorrect. Contrary to option D, NAT can be a great boon to security.

17. B, C. DHCP servers commonly deliver the client's IP address, network mask, gateway (router) address, DNS server address, hostname, and domain name. DHCP servers can also deliver more obscure data including the IP addresses of NetBIOS name servers and Network Time Protocol (NTP) servers. Options B and C are among this information and so are correct. DHCP doesn't deliver suggestions on default Web pages for Web browsers, so option A is incorrect. A computer's Ethernet hardware address is set at the factory and is not normally changed. Although DHCP relies on this address for initial communications, the protocol provides no means to change it, so option D is incorrect.

18. B. Option B describes the effect of the `myorigin` option in the main Postfix configuration file, so option B is correct. Option A describes the effect of the `mydestination` option. Option C describes the effects of masquerading, for which Postfix offers various options. Option D describes a fictitious feature and so is incorrect.

19. A. You use the `mail_location` setting to tell Dovecot where to store incoming mail and what format to use, and option A presents the correct syntax for the question's details, so option A is correct. Options B, C, and D all present fictitious option names and syntaxes and so are incorrect.

20. A. The `--chrooteveryone` option to Pure-FTPd does as option A specifies; `root` is the one exception to the `chroot` rule when this option is used. Because option A is correct, option B cannot be correct. Anonymous users and the account used to launch the server are not exceptions to the rule, contrary to options C and D.

21. B. The Xorg-X11 X server stores its current log file in `/var/log/Xorg.0.log`, so option B is correct. The remaining options are all fictitious files.

22. C. The main global login `bash` script is `/etc/profile`, and this script frequently executes scripts found in `/etc/profile.d`, enabling packages to add features to `bash` defaults by adding startup scripts to this directory. Thus, option C is correct. Options A and B describe fictitious software or features and so are incorrect. Option D is a partial description of the contents of the `/etc/fstab` file.

23. C. On a SysV-based distribution, text-mode virtual terminals are managed as described in option C. Virtual terminals are not managed via SysV startup scripts, so options A and B are incorrect. (GUI logins are sometimes managed via SysV startup scripts, though.) Although the kernel is ultimately responsible for input/output on each virtual terminal, kernel options do not tell the kernel how to use them in the way that option D specifies.

24. A. The `workgroup` option in `smb.conf` sets the NetBIOS workgroup *or domain* name. (Note that the NetBIOS domain name is unrelated to the DNS domain name.) Thus, option A is correct. Option B might be a correct entry in `/etc/resolv.conf`, to set the computer's DNS domain name, if that domain name is `picture.com`; however, the question is about Samba and Windows/NetBIOS domains, not DNS domains. Thus, option B is incorrect. Option C is a corruption of the correct answer, but you must use the `workgroup` parameter, not `domain`, when setting either the workgroup or the domain name, so option C is incorrect. To tell the server to use a domain controller, you must use the `security` parameter; however, it takes options of `Server`, `Domain`, or `ADS`, not the domain's name, so option D is incorrect.

25. B. The `no_root_squash` option causes `root`'s privileges on the client to be preserved on the server (ordinarily `root` is given restricted rights on the server). Thus, the client's (that is, `helpman`'s) `root` will be able to read and write all the files in `/home` on the server, as option B specifies. Option A is incorrect because none of the specified options prevents `root` (or any other authorized user) from mounting the export. Option C is incorrect because ordinary users' permissions are preserved by the NFS server; its permissions will remain applicable. (UIDs and GIDs may shift, however, which can change how permissions are applied.) None of the specified options affects where the client may mount the export, so option D is incorrect.

26. B. Option B presents the correct syntax for logging in using a different username than on the client system. (Alternatively, **ssh tesla.luna.edu -l mark** would work.) Option A would have the effect of attempting to use the username `samuel` on `tesla.luna.edu`, which would not work. Option C would attempt to log into the computer `user=mark` and run the command `tesla.luna.edu`, which would not work. Option D is close to an alternative method of specifying a username, but it's not quite right (you'd use `-l` rather than `--user`).

27. D. GRUB Legacy works with any 32- or 64-bit *x*86 or *x*86-64 CPU from any manufacturer and with any type of disk that can be read by the firmware. The only factor mentioned in any of the questions that is *not* compatible with GRUB Legacy is the Extensible Firmware Interface (EFI); GRUB Legacy is designed to work with the older (and more common) Basic Input/Output System (BIOS) firmware. Thus, option D is correct; such a computer can't use an unmodified GRUB Legacy. (The newer GRUB 2 is compatible with both BIOS and EFI.) GRUB Legacy will work with any of the systems described by options A, B, and C, provided no unmentioned factor causes problems.

28. C. Option C correctly describes the difference between these two `apache2ctl` subcommands. The remaining options are all fictitious explanations.

29. A. The `use_first_pass` option is recognized by most modules that perform password-based authentication in an `auth` stack. It does as the question specifies, so option A is correct. The `likeauth` option is recognized by many modules and causes the module to return the same information when called as part of a `password` stack as it would in an `auth` stack. This isn't what the question specifies, so option B is incorrect. Option C is an option that does something very similar to what the question asks, but if the password collected by an earlier module fails, the module will collect a new password. Because of this variance from what was asked, this option is incorrect. Option D describes a fictitious option.

30. C. The `iptables` program accepts packet identifications that can apply to incoming or outgoing packets to or from clients or servers. TCP Wrappers, by contrast, works only on the initial incoming connection to servers. Thus, option C is correct. Option A is backwards; `iptables` has no ability to match based on usernames, but TCP Wrappers does. Contrary to option B, neither TCP Wrappers nor `iptables` can cause an attacker's computer to shut down—and using such a feature if it did exist would be dubious at best from an ethical and legal point of view. Both `iptables` and TCP Wrappers can restrict access to both privileged and unprivileged ports, so option D is incorrect.

The LPI 201 Exam (60 Weights)

Chapter

1

System Startup and Advanced System Management

THE FOLLOWING LINUX PROFESSIONAL INSTITUTE OBJECTIVES ARE COVERED IN THIS CHAPTER:

✓ **202.1 Customizing system startup and boot processes (weight: 4)**

✓ **202.2 System recovery (weight: 4)**

✓ **205.4 Notify users on system-related issues (weight: 1)**

✓ **206.1 Make and install programs from source (weight: 4)**

An appropriate place to begin investigating advanced Linux system administration is with the way the computer starts. Therefore, this chapter covers that topic, including both boot loader configuration and use and the tools Linux uses to start its own core processes. Because a computer can't boot without any software installed, this chapter continues with a look at how to install software from source code, as opposed to using the package systems with which you're probably already familiar. Finally, this chapter describes tools you can use to notify users of important system events, such as likely sluggishness due to a major software package upgrade or an ongoing backup operation.

Exploring the Boot Process

Although the process normally proceeds smoothly once you press a computer's power button, booting a computer involves a large number of steps, ranging from hardware initialization to the launch of potentially dozens of programs. Some of these boot-time tasks include:

1. The CPU initializes itself.

2. The CPU examines a particular memory address for code to run. This address corresponds to part of the computer's firmware, which contains instructions on how to proceed.

3. The firmware initializes the computer's major hardware subsystems, performs basic memory checks, and so on.

4. The firmware directs the computer to look for boot code on a storage device, such as a hard disk, a removable disk, or an optical disc. This code, which is known as a *stage 1 boot loader*, is loaded and run.

5. The stage 1 boot loader code may direct the system to load additional stages of itself. Ultimately, the boot loader code loads the operating system's kernel and runs it. From this point on, the kernel is in control of the computer.

6. The kernel looks for its first process file. In Linux, this file is usually /sbin/init, and its process, once running, is known as init.

7. The init process reads one or more configuration files, which tell it what other programs it should launch.

8. Linux systems typically launch processes both directly from init and under the direction of *System V (SysV) startup scripts* or the *Upstart* system.

During the startup process, the computer mounts disks using the mount utility under direction of the /etc/fstab file. It may also perform disk checks using the fsck utility. Controlling these processes is described in detail in Chapter 3, "Basic Filesystem Management."

As part of the init-directed startup procedures (steps 7 and 8), Linux systems normally launch user login tools, such as the text-mode login or an X Display Manager (XDM) login screen. These programs enable ordinary users to log in and use the system. Server computers are normally configured to launch server programs, some of which provide similar login possibilities for remote users. Once users log in, they can of course launch additional programs.

Although Linux distributions are designed to start up correctly once they're installed, you must know how to change these configurations. You may need to adjust a boot loader configuration to boot a new kernel or to alter the options that the boot loader passes to the kernel, for instance. If you want to install server software, you may need to change the init or SysV startup procedures to launch the software automatically when the computer boots. The following pages describe how to make such changes.

 Real World Scenario

Computer Firmware Options

Since the 1980s, most *x86* and *x86-64* computers have used firmware known as the Basic Input/Output System (BIOS). This firmware has become rather dated, however, and so a shift is underway to a newer system, known as the Extensible Firmware Interface (EFI). Since 2005, the Unified EFI (UEFI) variant of EFI has been available. As of late 2010, EFI-based systems are still rare, although Intel-based Apple Macintoshes use EFI, and a few UEFI-based *x86-64* systems are available. Some hardware manufacturers expect to begin using UEFI in more systems beginning in 2011. Computers using CPUs other than the common *x86* and *x86-64* use non-BIOS firmware, such as OpenFirmware or EFI.

The details of how firmware-mediated portions of the boot process can be altered vary with the type of firmware installed on a computer. Even within a single type, such as BIOS, there can be substantial variation from one computer to another. Typically, you use a special keypress, such as F10, F12, or Delete, to enter a configuration utility that's built into the firmware. You can then set options such as which disk devices to use to boot the computer and which built-in hardware components to activate. You should consult a computer's manual to learn the details of its firmware configuration.

Booting Linux

As just described, a computer must proceed through a series of steps before an OS, such as Linux, can take control. The first step that's likely to be different on a Linux system than on a computer that runs Windows, Mac OS, or some other OS, is the boot loader, which is responsible for loading the kernel into memory. Several boot loaders are available that can load Linux, including the Grand Unified Bootloader (GRUB), the Linux Loader (LILO), and SysLinux. Most Linux installations use GRUB, which can also directly load some non-Linux kernels or redirect the boot process to a boot loader for Windows. Thus, GRUB can launch several OSs, should a computer have more than one installed. To configure GRUB, you must edit its configuration files. You can also interact with the boot loader at boot time, both to select your OS and to make on-the-fly changes, should you need to customize the way the OS boots on a one-time basis.

Configuring GRUB

Two major versions of GRUB exist: The original GRUB, now known as GRUB Legacy, has been frozen at version 0.97; and a new version, GRUB 2, is at version 1.98 as I write. GRUB Legacy is no longer being actively developed. GRUB 2 is under active development, and some features may change by the time you read this. The two versions are similar in broad details and in how users interact with them at boot time; however, they differ in some important configuration details. I therefore describe GRUB Legacy and then describe how GRUB 2 differs from GRUB Legacy.

Configuring GRUB Legacy

The usual location for GRUB Legacy's configuration file is /boot/grub/menu.1st. Some distributions, such as Fedora, Red Hat, and Gentoo, use the filename grub.conf rather than menu.1st. GRUB Legacy can read its configuration file at boot time, which means you needn't reinstall the boot loader to the boot sector when you change the configuration file. The GRUB Legacy configuration file is broken into global and per-image sections, each of which has its own options. Before getting into section details, though, you should understand a few GRUB quirks.

GRUB Legacy Nomenclature and Quirks

Listing 1.1 shows a sample GRUB Legacy configuration file. It can boot several OSs and kernels—Fedora on /dev/hda5, Debian on /dev/hda6, and Windows on /dev/hda2. Fedora and Debian share a /boot partition (/dev/hda1), on which the GRUB configuration resides.

Listing 1.1: A sample GRUB legacy configuration file

```
# grub.conf/menu.1st
#
# Global Options:
#
default=0
timeout=15
splashimage=/grub/bootimage.xpm.gz
#
# Kernel Image Options:
#
title Fedora (2.6.32)
    root (hd0,0)
    kernel /vmlinuz-2.6.32 ro root=/dev/hda5 mem=2048M
    initrd /initrd-2.6.32
title Debian (2.6.36-experimental)
    root (hd0,0)
    kernel (hd0,0)/bzImage-2.6.36-experimental ro root=/dev/hda6
#
# Other operating systems
#
title Windows
    rootnoverify (hd0,1)
    chainloader +1
```

GRUB Legacy refers to disk drives by numbers preceded by the string hd and enclosed in parentheses, as in (hd0) for the first hard disk GRUB detects. GRUB doesn't distinguish between Parallel Advanced Technology Attachment (PATA), Serial ATA (SATA), and SCSI drives. On a mixed system, ATA drives normally receive the lower numbers, although this isn't always the case. GRUB Legacy's drive mappings can be found in the /boot/grub/device.map file.

Additionally, GRUB Legacy numbers partitions on a drive starting at 0 instead of 1, which is used by Linux. GRUB separates partition numbers from drive numbers with a comma, as in (hd0,0) for the first partition on the first disk or (hd0,4) for the first logical partition on the first disk. Floppy devices are referred to as (fd0), or conceivably (fd1) or higher if you have more than one floppy drive. Floppy disks aren't partitioned, so they don't receive partition numbers.

GRUB Legacy defines its own root partition, which can be different from the Linux root partition. GRUB's root partition is the partition in which its configuration file (menu.1st or grub.conf) resides. Because this file is normally in Linux's /boot/grub/ directory, the GRUB Legacy root partition will be the same as Linux's root partition if you do *not* use a separate /boot or /boot/grub partition. If you split off /boot into its own partition, as is fairly common, GRUB's root partition will be the same as Linux's /boot partition. You must keep this difference in mind when referring to files in the GRUB configuration directory.

Essential Global GRUB Legacy Options

GRUB Legacy's global section precedes its per-image configurations. A handful of GRUB Legacy global configuration options are most important:

Default OS   The default= option tells GRUB Legacy which OS to boot. Listing 1.1's default=0 causes the first listed OS to be booted (remember, GRUB indexes from 0). If you want to boot the second listed operating system, use default=1, and so on, through all your OSs.

Timeout   The timeout= option defines how long, in seconds, to wait for user input before booting the default operating system.

Background Graphic   The splashimage= line points to a graphics file that's displayed as the background for the boot process. This line is optional, but most Linux distributions point to an image to spruce up the boot menu. The filename reference is relative to the GRUB Legacy root partition, so if /boot is on a separate partition, that portion of the path is omitted. Alternatively, the path may begin with a GRUB device specification, such as (hd0,5) to refer to a file on that partition.

Essential Per-Image GRUB Legacy Options

GRUB Legacy's per-image options are typically indented after the first line, but this is a convention, not a requirement of the file format. The options begin with an identification and continue with options that tell GRUB Legacy how to handle the image:

Title   The title line begins a per-image stanza and specifies the label to display when the boot loader runs. The GRUB Legacy title can accept spaces and is conventionally fairly descriptive, as shown in Listing 1.1.

GRUB Legacy Root   The root option specifies the location of GRUB Legacy's root partition. This is the /boot partition if a separate one exists; otherwise, it's usually the Linux root (/) partition. GRUB *can* reside on a FAT partition, on a floppy disk, or on certain other OSs' partitions, though, so GRUB's root could conceivably be somewhere more exotic.

Kernel Specification   The kernel setting describes the location of the Linux kernel as well as any kernel options that are to be passed to it. Paths are relative to GRUB Legacy's root partition. As an alternative, you can specify devices using GRUB's syntax, such as kernel (hd0,5)/vmlinuz ro root=/dev/hda5. Note that you pass most kernel options on this line. The ro option tells the kernel to mount its root filesystem read-only (it's later remounted read/write), and the root= option specifies the *Linux* root filesystem. Because these options are being passed to the kernel, they use Linux-style device identifiers, when necessary, unlike other options in the GRUB Legacy configuration file.

Initial RAM Disk   Use the `initrd` option to specify an initial RAM disk. Most distributions use initial RAM disks to store loadable kernel modules and some basic tools used early in the boot process; however, it's often possible to omit an initial RAM disk if you compile your own kernel.

Non-Linux Root   The `rootnoverify` option is similar to the `root` option except that GRUB won't try to access files on this partition. It's used to specify a boot partition for OSs for which GRUB Legacy can't directly load a kernel, such as DOS and Windows.

Chain Loading   The `chainloader` option tells GRUB Legacy to pass control to another boot loader. Typically, it's passed a +1 option to load the first sector of the root partition (usually specified with `rootnoverify`) and to hand over execution to this secondary boot loader.

To add a kernel to GRUB, follow these steps:

1.   As root, load the `menu.lst` or `grub.conf` file into a text editor.

2.   Copy a working configuration for a Linux kernel.

3.   Modify the `title` line to give your new configuration a unique name.

4.   Modify the `kernel` line to point to the new kernel. If you need to change any kernel options, do so.

5.   If you're adding, deleting, or changing a RAM disk, make appropriate changes to the `initrd` line.

6.   If desired, change the global `default` line to point to the new kernel.

7.   Save your changes, and exit the text editor.

At this point, GRUB Legacy is configured to boot your new kernel. When you reboot, you should see it appear in your menu, and you should be able to boot it. If you have problems, boot a working configuration to debug the issue.

WARNING   Don't eliminate a working configuration for an old kernel until you've determined that your new kernel works correctly.

Configuring GRUB 2

In principle, configuring GRUB 2 is much like configuring GRUB Legacy; however, some important details differ. First, the GRUB 2 configuration file is `/boot/grub/grub.cfg`. GRUB 2 adds a number of features, such as support for loadable modules for specific filesystems and modes of operation, that aren't present in GRUB Legacy. (The `insmod` command in the GRUB 2 configuration file loads modules.) GRUB 2 also supports conditional logic statements, enabling loading modules or displaying menu entries only if particular conditions are met.

If you merely want to add or change a single OS entry, you'll find the most important changes are to the per-image options. Listing 1.2 shows GRUB 2 equivalents to the image options shown in Listing 1.1.

Listing 1.2: GRUB 2 image configuration examples

```
#
# Kernel Image Options:
#
menuentry "Fedora (2.6.32)" {
    set root=(hd0,1)
    linux /vmlinuz-2.6.32 ro root=/dev/hda5 mem=2048M
    initrd /initrd-2.6.32
}
menuentry "Debian (2.6.36-experimental)" {
    set root=(hd0,1)
    linux (hd0,1)/bzImage-2.6.36-experimental ro root=/dev/hda6
}
#
# Other operating systems
#
menuentry "Windows" {
    set root=(hd0,2)
    chainloader +1
}
```

Important changes compared to GRUB Legacy include the following:

- The title keyword is replaced by menuentry.
- The menu title is enclosed in quotation marks.
- An opening curly brace ({) follows the menu title, and each entry ends with a closing curly brace (}).
- The set keyword precedes the root keyword, and an equal sign (=) separates root from the partition specification.
- The rootnoverify keyword has been eliminated; you use root instead.
- Partitions are numbered starting from 1 rather than from 0. A similar change in disk numbering is *not* implemented. This change can be very confusing. The most recent versions of GRUB 2 also support a more complex partition identification scheme to specify the partition table type or partitions that are embedded within other partitions, as are often used on Solaris or Berkeley Standard Distribution (BSD) OS installations.

GRUB 2 makes further changes, in that it employs a set of scripts and other tools that help automatically maintain the /boot/grub/grub.cfg file. The intent is that system administrators need never explicitly edit this file. Instead, you would edit files in /etc/grub.d, and the /etc/default/grub file, to change your GRUB 2 configuration.

Files in `/etc/grub.d` control particular GRUB OS probers. These scripts scan the system for particular OSs and kernels and add GRUB entries to `/boot/grub/grub.cfg` to support those OSs. You can add custom kernel entries, such as those shown in Listing 1.2, to the `40_custom` file to support your own locally compiled kernels or unusual OSs that GRUB doesn't automatically detect.

The `/etc/default/grub` file controls the defaults created by the GRUB 2 configuration scripts. For instance, if you want to adjust the timeout, you might change the following line:

```
GRUB_TIMEOUT=10
```

A distribution that's designed to use GRUB 2, such as recent versions of Ubuntu, will automatically run the configuration scripts after certain actions, such as installing a new kernel with the distribution's package manager. If you need to make changes yourself, you can type **update-grub** after you've edited `/etc/default/grub` or files in `/etc/grub.d`. This command re-reads these configuration files and writes a fresh `/boot/grub/grub.cfg` file.

Installing the GRUB Boot Loader

The command for installing both GRUB Legacy and GRUB 2 is `grub-install`. Also, you must specify the boot sector by device name when you install the boot loader. The basic command looks like:

```
# grub-install /dev/hda
```

or

```
# grub-install '(hd0)'
```

Either command will install GRUB into the first sector of your first hard drive. On many systems, you would use `/dev/sda` rather than `/dev/hda` in the first example. In the second example, you need single quotes around the device name. If you want to install GRUB in the boot sector of a partition rather than in the MBR, you include a partition identifier, as in `/dev/hda1` or `(hd0,0)`. This option doesn't always work well with GRUB 2, however.

Remember that you do *not* need to reinstall GRUB after making changes to its configuration file! (You may need to run **update-grub** after updating GRUB 2's `/etc`-based configuration files, though.) You need to install GRUB this way only if you make certain changes to your disk configuration, such as resizing or moving the GRUB root partition, moving your entire installation to a new hard disk, or possibly reinstalling Windows (which tends to wipe out MBR-based boot loaders). In some of these cases, you may need to boot Linux via a backup boot loader, such as GRUB installed to floppy disk. (Type **grub-install /dev/fd0** to create one and then label it and store it in a safe place.)

Interacting with GRUB at Boot Time

The first screen the GRUB Legacy or GRUB 2 boot loader shows you is a list of all the operating systems you specified with the `title` or `menuentry` option in your GRUB configuration file. You can wait for the timeout to expire for the default operating system to boot. To select an alternative, use your arrow keys to highlight the operating system that you want to boot. Once your choice is highlighted, press the Enter key to start booting.

Follow these steps when you want to change or pass additional options to your operating system:

1. Use your arrow keys to highlight the operating system that most closely matches what you want to boot.

2. Press the E key to edit this entry. You'll see a new screen listing all the options for this entry.

3. Use your arrow keys to highlight the kernel or linux option line.

4. In GRUB Legacy, press the E key to edit the kernel options. This step is not necessary in GRUB 2.

5. Edit the kernel or linux line to add any options, such as 1 to boot to single-user mode. GRUB will pass the extra option to the kernel when you boot.

6. Press the Enter key to complete the edits. This step is not necessary in GRUB 2.

7. Press the B key to start booting GRUB Legacy, or press Ctrl+X to start booting GRUB 2.

You can make whatever changes you like in step 5, such as using a different init program. You do this by appending init=/bin/bash (or whatever program you want to use) to the end of the kernel line.

More advanced boot-time interactions are possible by entering GRUB's interactive mode. You do this by pressing the C key at the GRUB menu. You can then type a variety of commands that are similar to Linux shell commands, such as ls to view files. If you type ls alone at the grub> prompt, you'll see a list of partitions, using GRUB's partition nomenclature. You can add a partition identifier and a slash, as in ls (hd0,3)/, to view the contents of that partition. By working your way through the partitions, you can probably identify your kernel file and, if your system uses it, an initial RAM disk file. This information, along with the identification of your root filesystem, should enable you to build up a working GRUB entry for your system.

Customizing System Startup

Linux relies on *runlevels* to determine what features are available. Runlevels are numbered from 0 to 6, and each one is assigned a set of services that should be active. Upon booting, Linux enters a predetermined runlevel, which you can set. Knowing what these functions are, and how to manage runlevels, is important if you're to control the Linux boot process and ongoing operations. Toward this end, you must understand the purpose of runlevels, be able to identify the services that are active in a runlevel, be able to adjust those services, be able to check your default and current runlevels, and be able to change the default and current runlevels. Complicating matters, two major startup systems, SysV startup scripts and Upstart, are available, and each provides different ways of doing these practical tasks, although both employ similar runlevel concepts.

Understanding Runlevels

Earlier in this chapter, I mentioned single-user mode, which is a special mode in which Linux permits only root to log in. To get to this mode when booting Linux, you use the number 1, the letter S or s, or the word single as an option passed to the kernel by the boot loader. Single-user mode is simply an available runlevel for your system. The available runlevels on most systems are the numbers 0 through 6. The letters S and s are synonymous with runlevel 1 as far as many utilities are concerned.

Runlevels 0, 1, and 6 are reserved for special purposes; the remaining runlevels are available for whatever purpose you or your Linux distribution provider decide. Table 1.1 summarizes the conventional uses of the runlevels. Other assignments—and even runlevels outside the range of 0 to 6—are possible, but such configurations are rare. (Gentoo uses an unusual runlevel system, as described shortly.) If you run into peculiar runlevel numbers, consult /etc/inittab—it defines them and often contains comments explaining the various runlevels.

TABLE 1.1   Runlevels and their purposes

Runlevel	Purpose
0	A transitional runlevel, meaning that it's used to shift the system from one state to another. Specifically, it shuts down the system. On modern hardware, the system should completely power down. If not, you're expected to either reboot the computer manually or power it off.
1, s, or S	Single-user mode. What services, if any, are started at this runlevel varies by distribution. It's typically used for low-level system maintenance that may be impaired by normal system operation, such as resizing partitions. Typically, s or S produces a root shell without mounting any filesystems, whereas 1 does attempt to mount filesystems and launches a few system programs.
2	On Debian and its derivatives (including Ubuntu), a full multi-user mode with X running and a graphical login. Most other distributions leave this runlevel undefined.
3	On Fedora, Mandriva, Red Hat, and most other distributions, a full multi-user mode with a console (non-graphical) login screen.
4	Usually undefined by default and therefore available for customization.
5	On Fedora, Mandriva, Red Hat, and most other distributions, the same behavior as runlevel 3 with the addition of having X run with an XDM (graphical) login.
6	Used to reboot the system. This runlevel is also a transitional runlevel. Your system is completely shut down, and then the computer reboots automatically.

WARNING   Don't configure your default runlevel to 0 or 6. If you do, your system will immediately shut down or reboot once it finishes powering up. Runlevel 1 could conceivably be used as a default, but chances are you'll want to use 2, 3, or 5 as your default runlevel, depending on your distribution and use for the system.

As a general rule, distributions have been drifting toward Red Hat's runlevel set; however, there are some exceptions and holdouts, such as Debian and Ubuntu. Gentoo also deserves special attention. Although it uses numbered runlevels at its core, Gentoo builds on this by enabling an arbitrary number of *named* runlevels. The default runlevel is called, appropriately enough, `default`. Gentoo's system permits you to create named runlevels for, say, connecting a laptop to half a dozen different networks, each with its own unique network configuration requirements. When you move from one network to another, enter the appropriate runlevel, as described in "Changing Runlevels on a Running System."

NOTE   Many of the files and file locations described in this chapter are based on the *Linux Standards Base (LSB)*, which is a specification of various standards for the locations of files, the existence of particular libraries, and so on. The LSB is designed to ensure a minimal level of compatibility across common Linux distributions.

Configuring SysV Startup Scripts

In the past, most Linux distributions have used *System V (SysV) startup scripts*, which are named after the System V version of Unix on which they originated. In the Linux implementation of SysV startup scripts, the kernel launches a process called `init`, which reads its configuration file and, in following its instructions, launches a series of scripts that can vary from one runlevel to another. As described later, in "Configuring Upstart," a competing startup system is becoming common on Linux.

Identifying the Services in a Runlevel

There are two main ways to affect what programs run when you enter a new runlevel. The first is to add or delete entries in `init`'s configuration file, `/etc/inittab`. A typical `/etc/inittab` file contains many entries, and except for a couple of special cases, inspecting or changing the contents of this file is best left to experts. Once all the entries in `/etc/inittab` for your runlevel are executed, your boot process is complete, and you can log in. The second way to alter programs run in a given runlevel is to edit the SysV or Upstart startup scripts.

Editing the */etc/inittab* File

Entries in /etc/inittab follow a simple format. Each line consists of four colon-delimited fields:

`id:runlevels:action:process`

Each of these fields has a specific meaning, as identified in Table 1.2. In a traditional configuration, /etc/inittab includes lines that launch the SysV startup scripts for each runlevel, as described shortly.

TABLE 1.2   Contents of a /etc/inittab entry

Code	Purpose
id	This field consists of a sequence of one to four characters that identifies the entry's function.
runlevels	This field consists of a list of runlevels for which this entry applies. For instance, 345 means the entry is applicable to runlevels 3, 4, and 5.
action	Specific codes in this field tell init how to treat the process. For instance, wait tells init to start the process once when entering a runlevel and to wait for the process's termination, and respawn tells init to restart the process whenever it terminates (which is great for login processes). Several other actions are available; consult the man page for inittab for details.
process	This field specifies the process to run for this entry, including any options and arguments that are required.

The upcoming section "Checking and Changing Your Default Runlevel" describes how to tell init what runlevel to enter when the system boots.

If you alter the /etc/inittab file, the changes won't take effect until you reboot the computer or type a command such as **telinit Q** to have it reread this file and implement its changes. Thus, when making changes, you should keep them simple or test their effects, lest problems occur later, after you've forgotten about changes to this file.

Understanding SysV Startup Scripts

The /etc/init.d/rc or /etc/rc.d/rc script performs the crucial task of running all the scripts associated with the runlevel. The runlevel-specific scripts are stored in /etc/

rc.d/rc?.d, /etc/init.d/rc?.d, /etc/rc?.d, or a similar location. (The precise location varies between distributions.) In all these cases, ? is the runlevel number. When entering a runlevel, rc passes the start parameter to all the scripts with names that begin with a capital S and passes the stop parameter to all the scripts with names that begin with a capital K. These SysV startup scripts start or stop services depending on the parameter they're passed, so the naming of the scripts controls whether they're started or stopped when a runlevel is entered. These scripts are also numbered, as in S10network and K35smb; the numbers control the order in which services are started or stopped.

The rc program runs SysV startup scripts in numeric order. This feature enables distribution designers to control the order in which scripts run by giving them appropriate numbers. This control is important because some services depend on others. For instance, network servers must normally be started after the network is brought up.

In reality, the files in the SysV runlevel directories are symbolic links to the main scripts, which are typically stored in /etc/rc.d, /etc/init.d, or /etc/rc.d/init.d (again, the exact location depends on the distribution). These original SysV startup scripts have names that lack the leading S or K and number, as in smb instead of K35smb.

To determine which services are active in a runlevel, search the appropriate SysV startup script directory for scripts with filenames that begin with an S. Alternatively, you can use a runlevel management tool, as described next.

 You can start services by hand. Run them with the start option, as in /etc/init.d/smb start to start the smb (Samba) server. Other useful options are stop, restart, and status. Most scripts support all these options.

Most distributions place useful information, such as the runlevels in which scripts run by default, in comments near the start of each SysV startup script. These comments can be helpful if you need to manually restore a system to its default configuration.

Managing Runlevel Services

The SysV startup scripts in the runlevel directories are symbolic links back to the original script. This is done so you don't need to copy the same script into each runlevel directory. Instead, you can modify the original script without having to track down its copies in all the SysV runlevel directories. Using a single linked-to file also simplifies system updates.

You can also modify which programs are active in a runlevel by editing the link filenames. Numerous utility programs are available to help you manage these links, such as chkconfig, ntsysv, update-rc.d, and rc-update. I describe chkconfig and update-rc.d tools because they are supported on many distributions. If your distribution doesn't support these tools, you should check distribution-centric documentation.

Using *chkconfig*

To list the services and their applicable runlevels with chkconfig, use the --list (or, usually, -l) option. The output looks something like this but is likely to be much longer:

```
# chkconfig --list
pcmcia            0:off    1:off    2:on     3:on     4:on     5:on     6:off
nfs-common        0:off    1:off    2:off    3:on     4:on     5:on     6:off
xprint            0:off    1:off    2:off    3:on     4:on     5:on     6:off
setserial         0:off    1:off    2:off    3:off    4:off    5:off    6:off
```

This output shows the status of the services in all seven runlevels. For instance, you can see that nfs-common is inactive in runlevels 0–2, active in runlevels 3–5, and inactive in runlevel 6.

On Red Hat, Fedora, and some other distributions, chkconfig can manage servers that are handled by xinetd as well as SysV startup scripts. The xinetd-mediated servers appear at the end of the chkconfig listing.

If you're interested in a specific service, you can specify its name:

```
# chkconfig --list nfs-common
nfs-common        0:off    1:off    2:off    3:on     4:on     5:on     6:off
```

To modify the runlevels in which a service runs, use a command like this:

```
# chkconfig --level 23 nfs-common on
```

The previous example is for Debian-based systems. On Red Hat and similar systems, you would probably want to target runlevels 3, 4, and 5 with something like --level 345 rather than --level 23.

You can set the script to be on (to activate it), off (to deactivate it), or reset (to set it to its default value).

If you've added a startup script to the main SysV startup script directory, you can have chkconfig register it and add appropriate start and stop links in the runlevel directories. When you do this, chkconfig inspects the script for special comments to indicate default runlevels. If these comments are in the file and you're happy with the suggested levels, you can add it to these runlevels with a command like this:

```
# chkconfig --add nfs-common
```

This command adds the nfs-common script to those managed by chkconfig. You would, of course, change nfs-common to your script's name. This approach may not work if the script lacks the necessary comment lines with runlevel sequence numbers for chkconfig's benefit.

Using *update-rc.d*

The update-rc.d program is most common on Debian and some of its derived distributions. It fills much the same role as chkconfig; however, details of its operation are quite different. Its basic syntax is:

update-rc.d [*options*] *name action*

The most common option is -n, which causes the program to report what it would do without taking any real action. The *name* is the name of the service to be modified. The *action* is the name of the action to be performed, along with any action-specific options. Common actions are summarized in Table 1.3.

TABLE 1.3 Contents of a /etc/inittab entry

Action code	Effect
remove	Removes links in runlevel-specific directories to the named service. The service's main script must not exist. This option is intended to clean up the SysV startup scripts after a service has been completely removed from the system.
defaults	Creates links to start the service in runlevels 2, 3, 4, and 5, and to stop it in runlevels 0, 1, and 6.
start *NN runlevels*	Creates a link to start the service in the specified *runlevels*, using the sequence number *NN*.
stop *NN runlevels*	Creates links to stop the service in the specified *runlevels*, using the sequence number *NN*.
enable [*runlevel*]	Modifies existing runlevel links to enable the service in the specified runlevel. If no runlevel is specified, runlevels 2, 3, 4, and 5 are modified.
disable [*runlevel*]	Modifies existing runlevel links to disable the service in the specified runlevel. If no runlevel is specified, runlevels 2, 3, 4, and 5 are modified.

As an example of rc-update.d in action, consider the following two commands:

```
# update-rc.d samba defaults
# update-rc.d gdm disable 234
```

The first of these examples sets the Samba server to run in the default runlevels. The second causes the GNOME Display Manager (GDM) login server to not run in runlevels 2, 3, and 4.

Configuring Upstart

Several modern Linux distributions, including recent versions of Ubuntu and Fedora, now use an `init` process called Upstart (http://upstart.ubuntu.com) rather than the venerable SysV startup system. Broadly speaking, Upstart does the same job as the SysV scripts, but Upstart is designed to better handle today's dynamically changing *hot-plug* hardware, which can be connected to and disconnected from a computer while it's still running. Upstart provides SysV compatibility features, so you should be familiar with the SysV methods described earlier; however, it also has its own unique scripts and differs in some important ways. In particular, Upstart does away with /etc/inittab, instead providing an integrated set of startup scripts that can, in principle, completely replace the SysV-style /etc/inittab and runlevel-specific startup scripts. Upstart scripts also support starting or stopping services based on a wider variety of actions than do SysV startup scripts; for instance, Upstart can launch a service whenever a particular hardware device is attached.

Using Upstart-Native Methods

A system that uses nothing but Upstart and its native scripts replaces both /etc/inittab and the runlevel-specific SysV startup script directories with scripts in the /etc/init directory. (This directory was called /etc/event.d on earlier versions of Upstart.) You may want to check the contents of this directory on your own Upstart-based system.

 As I write, Upstart is under heavy development, and its configuration file format is subject to change. Thus, you may find differences from what is described in these pages.

To change the runlevels in which a particular service runs, you'll have to edit its configuration file in a text editor. Locate the script (typically /etc/init/*name*.conf, where *name* is the name of the service), and load it into a text editor. Look for lines that include the text `start on` and `stop on`, as in the following example:

```
start on (filesystem
          and started hal
          and tty-device-added KERNEL=tty7
          and (graphics-device-added or stopped udevtrigger))
stop on runlevel [016]
```

Locate any `runlevel` specification and adjust it for your needs. For instance, you might change the preceding example's `stop on runlevel` specification to read `stop on runlevel [0126]` to include runlevel 2 in the list of runlevels on which the service is to be stopped.

After you make such a change, you can use the start or stop command to immediately start or stop the service, as in **stop gdm** to shut down the gdm server. Before changing your runlevel (as described shortly, in "Changing Runlevels on a Running System"), you should type **initctl reload** to have Upstart reread its configuration files.

 If you upgrade the package that provides the Upstart configuration script, you may need to reconfigure again.

Using SysV Compatibility Methods

Because the SysV startup script system has been so common for so long, a large number of software packages include SysV startup scripts. In order to accommodate such packages, Upstart provides a compatibility mode: It runs SysV startup scripts in the usual locations (/etc/rc.d/rc?.d, /etc/init.d/rc?.d, /etc/rc?.d, or a similar location). Thus, if you install a package that doesn't yet include an Upstart configuration script, it should still launch in the usual way. Furthermore, if you've installed utilities such as chkconfig, you should be able to use them to manage your SysV-based services just as you would on a SysV-based system.

You may find, however, that chkconfig and other SysV-based tools no longer work for some services. As time goes on, this is likely to be true for more and more services, because the developers of distributions that favor Upstart may convert their packages' startup scripts to use Upstart-native methods.

Checking Your Runlevel

Sometimes it's necessary to check your current runlevel. Typically, you'll do this prior to changing the runlevel or to check the status if something isn't working correctly. Two different runlevel checks are possible: checking your default runlevel and checking your current runlevel.

Checking and Changing Your Default Runlevel

On a SysV-based system, you can determine your default runlevel by inspecting the /etc/inittab file with the less command or opening it in an editor. Alternatively, you may use the grep command to look for the line specifying the initdefault action. You might see something like this:

```
# grep :initdefault: /etc/inittab
id:5:initdefault:
```

You may notice that this line does not define a process to run. In the case of the initdefault action, the process field is ignored.

If you want to change the default runlevel for the next time you boot your system, edit the initdefault line in /etc/inittab and change the runlevel field to the value that you want. If your system lacks a /etc/inittab file, as is common on Upstart-based systems, create one that contains *only* an initdefault line that specifies the runlevel you want to enter by default.

Determining Your Current Runlevel

If your system is up and running, you can determine your runlevel information with the runlevel command:

```
# runlevel
N 2
```

The first character is the previous runlevel. When the character is N, this means the system hasn't switched runlevels since booting. It's possible to switch to different runlevels on a running system with the init and telinit programs, as described next. The second character in the runlevel output is your current runlevel.

Changing Runlevels on a Running System

Sometimes you may want to change runlevels on a running system. You might do this to get more services, such as going from a console to a graphical login runlevel, or to shut down or reboot your computer. You can accomplish this with the init (or telinit), shutdown, halt, reboot, and poweroff commands.

Changing Runlevels with *init* or *telinit*

The init process is the first process run by the Linux kernel, but you can also use it to have the system reread the /etc/inittab file and implement changes it finds there or to change to a new runlevel. The simplest case is to have it change to the runlevel you specify. For instance, to change to runlevel 1 (the runlevel reserved for single-user or maintenance mode), you would type this command:

```
# init 1
```

To reboot the system, you can use init to change to runlevel 6 (the runlevel reserved for reboots):

```
# init 6
```

A variant of init is telinit. This program can take a runlevel number just like init to change to that runlevel, but it can also take the Q or q option to have the tool reread /etc/inittab and implement any changes it finds there. Thus, if you've made a change to the runlevel in /etc/inittab, you can immediately implement that change by typing **telinit q**.

The man pages for these commands indicate slightly different syntaxes, but telinit is sometimes a symbolic link to init, and in practice init responds just like telinit to the Q and q options.

Changing Runlevels with *shutdown*

Although you can shut down or reboot the computer with `init`, doing so has some problems. One issue is that it's simply an unintuitive command for this action. Another is that changing runlevels with `init` causes an immediate change to the new runlevel. This may cause other users on your system some aggravation because they'll be given no warning about the shutdown. Thus, it's better to use the `shutdown` command in a multi-user environment when you want to reboot, shut down, or switch to single-user mode. This command supports extra options that make it friendlier in such environments.

The `shutdown` program sends a message to all users who are logged into your system and prevents other users from logging in during the process of changing runlevels. The `shutdown` command also lets you specify when to effect the runlevel change so that users have time to exit editors and safely stop other processes they may have running.

When the time to change runlevels is reached, `shutdown` signals the `init` process for you. In the simplest form, `shutdown` is invoked with a time argument like:

```
# shutdown now
```

This changes the system to runlevel 1, the single-user or maintenance mode. The `now` parameter causes the change to occur immediately. Other possible time formats include *hh:mm*, for a time in 24-hour clock format (such as 6:00 for 6:00 a.m. or 13:30 for 1:30 p.m.), and *+m* for a time *m* minutes in the future.

You can add extra parameters to specify that you want to reboot or halt (that is, power off) the computer. Specifically, `-r` reboots the system, `-H` halts it (terminates operation but doesn't power it off), and `-P` powers it off. The `-h` option may halt or power off the computer, but usually it powers it off. For instance, you can type **shutdown -r +10** to reboot the system in 10 minutes.

To give people some warning about the impending shutdown, you can add a message to the end of the command:

```
# shutdown -h +15 "system going down for maintenance"
```

If you schedule a shutdown but then change your mind, you can use the `-c` option to cancel it:

```
# shutdown -c "never mind"
```

Changing Runlevels with the *halt, reboot,* and *poweroff* Commands

Three additional shortcut commands are `halt`, `reboot`, and `poweroff`. As you might expect, these commands halt the system (shut it down without powering it off), reboot it, or shut it down and (on hardware that supports this feature) turn off the power, respectively. Typically, two of these commands are symbolic links to a third; the single binary responds differently depending on the name used to call it.

Compile and Install Programs from Source

Both system startup utilities and users run software, and that software has to be installed in some way. The LPI Level 1 certification includes coverage of two common methods of installing software on Linux systems: the RPM Package Manager (RPM) and Debian packages. These tools are adequate and convenient for most common software packages; however, from time to time you'll have to install software that's not available in these forms. In such cases, you may need to compile and install the software from its original source code. The following pages describe this process, including the advantages and pitfalls of this approach, obtaining and unpacking source code, compiling the software, installing it, and uninstalling or upgrading it should it be necessary.

Chapter 2, "Linux Kernel Configuration," describes compiling the Linux kernel in greater detail. Many of the procedures and issues covered in this chapter apply to the kernel, but the kernel has its own special needs with respect to configuration, compilation, and installation.

Understanding Source Code Issues

Most Linux software is available in two forms: as *source code*, which programmers write and can subsequently modify; and as *object code* or *binary code*, which the computer runs. (Some software is written in *interpreted* computer languages, in which this distinction does not exist.) Software is converted from source code to binary code form by a program known as a *compiler*. Software in source code form can theoretically be compiled to run on any computer that provides the necessary compiler and associated tools. Binary code, on the other hand, is customized for one particular OS and hardware family. For instance, a Linux program in binary form for an $x86$-64 CPU can't run on a computer with a PowerPC CPU, even if that computer runs Linux; nor can the same binary run on MacOS X, even if it's running on an $x86$-64 CPU.

Tools such as QEMU (http://wiki.qemu.org/Main_Page) and Wine (http://www.winehq.org) provide ways to break some of these restrictions; they can run one CPU's or OS's binaries on another CPU or OS. CPU emulators such as QEMU work at the cost of speed; the code runs much slower under QEMU than it does on native hardware. WINE is useful only for running Microsoft Windows software under Linux or other Unix-like OSs, and it doesn't work with all Windows software.

If you don't have access to a binary package for your computer but want to run the software, you must compile the software yourself. This activity carries with it several prerequisites:

- You must have appropriate software development tools installed on your system. Typically, this means the GNU Compiler Collection (GCC), including the GCC package for the language in which the software was written, such as C or C++.

- You must have appropriate *development libraries* (also known as *header files*) installed on the computer. Note that development libraries are usually installed separately from their binary library equivalents; the latter are required for binaries to run, but to create the binaries, you need a separate development library. The development library is not required when you install a precompiled binary package.

- Several generic support tools are necessary, such as the `tar` program that's used to extract files from the source code package. These tools are usually installed by default on most Linux systems, but there may be exceptions to this rule.

Source code packages usually include documentation, described shortly, that summarizes its specific requirements. You may need to use your distribution's binary package management tools to locate and install various prerequisites.

Unfortunately, problems often occur while compiling software. Frequently, these problems can be overcome by installing missing packages, such as development libraries. Sometimes, though, the problems are more fundamental. Old programs may rely on equally old libraries that are no longer available; or the libraries may have been updated in such a way that the old program no longer compiles. Highly specialized programs may be written for a specific platform and simply won't compile under Linux, or they may need to be modified to compile properly. If you run into serious problems compiling software, you should study any error messages you encounter. A Web search on an error message may turn up a solution or at least help you to understand what's going wrong.

Fortunately, in many cases there are no problems at all. Linux is a popular enough platform that most open source programs for Unix-like OSs compile fine on Linux—provided you've installed the necessary development tools and libraries!

Preparing Source Code

The first step in compiling source code is to obtain it and understand the author's directions on using it. Source code can be obtained from a variety of places. Although there are some common practices in source code distribution, there are few rules that you can rely upon to be true in all cases. Therefore, you must be prepared to do different things to install different source packages, and it's very important that you read a package's documentation!

Obtaining Source Code

If you already know you want to install a particular package from source code, chances are you already know where and how to obtain it. If you're looking for software to perform some task but don't know its name, though, you may want to check out an open source repository site, such as SourceForge (https://sourceforge.net), Google Code (http://code.google.com), or Freshmeat (http://freshmeat.net). You could also try performing a Web search on key words relevant to the software you want to locate.

Sometimes program Web sites provide multiple packages intended for different platforms. Linux source code tarballs usually come in files with names that end in .tgz, .tar.gz, .tbz, .tbz2, or .tar.bz2. These filenames all denote tarballs—archive files created with the tar utility. The .tgz and .tar.gz extensions denote tarballs that have been compressed with gzip, while .tbz, .tbz2, and .tar.bz2 denote tarballs that have been compressed with bzip2. Occasionally you'll see source code distributed in PkZip .zip files, which can be extracted in Linux with the unzip utility. These files are not tarballs, but they serve the same function.

If you see a source RPM file, which has a name that ends in .src.rpm, and if you have an RPM-based distribution, you can download it and generate a binary RPM. Source RPMs are converted into binary RPMs by typing **rpmbuild --rebuild** *aprogram-1.2.3.src.rpm*, where *aprogram-1.2.3.src.rpm* is the source RPM's filename. The binary RPM will be stored in a location that is specified about a dozen lines above the end of the resulting output. You should not follow the normal source code compilation and installation instructions when installing a source RPM.

Unpacking Source Code

To uncompress any type of tarball, you use the tar utility, passing it the -x (or --extract) operation name along with either -z (--gzip) or -j (--bzip2) if the tarball was compressed and -f (--file) to specify the filename. You may want to add -v (--verbose) to see a list of filenames as they're extracted. The final command might look like this:

```
$ tar xvzf aprogram-1.2.3.tgz
```

The leading dash (-) can be, and often is, omitted when using single-character options with the tar program.

Some people prefer to call gunzip or bunzip2 separately, piping the result through tar:

```
$ gunzip -c aprogram-1.2.3.tgz | tar xv
```

Tarballs are conventionally built such that, when they're extracted, they create a subdirectory, usually with the same name as the tarball, and all files are placed within the new directory. This isn't always true, though, and it's often not true of .zip files. If you want to be sure that a tarball will extract neatly into a new subdirectory rather than litter the current directory with its files, you can use the -t (--list) operation, as in **tar tvzf aprogram-1.2.3.tgz**, to view its contents before extracting it.

You can extract a source tarball into your home directory and work on it there; however, if you intend to install a program on the system for all users' benefit, you may prefer to extract the tarball into a subdirectory of /usr/src. This directory exists to hold source code for programs that are locally compiled. You can then leave the source code in that location, ensuring that the necessary tools remain behind for uninstalling the software, should that become necessary. (The upcoming section "Uninstalling or Upgrading Software" describes how to uninstall locally compiled software.) By default, /usr/src is normally writeable only by root, so you may need to acquire superuser privileges to extract a tarball to this directory. It's usually possible to compile software as an ordinary user, so you may want to adjust permissions on the extracted directory to enable yourself to write to that directory tree as a non-root user. You will have to use root privileges to install the software, at least if you want to install it to a standard location for use by all users.

Reading Documentation

Once you've extracted the source code, you should type ls in the source code directory to view the files it contains. In most cases, you'll find several documentation files. Common files include COPYING (the license text), CHANGELOG (a history of technical changes to the software), NEWS (another history of changes, this one less technical), README (general documentation), and INSTALL (instructions on installing the software). Some packages come with additional or different files, and sometimes one or more of these common files may be missing. Documentation files like these usually have entirely uppercase names, but this isn't always true.

You should be sure to read the general documentation (README) and installation instructions (INSTALL) before proceeding with any source code compilation or installation procedure. Although most programs follow a similar procedure, the actions required are not completely standardized. You may find that the software you want to install requires some unusual steps, such as manual editing of a file or use of unusual syntax in its compilation commands. You may also discover that you need to install development libraries or tools that aren't already installed on your system.

Programs sometimes specify that they have special requirements or limitations on particular CPUs or with particular kernels. You can learn about both with the uname command, which displays information on the current CPU, kernel, and a few other system details. You can obtain various specific types of information by passing particular options to uname, but passing –a, as in uname –a, reveals all that the program can reveal. The kernel version number will be obvious. The string SMP, if present, denotes a symmetric multi-processing (SMP) CPU. A string such as i386 or x86_64 identifies a 32- or 64-bit kernel, respectively, on the x86/x86-64 platform.

Compiling Software

Once you've extracted the source code, read its documentation, and installed any additional tools you need to compile the software, you can begin configuring and compiling the software. Problems can occur at either of these steps, although most programs compile and install cleanly, provided you've satisfied all the prerequisites.

Configuring the Compilation

Simple programs require little or nothing in the way of configuration. More complex programs, however, ship with a tool that scans your system for available tools and libraries and adjusts the compilation process for your particular computer.

The most common method of performing this task is a script called `configure` located in the source code's main directory. You can type **./configure** to run this script. It will scan your system and adjust a file called `Makefile`, which controls the compilation process, to work optimally on your system.

The `configure` script often accepts parameters that enable you to set compile-time options for the software. These vary from one package to another; however, some common `configure` options are shown in Table 1.4. You might use these parameters to enable debugging features if you believe a program contains a bug or use them to set program-specific features such as support for specific third-party libraries.

TABLE 1.4   Common `configure` script parameters

Parameter	Effect
--help	Displays a summary of options.
--quiet	Displays fewer messages as the script does its work.
--prefix=*directory*	Sets the installation directory for architecture-independent files to *directory*. The default value is usually /usr/local.
--eprefix=*directory*	Sets the installation directory for architecture-dependent files to *directory*. The default value is usually /usr/local.
--enable-*FEATURE*	Enables a named *FEATURE*, which is program-specific.
--disable-*FEATURE*	Disables a named *FEATURE*, which is program-specific.
--enable-debug=*ARG*	Sets debugging symbols. *ARG* is yes, no, or full, with a default of no.
--disable-debug	Disables debugging output.
--with-*PACKAGE*[=*ARG*]	Enables support for a particular library or external tool, *PACKAGE*. By default, *ARG* is yes.
--without-*PACKAGE*	Disables support for a particular library or external tool, *PACKAGE*; equivalent to --with-*PACKAGE*=no.

When you run the configure script, it displays a series of lines that summarize what it's doing. These lines often begin with the word checking, and they report the status of a check. If the script discovers that you're missing some critical header files or software component, it will terminate and display an error message, such as the following:

```
checking for Qt... configure: error: Qt (>= Qt 3.0) (headers and
libraries) not found. Please check your installation!
```

```
For more details about this problem, look at the end of config.log.
```

Such a message tells you what you're missing that the program requires, but it may be a bit cryptic or incomplete. In many cases, you can resolve the problem by loading a high-level package management tool, such as Synaptic for Debian-based systems or Yumex on Fedora or Red Hat, and searching for a development package named after the missing tool. For instance, if you see the preceding message, you'd look for Qt development packages. Development packages usually include the string -devel, -develop, or -library in their names. Install any promising package and try again.

Some programs use other methods to configure the compilation. One such method, which is used by the Linux kernel, is to type **make config** or some variant of this command. In the case of the kernel, this command launches a tool that enables you to set various compile-time options. (Chapter 2 covers kernel configuration and compilation in more detail.)

A few programs suggest that you edit a file called Makefile to customize the program manually. Makefile is a configuration file for the make program, which controls the software compilation process. Typically, if you must edit Makefile yourself, the changes required are minor, such as changing the installation location or enabling support for one or two libraries or compile-time features. The documentation usually describes how to perform such changes; however, some developers assume you have a basic familiarity with programming. If you need help with technical terms or don't understand a description, try performing a Web search on the relevant terms.

Software that you compile yourself (that is, *locally*) is generally installed in /usr/local and its subdirectories. Installing software elsewhere can be dangerous, since you might easily overwrite the files installed by your distribution's package management tools; or such tools might subsequently replace files from a locally compiled program. It's generally a good idea to verify that the software is configured to install its files in /usr/local.

Compiling the Source Code

Once you've run the configure script and it's completed without errors, you can type **make** to compile the software. Software that doesn't use configure is also usually compiled in the same way, although you should double-check the documentation to be sure. The compilation process can take anywhere from a few seconds to several hours, depending on the size of the program. You'll see status lines appear on the screen during this process.

Depending on the package, these lines may be the individual compilation commands and their output or summaries. If you notice lines that contain the string `warning` along with scary-sounding messages about problems, don't be concerned; GCC generates warnings like this when programmers use commands in ways that might be a bit risky or that might be unsupported in the future. Such warnings seldom indicate real problems in release software. If the output created by `make` includes the word `error`, though, and terminates soon thereafter, this indicates a much more serious problem. An error prevents GCC from compiling the software, so there's no point in proceeding with installation until you've found the source of the problem.

To investigate, scroll upward until you locate the first `error` message. Frequently, one error results in another, which results in another, and so on. Fixing the last error is likely to be unproductive, but fixing the first error may eliminate all the subsequent errors. Compile-time errors in release software are often caused by missing header files or other programs. Ideally, `configure` will find such problems, but sometimes it doesn't. If the error message mentions a missing file or command, try doing a Web search on the name, or use your distribution's package manager to search for a package with a similar name. With any luck, this will lead you to a solution.

Sometimes, release programs don't compile because of changes in development tools—GCC might have stopped supporting a particular syntax that the programmer used, or changes in header files might require changes in the program. If you know enough about programming, you can tackle such problems yourself. If not, you'll have to contact the program's author or enlist the help of somebody with programming experience to solve the problem.

Installing Software

Once the program has finished compiling, you can install it. Typically, typing `make install` as `root` will do this: The binary program will be copied to a suitable location, such as `/usr/local/bin`, and the program's man pages and support files will also be copied to reasonable locations, usually in the `/usr/local` directory tree. If the program is a normal user program, you should then be able to launch it by typing its name, just as you'd run a program installed via a package manager.

Some programs don't provide an `install` target to make—that is, if you type `make install`, nothing useful will happen. For such programs, you must copy the program file manually. You may need to copy man pages or other support files, too; consult the program's documentation for details. Typically, typing `cp progname /usr/local/bin` (to copy the *progname* binary) as `root` will do the job; however, the `install` program does the copy job and will automatically adjust ownership and permissions for binaries. Typing `install progname /usr/local/bin` as `root` copies *progname* to /usr/local/bin, changing its ownership to the current effective user ID (`root`) and its permissions to 0755. Table 1.5 summarizes several common `install` options. Consult its man page for more advanced options.

TABLE 1.5   Common install options

Option	Effect
-b or --backup	Creates a backup of every destination file.
-g *GROUP* or --group=*GROUP*	Changes the group of the installed files to *GROUP* rather than to the current group ID.
-m *MODE* or --mode=*MODE*	Changes the installed files' mode to *MODE*.
-o *OWNER* or --owner=*OWNER*	Changes the owner of the installed files to *OWNER* rather than to the current user ID.
-s or --strip	Strips symbol tables; reduces a binary's size, but makes debugging harder.
-T or --no-target-directory	Treats the destination location as a file rather than as a directory.
-v or --verbose	Displays the names of all files and directories as they're being copied.

If the program is a server or other system utility that should be launched automatically, you'll need to perform additional configuration steps. For instance, you may need to create a unique SysV startup script, launch the program via a line in /etc/rc.local or some other generic system startup script, create an inetd or xinetd entry for the program, or create an entry in /etc/profile or some other user-level startup script to launch the program for individual users. Consult the program's documentation if you're unsure how to proceed. It may include suggestions or sample configurations you can modify for your system.

After you install software, you can type **make clean** to remove files generated during the compilation process. This can save disk space, but if you need to reinstall the software, you'll need to recompile it from scratch. You can, of course, completely remove the source code directory to save even more space; however, doing so will make it harder to uninstall the software, should you decide to do so in the future.

Uninstalling or Upgrading Software

If you decide you don't need the software after all or if you decide to install it from a binary package for your distribution, you should uninstall it. Many source packages support an uninstall target to make so that you can type **make uninstall** as root in the original source code directory to remove the software from the computer.

WARNING   Typing **make uninstall** will remove the software, much like using the uninstall feature of RPM or the Debian package manager. The make utility doesn't maintain a package database, though; it blindly removes whatever files are specified in Makefile. Thus, if you use the Makefile from a different version of the program than you have installed, you might not remove the right files. If the Makefile is configured to install the program outside of /usr/local, you might even delete files that were installed via a package manager.

If the software doesn't support a make uninstall operation, you'll have to delete the files manually. This shouldn't be too tedious for small programs that install just a handful of files, but it can become difficult for bigger programs. Fortunately, most big programs support the uninstall target.

To upgrade software installed from source using another source distribution, it's generally best to compile the new version, uninstall the old software, and then install the new version. This procedure ensures that you'll remove all the old files and install the relevant new files. Be sure to back up any configuration files and verify that your configuration is correct after you install the new version, though.

In Exercise 1.1, you will practice compiling and installing software from source code.

EXERCISE 1.1

Compiling and Installing Software from Source Code

This exercise gives you hands-on experience with software compilation procedures, using the JED editor (http://www.jedsoft.org/jed/) as an example. This editor is a small editor that provides features similar to those of the much larger Emacs package. To compile and install JED, follow these steps:

1. Like most open source programs, JED is available as a precompiled binary for many distributions. Type **jed** to see if the program is installed; if it is, it will launch a text-mode editor that you can exit by typing Ctrl+X Ctrl+C. If it's already installed on your system, you may want to uninstall it by typing **rpm -e jed, dpkg -r jed**, or some other distribution-specific command as root.

2. Download the source code from ftp://space.mit.edu/pub/davis/jed/v0.99/; or consult the main JED Web page for a more recent version. This exercise uses JED version 0.99-19 from the jed-0.99-19.tar.bz2 source code file as a model.

3. Change to a convenient location in your home directory or to /usr/src and ensure you have write permission to this directory. If necessary, use chmod as root or perform the following steps as root.

4. Type `tar xvjf ~/jed-0.99-19.tar.bz2`, adjusting the path to the source tarball as necessary. The result should be a list of files extracted into the jed-0.99-19 subdirectory.

5. Change into the jed-0.99-19 subdirectory and examine its contents. Consult the README and INSTALL.unix files.

6. As directed by the INSTALL.unix file, use your package manager to ensure that the slang development libraries are installed. These are likely to be called slang-devel, libslang2-dev, or something similar.

7. Type `./configure` to configure the build for your environment. Note that the INSTALL.unix file specifies use of the --prefix=/usr/local option, but this is the default and so is unnecessary. You may need to point the script to the slang libraries by using --with-slang=/usr/include (or some other path to slang.h).

8. Type `make clean` to ensure any stray files from old compilation attempts are removed.

9. Type `make` to build the text-mode binary.

10. If you want it, type `make xjed` to build a minimally X-enabled version of the program.

11. As root, type `make install` to install the program.

12. Test the program by using it to review a text file; for instance, by typing `jed INSTALL.unix`. You can test the xjed binary in a similar way. If you removed a binary package provided by your distribution in step #1, you may need to type the complete path to the binary, as in `/usr/local/bin/jed INSTALL.unix`. When you log out and back in again, this will no longer be necessary, provided /usr/local/bin is on your PATH environment variable.

13. JED provides no uninstall target in its Makefile, so if you want to remove the software, you must do so manually, by deleting the /usr/local/jed directory tree and the jed, jed-script, and xjed binary files from /usr/local/bin.

If any of the preceding steps fails, you will have to debug it, as described earlier in this chapter. Chances are you can overcome the problem by installing a suitable software package, such as gcc or make.

Notify Users of System-Related Issues

Computers are used by people, and people can become annoyed if their computers shut down or otherwise behave strangely at unexpected times. Thus, you should know how to communicate such issues with the users of a computer. Sometimes this task can be accomplished by setting login messages, but other times you must send messages to users in real time.

Setting Login Messages

When users log in via a text-mode login prompt, either at the console or remotely, the computer displays various messages. The login: prompt itself is one such message, but you can manipulate some others:

Local Login Messages   The /etc/issue file holds a message that's displayed above the login: prompt at a text-mode console. Typically, this message identifies the computer. It can contain variables that are replaced with the computer's hostname, the kernel version number, the time, and so on, as described shortly.

Network Login Messages   The /etc/issue.net file is similar to /etc/issue, but it holds information that's displayed by the Telnet server just before it presents the login: prompt to the remote Telnet client. This file does *not* influence logins via the Secure Shell (SSH) server, though.

Message of the Day   The message of the day (MOTD) is a message that's stored in /etc/motd. This file, if it exists, typically holds information you want to communicate to users about upcoming events or changes, such as scheduled downtime for system upgrades or changes to system use policies. Because users see its contents only when they log in, it's not very useful for notifying users of events that will occur in a matter of minutes. Most text-mode login methods, including console logins, Telnet, and SSH, display the MOTD. GUI login methods typically don't display it, though.

Fortunes   Some system administrators like to spice up the login experience with a pithy saying. You can do this with the help of the fortune program. Add a call to this program to the /etc/bashrc file to give users a new saying each day. You should be sure to call fortune only within an if clause, though, as shown in Listing 1.3; a direct call will interfere with some programs, such as scp. Note that the fortune program doesn't ship with all distributions.

Listing 1.3: Code to call fortune from /etc/bashrc

```
if [ $TERM != "dumb" ]; then
    fortune
fi
```

WARNING   The database used by fortune includes sayings that some people may find offensive. Sayings that are most likely to be considered offensive aren't generated by default, though; they appear only if you use the -a or -o option to the program. You should be very cautious when using these options to fortune, lest you provoke the ire of (or even a lawsuit from) an employer, employee, client, or other viewer of the fortunes.

The /etc/issue and /etc/issue.net files support variables that you can use to substitute information that might vary from one login to another or from one system to another (thus enabling you to use one file on multiple systems). These include \n (the computer's hostname), \r (the kernel version number), \s (the OS name—Linux), \m (the platform, such as x86), and \t (the time when the message is printed).

> **WARNING**
> Be sure not to put too much information in system messages, particularly in /etc/issue and /etc/issue.net. Advertising too much about your system, such as its kernel version number and platform, can give information to attackers that they can abuse to gain entry to your system.

One problem with all of these communication methods is that they're all geared toward text-mode users. If your system supports local or remote X-based users, these methods won't help you communicate with them. The same is true for users of servers, such as Web servers or mail servers. Of course, you can always employ more generic communication techniques, such as email, instant messaging tools, bulletin boards, paper memos, and even word of mouth.

Sending Users Messages in Real Time

Two tools that enable you to send messages to users in real time, rather than when they log into the computer, are:

Shutdown Alerts   One particularly important type of user communication is the shutdown alert. You can pass a message to all text-mode users when you shut down the system via the shutdown command, as described previously in "Changing Runlevels with shutdown." Specifically, text after all other parameters is treated as a shutdown alert message. For instance, shutdown -h +10 "System going down for maintenance" displays the message System going down for maintenance to all users with increasing frequency until the system shuts down.

Writing to All Terminals   The Unix and Linux wall command writes a message to all active terminals—that is, to all text-mode logins. The wall command may be invoked by any user, but its exact usage differs from one distribution to others. Sometimes, you type the command name followed by a message, as in wall Network access going down at 5:00 to display that message on all users' terminals. Other versions of wall require you to place the message in a file and then pass it to the program or accept input from standard input rather than on the command line. To use this latter form, you'd type wall and then type the message followed by Ctrl+D; or you could put the message in a file and pass the filename to the program. Users can block wall messages by using the mesg command, as in mesg n to block messages or mesg y to re-enable messages.

As with login messages, these messages are normally displayed only to users of text-mode logins or shells. A GUI-only user who doesn't have a text-mode shell open won't see such messages.

Summary

When a computer is first turned on, it proceeds through a series of system-specific checks and then passes control to the boot loader, which in turn loads the OS's kernel. The most common boot loader on Linux systems is GRUB, which is controlled through the menu.lst, grub.conf, or grub.cfg file in the /boot/grub directory. You can edit the configuration file, or scripts that re-create it when other commands run, in order to set certain boot-time options, add a new kernel to the system, or make other boot-time changes. Once the kernel has taken control of the system, it runs the init program, which reads its configuration file and uses a series of scripts to launch login processes, servers, and other basic system services. Traditionally, Linux has used a SysV startup system, which uses symbolic links in runlevel-specific directories to control what services are started in each runlevel. Recently, though, the Upstart system has become popular. Upstart supplements (and can theoretically completely replace) the runlevel-specific directories with Upstart-specific startup scripts that contain within them information on what conditions trigger the launch or termination of specific services.

The programs launched by startup systems or users can be installed by package management tools or by compiling the software locally. Few rules concerning the latter apply with certainty; software can be written in a variety of languages and may be prepared and installed in a variety of ways. Typically, though, the software must be configured for your particular system and then installed. Both tasks are performed by special scripts or by a file called Makefile, which is used by the make program.

You should endeavor to keep users informed of changes in system software or of impending system shutdowns or other actions that may impact their ability to use the computer. Several tools, such as options to shutdown, /etc/issue, /etc/motd, and wall, can be used to help you communicate with users. Because many modern systems are used primarily via a GUI, though, you may need to employ other methods, such as email or a telephone, to alert users before making disruptive changes to the system.

Exam Essentials

Describe the boot process, in overview.   When a computer first powers up, it reads instructions from firmware, which initiates a series of self-checks and further actions to be taken. One of these actions is to load and execute code from the computer's hard disk or other storage hardware. This code, the *boot loader*, further directs the boot process by loading the OS's kernel, which runs regular OS programs (beginning with init, in the case of Linux). These programs bring up the OS's usual array of software, culminating in a login prompt or an otherwise functional system.

Explain how a user may provide boot-time parameters to Linux.   The Grand Unified Bootloader (GRUB) uses configuration files to control the initial stages of the boot process.

These files provide default options for the system; however, by selecting a GRUB menu option and then pressing the E key, a user may edit the default options on a one-time basis.

Summarize the differences between SysV and Upstart.   The traditional System V (SysV) startup script relies on a handful of *runlevels*, each of which includes a number of services that can be started by fixed startup scripts stored in specific directories. Upstart provides backward compatibility for SysV startup scripts, but Upstart-native startup scripts enable starting or stopping services based on a wider variety of conditions, which can be helpful in designing systems to use modern hot-plug hardware.

Describe how to change runlevels in Linux.   The default runlevel is set by the id line in the /etc/inittab file. (This file is often absent on Upstart-based systems, but Upstart honors this one /etc/inittab line, if it's present.) You can change runlevels temporarily by passing the runlevel number to telinit or init, as in **telinit 3** to change to runlevel 3.

Explain how to change what services run in a given runlevel on a SysV system.   Scripts (or, more commonly, links to scripts) in /etc/rc.d/rc?.d, /etc/init.d/rc?.d, /etc/rc?.d, or a similar location, where ? is a runlevel number, determine what services are started or stopped in any given runlevel. Scripts in these directories should be renamed to start with K to stop them in the runlevel or to start with S to start them. Tools such as update-rc.d and chkconfig can help simplify this task.

Provide an overview of the process of installing software from source code.   Source code programs must be downloaded (usually in the form of a tarball) and extracted. Most programs provide a configure script, although some require no configuration or must be configured in some other way. Typing **make** typically compiles the software, and typing **make config** as root installs it. There is enough variability that reading the program's documentation prior to configuring it is advisable.

Describe important directories for locally compiled software.   The /usr/src directory tree is the usual location for source code that has been or is being compiled and installed on the system, with each package having its own directory, such as /usr/src/samba-3.5.4 for Samba version 3.5.4. Working files and copies of the binaries may be held here, too, although such files are often removed to save space after the software is installed. The binaries are usually stored in the /usr/local directory; this directory holds functional subdirectories, such as /usr/local/bin for binaries and /usr/local/lib for libraries.

Summarize tools used to communicate with users.   The /etc/issue and /etc/issue .net files contain text that's shown to local and remote text-mode users, respectively, as part of the login prompt, while /etc/motd holds a message that's shown after a successful text-mode login. The shutdown command includes an option to pass a message to users explaining an impending system shutdown, and wall enables you to send similar messages even if the system isn't about to be shut down.

Review Questions

1. What is the first program the Linux kernel runs once the kernel itself is running, assuming a normal Linux startup procedure?

    A. `begin`

    B. `startx`

    C. `Startup`

    D. `init`

2. You have accidentally renamed your system's kernel file and rebooted the computer, with the result that GRUB won't start the computer. If you remember the name you used when renaming the kernel file, how can you start the computer in a simple way?

    A. Select the misbehaving kernel entry in GRUB, press the D key to have it detect your kernels, and select the correct one from the list.

    B. Select the misbehaving kernel entry in GRUB, press the E key, and edit the kernel's name.

    C. Hold down the Shift key while booting to enter the Recovery Console and select the correct kernel within that tool.

    D. You can't; this error is severe enough that the only corrective measure is to reinstall Linux.

3. How can you boot Linux directly into single-user mode?

    A. In GRUB, select the kernel image you want to boot, press E, and add 1 or `single` to the `kernel` or `linux` line.

    B. In GRUB, select the kernel image you want to boot, press the 1 key, and confirm your intentions by responding **yes** to the prompt.

    C. In GRUB, type **single** at the `boot:` prompt to boot the kernel while passing it the parameter `single`.

    D. In GRUB, type **boot-single-user; true; boot-now** to boot the default kernel in single-user mode.

4. In what file is the system's initial runlevel specified on a SysV system?

    A. `/etc/fstab`

    B. `/etc/init.d/runlevel`

    C. `/etc/inittab`

    D. `/etc/runlevel`

5. How can you enter GRUB's interactive recovery mode?

   A. Press the I key at the GRUB main menu.

   B. Press the R key at the GRUB main menu.

   C. Press the M key at the GRUB main menu.

   D. Press the C key at the GRUB main menu.

6. What file would you edit to add an unusual operating system to a GRUB 2 boot menu?

   A. `/boot/grub/custom`

   B. `/boot/grub/menu.1st`

   C. `/etc/grub.d/40_custom`

   D. `/boot/grub/grub.conf`

7. The following line is present in a Linux computer's `/etc/inittab` file. What can you say about it?

`id:3:initdefault:`

   A. The computer boots into runlevel 3.

   B. The computer starts in text mode (X isn't run).

   C. The computer shuts down as soon as it boots.

   D. The computer uses the Upstart startup system.

8. What might you find in the `/etc/init.d` directory?

   A. Upstart startup scripts

   B. SysV startup scripts

   C. User login scripts

   D. System login scripts

9. Where might you find runlevel-specific symbolic links to SysV startup scripts? (Choose all that apply.)

   A. `/etc/inittab`

   B. `/etc/init`

   C. `/etc/init.d/rc?.d`

   D. `/etc/rc?.d`

10. You want to check the configuration of a server called `waiter` on a Fedora system, to see in which runlevels it runs. What might you type to do this?

   A. `chkconfig --list waiter`

   B. `info waiter`

   C. `ps ax | grep waiter`

   D. `runlevel waiter`

11. Which of the following might you reasonably use as a default runlevel? (Choose all that apply.)

A. 0

B. 2

C. 3

D. 5

12. An administrator of a Debian system types the following command as `root`. What will be the effect, assuming that the appropriate software is installed?

`update-rc.d enable disable 23`

A. The `disable` service will be enabled in runlevels 2 and 3.

B. The `disable` service will be enabled except in runlevels 2 and 3.

C. The `enable` service will be disabled except in runlevels 2 and 3.

D. The `enable` service will be disabled in runlevels 2 and 3.

13. You've taken over administration of a Fedora Linux system that's been running for more than a year. You discover that the `dostuff` program was installed from source code and resides in `/usr/local/bin` and related directories. You want to uninstall this program and install a newer version from a precompiled binary package. Where is the best location for you to look for the original source code directory so you can use its uninstall feature?

A. The `/usr/portage/distfiles` directory

B. The `/var/lib/rpm` directory

C. A subdirectory of `/usr/src`, probably `/usr/src/dostuff` or a related name

D. The `/opt/dostuff` directory or a directory with a related name.

14. Once you've located the original source code directory for a program (`dostuff`) that was previously compiled and installed locally, what is a common and effective way to uninstall the software?

A. Type `rm -r /usr/local/bin` as root.

B. Type `rm -r /usr/src/dostuff`, where *dostuff* is the original source directory.

C. Type `rpm -e dostuff` as root in the original source directory.

D. Type `make uninstall` as root in the original source directory.

15. You want to compile and install a program from source code on a Debian system. You've located the program's home page, where several files are listed in the download section. Which of these files is *most* likely to be a source code tarball, based on its filename?

A. `theprogram-7.2.12.pkg`

B. `theprogram-7.2.12.zip`

C. `theprogram-7.2.12.tgz`

D. `theprogram-7.2.12.src.rpm`

16. Which of the following options describes the most common sequence for installing software from source code?

    A. Unpack tarball; type `make install`; type `./configure`; type `make clean` as root.

    B. Unpack tarball; type `./configure`; type `make`; type `make install` as root.

    C. Unpack tarball; type `make`; type `make cloneconfig`; type `make uninstall` as root.

    D. Unpack tarball; type `make`; type `make install`; type `make uninstall` as root.

17. You want to compile software from source code and install it in the /opt directory tree (an unusual location). The source code includes a configure script. How might you run this script to achieve this goal?

    A. `./configure --prefix=/opt`

    B. `./configure --install=/opt`

    C. `./configure --dir=/opt`

    D. `./configure --goto=/opt`

18. A source package's `Makefile` does not include an `install` target to make. You type `make` to create a binary file called `theprog`. How might you install the software, assuming you care only about installing this one program? (Choose all that apply.)

    A. `cp theprog /usr/local/bin`

    B. `rpm -i theprog`

    C. `install theprog /usr/local/bin`

    D. `make install theprog`

19. You want to deliver a message to would-be Telnet users that your system is for official use by employees of your company. What file would you edit to deliver this message before Telnet users see a `login:` prompt?

    A. `/etc/profile.net`

    B. `/etc/profile`

    C. `/etc/issue.net`

    D. `/etc/issue`

20. In reviewing files in /etc, you find that /etc/motd is completely empty. What does this mean?

    A. The system won't display a message of the day after users log in.

    B. Morton's Own Temporary Documentation is not installed on the system.

    C. The `motd.conf` file's name has become corrupted and its contents lost.

    D. Users will see no witty aphorisms appear on the screen after logging in.

Answers to Review Questions

1. D. By default, the kernel launches the `/sbin/init` program as its first process, as option D specifies. This program handles the rest of the system startup process, including launching SysV or Upstart startup scripts. Options A, `begin`, and C, Startup, are fictitious programs. Option B's `startx` is a user script that's used to start the X server after a text-mode login; it's not involved in the system startup process.

2. B. GRUB enables you to edit its entries on a one-time basis by selecting them and pressing the E key, as specified in option B. Options A and C both describe fictitious procedures. (Although Windows provides a tool called the Recovery Console, Linux does not.) Because option B is correct, option D cannot be—although of course reinstalling Linux *would* fix the problem but hardly in a simple way.

3. A. Option A describes one method of booting into single-user mode. (It's also possible to create a permanent GRUB entry for single-user mode that you can select more directly.) Options B, C, and D all describe fictitious actions that would have no effect. (Option C describes a `boot:` prompt, which is a feature of the older Linux Loader, LILO, not of GRUB.)

4. C. The `/etc/inittab` specifies the initial runlevel on its `id` line, as stated in option C. The `/etc/fstab` file of option A holds information on filesystems and their mount points. The `/etc/init.d/runlevel` and `/etc/runlevel` files of options B and D are both fictitious.

5. D. Pressing the C key enters GRUB's interactive mode, as option D specifies. The other options do not have this effect.

6. C. When a system uses GRUB 2, system administrators are encouraged to edit `/etc/grub.d/40_custom` to add custom GRUB configurations for locally compiled kernels or unusual OSs. After making such a change, you should type **update-grub** to update the GRUB runtime configuration file, `/boot/grub/grub.cfg`. Option A is a fictitious file. Options B and D are two names for the GRUB Legacy configuration file; editing them has no effect on GRUB 2.

7. A. The `id` line in `/etc/inittab` specifies the default runlevel, which in this example is 3, as specified in option A. Although runlevel 3 is a text-mode-only runlevel on Red Hat and related distributions, as option B specifies, this isn't true of all distributions; Debian, Ubuntu, Gentoo, and others control the startup of X in ways other than by the default runlevel. Thus, option B is not a correct answer. Option C describes the effect of setting the default runlevel to 0, not to 3, so it is incorrect. The `/etc/inittab` file is a standard part of the SysV startup system, and it's present on some Upstart-based systems. Thus, the presence of this file, or the presence of the specified line in this file, is not diagnostic of an Upstart-based system, and option D is incorrect.

8. B. The `/etc/init.d` directory holds SysV startup scripts on many Linux systems, as option B specifies. Upstart startup scripts reside in `/etc/init` or `/etc/event.d`, so option A is incorrect. User login scripts are stored in the users' home directories under various names, so option C is incorrect. System login names reside in `/etc` or subdirectories of it, usually under names related to the shell, but not in `/etc/init.d`, so option D is incorrect.

9. C, D. Options C and D both specify directories where runlevel-specific symbolic links to SysV startup scripts may reside (the *?* is a stand-in for a runlevel number), depending on the distribution in use. The /etc/inittab file is the configuration file for init in the SysV startup system, but it doesn't hold symbolic links, so option A is incorrect. The /etc/init directory holds Upstart scripts on Upstart-based systems, not SysV startup scripts or links to them, so option B is incorrect.

10. A. The chkconfig command displays information on or modifies the status of services started by SysV startup scripts. The --list option displays the status of a service by the specified name, so option A does as the question asks. The info command is a system documentation tool; option B displays the info page, if it's present, for the waiter command, which is not what the question asks. Option C displays process information on any processes called waiter or that include the string waiter in the command line. This won't reveal in what runlevels these processes run, so option C is incorrect. The runlevel command displays the current and previous runlevel, but it won't tell you in which runlevels a particular program runs, so option D is incorrect.

11. B, C, D. Runlevels 2, 3, and 5 are all reasonable default runlevels, because they all correspond to working multi-user modes. Debian and related distributions generally use runlevel 2 as a default, and runlevels 3 and 5 are generally used as defaults without and with X running, respectively, on Red Hat and related distributions. Runlevel 0 is not a reasonable default, since runlevel 0 corresponds to system shutdown; if you set it as the default, the system will shut down as soon as it boots. Thus, option A is not correct.

12. D. The update-rc.d utility affects the runlevels in which services run. It takes a service name, an action, and a runlevel or list of runlevels as arguments. Thus, enable is a service name, albeit a confusing one, and disable is a command to disable the service. This command is applied to runlevels 2 and 3. Option D describes this effect, and the remaining options do not.

13. C. Source code that's compiled locally is traditionally extracted to /usr/src, into a subdirectory named after the package to be installed. Thus, option C is correct, although there's no guarantee that the relevant directory will be found—it's possible the previous administrator deleted the files or used a non-standard location to compile them. Option A describes a temporary holding location for source tarballs on a Gentoo Linux system, but it's not a likely location for a source directory on a Fedora system, so this option is incorrect. The /var/lib/rpm directory is used by RPM to store its package database and related files, but it's not a likely location for an administrator to extract source code for local compilation, so option B is incorrect. Binaries that are distributed in tarball form are sometimes installed in /opt, but this isn't a standard location for source code, so option D is incorrect.

14. D. Many programs have an uninstall target to make, meaning that if you do as option D suggests, the software will be uninstalled. This action isn't guaranteed to work, but it is a common approach, as the question suggests. Option A is incorrect because it will delete any other unrelated binaries, it will miss any non-binary files (such as man pages), and it might not even uninstall the binary, if it was installed in a non-standard location. Option B will delete the source code directory, but unless the program was run directly from that location (an unusual configuration), it won't delete the installed binary program, so this option is incorrect. Option C is incorrect because it's a way to uninstall a package installed via the RPM Package Manager (RPM), not from a source tarball.

15. C. Tarballs are files archived with `tar` and, frequently, compressed with `gzip` or `bzip2`. They usually have filenames that end in `.tgz`, `.tar.gz`, `.tbz`, `.tbz2`, or `.tar.bz2`. Only option C describes such a file. Although the filename doesn't contain a hint that it contains source code, this is not uncommon for Unix and Linux source tarballs. Option A's `.pkg` filename extension identifies it as a probable Mac OS X binary package file, not a source tarball, so option A is incorrect. A `.zip` filename extension identifies a PkZip archive. Although such files are comparable to tarballs in features, they aren't technically tarballs. These files are more commonly used in the Windows world, so it's likely that option B contains a Windows binary. Even if it contains source code, its non-tarball nature means that this option is incorrect. Option D takes the form for a source RPM file. Although such files contain source code, they aren't source tarballs, as the question specifies, so option D is incorrect.

16. B. Option B provides a correct, if simplified, description of how to install many source code packages. Option A is likely to not build correctly, since the `make install` command precedes `./configure`. (It might work if the software includes no `configure` script, but most open source software uses such a script.) Option C will result in no software installation, since there is no call to `make install` or other software installation commands. Option D might install the software, but the `make uninstall` command will immediately uninstall it.

17. A. The `--prefix` option to a configure script usually sets the base of the installation directory tree. In this example, binary files will probably go in `/opt/bin`, libraries in `/opt/lib`, and so on. The `--install`, `--dir`, and `--goto` options are all fictitious.

18. A, C. Copying the compiled program with `cp`, as in option A, will install the software, thus satisfying the question; however, the ownership and permissions on the program file may not be optimal. The `install` program, used as in option C, changes ownership and permissions as the file is copied, so it is a superior answer to the question—but both A and C remain correct. The `rpm` command in option B will attempt to read `theprog` as an RPM file and install its contents; however, since `theprog` is a Linux binary program file, this won't work, and option B will fail. Option D won't work because the question specified that the `Makefile` does *not* include an `install` target, so typing **make install** (even with the additional parameter `theprog`) will not work.

19. C. The `/etc/issue.net` file contains text that's sent by the Telnet server to the remote Telnet client prior to Telnet's sending the `login:` prompt—precisely what the question requires. There is no standard `/etc/profile.net` configuration file, and `/etc/profile` is a configuration file for the `bash` shell, which won't help achieve the question's goals. The `/etc/issue` file is similar to `/etc/issue.net`, but it controls the message that's displayed on the local text-mode console.

20. A. The /etc/motd file holds the message of the day, which is displayed after users log in using text-mode tools such as text-mode consoles or SSH. An empty /etc/motd file simply means that no such message will appear, as option A describes. There is no such thing as Morton's Own Temporary Documentation, referred to in option B. There is no standard /etc/motd.conf file, as described in option C. Witty aphorisms are created by the fortune program, which is usually called in ways that don't involve /etc/motd. Although they might not be displayed, as option D suggests, there's no linkage between this and the empty /etc/motd file; fortunes are enabled or disabled in other ways.

Chapter

2

Linux Kernel Configuration

THE FOLLOWING LINUX PROFESSIONAL INSTITUTE OBJECTIVES ARE COVERED IN THIS CHAPTER:

- ✓ 201.1 Kernel Components (weight: 2)

- ✓ 201.2 Compiling a kernel (weight: 2)

- ✓ 201.3 Patching a kernel (weight: 1)

- ✓ 201.4 Customize, build, and install a custom kernel and kernel modules (weight: 2)

- ✓ 201.5 Manage/query kernel and kernel modules at runtime (weight: 3)

Modern operating systems are built up in layers, starting from the *kernel*—a piece of software that serves as a gatekeeper between the hardware and other software, that doles out memory and CPU time, that manages filesystems and network access, and that otherwise performs critical low-level tasks. On a Linux computer, the kernel is known as *Linux*—technically, that word applies *only* to the kernel. Everything else you might think of as being part of Linux, such as bash, the X Window System, or the Samba file server, is in fact not technically part of Linux. Most such tools, including all three just mentioned, are available on many other OSs, such as FreeBSD and Solaris.

Because the kernel handles low-level hardware and other critical tasks, its use and configuration are unusually important. This chapter covers these tasks, starting with obtaining and installing updated precompiled kernels. Linux's open source nature enables you to compile your own kernel from source code. This task is similar to compiling other programs' binaries, as described in Chapter 1, "System Startup and Advanced System Management"; however, the kernel is a complex enough piece of software, with enough options, that it deserves special consideration. This chapter concludes with a look at *kernel modules*—pieces of the kernel that can be loaded and unloaded on a running system. Many Linux hardware drivers take the form of kernel modules. Managing modules enables you to adjust how Linux treats your hardware and the availability of other kernel-level features, such as filesystems.

Understanding the Kernel

Most Linux systems work well with the default binary kernel provided by the distribution maintainer. Even when using such a kernel, though, you should understand certain kernel features, such as whether you're using a stable or development kernel, what drivers and other features a particular kernel provides, and what the kernel file is called.

Obtaining and Installing a Kernel

The home site for Linux kernels is the Linux Kernel Archives (http://www.kernel.org); however, if you're using a precompiled kernel provided with your distribution, chances are you obtained it with your distribution's installation medium or by downloading it from your distribution's package site using APT, YUM, or some other package maintenance tool.

Either way, Linux kernels have three or four dot-separated numbers, as in 2.6.35 or 2.6.35.4. In the past, kernels came in two forms: stable and unstable (or development). Stable kernels were intended to be usable for day-to-day work on production server and desktop systems, whereas unstable kernels contained experimental code to support new hardware or implement new features. Stable kernels had even second numbers (such as 2.4.*x*), whereas unstable kernels had odd second numbers (such as 2.5.*x*).

With the release of the 2.6.*x* series, the old stable/unstable distinction has become much blurrier. Some individuals and groups have created what they term "stable" kernel branches based on specific kernel versions, such as 2.6.16 and 2.6.27; however, in terms of mainstream development, numbering is no longer a clear guide to what is stable and what is not. The Linux Kernel Archives site provides a prominent link on the main page to enable users to download the latest stable kernel. If you want to run an unstable kernel, you'll need to dig through the links to the extended listing of all kernel files. In the current numbering system, changes to the third number represent kernels with major new features, while increments to the fourth number indicate bug fixes on this feature set.

Kernels provided by distribution maintainers often add another revision number to the main kernel number in order to track patches applied by the distribution maintainer rather than applied as part of the standard Linux kernel. How these additional revision numbers are applied varies from one distribution to another.

If you want to obtain the source for the kernel you're currently running, you can use the uname command, which returns information on the current kernel and architecture. Typing **uname -r** returns the current kernel number, and typing **uname -a** returns more information, including various details about your CPU, when the kernel was compiled, and so on.

The kernels supplied on the Linux Kernel Archives site come as source tarballs; you must compile them yourself, as described later in this chapter in "Preparing a Kernel" and "Compiling a Kernel." If you don't need to customize your kernel, you can probably use the kernel provided by your distribution maintainer. If you need to upgrade this kernel, the process is usually as simple as upgrading any other software package, using yum, apt-get, or some other package management tool. These installation tools often run scripts to update your boot loader configuration to use the new kernel; however, in some cases you may need to adjust your boot loader configuration, as described in "Adding a Kernel to GRUB." After upgrading a kernel, you must normally reboot your computer to use it.

If you manage a system that can't afford any downtime at all, you can upgrade your kernel without rebooting by employing a tool known as Ksplice (http://www.ksplice.com). This software freezes the execution of the programs that the kernel manages, swaps a new kernel into memory, and then resumes program operation. This process is transparent to the programs that are running.

Even if you don't want to compile your kernel from source code, you may want to have the kernel source code available for a couple of reasons. First, the source code includes a documentation directory, described shortly, that can help you discover hardware-specific options or deal with obscure kernel features. Second, some programs rely on header files contained in the kernel source tree to compile. Thus, you may need to have an installed kernel, or at least these critical header files, to compile some non-kernel software.

You can download and unpack the Linux kernel source code much as you would any other source code tarball, as described in Chapter 1. Download the linux-*version*.tar.gz or linux-*version*.tar.bz2 file, where *version* is the version number. The patch-*version*.gz and patch-*version*.bz2 files are patch files, which you can use to upgrade an immediately preceding version of the kernel to the latest version. The upcoming section "Applying Kernel Patches" describes how to patch a kernel.

Traditionally, the Linux kernel source code resides in /usr/src/linux-*version*, where *version* is the version number, such as 2.6.35.4. A few distributions place their kernels in the /usr/src/kernels/linux-*version* directory. A symbolic link from /usr/src/linux should point to the current kernel source directory. This way, you can have several source trees available, but when a source code file references something in /usr/src/linux, it will find what it needs. If you unpack the source tarball, this symbolic link won't be created automatically, so you should do so by typing:

```
# rm /usr/src/linux
# ln -s /usr/src/linux-version /usr/src/linux
```

WARNING   It's best to verify that /usr/src/linux is a symbolic link before doing anything with it. You can do this by typing **ls -ld /usr/src/linux**, which displays the current file as either a directory or a symbolic link, with an expansion of the symbolic link, if that's what it is, so that you can see to which directory it links. If you find that /usr/src/linux is a directory, you can rename it with mv rather than delete it with rm.

If you want to use kernel source that exactly matches that used by your distribution, you can install it using your package manager. Look for a package called linux-source, kernel-devel, or something similar. A package called linux-headers, kernel-headers, or something similar contains just the headers necessary to compile software.

Reading Kernel Documentation

Before upgrading a kernel, it's advisable to read the documentation for the new kernel. You can read /usr/src/linux/README for an overview of the kernel, including compilation instructions. Documentation on specific drivers and kernel subsystems is in the /usr/src/linux/Documentation directory tree. Unfortunately, the kernel is big enough that this directory tree is a bit cluttered. The 00-INDEX file contains an overview of what each file and subdirectory contains, so you may want to peruse this file before doing anything else.

Most of the kernel documentation is highly technical. Some of it is written for programmers and will be quite mysterious to non-programmers. Other kernel documentation, though, can be useful to system administrators. This type of documentation often specifies options that can be passed to kernel modules at load time or to the kernel itself when it boots.

Locating Kernel Binaries

Like many other programs, the kernel source code by itself is of limited use. Once it's compiled, the kernel yields quite a few files, the most important of which fall into two categories:

The Main Kernel File   This file holds the core parts of the kernel. It's loaded by the boot loader when the computer boots, and it is therefore very critical to the system's functioning.

Kernel Modules   Kernel modules reside outside the main kernel file, typically in the /lib/ modules directory tree. (Subdirectories in this directory correspond to different kernel versions.) Kernel modules can be loaded and unloaded after the system has booted, as described later in "Managing Kernel Modules at Runtime."

The main kernel file usually resides in /boot, but sometimes it's placed in the root directory (/). It can have any of several names, as detailed in Table 2.1. Sometimes the names in Table 2.1 are altered by adding on a kernel version, as in bzImage-2.6.35.4. This practice enables you to keep multiple kernel versions ready on a computer, which is useful if you're not sure whether a new kernel will work correctly—you can install the new kernel without destroying the old one, giving you a fallback in case of problems.

TABLE 2.1   Common kernel names

Name	Explanation
vmlinux	An uncompressed version of the Linux kernel file; usually generated as an intermediate step and not copied to /boot. This form of the kernel is not directly bootable, since it's missing a few features.
vmlinuz	A variant of vmlinux that's been compressed with any of several tools and rendered bootable by adding some features. Linux distribution providers typically use vmlinuz as the name for their precompiled binary kernels.
zImage	A largely obsolete format similar to the vmlinuz format. In the past, locally compiled kernels were traditionally given this name. As the kernel grew in size, though, zImage became inadequate on *x*86 systems, because zImage is limited in size to 512 KiB.
bzImage	A compressed version of the Linux kernel, similar to vmlinuz. It was created to overcome technical limitations of the zImage format. Locally compiled kernels are often given this name.
kernel	A generic name that's used on some systems that employ the GRUB 2 boot loader. It's typically a bzImage-style binary.

Preparing a Kernel

If you want to compile your own kernel, you must first engage in a couple of preparatory steps. The first of these, which is not always necessary, is to patch the kernel to add new features or upgrade its version. The second step, which is critical, is to configure the kernel for your hardware.

Applying Kernel Patches

Patching a kernel enables you to make changes to the kernel source you have. One reason to patch a kernel is to save on download time: You can obtain a patch-*version*.gz or patch-*version*.bz2 file from the Linux Kernel Archives site and apply it to a Linux source code directory you already have. Because patch files are much smaller than full kernel tarballs, this practice can save time and network bandwidth. You must, however, apply the correct patch file or files to the correct kernel version. Mainstream patches from the Linux Kernel Archives site are applied to the immediately preceding base kernel version. For instance, you could apply either the patch-2.6.35.4.bz2 or patch-2.6.36.bz2 patch file to a 2.6.35 kernel source tree (with three, not four, dot-separated version numbers).

Another reason to apply a patch is to use a third-party or experimental driver, bug fix, or feature. Such code may eventually find its way into the kernel, but if you need it now, patching a kernel may be the only way to go. When applying such a patch, be sure to read the author's documentation; it's possible that the procedure will vary slightly (or significantly!) from the one described here.

To apply a patch, you should change into the current Linux source directory and type one of the following two commands, depending on which file you downloaded:

```
# gzip -cd ../patch-version.gz | patch -p1
# bzip2 -dc ../patch-version.bz2 | patch -p1
```

Adjust the path to the patch file, if necessary. Instead of doing this work manually, you can use the patch-kernel script in /usr/src/linux/scripts:

```
# /usr/src/linux/scripts/patch-kernel linux
```

This command looks for patch files in the current directory and applies them to the kernel found in the directory you specify (linux in this example). Monitor the output of the command carefully; it should report that various files have been changed or added. If you see messages that certain files couldn't be changed, then something is wrong—perhaps you're trying to apply a patch against an inappropriate kernel version, or you might be using an incorrect option to the patch command.

If a patch operation doesn't succeed, you can undo it by including the -R (--reverse) option to patch, as in **patch -p1 -R** as part of the complete commands shown previously.

If you have a kernel with fixes (say, 2.6.35.4) and want to upgrade to patch the kernel to another version (say, 2.6.35.6 or 2.6.36), you can apply the patch for the version you have in reverse, using the –R option, and then apply the patch for the version you want without the –R option. The first step "downgrades" the kernel to the base version, and the second step patches the kernel to the version you want. If you want to upgrade by more than one version in the third position (say, 2.6.34 to 2.6.36), you will have to apply multiple patch files.

Assuming the patch process completes successfully, you should be able to proceed with configuring and building the kernel. If you've applied a third-party patch, be sure to pay attention to any configuration options related to that patch, as described in the patch's documentation.

As a practical matter, applying patches can be a modest time-saver; however, sloppy application of patches can cause problems. If you apply the wrong patch file, and especially if you don't properly fix this problem, you can end up with your kernel source code in a hopelessly inconsistent state. If you run into troubles, you can download the full kernel source tree and unpack it to start fresh.

Configuring the Kernel Source

Configuring the kernel can be a daunting task because of the vast number of kernel options available—2,994, as of version 2.6.35.4. If you're starting from your distribution's version of the kernel, though, chances are most of the options won't need to be changed; you should be able to home in on whatever options you want to change to achieve your goal in recompiling the kernel and leave the rest alone. If you're starting with a stock kernel, though, you'll have to be very careful, since there are many types of configuration options that, if set incorrectly, can lead to an unbootable kernel. You may need to know a great deal about your computer's hardware, and particularly its disk subsystem, to ensure the system can boot.

Investigating Your Hardware

Before you fire up the Linux kernel configuration utilities, you should learn something about the hardware on your system so that you'll know which hardware modules to install. You should also know what filesystems and other kernel-level features your system uses so that you can be sure to compile the necessary support into your new kernel.

If in doubt, compile a driver or feature as a module. Unnecessarily compiling a module adds a fraction of a second to several seconds to the kernel compile time and consumes some disk space but won't usually cause other problems. An unused kernel module consumes no memory or CPU time on a running system.

For the most part, the kernel includes drivers for hardware by the *chipset* it uses. The chipset is one or more chips that provide the functionality for the subsystem in question. The chipset is often manufactured by a company other than the one whose name appears on the product's box, which can make identifying your hardware difficult in some cases. Several approaches exist to solving this problem:

Using Hardware Manuals   Documentation for your hardware, or even advertising on its box, may identify the chipset it uses. Pay attention to both the manufacturer and model number; sometimes a manufacturer produces several products, each of which requires a different Linux driver. One problem with this approach is that the same device may go by several names or model numbers. If the manufacturer uses one name in a manual and another name is used in the kernel configuration, you might miss the importance of the device.

Checking PCI Devices   If you type `lspci` at a Linux shell prompt, you'll see a list of all the Peripheral Component Interconnect (PCI) and PCI Express (PCIe) devices on the computer. Most of the critical devices on a computer use the PCI or PCIe bus, so this can be a good way to identify what's on your computer.

Checking USB Devices   Typing `lsusb` reveals Universal Serial Bus (USB) devices connected to your computer. This command will work properly only if there's support for the USB hardware built into the motherboard or plugged into the motherboard.

Checking Loaded Modules   If you type `lsmod` at a Linux shell prompt, you'll see a list of the kernel modules that are currently loaded. Since most Linux distributions build as much hardware support as modules as is possible, this list is likely to be close to complete for your system; however, the module names (in the first column of output) can sometimes be cryptic. What is the r8169 driver, for instance? (It's a driver for a type of Ethernet card.) The driver names are referenced in the kernel configuration, but you need to know where to look for them. Also, if drivers are built directly into the kernel, they won't show up in the `lsmod` output, but they may be critical for normal system functioning.

Using a Working Kernel as a Model   If you have the kernel configuration file (`.config` in the kernel source directory) for a working kernel, you can use that file as a model. The next section, "Using Kernel make Targets," describes this approach in more detail.

Visual Inspection   You can sometimes tell what drivers you need by looking at the hardware. This usually requires opening the computer and examining the names and model numbers stamped on the large chips on the motherboard and any plug-in hardware. Unfortunately, such identifying information is sometimes obscured by stickers or heat sinks. Between this problem and the need to open the computer, this method of identifying hardware is usually one of last resort.

You should pay particular attention to the drivers for the hard disk controller, Ethernet adapter, USB controller, and video adapter used by your computer. Support for sound hardware, printers, and scanners is usually less critical, since the computer will boot and do its most important functions even if support for these devices is missing. Hard disks, optical drives, keyboards, mice, network hubs, and broadband modems seldom need special drivers, although there are exceptions to this rule.

Some devices, including video hardware, printers, and scanners, employ drivers outside of the kernel. In the case of video hardware, kernel drivers exist to enable changes to the size and style of text-mode fonts or for certain non-X graphical programs; however, the most important video drivers are used by the X server, not the kernel. Printers and scanners both require kernel drivers for the interface hardware (such as a USB or parallel port), but drivers for the specific model device reside outside the kernel—in Ghostscript and the Common Unix Printing System (CUPS) for printers or in the Scanner Access Now Easy (SANE) or other scanning software for scanners.

The computer's role can be important in deciding on what drivers to build. For instance, a desktop system is likely to require drivers for sound hardware, advanced video devices, and so on; but such drivers are likely to be unimportant for a server.

Using Kernel *make* Targets

Once you've identified your major hardware components, you can begin configuring the kernel. This is done with the help of one or more make targets, as detailed in Table 2.2. A few other obscure options are available; see the /usr/src/linux/README file for details. Additional make targets, described in later sections of this chapter, actually build the kernel and help you install it.

TABLE 2.2   Common Linux kernel configuration make targets

Target	Explanation
mrproper	Removes old configuration and temporary files.
oldconfig	Updates an old configuration file, updating only those items that are new.
silentoldconfig	Similar to oldconfig but reduces screen clutter.
defconfig	Creates a configuration file using default values for your platform.
allmodconfig	Creates a configuration file that uses modular configuration as much as possible.
config	Configures every item in the kernel using a text-based interface. Sluggish and impractical with modern kernels.
menuconfig	Configures the kernel using a text-based menu system. Adequate when using a text-based console.
xconfig	Similar to menuconfig, but configuration is done using a Qt-based GUI environment.
gconfig	Similar to xconfig but uses a GTK-based GUI environment.

Typing **make help** in the kernel source tree produces a list of **make** targets and brief descriptions of each one. This list includes much more than the configuration targets summarized in Table 2.2.

If you want to be sure that the kernel source tree is in a pristine state, you should begin by typing **make mrproper**. This action cleans out all the old temporary and configuration files. If you're building a new kernel and have the source code for a working one available, you can copy the hidden .config file (which holds the kernel configuration) from a working kernel's source directory to the current directory and then type **make oldconfig** or **make silentoldconfig**. The program will then prompt you about various new features, such as:

```
Prompt for development and/or incomplete code/drivers (EXPERIMENTAL) [Y/n/?] y
Cross-compiler tool prefix (CROSS_COMPILE) [] (NEW)
```

If you don't know how to respond to certain queries, using the default answer (which is capitalized in most cases) is usually the best approach. Most features accept yes (y) and no (n) answers to their configuration prompts. Many features can be built as modules; you type **m** to implement modular compilation. A few features, such as the cross-compiler one in the preceding example, require free-form responses. Pressing the Enter key specifies the default, which is usually acceptable.

If you have no working kernel source as a model, you might want to start by typing **make allmodconfig**. The result, if you were to build the kernel immediately thereafter, would be a kernel that compiles as many components as modules as possible. Given an appropriate initial RAM disk (described later, in "Preparing an Initial RAM Disk"), such a kernel will work on most computers; but it may not be optimal. It will also take longer to compile than an optimized kernel, since you'll be compiling modules for huge numbers of hardware devices you don't have on your computer.

Setting Kernel Configuration Options

At this point, you should probably optimize your configuration further by using the menuconfig, xconfig, or gconfig target. Figure 2.1 shows the display created by typing **make xconfig**. Kernel options are arranged in a hierarchical fashion. In Figure 2.1, the main categories are shown in the left panel, while the top-right panel displays sub-options for whatever main category you've selected. Confusingly, the highest-level categories have sub-categories that expand below them in the left panel, as well as sub-options that are accessible in the top-right panel. Explanatory notes on the options appear in the bottom-right panel. You can select options by clicking them. A check mark means that an option will be compiled directly into the kernel, while a dot means that the option will be compiled as a module. (The gconfig target doesn't support this feature; you must check for a Y, M, or N character to the right of the option selection area. The text-based menuconfig uses a similar convention.) Not all options can be compiled as modules; some just don't work that way, and some options control features that aren't meaningful as modules. Such features give Y or N options, but not M.

FIGURE 2.1   A general kernel configuration target, such as xconfig, enables you to view and adjust all your compile-time kernel options.

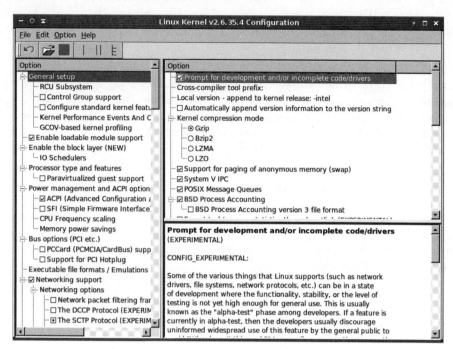

The kernel configuration options change fairly frequently with kernel development, and the huge number of options precludes describing them all. The major categories change relatively infrequently, though. As of the 2.6.35.4 kernel, they are:

General Setup   Miscellaneous and fairly high-level options appear in this category, including many that relate to how the system boots and what standards it supports.

Enable the Block Layer   This short category includes some obscure options related to disk devices and how the kernel manages input/output (I/O) scheduling. Select the default options unless you have specific reason to do otherwise.

Processor Type and Features   This section includes options that control how Linux manages the CPU, including several options that are CPU-specific. The Paravirtualized Guest Support subsection includes options that are important if you want to run certain types of virtualization software, which enables you to run another OS within your Linux system. (See also the Virtualization section, described shortly.)

Power Management and ACPI Options   Options in this area relate to hardware features designed to minimize power use, including support for suspend-to-RAM and suspend-to-disk (or hibernation) features that are particularly important on laptop computers.

Bus Options (PCI, etc.)   Over the course of Linux's history, several computer busses have been popular and then faded away. Old busses include the Industry Standard Architecture (ISA), the Extended ISA (EISA), the VESA Local Bus (VLB), Micro Channel Architecture (MCA), and NuBus. Depending on your platform, many of these obsolete busses may be available. You can trim your kernel size by removing them, if you're certain your hardware doesn't use them. This section also includes options related to PC Card (commonly used on laptops).

Executable File Formats/Emulations   Your kernel should almost certainly support the Executable and Linkable Format (ELF) file format for binaries. Support for the older a.out format is seldom necessary today unless you have some extremely old binary programs you need to run. Including support for miscellaneous binaries is usually a good idea. On $x86$-64 systems, including support for IA32 is usually wise.

Networking Support   This kernel configuration area is huge and includes a large number of options that can be confusing to the uninitiated. Note that low-level network hardware drivers do *not* reside in this area, but in the next one. You can usually greatly reduce compilation time and kernel (or at least module) size by perusing the options and removing unnecessary features. For instance, you're unlikely to need obscure networking stacks such as AppleTalk, DECnet, or IPX. On the other hand, if your local network uses one of these protocols, be sure it's installed!

Device Drivers   This configuration area is enormous. It includes options to support most of the hardware devices managed directly by the kernel, including hard disk controllers, network hardware drivers, multimedia devices (TV tuner cards and Webcams), video card framebuffer drivers, sound cards, and low-level USB devices. Many other options in this area relate to obscure or obsolete hardware. Follow the recommendations for specific devices or elect to compile the driver, at least as a module, if you're uncertain what to do.

File Systems   This category is extremely important, since it provides support for the filesystem used on your Linux boot device. Be sure to activate the appropriate filesystem, which is typically ext2fs, ext3fs, ext4fs, ReiserFS, XFS, JFS, or Btrfs on modern systems. CD-ROM, non-Linux, and other miscellaneous filesystems are listed in their own subcategories. The Partition Types subcategory is also important, since it controls what partitioning systems the kernel supports. On most systems, the PC BIOS (MS-DOS Partition Tables) Support option is most critical; this activates support for the Master Boot Record (MBR) system used on most $x86$ and $x86$-64 systems. The EFI GUID Partition Support option is important on Intel-based Macintoshes and is becoming important on other systems.

Kernel Hacking   You can set options that are mostly of interest to kernel developers in this section. Occasionally even a non-developer will need to adjust options in this area, particularly if you're using an older kernel patch. (The Enable __deprecated Logic option, for instance, is required by some third-party drivers.)

Security Options   A handful of security features can be controlled in this area.

Cryptographic API   Some kernel features and non-kernel software require cryptographic modules to be present in the kernel. You can enable or disable them here.

Virtualization   This category provides support for certain virtualization features, used to run another OS while Linux is running on the system.

Library Routines   This section includes a handful of features that are used by other kernel modules or by user-space programs. Stick with the default settings unless you know they should be changed.

A few kernel features are particularly important and therefore deserve special mention:

General Setup ➢ Local Version   You can add a string to the kernel version number using this option. This feature can be handy if you need to experiment with kernel options; you can build different kernels with different local version strings to signify different feature sets, thus keeping the kernels' module directories separated and producing different kernel identifiers when using uname or similar utilities.

General Setup ➢ Initial RAM Filesystem and RAM Disk (initramfs/initrd) Support   Be sure to activate this support if you intend to use an initial RAM disk (described shortly, in "Preparing an Initial RAM Disk").

General Setup ➢ Enable Loadable Module Support   Be sure this option is enabled, unless you intend to build a kernel with nothing but built-in drivers—a strange configuration with serious drawbacks on typical desktop or server configurations today.

Processor Type and Features ➢ Symmetric Multi-Processing Support   This option enables support for more than one CPU or CPU core. Most modern computers have two or more cores, so activating this support makes sense unless you're certain that your CPU has just one core.

Processor Type and Features ➢ Processor Family   If you're building a kernel for a specific computer, or for a set of identical computers, you can eke out a bit of extra performance by setting the correct CPU model in this option.

Processor Type and Features ➢ High Memory Support   This option is available for $x86$ CPUs, but not for $x86$-64 CPUs. You can use it to optimize performance based on how much RAM your computer has. If you have less than 1 GiB of RAM, select Off; if you have between 1 GiB and 4 GiB of RAM, select 4GB; and if you have more than 4 GiB of RAM, select 64GB. An incorrect selection can result in an inability to use all your system's memory.

Most modern computers have 64-bit $x86$-64 CPUs. On such computers, it's best to run a 64-bit version of Linux, particularly if the computer has more than 4 GiB of RAM. Although Linux can support up to 64 GiB of RAM on a 32-bit $x86$ CPU, this configuration imposes extra work on the kernel and creates some subtle limitations for applications. A 64-bit CPU, by contrast, directly supports much more memory, which is why the High Memory Support option isn't present when compiling a 64-bit kernel—it's needed only as a workaround for older 32-bit CPUs.

Networking Support ➢ Networking Options ➢ TCP/IP Networking   Almost all modern computers need this option, since the Transmission Control Protocol/Internet Protocol

(TCP/IP) is the basis of the Internet. This option contains a large number of suboptions. Peruse them and follow the suggestions or your judgment based on your knowledge of your local network and the computer's role in it. Note in particular the IPv6 Protocol suboption, which controls support for the next-generation version of TCP/IP, which is becoming a necessity in some areas.

Networking Support ➢ Networking Options ➢ Network Packet Filtering Framework   This option is critical if you want to configure a router or enable firewall rules on your computer.

Networking Support ➢ Networking Options ➢ Wireless   Be sure to enable this option if your computer uses a wireless network adapter.

Device Drivers ➢ SCSI Device Support   The Small Computer Systems Interface (SCSI) standard is a high-end disk interface. (It's also used by some scanners, printers, and other devices.) Although it's rare in modern computers, Linux uses a SCSI emulation layer for many devices, including drivers for the more common Serial Advanced Technology Attachment (SATA) disk interface and USB storage devices. Therefore, you must enable SCSI support, including support for SCSI disks and, usually, SCSI CD-ROMs, on most systems. If your system lacks true SCSI devices, though, you can usually uncheck the SCSI Low-Level Drivers section, omitting the large number of SCSI drivers from your build.

Device Drivers ➢ Serial ATA and Parallel ATA Drivers   This section includes drivers for most modern and many older SATA and PATA disk controllers. Enable the overall section and peruse it until you find your disk controller. Note that many controller chipsets include both SATA and PATA support, but these are often listed separately in this driver section. Thus, you may need to enable both SATA and PATA drivers. If you're building a kernel for a specific computer with a known chipset, I recommend building these drivers directly into the kernel, rather than as modules.

Device Drivers ➢ Multiple Devices Driver Support   This section includes options for Redundant Array of Independent Disks (RAID) and Logical Volume Manager (LVM) configurations, which are advanced disk management tools described in Chapter 4, "Advanced Disk Management."

Device Drivers ➢ Graphics Support   On most *x*86 and *x*86-64 systems, the features in this section are optional; however, enabling framebuffer support for your video chipset and framebuffer console support will provide you with advanced options for adjusting text-mode consoles. On some other platforms, you *must* include framebuffer support to get a text-mode console, and sometimes even for X.

Proprietary X Window System video drivers from AMD and nVidia include kernel modules that are compiled separately from the kernel. The standard kernel framebuffer drivers are incompatible with at least some proprietary X drivers, so be cautious about compiling the framebuffer drivers directly into the kernel if you intend to use the proprietary drivers. (Compiling the framebuffer drivers as modules should be safe, though.) You should consult the proprietary driver's documentation for details.

Device Drivers ➤ USB Support   This area includes both drivers for low-level USB hardware (typically built into the motherboard or on a plug-in card) and for a few USB devices or device categories, such as USB Mass Storage Support, which is used to interface with USB flash drives and other plug-in media. Many USB devices require support in other areas of the kernel, too.

Once you've checked all the kernel options you care to examine, you can exit from the configuration tool. It will save a new `.config` file, which will then guide `make` in determining what kernel features to compile.

Compiling a Kernel

With configuration out of the way, you can compile your kernel and prepare the system to use it. The build process is fairly straightforward, but you must then copy the kernel file to /boot, install kernel modules, prepare an initial RAM disk, and modify your GRUB configuration to point to the new kernel. You may also want to prepare a package file in some situations.

Building a Kernel

To build a kernel, type **make** in the kernel's source directory. Assuming you have the necessary development tools installed and that your kernel configuration contains no glaring errors, the build process will proceed smoothly. This process requires no additional input from you, but it will take a while—several minutes to more than an hour, depending on the speed of the computer and how many kernel features you're compiling. As the process proceeds, you'll see summary lines displayed on the screen:

```
CC      kernel/time/tick-sched.o
LD      kernel/time/built-in.o
CC      kernel/futex.o
```

These lines summarize what's being done in the process. For the most part, you need only be concerned that the compilation is proceeding. If the output ceases, something may be wrong—or perhaps the file being compiled is unusually large.

 NOTE   The default make target for the Linux kernel builds both the main kernel file and all the separate kernel modules. This is equivalent to typing **make all**. You can build the kernel and modules separately by typing **make bzImage** to build the kernel or **make modules** to build the modules. On some platforms, you can type **make zImage** instead of **make bzImage**.

On rare occasions, compilation will fail and you'll see an error message. This can happen because you're using a newer or older compiler than the Linux kernel developers expect or because of a glitch in the configuration. There are no certain rules for how to proceed, but you can try several approaches to fix the problem:

- If the error occurred when compiling a feature that's not absolutely necessary for your system, you can go back into the configuration tool and remove it.
- If the feature is required, you might get better results changing it from being built as a module to being built into the kernel, or vice versa.
- Sometimes you'll need to track down a feature upon which the failed one depends; normally the developers correctly flag such dependencies, but on occasion something gets overlooked.
- If you've patched the kernel, review your patching procedure. Be sure you applied the patch to the correct kernel version, and double-check that the patch was applied successfully. You might try compiling an unpatched version of the kernel for comparison.
- If you have more than one version of the GNU Compiler Collection (GCC) installed, try using a different version to compile the kernel.
- Try compiling a different version of the kernel. Even if you need a specific version, you might find a clue to the source of the problem when you compile another kernel.

 You can pipe make's output through grep to search for the string error, as in **make | grep -iw "error"**, to reduce the clutter of make's output and view only error messages.

A successful kernel compilation terminates with no error messages. If you typed **make bzImage**, you should see a message similar to the following:

```
Kernel: arch/x86/boot/bzImage is ready  (#1)
```

If you typed **make** to build both the main kernel file and all modules, that message will be buried quite a way up in the output, and the final lines will likely be simple status messages relating to the compilation of the last few kernel modules.

Installing a Kernel Binary

With the kernel compiled, you can install it. In other words, you can copy it from its location in the kernel source tree to the /boot directory. On most platforms, the compiled and ready-to-use kernel binary is called bzImage, but it could have another name on some platforms. (Consult Table 2.1 for details.) If you're compiling a kernel for an *x86* or *x86-64* system, it will be in the arch/x86/boot subdirectory of the kernel source tree, as specified near the end of the compilation messages. On other platforms, the location should be similar, although the x86 portion will reflect your CPU architecture.

Some distributions and administrators maintain a separate /boot partition and keep it unmounted most of the time in order to prevent accidental damage to critical boot files. If this is true of your system, be sure to mount the /boot partition before you copy your new kernel there. If you don't, the kernel won't reside where it should and your system won't boot correctly.

You can copy the bzImage file to /boot just as you would any other file, although you must normally be root to do the job. You may want to rename the file, adding its version number so as to enable multiple kernels to coexist:

```
# cp arch/x86/boot/bzImage /boot/bzImage-2.6.35.4
```

Remember the filename you give to the kernel file, since you'll need it later, when you add the kernel to your GRUB configuration.

In addition to the kernel file, you may want to copy the System.map file. This file contains pointers to functions in the kernel and is used for debugging kernel problems. Thus, copying it isn't critical, but it can be helpful. Once the system is running, /boot/System.map should be a symbolic link to the current System.map file. Thus, completely copying and setting up this file takes three commands:

```
# cp System.map /boot/System.map-2.6.35.4
# rm /boot/System.map
# ln -s /boot/System.map-2.6.35.4 /boot/System.map
```

You can put off these commands until after you've booted into your new kernel, if you like.

Typing **make install** serves as a shortcut for copying the kernel file, copying the System .map file, and often creating an initial RAM disk and modifying the GRUB configuration for the new kernel. The details vary from one distribution to another, though, since the install target relies on the installkernel script, which many distribution providers customize. This option can be a useful way to minimize kernel preparation effort; however, if you need to customize your installation or if you're not sure what your distribution's scripts do, you may prefer to perform the individual tasks manually instead.

Installing Kernel Modules

Installing kernel modules is easy: As root, type **make modules_install**. The make utility will create a subdirectory in /lib/modules named after the kernel version number, such as /lib/modules/2.6.35.4, and then copy the kernel modules into this subdirectory, creating additional levels of subdirectories for certain sets of modules.

If you forget to install the kernel modules, the computer might not boot into the new kernel. If the computer does boot, any hardware or other feature managed by a modular driver won't work.

In operation, Linux requires information on the dependencies between kernel modules. These dependencies are stored in a file called modules.dep, which is stored in the kernel modules directory. You can regenerate this file for the currently running kernel by typing **depmod** as root. As part of the module installation process, depmod is called to generate a modules.dep file for the new kernel modules.

> Objective 201.4 refers to a depmod target to make. Such a target does not exist, as of the 2.6.35.4 kernel; however, as just noted, the modules_install target does call the depmod utility.

Preparing an Initial RAM Disk

An initial RAM disk (aka an initial RAM filesystem) is a collection of critical kernel modules and a handful of system utilities that the boot loader reads from disk and passes to the kernel at boot time. The kernel accesses them in memory as if they were on disk, loading modules and running scripts and programs from the RAM disk in order to mount the root filesystem. Thereafter, additional tools can be accessed from the hard disk using the drivers that are built into the kernel or that the kernel loaded from the RAM disk.

When Should You Prepare an Initial RAM Disk?

If your kernel includes all the drivers it needs to boot within the main kernel file, an initial RAM disk isn't usually necessary; however, it's easy to overlook a critical module. If your system uses an advanced disk management system, such as a software RAID or LVM configuration, or a storage area network (SAN), an initial RAM disk may also be required to fully activate these subsystems.

> Support for an initial RAM disk must be built into the kernel, as described earlier in "Setting Kernel Configuration Options." You can specify a cpio archive to use as an initial RAM disk when you build the kernel, but it's more common to pass the filename to the kernel via a GRUB menu entry, as described later in "Adding a Kernel to GRUB."

Unfortunately, the tools and procedures needed to build an initial RAM disk vary from one distribution to another, so there is no one procedure that works on all systems. Two tools are common, though: mkinitrd and mkinitramfs. Some distributions ship with still other tools, some of which are built atop these. For instance, Gentoo Linux provides a tool called genkernel, which can help automate various kernel generation steps. Typing **genkernel initramfs** builds an initial RAM disk for the current kernel (that is, the one to which /usr/src/linux points).

Using *mkinitrd*

The mkinitrd program is common on Red Hat, Fedora, and related distributions. To use it, you must pass it an initial RAM disk image name and a kernel version number, as in:

```
# mkinitrd /boot/initrd-2.6.35.4.img 2.6.35.4
```

This command creates the `/boot/initrd-2.6.35.4.img` file using kernel modules for the 2.6.35.4 kernel. The `mkinitrd` utility supports a number of options, which are summarized in Table 2.3.

TABLE 2.3 Options to `mkinitrd`

Option	Explanation
`--version`	Displays the `mkinitrd` version number.
`-v`	Displays verbose information on actions as they're being performed.
`--preload=module`	Loads the module before the SCSI modules on system boot. This option may be repeated for as many modules as desired.
`--with=module`	Loads the module after the SCSI modules on system boot. This option may be repeated for as many modules as desired.
`--builtin=module`	Causes `mkinitrd` to behave as if the specified module were built into the kernel, even if it isn't.
`-f`	Enables overwriting an existing image file. Ordinarily, `mkinitrd` aborts its operation if an image file of the specified name exists.
`--fstab=filename`	Probes `filename` to determine what filesystem support is necessary. If this option is omitted, `/etc/fstab` is used.
`--image-version`	Appends the kernel version number to the `initrd` image path before the image is created.
`--nocompress`	Causes the image file to be uncompressed. (Normally, it's compressed with `gzip`.)
`--nopivot`	Causes the image to *not* use the `pivot_root` system call in the initial RAM disk. This enables the system to work with old 2.2.*x* kernels, but some filesystems (such as ext3fs) won't work. This option is scheduled to be removed in the future.
`--omit-lvm-modules`	Omits LVM modules from the image, even if `/etc/fstab` makes them seem necessary.
`--omit-raid-modules`	Omits RAID modules from the image, even if `/etc/fstab` makes them seem necessary.
`--omit-scsi-modules`	Omits SCSI modules from the image.

Using *mkinitramfs*

If your system doesn't include mkinitrd, it may rely on the similar mkinitramfs. It works in a similar way, except that you must use -o to specify the output filename for the RAM disk file:

```
# mkinitramfs -o /boot/initramfs-2.6.35.4.img 2.6.35.4
```

As with mkinitrd, various options are available that can modify the program's actions. These are summarized in Table 2.4.

TABLE 2.4 Options to mkinitramfs

Option	Explanation
-d *confdir*	Sets the configuration file directory for the program. The default is /etc/initramfs-tools.
-k	Causes the program to retain the temporary directory used to create the image. (This directory is normally deleted after image creation.)
-o *outfile*	Sets the output image filename.
-r *root*	Sets the Linux system's root partition. This is normally passed by the boot loader.
-v	Creates verbose output of actions as mkinitrd performs them.
--supported-host-version=*version*	Queries if the program can create a RAM disk image for a running kernel of the specified *version*.
--supported-target-version=*version*	Queries if the program can create a RAM disk image for a kernel of the specified *version*.
version	Sets the kernel version number; 2.6.35.4 in the preceding example. If this option is omitted, the currently running kernel version is used.

Preparing a Kernel Package

If you maintain many Linux systems, you might want to prepare a kernel once for all of them. To simplify maintenance, you may then want to package your kernel into an RPM Package Manager (RPM) or Debian package. These tasks can be accomplished with the rpm-pkg, binrpm-pkg, and deb-pkg targets to make in the Linux kernel source directory. These targets create a source and binary RPM, a binary RPM only, and a Debian binary package, respectively. These targets require that the computer have the appropriate package tools installed, of course. The packages built in this way will be available in your usual RPM build directory for the RPM build targets or in the /usr/src directory for the Debian target.

You can copy the binary package to any computer with a compatible architecture and hardware and install it just as you'd install a binary kernel package provided by the distribution maintainer. You should be sure, however, that the kernel includes *all* the necessary drivers and features used by *all* of the computers on which you intend to install it. If you're maintaining many identical computers, this task isn't too hard; you can test the kernel on one system and then, if it works, package it up for the others. The task of ensuring compatibility is harder if you're maintaining computers with different motherboards, video cards, network interfaces, and other features. In this case, it's entirely possible that the kernel will work fine on one computer but fail completely on another.

On an RPM-based system, install a new kernel with the -i option to rpm, rather than -U. Using -i installs the new kernel without replacing the old one. If you use -U, the old kernel will be removed, which can result in an unbootable system if the new kernel lacks a key driver.

Adding a Kernel to GRUB

With your new kernel built and all its files in place, it's time to add your new kernel to your boot loader configuration. Chapter 1 describes both the GRUB Legacy and GRUB 2 boot loader configuration process, so you should consult if for details of what the various boot options mean.

If you installed a kernel in binary form from a distribution's package manager, chances are you won't need to explicitly edit your boot loader configuration. Binary installations of this type typically update your GRUB configuration automatically. If you built your kernel yourself, though, you will almost certainly have to edit your boot loader configuration to include the new kernel.

Adding a Kernel to GRUB Legacy

As a general rule, the easiest way to add a new kernel to a GRUB Legacy configuration is to copy an existing entry and then modify it for your new kernel. A typical configuration looks something like this:

```
title Fedora (2.6.32)
    root (hd0,0)
    kernel /vmlinuz-2.6.32 ro root=/dev/sda5
    initrd /initrd-2.6.32
```

To add a new kernel, you should first copy this entry and then modify it. Pay particular attention to three details:

■ Change the `title` line so that you can uniquely identify your new kernel.

■ Change the kernel filename listed on the `kernel` line to match your new kernel. Remember that the kernel filename is specified relative to the *partition*'s root, not the Linux filesystem's root. In this example, the kernel is probably located on a separate `/boot` partition.

■ If the new kernel uses an initial RAM disk, adjust the `initrd` line to point to the new file, or add an `initrd` line if it isn't present in the original entry. If the new kernel does not use an initial RAM disk, be sure to remove any `initrd` line that's present in the model entry.

The GRUB entries provided by distribution maintainers often include additional options on the `kernel` line or other features. In most cases, it's best to keep those additional features in place in your copy of the entry. Sometimes removing an option you don't understand won't do any real harm; however, sometimes it's critical to making the system boot.

You can research options passed to the kernel on the `kernel` line using the Linux kernel documentation, as described previously in "Reading Kernel Documentation."

As described in Chapter 1, GRUB Legacy uses a `default` line to specify which kernel to boot by default. When you add your new kernel, you can place it before or after your existing kernel configuration, as you see fit. You may then want to modify the `default` line to point to the new kernel; however, if you do this and the new kernel doesn't work properly, you'll have to manually select another kernel when you reboot to fix the problem.

Do not replace your most recent working kernel entry when you first create your new kernel entry! If the new kernel doesn't work and there are no other options, your system will be difficult to recover. If you want to keep your boot options uncluttered, you can remove old kernel entries from the configuration, but you should wait until after you've tested your new kernel before doing so.

Adding a Kernel to GRUB 2

Before you proceed with any GRUB 2 reconfiguration, I recommend backing up `/boot/grub/grub.cfg`. If you encounter serious problems booting your new system, you can use an emergency boot disc to restore the old but working file over the new but broken one.

In some cases, adding a kernel to GRUB 2 is easier than adding one to GRUB Legacy. This is because GRUB 2 includes system probe scripts, such as update-grub or grub-mkconfig, to scan the computer for Linux kernels and non-Linux OSs and to update the actual boot-time GRUB configuration file (/boot/grub/grub.cfg). Thus, after you create and install a new kernel, you should type **update-grub** as root. (If grub-mkconfig is present, you can try it if update-grub doesn't work.) Check the output of this script, or the /boot/grub/grub.cfg file, for references to your new kernel. If they're present, chances are these entries will work, so you can reboot and try the new system.

If the automatic scripts don't detect your kernel, sometimes you can overcome the problem by renaming the kernel in a way that the script will understand. Sometimes the scripts look only for kernels with names that begin with vmlinuz or kernel, so you can try renaming your kernel to match that pattern and try again. If that doesn't work or if you prefer to create a custom GRUB 2 configuration by hand, you can edit the /etc/grub.d/ 40_custom file and create an entry for your new kernel, as described in Chapter 1. An example entry looks like this:

```
menuentry "Fedora (2.6.35.4)" {
    set root=(hd0,1)
    linux /vmlinuz-2.6.35.4 ro root=/dev/sda5
    initrd /initrd-2.6.35.4
}
```

If your existing /etc/grub.d/40_custom file already contains such an entry, use it as a model; copy it and modify the menuentry name, the kernel filename on the linux line, and the initial RAM disk filename on the initrd line—the same three critical details you must modify when adapting a GRUB Legacy entry (although GRUB 2 changes two of the keywords used to identify these items).

If your system lacks a /etc/grub.d/40_custom file or if it contains no entries, you can use the preceding example as a bare-bones model, or you can peruse /etc/grub/grub.cfg for models. The latter is likely to provide more complex models with additional options, which may or may not work better than the simple example shown here. If in doubt, you can create two or more entries and try each one, then delete any non-functional or unnecessary entries once you've determined what works best.

To change the default kernel, you must edit the /etc/default/grub file and change the GRUB_DEFAULT entry:

```
GRUB_DEFAULT=0
```

Unfortunately, the number of the default entry can be difficult to determine until you've generated a /boot/grub/grub.cfg file by typing **update-grub** or **grub-mkconfig**. Thus, you may need to type this command, then count the entries in the final file to determine which one you want to use as a default, then modify /etc/default/grub, and finally type

update-grub or **grub-mkconfig** again. Alternatively, you can locate the default entry in /boot/grub/grub.cfg and modify it directly:

```
set default="0"
```

This change will not, however, be retained when you (or some automated script) rebuild the /boot/grub/grub.cfg file.

Managing Kernel Modules at Runtime

Early Linux kernels consisted of a single file, which was loaded into memory by the boot loader. Although modern kernels still use this primary kernel file, Linux has supported kernel modules for several years. Placing most drivers in modules helps keep the size of the main kernel file down, enables the use of a single "generic" kernel on many computers without bloating the kernel's size too much, and gives users control over when and how drivers are loaded. This approach does require learning something about how modules are controlled, though. To begin, you must know how to obtain information on your kernel version and the modules that are currently loaded. Loading modules is also important for their use, and this task can be accomplished both by configuring boot files for modules you want to be used frequently and by using one-off commands. Similarly, unloading kernel modules can be important in some cases. Finally, some tools can help you maintain your kernel modules, such as changing default options and updating system information about available modules.

Obtaining Information About the Kernel and Its Modules

Before tweaking your kernel modules, you should know something about the kernel and the already installed modules. This information can be helpful because it can inform your decision of whether loading a new module is necessary, what modules are being used by other modules, and so on.

Learning About the Kernel

You can obtain the most important information about the kernel via the uname command:

```
$ uname -a
Linux nessus 2.6.35.4 #3 SMP PREEMPT Sun Sep 26 23:32:11 EDT 2010 x86_64
AMD Athlon(tm) 64 X2 Dual Core Processor 5400+ AuthenticAMD GNU/Linux
```

This program provides several types of information, and you can tell it what information to provide with various options, as summarized in Table 2.5.

TABLE 2.5   Options to uname

Short option name	Long option name	Explanation
-a	--all	Provides all available information. This is usually a safe option to use, although if you know precisely what information you need, you can create a less cluttered display by using a more specific option or set of options.
-s	--kernel-name	Produces the name of the kernel, which is normally Linux.
-n	--nodename	Displays the network node's hostname (nessus in the preceding example). This name is the one that's locally configured; depending on network Domain Name System (DNS) server configurations and client options, the computer might or might not actually be reachable by this name.
-r	--kernel-release	Displays the kernel release number (2.6.35.4 in the preceding example). This information is often very important because it can influence what driver modules may be used with the kernel.
-v	--kernel-version	Displays additional kernel version information. This information does *not* include the kernel version number, though, as displayed by the -r option. It does include the kernel build date and time (#3 SMP PREEMPT Sun Sep 26 23:32:11 EDT 2010 in the preceding example).
-m	--machine	Displays a code for the CPU—x86_64 in the preceding example, referring to an *x86-64* (aka AMD64 or EM64T) CPU.
-p	--processor	Displays a description of the CPU, as in AMD Athlon(tm) 64 X2 Dual Core Processor 5400+ in the preceding example. This information is often quite helpful if you need to know what specific CPU hardware you're using.
-i	--hardware-platform	Displays an identification string provided by the CPU—AuthenticAMD in the preceding example.
-o	--operating-system	Displays the name of the OS (GNU/Linux in the preceding example). This is distinct from the kernel name (the -k option) because it refers to the OS as a whole, not just the kernel.
N/A	--help	Displays a summary of the program's options.
N/A	--version	Displays the uname version number.

Some of these options may seem odd. After all, you probably know perfectly well that you're running Linux, so why use a -k or -o option? The uname tool is available on non-Linux Unix-like OSs, though, and so it's a handy way for cross-platform scripts to learn something about the OS on which they're running. The scripts can then adjust themselves to work correctly on Linux, FreeBSD, Solaris, Mac OS X, or other environments. If you write such a script, be aware that some OSs support only the long forms of the options (say, --operating-system rather than -o), so you should use the long form in scripts that might run on non-Linux systems.

For your own use, the kernel release information is likely to be the most important. Some third-party kernel modules come in precompiled forms that work only with certain kernels, so if your kernel version doesn't match, you may need to rebuild the right version, as described earlier in "Compiling a Kernel." The architecture and CPU data can also be important if you don't already know this information. Some programs work only with certain CPUs, and if you need to evaluate the speed of a system you've not used before, this can provide you with some important basic data. Precompiled kernel modules also typically work only with one type of CPU. For instance, you couldn't load a binary module for an *x86* CPU on an *x86-64* kernel such as the one that produced the preceding example output.

 Real World Scenario

Kernel Information and Control

The /proc directory houses a variety of files that provide information on, and enable control of, many different Linux subsystems. This directory isn't an ordinary disk directory; it's a *virtual filesystem*, meaning that it's generated on the fly as a means of interfacing with programs and users. (The /dev and /sys directories are two other examples of virtual filesystems in Linux.)

Of particular interest to the kernel is the /proc/sys/kernel subdirectory, which contains a large number of files that enable you to view and adjust kernel settings. As a practical matter, you're unlikely to need to use this directory very often, since command-line tools provide a more convenient interface. For instance, uname provides access to various files in this directory, such as /proc/sys/kernel/ostype (uname -s) and /proc/sys/kernel/version (uname -v).

Learning About the Kernel Modules

You can learn about the modules that are currently loaded on your system by using lsmod, which takes no options and produces output like this:

```
$ lsmod
Module                 Size  Used by
usblp                  9283  0
e100                  26134  0
r8169                 31795  0
bridge                40462  0
snd_hda_intel         17848  2
sr_mod                10922  0
cdrom                 28375  1 sr_mod
dm_mirror             10907  0
dm_region_hash         6280  1 dm_mirror
dm_log                 7344  2 dm_mirror,dm_region_hash
```

 This output has been edited for brevity. Although outputs this short are possible with certain configurations, they're rare.

The most important column in this output is the first one, labeled Module; this column specifies the names of all the modules that are currently loaded. You can learn more about these modules with modinfo, as described shortly, but sometimes their purpose is fairly obvious. For instance, the cdrom module provides access to the CD-ROM (or other optical disc) drive.

The Used by column of the lsmod output describes what's using the module. All the entries have a number, which indicates the number of other modules or processes that are using the module. For instance, in the preceding example, the usblp module (used to access USB printers) is not currently in use, as revealed by its 0 value, but the snd_hda_intel module (used to access sound hardware) is being used, as shown by its value of 2. If one of the modules is being used by another module, the using module's name appears in the Used by column. For instance, the sr_mod module relies on the cdrom module, so the latter module's Used by column includes the sr_mod module name. This information can be useful when managing modules. For instance, if your system produced the preceding output, you couldn't directly remove the cdrom module because it's being used by the sr_mod module, but you could remove the sr_mod module, and after doing so you could remove the cdrom module. (Both modules would need to be added back to read optical discs, though.)

 The lsmod command only displays information on kernel modules, not on drivers that are compiled directly into the Linux kernel. For this reason, a module might need to be loaded on one system but not on another to use the same hardware because the second system might compile the relevant driver directly into the kernel.

You can learn still more about kernel modules with the help of the `modinfo` command. Normally, you type this command followed by the name of the module in which you're interested:

```
$ modinfo sr_mod
filename:        /lib/modules/2.6.35.4/kernel/drivers/scsi/sr_mod.ko
license:         GPL
alias:           scsi:t-0x04*
alias:           scsi:t-0x05*
alias:           block-major-11-*
license:         GPL
description:     SCSI cdrom (sr) driver
srcversion:      8B17EBCB6C3BD4B1608CC70
depends:         cdrom
vermagic:        2.6.35.4 SMP preempt mod_unload modversions
parm: xa_test:int
```

The information returned usually includes the filename, its license name, aliases by which it's known, a brief description, the names of any modules upon which it depends, some kernel version information, and parameters that can be passed to the module. The exact information returned depends on the module, though; some omit some of these fields or add others. If you're interested in only one field, you can specify it with the `-F` *fieldname* option, as in `modinfo -F description sr_mod` to obtain the description for the `sr_mod` module.

The `modinfo` utility is most useful for learning a bit about modules you've seen in `lsmod` output that you can't readily identify. Unfortunately, many modules lack the helpful description field, so in practice, `modinfo` is often less helpful than it might be.

Loading Kernel Modules

Linux enables you to load kernel modules with two programs: `insmod` and `modprobe`. The `insmod` program inserts a single module into the kernel. This process requires that any modules upon which the module you're loading relies are already loaded. The `modprobe` program, by contrast, automatically loads any depended-on modules and so is generally the preferred way to do the job.

In practice, you may not need to use `insmod` or `modprobe` to load modules because Linux can load them automatically. This ability relies on the kernel's module auto-loader feature, which must be compiled into the kernel, and on various configuration files, which are also required for `modprobe` and some other tools. Using `insmod` and `modprobe` can be useful for testing new modules or for working around problems with the auto-loader, though.

In practice, `insmod` is a fairly straightforward program to use; you type it followed by the module filename:

```
# insmod /lib/modules/2.6.35.4/kernel/drivers/cdrom/cdrom.ko
```

This command loads the `cdrom.ko` module, which you must specify by filename. Modules have module names, too, which are usually the same as the filename but without the extension, as in `cdrom` for the `cdrom.ko` file. Unfortunately, `insmod` requires the full module filename, which can be tedious to type—or even to locate the file!

You can pass additional module options to the module by adding them to the command line. Module options are highly module-specific, so you must consult the documentation for the module to learn what to pass. Examples include options to tell an RS-232 serial port driver what interrupt to use to access the hardware or to tell a video card framebuffer driver what screen resolution to use.

Some modules depend on other modules. In these cases, if you attempt to load a module that depends on others and those other modules aren't loaded, `insmod` will fail. When this happens, you must either track down and manually load the depended-upon modules or use `modprobe`. In the simplest case, you can use `modprobe` just as you use `insmod`, by passing it a module name:

```
# modprobe cdrom
```

As with `insmod`, you can add kernel options to the end of the command line. Unlike `insmod`, you specify a module by its module name rather than its module filename when you use `modprobe`. Generally speaking, this helps make `modprobe` easier to use, as does the fact that `modprobe` automatically loads dependencies. This greater convenience means that `modprobe` relies on configuration files, as described shortly in "Maintaining Kernel Modules." It also means that you can use options (placed between the command name and the module name) to modify `modprobe`'s behavior, as summarized in Table 2.6.

TABLE 2.6 Common options to modprobe

Short option name	Long option name	Explanation
-v	--verbose	This option displays extra information on modprobe's operation. Typically, this includes a summary of every insmod operation performed.
-C filename	--config filename	The modprobe program uses a configuration file called /etc/modprobe.conf. You can change the file by passing a new file with this option, as in **modprobe -C /etc/mymodprobe.conf cdrom**.
-n	--dry-run	This option causes modprobe to perform checks and all other operations *except* for the actual module insertions. You might use this option in conjunction with -v to see what modprobe would do without actually loading the module. This might be helpful in debugging, particularly if inserting the module is having some detrimental effect, such as disabling disk access.

TABLE 2.6   Common options to modprobe *(continued)*

Short option name	Long option name	Explanation
-r	--remove	This option reverses modprobe's usual effect; it causes the program to remove the specified module and any upon which it depends. (Depended-upon modules are *not* removed if they're in use, though.)
-f	--force	This option tells modprobe to force the module loading even if the kernel version doesn't match what the module specifies. This action is potentially dangerous, but it's occasionally required when using third-party binary-only modules.
N/A	--show-depends	This option shows all the modules upon which the specified module depends. This option doesn't install any of the modules; it's purely informative in nature.
-l	--list	This option displays a list of available options whose names match the wildcard you specify. For instance, typing **modprobe -l v*** displays all modules whose names begin with v. If you provide no wildcard, modprobe displays all available modules. Like --show-depends, this option doesn't cause any modules to be loaded.

Table 2.6's list of options is incomplete. The others are relatively obscure, so you're not likely to need them often. Consult modprobe's man page for more information.

Removing Kernel Modules

In most cases, you can leave modules loaded indefinitely; the only harm that a module does when it's loaded but not used is to consume a small amount of memory. (The lsmod program shows how much memory each module consumes.) Sometimes, though, you might want to remove a loaded module. Reasons include reclaiming that tiny amount of memory, unloading an old module so that you can load an updated replacement module, and removing a module that you suspect is unreliable.

The actual work of unloading a kernel module is done by the rmmod command, which is something of the opposite of insmod. The rmmod command takes a module name as an option, though, rather than a module filename:

```
# rmmod cdrom
```

This example command unloads the cdrom module. You can modify the behavior of rmmod in various ways, as summarized in Table 2.7.

TABLE 2.7   Options to rmmod

Short option name	Long option name	Explanation
-v	--verbose	This option causes rmmod to display some extra information about what it's doing. This might be helpful if you're troubleshooting a problem.
-f	--force	This option forces module removal even if the module is marked as being in use. Naturally, this is a very dangerous option, but it's helpful sometimes if a module is misbehaving in some way that's even more dangerous. This option has no effect unless the CONFIG_MODULE_FORCE_UNLOAD kernel option is enabled.
-w	--wait	This option causes rmmod to wait for the module to become unused, rather than return an error message, if the module is in use. Once the module is no longer being used (say, after an optical disc is unmounted if you try to remove the cdrom module), rmmod then unloads the module and returns. Until then, rmmod doesn't return, making it look like it's not doing anything.
-s	--syslog	You can send error messages to the system logger rather than to the standard error output if you use this option. This might be useful in scripts that are run in cron jobs.
-V	--version	This option displays the version number of the rmmod program.

Like insmod, rmmod operates on a single module. If you try to unload a module that's depended upon by other modules or is in use, rmmod will return an error message. (The -w option modifies this behavior, as just described.) If the module is depended upon by other modules, those modules are listed, so you can decide whether to unload them. If you want to unload an entire *module stack*—that is, a module and all those upon which it depends—you can use the modprobe command and its -r option, as described previously in "Loading Kernel Modules."

EXERCISE 2.1

Managing Kernel Modules

To learn about kernel modules, it's helpful to experiment. This exercise will give you some hands-on experience. It assumes you have a computer in which the cdrom driver is compiled as a module. If your computer's optical disc drivers are built directly into the kernel, or if you have no optical disc drive, you may have to select a different module for experimentation.

Before you begin, you should locate a data disc. Any data disc (CD-ROM, CD-R, DVD, or Blu-Ray, depending on your hardware's capabilities) will do. Music CDs will not work with this procedure as written. With the disc in hand, follow these steps:

1. Insert the disc in the drive and wait for the access light to go out.

2. Acquire root privileges by logging in as root or by typing **su** and entering the root password. You must type all the following commands as root.

3. Mount the disc by typing **mount /dev/cdrom /mnt/cdrom** as root. You may need to change the device filename or mount point, depending on your computer's configuration. Also, some Linux systems are configured to auto-mount optical discs, so this step may be unnecessary.

4. Type **lsmod | grep cdrom** to view the lsmod output related to the cdrom module, which should be in use unless the driver was compiled into the main kernel file. This command will also reveal the bus-specific driver associated with the optical disc device—typically sr_mod or ide_cd_mod.

5. Type **rmmod cdrom**. The program will reply that cdrom is in use by the bus-specific driver.

6. Type **rmmod sr_mod** (or change sr_mod to ide_cd_mod or whatever module was identified in step #5). The program will reply that the module is in use, but it won't say by what. This is because the module is in use by a non-module subsystem.

7. Type **umount /mnt/cdrom** (changing the mount point, if necessary).

8. Repeat steps #5 and #6. This time, step #6 will succeed. You can then type **rmmod cdrom** to unload that module, and it will succeed. This step illustrates removing a module stack the long way, by using rmmod on each individual module.

9. Type **modprobe -v sr_mod** to load the optical disc module stack again. (Change sr_mod, if necessary, for your system.) Both the sr_mod and cdrom modules will be loaded, as revealed by the output that the -v option generates.

10. Mount your optical disc again and check its contents with ls to verify that it's working.

11. Type **umount /mnt/cdrom** to unmount the optical disc.

12. Type **modprobe -v -r sr_mod** (changing sr_mod, if necessary). This action will unload both sr_mod and cdrom, illustrating unloading a module stack the quick way. In principle, other modules might be unloaded, as well, if they were used by sr_mod or cdrom and not by anything else.

13. Verify that cdrom is unloaded by typing **lsmod | grep cdrom**; the output will be empty.

14. Type **modprobe sr_mod** to restore the optical disc module stack to ensure that it works properly when you're finished with this exercise.

You can, of course, experiment with additional kernel modules; however, be cautious: Some modules are necessary for normal system operation and so should never be removed. In most such cases, neither rmmod nor modprobe will permit you to remove the module, so the risk is low. Sometimes, though, you'll remove a module only to discover that it's needed by something that's not immediately obvious. For instance, if you remove usblp, you might not notice a problem immediately, but if you subsequently attempt to print to a USB printer, the attempt may fail. In a worst-case scenario, rebooting the computer should restore it to normal functioning. Less radical steps, such as reloading the module and restarting any service that relies on it, can usually fix the problem.

Maintaining Kernel Modules

Tools such as lsmod, modprobe, and rmmod are very useful for managing kernel modules. These tools rely on configuration files, though, and knowing how to maintain these files is important for keeping your modules operating smoothly. Most of these files, and the tools that help modify them, need only be touched after you add or remove a module to your collection. Sometimes, though, you might want to change the way a module operates by passing it kernel options; this can be done even if you've not recompiled, added, replaced, or removed a module.

Kernel Module Maintenance Tools and Files

Two files help manage some important kernel module features:

Module Dependencies   Module dependencies are stored in the modules.dep file, which resides in your main modules directory, /lib/modules/*version*, where *version* is the kernel version number. (This number sometimes includes distribution-specific codes.) You don't normally edit this file directly; instead, you use depmod to work on it. Type **depmod** with no options as root will rebuild the modules.dep file for the modules in the current kernel's modules directory. This action also occurs automatically when you install kernel modules, as described earlier in "Installing Kernel Modules."

Module Configuration   The main module configuration file is /etc/modules.conf or /etc/modprobe.conf. This file holds module aliases (that is, alternate names for modules), module options, and more. This file's format is surprisingly complex, but most changes can be relatively simple, as described shortly in "Passing Options to Kernel Modules." Very old distributions called this file /etc/conf.modules, but this name has fallen out of favor.

 Rather than use a monolithic /etc/modules.conf or /etc/modprobe.conf file, many modern distributions place smaller configuration files in the /etc/modules.d or /etc/modprobe.d directory. Sometimes a utility, such as modules-update, generates a .conf file from the directory, but other times the files in the subdirectory are used directly. If you use such a distribution and want to change your module configuration, you should do so by editing the appropriate file in /etc/modules.d or /etc/modprobe.d or by creating a new file there. If you see a modules.conf or modprobe.conf file, you should then type **modules-update** as root.

Passing Options to Kernel Modules

You can pass options to kernel modules via insmod or modprobe; however, Linux will usually load a module automatically when it determines that you're trying to use a device. When this happens, you can't manually pass options to the kernel module. Instead, you must edit /etc/modules.conf or /etc/modprobe.conf (or a file in /etc/modules.d or /etc/modprobe.d) to tell the system about the options you want to pass. To do so, you must add an options line, such as this:

```
options sisfb mode=1280x1024 rate=75
```

This line specifies options for the sisfb module, which is the SiS framebuffer driver— that is, it handles text-based video modes for certain SiS video chipsets. (Framebuffer drivers can also be used by X via the X framebuffer driver, but X more often drives the video hardware more directly.) This example passes two options to the sisfb module: mode=1280x1024 and rate=75. These options tell the driver to run at a resolution of 1280 × 1024 with a refresh rate of 75Hz.

Unfortunately, driver options are very driver-centric. For instance, if you were to use the vesafb video driver (which works with many VESA-compatible video cards) rather than the sisfb driver, you wouldn't use mode= and rate= options; instead, you'd use a vga= option, which takes a numeric code to set the video mode. Your best bet to learn about the options you might want to use is to consult the driver's documentation, as described earlier in "Reading Kernel Documentation." If you need to pass options to a driver that didn't ship with a standard kernel, consult the documentation that came with it.

Once you make changes to this file, you should type **depmod**, and if the module whose behavior you want to affect is loaded, unload it. When you reload it, the new options should take effect. A few modules, such as framebuffer video drivers, cannot be easily removed once loaded, so you might need to reboot the computer to see your changes take effect.

Summary

Linux distributions typically provide precompiled kernels that you can use without modification for most purposes; however, sometimes it's necessary to upgrade the kernel. You can do this by using a kernel from your distribution provider if you just need to obtain an update that fixes a bug; however, if you need the features of a new kernel or if you need to apply a source code patch to obtain an unusual feature, you'll have to obtain the kernel source code, compile it, and install it manually. The most difficult part of this task is kernel configuration, because of the thousands of kernel options. Fortunately, you can use a working kernel's configuration as a template, and it's often possible to disable large groups of options when you know your system doesn't use any of them. Once the kernel configuration is done, building and installing the kernel is a matter of typing a handful of commands. Adding the kernel to your GRUB configuration requires more effort; this task usually involves copying one configuration and then modifying it for the new kernel.

Once a kernel is running, it can still require management. You can identify the kernel you're using with the uname command. You can also load and unload kernel modules, which manage specific hardware devices, filesystems, and other features, using the insmod, modprobe, and rmmod commands. Modules sometimes require options to adjust how they manage their duties. These can be passed on the insmod or modprobe command line, or they can be entered into module configuration files such as /etc/modprobe.conf, /etc/modules .conf, or a file in a subdirectory called /etc/modprobe.d or /etc/modules.d.

Exam Essentials

Summarize the common names and locations of kernel binaries.   Kernel binaries are usually located in /boot, although sometimes they're stored in the root (/) directory. Precompiled binaries are generally called vmlinuz or vmlinuz-*version*, where *version* is the kernel version number. Locally compiled kernels are frequently called zImage or zImage-*version* (on some obscure platforms or very old kernels) or bzImage or bzImage-*version* (on *x*86 and *x*86-64 systems). Occasionally the generic name kernel or kernel-*version* is used. The vmlinux file is a complete uncompressed kernel that is generated late in the build process; a few features are added, and it's compressed to create the other forms.

Describe where you can find documentation on kernel features.   Kernel documentation appears in the /usr/src/linux/Documentation directory tree. Much of this documentation is highly technical programming information, but some of it describes kernel and module options of use to a system administrator. Most kernel features also include brief summary descriptions that appear when you click the relevant option in an X-based configuration tool (or by selecting the Help item when running make menuconfig). This configuration tool help is useful in deciding whether to compile a feature or set of features.

Describe why you might want to recompile your kernel.   Recompiling your kernel enables you to upgrade to the latest kernel and optimize your kernel for your system. Locally compiled kernels can include precisely those drivers and other features that you need and can also be compiled with CPU features to suit your system.

Explain the function of a kernel patch file.   A kernel patch file is a single file that encodes changes between two versions of a kernel. Patch files from the main kernel site enable quick and low-bandwidth downloads of changes to the kernel, should you have a recent version available and want to upgrade to a newer version. Patches from third parties enable you to add unusual or under-development drivers or features to the kernel.

Summarize the kernel compilation process.   To compile a kernel, you must download the kernel source code, extract the source code, type `make xconfig` (or a similar command) to configure the kernel for your system, type `make` to build the kernel, type `make modules_install` to install the kernel modules, and then copy the kernel file to a convenient location (typically /boot). You must then reconfigure your boot loader to boot the new kernel and reboot the system.

Describe the common `make` targets for the Linux kernel.   The `mrproper` target removes all temporary and configuration files, while `clean` removes only the temporary files. The `oldconfig` target updates a `.config` file you've copied from an old build to include options for the current kernel. The `config`, `menuconfig`, `xconfig`, and `gconfig` options enable you to adjust the kernel options that will be built. The `zImage` and `bzImage` targets build the kernel itself, while `modules` build kernel modules. The `modules_install` target installs the kernel modules in `/lib/modules`.

Explain how you can create an initial RAM disk.   Initial RAM disks can be created using `mkinitrd`, `mkinitramfs`, or a similar utility. You must pass the RAM disk's filename and the kernel version number to the utility, and optionally other command-line options to control the program's activities.

Summarize the tools used to load and unload kernel modules.   The `insmod` and `modprobe` tools load kernel modules. The `insmod` tool loads a single kernel module by filename, while `modprobe` loads a module and all those upon which it depends by module name. The `rmmod` command removes a single kernel module, provided it's not in use, while `modprobe` can remove a module stack if it's called with its `-r` option.

Describe how to learn what options a module accepts.   You can use the `modinfo` tool, as in `modinfo cdrom`, to obtain technical information on a module, including the options it accepts. The parameters listed by this tool may be a bit cryptic, though. For a clearer explanation, you should look for documentation in `/usr/src/linux/Documentation`.

Explain how to learn what modules are installed on your system.   The `lsmod` command displays information on the currently loaded modules, including their names, memory consumed, whether they're in use, and what other modules rely on them. Note that drivers built directly into the kernel do *not* appear in this list!

Review Questions

1. What is the conventional name for a locally compiled, bootable Linux kernel on an *x86* system?

   A. /boot/vmlinux-*version*

   B. /boot/vmlinuz

   C. /boot/bzImage-*version*

   D. /usr/src/linux-*version*

2. Which of the following statements about /usr/src/linux is usually true?

   A. It is a symbolic link to a directory holding the system's current kernel source code, or the version currently being prepared.

   B. It holds subdirectories, each of which contains the source code for a different version of the Linux kernel.

   C. It contains kernel binaries for *x86*, *x86-64*, PowerPC, Alpha, and several other CPU architectures.

   D. Because of its sensitive contents, it should never be accessed by anybody but the system's superuser (root).

3. In what directory might you look for information on options that can be applied to your computer's Ethernet driver module?

   A. /usr/src/linux/Documentation

   B. /lib/modules/options

   C. /usr/share/doc/modules

   D. /etc/modules.conf

4. Which type of kernel image has been largely abandoned on *x86* computers in favor of the bzImage format?

   A. vmlinux

   B. zImage

   C. initramfs

   D. initrd

5. Which of the following commands, when typed in /usr/src/linux after configuring the kernel, compile the main Linux kernel file and its modules?

   A. make bzImage

   B. make modules

   C. make xconfig

   D. make

6. Which *two* of the following kernel features should you compile into the main kernel file of a regular disk-based *x86-64* installation to simplify booting the system? (Select two.)

    A. Drivers for your boot disk's ATA controller or SCSI host adapter

    B. Support for your root (/) filesystem

    C. Drivers for your USB port

    D. Framebuffer drivers for your video card

7. You've compiled and installed a new kernel, of version 2.6.35.4. You now want to prepare an initial RAM disk. Which *two* of the following commands will do so, depending on your distribution? (Select two options.)

    A. `mkinitrd -o /boot/initrd-2.6.35.4 2.6.35.4`

    B. `mkinitrd /boot/initrd-2.6.35.4 2.6.35.4`

    C. `mkinitramfs /boot/initramfs-2.6.35.4 2.6.35.4`

    D. `mkinitramfs -o /boot/initramfs-2.6.35.4 2.6.35.4`

8. Which of the following commands might you type while in `/usr/src/linux`, after copying the configuration file from an old kernel, to use the old kernel's options and update the configuration for new options in the new kernel?

    A. `make config`

    B. `make allmodconfig`

    C. `make oldconfig`

    D. `make mrproper`

9. In which of the following circumstances would it make the *least* sense to patch a kernel?

    A. You have recent stable kernel source code and you need to add support for a new kernel feature that's not in that version.

    B. You have recent kernel source, but it has a buggy driver. A fix is available in a later kernel and is available as a patch for your current kernel.

    C. You have the 2.6.36 kernel source and you want to upgrade to a 2.6.36.1 kernel.

    D. You have kernel source from your distribution maintainer and you want to compile a "generic" kernel for your system.

10. You've downloaded the `patch-2.6.35.4.bz2` file. What program will you use as part of the patch operation to handle this file's compression?

    A. `bunzip2`

    B. `gunzip`

    C. `tar`

    D. `cpio`

11. Which of the following commands would you type to configure a Linux kernel using an interactive text-mode tool?

    A. `make xconfig`

    B. `make menuconfig`

    C. `make config`

    D. `make textconfig`

12. You've configured and compiled your new kernel, version 2.6.35.4. You now type **make modules_install**. Where can you expect to find the module files?

    A. `/lib/modules/modules-2.6.35.4`

    B. `/usr/src/linux/2.6.35.4`

    C. `/lib/modules/2.6.35.4`

    D. `/usr/lib/2.6.35.4`

13. In what file in the Linux kernel source tree are configuration options stored?

    A. `kernel.conf`

    B. `configure`

    C. `.config`

    D. `linux.conf`

14. After copying an existing GRUB Legacy configuration entry, what three features are most important to alter to get the new entry to work with a new kernel?

    A. The `title`, the `kernel` filename, and the `initrd` filename

    B. The `title`, the `kernel` filename, and the kernel's `root` entry

    C. The `kernel` options, the `initrd` filename, and the `initrd` options.

    D. The `kernel` filename, the `kernel` options, and the `initrd` options.

15. What would you expect to see if you type **uname -a**?

    A. Information on the username of the current user, including the user's real name

    B. Information on the running system, such as the OS, the kernel version, and the CPU type

    C. Information on the computer's hostname, as it's defined locally

    D. Information on the loaded kernel modules, including the modules upon which they depend

16. What is the most important practical difference between `insmod` and `modprobe`?

    A. `insmod` unloads a single module, whereas `modprobe` loads a single module.

    B. `insmod` loads a single module, whereas `modprobe` loads a module and all those upon which it depends.

    C. `insmod` isn't a real Linux command, but `modprobe` loads a module and all those upon which it depends.

    D. `insmod` loads a single module, whereas `modprobe` displays information about modules.

17. You type the command **rmmod ide_core**, but the system responds with the message ERROR: Module ide_core is in use by via82cxxx,ide_cd,ide_disk. What is the meaning of this response?

    A.   The via82cxxx, ide_cd, and ide_disk modules all rely on ide_core, so ide_core can't be unloaded without first unloading these other modules.

    B.   The ide_core module relies on via82cxxx, ide_cd, and ide_disk modules, so they can't be unloaded without first unloading ide_core.

    C.   The ide_core module is a core module, meaning that it can never be unloaded once it's loaded.

    D.   The ide_core module is buggy or the rmmod utility is broken; it should never return an error message.

18. What file or files might you edit to change the options that are automatically passed to kernel modules? (Select all that apply.)

    A.   Files in the /etc/modules.d directory

    B.   modules.dep in the modules directory

    C.   .config in the kernel directory

    D.   /etc/modules.conf

19. You have two computers, both of which have identical motherboards and DVD drives. Both run the 2.6.35.4 kernel, which was configured and compiled independently on each system. On one (computera), typing **lsmod** produces output that includes the cdrom module. On the other (computerb), typing **lsmod** does *not* produce output that includes a module called cdrom, even when the DVD drive is in use. What might account for this difference?

    A.   The cdrom driver is used to access CD-ROM devices, not DVD drives, so its presence on computera but not computerb is unimportant.

    B.   The "DVD" drive in computera is clearly a counterfeit, since its use should not trigger loading of the cdrom driver.

    C.   The cdrom driver is built as a module on computera, but it's built into the main kernel file on computerb.

    D.   You must type **insmod cdrom** before using the drive on computerb, else data transfers will be corrupted.

20. Which of the following files contains the same information as can be obtained by typing **uname -v**?

    A.   /usr/src/linux/Documentation/variables

    B.   /lib/modules/verbose

    C.   /etc/kernel/verbose

    D.   /proc/sys/kernel/version

Answers to Review Questions

1. C. Locally compiled Linux kernels are usually called /boot/bzImage or /boot/bzImage-*version*, where *version* is the version number. The vmlinux file is a complete but unbootable kernel image used to generate other image file formats, so option A is incorrect. The /boot/vmlinuz or /boot/vmlinuz-*version* file is the stock distribution's kernel, not a locally compiled kernel, so option B is incorrect. The /usr/src/linux-*version* name is held by the Linux kernel source directory, not a compile kernel file, so option D is incorrect.

2. A. Option A correctly describes the usual state of /usr/src/linux. Option B is incorrect because /usr/src/linux usually points to just one version of the Linux kernel. Option B might be true of /usr/src, though. Option C is incorrect because, although the Linux kernel source tree can be used to build binaries for a wide range of CPUs, it's rare to build them all on one computer. Option D is incorrect because the kernel source tree is readily available from the Internet; there's nothing particularly sensitive about it or about the intermediate files or final binaries produced. Furthermore, access to some kernel header files is required by ordinary users who need to compile software.

3. A. The /usr/src/linux/Documentation directory tree holds files that describe the features of many Linux kernel subsystems and modules, including Ethernet drives. Thus, this directory is a good place to look for the specified information. Options B and C both describe fictitious locations. Option D is one common name for a modules configuration file. Although you might find your system's current Ethernet options in this file, they might not be well documented. Furthermore, the question asks for a *directory*, and /etc/modules.conf is a *file*. Thus, option D is incorrect.

4. B. The zImage format was once common on *x*86 computers but has largely been abandoned on that platform, as the question specifies. Option A, vmlinux, is the name used by a complete but unbootable form of the Linux kernel generated as an intermediate step in preparing other kernel formats. Options C and D are names given to initial RAM disks, not kernel images.

5. D. Typing **make** alone will build both the main kernel file and all the kernel modules, so option D is correct. Alternatively, you could type the commands specified by *both* options A and B; however, these options build the kernel file and the modules alone, respectively, so neither one alone is adequate and both options are incorrect. Option C specifies one of several kernel configuration commands; it won't build a kernel or its modules and so is incorrect.

6. A, B. The Linux kernel needs to be able to access your hard disk to continue past the most basic boot stage, so it needs drivers for your hard disk's ATA controller or SCSI host adapter as well as support for whatever filesystem you use on your root (/) partition in the kernel itself. Alternatively, these drivers can be placed on an initial RAM disk, but this configuration requires more work. The USB port isn't needed during the boot process, so option C is incorrect. (CD-ROM drivers are, of course, needed for CD-ROM-based distributions, but the question specified a hard-disk-based installation.) Although video card support is required by most installations, basic text-mode video support is standard, and drivers in the X Window System handle GUI video. The framebuffer drivers specified in option D are definitely optional on the *x*86 and *x*86-64 platforms, making option D incorrect.

7. B, D. The `mkinitrd` and `mkinitramfs` utilities both generate initial RAM disks. The four options use each of these two commands, varying in which ones use a `-o` parameter prior to the initial RAM disk filename and which ones do not. Since the `mkinitrd` command does *not* use a `-o` parameter but `mkinitramfs` *does* require this parameter, that makes options B and D correct, while options A and C are incorrect.

8. C. In the Linux kernel, the `oldconfig` target to `make` does as the question specifies, so option C is correct. Option A is used to query the user in text mode about every kernel option. This differs from the action of the `oldconfig` option in that `oldconfig` omits options that are already present in the old configuration file, greatly shortening the configuration process. Option B is incorrect because it discards the old configuration file and builds a new one with as many options being specified as modular build as possible. Option D causes all the intermediate files and configuration files to be deleted.

9. D. Kernel source code from distribution maintainers is usually heavily patched, making application of new patches to create a "generic" kernel difficult. Thus, option D is a poor choice for patching; it's probably better to download the desired kernel version directly in this case. Options A and B both describe cases in which patching is reasonable: You must apply a third-party patch for a new kernel feature (option A) or an updated driver (option B). In the case of option B, you could elect to upgrade to the newer kernel (by downloading the whole thing or by applying a patch) or simply apply the patch for the fix, but a patch is a reasonable approach in any case. Option C describes a good candidate for patching; you're upgrading over a very small version difference, which is likely to be an easy patch to apply.

10. A. The `.bz2` filename extension indicates that the patch file is compressed with `bzip2`. Such files can be uncompressed with `bunzip2`, as option A specifies. Option B's `gunzip` program is used to uncompress files compressed with `gzip`; such files typically have `.gz` extensions, so this option is incorrect. The `tar` and `cpio` programs specified by options C and D handle archive files, but patch files are not archive files, so these options are both incorrect.

11. B. The `make menuconfig` kernel configuration command starts a text-based interactive menu configuration tool. This tool provides the same capabilities as the X-based tool that's started by `make xconfig`. Both of these tools are more flexible than the bare-bones text-mode `make config`. There is no `make textconfig` target.

12. C. Option C specifies the usual location for kernel modules for the 2.6.35.4 kernel. (If you use the General Setup ➢ Local Version option, the version number, and hence the directory name in /lib/modules, may be expanded.) Since there is no `modules-` prefix to the kernel version number in the modules directory name, option A is incorrect. Although the individual module files can be found in the Linux source tree as well as in the installed file location, these files do not appear in a subdirectory named after the kernel version, so option B is incorrect. Linux kernel modules do not normally appear anywhere in the /usr/lib directory tree, so option D is incorrect.

13. C. The `.config` file holds configuration options for the kernel. Options A, B, and D all describe fictitious files. (Note that many non-kernel packages include a `configure` file, but this is a script that's used to configure the software for your system.)

14. A. The `title` should be changed so that you can identify the new kernel when you reboot and the filenames for both the kernel and the `initrd` file (if present) must be changed to boot the correct kernel with the correct RAM disk image. Thus, option A is correct. Some of these three items are repeated in options B, C, and D, but none of these options includes them all, and each includes items that do not normally need to be changed. The `kernel`'s `root` entry and other options don't normally need adjusting, and the `initrd` entry doesn't normally have options, aside from the RAM disk image's filename.

15. B. The `uname` command displays system information, and the `-a` option to that command causes it to display all the information it's designed to summarize. Options A, C, and D are all incorrect, although other utilities will produce these results: `whoami`, `hostname`, and `lsmod` do the jobs described by options A, C, and D, respectively.

16. B. Option B correctly summarizes the main actions of both of these commands. Option A states that `modprobe` loads a single module. This is only partially correct; `modprobe` loads the module you specify *and* those upon which it depends. Option A also states that `insmod` unloads a module, when in fact it loads a module. Option C says that `insmod` isn't a real command, but it is. Option D says that `modprobe` displays information about modules, but it doesn't; that function is handled by `modinfo`.

17. A. The `rmmod` utility can only remove modules that are not being used by other modules or by other system software. The error message in this case indicates that the other specified modules rely on `ide_core`, so you can't unload `ide_core` until that dependency is broken by unloading these other modules. Option B specifies this dependency backwards. Although some modules are hard to remove once loaded, they aren't called "core modules," as option C specifies. The `rmmod` utility can and does return error messages when you ask it to do something it can't do, contrary to what option D says.

18. A, D. The `/etc/modules.conf` file controls automatic module loading and options passed to modules automatically. On most distributions, you edit this file directly; however, some require you to edit files in `/etc/modules.d` and then type **modules-update** to have the system update `modules.conf` itself. The `modules.dep` file referred to in option B specifies module dependencies, not module options passed to the modules. The kernel's `.config` file controls what kernel features are compiled; it doesn't specify options passed to the modules.

19. C. The `lsmod` command displays information on kernel modules, but not on drivers that are built into the kernel file. Given the evidence presented in the question, it's safe to conclude that the `cdrom` driver is built into the main kernel file used by `computerb`, as option C states. The `cdrom` driver is used to access both CD-ROM and DVD drives, contrary to options A and B. Although typing **insmod cdrom**, as option D suggests, might be required in some situations, the question specified that the drive was in use, so this clearly was not necessary on `computerb`. Furthermore, failure to type **insmod cdrom**, if it's necessary, will result in a failure to access the drive, not data corruption.

20. D. The `/proc/sys/kernel` directory tree holds information on many critical kernel features. Many of these features are accessible or changeable via specialized utilities, including **uname**, and the specified command displays the contents of the file specified in option D. The files specified in options A, B, and C are all fictitious.

Chapter

3

Basic Filesystem Management

THE FOLLOWING LINUX PROFESSIONAL
INSTITUTE OBJECTIVES ARE COVERED IN
THIS CHAPTER:

- ✓ 203.1 Operating the Linux filesystem (weight: 4)

- ✓ 203.2 Maintaining a Linux filesystem (weight: 3)

- ✓ 203.3 Creating and configuring filesystem options (weight: 2)

- ✓ 203.4 udev Device Management (weight: 1)

Linux files are stored in one or more *filesystems*, which are large data structures that enable access to stored files by name. Filesystems require a certain amount of effort to manage and maintain. Specific areas that must be attended to include *mounting* filesystems (that is, making disk filesystems accessible by attaching them to the Linux directory tree), creating filesystems, repairing errors in filesystems, and tuning them for optimal performance.

Several special-case filesystems and variants on filesystems also exist. *Swap space* isn't technically a filesystem, but it is disk storage space and so is covered in this chapter. Optical discs use their own special filesystems, which have unique methods of creation. Finally, the Linux udev tool creates a special filesystem that's used to access hardware devices. You can write udev rules that adjust the names and other characteristics of the files Linux creates to enable program access to hardware.

The word *filesystem* has two meanings. This first, as just described, refers to the low-level disk data structures associated with the storage areas for files. The second meaning is that of an entire Linux directory tree, as in "the /etc directory in the Linux filesystem holds configuration files." Not every filesystem in the sense of a low-level data structure has an /etc directory, but every high-level Linux root filesystem does have such a directory. This distinction is usually clear from context, but when there might be confusion, I use additional or different terms to clarify matters; for instance, I might use the terms *low-level* or *high-level* to refer to a specific meaning of the word *filesystem*, or I might use the term *directory tree* rather than *filesystem* when referring to the high-level structure. This chapter is concerned with low-level filesystems.

Making Filesystems Available

Filesystems are useless unless they are accessible, so this chapter begins with a look at how filesystems may be mounted in Linux. This task begins with a tally of filesystem types. You can then look into methods of mounting a filesystem, either on a one-time basis or permanently (so that a filesystem will reappear when you reboot the computer). You may also want to use an *automounter*, which is a software component that automatically mounts filesystems you have not explicitly described. Automounters are especially useful with removable media. No matter how particular filesystems were mounted, you should be able to determine what filesystems are currently mounted. You should also be able to unmount filesystems.

Identifying Filesystem Types

Linux supports quite a few different filesystems, both Linux native and those intended for other OSs. Some of the latter barely work under Linux, and even when they do work reliably, they usually don't support all the features that Linux expects in its native filesystems. Thus, when preparing a Linux system, you'll use one or more of its native filesystems for most or all partitions:

Ext2fs The *Second Extended File System* (ext2fs or ext2) is the traditional Linux native filesystem. It was created for Linux and was the dominant Linux filesystem throughout the late 1990s. Ext2fs has a reputation as a reliable filesystem. It has since been eclipsed by other filesystems, but it still has its uses. In particular, ext2fs can be a good choice for a small /boot partition, if you choose to use one, and for small (sub-gibibyte) removable disks. On such small partitions, the size of the journal used by more advanced filesystems can be a real problem, so the non-journaling ext2fs is a better choice. (Journaling is a feature that enables quicker recovery after a power outage, system crash, or other uncontrolled disconnection of the hard disk from the computer.) The ext2 filesystem type code is ext2.

Ext3fs The *Third Extended File System* (ext3fs or ext3) is basically ext2fs with a journal added. The result is a filesystem that's as reliable as ext2fs but that recovers from power outages and system crashes much more quickly. The ext3 filesystem type code is ext3.

Ext4fs The *Fourth Extended File System* (ext4fs or ext4) is the next-generation version of this filesystem family. It adds the ability to work with very large disks (those over 32 tebibytes) or very large files (those over 2 tebibytes), as well as extensions intended to improve performance. Its filesystem type code is ext4.

ReiserFS This filesystem was designed from scratch as a journaling filesystem for Linux and is a popular choice in this role. It's particularly good at handling filesystems with large numbers of small files (say, smaller than about 32KiB) because ReiserFS uses various tricks to squeeze the ends of files into each other's unused spaces. This small savings can add up to a large percentage of file sizes when files are small. You should use reiserfs as the type code for this filesystem.

As of Linux kernel version 2.6.35.4, ReiserFS version 3.*x* is current. A from-scratch rewrite of ReiserFS, known as Reiser4, is being developed but has not yet been integrated into the mainstream kernel.

JFS IBM developed the *Journaled File System* (JFS) for its AIX OS and later re-implemented it on OS/2. The OS/2 version was subsequently donated to Linux. JFS is a technically sophisticated journaling filesystem that may be of particular interest if you're familiar with

AIX or OS/2 or want an advanced filesystem to use on a dual-boot system with one of these OSs. As you might expect, this filesystem's type code is jfs.

XFS   Silicon Graphics (SGI) created its *Extents File System* (XFS) for its IRIX OS and, like IBM, later donated the code to Linux. Like JFS, XFS is a very technically sophisticated filesystem. XFS has gained a reputation for robustness, speed, and flexibility on IRIX, but some of the XFS features that make it so flexible on IRIX aren't supported well under Linux. Use xfs as the type code for this filesystem.

Btrfs   This filesystem (pronounced "butter eff ess" or "bee tree eff ess") is an advanced filesystem with features inspired by those of Sun's Zettabyte File System (ZFS). Like ext4fs, JFS, and XFS, Btrfs is a fast performer and is able to handle very large disks and files. As of the 2.6.35.4 kernel, Btrfs is considered experimental; however, its advanced features make it a likely successor to the current popular filesystems.

In practice, most administrators choose ext3fs, ext4fs, or ReiserFS as their primary filesystems; however, JFS and XFS also work well, and some administrators prefer them, particularly on large disks that store large files. (Ext4fs also handles large files, but it's newer and therefore less trusted than JFS and XFS.) Hard data on the merits and problems with each filesystem are difficult to come by, and even when they do exist, they're suspect because filesystem performance interacts with so many other factors. For instance, as just noted, ReiserFS can cram more small files into a small space than can other filesystems, but this advantage isn't very important if you'll be storing mostly larger files.

If you're using a non-*x*86 or non-*x*86-64 platform, be sure to check filesystem development on that platform. A filesystem may be speedy and reliable on one CPU but sluggish and unreliable on another.

In addition to these Linux-native filesystems, you may need to deal with some others from time to time, including the following:

FAT   The *File Allocation Table* (FAT) filesystem is old and primitive—but ubiquitous. It's the only hard disk filesystem supported by DOS and Windows 9*x*/Me. For this reason, every major OS understands FAT, making it an excellent filesystem for exchanging data on removable disks. FAT varies on two major orthogonal dimensions: the size of the FAT data structure after which the filesystem is named (12-, 16-, or 32-bit pointers), and support (or lack thereof) for long filenames. Linux automatically detects the FAT size, so you shouldn't need to worry about this. To use the original FAT filenames, which are limited to eight characters with an optional three-character extension (the so-called *8.3 filenames*), use the Linux filesystem type code of msdos. To use Windows-style long filenames, use the filesystem type code of vfat. A Linux-only long filename system, known as umsdos, supports additional Linux features—enough that you can install Linux on a FAT partition. The umsdos driver was removed from the Linux kernel with version 2.6.11 because of lack of maintenance.

NTFS   The *New Technology File System* (NTFS) is the preferred filesystem for Windows NT/200*x*/XP/Vista. Unfortunately, Linux's NTFS support is rather rudimentary. As of the

2.6.*x* kernel series, Linux can reliably read NTFS and can overwrite existing files, but the Linux kernel can't write new files to an NTFS partition.

> If you must have good NTFS read/write support for a dual-boot system, look into NTFS-3G, which is available in both proprietary and open source ("community edition") versions from Tuxera (http://www.tuxera.com). This is a read/write NTFS driver that resides in user space rather than in kernel space. It's used as the default NTFS driver by some Linux distributions.

HFS and HFS+　Apple has long used the *Hierarchical File System* (HFS) with its Mac OS, and Linux provides full read/write HFS support. This support isn't as reliable as Linux's read/write FAT support, though, so you may want to use FAT when exchanging files with Mac users. Apple has extended HFS to better support large hard disks and many Unix-like features with its HFS+ (a.k.a. Extended HFS), which is the default filesystem on Mac OS X systems. Linux 2.6.*x* adds limited HFS+ support; but write support works only with the HFS+ journal disabled.

ISO-9660　The standard filesystem for CD-ROMs has long been *ISO-9660*. This filesystem comes in several levels. Level 1 is similar to the original FAT in that it supports only 8.3 filenames. Levels 2 and 3 add support for longer 32-character filenames. Linux supports ISO-9660 using its iso9660 filesystem type code. Linux's ISO-9660 support also works with the *Rock Ridge extensions*, which are a series of extensions to ISO-9660 to enable it to support Unix-style long filenames, permissions, symbolic links, and so on. If a disc includes Rock Ridge extensions, Linux will automatically detect and use them.

Joliet　This filesystem is used much like Rock Ridge, as an extension to ISO-9660. *Joliet* was created by Microsoft for use by Windows, so it emphasizes Windows filesystem features rather than Unix/Linux filesystem features. Linux supports Joliet as part of its iso9660 driver; if a disc contains Joliet but not Rock Ridge, Linux uses the Joliet filesystem.

UDF　The *Universal Disc Format* (UDF) is the next-generation filesystem for optical discs. It's commonly used on DVD-ROMs and recordable optical discs. Linux supports it, but read/write UDF support is still in its infancy.

As a practical matter, if you're preparing a hard disk for use with Linux, you should probably use Linux filesystems only. If you're preparing a disk that will be used for a dual-boot configuration, you may want to set aside some partitions for other filesystem types. For removable disks, you'll have to be the judge of what's most appropriate. You might use ext2fs for a Linux-only removable disk, FAT for a cross-platform disk, or ISO-9660 (perhaps with Rock Ridge and Joliet) for a CD-R or recordable DVD.

> ISO-9660 and other optical disc filesystems are created with special tools intended for this purpose, as described in the upcoming section "Managing Optical Discs."

In addition to these disk filesystem types, several other filesystem types exist. Network filesystems, such as the Server Message Block/Common Internet Filesystem (SMB/CIFS) and the Network Filesystem (NFS), enable one computer to access another's disks. These protocols are described in Chapter 8, "Configuring File Servers." Virtual filesystems give file-like access to kernel features or hardware. The udev filesystem, described in the section "Managing Devices with udev," is an important example of a virtual filesystem.

Mounting a Filesystem Once

Linux provides the mount command to mount a filesystem to a mount point. In practice, using this command is usually fairly simple, but it supports a large number of options.

Understanding *mount*

The syntax for mount is as follows:

```
mount [-alrsvw] [-t fstype] [-o options] [device]  [mountpoint]
```

Common parameters for mount support a number of features, as outlined in Table 3.1. Ordinarily, a device filename (such as /dev/sda5) and a mount point (such as /mnt/somedisk) are required when you use mount. As described shortly, though, there are exceptions to this rule. The list of mount parameters in Table 3.1 isn't comprehensive; consult mount's man page for some of the more obscure options.

TABLE 3.1   Options to mount

Short option name	Long option name	Explanation
-a	--all	This parameter causes mount to mount all the filesystems listed in the /etc/fstab file, which specifies the most-used partitions and devices. The upcoming section "Permanently Mounting Filesystems" describes this file's format.
-r	--read-only	This parameter causes Linux to mount the filesystem read-only, even if it's normally a read/write filesystem.
-v	--verbose	As with many commands, this option produces verbose output—the program provides comments on operations as they occur.
-w	--rw	This parameter causes Linux to attempt to mount the filesystem for both read and write operations. This is the default for most filesystems, but some experimental drivers default to read-only operation. The -o rw option has the same effect.

Short option name	Long option name	Explanation
-t *fstype*	--types *fstype*	Use this parameter to specify the filesystem type. Common filesystem types are described earlier in "Identifying Filesystem Types." If this parameter is omitted, Linux will attempt to auto-detect the filesystem type.
-L *label*	N/A	You can specify a filesystem by its human-readable label rather than by a device filename if you use this option.
-U *uuid*	N/A	You can specify a filesystem by a special numeric code by using this option.
-o *options*	--options *options*	You can pass additional or filesystem-specific options using this parameter.

Linux requires support in the kernel or as a kernel module to mount a filesystem of a given type. If this support is missing, Linux will refuse to mount the filesystem in question.

The most common applications of mount use few parameters because Linux generally does a good job of detecting the filesystem type and the default parameters work reasonably well. For instance, consider this example:

```
# mount /dev/sdb7 /mnt/shared
```

This command mounts the contents of /dev/sdb7 on /mnt/shared, auto-detecting the filesystem type and using the default options. Ordinarily, only root may issue a mount command; however, if /etc/fstab specifies the user, users, or owner option, an ordinary user may mount a filesystem using a simplified syntax in which only the device *or* mount point is specified, but not both. For instance, a user may type mount /mnt/cdrom to mount a CD-ROM if /etc/fstab specifies /mnt/cdrom as its mount point and uses the user, users, or owner option.

Most Linux distributions ship with auto-mounter support, which causes the OS to automatically mount removable media when they're inserted. In GUI environments, a file browser may also open on the inserted disk. In order to eject the disk, the user will need to unmount the filesystem by using umount, as described shortly, or by selecting an option in the desktop environment.

The mount point is ordinarily an *empty* directory. If you specify a directory with files as the mount point, those files will seem to disappear when you mount the filesystem on the directory. Those files will still exist, though; they'll just be hidden by the mounted filesystems. To access the hidden files, you must unmount the filesystem that obscures them.

Knowing *mount* Options

When you need to use special parameters, it's usually to add filesystem-specific options. Table 3.2 summarizes the most important filesystem options. Some of these are meaningful only in the /etc/fstab file, which is described later in "Permanently Mounting Filesystems."

TABLE 3.2 Important filesystem options for the mount command

Option	Supported filesystems	Description
defaults	All	Causes the default options for this filesystem to be used. It's used primarily in the /etc/fstab file to ensure that the file includes an options column.
loop	All	Allows you to mount a file as if it were a disk partition. For instance, **mount -t vfat -o loop image.img /mnt/image** mounts the file image.img as if it were a disk.
auto or noauto	All	Mounts or doesn't mount the filesystem at boot time or when root issues the **mount -a** command. The default is auto, but noauto is appropriate for removable media. Used in /etc/fstab.
user or nouser	All	Allows or disallows ordinary users to mount the filesystem. The default is nouser, but user is often appropriate for removable media. Used in /etc/fstab. When included in this file, user allows users to type **mount /mountpoint** (where /mountpoint is the assigned mount point) to mount a disk. Only the user who mounted the filesystem may unmount it.
users	All	Similar to user, except that any user may unmount a filesystem once it's been mounted.
owner	All	Similar to user, except that the user must own the device file. Some distributions assign ownership of some device files (such as /dev/fd0 for the floppy disk) to the console user, so this can be a helpful option.

Option	Supported filesystems	Description
remount	All	Changes one or more mount options without explicitly unmounting a partition. To use this option, you issue a mount command on an already-mounted filesystem but with remount along with any options you want to change. This feature can be used to enable or disable write access to a partition, for example.
ro	All	Specifies a read-only mount of the filesystem. This is the default for filesystems that include no write access and for some with particularly unreliable write support.
rw	All read/write filesystems	Specifies a read/write mount of the filesystem. This is the default for most read/write filesystems.
uid=*value*	Most filesystems that don't support Unix-style permissions, such as vfat, hpfs, ntfs, and hfs	Sets the owner of all files. For instance, uid=500 sets the owner to whoever has Linux user ID 500. (Check Linux user IDs in the /etc/passwd file.)
gid=*value*	Most filesystems that don't support Unix-style permissions, such as vfat, hpfs, ntfs, and hfs	Works like uid=*value*, but sets the group of all files on the filesystem. You can find group IDs in the /etc/group file.
umask=*value*	Most filesystems that don't support Unix-style permissions, such as vfat, hpfs, ntfs, and hfs	Sets the umask for the permissions on files. *value* is interpreted in binary as bits to be removed from permissions on files. For instance, umask=027 yields permissions of 750, or -rwxr-x---. Used in conjunction with uid=*value* and gid=*value*, this option lets you control who can access files on FAT, HPFS, and many other foreign filesystems.
dmask=*value*	Most filesystems that don't support Unix-style permissions, such as vfat, hpfs, ntfs, and hfs	Similar to umask, but sets the umask for directories only, not for files.

TABLE 3.2 Important filesystem options for the mount command *(continued)*

Option	Supported filesystems	Description
fmask=*value*	Most filesystems that don't support Unix-style permissions, such as vfat, hpfs, ntfs, and hfs	Similar to umask, but sets the umask for files only, not for directories.
conv=*code*	Most filesystems used on Microsoft and Apple OSs: msdos, umsdos, vfat, hpfs, and hfs	If *code* is b or binary, Linux doesn't modify the files' contents. If *code* is t or text, Linux auto-converts files between Linux-style and DOS- or Macintosh-style end-of-line characters. If *code* is a or auto, Linux applies the conversion unless the file is a known binary file format. It's usually best to leave this at its default value of binary because file conversions can cause serious problems for some applications and file types.
norock	iso9660	Disables Rock Ridge extensions for ISO-9660 CD-ROMs.
nojoliet	iso9660	Disables Joliet extensions for ISO-9660 CD-ROMs.

Some filesystems support additional options that aren't described here. The man page for mount covers some of these, but you may need to look at the filesystem's documentation for some filesystems and options. This documentation may appear in /usr/src/linux/Documentation/filesystems or /usr/src/linux/fs/*fsname*, where *fsname* is the name of the filesystem.

Permanently Mounting Filesystems

The /etc/fstab file controls how Linux provides access to disk partitions and removable media devices. Linux supports a unified directory structure in which every disk device (partition or removable disk) is mounted at a particular point in the directory tree. For instance, you might access a USB flash drive at /media/usb. The root of this tree is accessed from /. Directories off this root may be other partitions or disks, or they may be ordinary directories. For instance, /etc should be on the same partition as /, but many other directories, such as /home, may correspond to separate partitions. The /etc/fstab file describes how these filesystems are laid out. (The filename fstab is an abbreviation for *filesystem table*.)

The /etc/fstab file consists of a series of lines that contain six fields each; the fields are separated by one or more spaces or tabs. A line that begins with a hash mark (#) is a comment and is ignored. Listing 3.1 shows a sample /etc/fstab file.

Listing 3.1: Sample /etc/fstab file

```
#device        mount point  filesystem options        dump fsck
/dev/sda1      /            ext3       defaults          1 1
UUID=3631a288-673e-40f5-9e96-6539fec468e9 ↲
               /usr         reiserfs   defaults          0 0
LABEL=/home    /home        reiserfs   defaults          0 0
/dev/sdb5      /windows     vfat       uid=500,umask=0 0 0
/dev/cdrom     /media/cdrom iso9660    users,noauto      0 0
/dev/sdb1      /media/usb   auto       users,noauto      0 0
server:/home   /other/home  nfs        users,exec        0 0
//winsrv/shr   /other/win   cifs       users,credentials=/etc/creds 0 0
/dev/sda4      swap         swap       defaults          0 0
```

The meaning of each field in this file is as follows:

Device   The first column specifies the mount device. These are usually device filenames that reference hard disks, floppy drives, and so on. Most distributions now specify partitions by their labels or Universally Unique Identifiers (UUIDs), as in the LABEL=/home and UUID=3631a288-673e-40f5-9e96-6539fec468e9 entries in Listing 3.1. When Linux encounters such an entry, it tries to find the partition whose filesystem has the specified name or UUID and mount it. This practice can help reduce problems if partition numbers change, but some filesystems lack these labels. It's also possible to list a network drive, as in server:/home, which is the /home export on the computer called server; or //winsrv/shr, which is the shr share on the Windows or Samba server called winsrv.

> Each filesystem's UUID is theoretically unique in the world and so makes a good identifier for use in /etc/fstab. Device filenames, by contrast, can change if you repartition the disk, add a disk, or remove a disk. The blkid program returns the UUID and filesystem type of a partition, which can be useful if you want to use the UUID specification yourself. Type **blkid** *device*, where *device* is a device specification such as /dev/sda1.

Mount Point   The second column specifies the mount point; in the unified Linux filesystem, this is where the partition or disk will be mounted. This should usually be an empty directory in another filesystem. The root (/) filesystem is an exception. So is swap space, which is indicated by an entry of swap.

Filesystem Type   The filesystem type code is the same as the type code used to mount a filesystem with the mount command. You can use any filesystem type code you can use directly with the mount command. A filesystem type code of auto lets the kernel auto-detect the filesystem type, which can be a convenient option for removable media devices. Auto-detection doesn't work with all filesystems, though.

Mount Options   Most filesystems support several mount options, which modify how the kernel treats the filesystem. You may specify multiple mount options, separated by commas, as in the users,noauto options for /media/cdrom and /media/usb in Listing 3.1. Table 3.2 summarizes the most common mount options. Type **man mount** or consult filesystem-specific documentation to learn more.

Backup Operation   The next-to-last field contains a 1 if the dump utility should back up a partition or a 0 if it shouldn't. If you never use the dump backup program, this option is essentially meaningless. (The dump program was once a common backup tool, but it is much less popular today.)

Filesystem Check Order   At boot time, Linux uses the fsck program to check filesystem integrity. The final column specifies the order in which this check occurs. A 0 means that fsck should *not* check a filesystem. Higher numbers represent the check order. The root partition should have a value of 1, and all others that should be checked should have a value of 2. Some filesystems, such as ReiserFS, shouldn't be automatically checked and so should have values of 0.

If you add a new hard disk or have to repartition the one you have, you may need to modify /etc/fstab, particularly if you use device filenames to refer to partitions. (Using LABEL and UUID codes can obviate the need for such changes, which is why many modern distributions use these methods of specifying partitions today.) You may also need to edit /etc/fstab to alter some of its options. For instance, setting the user ID or umask on Windows partitions mounted in Linux may be necessary to let ordinary users write to the partition.

 Real World Scenario

Managing User-Mountable Media

You may want to give ordinary users the ability to mount certain partitions or removable media, such as floppies, CD-ROMs, and USB flash drives. To do so, create an ordinary /etc/fstab entry for the filesystem, but be sure to add the user, users, or owner option to the options column. Table 3.2 describes the differences between these three options. Listing 3.1 shows some examples of user-mountable media: /media/cdrom, /media/usb, /other/home, and /other/win. The first two of these are designed for removable media and include the noauto option, which prevents Linux from wasting time trying to mount them when the OS first boots. The second pair of mount points are network file shares that are mounted automatically at boot time; the users option on these lines enables ordinary users to unmount and then remount the filesystem, which might be handy if, say, ordinary users have the ability to shut down the server.

As with any filesystems you want to mount, you must provide mount points—that is, create empty directories—for user-mountable media. Removable media are usually mounted in subdirectories of /mnt or /media.

Many modern distributions include auto-mount facilities that automatically mount removable media when they're inserted. The upcoming section "Using an Automounter" describes automounter configuration in more detail.

The credentials option for the /other/win mount point in Listing 3.1 deserves greater elaboration. Ordinarily, most SMB/CIFS shares require a username and password as a means of access control. Although you can use the username=*name* and password=*pass* options to smbfs or cifs, these options are undesirable, particularly in /etc/fstab, because they leave the password vulnerable to discovery—anybody who can read /etc/fstab can read the password. The credentials=*file* option provides an alternative—you can use it to point Linux at a file that holds the username and password. This file has labeled lines:

```
username=hschmidt
password=yiW7t9Td
```

Of course, the file you specify (/etc/creds in Listing 3.1) must be well protected—it must be readable only to root and perhaps to the user whose share it describes.

Using an Automounter

Several *automounters* exist for Linux. These are programs that automatically mount a filesystem when certain conditions are met. Broadly speaking, automounters fall into two categories: those that mount local storage when it's inserted into the computer and those that mount filesystems (typically network filesystems) when a user accesses their mount points. These two types of automounter are described in the following pages.

Using a File Manager's Automounter

When you insert a physical medium, such as a DVD or USB flash drive, into a Linux computer that's running a desktop environment, the computer is likely to create a desktop icon, mount the disk and display its contents in a file browser, or pop up a notification with options for the user. This seemingly simple response actually involves several software components. On a low level, a system utility must monitor for hardware changes, such as the insertion of a disk, and can take actions or notify other programs of hardware changes. On a higher level, the desktop environment (or more precisely, the file manager that's part of the desktop environment) receives messages relating to hardware changes and mounts filesystems when its configuration files dictate that it do so.

The low-level software in this stack has traditionally been the Hardware Abstraction Layer (HAL) Daemon (HALD). This software is configured through files in the /etc/hal and /usr/share/hal/fdi/policy/10osvendor/ directories. You can sometimes edit these files to effect changes in how removable media are treated. Unfortunately, the relevant files vary from one distribution to another, although they usually include the string storage in their filenames.

In 2009, distributions began shifting away from HAL. The intent is to use udev more directly for triggering automounter and other responses to hardware changes. The upcoming section "Managing Devices with udev" describes udev in more detail.

Once HAL or udev has notified a file manager about an inserted disk, the user's file manager settings take over. Details vary greatly from one file manager to another. As an illustration, consider Thunar, which is the default file manager for Xfce. (Other file managers have similar adjustment options, but Thunar provides more automounter options than most, which is why I'm describing Thunar here.) To adjust Thunar's settings, select Edit ➢ Preferences from a Thunar window. This action produces the File Manager Preferences dialog box. Click the Advanced tab, and check the Enable Volume Management check box. (If you want to disable the automounter, you can uncheck this box.) You can then click Configure to bring up the main configuration options, which are shown in Figure 3.1.

FIGURE 3.1 File managers provide options to enable you to fine-tune how removable disk insertions are handled.

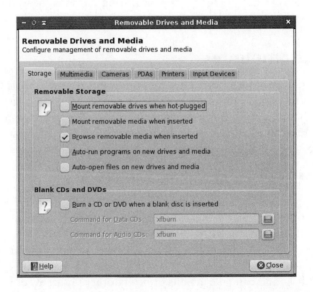

You can check or uncheck specific options to adjust how Thunar handles particular events. For instance, if you want CD-ROMs or DVDs to be automatically mounted, be sure the Mount Removable Media When Inserted option is checked. You can use this same dialog box to specify applications to use when audio CDs, cameras, and some other devices are attached to the computer; click the relevant tabs to adjust these settings.

> In Thunar's terms, *removable media* are media, such as floppy disks, CD-ROMs, and DVDs, that can be inserted into and removed from drives. *Removable disks*, by contrast, are hard disks or similar devices that can be attached or detached from the computer while it's running. Examples include USB flash drives and external hard disks.

Broadly speaking, Thunar and KDE's file manager, Konqueror, provide the most options for configuring automount options. GNOME's default file manager, Nautilus, automatically mounts all media, including both removable and non-removable disks; that is, if you use GNOME, you're likely to see hard disk partitions you don't configure in GNOME appear on your desktop.

File manager automounters typically create mount points in the /media directory. These mount points may be named after the media type, such as /media/cdrom; after the filesystem's label; or after the filesystem's UUID.

> If you see UUIDs or other unhelpful names for filesystems that are auto-mounted, consider adding a filesystem label to the device. This task is most easily accomplished when creating a filesystem; however, it's sometimes possible to alter the filesystem's label after the fact with tools such as tune2fs.

Filesystems mounted by a file manager's automounter can usually be unmounted by an ordinary user, as described shortly, in "Unmounting a Filesystem." The file manager also usually provides some way to unmount the filesystems it has mounted, typically by right-clicking an icon for the filesystem and selecting an option to unmount, eject, or remove the filesystem.

Using *autofs*

Network filesystems, such as SMB/CIFS and NFS, enable users of one computer to access files stored on another computer. This is a very useful ability, but there are certain risks and problems associated with it. One of these problems is that, if you mount a remote filesystem as soon as the computer boots and leave it mounted all the time, you may experience strange problems if the server becomes unavailable—certain tools, such as df, may pause for extended periods as they repeatedly try and fail to poll the server. Keeping remote filesystems mounted permanently also consumes some network bandwidth, which may be unacceptable if a server has a large number of clients.

The autofs automounter exists to resolve, or at least minimize, such problems. Unlike a GUI file manager's automounter, autofs is a purely system-level tool with no user-level configuration. It's not always installed by default, so you should first ensure that you've installed it on your system. (Unsurprisingly, it usually has the package name autofs.)

The /etc/auto.master file is the main configuration file for autofs. Your distribution will have a default file that probably doesn't define any mount points, although it may include lines that point to script files (/etc/auto.smb and /etc/auto.net) that come with the package. These scripts set up /smb and /net directory trees that can work on a variety of networks, as described shortly. To define directories that autofs should monitor for user activity, you should specify a base directory and a configuration file for that directory at the end of /etc/auto.master:

```
/remote   /etc/auto.servers   --timeout=60
```

In this example, the /etc/auto.servers file controls the /remote mount point. After a server is mounted, it will be unmounted after 60 seconds (the timeout value). You must now create the /etc/auto.servers file, which specifies subdirectories (relative to the mount point in /etc/auto.master—/remote in this example) and the servers to which they connect:

```
music                        louis.example.com:/home/armstrong/music
research   -fstype=nfs4  albert.example.com:/home/einstein/data
```

These examples, in conjunction with the /etc/auto.master entry shown earlier, enable access to the /home/armstrong/music directory on louis.example.com via /remote/music, and to the /home/einstein/data directory on albert.example.com via /remote/research. The first line uses NFS defaults, but the second adds an option that forces use of NFSv4.

The /etc/auto.net and /etc/auto.smb files are scripts that can be called like other autofs configuration files. They provide dynamic configurations that enable access to servers via their hostnames and export names. For instance, suppose you include the following line in /etc/auto.master:

```
/network   /etc/auto.net
```

If your local network includes a server called multi that exports the directories /opt and /home via NFS, those directories could then be accessed as /network/multi/opt and /network/multi/home, respectively, without further configuration. The /etc/auto.smb file theoretically provides similar functionality for SMB/CIFS shares; however, the SMB/CIFS security model requires a username and a password, and the auto.smb file delivered with most distributions lacks support for this basic SMB/CIFS requirement. A variant of auto.smb, called auto.cifs, is available at http://www.howtoforge.com/accessing_windows_or_samba_shares_using_autofs and provides better username and password support.

Although autofs is intended primarily to manage network filesystems, you can also configure it to mount local hardware devices. The /etc/auto.misc file on most distributions provides some examples, such as:

```
boot          -fstype=ext2             :/dev/hda1
floppy        -fstype=auto             :/dev/fd0
```

To use such configurations, you would reference /etc/auto.misc in /etc/auto.master. These two lines would then cause /dev/hda1 to be mounted at the boot subdirectory, and /dev/fd0 to be mounted at the floppy subdirectory of the directory specified in /etc/auto .master. Although a file browser's automount features are probably more convenient for most users, this type of autofs configuration could be useful for purely text-mode users or to enable automounting for non-login programs such as servers.

With your configuration files in place, you can launch autofs, typically via a SysV or Upstart script, as described in Chapter 1. You can then begin testing it by accessing the directories that autofs manages. Once autofs is running, you can change its configuration without restarting it; the tool will detect the changes and implement them immediately.

When you begin experimenting with autofs, you'll discover one of the features of the tool: After a period of inactivity (specified by the --timeout parameter in /etc/auto .master), the filesystem is unmounted. This feature can minimize problems such as those noted at the beginning of the section.

Determining What Is Mounted

When Linux mounts a filesystem, it ordinarily records this fact in /etc/mtab. This file has a format similar to that of /etc/fstab and is stored in /etc, but it's not a configuration file that you should edit. You might examine this file to determine what filesystems are mounted, though. The /proc/mounts virtual file serves a role that's similar to /etc/mstab, although the two files differ in certain ways. Prior to the 2.6.26 kernel, /proc/mounts included less information than /etc/mtab; but with 2.6.26 and later kernels, /proc/mounts contains more information. In principle, /etc/mtab can be a symbolic link to /proc/ mounts, at least with recent kernels.

The df command is another way to learn what filesystems are mounted. This command shows additional information, such as how large each filesystem is and how much of that space is in use:

```
$ df
Filesystem          1K-blocks      Used Available Use% Mounted on
/dev/sda2           20642428   9945008   9648844  51% /
udev                 1479784       668   1479116   1% /dev
/dev/sda3            198337     94543     93554  51% /boot
/dev/sdb2           29931580  26075996   2335440  92% /home
```

Unmounting a Filesystem

The umount command unmounts a filesystem. (Yes, it's spelled correctly; the command is missing the first n.) This command is simpler than mount. The basic umount syntax is as follows:

```
umount [-afnrv] [-t fstype] [device | mountpoint]
```

Most of these parameters have meanings similar to their meanings in mount, but some differences deserve mention:

Unmount All Rather than unmount partitions listed in /etc/fstab, the -a option causes the system to attempt to unmount all the partitions listed in /etc/mtab. On a normally running system, this operation is likely to succeed only partly because it won't be able to unmount some key filesystems, such as the root partition.

Force Unmount You can use the -f option to tell Linux to force an unmount operation that might otherwise fail. This feature is sometimes helpful when unmounting NFS mounts shared by servers that have become unreachable.

Fall Back to Read-Only The -r option tells umount that if it can't unmount a filesystem, it should attempt to remount it in read-only mode.

Unmount Partitions of a Specific Filesystem Type The -t *fstype* option tells the system to unmount only partitions of the specified type. You can list multiple filesystem types by separating them with commas.

The Device and Mount Point You need to specify only the *device* or only the *mountpoint*, not both.

As with mount, normal users can't ordinarily use umount. The exception is if the partition or device is listed in /etc/fstab and specifies the user, users, or owner option, in which case normal users can unmount the device. (In the case of user, only the user who mounted the partition may unmount it; in the case of owner, the user issuing the command must also own the device file, as with mount.) These options are most useful for removable-media devices.

Be cautious when removing floppy disks or unplugging USB disk-like devices (USB flash drives or external hard disks). Linux caches accesses to most filesystems, which means that data may not be written to the disk until some time after a write command. Because of this, it's possible to corrupt a disk by ejecting or unplugging it, even when the drive isn't active. You must *always* issue a umount command before ejecting a mounted disk. (GUI unmount tools do this behind the scenes, so using a desktop's unmount or eject option is equivalent to using umount.) After issuing the umount command, wait for the command to return, and if the disk has activity indicators, wait for them to stop blinking to be sure Linux has finished using the device. This isn't an issue for most internal removable media, such as DVD drives, because Linux can lock their eject mechanisms, preventing this sort of problem. Another way to write the cache to disk is to use the sync command; but because this command does *not* fully unmount a filesystem, it's not a substitute for umount.

You can't always unmount a filesystem. Most notably, if any files are open on the filesystem, your umount command will fail:

```
# umount /home
umount: /home: device is busy.
        (In some cases useful info about processes that use
         the device is found by lsof(8) or fuser(1))
```

If you want to unmount the filesystem, you should track down whatever process is using it and terminate that process. As the error message notes, the lsof and fuser commands can sometimes be useful in this task; they list open files and list processes that use files, respectively. If it's impossible to unmount a filesystem, you can sometimes remount it read-only using the remount option to mount:

```
# mount -o remount,ro /home
```

If successful, this action will make it safe to use some filesystem check utilities and will make it less likely that the disk will suffer damage should you be forced to shut down without unmounting.

Maintaining Filesystems

Filesystems don't just spring into being and maintain themselves by magic; these tasks must be performed by utility programs, and you must know how to operate these programs. The following pages describe these tasks, including filesystem creation, checking for and repairing filesystem errors, and fine-tuning filesystem performance parameters. I also describe the creation and use of swap space, which isn't technically a filesystem but is an important data structure that can be stored on a partition much like a filesystem.

Creating Filesystems

Most filesystems, including all Linux-native filesystems, have Linux tools that can create the filesystem on a partition. Typically, these tools have filenames of the form mkfs.*fstype*, where *fstype* is the filesystem type code. These tools can also be called from a front-end tool called mkfs; you pass the filesystem type code to mkfs using its -t option:

```
# mkfs -t ext3 /dev/sda6
```

For ext2, ext3, and ext4 filesystems, the mke2fs program is often used instead of mkfs. The mke2fs program is just another name for mkfs.ext2.

This command creates an ext3 filesystem on /dev/sda6. Depending on the filesystem, the speed of the disk, and the size of the partition, this process can take anywhere from a fraction of a second to more than a minute. Most filesystem-build tools support additional options, some of which can greatly increase the time required to build a filesystem. In particular, the -c option is supported by several filesystems. This option causes the tool to perform a bad-block check by using the badblocks program—every sector in the partition is checked to be sure it can reliably hold data. If it can't, the sector is marked as bad and isn't used.

 If you perform a bad-block check and find that some sectors are bad, chances are the entire hard disk doesn't have long to live. Sometimes this sort of problem can result from other issues, though, such as bad cables.

Of the common Linux filesystems, ext2fs, ext3fs, and ext4fs provide the most options in their mkfs tools. (In fact, these tools are one and the same; the program simply creates a filesystem with the appropriate features for the name that's used to call it.) You can type **man mkfs.ext2** to learn about these options, most of which deal with obscure or unimportant features. One option that does deserve mention is -m *percent*, which sets the reserved-space percentage. The idea is that you don't want the disk to completely fill up with user files; if the disk starts getting close to full, Linux should report that the disk *is* full before it really is, at least for ordinary users. This gives the root user the ability to log in and create new files, if necessary, to recover the system.

The ext2fs/ext3fs/ext4fs reserved-space percentage defaults to 5 percent, which translates to quite a lot of space on large disks. You may want to reduce this value (say, by passing -m 2 to reduce it to 2 percent) on your root (/) filesystem and perhaps even lower (1 percent or 0 percent) on some, such as /home. Setting -m 0 also makes sense on removable disks, which aren't likely to be critical for system recovery and may be a bit cramped to begin with.

If a filesystem is to be used on removable media, you may want to give it a descriptive label so that automounters can use the label as the mount point, as described earlier in "Using a File Manager's Automounter." Most filesystem-specific filesystem creation tools use -L *label* to set the filesystem's label. ReiserFS and FAT are exceptions to this rule; mkreiserfs (aka mkfs.reiserfs) uses a lowercase option, as in -l *label*, while mkdosfs (aka mkfs.msdos or mkfs.vfat) uses -n *label*.

In addition to providing filesystem-creation tools for Linux-native filesystems, Linux distributions usually provide such tools for various non-Linux filesystems. The most important of these may be for FAT. The main tool for this task is called mkdosfs, but it's often linked to the mkfs.msdos and mkfs.vfat names, as well. This program automatically adjusts the size of the FAT data structure to 12, 16, or 32 bits depending on the device size. No special options are required to create a FAT filesystem that can handle Windows-style (VFAT) long filenames; these are created by the OS. The mkfs.msdos and mkfs.vfat variant names for the utility have no effect on the long filename capabilities of the created filesystem.

In Exercise 3.1, you'll practice creating filesystems using mkfs and related utilities.

EXERCISE 3.1

Creating Filesystems

Try creating some filesystems on a spare partition or a removable disk. Even a floppy disk will do, although you won't be able to create journaling filesystems on a floppy disk. The following steps assume you're using a USB flash drive with at least one partition, /dev/sdc1; change the device specification as necessary. *Be sure to use an empty partition!* Accidentally entering the wrong device filename could wipe out your entire system!

This exercise uses a few commands that are described in more detail later in this chapter. To create some filesystems, follow these steps:

1.   Log in as root.

2.   Use **parted** to verify the partitions on your target disk by typing **parted /dev/sdc print**. You should see a list of partitions, including the one you'll use for your tests.

3.   Verify that your test partition is **not** currently mounted. Type **df** to see the currently mounted partitions and verify that /dev/sdc1 is not among them.

4.   Type **mkfs -t ext2 /dev/sdc1**. You should see several lines of status information appear.

5.   Type **mount /dev/sdc1 /mnt** to mount the new filesystem to /mnt. (You may use another mount point, if you like.)

6.   Type **df /mnt** to see basic accounting information for the filesystem. Note the values in the Size, Used, and Avail columns. Given the default values for ext2fs, the Avail column's value will be slightly less than 95% of the Size column's value. Most of this difference is a result of the 5% reserved blocks percentage; but some of it is because of space allocated to low-level filesystem data structures.

7.   Type **umount /mnt** to unmount the filesystem.

8.   Type **mkfs -t ext2 -m 0 /dev/sdc1** to create a new ext2 filesystem on the device, but without any reserved space.

9.   Repeat steps 5–7. Note that the available space has increased. The available space plus the used space should now equal the total space.

10. Repeat steps 4–7, but use a filesystem type code of ext3 to create a journaling filesystem. (This won't be possible if you use a floppy disk.) Note how much space is consumed by the journal.

11. Repeat steps 4–7, but use another filesystem, such as JFS or ReiserFS. Note how the filesystem-creation tools differ in the information they present and in their stated amounts of available space.

Be aware that, because of differences in how filesystems store files and allocate space, a greater amount of available space when a filesystem is created may not translate into a greater capacity to store files.

Checking Filesystems for Errors

Human error, bugs, power outages, cats playfully yanking external hard drive cables, and other events can all cause errors to creep into the complex data structures that are filesystems. When this happens, the result can be data loss. In some cases, Linux will refuse to mount a damaged filesystem. To minimize data lost to damaged filesystems and to enable Linux to mount a filesystem after it's been damaged, filesystem check tools exist. The main tool you'll use for this purpose is called fsck. This program is actually a front end to other tools, such as e2fsck or XFS's xfs_check (which checks for problems) and xfs_repair (which repairs problems). Filesystem-specific helper programs can also be called by the name fsck.*fstype*, where *fstype* is the filesystem type code. The syntax for fsck is as follows:

```
fsck  [-sACVRTNP] [-t fstype] [--] [fsck-options]  filesystems
```

The more common parameters to fsck enable you to perform useful actions, as summarized in Table 3.3. Normally, you run fsck with only the filesystem device name, as in **fsck /dev/sda6**. You can add options as needed, however. Check fsck's man page for less common options.

TABLE 3.3 Common options to fsck

Option name	Explanation
-A	This option causes fsck to check all the filesystems marked to be checked in /etc/fstab. This option is normally used in system startup scripts.
-C	This option displays a text-mode progress indicator of the check process. Most filesystem check programs don't support this feature, but e2fsck does.
-V	You can obtain a verbose progress summary by using this option.
-N	This option tells fsck to display what it would normally do without actually doing it.
-t *fstype*	Normally, fsck determines the filesystem type automatically. You can force the type with the -t *fstype* flag, though. Used in conjunction with -A, this causes the program to check only the specified filesystem types, even if others are marked to be checked. If *fstype* is prefixed with no, then all filesystems *except* the specified type are checked.
fsck-options	Filesystem check programs for specific filesystems often have their own options. The fsck command passes options it doesn't understand or those that follow a double dash (--) to the underlying check program. Common options include -a or -p (perform an automatic check), -r (perform an interactive check), and -f (force a full filesystem check even if the filesystem initially appears to be clean).
filesystems	The final parameter is usually the name of the filesystem or filesystems being checked, such as /dev/sda6.

WARNING Run fsck *only* on filesystems that are not currently mounted or that are mounted in read-only mode. Changes written to disk during normal read/ write operations can confuse fsck and result in filesystem corruption.

Linux runs fsck automatically at startup on partitions that are marked for this in /etc/fstab, as described earlier in "Permanently Mounting Filesystems." The normal behavior of e2fsck causes it to perform just a quick cursory examination of a partition if it's been unmounted cleanly. The result is that the Linux boot process isn't delayed because of a filesystem check unless the system wasn't shut down properly. This rule has a couple of exceptions, though: e2fsck forces a check if the disk has gone longer than a certain amount of time without checks (normally six months) or if the filesystem has been mounted more than a certain number of times since the last check (normally 20). You can change these options using tune2fs, as described later in "Adjusting Tunable Filesystem Parameters." Therefore, you'll occasionally see automatic filesystem checks of ext2fs and ext3fs partitions even if the system was shut down correctly.

Journaling filesystems do away with full filesystem checks at system startup even if the computer wasn't shut down correctly. Nonetheless, these filesystems still require check programs to correct problems introduced by undetected write failures, bugs, hardware problems, and the like. If you encounter odd behavior with a journaling filesystem, you might consider unmounting it and performing a filesystem check—but be sure to read the documentation first. Some Linux distributions do odd things with some journaling filesystem check programs. For instance, Mandriva uses a symbolic link from /sbin/fsck .reiserfs to /bin/true. This configuration speeds system boot times should ReiserFS partitions be marked for automatic checks, but it can be confusing if you need to manually check the filesystem. If this is the case, run /sbin/reiserfsck to do the job. Similarly, /sbin/fsck.xfs is usually nothing but a script that advises the user to run xfs_check or xfs_repair.

Tuning Filesystems

Filesystems are basically just big data structures—they're a means of storing data on disk in a way that makes it easy to locate the data later. Like all data structures, filesystems include design compromises. For instance, a design feature might speed up disk checks but consume disk space. In many cases, you have no choice concerning these compromises, but some filesystems include tools that enable you to set filesystem options that affect performance. This is particularly true of ext2fs and the related ext3fs and ext4fs, although tools for XFS, ReiserFS, and others are also available. The following pages describe tools that you can use to obtain information about filesystems, tune filesystem performance, and interactively debug filesystems.

Obtaining Filesystem Information

Before you begin tuning filesystem parameters, it's often important to learn about the current state of your filesystems. Various utilities can help accomplish this goal, particularly for the ext2fs/ext3fs/ext4fs family, XFS, and ReiserFS.

Learning About Ext2, Ext3, or Ext4 Filesystems

You can learn a lot about your ext2, ext3, or ext4 filesystem with the `dumpe2fs` command. This command's syntax is fairly straightforward:

```
dumpe2fs [options] device
```

The *device* is the filesystem device file. This command accepts several *options*, most of which are rather obscure. The most important option is probably `-h`, which causes the utility to omit information about group descriptors. (This information is helpful in very advanced filesystem debugging but not for basic filesystem tuning.) For information about additional options, consult the `man` page for `dumpe2fs`.

Unless you're a filesystem expert and need to debug a corrupted filesystem, you will likely want to use `dumpe2fs` with the `-h` option. The result is about three dozen lines of output, each specifying a particular filesystem option, like these:

```
Filesystem volume name:    <none>
Last mounted on:           <not available>
Filesystem UUID:           2e53147d-16ea-4e69-b6d3-07e897ab7ed1
Filesystem features:       has_journal ext_attr resize_inode dir_index filetype
extent flex_bg sparse_super huge_file uninit_bg dir_nlink extra_isize
Filesystem state:          clean
Inode count:               128016
Block count:               512000
Last checked:              Mon Sep 20 21:30:42 2010
Check interval:            15552000 (6 months)
Next check after:          Sat Mar 19 21:30:42 2011
```

Some of these options' meanings are fairly self-explanatory; for instance, the filesystem was last checked (with `fsck`, described in "Checking Filesystems") on September 20. Other options aren't so obvious; for instance, the `Inode count` line may be puzzling. (It's a count of the number of *inodes* supported by the filesystem. Each inode contains information for one file, so the number of inodes effectively limits the number of files you can store.)

Later sections of this chapter describe some of the options you may want to change. For now, you should know that you can retrieve information about how your filesystems are currently configured using `dumpe2fs`. You can then use this information when modifying the configuration; if your current settings seem reasonable, you can leave them alone, but if they seem ill adapted to your configuration, you can change them.

Unlike many low-level disk utilities, you can safely run dumpe2fs on a filesystem that's currently mounted. This can be handy when you're studying your configuration to decide what to modify.

Learning About XFS

Most other filesystems lack an equivalent to dumpe2fs, but XFS provides something with at least some surface similarities: xfs_info. To invoke it, pass the command the name of the partition that holds the filesystem you want to check:

```
# xfs_info /dev/sda7
meta-data=/dev/sda7     isize=256      agcount=88, agsize=1032192 blks
         =              sectsz=512     attr=0
data     =              bsize=4096     blocks=89915392, imaxpct=25
         =              sunit=0        swidth=0 blks, unwritten=1
naming   =version 2     bsize=4096
log      =internal      bsize=4096     blocks=8064, version=1
         =              sectsz=512     sunit=0 blks
realtime =none          extsz=65536    blocks=0, rtextents=0
```

Instead of the partition name, you can pass the mount point, such as /home or /usr/local. Unlike most filesystem tools, xfs_info requires that the filesystem be mounted. The information returned by xfs_info is fairly technical, mostly related to block sizes, sector sizes, and so on.

Another XFS tool is xfs_metadump. This program copies the filesystem's metadata (filenames, file sizes, and so on) to a file. For instance, xfs_metadump /dev/sda7 ~/dump-file copies the metadata to ~/dump-file. This command doesn't copy actual file contents and so isn't useful as a backup tool. Instead, it's intended as a debugging tool; if the filesystem is behaving strangely, you can use this command and send the resulting file to XFS developers for study.

Learning About ReiserFS

ReiserFS provides a tool known as debugreiserfs that can display critical ReiserFS data. The program's syntax is:

```
debugreiserfs [ -JpuqS ] [ -B file ] [ -1 blocknum ] device
```

Table 3.4 summarizes the debugreiserfs options. The -J option is likely to be the most useful to system administrators; however, if you encounter a problem and need help debugging it, -p can be a good way to get that help. By sending the filesystem metadata (filenames, date stamps, and so on, without the actual file contents), a programmer can reproduce your filesystem's structure to study any problem you might have.

TABLE 3.4 Common options to debugreiserfs

Option name	Explanation
-J	Displays the journal header, which includes assorted filesystem details.
-p	Extracts the filesystem's metadata to standard output. You can redirect the output to a file and send it to the ReiserFS developers if you think you've found a ReiserFS bug.
-u	Accepts a ReiserFS metadata image (created with the program's -p option) for insertion into the *device*. This option is normally only used by developers attempting to re-create a user's problem filesystem.
-q	Modifies the action of -p to suppress the default progress indicator.
-S	Modifies the action of -p to create a more complete metadata image.
-B *file*	Creates a file with a list of the blocks that are flagged as being bad in the filesystem.
-1 *blocknum*	Displays the contents of the specified disk block number.

Adjusting Tunable Filesystem Parameters

Several filesystems provide tools that enable you to adjust their performance parameters. Although the defaults work well enough for many purposes, you may want to adjust these options if you have particular needs.

Tuning Ext2fs, Ext3fs, or Ext4fs

The tune2fs program enables you to change many of the filesystem parameters that are reported by dumpe2fs. This program's syntax is fairly simple, but it hides a great deal of complexity:

```
tune2fs [options] device
```

The complexity arises because of the large number of *options* that the program accepts. Each feature that tune2fs enables you to adjust requires its own option, as summarized in Table 3.5. The options described here are the ones that are most likely to be useful. Several other options are available; consult tune2fs's man page for details.

TABLE 3.5   Common options to `tune2fs`

Option name	Explanation
`-c` *mounts*	Ext2fs, ext3fs, and ext4fs require a periodic disk check with `fsck`. This check is designed to prevent errors from creeping onto the disk undetected. You can adjust the maximum number of times the disk may be mounted without a check with this option, where *mounts* is the number of mounts.
`-C` *mounts*	You can trick the system into thinking the filesystem has been mounted a certain number of times with the (uppercase) `-C` *mounts* option; this sets the mount counter to *mounts*.
`-i` *interval*	Periodic disk checks are required based on time as well as the number of mounts. You can set the time between checks with this option, where *interval* is the maximum time between checks. Normally, *interval* is a number with the character d, w, or m appended, to specify days, weeks, or months, respectively.
`-j`	This option adds a journal to the filesystem, effectively converting an ext2 filesystem into an ext3 filesystem.
`-m` *percent*	This option sets the percentage of disk space that's reserved for use by root. The default value is 5, but this is excessive on multi-gigabyte hard disks, so you may want to reduce it. You may want to set it to 0 on removable disks intended to store user files.
`-r` *blocks*	This option is similar to `-m`, but it sets the reserved blocks to an absolute number of disk blocks, rather than to a percentage of disk space.
`-L` *label*	You can change the filesystem's label with this option. The label cannot exceed 16 characters in length.
`-U` *uuid*	You can change a filesystem's UUID value with this option. You'll normally set the UUID to a known value (such as the UUID the partition used prior to it being reformatted); or you can use `clear` as the *uuid* value to have `tune2fs` create an all-0 UUID, random to generate a random UUID, or time to generate a UUID based on the current time. You should *not* set the UUID to a value that's in use on another partition!

As with most low-level disk utilities, you shouldn't use `tune2fs` to adjust a mounted filesystem. If you want to adjust a key mounted filesystem, such as your root (/) filesystem, you may need to boot up an emergency disk system, such as SystemRescueCd (http://www.sysresccd.org). Many distributions' install discs can be used in this capacity, as well.

Tuning XFS

If you use XFS, the `xfs_admin` command is the rough equivalent of `tune2fs`. Table 3.6 summarizes some of the `xfs_admin` options you may want to adjust.

TABLE 3.6 Common options to xfs_admin

Option name	Explanation
-j	This option enables version 2 log (journal) format, which can improve performance in some situations.
-l	You can find the filesystem's label with this option.
-L *label*	You can change the filesystem's label with this option. The label cannot exceed 12 characters in length.
-u	This option reports the disk's UUID value. (The blkid utility also reports the UUID for any filesystem that uses one.)
-U *uuid*	You can change a filesystem's UUID value with this option. You'll normally set the UUID to a known value (such as the UUID the partition used prior to it being reformatted); or you can use generate as the *uuid* value to have xfs_admin create a new UUID. You should *not* set the UUID to a value that's in use on another partition!

In use, xfs_admin might look something like this:

```
# xfs_admin -L av_data /dev/sda7
writing all SBs
new label = "av_data"
```

This example sets the name of the filesystem on /dev/sda7 to av_data. As with tune2fs, xfs_admin should be used only on unmounted filesystems.

Tuning ReiserFS

The utility for tuning ReiserFS features is called reiserfstune. It is used much like tune2fs or xfs_admin, by passing one or more options and a device filename. Table 3.7 summarizes the more useful reiserfstune options. Consult its man page for more obscure options.

TABLE 3.7 Common options to reiserfstune

Short option name	Long option name	Explanation
-u *uuid*	--uuid *uuid*	You can change a filesystem's UUID value with this option. You'll normally set the UUID to a known value (such as the UUID the partition used prior to it being reformatted). You should *not* set the UUID to a value that's in use on another partition!
-l *label*	--label *label*	You can change the filesystem's label with this option.

Short option name	Long option name	Explanation
-m *mounts*	--max-mnt-count *mounts*	ReiserFS requires a periodic disk check with fsck. This check is designed to prevent errors from creeping onto the disk undetected. You can adjust the maximum number of times the disk may be mounted without a check with this option, where *mounts* is the number of mounts, use disable to disable the feature, or use default to restore the compile-time default. This option works only with kernel 2.6.25 and later.
-c *interval*	--check-interval *interval*	Periodic disk checks are required based on time as well as the number of mounts. You can set the time between checks with this option, where *interval* is the maximum time between checks, in days, or with disable to disable this feature.
-C *timestamp*	--time-last-checked *timestamp*	You can set the time and date code for the last filesystem check with this option. The *timestamp* can be now to signify the present time or a time in YYYYMMDD[HH[MM[SS]]] format.

Interactively Debugging a Filesystem

The debugfs program is an interactive tool for ext2, ext3, and ext4 filesystems that provides the features of many other filesystem tools rolled into one. To use the program, type its name followed by the device filename corresponding to the filesystem you want to manipulate. You'll then see the debugfs prompt:

```
# debugfs /dev/hda11
debugfs:
```

Despite their similar names, debugfs and debugreiserfs are very different programs. As described earlier, debugreiserfs is a tool that provides some basic ReiserFS data and can extract ReiserFS metadata to a file for delivery to ReiserFS developers.

You can type commands at this prompt to achieve specific goals:

Display Filesystem Superblock Information   The show_super_stats or stats command produces superblock information, similar to what dumpe2fs displays.

Display Inode Information   You can display the inode data on a file or directory by typing **stat *filename***, where *filename* is the name of the file.

Undelete a File   You can use debugfs to undelete a file by typing **undelete *inode name***, where *inode* is the inode number of the deleted file and *name* is the filename you want to give to it. (You can use undel in place of undelete if you like.) This facility is of limited utility because you must know the inode number associated with the deleted file. You can obtain a list of deleted inodes by typing **lsdel** or **list_deleted_inodes**, but the list may not provide enough clues to let you zero in on the file you want to recover.

Extract a File   You can extract a file from the filesystem by typing **write *internal-file external-file***, where *internal-file* is the name of a file in the filesystem you're manipulating and *external-file* is a filename on your main Linux system. This facility can be handy if a filesystem is badly damaged and you want to extract a critical file without mounting the filesystem.

Manipulate Files   Most of the commands described in Chapter 4, "Advanced Disk Management," work within debugfs. You can change your directory with cd, create links with ln, remove a file with rm, and so on.

Obtain Help   Typing **list_requests, lr, help**, or **?** produces a summary of available commands.

Exit   Typing **quit** exits from the program.

This summary just scratches the surface of debugfs's capabilities. In the hands of an expert, this program can help rescue a badly damaged filesystem or at least extract critical data from it. To learn more, consult the program's man page.

> Although debugfs is a useful tool, it's potentially dangerous. Don't use it on a mounted filesystem, don't use it unless you have to, and be very careful when using it. If in doubt, leave the adjustments to the experts. Be aware that the LPIC 201 exam objectives do include debugfs, though.

The closest XFS equivalent to debugfs is called xfs_db. Like debugfs, xfs_db provides an interactive tool to access and manipulate a filesystem; but xfs_db provides fewer tools that are amenable to novice or intermediate use. Instead, xfs_db is a tool for XFS experts.

Manipulating Swap Space

Some partitions don't hold files. Most notably, Linux can use a *swap partition*, which is a partition that Linux treats as an extension of memory. (Linux can also use a *swap file*, which is a file that works in the same way. Both are examples of *swap space*.) If you run enough programs that your computer's memory fills up, Linux copies some memory contents to the swap space, thus enabling you to run more programs than you could otherwise. Sometimes Linux does this even if you have enough memory to hold all your programs in order to free up memory for use in disk buffers, which can improve disk access time. A secondary use for swap space is to hold an image of system memory if you use a *suspend-to-disk* (aka *hibernate*) mode, which is a way of powering off the computer without going through the normal shutdown sequence. To use this feature, your swap space must be at least as large as your system's memory.

> Linux swap partitions normally use an MBR type code of 0x82. Unfortunately, Solaris for *x86* also uses an MBR partition type code of 0x82, but in Solaris, this code refers to a Solaris partition. If you dual-boot between Solaris and Linux, this double meaning of the 0x82 partition type code can cause confusion. This is particularly true when installing the OSs. You may need to use Linux's fdisk to temporarily change the partition type codes to keep Linux from trying to use a Solaris partition as swap space or to keep Solaris from trying to interpret Linux swap space as a data partition.

Although swap space doesn't hold a filesystem *per se* and isn't mounted in the way that filesystem partitions are mounted, swap space does require preparation similar to that for creation of a filesystem. This task is accomplished with the mkswap command, which you can generally use by passing it nothing but the device identifier:

```
# mkswap /dev/sda7
```

This example turns /dev/sda7 into swap space. Several options to mkswap exist, but most are very obscure or dangerous. The -L *label* and -U *uuid* options are the ones you're most likely to use; these options enable you to set the label and UUID of the swap space so that you can reference swap space by label or UUID in /etc/fstab or elsewhere. If you don't use the -U option, mkswap generates a UUID itself. You can find a swap partition's UUID using blkid.

Although swap space is often created on partitions, you can turn an ordinary file into swap space using mkswap. You can then reference the file in /etc/fstab or enable it with swapon, as described shortly. A swap file can be convenient if you run out of swap space; you can create a swap file quickly and without adjusting your system's partitions. Swap files can be created on most Linux-native filesystems, but some filesystems aren't suitable for holding swap files. NFS, for instance, can't hold a swap file. (Even if it could, placing swap on a network mount would produce very poor performance.)

> If you create a swap file and subsequently back up the partition on which it resides, try to avoid backing up the swap file; it will be a waste of space on the backup medium. Likewise, there's no point in backing up swap partitions.

To use the swap space, you must activate it with the swapon command:

```
# swapon /dev/sda7
```

Table 3.8 summarizes several swapon options. To permanently activate swap space, you must create an entry for it in /etc/fstab, as described previously in "Permanently Mounting Filesystems."

TABLE 3.8 Common options to swapon

Short option name	Long option name	Explanation
-a	--all	Activates all swap devices specified in /etc/fstab.
-e	--ifexists	Skips devices that don't exist without displaying error messages.
-L *label*	N/A	Mounts swap space by its label rather than by its device filename.
-p *priority*	--priority *priority*	Sets a priority value from 0 to 32767. Swap space with a higher priority is used preferentially. You might use this feature if you have swap space on disks of differing speeds; setting a higher priority to the faster disk will improve performance. Priorities may be set in /etc/fstab by setting the pri=*priority* option.
-s	--summary	Displays summary information on swap space use.
-U *uuid*	N/A	Mounts swap space by UUID rather than by its device filename.

To deactivate swap space, you can use **swapoff**:

```
# swapoff /dev/sda7
```

You can use the -a option with swapoff to have it deactivate all swap space. If you deactivate a swap file and intend to never use it again, remember to delete it to save disk space.

Managing Optical Discs

Optical media are a popular means of exchanging moderately large files. Most CD-R and CD-RW media hold 700MB of files (older discs held 650MB), recordable DVD formats have capacities of 4.7–8.5GB, and Blu-ray discs hold 25–50GB. Plain write-once CDs and

DVDs cost $0.10 to $1 and are likely to remain readable for several years to decades, given proper storage. You don't normally mount an optical disc and write files to it as you would a floppy disk, though; you must create a complete filesystem and then copy (or "burn") that filesystem to the disc. (The upcoming section "Reading and Writing UDF Discs" describes an exception to this rule.) This process requires using two tools, mkisofs and cdrecord, or requires variants of or front-ends to these tools.

Linux Optical Disc Tools

The Linux optical disc creation process involves three steps:

1. Collect source files. You must first collect source files in one location, typically a single subdirectory of your home directory.

2. Create a filesystem. You point a filesystem-creation program, mkisofs, at your source directory. This program generates an ISO-9660 filesystem in an image file. Recently, mkisofs has been renamed genisofs; however, the mkisofs name is retained as a symbolic link to genisofs. Because the LPIC 201 objectives refer to mkisofs, I use that command name in this chapter.

3. Burn the disc. You use an optical disc–burning program, such as cdrecord, to copy the image file to the optical device.

> Recent Linux distributions provide both mkisofs and cdrecord in a single package called cdrtools or cdrkit; or they may be split into the genisoimage and wodim packages, respectively.

The growisofs program (typically installed in the dvd+rw-tools package) combines the functionality of mkisofs and cdrecord, but growisofs works only with DVDs and Blu-ray discs, not with the smaller CD-Rs. In turn, many versions of cdrecord won't work with the larger DVDs and Blu-ray discs!

Another approach to optical disc creation is to use GUI front-ends to the text-mode tools. These GUI tools provide a point-and-click interface, eliminating the need to remember obscure command-line parameters. Popular GUI Linux optical disc creation tools include X-CD-Roast (http://www.xcdroast.org), GNOME Toaster (http://freshmeat .net/projects/gnometoaster/), and K3B (http://k3b.sourceforge.net).

All of these optical disc tools provide a dizzying array of options. For the most part, the default options work quite well, although you may need to provide information to identify your drive and burn speed, as described in the next section. Some mkisofs options can also be important in generating image files that can be read on a wide variety of OSs, as described later in "Creating Cross-Platform Discs."

A Linux Optical Disc Example

To begin creating optical discs, starting with mkisofs makes sense:

```
$ mkisofs -J -r -V "volume name" -o ../image.iso ./
```

This command creates an image file called *image.iso* in the parent of the current directory, placing files from the current working directory (./) in the resultant image file. The -J and -r options enable Joliet and Rock Ridge extensions, respectively, and the -V option sets the volume name to whatever you specify. Dozens of other options and variants on these are available; check mkisofs's man page for details.

Once you've created an image file, you can burn it with a command such as the following:

```
$ cdrecord dev=/dev/dvdrw speed=4 ../image.iso
```

The device (dev=*/dev/dvdrw*) must exist and be your optical drive. (This may be /dev/dvdrw or something similar even if you're burning a CD-R. Details vary depending on your distribution and hardware.) The write speed is set using the speed option, and the final parameter specifies the source of the file to be burned. As with mkisofs, cdrecord supports many additional options; consult its man page for details. If the SUID bit isn't set on this program, with ownership set to root, you must run it as root.

You can mount an image file using the loopback option to verify its contents before burning it. For instance, typing **mount -t iso9660 -o loop** *image.iso* */mnt/cdrom* mounts the *image.iso* file to */mnt/cdrom*. You can then check that all the files that should be present are present. You must be root to use this option, or you must have created an appropriate */etc/fstab* entry.

When burning DVDs or Blu-ray discs, you may need to use growisofs, which combines the features of both mkisofs and cdrecord:

```
$ growisofs -speed=4 -Z /dev/dvdrw -J -r -V "volume name" ./
```

The -speed option of growisofs is equivalent to the speed option of cdrecord. You specify the target device using -Z rather than dev=. Options following the device are the same as those used by mkisofs. The growisofs approach eliminates the need for a temporary image file, which is particularly helpful with larger discs. If you prefer, though, you can create such a file with mkisofs or some other utility and then burn it with growisofs by adding the source file to the -Z option:

```
$ growisofs -speed=4 -Z /dev/dvdrw=source-file.iso
```

This form of growisofs is also useful for burning a DVD image file you've obtained from another source, such as a Linux installation DVD image you've downloaded from the Internet.

Creating Cross-Platform Discs

You may want to create a disc that works on many different OSs. If so, you may want to use a wide range of filesystems and filesystem extensions. Such discs contain just one copy of each file; the filesystems are written in such a way that they all point their unique directory structures at the same files. Thus, the extra space required by such a multiplatform disc is minimal. Features you may want to use on such a disc include the following:

Following Symbolic Links   The -f option to mkisofs causes the tool to read the files that symbolic links point to and include them on the CD-R, rather than to write symbolic links as such using Rock Ridge extensions. Following symbolic links can increase the disk space used on a CD-R, but this option is required if you want symbolic links to produce reasonable results on OSs that don't understand Rock Ridge, such as Windows.

Long ISO-9660 Filenames   Normally, mkisofs creates only short filenames for the base ISO-9660 filesystem. Long filenames are stored in Rock Ridge, Joliet, or other filesystem extensions. You can increase the raw ISO-9660 name length to 31 characters with the -1 (that's a lowercase *L*) option.

Joliet Support   The -J option to mkisofs, as noted earlier, creates an image with Joliet extensions. These extensions do *not* interfere with reading the disc from OSs that don't understand Joliet.

Rock Ridge Support   The -R and -r options both add Rock Ridge extensions. The -R option adds the extensions, but files are stored using their original ownership and permissions, which might be inappropriate on another computer. Using -r works the same, except that it changes ownership of all files to root, gives all users read access to the files, and removes write permissions. These features are usually desirable on a disc that's to be used on any but the original author's computer.

UDF Support   You can add support for the UDF filesystem by including the -udf option. UDF is the "up and coming" optical disc filesystem and is the preferred filesystem for DVDs. Most modern OSs, including recent versions of Linux, Windows, and Mac OS, understand UDF.

HFS Support   To create a disc that includes Mac OS HFS support, add the -hfs option. When you insert the resulting disc into a Macintosh, the computer will read the HFS filenames. A slew of options are related to this one.

Bootable Discs   Although it's not really a cross-platform issue, bootable discs can be important. The standard for bootable discs is known as the *El Torito* specification. To create an El Torito disc, you must pass a bootable image to mkisofs using the -b *image-file* option, where *image-file* is the filename of a bootable disk image, relative to the directory that's used to create the disc image. Typically the disk image is a floppy disk image; when the computer boots, it acts as if it were booting from a floppy disk. If the boot image is of a complete hard disk, add the -hard-disk-boot parameter; if it's of a disk partition, use the -no-emul-boot parameter. You can create a disk image file by copying from the original source using dd, as in **dd if=/dev/fd0 of=floppy.img** to create an image of a floppy disk.

Reading and Writing UDF Discs

You can create a UDF disc using the -udf option to mkisofs, as just described; however, mkisofs creates UDF as an addition to the ISO-9660 filesystem, and the disc must be created using the same basic process as an ISO-9660 disc. A disc created in this way may be mounted as UDF, but it will be a read-only filesystem.

Full random read/write access to an optical disc, similar to the access you have to USB flash drives or other disks, is referred to as *packet writing*. To obtain this support, you may use the Linux kernel driver for UDF, the kernel's packet writing support, and the udftools package. This combination gives you access to DVD+RW drives as if they were regular hard disks. CD-RW media cannot be mounted in a read/write manner using these tools, although you can mount CD-RW UDF media for read-only access.

To begin using packet writing features, you should first ensure that you have the relevant kernel drivers and udftools package installed. (The kernel drivers are included with most distributions' standard kernels.) You can then create a UDF filesystem on your DVD+RW disc:

```
# mkudffs /dev/dvdrw
```

Change the device filename as necessary. You can then mount the disc, copy files to it, delete files from it, and otherwise use it much as you'd use a hard disk. Writing to UDF discs tends to be quite slow, so be prepared to wait if you're copying many or large files to the disc. Like ISO-9660 with Rock Ridge, UDF supports Linux-style ownership and permissions, so you should bear this in mind and set ownership and permissions appropriately if the disc will be read on other Linux or UNIX computers.

Unlike discs created with mkisofs or growisofs, discs created with mkudffs contain no ISO-9660 filesystem. Therefore, older OSs that have no UDF support won't be able to read mkudffs-created discs. Likewise, if you specify an optical disc mount point in /etc/fstab with a filesystem type of iso9660, you won't be able to mount such discs in Linux unless you manually specify the filesystem type or mount the disc in some other location. You can use a filesystem specification of udf or auto in /etc/fstab to ensure that UDF-only discs can be mounted.

Managing Devices with *udev*

Most filesystems provide access to files stored on physical media—hard disks, optical discs, USB flash drives, and so on. A few filesystems, however, are virtual—they provide access to information or non-disk data in file-like form. One virtual filesystem that you may need to configure is udev, which controls the device files in the /dev directory tree. These files give programs access to the computer's hardware—the keyboard, mouse, printer, and even hard disks and partitions in a "raw" form.

Configuring udev requires understanding what it does. You can then create rules that modify how udev operates. If you have problems, you may need to use utilities to monitor udev's operation as you attach and detach devices or load and unload relevant kernel modules.

Understanding *udev*

When a Linux computer boots, the kernel scans the hardware to see what is available. The udev subsystem then creates entries in the /dev virtual filesystem for most hardware devices. This approach to device file maintenance enables the system to adapt to a wide variety of hardware and keeps the /dev directory uncluttered—prior to udev, Linux systems frequently had a fixed set of /dev directory entries for all common hardware devices, even if those devices did not exist on the computer.

NOTE   Not all hardware devices get /dev directory entries. Network devices, such as Ethernet and WiFi ports, are notable exceptions. Nonetheless, udev handles these devices; you can use it to rename network devices or ensure consistent naming of network devices across boots.

Standards exist for naming devices in /dev. For instance, most hard disks take names of the form /dev/sd*A*, where *A* is a letter. Partitions on hard disks take the same name with a number added. Thus, /dev/sda is the first hard disk, /dev/sdb is the second hard disk, /dev/sda1 is the first partition on the first hard disk, and so on. The /dev directory also holds subdirectories, which are used to hold entire categories of device files. Table 3.9 presents some important Linux device filenames. In this table, *A* refers to a letter, # refers to a number, and * refers to whole filenames or subdirectories. Table 3.9 is incomplete; many other devices are available. There are also variations from one distribution to another in what device nodes are created, even on identical hardware.

TABLE 3.9   Common Linux device filenames

Device filename pattern	Explanation
/dev/sd*A*	A whole hard disk, accessible using the Small Computer System Interface (SCSI) subsystem. (Many non-SCSI disks use this subsystem on modern computers.)
/dev/hd*A*	A whole hard disk or optical disc, accessible by using the Integrated Device Electronics (IDE) subsystem. IDE addressing is becoming rare.
/dev/sd*A*#	A hard disk partition on a disk that uses the SCSI subsystem.

TABLE 3.9   Common Linux device filenames *(continued)*

Device filename pattern	Explanation
/dev/hd*A*#	A hard disk partition on a disk that uses the IDE subsystem.
/dev/fd#	A floppy disk.
/dev/sr#	An optical disc, accessible by using the SCSI subsystem. One or more symbolic links called /dev/cdrom, /dev/cdrw, /dev/dvd, and /dev/dvdrw are also likely to exist.
/dev/lp#	A parallel port.
/dev/usb/lp#	A USB printer.
/dev/ttyS#	An RS-232 serial port.
/dev/tty#	A text-mode login console.
/dev/pts/#	A text-mode session in a pseudo-terminal, which is a remote login session, X text-mode console, or similar login tool.
/dev/bus/usb/*	This directory tree provides access to USB devices. The names are normally very uninformative.
/dev/snd/*	These files provide access to your sound hardware.
/dev/input/*	Human input devices (primarily mice) are accessed via these files. /dev/input/mice provides access to any and all mice, while /dev/input/mouse# provides access to specific mice.
/dev/zero	When read, this device file produces an endless string of binary 0 values. It may be used as a source to completely blank out a file or partition.
/dev/null	This file is intended for writing, but it's connected to nothing; any data sent to /dev/null disappears.

Most devices in /dev are *character devices*, which means you can read or write data one character (byte) at a time. Examples include printer ports, mice, and consoles. Some devices, however, are *block devices*, which means you must read or write data in multibyte chunks. The most common block devices are disk devices. Most disks have 512-byte blocks, but some use larger block sizes.

Like all files in Linux, the files in /dev have owners, group owners, and permissions. These features control who may access a device. In most cases, you don't want ordinary users to have full read/write access to the raw disk devices; however, ordinary users may require access to the sound hardware devices. One of the key features of udev is that you can alter the default ownership and permissions associated with device files, thus giving access to the hardware to those users who require it.

Preparing to Create *udev* Rules

The /etc/udev/rules.d directory holds one or more files that contain udev rules. These files normally have names of the form ##-*description*.rules, where ## is a sequence number and *description* is a short description of what type of rules reside in the file. The sequence number controls the order in which the udev rules are executed when the system boots or when a device is attached to or detached from the computer.

   To control udev, you must know the names for various kernel attributes related to your hardware. One way to learn the relevant attribute names is with the udevadm command, which has various subcommands that can be used to examine or manipulate the udev subsystem. Of particular relevance to start with is the info subcommand, which can be used with various parameters to reveal the attributes associated with any given device file. The following command demonstrates this use, producing the attributes associated with /dev/input/mouse1:

```
$ udevadm info -a -p $(udevadm info -q path -n /dev/input/mouse1)
```

```
Udevadm info starts with the device specified by the devpath and then
walks up the chain of parent devices. It prints for every device
found, all possible attributes in the udev rules key format.
A rule to match, can be composed by the attributes of the device
and the attributes from one single parent device.

  looking at device '/class/input/input6/mouse1':
    KERNEL=="mouse1"
    SUBSYSTEM=="input"
    DRIVER==""

  looking at parent device '/class/input/input6':
    KERNELS=="input6"
    SUBSYSTEMS=="input"
    DRIVERS==""
    ATTRS{name}=="Logitech Trackball"
    ATTRS{phys}=="usb-0000:00:13.0-3/input0"
    ATTRS{uniq}==""
    ATTRS{modalias}=="input:b0003v046DpC404e0110-e0,1,2,4,k110,111,112,r0,1,8,
am4,lsfw"

  looking at parent device '/class/input':
    KERNELS=="input"
    SUBSYSTEMS=="subsystem"
    DRIVERS==""
```

Older versions of the udev utilities employed a separate program for each udevadm action. The udevinfo command took the place of udevadm info. If you're using an older distribution, you might have to make this substitution.

If you want to tweak a udev rule, you should locate features that distinguish the device you want to affect from other devices. For instance, in the preceding output, the ATTRS{name} field might be unique on your system. Some devices report serial numbers, driver names, vendor ID codes, or other features that can help you uniquely identify a device.

Rules in a udev rules file consist of a series of comma-separated key/value pairs, with the key and value separated by an operator, as specified in Table 3.10. Operators come in two types: matching and assignment. Matching operators are used to specify conditions for the assignment operators to be applied—that is, the assignment operators in a rule are activated if and only if all the matching operators evaluate as true.

TABLE 3.10   udev operators

Operator	Type	Explanation
==	Matching	Compares for equality
!=	Matching	Compares for inequality
=	Assignment	Assigns the value to the key, replacing the old value
+=	Assignment	Adds the value to the existing set of key values
:=	Assignment	Assigns the value to the key and disallow future changes

Pay careful attention to the difference between the == matching operator and the = assignment operator! This single-character difference is easy to overlook, and if you get it wrong, your udev rules will not work as you intended.

Table 3.11 specifies some common udev keys. (Consult udev's man page for additional options.) Some of these appear in the preceding example output. When you specify a key in a matching operator, you can use wildcards, such as * to match any string, ? to match any single character, or [abc] to match any one character in the set abc.

TABLE 3.11 Common udev keys

Key	Type	Explanation
LABEL	Control	A name set to manage the flow of matches within a udev rules file.
GOTO	Control	A statement that can redirect the flow of matching operations within a udev rules file.
WAIT_FOR	Control	Causes matching to be paused until the specified file is created.
ACTION	Matching	The name of an action that udev has taken, such as add to add a device file.
KERNEL	Matching	The kernel's name for the device, such as sd* for any SCSI disk device.
DEVPATH	Matching	The kernel's device path, such as /devices/*.
SUBSYSTEM	Matching	The kernel's name for the device subsystem, such as sound or net.
DRIVER	Matching	The name of a device driver.
PROGRAM	Matching	Executes an external program. When used with a matching key, the key is considered true if the program returns a 0 value.
RESULT	Matching	The standard output of the most recent PROGRAM call.
ATTR{*string*}	Matching or Assignment	An arbitrary name that can be set for the device.
NAME	Assignment	The name of a device file to be created, relative to /dev. (A device node is not created for network devices, but NAME may still be used to specify the device's name.)
SYMLINK	Assignment	The name of a symbolic link to be created, relative to /dev.
OWNER	Assignment	The owner of the device file.
GROUP	Assignment	The group of the device file.
MODE	Assignment	The permissions of the device file.
RUN	Assignment	The name of an external program (in /lib/udev if the name is specified without a full path) to be executed. Such programs must execute quickly; if they don't, they'll cause delays in udev processing.
OPTIONS	Assignment	Sets device-specific options, such as all_partitions to create partitions for disk devices.

Earlier versions of udev used SYSFS{*string*} rather than ATTR{*string*}. Many of the keys used for matching can be turned into plural forms (such as SUBSYSTEM to SUBSYSTEMS or ATTR{*string*} to ATTRS{*string*}) to search in multiple layers of the device path. That is, in the udevadm info output you'll find keys associated with several levels of drivers. Using the singular matching rules matches only one layer, whereas the plural form matches all devices higher in the tree from the match.

Creating *udev* Rules

A simple example, shown in Listing 3.2, demonstrates how udev may be used to adjust several device nodes. You might create such a file as /etc/udev/rules.d/99-my.rules. In most cases, you should *not* modify the standard udev rules files, since they're likely to be replaced by system upgrades.

Listing 3.2: Sample udev rules file

```
SUBSYSTEM!="usb_device", ACTION!="add", GOTO="minolta_rules_end"

# Minolta|DiMAGE Scan Elite 5400
ATTR{idVendor}=="0686", ATTR{idProduct}=="400e", SYMLINK+="scan5400"↩
 MODE="0660", OWNER="lisa", GROUP="scanner"

LABEL="minolta_rules_end"

# PCI device 0x8086:0x1030 (e100)
SUBSYSTEM=="net", ACTION=="add", ATTR{address}=="00:03:47:b1:e3:d8",↩
 KERNEL=="eth*", NAME="eth0"

# PCI device 0x10ec:0x8168 (r8169)
SUBSYSTEM=="net", ACTION=="add", ATTR{address}=="00:e0:4d:a3:22:c5",↩
 KERNEL=="eth*", NAME="eth1"
```

The first line in Listing 3.2, which includes a GOTO statement, is designed to keep the first rule from executing except when USB devices are added. This line is not very important in this example, but you use a similar configuration to bypass many or slow-executing rules to improve udev speed. If a USB device is not being added, everything between the first line and the LABEL="minolta_rules_end" line is ignored.

The first rule in Listing 3.2 adjusts permissions and sets up a symbolic link for a specific device, identified in the comment line (denoted by a leading hash mark, #) as a Minolta DiMAGE Scan Elite 5400 film scanner. This device can be identified by its unique ATTR{idVendor} and ATTR{idProduct} keys. The main purpose of this rule is to adjust the ownership, group ownership, and permissions of the device node, enabling the user lisa and members of the scanner group to access the device. The rule also creates a symbolic link, /dev/scan5400, to point to the original device node. Note that the MODE, OWNER, and GROUP keys all use the = operator, since files can have but one mode, owner, and group; but the SYMLINK key uses the += operator, since multiple symbolic links can point to a single device node, and if you used =, your rule would override any other symbolic links that might be created by other rules—something you probably don't want to do.

The next two rules are similar to one another; they both specify names for particular Ethernet devices, using their hardware addresses as keys. Rules like this are common on computers with multiple devices of the same type. Without these rules, there's no guarantee that a given device will have the same identifier each time the computer boots—that is, eth0 today might become eth1 if you reboot the computer tomorrow. Although such inconsistency isn't a big problem for some devices, it can be disastrous for others. A computer with two Ethernet interfaces might be used as a router, for instance, and you might configure the system with a specific address on each interface. Other devices you might need to distinguish in this way include optical discs, hard disks, printers, television tuners, and scanners.

Modern Linux distributions often create rules similar to the last two rules in Listing 3.2 for network devices and optical discs. These rules typically appear in the 70-persistent-net.rules and 70-persistent-cd.rules files in /etc/udev/rules.d. If you swap hardware, you can end up with new Ethernet device names or optical disc device nodes, which may not be a desirable effect. If this happens, you should be able to edit these files to produce the desired node naming. (Editing these files is an exception to the rule of not editing your distribution's pre-existing udev rules files.) These files may be updated again in the future, but your changes will normally persist.

Sometimes you might prefer to create a symbolic link with a distinctive name rather than specify a conventional name for a device. Such a configuration would closely resemble the Minolta scanner example in Listing 3.2. You could then refer to the device by a distinctive name, such as /dev/scan5400, in software.

Monitoring *udev* Activity

Once you've created new udev rules, you'll want to test them. You don't need to reboot or even restart any programs to enable your rules; just save the new rules file. You will, however, have to reload the device to have your rule take effect. If the device is hot-pluggable (that is, if it can be safely disconnected and reconnected), like a USB device, you can unplug it and plug it back in again, or perhaps power it off and then back on again. If the device is not hot-pluggable, you may be able to cause the udev rules to be re-interpreted by unloading and reloading a relevant kernel module, as described in Chapter 2, "Linux

Kernel Configuration." If this is impossible, you may have to enter runlevel S or s, or even reboot the computer, to test the new udev configuration.

If you have problems, you may find some clues by using udevadm, this time with its monitor option. (This action used to be enabled via the separate udevmonitor program; the LPI objectives refer to it as such.) The result is likely to be a series of lines like the following when you activate a device:

```
KERNEL[1285302053.747736] add        /class/input/input7 (input)
KERNEL[1285302053.747891] add        /class/input/input7/mouse1 (input)
KERNEL[1285302053.748003] add        /class/input/input7/event5 (input)
KERNEL[1285302053.748089] add        /class/hidraw/hidraw1 (hidraw)
```

These lines summarize the information files (in /class and /devices, but not in /dev) that are being created for each device. When a device is removed, a similar line, but with remove rather than add, is displayed.

Summary

Proper management of a Linux computer's filesystems is necessary for the computer's ongoing utility. The most basic aspect of this management is making filesystems available, which is usually done by mounting them. The mount command mounts a filesystem to a mount point, while the umount command undoes this association. You can also permanently mount a filesystem by editing the /etc/fstab file, which controls how filesystems are mounted when the computer boots.

Of course, you can't mount a filesystem if it hasn't been created or if it's been badly damaged, and Linux provides tools to enable you to create and repair filesystems. Specifically, mkfs creates filesystems, while fsck checks them for errors and repairs any errors it finds. (Both programs are actually front-ends; the real work is done by filesystem-specific tools, which you can call directly if you prefer.) Various filesystem-specific tools enable you to fine-tune filesystem operations, such as adjusting the amount of space reserved for root or altering journal functioning. The filesystems used on optical discs (ISO-9660 and its extensions, as well as the newer UDF) require special attention because they're created using special tools, such as mkisofs. These filesystems are also written to optical discs in a special way, using cdrecord or growisofs, although once they're prepared, optical discs are mounted and used much like other filesystems. Although it isn't a filesystem, swap space is managed in a similar way, and you should be familiar with the mkswap, swapon, and swapoff tools that handle swap space.

One special filesystem deserves special attention: udev. This tool creates device nodes, which provide programs with access to hardware—text-mode consoles, printers, scanners, and even raw disk devices. Although Linux distributions ship with basically functional udev configurations, you may need to tweak the standard configuration to ensure consistent naming of devices, to adjust ownership or permissions so that users can access hardware, or for other reasons.

Exam Essentials

Describe the command that's used to mount a filesystem.   The mount command mounts a filesystem. Normally, it's passed a device node and mount point, as in **mount /dev/sda2 /mnt/data** to mount the filesystem on /dev/sda2 on /mnt/data. You can pass additional options to fine-tune its operation. If a filesystem is defined in /etc/fstab with the user, users, or owner options, ordinary users may use mount, passing only the device node or mount point, as in **mount /mnt/data**.

Summarize the /etc/fstab file format.   The /etc/fstab file consists of lines, each of which defines a single mount. (Comment lines may also be present; they begin with hash marks, #.) Each line consists of six fields separated by spaces or tabs: the device filename, the mount point, the filesystem type code, the mount options, the dump code, and the filesystem check order.

Explain how filesystems may be unmounted.   The umount command unmounts filesystems. This command takes a device name or mount point of a mounted filesystem as an argument. Various options can modify its behavior. Ordinarily, only root may use this command, although if /etc/fstab contains a relevant entry, ordinary users may unmount a filesystem.

Describe how filesystems are created.   The mkfs utility is used to create filesystems. At a minimum, you pass the filesystem type code using the -t option and the device filename. For instance, **mkfs -t ext4 /dev/sda8** creates an ext4 filesystem on /dev/sda8. The mkfs program relies on helper programs for each filesystem, and you may call the helper programs directly if you prefer, as in **mkfs.ext4 /dev/sda8**. Although mkfs and its helpers may be used by ordinary users, normally only root has write access to the device files, so in practice only root may use these programs on most disk devices.

Describe how filesystems are checked for errors.   The fsck utility checks a filesystem for errors and repairs any errors that are found. At a minimum, you pass fsck the name of a device that should be checked, as in **fsck /dev/sda8**. (That device should *not* be mounted!) Like mkfs, fsck actually relies on helper programs that you can call directly. Both fsck and its helper programs support options that modify how the check proceeds; for instance, you might force a more complete check even if a quick check suggests the filesystem is clean.

Summarize how swap space is created and managed.   The mkswap program creates swap space, as in **mkswap /dev/sda9**. Once created, swap space can be activated with swapon or deactivated with swapoff. To permanently add swap space to a system, you can create an entry in /etc/fstab, using a filesystem type code of swap and a mount point of swap.

Describe the tools used to create optical discs.   The mkisofs (aka genisoimage) program creates an ISO-9660 filesystem in a file, optionally including the Rock Ridge or Joliet filesystem extensions or an HFS or UDF filesystem. The image file may then be written to an optical disc using the `cdrecord` or `wodim` programs (for CD media) or the `growisofs` program (for DVD and Blu-ray media). Alternatively, `growisofs` incorporates `mkisofs` features, which can streamline creation of optical discs; or you can use any of several GUI front-ends that enable point-and-click optical disc creation.

Explain how `udev` is configured   You can find `udev` configuration files in `/etc/udev/rules.d`; each file has a filename that ends in `.rules`. These files contain key/value pairs separated by operators. The operators can perform matching tasks (which collectively determine whether a rule is applied) or can signify assignment (in which a device node is created or modified or some other action is taken). Using these rules, you can adjust permissions of nodes, create symbolic links, run external helper scripts, or perform other tasks to help manage your system's device nodes.

Review Questions

1. What mount point should you associate with swap partitions?

    A. /

    B. /swap

    C. /boot

    D. None

2. To access files on a USB pen drive, you type **mount /dev/sdc1 /media/pen** as root. Which types of filesystems will this command mount, provided the filesystem support exists in the kernel?

    A. Ext2fs

    B. FAT

    C. HFS

    D. All of the above

3. Which of the following /etc/fstab entries will mount /dev/sdb2 as the /home directory at boot time?

    A. /dev/sdb2 reiserfs /home defaults 0 0

    B. /dev/sdb2 /home reiserfs defaults 0 0

    C. /home reiserfs /dev/sdb2 noauto 0 0

    D. /home /dev/sdb2 reiserfs noauto 0 0

4. What filesystem options might you specify in /etc/fstab to make a removable disk (USB pen drive, Zip disk, floppy disk, and so on) user-mountable? (Select all that apply.)

    A. user

    B. users

    C. owner

    D. owners

5. Your /etc/fstab file contains the following entry:

    ```
    /dev/sdc5  /  ext4  defaults  1 1
    ```

    Unfortunately, the order in which your three hard disks is detected varies randomly from one boot to another, which makes this entry problematic. How might you change the entry to fix this problem?

    A. Replace /dev/sdc5 with a drive letter specification, such as DRIVE=D:, obtaining the drive letter from GNOME's file browser, Nautilus.

    B. Replace /dev/sdc5 with a UUID specification, such as UUID=8b4cdbdd-b9b3-404a-9a54-c1691f1f1483, obtaining the UUID value using blkid.

    C. Replace the mount point, /, with the drive-independent mount point specification of //rootdevice//; and change defaults to rootdrive.

    D. Replace the mount point, /, with an appropriate LABEL= specification, such as LABEL=root, obtaining the LABEL value using dumpe2fs.

6. You've just repartitioned a non-boot disk, added a swap partition to it (/dev/sdb7), created swap space on the partition, and added a suitable entry to /etc/fstab for the new swap partition. How can you activate the new swap partition? (Select all that apply.)

    A. mount /dev/sdb7

    B. mkswap /dev/sdb7

    C. swapon /dev/sdb7

    D. swapon -a

7. What is the purpose of the /etc/mtab file?

    A. It describes the filesystems that are currently mounted, using syntax similar to that of /etc/fstab.

    B. It controls the filesystems that the automounter mounts in response to attempts to access empty subdirectories.

    C. It provides information on the UUID values and filesystem types contained in all partitions.

    D. It summarizes the filesystems currently available to the Linux kernel—that is, those you can mount.

8. A network file server has become unavailable while your Linux computer was accessing it at /mnt/remote. Now you want to unmount that share, but because the server has disappeared, umount complains. Which of the following commands is most likely to successfully unmount this unresponsive mount?

    A. umount -f /mnt/remote

    B. umount -a

    C. mount -o remount,ro /mnt/remote

    D. umount --kill /mnt/remote

9. What does the following command accomplish?

    # mkfs.ext2 /dev/sda4

    A. It sets the partition table type code for /dev/sda4 to ext2.

    B. It converts a FAT partition into an ext2fs partition without damaging the partition's existing files.

    C. It creates a new ext2 filesystem on /dev/sda4, overwriting any existing filesystem and data.

    D. It checks the ext2 filesystem on /dev/sda4 for errors, correcting any that it finds.

10. Which of the following options is used with `fsck` to force it to use a particular filesystem type?

   A.   -A

   B.   -N

   C.   -t

   D.   -C

11. What is an advantage of a journaling filesystem over a conventional (non-journaling) filesystem?

   A.   Journaling filesystems are older and better tested than non-journaling filesystems.

   B.   Journaling filesystems never need to have their filesystems checked with `fsck`.

   C.   Journaling filesystems support Linux ownership and permissions; non-journaling filesystems don't.

   D.   Journaling filesystems require shorter disk checks after a power failure or system crash.

12. Which of the following features can you adjust with `tune2fs`? (Select all that apply.)

   A.   The presence of a journal

   B.   The size of the filesystem

   C.   The filesystem's UUID value

   D.   The owner of all the files on the filesystem

13. You have accidentally deleted a file on an ext3fs partition. To recover it, you first enter debugfs, specifying the partition's device node. How can you recover the file?

   A.   Type **restore** and then select the file from the list that appears.

   B.   Type **undelete *inode***, where *inode* is the file's inode number.

   C.   Type **restore */path/filename***, where *path* is the complete path to the file and *filename* is its filename.

   D.   Type **undelete *path/filename***, where *path* is the complete path to the file and *filename* is its filename.

14. An ext4 filesystem on /dev/sda3 is being checked every time you reboot your computer. You suspect it may have an incorrect value set that's causing the system to check it after every mount operation. How can you test this hypothesis?

   A.   Type **dumpe2fs -h /dev/sda3** and examine the maximum mount count and maximum check interval values.

   B.   Type **tune2fs -c 26 /dev/sda3** and examine the filesystem check values.

   C.   Type **tune4fs -c 26 /dev/sda3** and examine the filesystem check values.

   D.   Type **resize2fs /dev/sda3** and examine the inode count and disk percentage values.

15. What option to mkisofs would you use if you want a computer running Microsoft Windows 7 to be able to read long filenames on a CD-R or DVD created with Linux? (Choose all that apply.)

    A. -J

    B. -r

    C. -hfs

    D. -udf

16. You've downloaded the latest version of your Linux distribution as a 4 GB DVD image file (distrib.iso). Which of the following commands will burn this file to a blank DVD, assuming your DVD drive can be accessed as /dev/dvdrw?

    A. growisofs -Z /dev/dvdrw distrib.iso

    B. cdrecord -Z /dev/dvdrw distrib.iso

    C. growisofs -Z /dev/dvdrw=distrib.iso

    D. mkisofs -o /dev/dvdrw -i distrib.iso

17. You want to write files to a DVD+RW disc over a period of several days, retaining the ability to read the disc on another computer at a moment's notice. How can you accomplish this task?

    A. Use mke2fs to create an ext2 filesystem on the disc, mount it as if it were a hard disk, and write files to it.

    B. Use growisofs with its -J option to create a Joliet filesystem on the disc, mount it as if it were a hard disk, and write files to it.

    C. Use growisofs with its -udf option to create a UDF filesystem on the disc, mount it as if it were a hard disk, and write files to it.

    D. Use mkudffs to create a UDF filesystem on the disc, mount it as if it were a hard disk, and write files to it.

18. The /etc/auto.master file on ganymede.example.com contains the following line:

    /mnt/net   /etc/auto.servers

    The /etc/auto.servers file includes the following line:

    templates   europa.example.com:/data/templates

    What file should a user on ganymede.example.com access to read the /data/templates/iceflow.txt file on europa.example.com?

    A. /mnt/net/iceflow.txt

    B. /mnt/net/templates/iceflow.txt

    C. /data/templates/iceflow.txt

    D. /data/templates/mnt/net/iceflow.txt

19. What is the effect of the following udev rule, when placed in the /etc/udev/rules.d/
99-my.rules file?

    KERNEL=="video*", DRIVER=="saa7134", SYMLINK+="video-A180"

    A. It forces loading of the saa7134 driver for a video device for which a symbolic link
    called /dev/video-A180 exists.

    B. It creates a symbolic link called /dev/video-A180 that points to the primary device
    file for a video device that has a driver called saa7134.

    C. It registers the name of a driver as saa7134 for all video devices.

    D. It links the existing /dev/video-A180 device file to the hardware that's managed by
    the saa7134 driver.

20. You're using a third-party Linux driver that creates device files called /dev/pd-c0-ain,
/dev/pd-c0-aout, /dev/pd-c0-din, and several more of this form. You want to give users
in the exper group full read/write access to these devices, while keeping other users from
accessing them. What udev rule can accomplish this goal?

    A. KERNEL=="pd-c?-*", GROUP="exper", MODE="0660"

    B. KERNEL=="pd-c?-*", GROUP=="exper", MODE="0660"

    C. KERNEL=="pd-c0-*", GROUP=="exper", MODE=="0660"

    D. KERNEL=="pd-c0-*", GROUP=="exper", MODE="0666"

Answers to Review Questions

1. D. Swap partitions aren't mounted in the way filesystems are, so they have no associated mount points.

2. D. When typed without a filesystem type specification, mount attempts to auto-detect the filesystem type. If the media contains any of the specified filesystems, it should be detected and the disk mounted.

3. B. The /etc/fstab file consists of lines that contain the device identifier, the mount point, the filesystem type code, filesystem mount options, the dump flag, and the filesystem check frequency, in that order. Option B provides this information in the correct order and so will work. Option A reverses the second and third fields but is otherwise correct. Options C and D both scramble the order of the first three fields and also specify the noauto mount option, which causes the filesystem to not mount automatically at boot time.

4. A, B, C. The user, users, and owner options in /etc/fstab all enable ordinary users to mount a filesystem, but with slightly different implications: user enables anybody to mount a filesystem, and only that user may unmount it; users enables anybody to mount a filesystem, and anybody may unmount it; and owner enables only the owner of the mount point to mount or unmount a filesystem. Any of these is likely to be accompanied by noauto, which prevents Linux from attempting to mount the filesystem at boot time. The owners parameter of option D doesn't exist.

5. B. The UUID method of specifying a filesystem can protect against changes in device node names such as those described in the question. Option B correctly describes an appropriate change, although of course the exact UUID value you use will depend on your system. Linux doesn't recognize drive letters as described in option A; those are DOS and Windows constructs. Thus, option A is incorrect. Option C is a completely fictitious solution with no correct elements. Option D is a distortion of a possible correct solution; however, to be correct you would need to replace the device specification (/dev/sdc5), not the mount point. Thus, option D is incorrect.

6. C, D. The swapon command is the usual way to activate swap space. Option C's use of the command activates a single swap partition, /dev/sdb7, and so satisfies the question's requirements. Option D's use of swapon activates all the swap spaces that are defined in /etc/fstab. Since the question specifies that such an entry has been created, option D will also work. Option A's mount command is used to mount filesystems; it's useless with swap space, and so is incorrect. Option B's mkswap command creates swap space, which the question specifies has already been done. Therefore, this option is unnecessary, and since it doesn't activate the swap space, it's incorrect.

7. A. Option A correctly describes the purpose of /etc/mtab. Option B describes the purpose of /etc/auto.master and other autofs configuration files, so this option is incorrect. Option C describes information that can be obtained from the blkid utility, but /etc/mtab will contain, at best, partial information of this type (it will specify filesystems used on *mounted* partitions, not all of them, and it won't have UUID information). Thus, option C is incorrect. Option D doesn't describe information contained in any Linux configuration file; however, typing lsmod will show loaded kernel filesystem modules (among other modules). In any event, option D is incorrect.

8. A. The -f option to umount forces an unmount operation when a remote server is inaccessible, so it's the appropriate response to the condition described in the question. Option B's command will unmount all filesystems in /etc/fstab, but it's no more likely to work at unmounting /mnt/remote than umount /mnt/remote. Unmounting all filesystems is also likely to have undesirable side effects. Option C's command will remount the network filesystem in read-only mode. If successful, this might be better than leaving it as-is, but it won't unmount the filesystem. Option D is fictitious; there is no --kill option to umount.

9. C. The mkfs command creates a new filesystem, overwriting any existing data and therefore making existing files inaccessible. This command doesn't set the partition type code in the partition table. The fsck utility and its helpers check filesystems for errors.

10. C. The -t option is used to tell fsck what filesystem to use. Normally, fsck determines the filesystem type automatically. The -A option causes fsck to check all the filesystems marked to be checked in /etc/fstab. The -N option tells fsck to take no action and to display what it would normally do without doing it. The -C option displays a text-mode progress indicator of the check process.

11. D. The journal of a journaling filesystem records pending operations, resulting in quicker disk checks after an uncontrolled shutdown. Contrary to option A, journaling filesystems are, as a class, newer than non-journaling filesystems; in fact, the journaling ext3fs is built upon the non-journaling ext2fs. Although disk checks are quicker with journaling filesystems than with non-journaling filesystems, journaling filesystems do have fsck utilities, and these may still need to be run from time to time. All Linux native filesystems support Linux ownership and permissions; this isn't an advantage of journaling filesystems, contrary to option C.

12. A, C. The tune2fs utility enables you to adjust various filesystem metadata, such as journal parameters (including the journal's presence, as option A indicates), mount count options, and the UUID value (as option C specifies). You cannot adjust the filesystem's size with tune2fs, though; that task requires resize2fs, so option B is incorrect. Because file ownership is a characteristic of individual files, not of the filesystem itself, option D is incorrect. (File ownership for all files can be adjusted by mount options for some non-Linux filesystems, though.)

13. B. Unfortunately, the undelete feature of debugfs requires you to know the inode number of a file in order to restore it; option B is correct. Although options A, C, and D would all be easier to perform, none of them can accomplish the stated task.

14. A. The dumpe2fs program displays various filesystem metadata, including maximum mount count and maximum check interval values, so option A is correct. (The -h option to dumpe2fs suppresses some lengthy information that's irrelevant to the question at hand.) Option B's command will change the maximum mount count value to 26, which might correct the problem if the hypothesis is correct; but it won't report the current value, so it won't enable you to test your hypothesis. Option C is like option B, but it specifies the fictitious tune4fs program; despite the 2 in the names, dumpe2fs, tune2fs, resize2fs, and other *2fs programs work with ext2fs, ext3fs, and ext4fs. Option D will resize the filesystem to fill its current partition, but it won't change or display the maximum mount count value.

15. A, D. The -J option creates a disc with Joliet extensions, and -udf creates one with the UDF filesystem. Recent versions of Windows understand both of these extensions. The -r option creates a disc with Rock Ridge extensions, while -hfs creates one with Apple's HFS. Windows won't understand either of these without special drivers, although Windows will still be able to read the underlying ISO-9660 filesystem (with 8.3 filenames).

16. C. The growisofs program is generally used to burn DVDs, since many versions of cdrecord lack DVD support. Of the two growisofs command options, C presents the correct syntax; option B is missing a critical equal sign (=) between the device filename and the image filename. Even if your version of cdrecord supports DVDs, option B's syntax is incorrect; cdrecord uses dev= rather than -Z to specify the target device. The mkisofs command is used to create an image file, not to burn one to disc; and option D's syntax is incorrect in any event.

17. D. Producing full random-access read/write features on a DVD+RW disc requires using mkudffs to create a pure UDF filesystem on the disc, as option D specifies. Because of hardware differences between hard disks and optical discs, ext2fs cannot be used as a full read/write filesystem on optical discs, so option A won't work. Options B and C won't work because growisofs creates read-only filesystems, not read/write filesystems. Option B's Joliet is inherently read-only, and even though the UDF filesystem created by option C *can be* read/write (as it is when created by mkudffs), growisofs creates a read-only UDF filesystem (along with a read-only ISO-9660 filesystem).

18. B. The first column in the /etc/auto.master files' lines specifies the main directory where the automounter will mount specific subdirectories corresponding to its managed mounts. The specific configuration file (/etc/auto.servers in this case) includes the subdirectories within the specific directories that will be used as mount points. Thus, given the specified files, /mnt/net/templates will be the mount point. This mount point corresponds to the NFS export corresponding to /data/templates on europa.example.com. Thus, /data/templates/iceflow.txt on that server can be read from /mnt/net/templates/iceflow.txt on the client, as option B specifies.

19. B. The udev rule includes two matching conditions (KERNEL=="video*", which matches drivers with generic names that begin with video; and DRIVER=="saa7134", which matches devices that use the saa7134 driver) and one assignment operator (SYMLINK+="video-A180", which creates a symbolic link). Option B correctly describes this configuration. Options A, C, and D all confuse matching and assignment actions in the udev rules.

20. A. Option A's udev rule will accomplish the stated goal. Option B looks almost identical, but it mistakenly uses the matching operator == rather than the assignment operator = in the GROUP=="exper" portion of its rule. Option C makes the same mistake and compounds it by replicating this mistake in its MODE=="0660" option. Option D is like option B, but it uses 0666 as the mode. Even if it weren't for the error in the GROUP comparison, option D would set the mode incorrectly, enabling *all* users to access the hardware.

Chapter

4

Advanced Disk Management

THE FOLLOWING LINUX PROFESSIONAL INSTITUTE OBJECTIVES ARE COVERED IN THIS CHAPTER:

- ✓ 204.1 Configuring RAID (weight: 2)
- ✓ 204.2 Adjusting Storage Device Access (weight: 1)
- ✓ 204.3 Logical Volume Manager (weight: 3)
- ✓ 206.2 Backup Operations (weight: 3)

Chapter 3, "Basic Filesystem Management," describes how to create and manage filesystems. The topic of managing filesystems is tied closely to the topic of managing the data structures that contain them. Most commonly, these data structures are *partitions*—contiguous collections of sectors on a hard disk. Partition management is covered in the LPIC-1 exams. LPIC-2, and therefore this chapter, emphasizes more advanced filesystem container management: *Redundant Array of Independent Disks (RAID)*, which enables merging multiple disks together to improve performance or security; and *Logical Volume Manager (LVM)*, which enables combining partitions or disks into a storage area that can be managed more flexibly than conventional partitions. Although the LPIC-2 exam emphasizes these topics, the fact that they rely on simple partitions means that this chapter begins with information on conventional partitioning.

This chapter also covers additional disk-related topics. The first of these is adjusting hardware parameters for optimal performance. Typically, Linux performs reasonably well with no modifications; however, it's sometimes possible to improve performance by using various utilities. Another important topic is that of backing up your data. Without a backup, a failure of disk hardware or corruption of filesystem data structures can make for a very bad day, so preparing for such a problem is extremely important.

Partitioning Disks

Hard disks are typically broken into segments, known as *partitions*, that can be used for various purposes. In Linux, most partitions (or, to be more precise, the filesystems they contain) are *mounted* at specific directories. Swap partitions are an exception to this rule; they are accessed as an adjunct to system memory. Although Chapter 3 describes filesystem and swap space management, it doesn't describe partition management. The next few pages describe this topic, including both the important principles and partition types and the basic operation of the tools used to create partitions.

Understanding Partitions

Partitions are described in a data structure that is known generically as a *partition table*. The partition table is stored in one or more sectors of a hard disk, in locations that are defined by the partition table type. Over the years, several different partition table types have been developed. In 2010, three partition table types are most important:

Master Boot Record (MBR)   This partition table type is the most common one on disks under 2 TiB in size. It was used by Microsoft's Disk Operating System (DOS) and has been adopted by most OSs that run on the same hardware as DOS and its successor, Windows. Unfortunately, MBR suffers from many limitations, as described shortly, and so is being slowly abandoned. MBR is known by various other names, including MS-DOS partitions and BIOS partitions.

Apple Partition Map (APM)   Apple used this partition table type on its 680x0- and PowerPC-based Macintoshes, and it's been adopted by a few other computer types. Because Mac OS has never dominated the marketplace, APM is uncommon except on older Mac hardware; however, you may occasionally run into a removable disk that uses APM.

GUID Partition Table (GPT)   This partition table type is described in the Extensible Firmware Interface (EFI) definition, but it can be used on non-EFI systems. Apple switched to GPT for its Macintosh computers when it adopted Intel CPUs. GPT overcomes many of the problems of the older MBR and APM partition tables, particularly their disk size limits, and so GPT seems likely to become increasingly important as disk sizes rise.

Most Linux computers use MBR partitions; however, if you're running Linux on a PowerPC-based Mac, it probably uses APM. Newer Macs, and some non-Mac systems, use GPT.

As just noted, MBR has a number of limitations. The most important of these is that it uses 32-bit pointers to refer to disk sectors. Given a sector size of 512 bytes, this works out to a limit on partition size of precisely 2 TiB ($2^{32} \times 512$ bytes = 2.2×10^{12} bytes, or 2 TiB). APM shares the same limit. GPT, by contrast, uses 64-bit sector pointers, so it can handle disks of up to 9.4×10^{21} bytes—8 ZiB (zebibytes).

Disk manufacturers are beginning to transition away from 512-byte sectors to 4096-byte sectors. This change may extend the useful life of MBR, since its limit is raised to 16 TiB with 4096-byte sectors.

MBR has some other quirks that deserve mention. The first of these is that the original MBR specification provided for just four partitions. When this limit became troublesome, a workaround was devised: One of the original four partitions (now known as *primary partitions*) was allocated as a placeholder (an *extended partition*) for an arbitrary number of additional partitions (*logical partitions*). Although this is an effective workaround, it can be limiting. All logical partitions must reside within a single extended partition, which means that primary partitions cannot exist between logical partitions. As a disk is used, it's common to want to delete, add, move, and resize partitions, and these operations can become awkward when working around the primary/extended/logical partition requirements. Furthermore, some OSs, such as Microsoft Windows, must boot from a primary partition. (Linux is not so limited.) In Linux, primary partitions are numbered from 1 to 4, while logical partitions are numbered 5 and up.

GPT uses a different set of data structures than does MBR, so GPT's limits and quirks are different. Under GPT, there is no distinction between primary, extended, and logical partitions. Instead, GPT supports a fixed number of partitions (128 by default), all of which are defined in the main partition table. GPT and MBR support slightly different meta-data—for instance, GPT supports a partition name, which MBR doesn't support.

No matter what partitioning system you use, you should be aware of one critical limitation of partitions: They are composed of contiguous sets of sectors. Thus, if you want to change the way partitions are laid out, you may need to move all the data on one or more partitions. This is one of the limitations that LVM is designed to overcome, as described later in "Configuring LVM."

Creating Partitions

Several Linux tools are available to partition MBR and GPT disks in Linux:

The libparted Tools   The GNU Project's libparted (http://www.gnu.org/software/parted/), which comes with the parted text-mode program, is a popular tool that can handle MBR, GPT, APM, and several other partition table formats. GUI tools, such as GNOME Partition Editor (aka GParted; http://gparted.sourceforge.net), have been built upon libparted. The greatest strength of these tools is the ability to move and resize both partitions and the filesystems they contain. They can also create filesystems at the same time you create partitions.

The fdisk Family   The Linux fdisk program is named after the DOS FDISK program. Although the two are very different in operation, they do the same basic job: They create and manipulate MBR partition tables. In Linux, fdisk is the basic program, with a simple text-mode interactive user interface. The sfdisk program can do similar jobs, but it's designed to be used in a non-interactive way via command-line options. It's therefore useful in scripts. The cfdisk program uses a more sophisticated text-mode interface similar to that of a text editor. These programs ship with the standard util-linux or util-linux-ng packages.

GPT fdisk   This package, consisting of the gdisk and sgdisk programs, is designed as a workalike to fdisk but for GPT disks. The gdisk program is modeled on fdisk. Although sgdisk is designed for shell-based interaction, it bears little resemblance to sfdisk in its operational details. You can learn more at http://www.rodsbooks.com/gdisk/.

Partitions can be created, deleted, and otherwise manipulated using any of these programs (or other programs for other partition table types). In most cases, you launch the program by typing its name followed by a disk device filename, such as /dev/sda. You'll then see a command prompt, such as the following for fdisk:

```
Command (m for help):
```

 WARNING   If fdisk displays a message to the effect that GPT was detected on the disk, *exit immediately* by typing **q**! You should use GPT fdisk or a libparted-based tool on such disks. Attempting to use fdisk on a GPT disk is likely to cause serious problems.

Pass fdisk the -u option to have it use sectors rather than cylinders as the default units of measure. Passing -c affects where fdisk starts its first partition. As a general rule, both options are desirable on modern disks, so you should generally launch it as **fdisk -uc /dev/sda** (changing the device filename, if necessary).

Table 4.1 summarizes the most important fdisk commands that can be typed at this prompt. Some of these commands silently do something, but others require interaction. For instance, typing **n** results in a series of prompts for the new partition's type (primary, extended, or logical), start point, and size or end point. (If you must edit a GPT disk, gdisk supports all the commands shown in Table 4.1 except u, although some of the details of subsequent interactions differ slightly.)

TABLE 4.1 Common fdisk commands

Command	Explanation
d	Deletes a partition
l	Displays a list of partition type codes
n	Creates a new partition
o	Destroys the current partition table, enabling you to start fresh
p	Displays the current partition table
q	Exits without saving changes
t	Changes a partition's type code
u	Toggles units between sectors and cylinders
v	Performs checks on the validity of the disk's data structures
w	Saves changes and exits

The l and t commands deserve elaboration: MBR supports a 1-byte type code for each partition. This code helps identify what types of data are supposed to be stored on the partition. For instance, in hexadecimal, 0x07 refers to a partition that holds High Performance Filesystem (HPFS) or New Technology Filesystem (NTFS) data, 0x82 refers to a Linux swap partition, and 0x83 refers to a Linux data partition. For the most part, Linux ignores partition type codes; however, Linux installers frequently rely on them, as do other OSs. Thus, you should be sure your partition type codes are set correctly. Linux fdisk creates 0x83 partitions by default, so you should change the code if you create anything but a Linux partition.

> If you just want to view the partition table, type `fdisk -lu /dev/sda`. This command displays the partition table, using units of sectors, and then exits. You can change the device filename for the device in which you're interested, of course.

GPT also supports partition type codes, but these codes are 16-byte GUID values rather than 1-byte MBR type codes. GPT fdisk translates the 16-byte GUIDs into 2-byte codes based on the MBR codes; for instance, the GPT code for a Linux swap partition becomes 0x8200. Unfortunately, Linux and Windows use the same GUID code for their partitions, so GPT fdisk translates both to 0x0700. Programs based on `libparted` don't give direct access to partition type codes, although they use them internally. Several GPT type codes are referred to as "flags" in `libparted`-based programs; for instance, the "boot flag" refers to a partition with the type code for an EFI System Partition on a GPT disk.

Configuring RAID

In a RAID configuration, multiple disks are combined together to improve performance, reliability, or both. The following pages describe RAID in general, Linux's RAID subsystem, preparing a disk for use with RAID, initializing the RAID structures, and using RAID disks.

Understanding RAID

The purpose of RAID depends on its specific *level*:

Linear Mode   This isn't technically RAID, but it's handled by Linux's RAID subsystem. In linear mode, devices are combined together by appending one device's space to another's. Linear mode provides neither speed nor reliability benefits, but it can be a quick way to combine disk devices if you need to create a very large filesystem. The main advantage of linear mode is that you can combine partitions of unequal size without losing storage space; other forms of RAID require equal-sized underlying partitions and ignore some of the space if they're fed unequal-sized partitions.

RAID 0 (Striping)   This form of RAID combines multiple disks to present the illusion of a single storage area as large as all the combined disks. The disks are combined in an interleaved manner so that a single large access to the RAID device (for instance, when reading or writing a large file) results in accesses to all the component devices. This configuration can improve overall disk performance; however, if any one disk fails, data on the remaining disks will become useless. Thus, reliability actually *decreases* when using RAID 0, compared to conventional partitioning.

 LVM provides a striping feature similar to RAID 0. Thus, if you want to use striping and LVM, you can skip the RAID configuration and use LVM alone. If you're interested only in striping, you can use either RAID 0 or LVM.

RAID 1 (Mirroring)   This form of RAID creates an exact copy of one disk's contents on one or more other disks. If any one disk fails, the other disks can take over, thus improving reliability. The drawback is that disk writes take longer, since data must be written to two or more disks. Additional disks may be assigned as *hot standby* or *hot spare* disks, which can automatically take over from another disk if one fails. (Higher RAID levels also support hot standby disks.)

 Hot spare disks are normally inactive; they come into play only in the event another disk fails. As a result, when a failure occurs, the RAID subsystem must copy data onto the hot spare disk, which takes time.

RAID 4   Higher levels of RAID attempt to gain the benefits of both RAID 0 and RAID 1. In RAID 4, data are striped in a manner similar to RAID 0; but one drive is dedicated to holding checksum data. If any one disk fails, the checksum data can be used to regenerate the lost data. The checksum drive does not contribute to the overall amount of data stored; essentially, if you have n identically sized disks, they can store the same amount of data as $n-1$ disks of the same size in a non-RAID or RAID 0 configuration. As a practical matter, you need at least three identically sized disks to implement a RAID 4 array.

RAID 5   This form of RAID works just like RAID 4, except that there's no dedicated checksum drive; instead, the checksum data are interleaved on all the disks in the array. RAID 5's size computations are the same as those for RAID 4; you need a minimum of three disks, and n disks hold $n-1$ disks worth of data.

RAID 6   What if two drives fail simultaneously? In RAID 4 and RAID 5, the result is data loss. RAID 6, though, increases the amount of checksum data, therefore increasing resistance to disk failure. The cost, however, is that you need more disks: four at a minimum. With RAID 6, n disks hold $n-2$ disks worth of data.

RAID 10   A combination of RAID 1 with RAID 0, referred to as RAID 1 + 0 or RAID 10, provides benefits similar to those of RAID 4 or RAID 5. Linux provides explicit support for this combination to simplify configuration.

Additional RAID levels exist; however, the Linux kernel explicitly supports only the preceding RAID levels. If you use a hardware RAID disk controller, as described shortly in the Real World Scenario "Software vs. Hardware RAID," you might encounter other RAID levels.

Linux's implementation of RAID is usually applied to partitions rather than to whole disks. Partitions are combined by the kernel RAID drivers to create new devices, with names of the form /dev/md#, where # is a number from 0 up. This configuration enables you to combine devices using different RAID levels, to use RAID for only some partitions, or even to use RAID with disks of different sizes. For instance, suppose you have two 1.5 TiB disks and one 2 TiB disk. You could create a 2 TiB RAID 4 or RAID 5 array using 1 TiB partitions on each of the disks, a 1 TiB RAID 0 array using 0.5 TiB from one of the 1.5 TiB disk and the 2 TiB disk, and a 0.5 TiB RAID 1 array using 0.5 TiB from the second 1.5 TiB disk and the 2 TiB disk.

When using Linux's software RAID, you should realize that boot loaders are sometimes unable to read RAID arrays. GRUB Legacy, in particular, can't read data in a RAID array. (RAID 1 is a partial exception; because RAID 1 partitions are duplicates of each other, GRUB Legacy can treat them like normal partitions for read-only access.) GRUB 2 includes Linux RAID support, however. Because of this limitation, you may want to leave a small amount of disk space in a conventional partition or used as RAID 1, for use as a Linux /boot partition.

When you partition a disk for RAID, you should be sure to assign the proper partition type code. On an MBR disk, this is 0xFD. If you edit a GPT disk using GPT fdisk, the equivalent code is 0xFD00. If you use a libparted-based tool with either MBR or GPT disks, a RAID partition is identified as one with the RAID flag set.

RAID relies on Linux kernel features. Most distributions ship with kernels that have the necessary support. If you compile your own kernel, however, as described in Chapter 2, "Linux Kernel Configuration," you should be sure to activate the RAID features you need. These can be found in the Device Drivers ➤ Multiple Devices Driver Support (RAID and LVM) ➤ RAID Support area. Enable the main RAID Support area along with support for the specific RAID level or levels you intend to use. It's best to compile this support directly into the kernel, since this can sometimes obviate the need to create an initial RAM disk.

 Real World Scenario

Software vs. Hardware RAID

This chapter emphasizes Linux's software RAID subsystem; however, RAID can also be implemented by special disk controllers with hardware RAID support. When using such a controller, multiple hard disks appear to Linux to be single disks with a conventional disk device filename, such as /dev/sda.

Generally speaking, hardware RAID implementations are more efficient than software RAID implementations. This is particularly true of RAID 1; a hardware RAID controller is likely to enable true parallel access to both drives, with no extra overhead. Hardware RAID also computes the checksums required for higher RAID levels, removing this burden from the CPU.

Be aware that many motherboards claim to have built-in RAID support. Most of these, however, implement their own proprietary form of software RAID, which some people refer to as *fake RAID*. These implementations require special drivers, which may or may not be available for Linux. As a general rule, it's better to use Linux's own software RAID implementations. If you want the benefits of true hardware RAID, you will probably have to buy a new disk controller. Be sure that the Linux kernel supports any hardware RAID controller you buy.

If you have a true hardware RAID controller, you should consult its documentation to learn how to configure it. Once it's set up, it should present the illusion of one disk that's larger than any of your individual disks. There is then no need to apply Linux's software RAID features; you can partition and use the hardware RAID array as if it were a single conventional disk.

Disks in a hardware RAID array are accessed in blocks, typically between 16 KiB and 256 KiB in size. This block size is larger than the 512-byte sector size, and this fact can have performance implications. In particular, if partitions do not start on multiples of the RAID array allocation block, performance can be degraded by 10–30 percent. The latest versions of Linux partitioning software provide options to align partitions on 1 MiB boundaries, which is a safe default for such devices. Be sure you use such an option if you use a hardware RAID controller.

Preparing a Disk for Software RAID

The first step in software RAID configuration is partitioning the disk. As noted earlier, you should give the partitions the correct type code in fdisk or any other partitioning software you're using. Two methods of partitioning for RAID are possible:

- You can create a single RAID partition on each disk and then, when you've defined the full array, create partitions in it as if the RAID array were a hard disk.
- You can create multiple partitions on the underlying disk devices, assembling each into a separate RAID device that will be used to store a filesystem.

The first method can simplify the initial RAID configuration, but the second method is more flexible; using the second method enables you to use different RAID levels or even combine disks of unequal size into your RAID configuration.

When you define RAID partitions, be sure that the partitions to be combined on multiple disks are as equal in size as possible. If the component partitions are of unequal size, only the amount of space in the smallest partition will be used in all the others. For instance, if you combine an 800 MiB partition on one disk with two 900 MiB partitions on two other disks, you'll be throwing away 100 MiB of space on each of the two disks with 900 MiB partitions. Sometimes a small amount of waste is acceptable if your disks have slightly different sizes. If the amount of wasted space is significant, though, you might want to use the otherwise wasted space as conventional (non-RAID) partitions.

Normally, disks to be combined using RAID will be of the same size. If you're stuck with unequal-sized disks, you can leave some space on the larger disks outside of the RAID array or, with enough disks, find ways to combine segments from subsets of the disks. (Linear mode enables combining disks of unequal size.)

If you're using older Parallel Advanced Technology Attachment (PATA) disks, which enable two disks to be connected via a single cable, it's best to combine devices on different cables into a single RAID array. The reason is that PATA bandwidth is limited on a per-channel basis, so combining two devices on a single channel (that is, one cable) will produce a smaller performance benefit than combining devices on different channels. Newer Serial ATA (SATA) disks don't have this problem because SATA supports one device per channel. Small Computer Systems Interface (SCSI) devices multitask well even on a single channel.

Assembling a RAID Array

Once you've set up the partitions that are to be included in a RAID array, you may use the mdadm tool to define how the devices should be assembled. (This tool's name is short for *multiple device administration*.) This command's syntax is:

mdadm [*mode*] *raid-device* [*options*] *component-devices*

Table 4.2 summarizes the *mode* values you may use, while Table 4.3 summarizes the most important *options*. Most of your use of mdadm will employ the --create mode; other options are intended for troubleshooting, advanced use, or reconfiguring an already-created RAID array. (The --auto-detect mode is called by startup scripts when the system boots.) If no *mode* is specified, the command is in *manage* mode or *misc* mode; various miscellaneous tasks can be performed in these modes.

TABLE 4.2 Common *mode* values for mdadm

Long *mode* name	Short *mode* name	Explanation
--assemble	-A	Assembles the components of a previously assembled array. Most useful in troubleshooting or activating an array transferred from another computer.
--build	-B	Builds an array from devices that lack RAID metadata. Only experts should use this mode.
--create	-C	Creates an array, including the necessary metadata to help mdadm manage the array.
--follow or --monitor	-F	Monitors an array for state changes.
--grow	-G	Grows, shrinks, or otherwise modifies an array. Used to add partitions to an array or notify mdadm about changes to the size of underlying partitions.
--incremental	-I	Adds a single device to an array.
--auto-detect	N/A	Causes the kernel to scan for RAID devices and activates any that can be activated by the kernel.

TABLE 4.3 Common *options* for mdadm

Long option name	Short option name	Used with modes	Explanation
--help	-h	all	Presents basic help information.
--version	-V	all	Displays version information.
--verbose	-v	all	Displays extra information about what the program does.
--force	-f	all	Be more forceful; can override certain conditions that might otherwise cause an operation to abort.

TABLE 4.3 Common *options* for mdadm *(continued)*

Long option name	Short option name	Used with modes	Explanation
--config=*file*	-c *file*	all	Specifies configuration file. The default is /etc/mdadm.conf or, if that file is not present, /etc/mdadm/mdadm.conf.
--scan	-s	all	Obtains missing information from the configuration file.
--metadata=*level*	-e *level*	all	Sets the style of the metadata. The default is 0.90 when creating arrays or to guess for other operations. The 0.90 format limits arrays to 28 components and limits component partitions to 2 TiB. 1, 1.0, 1.1, and 1.2 raise these limits.
--raid-devices=*num*	-n *num*	create, build, or grow	Sets the number of active devices in the array. This value plus the number of spare devices must equal the total number of devices.
--spare-devices=*num*	-x *num*	create, build, or grow	Sets the number of spare (extra) devices in the array.
--chunk=*size*	-c *size*	create, build, or grow	Sets the size, in kibibytes, of data blocks for RAID levels 0, 4, 5, 6, and 10. The default is 64.
--level=*level*	-l *level*	create or build	Sets the RAID level. Valid options are linear, raid0, 0, stripe, raid1, 1, mirror, raid4, 4, raid5, 5, raid6, 6, raid10, 10, multipath, mp, faulty, and container.
--name=*name*	-N *name*	create, build, grow, or assemble	Sets a name for the array, which can be used to identify array components. This requires a version-1 superblock (metadata level).
--add	-a	manage	Adds a new device to the array.
--re-add	N/A	manage	Adds a device that had been removed back to the array.

Long option name	Short option name	Used with modes	Explanation
`--remove`	`-r`	manage	Removes a device from the array. This device must be flagged as a spare or failed device.
`--fail` or `--set-faulty`	`-f`	manage	Flags a device as failed.
`--stop`	`-S`	misc	Deactivates the array.

Table 4.3 is incomplete; `mdadm` is an extremely complex program with many options, most of which are highly technical in nature. You should consult its `man` page for further details.

Despite the complexity of RAID, its basic configuration is fairly straightforward. To create a RAID array, you begin by using `mdadm` with `--create`. You must then pass it the name of a RAID device (typically /dev/md0 for the first device), the RAID level, the number of RAID devices, and the device filenames for all the component devices:

```
# mdadm --create /dev/md0 --level=5 --raid-devices=3 ↵
  /dev/sda6 /dev/sdc1 /dev/sdd1
```

This example creates a RAID 5 array using /dev/sda6, /dev/sdc1, and /dev/sdd1 as the component devices. If there are no problems, you'll see a /dev/md0 device appear, which you can then use as if it were a disk device or partition, as described shortly.

Using a RAID Array

Once you've created a RAID array, you can begin using it. As noted earlier, you can either treat your RAID devices (/dev/md0 and so on) as if they were partitions or further subdivide them by placing partition tables on them or using them as physical volumes in an LVM configuration.

Creating Filesystems on a RAID Array

The simplest way to use a RAID array is to do so directly: You can create a filesystem on it as if it were a partition. To do this, treat the RAID device file like a partition's device file with `mkfs`, `mount`, and the other filesystem-related tools described in Chapter 3:

```
# mkfs -t ext4 /dev/md0
# mount /dev/md0 /mnt
```

You can also create /etc/fstab entries, substituting /dev/md0 and other RAID device filenames for partition filenames such as /dev/sda1. When you do so, your RAID devices should mount automatically when you reboot the computer.

If you're planning to move critical system files, such as the contents of /usr, onto RAID devices, you may need to rebuild your initial RAM disk so that it includes RAID support. Modify your /etc/fstab file to refer to the RAID device and then rebuild the initial RAM disk. The initrd or initramfs utility should note the use of RAID and build in the necessary support. Chapter 2 describes initial RAM disk configuration in more detail.

Subdividing a RAID Array

If you've created a massive RAID array with the intention of subdividing it further, now is the time to do so. You can use fdisk or other disk partitioning tools to create partitions within the RAID array; or you can use the RAID device file as a component device in an LVM configuration, as described shortly.

If you subdivide your RAID array using partitions, you should see new device files appear that refer to the partitions. These files have the same name as the parent RAID device file, plus p and a partition number. For instance, if you create three partitions on /dev/md0, they might be /dev/md0p1, /dev/md0p2, and /dev/md0p3. You can then treat these RAID partitions as if they were partitions on regular hard disks.

Another method of subdividing a RAID array is to deploy LVM atop it. The upcoming section "Configuring LVM" describes configuring LVM generically. You can use a RAID device file, such as /dev/md0, as if it were a partition for purposes of LVM configuration.

Reviewing a RAID Configuration

Once you have your RAID array set up, you can review the details by examining the /proc/mdstat pseudo-file. A simple example looks something like this:

```
Personalities : [raid6] [raid5] [raid4]
md0 : active raid5 sdd1[2] sdc1[1] sda6[0]
      321024 blocks level 5, 64k chunk, algorithm 2 [3/3] [UUU]


unused devices: <none>
```

The Personalities line reveals what RAID level a given device uses; however, this line groups several different types of RAID, as shown here.

Following the Personalities line, you'll see additional groups of lines, one for each RAID device. This example shows just one, md0 for /dev/md0. Information included here includes the status (active in this case), the exact RAID type (raid5), the devices that make up the array (sdd1, sdc1, and sda6), the size of the array (321024 blocks), and some additional technical details. The numbers in square brackets following the component device names (sdd1, sdc1, and sda6 in this example) denote the role of the device in the array. For RAID 5, three devices are required for basic functionality, so roles 0 through 2 are basic parts of the array. If a fourth device were added, it would have a role number of 3, which would make it a spare drive—if another drive were to fail, the RAID subsystem would automatically begin copying data to the spare drive and begin using it.

Configuring Logical Volume Manager

LVM is similar to RAID in some ways, but the primary reason to use LVM is to increase the flexibility and ease of manipulating low-level filesystems by providing a more flexible container system than partitions. Unfortunately, to achieve this greater flexibility, more complexity is required, involving three levels of data structures: physical volumes, volume groups, and logical volumes. Despite this complexity, a basic LVM configuration can be set up with just a few commands; however, using LVM effectively requires an appreciation for LVM's capabilities.

> The Enterprise Volume Management System (EVMS) is a system for managing RAID, LVM, and other types of partitioning and volume management systems using a single set of tools. See http://evms .sourceforge.net for more details.

Understanding Logical Volume Manager

Partitions, as traditionally used on most computers, are inflexible. A partition begins at a particular sector on the disk, ends at another sector on the disk, and contains all the sectors between those two, in sequential order. To understand how inflexible this configuration is, consider Figure 4.1, which shows the GParted partitioning program's view of a small hard disk. Suppose you wanted to create a new 4 GiB partition on this disk. There's enough room, located in two 2 GiB segments on either side of /dev/sdc3. That's the problem, though: The free space is broken into *two parts*, but partitions must be composed of *contiguous* sets of sectors.

FIGURE 4.1 Partitions must be contiguous sector sets, which can make consolidating free space that's discontinuous awkward and risky.

Partition	File System	Mount Point	Size	Used	Unused	Flags
unallocated	unallocated		1.00 MiB	---	---	---
/dev/sdc1	ext4	/mnt/usb	5.00 GiB	218.37 MiB	4.79 GiB	
unallocated	unallocated		2.00 GiB	---	---	
/dev/sdc3	reiserfs		2.00 GiB	32.14 MiB	1.97 GiB	
unallocated	unallocated		2.00 GiB	---	---	
/dev/sdc4	xfs		3.00 GiB	10.08 MiB	2.99 GiB	
/dev/sdc5	linux-swap		1.06 GiB	---	---	

You can use partition and filesystem management tools such as GParted to manipulate existing partitions to produce contiguous disk space. For instance, GParted can move Figure 4.1's /dev/sdc3 to the left or right, creating a single 4 GiB section of free disk space. Unfortunately, this type of operation is likely to be time-consuming and risky. Data must be physically copied from one location to another on the disk, and if there's a power failure, system crash, invalid data on the disk, a bug in the program, or other problems, you could lose all the data on the partition being moved.

LVM exists, in part, to solve this type of problem. In an LVM configuration, *logical volumes*, which are the LVM equivalent of partitions, are allocated much like files in a filesystem. When you create a file, you needn't worry about what sectors it's occupying or whether there's enough contiguous space left to hold a large file. The filesystem deals with those details and enables files to be broken into pieces to fit into multiple small chunks if there isn't enough contiguous free space. LVM goes further, though: LVM enables logical volumes to span multiple partitions or even hard disks, thus enabling consolidation of space much like a linear RAID or RAID 0 configuration.

To do its work, LVM uses data structures at three different levels:

Physical Volumes   In most cases, *physical volumes* are conventional partitions; however, LVM can be built atop entire disk devices if desired. Using partitions as physical volumes enables you to use partitions when they have advantages. For instance, GRUB Legacy can't read logical volumes, so you may want to put the Linux /boot directory on a partition and use another partition as an LVM physical volume.

Volume Groups   A *volume group* is a collection of one or more physical volumes, which are managed as a single allocation space. The use of volume groups as an intermediate level of organization enables you to create larger filesystems than any individual device could handle by itself. For instance, if you combine two 1 TiB disks into a single volume group, you can create a filesystem of up to 2 TiB.

Logical Volumes   As stated earlier, logical volumes are the ultimate goal of LVM. They're created and managed in volume groups much like you create and manage files in a filesystem. Unlike partitions on a disk, logical volumes are created without reference to device sector numbers, and the LVM subsystem can create logical volumes that span multiple disks or that are discontiguous.

Because logical volumes are created and managed like files, LVM is a powerful disk management tool, particularly if you regularly create, delete, or resize your filesystems. Consider Figure 4.1 again. Although GParted doesn't manage LVMs, if a similar configuration existed within an LVM, you could create a new 4 GiB logical volume without adjusting the existing volumes. The new logical volume would simply be split across the available free space.

The biggest drawback to LVMs is their added complexity. To use LVMs, you normally create partitions, much like you would without LVM; however, you're likely to create fewer partitions with LVM than you would in a conventional setup. You must then use several LVM utilities to prepare the physical volumes to hold data, to "glue" the physical volumes together into a volume group, and to create logical volumes within your volume group. The tools to read the LVM configuration must also be present in your initial RAM disk and kernel, or it won't work when you reboot.

Another drawback to LVMs is that they can be more dangerous. If you glue multiple disks together in an LVM, a failure of one disk means loss of all data in the LVM, similar to a linear RAID or RAID 0 configuration. Even in a single-disk configuration, the LVM data structures are necessary to access the files stored on the filesystems in the logical volume. Thus, if the LVM data structures are damaged, you can lose access to your data.

Building LVM atop a RAID 1 or higher configuration reduces the risks associated with LVM. Although this configuration also adds complexity, it can be a worthwhile way to configure disk space on large servers or other systems with significant or frequently changing storage requirements.

Despite these drawbacks, LVM's advantages in terms of increased flexibility often make it worth using, particularly if your system sees much in the way of filesystem changes— adding disks, changing the sizes of filesystems, and so on.

Creating and Manipulating Physical Volumes

If you want to use LVM, the first step is to prepare physical volumes. There are actually two substeps to this step. The first substep is to flag your physical volumes as being for LVM use. (This is necessary if you use partitions as physical volumes, but not if you use whole unpartitioned disks or RAID devices.) The MBR type code for LVM partitions is 0x8E, so if you use fdisk, be sure to enter that as the type code for your physical volumes. If you use GPT disks and manipulate them with gdisk, use a type code of 0x8E00. When you use libparted-based tools with either MBR or GPT disks, set the lvm flag.

The second substep is to begin manipulating the contents of your properly labeled physical volumes. This is done with a series of tools whose names begin with pv, as summarized in Table 4.4. (Alternatively, these commands can be accessed as subcommands of the lvm program.) Although a complete description of all these tools is well beyond the scope of this book, you should know some of the most important uses for the most common commands. Consult each command's man page for additional details.

TABLE 4.4   Tools for physical volume manipulation

Command	Explanation
pvchange	Changes allocation permissions on a physical volume. You might disallow new allocations if you're making changes on other volumes and intend to delete one immediately thereafter.
pvck	Checks the physical volume for errors; similar to fsck for filesystems.

TABLE 4.4   Tools for physical volume manipulation *(continued)*

Command	Explanation
pvcreate	Initializes a partition or other device for use by LVM; similar to mkfs for filesystems.
pvdisplay	Displays information on a physical volume, including the name of the volume group to which it belongs, its capacity, and how much of its capacity is not yet consumed by logical volumes.
pvmove	Moves data from one physical volume to another one. You might use this prior to retiring a disk to move data off it.
pvremove	Removes physical volume data structures from a partition; essentially the opposite of pvcreate. *Do not* use this command until you've moved data off the physical volume and removed it from the volume group (using vgreduce).
pvresize	Resizes the physical volume data structures. This command does *not* resize the partition in which it resides; that must be done before (when enlarging) or after (when shrinking) using pvresize, typically with fdisk.
pvs	Summarizes information about physical volume. Similar to pvdisplay, but more succinct.
pvscan	Scans disk partitions for LVM data structures.

When preparing an LVM configuration, pvcreate is the most important command. This command supports a number of options, most of which are highly technical. (Consult its man page for details.) In most cases, you need to pass it the device filename of a disk device:

pvcreate /dev/sda2

This example creates a physical volume on /dev/sda2. You must, of course, create physical volumes on all the partitions or other devices you intend to use in your LVM setup.

After you've finished your LVM configuration, you may want to use additional commands from Table 4.4 to monitor and maintain your LVM setup. The most important of these are likely to be pvdisplay and pvs to ascertain how much space remains unallocated in your physical volumes, pvmove to move data between physical volumes, and pvremove to clean up after you completely remove a physical volume from a volume group.

The pvdisplay and pvs commands can both be used either with no parameters, in which case they display information on all your physical volumes, or with a device filename specification, in which case they display information on only that device. The pvs command displays simpler information:

```
# pvs
PV          VG      Fmt  Attr PSize   PFree
/dev/sda8   speaker lvm2 a-   141.25g 2.03g
/dev/sdb9   speaker lvm2 a-   29.78g  0
```

This example shows two physical volumes, /dev/sda8 and /dev/sdb9, that together constitute the speaker volume group. The sizes of the volumes are listed under the PSize column, and PFree shows how much free space exists in each physical volume. From this output, you can see that about 2 GiB is available for allocation, all on /dev/sda8.

For more information, pvdisplay does the job:

```
# pvdisplay /dev/sda8
  --- Physical volume ---
  PV Name               /dev/sda8
  VG Name               speaker
  PV Size               141.27 GiB / not usable 23.38 MiB
  Allocatable           yes
  PE Size               32.00 MiB
  Total PE              4520
  Free PE               65
  Allocated PE          4455
  PV UUID               tZ7DqF-Vq3T-VGqo-GLsS-VFKN-ws0a-nToP0u
```

Most of this additional information is not very useful; however, technical details like the extents size (PE Size) and UUID might be important in some debugging operations. The PV Size line includes information about the amount of space that's unusable because the partition's size isn't an even multiple of the extents size.

If you want to remove a disk from an LVM, you should first use the pvmove command:

```
# pvmove /dev/sdb7 /dev/sda2
```

This example moves all the data from /dev/sdb7 to /dev/sda2, providing /dev/sda2 is large enough. You can then use the vgreduce command, described shortly in "Creating and Manipulating Volume Groups." Once this is done, you can use pvremove to ensure that the physical volume isn't picked up on future scans of the system for physical volumes.

Creating and Manipulating Volume Groups

Table 4.5 summarizes the commands that manipulate volume groups. Consult the individual commands' man pages for details on their operation.

TABLE 4.5 Tools for volume group manipulation

Command	Explanation
vgcfgbackup	Backs up volume group metadata, by default to files in /etc/lvm/backup.
vgcfgrestore	Restores volume group metadata, by default from files in /etc/lvm/backup.
vgchange	Changes certain volume group attributes. Most importantly, it may be used to manually activate or deactivate a volume group.
vgck	Checks volume group metadata; similar to fsck for filesystems.
vgconvert	Converts volume group metadata from one version to another. LVM version 2 (LVM2) is the current version in 2011 and has been for some time.
vgcreate	Creates a volume group, starting with one or more physical volumes you specify.
vgdisplay	Displays information on your volume groups, including information on the number of physical devices and logical volumes as well as the total and free space.
vgexport	Makes a volume group unknown to the system, enabling it to be moved to another computer for integration into its LVM configuration.
vgextend	Adds physical volumes to an existing volume group.
vgimport	Makes a volume group known to the system.
vgimportclone	Imports a volume group, renaming conflicting logical volumes. This may be used if you've cloned a volume group for backup purposes and find you need to access the backup.
vgmerge	Merges two volume groups, one of which must be inactive.
vgmknodes	Updates the device files in /dev that refer to logical volumes. Normally not called manually.

Command	Explanation
vgreduce	Removes one or more unused physical volumes from a volume group.
vgremove	Completely removes a volume group from the computer; effectively the opposite of vgcreate.
vgrename	Renames a volume group.
vgs	Displays summary information about a volume group; similar to vgdisplay but with more terse output.
vgscan	Scans the system for volume groups. Normally unneeded but may be helpful after hot-swapping a new disk.
vgsplit	Splits a volume group into two; effectively the opposite of vgmerge.

The most commonly used commands from Table 4.5 are vgchange, vgcreate, vgdisplay, vgextend, vgreduce, vgremove, and vgs.

When creating a volume group, you will of course start with vgcreate, once you've created one or more physical volumes. This command takes quite a few arguments (consult its man page for detail), but normally, you pass it a volume group name followed by the filenames of one or more physical volumes:

```
# vgcreate speaker /dev/sda8 /dev/sdb9
```

This example creates a volume group, to be called speaker, using the physical volumes /dev/sda8 and /dev/sdb9 as constituents.

Once a volume group is created, you can display information about it using vgs and vgdisplay. As with their physical volume counterparts, these commands display terse and not-so-terse summaries of volume group information:

```
# vgs
  VG       #PV #LV #SN Attr   VSize   VFree
  speaker   2   6   0 wz--n- 171.03g 2.03g
# vgdisplay
  --- Volume group ---
  VG Name               speaker
  System ID
  Format                lvm2
  Metadata Areas        2
  Metadata Sequence No  33
  VG Access             read/write
```

```
VG Status          resizable
MAX LV             0
Cur LV             6
Open LV            3
Max PV             0
Cur PV             2
Act PV             2
VG Size            171.03 GiB
PE Size            32.00 MiB
Total PE           5473
Alloc PE / Size    5408 / 169.00 GiB
Free  PE / Size    65 / 2.03 GiB
VG UUID            gQOoBr-xhM9-IOPd-dOvp-woOT-oKnB-7vZ1U5
```

The vgextend, vgreduce, and vgremove commands are useful when increasing the size of, decreasing the size of, or completely deleting a volume group, respectively. To use vgextend, pass it a volume group name followed by the filenames of one or more physical volumes you want to add:

vgextend speaker /dev/sdc2

The vgreduce command is similar, except that the physical volume device filename is optional—if you omit it, the command removes all the empty physical volumes from the volume group. The vgremove command can be used without any parameters; but if you have more than one volume group defined, you can pass that name to remove only that volume group.

You won't normally need to use the vgchange command; however, it's very important in some emergency situations. If you need to access a volume group from an emergency boot CD, you may need to use vgchange to activate your volume group:

vgchange -ay

This command makes the volume group's logical volumes available. If it's not executed, either explicitly by you or in a system startup script, you won't find any device files in /dev for your logical volumes, and therefore you won't be able to access them.

Creating and Manipulating Logical Volumes

Once you've created physical volumes and volume groups, it's time to create logical volumes. These can be created and manipulated by the commands listed in Table 4.6. These commands all support multiple options; consult their man pages for details.

TABLE 4.6 Tools for logical volume manipulation

Command	Explanation
lvchange	Changes attributes of a logical volume, such as whether it must be allocated to contiguous sectors and whether it can be written.
lvconvert	Converts between linear, mirror, and snapshot status.
lvcreate	Creates a logical volume.
lvdisplay	Displays verbose information about logical volumes.
lvextend	Expands the size of a logical volume. (This does *not* expand the contained filesystem, though.)
lvreduce	Shrinks a logical volume. (This does *not* shrink the contained filesystem, though.)
lvremove	Deletes a logical volume.
lvrename	Renames a logical volume.
lvresize	Resizes a logical volume; does the jobs of both lvextend and lvreduce. (This does *not* shrink the contained filesystem, though.)
lvs	Displays a terse summary of logical volume information
lvscan	Scans all disks for logical volumes.

To create a logical volume, you will of course use lvcreate. This command takes a large number of options, but chances are you'll need just a few:

```
# lvcreate -L 20G -n deb_root speaker
```

This command creates a 20 GiB logical volume (-L 20G) called deb_root (-n deb_root) on the speaker volume group. One additional option deserves attention: -i (or --stripes). This option specifies the number of stripes used to create the volume. If your volume group spans multiple physical volumes on different physical disks, you can improve performance by striping the logical volume across different physical disks, much like a RAID 0 array. Specifying -i 2 will spread the logical volume across two devices. Whether or not you stripe your logical volume, you can specify particular devices the logical volume is to occupy by adding the device filenames to the command:

```
# lvcreate -L 20G -i 2 -n deb_root speaker /dev/sda8 /dev/sdc2
```

Once a logical volume is created, it becomes accessible through at least two device files. One is in /dev/mapper, and it takes the name *groupname-logname*, where *groupname* is the volume group name and *logname* is the logical volume name. The second name is /dev/*groupname*/*logname*. For instance, the preceding lvcreate command creates device files called /dev/mapper/speaker-deb_root and /dev/speaker/deb_root. Typically, the device file in /dev/mapper is the true device node, while the file in /dev/*groupname* is a symbolic link to the file in /dev/mapper; however, some distributions create a true device node under some other name, such as /dev/dm-0, and both the /dev/mapper files and those in /dev/*groupname* are symbolic links to this other file.

No matter how the device files are arranged, you can use them much as you would use partition device files; you can create filesystems on them using mkfs, mount them with mount, list them in the first column of /etc/fstab, and so on.

If you want to manipulate your logical volumes after you create them, you can use additional commands from Table 4.6. The lvs and lvdisplay commands produce terse and verbose information about the logical volumes:

```
# lvs
  LV               VG       Attr    LSize  Origin Snap% Move Log Copy% Convert
  PCLOS            speaker  -wi-ao  30.00g
  gentoo_root      speaker  -wi-ao  10.00g
  gentoo_usr       speaker  -wi-a-  15.00g
  gentoo_usrlocal  speaker  -wi-a-   4.00g
  home             speaker  -wi-ao  80.00g
# lvdisplay /dev/speaker/PCLOS
  --- Logical volume ---
  LV Name                /dev/speaker/PCLOS
  VG Name                speaker
  LV UUID                b1fnJY-o6eD-Sqpi-Ont7-11pp-y7Qf-EGUaZH
  LV Write Access        read/write
  LV Status              available
  # open                 1
  LV Size                30.00 GiB
  Current LE             960
  Segments               2
  Allocation             inherit
  Read ahead sectors     auto
  - currently set to     256
  Block device           253:5
```

If you find that a logical volume has become too small, you can expand it with lvextend or lvresize:

```
# lvextend -L +10G /dev/speaker/PCLOS
```

The plus sign (+) preceding the size indicates that the logical volume is to be expanded by that much; omitting the plus sign lets you specify an absolute size. Of course, you can only increase the size of a logical volume if the volume group has sufficient free space. After you resize a logical volume, you must normally resize the filesystem it contains:

```
# resize2fs /dev/speaker/PCLOS
```

The resize2fs program resizes a filesystem to match the container, or you can specify a size after the device filename. You should, of course, use whatever filesystem resizing tool is appropriate for the filesystem you use. If you want to shrink a logical volume, you must resize the filesystem *first*, and you must explicitly specify a size for the filesystem:

```
# resize2fs /dev/speaker/PCLOS 20G
```

You can then resize the logical volume to match this size:

```
# lvresize -L 20G /dev/speaker/PCLOS
```

Be very careful to set the size precisely and correctly when shrinking a logical volume to match a reduced filesystem size. You can add a safety margin by shrinking the filesystem to a smaller-than-desired size, resizing the logical volume to the desired size, and then using the automatic size-matching feature of resize2fs or a similar tool to match the logical volume's size.

If you want to change the role of a logical volume, you can use lvrename to give it a new name:

```
# lvrename speaker PCLOS SUSE
```

This command changes the name of the PCLOS logical volume in the speaker volume group to SUSE. If a logical volume is no longer necessary, you can remove it with lvremove:

```
# lvremove /dev/speaker/SUSE
```

The text-mode tools for managing LVM are flexible but complex. As a practical matter, it's sometimes easier to manage an LVM using a GUI tool, such as Kvpm (https://launchpad.net/kvpm) or system-config-lvm (http://fedoraproject.org/wiki/SystemConfig/lvm). These tools present GUI front-ends to LVM and help integrate filesystem resizing into the process, which can be particularly helpful when resizing logical volumes.

Exercise 4.1 guides you through the entire process of creating and using an LVM configuration, albeit on a small scale.

Creating and Using an LVM

In order to perform this exercise, you must have a spare hard disk partition. Storage space on a USB flash drive will work fine, if you have no other disk space available. Be sure you've removed all the valuable data from whatever partition you intend to use before proceeding. To set up your test LVM, proceed as follows:

1. Log into the computer as root, acquire root privileges by using su, or be prepared to issue the following commands using sudo.

2. If you're using a USB flash drive or external hard disk, connect it to the computer and wait for its activity light to stop flashing.

3. This activity assumes you'll be using /dev/sdb1 as the target partition. You must first mark the partition as having the correct type using fdisk, so type **fdisk /dev/sdb** to begin. (You can use gdisk instead of fdisk if your disk uses GPT rather than MBR.)

4. In fdisk, type **p** and review the partition table to verify that you're using the correct disk. If not, type **q** and try again with the correct disk.

5. In fdisk, type **t** to change the type code for the partition you intend to use. If the disk has more than one partition, you'll be prompted for a partition number; enter it. When prompted for a hex code, type **8e**. (Type **8e00** if you're using gdisk and a GPT disk.)

6. In fdisk, type **p** again to review the partition table. Verify that the partition you want to use now has the correct type code. If it does, type **w** to save your changes and exit.

7. At your shell prompt, type **pvcreate /dev/sdb1** (changing the device filename, as necessary). The program should respond Physical volume "/dev/sdb1" successfully created.

8. Type **vgcreate testvg /dev/sdb1**. The program should respond Volume group "testvg" successfully created.

9. Type **pvdisplay** to obtain information on the volume group, including its size.

10. Type **lvcreate -L 5G -n testvol testvg** to create a 5 GiB logical volume called testvol in the testvg volume group. (Change the size of the logical volume as desired or as necessary to fit in your volume group.) The program should respond Logical volume "testvol" created.

11. Type **ls /dev/mapper** to verify that the new volume group is present. You should see a control file, a file called testvg-testvol, and possibly other files if your computer already uses LVM for other purposes.

12. Type **lvdisplay /dev/testvg/testvol** to view information on the logical volume. Verify that it's the correct size. (You can use the filename /dev/mapper/testvg-testvol instead of /dev/testvg/testvol, if you like.)

13. Type `mkfs -t ext3 /dev/mapper/testvg-testvol` to create a filesystem on the new logical volume. (You can use another filesystem, if you like.) This command could take several seconds to complete, particularly if you're using a USB 2.0 disk device.

14. Type `mount /dev/mapper/testvg-testvol /mnt` to mount your new logical volume. (You can use a mount point other than /mnt, if you like.)

15. Copy some files to the logical volume, as in `cp /etc/fstab /mnt`. Read the files back with `less` or other tools to verify that the copy succeeded.

16. Type `df -h /mnt` to verify the size of the logical volume's filesystem. It should be the size you specified in step #10, or possibly a tiny bit smaller.

17. Type `umount /mnt` to unmount the logical volume.

18. Type `vgchange -an testvg` to deactivate the logical volume.

19. If you used a USB disk, you can now safely disconnect it.

If you don't want to experiment with LVM on this disk any more, you can now use `vgremove`, `pvremove`, and `mkfs` to remove the LVM data and create a regular filesystem on the partition. You must also use `fdisk` or `gdisk` to change its type code back to 0x83 (or 0x0700 for GPT disks), or some other value that's suitable for whatever filesystem you use. Alternatively, if you want to use LVM in a production environment, you can type `vgchange -ay` to reactivate the volume group, create suitable logical volumes, and add them to /etc/fstab.

Using LVM Snapshots

LVM provides a useful feature known as a *snapshot*. A snapshot is a logical volume that preserves the state of another logical volume, enabling you to make changes to the original while retaining the original state of the volume. Snapshots are created very quickly, so you can use them to back up a disk at one moment in time, or you can use a snapshot as a quick "out" in case a major system change doesn't work out. For instance, you can create a snapshot and then install major package upgrades that you suspect might cause problems. If the package upgrades don't work to your satisfaction, you can use the snapshot to restore the system to its original state.

 The latest Linux filesystem, Btrfs, includes its own snapshot feature. LVM snapshots work with any filesystem that's stored on a logical volume.

To create a snapshot, use the `lvcreate` command with its -s (--snapshot) option:

```
# lvcreate -L 10G -s -n snappy /dev/speaker/PCLOS
```

This example creates a new logical volume, snappy, that duplicates the current contents of /dev/speaker/PCLOS. The snapshot's size (10 GiB in this example) can be substantially smaller than the source volume's size. For most purposes, a snapshot can be just 10 or 20 percent of the original logical volume's size. When mounted, the snapshot will appear to be as large as the original volume. The lvs and lvdisplay commands reveal how much of the snapshot volume's capacity is being used, under the Snap% column of lvs or the Allocated to snapshot line of lvdisplay.

You can mount and use the snapshot volume much as you would any other logical volume. Used in this way, a snapshot volume can be a useful backup tool. Ordinary backup operations can take minutes or hours to complete, which means that on a heavily used system the backup may be inconsistent—related files created or changed within milliseconds of each other may be backed up at different times, one before and one after a near-simultaneous change. A snapshot avoids such problems: The snapshot reflects the state of the filesystem at one moment in time, enabling a more consistent backup.

Another use of snapshots is to provide a way to revert changes made to the original filesystem. To do this, you create the snapshot in exactly the way just described. If the changes you've made don't work out, you will then use the snapshot to restore the original filesystem. If the original filesystem isn't critical to normal system functioning, you can do this from a normal system boot; however, this type of operation often involves the main system, which can't be unmounted. You can still perform the merge operation, but it will be deferred until you unmount the mounted filesystem, which normally means until you reboot the computer. The merge uses the --merge option to lvconvert:

```
# lvconvert --merge /dev/speaker/snappy
```

Once this operation completes, the original state of the original logical volume will be restored. The merge will also automatically delete the snapshot volume, so if you want to attempt again whatever operation prompted these actions, you'll have to re-create the snapshot volume.

The ability to merge snapshots is fairly recent; it originated in the 2.6.33 kernel and the LVM tools version 2.02.58. If you want to attempt snapshot merging with older software, you'll have to upgrade first.

Tuning Disk Access

Like most computer hardware, hard disks have undergone major changes over the years. The result is that there are a large number of disk types and drivers for all these disks and their interface hardware. This wealth of hardware means that it's sometimes necessary to fine-tune disk access to optimize Linux's disk performance. To do this, you must first understand the various disk devices so that you can correctly identify your own disk hardware and learn what resources it uses. You can then employ any of a handful of utilities to optimize the way your system accesses the disks.

Some disk tuning operations can be handled by higher-level utilities than those described here. Filesystem tuning, for instance, is done via tools such as tune2fs, which adjusts ext2, ext3, and ext4 filesystem features. These tools are described in Chapter 3.

Understanding Disk Hardware

Hard disks can be classified in many ways; however, from a Linux point of view, the most important distinction between disk types is how the disks interface with the computer. Four interfaces are common today:

PATA   The *Parallel Advanced Technology Attachment (PATA)* interface was once king of the PC marketplace. Previously known as ATA, *Integrated Device Electronics (IDE)*, or *Enhanced IDE (EIDE)*, PATA devices are characterized by wide 40- or 80-pin ribbon cables for data transfer. These cables can connect up to two disks to a single connector on a motherboard or plug-in PATA card. In years past, PATA drives had to be configured as *master* or *slave* via a jumper; but modern PATA drives have an auto-configure setting that works well in most cases. The term *ATA* today often refers to either PATA or the more recent SATA (described next). A data format associated with ATA, the *ATA Packet Interface (ATAPI)*, enables ATA to be used for devices other than hard disks, such as optical discs.

SATA   The *Serial ATA (SATA)* interface is the successor to PATA. SATA drives use much slimmer cables than do PATA drives, as shown in Figure 4.2. Each SATA cable connects one device to the motherboard or SATA controller card, obviating the need for jumper configuration related to the drive identification. (Some SATA drives have jumpers for other purposes, though.) Although most SATA devices are internal to the computer, an external variant of the protocol, known as eSATA, is used by some external drives.

FIGURE 4.2   SATA (left) features much slimmer connecting cables than the older PATA (right).

SCSI   The *Small Computer System Interface (SCSI)* standard physically resembles PATA, in that it uses ribbon cables, although they're slightly wider, with 50 pins. SCSI supports up to 8 or 16 devices per cable, depending on the SCSI version, but the SCSI host adapter in the computer counts as a device, so the limit on the number of disks is seven or fifteen. In the past, SCSI was the favorite for servers and high-end workstations. Today, SCSI has faded in popularity, but SCSI devices are still available. A next-generation SCSI interface, known as *Serial Attached SCSI (SAS)*, is also available. In addition to being the next-generation SCSI interface, SAS is a step toward integrating the SCSI and ATA lines.

USB   The *Universal Serial Bus* is a popular method of interfacing external devices, including portable hard disks and USB flash drives. The first and second generations of USB are poor performers compared to all but rather elderly dedicated hard disk interfaces, but USB 3.0 greatly improves USB speed.

In addition to these four interfaces, various others are or have been used. These alternative interfaces are either modern but rare (such as IEEE-1394, aka FireWire) or obsolete interfaces.

From a Linux software perspective, all but the most obscure hard disk hardware uses one of two driver sets:

PATA   The PATA drivers, identified in the kernel as ATA/ATAPI/MFM/RLL, are officially deprecated with the most recent kernels, meaning that these drivers are still supported but are likely to be removed in the future. These drivers are most often used with PATA disks; however, this driver set includes support for some SATA hardware. Devices using these drivers receive names of the form /dev/hda, /dev/hdb, and so on. The first of these (/dev/hda) is reserved for the master drive on the first controller, /dev/hdb is the slave drive on the first controller, /dev/hdc is the master drive on the second controller, and so on. Thus, depending on how drives are connected, letters may be skipped—a computer can have /dev/hda and /dev/hdc but not /dev/hdb. PATA optical drives receive the same types of identifiers, although they can also usually be accessed as /dev/cdrom and other similar names.

SCSI   The Linux kernel's SCSI subsystem, originally used by SCSI devices, has slowly adopted other disk device types, including most SATA devices, USB devices, and today even many PATA devices. Hard disks managed by Linux's SCSI drivers receive names of /dev/sda, /dev/sdb, and so on. Gaps in the sequence don't normally exist for internal hard disks, but they can develop when USB or other external disks are removed. Optical disks managed by these drivers use names of /dev/sr0, /dev/sr1, and so on, with symbolic links using /dev/cdrom, /dev/dvd, and similar names.

It's important to realize that Linux's disk drivers are written for the controller circuitry on the motherboard or disk controller card; individual disks need no driver per se, since disk hardware is standardized within each category. The techniques and utilities described in the next few pages, however, enable you to tweak disk access methods in case a particular disk's needs aren't properly auto-detected.

Most modern computers include connectors for at least four disk devices on the motherboard. In most cases, the motherboard's main chipset provides the disk controller circuitry. In some cases, particularly on motherboards that support more than four disks, two different disk controllers are used. Plug-in cards are available to expand the number or type of disk devices a computer can use.

> In some cases, connecting a disk to a different motherboard controller port can overcome performance problems. This can be true if switching ports moves the disk from one disk controller to another one; sometimes the Linux drivers for one controller are deficient, or there may be disk/ controller hardware incompatibilities that impede performance. Such a swap is usually easy to implement once you've opened the computer's case, so it can be a good thing to try if you're having disk problems.

From a Linux configuration perspective, the nature of the technology used to store data—spinning platters on a hard disk, magneto-optical (MO) devices, solid state device (SSD) hardware, or something else—is mostly irrelevant. Such devices all present the same type of interface to Linux, using the PATA or SCSI drivers to enable the kernel and higher-level tools to read and write data from and to the disk. Some devices have subtle quirks, such as a need to align partitions in particular ways (as described in the Real World Scenario "Software vs. Hardware RAID"), but fundamentally they're the same. Optical drives (CD-ROMs, DVDs, and Blu-ray discs) are an exception; as described in Chapter 3, these devices must be accessed in different ways, particularly for writing.

Identifying Disk Resource Use

Disk controllers, like all hardware devices, use hardware resources. For the most part, resource use is managed automatically by the Linux kernel and its drivers; however, you may want to check on, and perhaps adjust, some details.

One important hardware resource is the *interrupt request* (*IRQ*, or *interrupt*) used by the device. Whenever some event occurs in the hardware device, such as the user pressing an eject button on a removable disk, the hardware signals this event to the computer via an interrupt. The traditional *x*86 architecture supports 16 interrupts, numbered 0–15; however, modern computers support more interrupts than this.

In the traditional *x*86 scheme, IRQs 14 and 15 are dedicated to the primary and secondary PATA controllers. Today, though, these interrupts might not be used. You can learn how your interrupts are allocated by examining the /proc/interrupts pseudo-file:

```
$ cat /proc/interrupts
          CPU0      CPU1
   0:      127      2550    IO-APIC-edge      timer
   1:     1048    574249    IO-APIC-edge      i8042
   7:        1         0    IO-APIC-edge      parport0
```

```
 8:          0         275   IO-APIC-edge      rtc0
 9:          0           0   IO-APIC-fasteoi   acpi
12:       9519     4373252   IO-APIC-edge      i8042
16:        118       37123   IO-APIC-fasteoi   ohci_hcd:usb3, ohci_hcd:usb4, ↵
hda_intel
17:         16        4753   IO-APIC-fasteoi   ehci_hcd:usb1
18:          8        6696   IO-APIC-fasteoi   ohci_hcd:usb5, ohci_hcd:usb6, ↵
ohci_hcd:usb7, radeon@pci:0000:01:05.0
19:         76       44026   IO-APIC-fasteoi   ehci_hcd:usb2, hda_intel
20:      38739    77465820   IO-APIC-fasteoi   cx88[0], cx88[0]
21:      34021    21279132   IO-APIC-fasteoi   eth0
22:       3846     1959346   IO-APIC-fasteoi   ahci
40:        136       89933   PCI-MSI-edge      eth1
NMI:        0           0   Non-maskable interrupts
LOC: 197186178  205069577   Local timer interrupts
SPU:        0           0   Spurious interrupts
PMI:        0           0   Performance monitoring interrupts
PND:        0           0   Performance pending work
RES: 194455575  191841607   Rescheduling interrupts
CAL:      381         346   Function call interrupts
TLB:   136306      146018   TLB shootdowns
THR:        0           0   Threshold APIC interrupts
MCE:        0           0   Machine check exceptions
MCP:     2557        2557   Machine check polls
ERR:        1
MIS:        0
```

Scan the output's last column for a driver related to disk access. In this example, IRQs 16 and 19 are both associated with hda_intel, a disk driver; and IRQ 22 is linked with ahci, a modern disk-access method. IRQs 16 and 19 in this example are shared—multiple devices use the same interrupt. This seldom causes problems on modern hardware, but if you suspect your disk accesses are being impaired by a shared interrupt, you can look into driver module options to change how interrupts are assigned. Research the drivers for both your disk devices and whatever is sharing the interrupts with them, as described in Chapter 2. You can also review your computer's firmware options; these may enable you to adjust IRQ assignment. Finally, the sysctl utility and its configuration file, /etc/sysctl.conf, can often be used to adjust IRQ assignments. Try typing **sysctl -a | grep irq** to learn about relevant options and then change any you find in /etc/sysctl.conf.

A second type of hardware resource you might want to adjust is direct memory access (DMA) allocation. In a DMA configuration, a device transfers data directly to and from an area of memory, as opposed to passing data through the computer's CPU. DMA can speed access, but if two devices try to use the same DMA channel, data can be corrupted. You can examine /proc/dma to review DMA address assignments:

```
$ cat /proc/dma
 3: parport0
 4: cascade
```

DMA problems are extremely rare on modern computers. If you need to adjust them, though, you can review your driver documentation and sysctl settings much as you would for IRQ conflicts to find a way to reassign a device to use a new DMA channel.

Testing Disk Performance

If you suspect disk problems, you should first try to quantify the nature of the problem. The hdparm utility can be useful for this. Pass it the -t parameter to test uncached read performance on the device:

```
# hdparm -t /dev/sda

/dev/sda:
 Timing buffered disk reads:  264 MB in  3.00 seconds =  87.96 MB/sec
```

 Using an uppercase –T instead of a lowercase –t tests the performance of the disk cache, which is mostly a measure of your computer's memory performance. Although this measure isn't very interesting in terms of real disk performance, many people habitually do both tests at the same time, as in **hdparm -tT /dev/sda**. For best results, run the hdparm test two or three times on an unloaded system.

As a general rule, conventional disks in 2011 should produce performance figures in the very high tens of megabytes per second and above. You can try to track down specifications on your disk from the manufacturer; however, disk manufacturers like to quote their disk interface speeds, which are invariably higher than their platter transfer rates (aka their internal transfer rates). Even if you can find an internal transfer rate for a drive, it's likely to be a bit optimistic.

SSD performance can be significantly better than that of conventional spinning disks, at least when using a true disk interface such as SATA. (USB flash drives tend to be quite slow.) If you apply hdparm to a RAID 0, 4, 5, 6, or 10 array, you're likely to see very good transfer rates, too.

Be aware that performance in actual use is likely to be lower than that produced by hdparm; this utility reads a large chunk of data from the drive without using the filesystem. In real-world use, the filesystem will be involved, which will degrade performance because of extra CPU overhead, the need to seek to various locations to read filesystem data, and other factors. Write performance may also be lower than read performance.

Adjusting Disk Parameters

If you use a device via a Linux PATA driver, the hdparm utility can be used to tweak disk access parameters, not just to measure performance. Table 4.7 summarizes the most important performance-enhancing features of hdparm, including one for power saving. Consult the program's man page for more hdparm options.

TABLE 4.7 hdparm options for enhancing performance

Option	Explanation
-d*n*	PATA devices can be run in either Programmed Input/Output (PIO) mode or in DMA mode. DMA mode produces lower CPU loads for disk accesses. Using -d0 enables PIO mode, and -d1 enables DMA mode. The -d1 option is generally used in conjunction with -X (described shortly). This option doesn't work on all systems; Linux requires explicit support for the DMA mode of a specific ATA chipset if you're to use this feature.
-p *mode*	This parameter sets the PIO mode, which in most cases varies from 0 to 5. Higher PIO modes correspond to better performance.
-c *mode*	Queries or sets 32-bit transfer status. Omit *mode* to query the status, set *mode* to 0 to disable 32-bit support, set *mode* to 1 to enable 32-bit support, or set *mode* to 3 to enable 32-bit support using a special sequence needed by some chipsets.
-S *timeout*	This option sets an energy-saving feature: the time a drive will wait without any accesses before it enters a low-power state. It takes a few seconds for a drive to recover from such a state, so many desktops leave *timeout* at 0, which disables this feature. On laptops, though, you may want to set *timeout* to something else. Values between 1 and 240 are multiples of 5 seconds (for instance, 120 means a 600-second, or 10-minute, delay); 241–251 mean 1–11 units of 30 minutes; 252 is a 21-minute timeout; 253 is a drive-specific timeout; and 255 is a 21-minute and 15-second timeout.
-v	You can see assorted disk settings with this option.
-X *transfermode*	This option sets the DMA transfer mode used by a disk. The *transfermode* is usually set to a value of sdma*x*, mdma*x*, or udma*x*. These values set simple DMA, multiword DMA, or Ultra DMA modes, respectively. In all cases, *x* represents the DMA mode value, which is a number. On modern hardware, you should be able to use a fairly high Ultra DMA mode, such as -X udma5 or -X udma6. Use this option with caution; setting an improper mode can cause the disk to become inaccessible, which in turn can cause your system to hang.

Although hdparm is useful for tuning PATA disks, most of its options have no effect on SCSI disks, including most SATA, USB, and even PATA disks that use the new SCSI interface for PATA. Fortunately, this isn't usually a problem, since true SCSI disks and the newer devices that are managed through the SCSI subsystem are generally configured optimally by default.

The sdparm utility, despite the name's similarity to hdparm, isn't really a SCSI equivalent of hdparm. Nonetheless, you can use sdparm to learn about and even adjust your SCSI devices. Table 4.8 summarizes the most important sdparm options; consult its man page for more obscure sdparm options. To use it, pass one or more options followed by a device name, such as /dev/sr0 or /dev/sda.

TABLE 4.8   Common sdparm options

Long option name	Short option name	Explanation
--all	-a	Displays a variety of technical information on the device.
--enumerate	-e	Displays information on the pages and fields that can be adjusted by sdparm. Ignores the device specification.
--flexible	-f	Corrects for problems in interpreting responses that can be caused by buggy devices or drivers.
--get *field*	-g *field*	Retrieves an individual *field* of technical data.
--inquiry	-i	Displays inquiry mode pages for the device.
--long	-l	Creates additional output with many commands.
--set=*STR=n*	-s *STR=n*	Sets a field to a specified value. Use with extreme caution!
--six	-6	Uses a 6-byte interface mode, rather than the newer 10-byte mode. Useful with older SCSI devices.

Many sdparm features enable sending low-level SCSI signals to your SCSI devices. This ability is potentially very dangerous. You should not experiment with random sdparm options.

Monitoring a Disk for Failure

Modern hard disks provide a feature known as Self-Monitoring, Analysis, and Reporting Technology (SMART), which is a self-diagnostic tool that you can use to predict impending failure. Periodically checking your drives for such problems can help you avoid costly incidents; if a SMART tool turns up a problem, you can replace the disk before you lose any data!

Several SMART-monitoring tools for Linux are available. One of these is smartctl; you can obtain a SMART report on a drive by typing **smartctl -a /dev/sda**, where */dev/sda* is the disk device node. Much of the output will be difficult to interpret, but you can search for the following line:

```
SMART overall-health self-assessment test result: PASSED
```

The smartctl output is wider than the standard 80 columns. You'll find it easier to interpret if you run it from a console that's at least 90 columns wide. If you run it from an X-based terminal, widen it before you run smartctl.

Of course, if the report indicates a failure, you should peruse the remainder of the report to learn what the problem is. You can also use smartctl to run active tests on a drive; consult its man page for details.

If you prefer a GUI tool, the GSmartControl utility (http://gsmartcontrol.berlios.de) may be what you need. Launch it, click an icon corresponding to a hard disk, and you'll see a window similar to the one in Figure 4.3. The final summary line on the Identity tab reveals the drive's overall health. If that line indicates problems or if you want to peruse the details, you can click the other tabs. The Perform Tests tab enables you to run active tests on the drive.

FIGURE 4.3   A SMART monitoring tool enables you to identify failing disk hardware before it causes you grief.

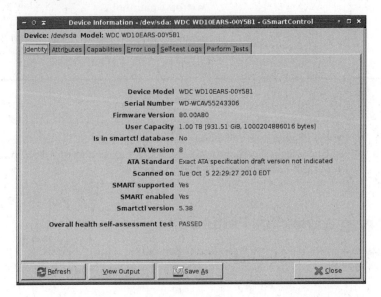

If a SMART test reveals problems, you should replace the drive immediately. You can transfer data by partitioning the new disk and creating filesystems on it and then using `tar` or `cpio` to copy data, or you can use a backup and data transfer tool such as CloneZilla (`http://clonezilla.org`).

Backing Up and Restoring a Computer

Many things can go wrong on a computer that might cause it to lose data. Hard disks can fail, you might accidentally enter some extremely destructive command, a cracker might break into your system, or a user might accidentally delete a file, to name just a few possibilities. To protect against such problems, it's important that you maintain good backups of the computer. To do this, select appropriate backup hardware, choose a backup program, and implement backups on a regular schedule. You should also have a plan in place to recover some or all of your data should the need arise.

Choosing Backup Hardware

Just about any device that can store computer data and read it back can be used as a backup medium. The best backup devices are inexpensive, fast, high in capacity, and reliable. They don't usually need to be *random-access* devices, though. Random-access devices are capable of quickly accessing any piece of data. Hard disks, CD-ROMs, and DVDs are all random-access devices. These devices contrast with *sequential-access* devices, which must read through all intervening data before accessing the sought-after component. Tapes are the most common sequential-access devices. Table 4.9 summarizes critical information about the most common types of backup device. For some such as tape, there are higher-capacity (and more expensive) devices for network backups.

TABLE 4.9   Vital statistics for common backup devices

Device	Cost of drive	Cost of media	Uncompressed capacity	Speed	Access type
Tape	$150–$4000	$0.25–$3.00/ GB	36GB–1.5TB	3–140MB/s	Sequential
Internal hard disks	$100 (for removable mounting kit)	$0.20/GB (including mounting frame)	80GB–2TB	50–100MB/s	Random

TABLE 4.9   Vital statistics for common backup devices *(continued)*

Device	Cost of drive	Cost of media	Uncompressed capacity	Speed	Access type
External hard disks	$50–$7000	$0.20–$2.00/ GB	80GB–16TB[1]	12–100MB/s	Random
Optical	$25–$200	$0.04–$0.50/ GB	650MB–50GB	1–45MB/s	Random

[1] External hard disk capacities can be greater than internal because some external hard disks include built-in RAID controllers and multiple physical disks in a single enclosure.

Numbers are approximate as of late 2010. Prices on all storage media have historically fallen rapidly, and capacities have risen. Costs are likely to be lower, and capacities higher, in the future.

The types of devices that appear in Table 4.9 are those most often used for backing up Linux systems. The pros and cons of using specific devices are:

Tapes   Tape drives have historically been the most popular choice for backing up entire computers. Their sequential-access nature is a hindrance for some applications, but it isn't a problem for routine backups. The biggest problem with tapes is that they're less reliable than some backup media, although reliability varies substantially from one type of tape to another, and the best are reasonably reliable.

Hard Disks   It's possible to use hard disks for backup purposes. If your computer is equipped with a kit that enables a drive to be quickly removed from a computer, you can swap hard disks in and out and move them off-site for storage, if desired. Similar comments apply to external hard disks. Internal hard disks without a removable disk bay, however, are susceptible to theft or damage along with the computer they're meant to back up.

Optical   Optical media are reliable in the short term, but less reliable in the long term than once believed. High-quality media, properly stored, can theoretically last decades; but in practice, failures sometimes occur after only a year or two. Some optical media are large enough to back up entire small systems, but for really large jobs, the higher capacity of tapes or hard disks is desirable. The need to use special tools, such as cdrecord, to write to optical devices can complicate backup plans, but this isn't an insurmountable hurdle.

In the past, the best backup devices for entire computers and networks have been tapes. The low cost and high capacity of tapes made them well suited to performing multiple backups of entire computers. In recent years, though, hard disks have plummeted in price, making removable or external hard disks more appealing than tapes for many applications. It's sometimes desirable to supplement tape or removable hard disk backups with optical backups.

It's generally wise to keep multiple backups and to store some of them away from the computers they're meant to protect. Such off-site storage protects your data in case of fire, vandalism, or other major physical traumas. Keeping several backups makes it more likely you'll be able to recover something, even if it's an older backup, should your most recent backup medium fail. Some administrators like to follow the *3-2-1 strategy* for backups, which involves keeping three copies of the data on at least two different types of media with at least one copy off-site.

Tape devices are accessed in Linux using the /dev/st0 (SCSI) or /dev/ht0 (PATA) device filenames. The /dev/nst0 and /dev/nht0 filenames are non-rewinding variants of these names—when using /dev/st0 or /dev/ht0, the tape rewinds automatically after every operation; but when using /dev/nst0 or /dev/nht0, the tape does not rewind. If a computer has more than one tape drive of a particular type, the number at the end of the device filename is incremented for each additional drive, as in /dev/st1 for the second SCSI tape drive.

If you decide to use hard disks in removable mounts as a backup medium, you'll need ordinary internal drives and mounting hardware. The hardware comes in two parts: a mounting bay that fits in the computer and a frame in which you mount the hard drive. To use the system, you slide the frame with hard drive into the mounting bay. You can get by with one of each component, but it's best to buy one frame for each hard drive, which effectively raises the media cost. From a Linux software point of view, removable hard disk systems work like regular hard disks or other removable disk systems, like USB flash drives. Most of these systems use SATA disks, which you'll access as /dev/sdb, /dev/sdc, or some other SCSI device identifier. The disks are likely to be partitioned, and the partitions are likely to hold ordinary Linux filesystems.

External disks with USB or eSATA interfaces are very common and can make good backup media; however, you'll need to buy several of them for optimum backup security. Alternatively, you can use an external caddy or cable, to which you can easily attach a bare hard disk. Buying one caddy and several hard disks enables you to keep multiple backups. For optimum speed, get a USB 3.0 or eSATA drive—and be sure your computer supports this high-performance interface!

Choosing Backup Software

Linux supports several backup programs. Some are tools designed to back up individual files, directories, or computers. Others build on these simpler tools to provide network backup facilities. Basic backup programs include tar, cpio, dump, and dd. ARKEIA (http://www.arkeia.com) and BRU (http://www.tolisgroup.com) are two commercial backup packages that provide explicit network support and GUI front-ends. AMANDA (http://www.amanda.org), Bacula (http://www.bacula.org), and BackupPC (http://backuppc.sourceforge.net) are network-capable backup packages that can perform a backup of an entire network. The rsync utility is a relatively simple program for performing network data transfers. When dealing with tapes, the mt program is useful for controlling the tape hardware.

This section provides a look at tar, cpio, dd, rsync, and mt as examples of how to back up a Linux system.

Using *tar*

The tar program's name stands for "tape archiver." Despite this, you can use tar to archive data to other media. In fact, *tarballs* (archive files created by tar and typically compressed with gzip or bzip2) are often used for transferring multiple files between computers in one step, such as when distributing source code. (Chapter 1 describes the use of tar in this context.)

The tar program is a complex package with many options, but most of what you'll do with the utility can be covered with a few common commands. Table 4.10 lists the primary tar commands, and Table 4.11 lists the qualifiers that modify what the commands do. Whenever you run tar, you use exactly one command, and you usually use at least one qualifier.

TABLE 4.10 tar commands

Command	Abbreviation	Description
--create	c	Creates an archive
--concatenate	A	Appends tar files to an archive
--append	r	Appends non-tar files to an archive
--update	u	Appends files that are newer than those in an archive
--diff or --compare	d	Compares an archive to files on disk
--list	t	Lists an archive's contents
--extract or --get	x	Extracts files from an archive

TABLE 4.11 tar qualifiers

Qualifier	Abbreviation	Description
--directory *dir*	C	Changes to directory *dir* before performing operations
--file [*host:*]*file*	f	Uses the file called *file* on the computer called *host* as the archive file

Qualifier	Abbreviation	Description
`--listed-incremental` *file*	g	Performs an incremental backup or restore, using *file* as a list of previously archived files
`--one-file-system`	l (on older versions of tar)	Backs up or restores only one filesystem (partition)
`--multi-volume`	M	Creates or extracts a multi-tape archive
`--tape-length` *N*	L	Changes tapes after *N* kilobytes
`--same-permissions`	p	Preserves all protection information
`--absolute-paths`	P	Retains the leading / on filenames
`--verbose`	v	Lists all files read or extracted when used with `--list`; displays file sizes, ownership, and time stamps
`--verify`	W	Verifies the archive after writing it
`--exclude` *file*	(none)	Excludes *file* from the archive
`--exclude-from` *file*	X	Excludes files listed in *file* from the archive
`--gzip` or `--ungzip`	z	Processes an archive through gzip
`--bzip2`	j (some older versions used I or y)	Processes an archive through bzip2

Of the commands listed in Table 4.10, the most commonly used are `--create`, `--extract`, and `--list`. The most useful qualifiers from Table 4.11 are `--file`, `--listed-incremental`, `--one-file-system`, `--same-permissions`, `--gzip`, `--bzip2`, and `--verbose`. If you fail to specify a filename with the `--file` qualifier, tar will attempt to use a default device, which is often (but not always) a tape device file.

Using *cpio*

The cpio program is similar to tar in that it creates an archive file. That file can be stored on disk, or it can be directed straight to your tape device. This can be a convenient way to back up the computer, because it requires no intermediate storage. To restore data, you use cpio to read directly from the tape device file.

The `cpio` utility has three operating modes:

Copy-Out Mode   This mode, activated by use of the -o or --create option, creates an archive and copies files into it.

Copy-In Mode   You activate copy-in mode by using the -i or --extract option. This mode extracts data from an existing archive. If you provide a filename or a pattern to match, `cpio` will extract only the files whose names match the pattern you provide.

Copy-Pass Mode   This mode is activated by the -p or --pass-through option. It combines the copy-out and copy-in modes, enabling you to copy a directory tree from one location to another.

 The copy-out and copy-in modes are named confusingly.

In addition to the options used to select the mode, `cpio` accepts many other options, the most important of which are summarized in Table 4.12. To back up a computer, you'll combine the --create (or -o) option with one or more of the options in Table 4.12; to restore data, you'll do the same but use --extract (or -i). In either case, `cpio` acts on filenames that you type at the console. In practice, you'll probably use the redirection operator (<) to pass a filename list to the program.

TABLE 4.12   Options for use with cpio

Option	Abbreviation	Description
--reset-access-time	-a	Resets the access time after reading a file so that it doesn't appear to have been read.
--append	-A	Appends data to an existing archive.
--pattern-file=*filename*	-E *filename*	Uses the contents of *filename* as a list of files to be extracted in copy-in mode.
--file=*filename*	-F *filename*	Uses *filename* as the cpio archive file; if this parameter is omitted, cpio uses standard input or output.
--format=*format*	-H *format*	Uses a specified format for the archive file. Common values for *format* include bin (the default, an old binary format), crc (a newer binary format with a checksum), and tar (the format used by tar).

Option	Abbreviation	Description
N/A	-I `filename`	Uses the specified `filename` instead of standard input. (Unlike -F, this option does not redirect output data.)
--no-absolute-filenames	N/A	In copy-in mode, extracts files relative to the current directory, even if filenames in the archive contain full directory paths.
N/A	-O `filename`	Uses the specified `filename` instead of standard output. (Unlike -F, this option does not redirect input data.)
--list	-t	Displays a table of contents for the input.
--unconditional	-u	Replaces all files, without first asking for verification.
--verbose	-v	Displays filenames as they're added to or extracted from the archive. When used with -t, displays additional listing information (similar to `ls -l`).

Using *dd*

The dd utility is a low-level file copying tool, with the ability to apply certain transformations at the same time. As a backup tool, dd is useful for backing up an entire raw filesystem—even one that Linux doesn't support or one that's been badly damaged. Table 4.13 summarizes the dd options you're most likely to use when backing up a filesystem using this tool. Consult the program's man page for additional options.

TABLE 4.13 Common dd operands

Operand	Description
bs=*size*	Operates on chunks (blocks) of *size* bytes at a time.
count=*blocks*	Copies the specified number of blocks.
if=*file*	Uses *file* as the source (input) file. If this operand is omitted, standard input is assumed.
of=*file*	Writes output to the specified *file*. If this operand is omitted, standard output is assumed.

TABLE 4.13   Common dd operands *(continued)*

Operand	Description
skip=*blocks*	Skips the specified number of blocks on input.
seek=*blocks*	Starts writing the specified number of blocks into the output file.
conv=*conversions*	Applies conversion rules from a list. From a backup perspective, noerror is the most interesting conversion rule; this causes the program to continue if it encounters an input/output error, enabling backup (albeit possibly corrupted) even from or to faulty hardware.

To use dd to back up a partition, you specify the original partition's device filename with if= and a backup partition, file, or device with of=. For instance, if you want to back up /dev/sda2 to a file on an external hard disk that's mounted at /media/backups, you might type the following:

```
# dd if=/dev/sda2 of=/media/backups/sda2-back.img
```

If you wanted to restore the backup, you would reverse the if= and of= operands.

WARNING   You should back up or restore only *unmounted* filesystems using dd. Backing up a mounted filesystem can produce an inconsistent filesystem. Restoring to a mounted partition can produce severe disk corruption. If you need to back up a running system using dd and if the device in question is part of an LVM, you can use the LVM snapshot feature, as described earlier in "Using LVM Snapshots," and back up the snapshot volume.

If you want to apply compression, you can omit the of= (on backup) or if= (on restore) option and use dd with a compression program in a pipe:

```
# dd if=/dev/sda2 | gzip -9 > /media/backups/sda2-back.img.gz
# gunzip /media/backups/sda2-back.img.gz - | dd of=/dev/sda2
```

The first command backs up /dev/sda2; the second command restores that partition.

The greatest strength of dd is its filesystem independence; you can back up anything with dd, even if Linux provides limited or no support for the filesystem. You can also back up a damaged filesystem with dd, which is useful if you want to attempt a repair but fear causing further damage to the original filesystem. The biggest problem with dd is that, because it backs up everything on a byte-by-byte basis, it wastes time and disk space backing up unused space in the filesystem. If you have a 20 GiB partition, it will take 20 GiB of backup storage space if backed up uncompressed, even if the partition holds just 2 KiB of files.

Applying compression can minimize this problem, but in some cases, unused parts of a filesystem actually hold old data, so the backup can still be larger than necessary.

> The dcfldd utility (http://dcfldd.sourceforge.net) is a dd variant with additional features, such as a progress indicator. The ddrescue utility (http://www.gnu.org/software/ddrescue/ddrescue.html), although dissimilar from dd and dcfldd in usage details, tries extra hard to recover data from bad media, which is sometimes vitally important.

Using *rsync*

For small network backup tasks, rsync may be all you need. This program is designed to copy data from one computer to another on a network, keeping two network directories synchronized. The program supports a large number of options and variant machine specifications; however, a general use looks something like this:

```
$ rsync -av ./ user@remote:~/backups/
```

This command copies all the files in the current directory to the *remote* computer, using the username *user*, and places the files in the *~/backups* directory on that system.

As shown here, rsync can be used by ordinary users. Alternatively, it can be used by a backup script to do its transfers. In either case, rsync relies on another network file-transfer tool, such as ssh. In some cases, this tool may require a password, so you may need to be present to type it; or you can configure the computers to enable password-free file transfers.

Although rsync doesn't transfer data directly to a backup medium unless it's a hard disk that's mounted, it can be useful for network data transfers. Users can copy their files to a central backup server, or the backup server can use rsync to grab files from backup client computers. In either case, the backup server computer can then back the files up to tape or some other storage medium.

Using *cpio* or *tar* to Back Up a Computer

The preceding sections describe the basic features of several common backup utilities. It is informative to see how these tools are used in practice, though. Therefore, this section illustrates how to use cpio or tar to back up a computer.

It's often desirable to compress backups, but the cpio and tar programs don't compress data themselves. To do this, these programs rely on an external program, such as gzip or bzip2, to compress an entire cpio or tar archive. The problem with this approach is that if an error occurs while restoring the compressed archive, all the data from that error onward will be lost. This makes compressed cpio or tar archives risky for backup. Fortunately, most tape drives support compression in their hardware, and these use more robust compression algorithms. Therefore, if your tape drive supports compression, you should *not* compress a cpio or tar backup. Let the tape drive do that job, and if there's a read error at restore, you'll probably lose just one or two files. If your tape drive doesn't include built-in compression features, you should either not compress your backups or use another utility, most of which don't suffer from this problem.

To back up a computer with cpio, a command like the following will do the job:

```
# find / | cpio -oF /dev/st0
```

Because cpio expects a list of files on standard input, this command uses the find command and a pipe to feed this information to cpio. The -o option then tells cpio to create an archive, and -F specifies where it should be created—in this case, it uses /dev/st0 to create the archive on the tape device.

This command, though, has some negative effects. Most notably, it backs up everything, including the contents of the /proc filesystem and any mounted removable disks that might be present. You can use the -xdev option to find to have that program omit mounted directories from its search, but this means you'll have to explicitly list each partition you want to have backed up. For instance, you might use a command like the following to back up the /home, root (/), /boot, and /var partitions:

```
# find /home / /boot /var -xdev | cpio -oF /dev/st0
```

This command lists directories in a particular order. Because tape is a sequential-access medium, the system will restore items in the order in which they were backed up. Therefore, for the fastest partial restores, list the filesystems that you most expect to have to restore first. In this example, /home is listed first because users sometimes delete files accidentally. Backing up /home first, therefore, results in quicker restoration of such files.

Depending on the filesystem you use, you may see a string of truncating inode number messages. This happens when you use an old cpio format with a filesystem that uses inode numbers greater than 65,536. To overcome this problem, specify another format, such as crc, using -H.

The procedure for backing up with tar is similar; however, tar doesn't need a list of files piped to it; you provide a list of files or directories on the command line:

```
# tar cvpf /dev/st0 --one-file-system /home / /boot /var
```

Ordinarily, tar descends the directory tree; the --one-file-system option prevents this, much like the -xdev option to find.

After creating a backup with tar, you may want to use the tar --diff (also known as --compare, or d) command to verify the backup you've just written against the files on disk. Alternatively, you can include the --verify (W) qualifier to have this done automatically. Verifying your backup doesn't guarantee it will be readable when you need it, but it should at least catch major errors caused by severely degraded tapes. On the other hand, the verification will almost certainly return a few spurious errors because of files whose contents have legitimately changed between being written and being compared. This may be true of log files, for instance.

Backing Up Using Optical Media

Optical media require special backup procedures. As described in Chapter 3, tools such as cdrecord or growisofs are required to write to these discs.

One option for backing up to optical discs is to use mkisofs and then cdrecord to copy files to a CD-R or use growisofs to copy files to a DVD or Blu-ray disc. If you copy files "raw" in this way, though, you'll lose some information, such as write permission bits. You'll have better luck if you create a cpio or tar file on disk, much as you would when you back up to tape. You would then use mkisofs/cdrecord or growisofs to copy this file to the disc. The result will be a CD-R that you can mount and that will contain an archive you can read with cpio or tar.

A somewhat more direct option is to create an archive file and burn it directly to the optical disc using cdrecord, bypassing mkisofs. Such a disc won't be mountable in the usual way, but you can access the archive directly by using the optical device file. On restoration, this works much like a tape restore, except that you specify the optical device filename (such as /dev/cdrom) instead of the tape device filename (such as /dev/st0).

Using *mt* to Control a Tape Drive

In cpio and tar terminology, each backup is a file. This file is likely to contain many files from the original system, but like an RPM or Debian package file, the archive file is a single entity. Sometimes an archive file is far smaller than the tape on which it's placed. If you want to store more than one archive file on a tape, you can do so by using the nonrewinding tape device filename. For instance, the following commands accomplish the same goal as the ones shown in the previous section, but in a somewhat different manner and with subtly different results:

```
# tar cvlpf /dev/nst0 /home
# tar cvlpf /dev/nst0 /
# tar cvlpf /dev/nst0 /boot
# tar cvlpf /dev/nst0 /var
```

After you issue these commands, the tape will contain four tar files, one for each of the four directories. To access each file after writing them, you need to use a special utility called mt. This program moves forward and backward among tape files and otherwise controls tape features. Its syntax is as follows:

```
mt -f device operation [count] [arguments]
```

The *device* parameter is the tape device filename. The mt utility supports many operations, as summarized in Table 4.14.

TABLE 4.14 Common mt operations

Operation	Description
fsf	Moves forward *count* files.
bsf	Moves backward *count* files.
eod or seod	Moves to the end of data on the tape.
rewind	Rewinds the tape.
offline or rewoffl	Rewinds and unloads the tape. (Unloading is meaningless on some drives but ejects the tape on others.)
retension	Rewinds the tape, winds it to the end, and then rewinds it again. This action improves reliability with some types of tape, particularly if the tape has been sitting unused for several months.
erase	Erases the tape. (This command usually doesn't actually erase the data; it just marks the tape as being empty.)
status	Displays information on the tape drive.
load	Loads a tape into the drive. Unnecessary with many drives.
compression	Enables or disables compression by passing an argument of 1 or 0, respectively.
datcompression	Also enables and disables compression.

 The compression and datcompression operations aren't identical; sometimes a tape drive works with one but not the other.

For instance, suppose you created a backup on a SCSI tape, but now you want to create another backup on the same tape without eliminating the first backup. You could issue the following commands to accomplish this task:

```
# mt -f /dev/nst0 rewind
# mt -f /dev/nst0 fsf 1
# tar cvlpf /dev/nst0 /directory/to/back/up
# mt -f /dev/nst0 offline
```

These commands rewind the tape, space past the first file, create a new backup, and then unload the tape. Such commands are particularly useful when performing incremental backups, as described shortly.

Planning a Backup Schedule

Regular computer backup is important, but precisely *how* regularly is a matter that varies from one system to another. If a computer's contents almost never change (as might be true of a dedicated router or a workstation whose user files reside on a file server), backups once a month or even less often might be in order. For critical file servers, once a day is not too often. You'll have to decide for yourself just how frequently your systems require backup. Take into consideration factors such as how often the data change, the importance of the data, the cost of recovering the data without a current backup, and the cost of making a backup. Costs may be measured in money, your own time, users' lost productivity, and perhaps lost sales.

Even the most zealous backup advocate must admit that creating a full backup of a big system on a regular basis can be a tedious chore. A backup can easily take several hours, depending on backup size and hardware speed. For this reason, most backup packages, including tar, support *incremental backups*. You can create these using the --listed-incremental *file* qualifier to tar, as shown in this example:

```
# tar cvplf /dev/st0 --listed-incremental /root/inc / /home
```

This command stores a list of the files that have been backed up (along with identifying information to help tar determine when the files have changed) in /root/inc. The next time the same command is issued, tar will not back up files that have already been backed up; it will back up only new files. Thus, you can create a schedule in which you do a full backup of the entire computer only occasionally—say, once a week or once a month. You'd do this by deleting the increment file and running a backup as usual. On intervening weeks or days, you can perform an incremental backup, in which only new and changed files are backed up. These incremental backups will take comparatively little time.

With cpio, the key to incremental backups is in the list of files fed to the program. You can perform an incremental backup by using find options to locate only new files or files that have changed since the last backup. For instance, the -newer *file* option to find causes that program to return only files that have been modified more recently than *file*.

Thus, you could create a file (perhaps a log of your backup activity) during each backup and use it as a way of determining what files have been modified since the last backup.

You can use incremental backups in conjunction with mt to store multiple incremental backups on one tape. Typically, you'll have two tapes for a backup set: one for a full backup and one for intervening incremental backups. Suppose you do a full backup on Monday. On Tuesday, you'd insert the incremental tape and perform the first incremental backup. On Wednesday, you'd insert this tape and type `mt -f /dev/nst0 fsf 1` to skip past Tuesday's incremental backup, and then perform another incremental backup. On Thursday, you'd type `mt -f /dev/nst0 fsf 2`, and so on.

Performing incremental backups has a couple of drawbacks. One is that they complicate restoration. Suppose you do a full backup on Monday and incremental backups every other day. If a system fails on Friday, you'll need to restore the full backup and several incremental backups. Second, after restoring an incremental backup, your system will contain files that you'd deleted since the full backup. If files have short life spans on a computer, this can result in a lot of "dead" files being restored when the time comes to do so.

Despite these problems, incremental backups can be an extremely useful tool for helping make backups manageable. They can also reduce wear and tear on tapes and tape drives, and they can minimize the time it takes to restore files if you know that the files you need to restore were backed up on an incremental tape.

WARNING   Whether you perform incremental backups or nothing but complete backups, you should maintain multiple backups. Murphy's Law guarantees that your backup will fail when you need it most, so having a backup for your backup (even if it's from a week or a month earlier) can help immensely. A typical backup plan includes a rotating set of backup tapes. For instance, you might have two tapes per week—one for a full backup on one day and one to hold several incremental backups. Eight tapes will then hold backups for four weeks.

Preparing for Disaster: Backup Recovery

Creating backups is advisable, but doing this isn't enough. You must also have some way to restore backups in case of disaster. This task involves two aspects: partial restores and emergency recovery.

Partial restores involve recovering just a few noncritical files. For instance, users might come to you and ask you to restore files from their home directories. You can do so fairly easily by using the --extract (x) tar command, as in:

```
# cd /
# tar xvpf /dev/st0 home/username/filename
```

This sequence involves changing to the root directory and issuing a relative path to the file or directory that must be restored. This is required because tar normally strips away the leading / in files it backs up, so the files are recorded in the archive as relative filenames. If you try to restore a file with an absolute filename, it won't work.

When you're using cpio, the procedure is similar, but you use the --extract (-i) option, along with other options to feed the name of the archive, and perhaps do other things:

```
# cd /
# cpio -ivF /dev/st0 home/username/filename
```

This cpio command uses –F to have cpio retrieve data from the specified file (/dev/st0) rather than from standard input. Alternatively, you could use redirection to do the job, as in **cpio -iv < /dev/st0 home/*username*/filename**.

Whether you're using tar or cpio, you'll need to know the exact name of the file or directory you want to restore in order to do this. If you don't know the exact filename, you may need to use the --list (t) command to cpio or tar to examine the entire contents of the tape, or at least everything until you see the file you want to restore.

If you use incremental backups, you can use the incremental file list to locate the filename you want to restore.

A much more serious problem is that of recovering a system that's badly damaged. If your hard disk has crashed or your system has been invaded by crackers, you must restore the entire system from scratch, without the benefit of your normal installation. You can take any of several approaches to this problem, including the following:

Distribution's Installation Disk   Most Linux distributions' installation disks have some sort of emergency recovery system. These systems are typically small but functional Linux installations with a handful of vital tools, such as fdisk, mkfs, Vi, and tar. Check your distribution's documentation or boot its boot media and study its options to learn more.

CD-Based Linux System   Several Linux systems are now available that boot from CD-ROM or DVD. Examples include Knoppix (http://www.knoppix.com), SystemRescueCd (http://www.sysresccd.org), and PartedMagic (http://partedmagic.com). All of these systems can be used to help recover or restore a corrupted Linux installation.

Emergency System on Removable Disk   You can create your own emergency system on a removable disk, such as a USB flash drive. A 16 GiB flash drive is sufficient to hold a fairly comfortable Linux installation, although it won't perform as quickly as an installation on a PATA, SATA, or SCSI hard disk.

Emergency Recovery Partition   If you plan ahead, you might create a small emergency installation of your preferred distribution alongside the regular installation. You should *not* mount this system in /etc/fstab. This system can be useful for recovering from some problems, such as software filesystem corruption, but it's not useful for others, such as a total hard disk failure.

Partial Reinstallation   You can reinstall a minimal Linux system and then use it to recover your original installation. This approach is much like the emergency recovery partition approach, but it takes more time at disaster recovery. On the other hand, it will work even if your hard disk is completely destroyed.

Whatever approach you choose to use, you should test it before you need it. Learn at least the basics of the tools available in any system you plan to use. If you use unusual backup tools (such as commercial backup software), be sure to copy those tools to your emergency system or have them available on a separate removable disk. If you'll need to recover clients via network links, test those setups as well.

You may not be able to *completely* test your emergency restore tools. Ideally, you should boot the tools, restore a system, and test that the system works. This may be possible if you have spare hardware on which to experiment, but if you lack this luxury, you may have to make do with performing a test restore of a few files and testing an emergency boot procedure—say, using Super GRUB Disk (http://www.supergrubdisk.org). Note that a freshly restored system will not be bootable; you'll need a tool such as Super GRUB Disk to boot the first time. You can then reinstall GRUB to restore the system's ability to boot from the hard disk.

Summary

Most Linux distributions create fairly conventional partition-based installations by default; however, advanced tools can be very useful alternatives to conventional partitioning schemes in certain situations. RAID enables you to combine multiple hard disks together to create larger filesystems, to improve speed, to improve reliability, or to do all these things. LVM can use a single storage area or multiple storage areas to create larger filesystems, to improve speed, to improve flexibility, or to do all of these things. You can combine RAID and LVM to gain all of these benefits. Both RAID and LVM, however, come at the cost of added complexity, and some configurations can reduce reliability.

Tuning disk access can improve disk performance. The most dramatic improvements are possible with older PATA disks, particularly if the default drivers and options are misconfigured for the disks. For more modern SCSI and SATA disks, dramatic performance improvements are unlikely, but you may want to test your disk's performance just to be sure it's reasonable. This includes using a SMART utility to verify that the disk hardware isn't on the verge of failing.

After you put effort into creating an ideal partitioning, RAID, or LVM setup; installing Linux; and tweaking the system, it would be a shame to throw away all that effort. Your users would say the same about their data on your computer. Thus, you should plan and deploy a backup strategy, backing up your data on a regular basis. If you do so, problems such as major user error, major software bugs, system intrusions, hardware failure, and even hardware theft can be overcome in a matter of minutes or hours by restoring a backup.

Exam Essentials

Explain the partitioning needs of a RAID configuration.   MBR partitions added to a Linux software RAID array must be of type 0xFD. On a GPT disk, the partition is flagged as type 0xFD00 in GPT fdisk or as having the raid flag set in libparted-based tools. A single disk may hold one or more RAID partitions, each of which is combined with a matched partition on another physical disk.

Summarize the major levels of RAID supported by Linux.   Linear RAID, although technically not RAID, combines devices in a simple one-after-the-other manner. RAID 0 combines two equal-sized devices in an interleaved manner to improve performance. RAID 1 creates a duplicate copy of one device on another one to improve reliability. RAID levels 4, 5, and 6 use checksums and one (two for RAID 6) extra device to improve both reliability and speed. RAID 10 is similar to RAID 4 and 5 in purpose, but it works by combining RAID 1 and RAID 0 features.

Explain the partitioning needs of an LVM configuration.   MBR partitions in a Linux LVM setup must be of type 0x8E. On a GPT disk, the partition is flagged as type 0x8E00 in GPT fdisk or as having the lvm flag set in libparted-based tools. A single disk may hold one or more LVM partitions, which can be combined together or with partitions on other disks to create a volume group.

Summarize the three levels of data structures employed by LVM.   Physical volumes are at the bottom of the LVM data structure hierarchy; these are partitions, RAID volumes, or other low-level devices that are suitably flagged and marked with basic LVM data structures. Physical volumes are combined into volume groups, which act as a pool of allocatable disk space. Logical volumes are created within this pool of disk space and can be used much like partitions; they typically hold filesystems or swap space.

Describe how LVM can improve backup operations.   You can create a snapshot of a logical volume—that is, a duplicate of the original logical volume that won't change even as accesses continue on the original. By backing up the snapshot rather than the original logical volume, you ensure that it will be in a consistent state, even if the original is being used heavily and therefore might yield a backup that contains slightly mismatched files.

Describe how PATA disk access speed can be optimized.   You can use the hdparm program to test raw disk read speed and to set various low-level disk access options. These include the use of DMA versus PIO mode, as well as the specific DMA or PIO transfer mode. These options are meaningful only for older PATA disks using the recently deprecated PATA drivers.

Summarize common backup hardware options.   Tape is the traditional backup medium, and it remains a good choice for large installations. Tape can be expensive for small systems, though. For such computers, a removable or external hard disk can be a good alternative. Optical media (CD-Rs, recordable DVDs, and recordable Blu-ray discs) can be a useful backup medium for smaller systems or for small amounts of data, but these media lack the capacity to back up very large installations.

Summarize common backup software options.   The tar and cpio programs are both popular file-based backup tools that are useful for backing up complete Linux installations. When backing up exotic filesystems that Linux might not fully support or when you need a low-level image prior to attempting repairs or modifications of a valuable filesystem, dd is a good choice. Commercial and network-based tools, such as BRU, ARKEIA, AMDANDA, Bacula, and BackupPC, are useful for backing up large systems or for performing backups of entire networks.

Explain common backup schedules.   A full backup backs up all the files on a computer or in a directory tree. Such backups are easy to restore but consume a great deal of space on the backup medium. To save time and space, incremental backups can be performed in between full backups. These backups store only the files that have changed since the last full or incremental backup. Typically, you'll perform a full backup every once in a while (perhaps once a month or once a week), with incremental backups more frequently. The optimum schedule depends on many factors, including how often your files change, how valuable your data are, and your available resources.

Review Questions

1. Typing **fdisk -lu /dev/hda** on a Linux computer with an MBR disk produces a listing of four partitions: /dev/hda1, /dev/hda2, /dev/hda5, and /dev/hda6. Which of the following is true?

    A. The disk contains two primary partitions and two extended partitions.

    B. Either /dev/hda1 or /dev/hda2 is an extended partition.

    C. The partition table is corrupted; there should be a /dev/hda3 and a /dev/hda4 before /dev/hda5.

    D. If you add a /dev/hda3 with fdisk, /dev/hda5 will become /dev/hda6, and /dev/hda6 will become /dev/hda7.

2. A new server is arriving at the end of the week. It will have four 1 TiB hard drives installed and configured in a RAID 5 array with no hot standby spare drives. How much data can be stored within this array?

    A. 4 TiB

    B. 3 TiB

    C. 2 TiB

    D. 1 TiB

3. You have been told by your manager that the server being moved from the test lab to production must have the two drives within it mirrored. What level of RAID is used for mirroring?

    A. RAID 6

    B. RAID 5

    C. RAID 1

    D. RAID 0

4. What can you conclude from the following line, which is found in /proc/mdstat?

    ```
    md0 : active raid4 sdd2[2] sdc1[1] sda8[0]
    ```

    A. The /dev/md0 RAID 4 device is built from the /dev/sda8, /dev/sdc1, and /dev/sdd2 partitions.

    B. The /dev/md0 RAID device is missing one partition; it should have four component partitions, given its RAID level (4).

    C. The /dev/md0 RAID device is badly misconfigured; the partition numbers of the component devices should match.

    D. None of the above.

5. Which of the following commands correctly assembles a RAID 1 array from the component devices /dev/sda1 and /dev/hda2?

    A. `mdadm --create --level=1 --raid-devices=2 /dev/sda1 /dev/hda2`

    B. `mdadm --level=1 --raid-devices=2 /dev/sda1 /dev/hda2`

    C. `mdadm --level=5 --raid-devices=2 /dev/sda1 /dev/hda2`

    D. `mdadm --create /dev/md0 --level=1 --raid-devices=2 /dev/sda1 /dev/hda2`

6. Once Linux is booted, which file can you view to see which IRQs are in use on the Linux computer?

    A. `/etc/interrupts`

    B. `/boot/interrupts`

    C. `/root/interrupts`

    D. `/proc/interrupts`

7. Why should you be cautious when using `hdparm`?

    A. The `hdparm` tool can set hardware options that are not supported by some hardware, thus causing data corruption.

    B. Because `hdparm` modifies partition tables, an error can result in loss of one or more partitions and all their data.

    C. By changing hardware device file mappings, you can become confused about which drive is /dev/hda and which is /dev/hdb.

    D. The `hdparm` tool can cause Linux to treat an ext2fs partition as if it were FAT, resulting in serious data corruption.

8. Which of the following tools is used to initialize a partition so that it may function as a physical volume in an LVM configuration?

    A. pvchange

    B. pvcreate

    C. lvcreate

    D. lvconvert

9. Which of the following device files might you reasonably include in a volume group, assuming they're properly flagged and prepared? (Select all that apply.)

    A. /dev/sdc

    B. /dev/md1

    C. /dev/sda7

    D. /dev/hdb2

10. Your computer has crashed because of filesystem corruption, and you must perform emergency recovery using an emergency boot disc. How can you activate your LVM devices, if they aren't activated automatically when you boot your emergency disc?

    A. vgscan

    B. vgimport

    C. vgchange -ay

    D. vgdisplay

11. Where are you likely to find device nodes for the MyGroup volume group?

    A. /dev/mapper

    B. /dev/mygroup

    C. /dev/lvm

    D. /dev/LVM/MyGroup

12. What is the appropriate procedure for increasing the size of a logical volume containing an ext3 filesystem? (Assume sufficient free space exists in the volume group.)

    A. Use resize2fs to resize the filesystem, and then lvresize to resize the logical volume, and then resize2fs again to make the filesystem fill the logical volume precisely.

    B. Use resize2fs to resize the filesystem followed by lvresize to resize the logical volume.

    C. Use GParted to move other logical volumes, if necessary, so that the logical volume may be resized, and then resize the target logical volume.

    D. Use lvresize to resize the logical volume followed by resize2fs to resize the filesystem.

13. You have an old Debian installation on the debian logical volume in the MyLVM volume group. You want to install a new version of Fedora Linux to replace this older Debian installation. The current debian logical volume is the right size for the new installation, but you want to give the logical volume a new name to avoid confusion. How can you do this?

    A. vgrename MyLVM -n fedora -o debian

    B. lvrename MyLVM debian fedora

    C. mv /dev/MyLVM/debian /dev/MyLVM/fedora

    D. lvadjust MyLVM -name debian,fedora

14. Which of the following commands are commonly used to create archive files? (Select all that apply.)

    A. restore

    B. tar

    C. tape

    D. cpio

15. Which of the following commands backs up the /home directory to an ATAPI tape drive?

    A. tar cvlpf /home /dev/st0

    B. tar cvlpf /home /dev/ht0

    C. tar cvf /dev/st0 /home

    D. tar cvf /dev/ht0 /home

16. What is wrong with the following commands, which are intended to record an incremental backup on a tape that already holds one incremental backup?

```
# mt -f /dev/st0 fsf 1
# tar cvpf /dev/st0 --listed-incremental /root/inc /home
```

    A. The mt command should terminate in 2, rather than 1, to skip to the second position on the tape.

    B. When backing up /home, the incremental file must reside in /home, not in /root.

    C. The device filename should be a nonrewinding name (such as /dev/nst0), not a rewinding name (/dev/st0).

    D. The incremental backup must include the root (/) directory; it cannot include only /home.

17. You need to restore some files that were accidentally deleted. Which of the following commands can be used to list the contents of an archive stored on a SCSI tape?

    A. cpio -itv > /dev/st0

    B. cpio -otv > /dev/st0

    C. cpio -otv < /dev/st0

    D. cpio -itv < /dev/st0

18. You arrive at work on Monday morning to find that the server has crashed. All indications point to the crash as occurring earlier that morning. Scripts automatically do a full backup of the server every Friday night and an incremental backup all other nights. Which tapes do you need to restore the data on a new server? (Choose all that apply.)

    A. Thursday's tape

    B. Friday's tape

    C. Saturday's tape

    D. Sunday's tape

19. A 20 GiB partition, /dev/sda1, holding your main Linux installation, has become damaged by improper use of a low-level disk utility. Before attempting to repair it with fsck, you decide to back it up to a currently unused 25 GiB partition, /dev/sdc6. How can you do this?

A. `dd if=/dev/sda1 of=/dev/sdc6`

B. `dd of=/dev/sda1 if=/dev/sdc6`

C. `dd if=/dev/sda1 of=/dev/sdc6 bs=1024 count=2048`

D. `dd of=/dev/sda1 if=/dev/sdc6 bs=1024 count=2048`

20. Which of the following is a sequential backup medium?

A. Tape

B. External hard disk

C. Recordable DVD

D. Recordable Blu-ray

Answers to Review Questions

1. B. Logical partitions are numbered from 5 and up, and they reside inside an extended partition with a number between 1 and 4. Therefore, one of the first two partitions must be an extended partition that houses partitions 5 and 6. Because logical partitions are numbered starting at 5, their numbers won't change if /dev/hda3 is subsequently added. The disk holds one primary, one extended, and two logical partitions.

2. B. In a RAID 5 array, the amount of data that can be stored is equal to the number of disks minus 1, since that amount of space will be used for holding parity information. (Hot standby spare drives further reduce available storage space, if used.) In this case, there are a total of four drives. Subtracting one means the amount of data space available is equal to three times the 1 TiB disk size, or a total of 3 TiB.

3. C. In a RAID 1 array, the disks are mirrored. RAID 5 is an implementation of disk striping with parity, while RAID 0 is disk striping without parity. RAID 6 is an experimental implementation of striping with parity that can survive the failure of two disks at a time.

4. A. Option A correctly summarizes some of the information encoded in the specified line. (The array is also flagged as being active, and the order of the devices is encoded in the numbers following their names.) Option B is incorrect because RAID 4 arrays can be built from as few as three devices; the RAID level does not specify the minimum number of component devices. Option C is incorrect because Linux's software RAID implementation does not require the component devices to have matched partition numbers. Because option A is correct, option D cannot be correct.

5. D. Option D is the correct command to do as the question asks. (This answer assembles the array to be accessible as /dev/md0; the question didn't specify a particular target device, but you must specify one with mdadm.) Option A is correct except that it's missing the device filename for the --create option. Options B and C are both missing the necessary --create option entirely, and option C incorrectly states the RAID level as being 5.

6. D. Once Linux is booted, you can check on resource consumption by examining files in the /proc filesystem. In particular, /proc/interrupts holds IRQ use information. The other choices listed do not exist as standard, dynamically updated files within Linux.

7. A. The hdparm program manipulates low-level options in ATA hard disk controllers, such as the use of DMA or PIO modes. If a controller is buggy or doesn't support a specified mode, the result can be data corruption or lost access to hard disks. The utility has nothing to do with partition tables, device file mappings, or filesystems per se.

8. B. The pvcreate utility lays out the basic data structures needed by LVM on a physical volume, so option B is correct. The pvchange utility changes physical volume attributes but doesn't prepare a partition as the question asks. Options C and D both operate on logical volumes, not physical volumes: lvcreate creates a new logical volume, and lvconvert converts between modes, as for example when merging a snapshot into its parent.

9. A, B, C, D. All of the listed devices can be included in an LVM configuration. Although using a whole disk, as in option A, is unusual, it is a valid choice. Option B denotes a RAID device, which you might include if you want to combine the benefits of both RAID and LVM. Options C and D are conventional LVM choices on partitions using SCSI and PATA disks, respectively.

10. C. The vgchange command with its -ay option, activates a volume group's devices, so option C is correct. The vgscan command scans for volume groups but does not activate the device nodes for the logical volumes it contains. The vgimport command is used to import (activate) a previously exported (deactivated) volume group; but the question specifies that the problems were caused by a system crash, not an improperly exported volume group, so option B is incorrect. The vgdisplay command displays information on the volume group; it doesn't activate the device nodes for its logical volumes.

11. A. The /dev/mapper directory holds device files for logical volumes, so option A is correct. (The files will take the form /dev/mapper/MyGroup-*lvname*, where *lvname* is the logical volume name.) Although /dev/*groupname*, where *groupname* is the volume group name, typically holds duplicates of logical volume device nodes, because Linux uses a case-sensitive filesystem, option B is incorrect. Neither /dev/lvm nor /dev/LVM is a standard location for logical volume device nodes, so options C and D are both incorrect. Note that any of these options could be made to be correct by creating custom udev rules; however, these aren't standard configurations.

12. D. Option D correctly summarizes the procedure. Options A and B are both possibilities when *shrinking* a logical volume, but the question asks about *growing* the logical volume. Option C correctly summarizes the procedure for adjusting partitions, but one of the key advantages of LVM is that it obviates the need for adjusting the sizes and positions of filesystem containers other than the one being adjusted.

13. B. Option B presents the correct command to do as the question asks. Option A's vgrename command is used to rename a volume group (MyLVM in this example), and the syntax in option A is incorrect, so this option is wrong. Although option C will temporarily change the name of the device file, the effect won't last across boots, and the logical volume name itself won't be changed. Option D's lvadjust command is fictitious.

14. B, D. The tar and cpio programs are common Linux archive-creation utilities. The restore command restores (but does not back up) data; its backup counterpart command is dump. There is no standard tape command in Linux.

15. D. The device filename for an ATAPI tape drive is /dev/ht0; /dev/st0 refers to a SCSI tape drive. The target device or filename must follow the --file (f) qualifier; the first two options try to back up the contents of the tape device to the /home file.

16. C. The /dev/st0 device (and /dev/ht0, for that matter) rewinds after every operation. Therefore, the first command as given will wind past the first incremental backup and then immediately rewind. The second command will therefore overwrite the first incremental backup.

17. D. With the cpio utility, the -i option is used to read in from an external source—in this case coming in (<) from /dev/st0. The -tv options are used to show the files on the tape and provide a listing of what is there.

18. B, C, D. To restore the data, you must restore the most recent full backup—which was done on Friday night. After the full restore, you must restore the incremental backups in the order in which they were done. In this case, two incrementals (Saturday's and Sunday's) were done after the full backup and they must be restored as well.

19. A. Option A presents the correct command to do as specified. Option B reverses the `if=` and `of=` options, the effect being that the currently empty `/dev/sdc6` will be duplicated onto `/dev/sda1`, completely wiping out your already damaged installation! Option C unnecessarily adds the block size (`bs=`) and `count=` options; and worse, it gets them wrong, so that only 2048 KiB (2 MiB) of the 20 GiB partition will be copied. Option D compounds the errors of both options B and C—which in fact is better than option B, since only 2 MiB of data will be lost from the target partition.

20. A. Tape is a sequential backup medium. Hard disks, DVDs, and Blu-ray discs are all random-access, not sequential, media.

Chapter

5

Networking Configuration

THE FOLLOWING LINUX PROFESSIONAL INSTITUTE OBJECTIVES ARE COVERED IN THIS CHAPTER:

- ✓ **205.1 Basic networking configuration (weight: 3)**

- ✓ **205.2 Advanced network configuration and troubleshooting (weight: 4)**

- ✓ **205.3 Troubleshooting network issues (weight: 5)**

Computers today are often useless without a network. People use computers to browse the Web, exchange email, store documents on remote computers, and even play games. Linux computers can be configured as network clients (which initiate connections), as servers (which respond to connection requests from clients), or both. For this reason, it's critical that you understand how to configure a network.

Network configuration begins with bringing up a network interface and assigning basic attributes. More advanced configurations involve more sophisticated diagnostics and routing configurations, including security measures that can enable users to exchange sensitive documents over insecure networks. Because network configurations often go awry, this chapter concludes with a look at network diagnostics and troubleshooting.

 This chapter emphasizes the Transmission Control Protocol/Internet Protocol (TCP/IP) set of networking tools. TCP/IP is the most common type of network today, and it's the basis of the world-spanning Internet. Other network types, such as AppleTalk, Internetwork Packet Exchange/ Sequenced Packet Exchange (IPX/SPX), and DECnet, exist and are still used in some environments. Linux supports many of these network *protocol stacks*, as they're called, but they must be configured differently from the TCP/IP tools described in this chapter and elsewhere in this book.

Performing Basic Network Configuration

Several basic network features must be configured before you can proceed to the more advanced tasks, including configuring the network tools that are the reasons you're connecting a computer to a network. (Most of these tools are described in subsequent chapters of this book.) If your network employs *wireless* (aka *Wi-Fi*) protocols, the first of these tasks is making these wireless connections. (On a wired network, the equivalent task is simply plugging a cable into the computer.) Once the low-level wired or wireless hardware is configured, you can proceed to connecting to a network (using either automatic or manual IP address settings), setting basic routing options, and using higher-level network scripts.

Connecting to a Wireless Network

To use a wireless network, you must first know something about the network. This knowledge can come from your own work in setting up the network, by asking others about it, or by scanning for public networks. With this knowledge in hand, you can activate your wireless device, linking it to the local wireless network. (This action does *not* make networking functions completely available, though; it's merely analogous to plugging a cable into a port. Subsequent sections describe how to activate TCP/IP networking.)

Configuring or Learning About a Network

To begin the process, you must first obtain information on your wireless network's settings. If you're using a wireless network set up by somebody else, such as your employer's network or a public access point, you should be able to get the relevant information from its maintainer. If you're using a network that you maintain yourself, such as a home network or one that you've set up for your employer, you can find the information from the configuration tools provided by your WAP or broadband router. This information can often be accessed via a Web server run on the device. For instance, Figure 5.1 shows the configuration screen for one broadband router. In this model, the Wireless options screen contains several tabs, each of which provides certain data. Pay particular attention to the radio band (802.11g in Figure 5.1), service set identifier (SSID; NoWires in Figure 5.1), channel (Channel 1 in Figure 5.1), authentication type, and authentication key. (These last two items are on the Security tab, which isn't shown in Figure 5.1.)

FIGURE 5.1   WAPs and broadband routers provide configuration tools in which you set wireless options for your network.

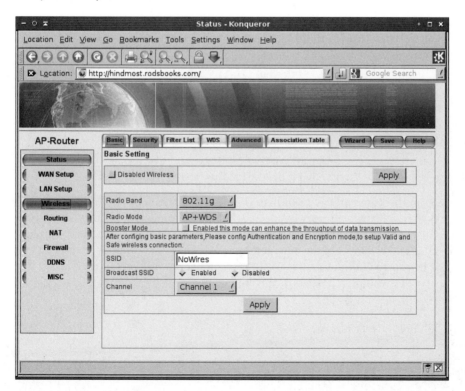

WARNING If you're configuring your own wireless network, be sure to enable the highest security level possible, Wi-Fi Protected Access 2 (WPA2). Earlier security systems, particularly Wired Equivalent Privacy (WEP), are extremely vulnerable. Using them enables anybody with modest skill to snoop on all your network traffic. Depending on your local security settings, intruders might be able to easily break into other wired or wireless computers on your network from outside your building using a notebook computer.

Before proceeding with network configuration, you may want to scan for the available local networks using the iwlist tool. If you've set up your own network, you should see it among the available options. If you're on the road, using wireless access provided by a coffee shop, hotel, or other party, you can use iwlist to locate the available networks. Pass the scan or scanning command to iwlist, optionally preceded by the network device (typically wlan0):

```
# iwlist wlan0 scan
wlan0     Scan completed :
          Cell 01 - Address: 00:27:81:A5:0C:10
                    ESSID:"NoWires"
                    Protocol:IEEE802.11N-24G
                    Mode:Master
                    Channel:11
                    Encryption key:on
                    Bit Rates:130 Mb/s
                    Extra: Rates (Mb/s): 1 2 5.5 6 9 11 12 18 24 36 48 54
                    Quality=65/100  Signal level=-58 dBm  Noise level=-102 dBm
                    IE: IEEE 802.11i/WPA2 Version 1
                        Group Cipher : CCMP
                        Pairwise Ciphers (1) : CCMP
                        Authentication Suites (1) : PSK
                    Extra: Last beacon: 122ms ago
```

If you run this command as an ordinary user, it will only display information on the networks to which you're already connected; but if you run it as root, the iwlist output includes all the nearby networks (or cells, in iwscan parlance). As a practical matter, the ESSID value and channel are the most important settings. If encryption is on, you must know, or be able to obtain, the password for the network; but if encryption is off, you can use the network without a password.

WARNING   Just because you *can* use an open network doesn't mean that you *should* do so. People sometimes misconfigure their network hardware so that it doesn't use encryption. On the other hand, some public wireless networks are configured in this way deliberately. Bear in mind that any data you send over an unencrypted wireless link can be easily monitored by third parties, so you should only use such networks for non-sensitive tasks or via tools with their own encryption, such as the Secure Shell (SSH) remote login protocol.

In addition to scanning for networks, the `iwlist` command can deliver information on the characteristics of a Wi-Fi network interface. To use it in this way, replace `scan` with another subcommand name, as summarized in Table 5.1. A few additional subcommands are available, but they either are extremely obscure or are deprecated (no longer officially supported).

TABLE 5.1   Common `iwlist` subcommands

Subcommand	Function
scan or scanning	Lists all the available networks (or those to which the interface is already linked, when run as an ordinary user)
freq, frequency, or channel	Lists all the available channels for the device
rate, bit, or bitrate	Lists all the speeds (bitrates) supported by the device
keys, enc, or encryption	Lists the encryption key sizes available
power	Lists power management modes available
txpower	Lists available transmit power settings for the device
retry	Lists the current retry setting
event	Lists wireless events supported by the device
auth	Lists the authentication parameters that are currently set
wpa or wpakeys	Lists the WPA keys set in the device
modu or modulation	Lists the modulation used by the device

Plugging Your Computer into a Local Wi-Fi Network

To initiate the basic connection to the local Wi-Fi network, you use the `iwconfig` command, passing it the relevant data using option names such as `essid` and `channel`, preceded by the wireless network device name (typically `wlan0`):

```
# iwconfig wlan0 essid NoWires channel 1 mode Managed key s:N1mP7mHNw
```

This example sets the options for `wlan0` to use the managed network on channel 1 with the SSID of `NoWires` and a password of `N1mP7mHNw`. The password requires a few extra comments. Ordinarily, `iwconfig` takes a password as a string of hexadecimal values, with optional dashes between 2-byte blocks, as in 0123-4567-89AB. Often, however, the password is given as a text string. The string `s:` must precede the password in this case, as shown in the example.

For details on additional `iwconfig` options, including some highly technical ones, consult its man page.

Once you've configured a wireless interface, you can check on its settings by using `iwconfig` with no options or with only the interface name:

```
# iwconfig wlan0
wlan0    IEEE 802.11g  ESSID:"NoWires"
         Mode:Managed  Frequency:2.462 GHz  Access Point: 08:10:74:24:1B:D4
         Bit Rate=54 Mb/s   Tx-Power=27 dBm
         Retry min limit:7   RTS thr:off   Fragment thr=2352 B
         Encryption key: 374E-503D-6d37-4E48-0A [2]
         Link Quality=100/100  Signal level=-32 dBm  Noise level=-94 dBm
         Rx invalid nwid:0  Rx invalid crypt:0  Rx invalid frag:0
         Tx excessive retries:0  Invalid misc:0    Missed beacon:0
```

In addition to providing information on settings, `iwconfig` provides some diagnostic information, such as the link quality, received (Rx) and transmitted (Tx) errors, and so on.

Using Wicd

The `iwlist` and `iwconfig` tools can manage Wi-Fi connections, but they can also be tedious and frustrating to use—a small error in copying an option from the information you're given or discovered using `iwlist` to `iwconfig` can result in an inability to connect to the network. Although it's not mentioned in the LPI objectives, one tool that can greatly simplify the maintenance of a Wi-Fi connection is Wicd (http://wicd.sourceforge.net). This package provides both text-mode (`wicd-cli` and `wicd-curses`) and GUI (`wicd-gtk`) tools for managing your network connections. Figure 5.2 shows a Wicd GUI in operation. Click the Connect or Disconnect button to manage connections, or click the Properties button to adjust details for each network.

FIGURE 5.2 Wicd enables point-and-click Wi-Fi management similar to that in other OSs.

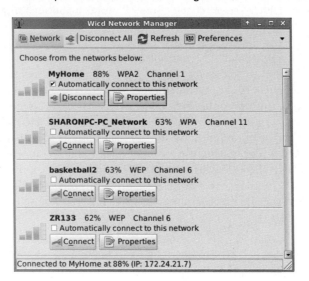

In addition to managing Wi-Fi features, Wicd can manage higher-level TCP/IP features, such as IP addresses, hostnames, and routing—the features described in the next few pages. In addition, Wicd can manage wired connections, including options that enable wired or wireless networks depending on which are available.

Connecting to a Network with DHCP

One of the easiest ways to configure a computer to use a TCP/IP network is to use the Dynamic Host Configuration Protocol (DHCP), which enables one computer on a network to manage the settings for many other computers. It works like this: When a computer running a DHCP client boots up, it sends a broadcast in search of a DHCP server. The server replies (using nothing but the client's hardware address) with the configuration information the client needs to enable it to communicate with other computers on the network—most important, the client's IP address and netmask and the network's gateway and Domain Name Service (DNS) server addresses. The DHCP server may also give the client a hostname and provide various other network details. The client then configures itself with these parameters. The IP address isn't assigned permanently; it's referred to as a *DHCP lease*, and if it's not renewed, the DHCP server may give the lease to another computer. Therefore, from time to time the client checks back with the DHCP server to renew its lease.

Linux can function as a DHCP server as well as a DHCP client. Chapter 7, "Advanced Network Configuration," describes DHCP server configuration.

Three DHCP clients are in common use on Linux: pump, dhclient, and dhcpcd (not to be confused with the DHCP server, dhcpd). Some Linux distributions ship with just one of these, but others ship with two or even all three. All distributions have a default DHCP client—the one that's installed when you tell the system you want to use DHCP at system installation time. Those that ship with multiple DHCP clients typically enable you to swap out one for another simply by removing the old package and installing the new one.

Ideally, the DHCP client runs at system bootup. This can be handled by its own SysV startup script or by an Upstart configuration file, as described in Chapter 1, "System Startup and Advanced System Management." In other cases, the DHCP client can be run as part of the main network configuration startup file (typically a SysV startup file called network or networking). The system often uses a line in a configuration file to determine whether to run a DHCP client. For instance, Red Hat and Fedora set this option in a file called /etc/sysconfig/network-scripts/ifcfg-eth0 (this filename may differ if you use something other than a single Ethernet interface). The line in question looks like this:

```
BOOTPROTO=dhcp
```

If the BOOTPROTO variable is set to something else, changing it as shown here will configure the system to use DHCP. It's usually easier to use a GUI configuration tool to set this option, though.

Ubuntu uses the /etc/network/interfaces file for a similar purpose, but the details differ. On a system that uses DHCP, a line like the following appears:

```
iface eth0 inet dhcp
```

Details may vary, of course; for instance, the interface name (eth0) may be something else. You may prefer to use the GUI system configuration tools to adjust these options.

Once a DHCP client is configured to run when the system boots, the configuration task is done—at least, if everything works as it should. On very rare occasions, you may need to tweak DHCP settings to work around client/server incompatibilities or to have the DHCP client do something unusual. Consult the man page for your DHCP client if you need to make changes. You'll then have to modify its SysV startup script or a file to which it refers in order to change its operation.

If you need to manually run a DHCP client, you can usually do so by typing its name (as root), optionally followed by a network identifier, as in **dhclient eth0** to have the DHCP client attempt to configure eth0 with the help of any DHCP server it finds on that network.

Connecting to a Network with a Static IP Address

If a network lacks a DHCP server, you must provide basic network configuration options manually. You can set these options using either configuration files or interactive commands.

Adjusting Network Configuration Files

To set a static IP address in the long term, you adjust a configuration file such as /etc/sysconfig/network-scripts/ifcfg-eth0 or /etc/network/interfaces. Listing 5.1 shows a typical ifcfg-eth0 file, configured to use a static IP address. (Note that this file's exact location and name may vary from one distribution to another.)

Listing 5.1: A sample network configuration file

```
DEVICE=eth0
BOOTPROTO=static
IPADDR=192.168.29.39
NETMASK=255.255.255.0
NETWORK=192.168.29.0
BROADCAST=192.168.29.255
GATEWAY=192.168.29.1
ONBOOT=yes
```

If you want the computer to have multiple IP addresses on a single network wire, you can do so. Define the first address in the usual way, then create a new one using the name eth0:0 (or eth1:0 or whatever variant is appropriate). The second address is called an *IP alias*.

Several specific items are required, or at least helpful, for static IP address configuration:

IP Address   You can set the IP address manually with the ifconfig command (described in more detail shortly) or with the IPADDR item in the configuration file.

Network Mask   You can set the netmask manually with the ifconfig command or with the NETMASK item in a configuration file.

Gateway Address   You can manually set the gateway with the route command. To set it permanently, you need to adjust a configuration file, which may be the same configuration file that holds other options or another file, such as /etc/sysconfig/network/routes. In either case, the option is likely to be called GATEWAY. The gateway isn't necessary on a system that isn't connected to a wider network—that is, if the system works *only* on a local network that contains no routers.

DNS Settings   For Linux to use DNS to translate between IP addresses and hostnames, you must specify at least one DNS server in the /etc/resolv.conf file. Precede the IP address of the DNS server by the keyword nameserver, as in nameserver 192.168.29.1. You can include up to three nameserver lines in this file. Adjusting this file is all you need to do to set the name server addresses; you don't have to do anything else to make the setting permanent. You can also set your computer's local domain name in this file using the domain option, as in domain luna.edu to set the domain to luna.edu.

The network configuration script may hold additional options, but most of these are related to others. For instance, Listing 5.1 has an option specifying the interface name (DEVICE=eth0), another that tells the computer to assign a static IP address (BOOTPROTO=static), and a third to bring up the interface when the computer boots (ONBOOT=yes). The NETWORK and BROADCAST items in Listing 5.1 are derived from the IPADDR and NETMASK items, but you can change them if you understand the consequences.

Unfortunately, these configuration details vary from one distribution to another. For instance, if you use Ubuntu, you would edit /etc/network/interfaces rather than /etc/sysconfig/network-scripts/ifcfg-eth0. The precise layout and formatting of information in the two files differs, but the same basic information is present in both of them. You may need to consult distribution-specific documentation to learn about these details. Alternatively, GUI tools are usually fairly easy to figure out, so you can look for these.

If you aren't sure what to enter for the basic networking values (the IP address, network mask, gateway address, and DNS server addresses), you should consult your network administrator. *Do not* enter random values or values you make up that are similar to those used by other systems on your network. Doing so is unlikely to work at all, and it can conceivably cause a great deal of trouble—say, if you mistakenly use an IP address that's reserved for another computer.

Using Interactive Commands

As just mentioned, the ifconfig program is critically important for setting both the IP address and the netmask. This program can also display current settings. Basic use of ifconfig to bring up a network interface resembles the following:

ifconfig *interface* up *addr* netmask *mask*

For instance, the following command brings up eth0 (the first Ethernet card) using the address 192.168.29.39 and the netmask 255.255.255.0:

ifconfig eth0 up 192.168.29.39 netmask 255.255.255.0

This command links the specified IP address to the card so that the computer responds to the address and claims to be that address when sending data. It doesn't, though, set up a route for traffic beyond your current network. For that, you need to use the route command:

route add default gw 192.168.29.1

Substitute your own gateway address for 192.168.29.1. Both ifconfig and route can display information on the current network configuration. For ifconfig, omit up and everything that follows; for route, omit add and everything that follows. For instance, to view interface configuration, you might issue the following command:

```
# ifconfig eth0
eth0   Link encap:Ethernet  HWaddr 00:A0:CC:24:BA:02
       inet addr:192.168.29.39  Bcast:192.168.29.255   Mask:255.255.255.0
       UP BROADCAST RUNNING MULTICAST  MTU:1500  Metric:1
       RX packets:10469 errors:0 dropped:0 overruns:0 frame:0
       TX packets:8557 errors:0 dropped:0 overruns:0 carrier:0
       collisions:0 txqueuelen:100
       RX bytes:1017326 (993.4 Kb)  TX bytes:1084384 (1.0 Mb)
       Interrupt:10 Base address:0xc800
```

When configured properly, ifconfig should show a hardware address (HWaddr), an IP address (inet addr), and additional statistics. There should be few or no errors, dropped packets, or overruns for both received (RX) and transmitted (TX) packets. Ideally, few (if any) collisions should occur, but some are unavoidable if your network uses a hub rather than a switch. If collisions total more than a few percent of the total transmitted and received packets, you may want to consider replacing a hub with a switch. To use route for diagnostic purposes, you might try the following command:

```
# route
Kernel IP routing table
Destination  Gateway      Genmask       Flags Metric Ref  Use Iface
192.168.29.0 *            255.255.255.0 U     0      0      0 eth0
127.0.0.0    *            255.0.0.0     U     0      0      0 lo
default      192.168.29.1 0.0.0.0       UG    0      0      0 eth0
```

> The -v option to route produces more verbose output. This is helpful when using route in certain ways, although it usually doesn't produce more output on a simple configuration such as the one shown in this example.

This command shows that data destined for 192.168.29.0 (that is, any computer with an IP address between 192.168.29.1 and 192.168.29.254) goes directly over eth0. The 127.0.0.0 network is a special interface that "loops back" to the originating computer. Linux uses this for some internal networking purposes. The last line shows the *default route*, which describes what to do with everything that doesn't match any other entry in the routing table. This line specifies the default route's gateway system as 192.168.29.1. If it's missing or misconfigured, some or all traffic destined for external networks, such as the Internet, won't make it beyond your local network segment.

As with DHCP configuration, it's almost always easier to use a GUI configuration tool to set up static IP addresses, at least for new administrators. The exact locations of the configuration files differ from one distribution to another, so the examples listed previously may not apply to your system.

The Coming of IPv6

The IP addresses emphasized in this chapter apply to version 4 of the IP portion of TCP/IP. This version has been current for many years. A major upgrade to IP is underway, however, and it goes by the name *IPv6*, for IP version 6. IPv6 adds several features and improvements to TCP/IP, including standard support for more secure connections and support for many more addresses. Check http://playground.sun.com/pub/ipng/html/ipng-main.html or http://www.ipv6forum.com for detailed information about IPv6.

TCP/IP supports a theoretical maximum of about 4 billion addresses. Although this may sound like plenty, those addresses have not been allocated as efficiently as possible. Therefore, as the Internet has expanded, the number of truly available addresses has been shrinking at a rapid rate. IPv6 raises the number of addresses to 2^{128}, or 3.4×10^{38}. This is enough to give every square millimeter of land surface on Earth 2.2×10^{18} addresses.

IPv6 is starting to emerge as a real networking force in many parts of the world. The United States, though, is lagging behind on IPv6 deployment. The Linux kernel includes IPv6 support, and most distributions now attempt to automatically configure IPv6 networking in addition to IPv4. Chances are that by the time the average office will need IPv6, it will be standard. Configuring a system for IPv6 is somewhat different from configuring it for IPv4, which is what this chapter emphasizes.

Using GUI Configuration Tools

Most distributions include their own GUI configuration tools for network interfaces. For instance, Fedora and Red Hat ship with a custom GUI tool called Network Configuration (system-config-network), and SUSE has a text-mode and GUI tool called YaST. The details of operating these programs differ, but the GUI configuration tool provides a means to enter the information described earlier.

Although the LPI exam doesn't cover GUI network configuration tools, they're generally easier to locate and use than the configuration files in which settings are stored. Thus, you may want to look for your distribution's tool and learn to use it. Once you understand the principles of network configuration (IP addresses, DHCP, and so on), you shouldn't have trouble entering the necessary information in the GUI fields.

The precise details of how to configure a Linux system using GUI tools differ from one distribution to another. For instance, SUSE's YaST doesn't lay out its options in precisely the same way as Fedora's Network Configuration tool. The basic principles are the same, though; you must choose whether to use static IP address assignment or an automatic system such as DHCP and enter a number of key options, depending on what configuration method you choose.

Using the *ifup* and *ifdown* Commands

Most Linux distributions today ship with two commands, ifup and ifdown, that combine the functions of several other network commands, most notably ifconfig and route. In their simplest forms, they bring interfaces up or shut them down based on information in whatever files your distribution uses to store network configuration data:

```
# ifup eth0
Determining IP information for eth0... done.
```

After you issue this command, eth0 will be fully configured, including all routing information, assuming you've properly configured it by using your distribution's network configuration tools or by manually editing configuration files such as /etc/network/interfaces and /etc/sysconfig/network-scripts/ifcfg-eth0. You can bring the interface down with equal ease by typing **ifdown eth0.**

The ifup and ifdown commands are useful for verifying that the network settings are configured properly for the next time the computer boots. They're also useful if you want to quickly take down the network or bring it back up again, because you can type fewer commands and you don't need to remember all the details of IP addresses, routes, and so on. If you need to experiment or debug a problem, though, using ifconfig and route individually is preferable, because they give you finer control over the process.

Configuring Hostnames

Computers "think" in terms of numbers, and so TCP/IP uses numbers to uniquely identify computers. Humans, though, work better with words. Thus, computers also usually have names, known as *hostnames*. Entire networks also have names, known as *domain names*. Hostnames typically appear as the first part of a *fully qualified domain name (FQDN)*. For instance, tsiolkovsky.luna.edu is an FQDN, tsiolkovsky is the hostname, and luna.edu is the domain name.

Hostnames are configured in a couple of ways:

On DNS   Your network administrator should be able to add an entry for your computer to your network's DNS server. This entry should make your computer addressable by name from other computers on your local network, and perhaps from the Internet at large. Alternatively, remote systems' /etc/hosts files can be modified to include your system.

On Your Local Computer   Various local programs should know your computer's name. For instance, you may want to have your hostname displayed as part of a command prompt or entered automatically in email programs. For this task, you must set your hostname locally. Note that this is entirely independent of your DNS hostname. In theory, you can set the two to very different values, but this practice is likely to lead to confusion and perhaps even failure of some programs to operate properly.

The most basic tool for setting your hostname locally is called, appropriately enough, hostname. Type the command alone to see what your hostname is, or type it with a new name to set the system's hostname to that name:

```
# hostname tsiolkovsky.luna.edu
```

Many Linux distributions look in the /etc/hostname or /etc/HOSTNAME file for a hostname to set at boot time. Thus, if you want to set your hostname permanently, you should look for these files, and if one is present, you should edit it. Fedora uses /etc/sysconfig/network for this purpose, among others. If you can't find one of these files, consult your distribution's documentation; it's conceivable that your distribution stores its hostname in some unusual location.

Real World Scenario

Using PPP with DSL

Broadband users, particularly those with Digital Subscriber Line (DSL) connections, sometimes have to use a variant of the Point-to-Point Protocol (PPP) to make their connections. PPP is a login-based way to access the Internet—you use a PPP utility to initiate a connection to a remote computer, which includes an exchange of a username and a password. A decade ago, PPP was used in dial-up Internet access (and it's still used in this capacity), but some DSL providers have adapted PPP for their own purposes. In the case of DSL, this configuration method is called PPP over Ethernet (PPPoE).

In many cases, the simplest way to use a PPPoE configuration is to purchase a broadband router. This device attaches to the DSL modem and makes the PPPoE connection. The broadband router then works just like an ordinary Ethernet or Wi-Fi router, as far as your local computers are concerned, so you can configure Linux as you would on any other local network.

If you must connect a Linux system directly to a DSL network that uses PPPoE, you must use a Linux PPPoE client. Most Linux distributions ship with such clients; but configuration details vary from one distribution to another. Your best bet is to look for your distribution's GUI network configuration tool; chances are, you'll be able to find a set of options that are clearly labeled as applying to DSL or PPPoE.

Checking Basic Connectivity

With your network configured and initialized, you can perform a basic test of its operation using one command: `ping`. This command sends an Internet Control Message Protocol (ICMP) packet to the system you name (via IP address or hostname) and waits for a reply. In Linux, `ping` continues sending packets once every second or so until you interrupt it with a Ctrl+C keystroke. (You can instead specify a limited number of tests via the `-c` *num* option.) Here's an example of its output:

```
$ ping -c 4 speaker
PING speaker (192.168.1.1) 56(84) bytes of data.
64 bytes from speaker.example.com (192.168.1.1): icmp_seq=1 ttl=64 time=0.194ms
64 bytes from speaker.example.com (192.168.1.1): icmp_seq=2 ttl=64 time=0.203ms
64 bytes from speaker.example.com (192.168.1.1): icmp_seq=3 ttl=64 time=0.229ms
64 bytes from speaker.example.com (192.168.1.1): icmp_seq=4 ttl=64 time=0.217ms

--- speaker ping statistics ---
4 packets transmitted, 4 received, 0% packet loss, time 3002ms
rtt min/avg/max/mdev = 0.194/0.210/0.229/0.022 ms
```

This command sent four packets and waited for their return, which occurred quite quickly (in an average of 0.210 ms) because the target system was on the local network. By pinging systems on both local and remote networks, you can isolate where a network problem occurs. For instance, if you can ping local systems but not remote systems, the problem is most probably in your router configuration. If you can ping by IP address but not by name, the problem is with your DNS configuration. If you have problems, consult the upcoming section "Troubleshooting Network Issues."

In Exercise 5.1, you'll familiarize yourself with some of the tools used to configure basic network settings. You'll use these tools both to study and to change your network configuration.

EXERCISE 5.1

Configuring a Network Connection

In this exercise, the assumption is that the computer is correctly configured to use an IPv4 Ethernet network, including both local network access and access to a larger network (probably the Internet) via a router.

Some of the procedures in this exercise can easily break your network connectivity if something goes wrong. If this happens, typing **ifdown** followed by **ifup** is one way to recover. If this fails, rebooting the computer is almost certain to work, although it's a radical solution.

To study and modify your system's network configuration, follow these steps:

1. Log into the Linux system as a normal user.

2. Launch an xterm from the desktop environment's menu system, if you used a GUI login method.

3. Acquire root privileges. You can do this by typing **su** in an xterm, by selecting Session ➢ New Root Console from a Konsole, or by using sudo (if it's configured) to run the commands in the following steps.

4. Type **ifconfig**. This command displays information about your local network settings for all your network interfaces. Most systems have both a loopback interface (lo) and an Ethernet interface (eth0). Look for a line in the Ethernet section that includes the string inet addr:. The following 4-byte number is your IP address. Write it down, as well as the value of your netmask (Mask:). Study the other information in this output, too, such as the number of received (RX) and transmitted (TX) packets, the number of errors, the number of collisions, and the Ethernet adapter's hardware address.

5. Type **route -n**. The output is your computer's routing table information. This normally includes information about the loopback network address (127.0.0.0/24), the local network address, and a default route (identified as the route for 0.0.0.0). Some systems may display fewer or additional lines, depending on local configuration. The default route includes an IP address under the Gateway column. Write down that address.

6. Use ping to test connectivity to both local and remote computers. You need the name or IP address of at least one local computer and at least one distant computer (beyond your local router). Type **ping address** where *address* is the name or IP address of each test machine. Perform this test for localhost or 127.0.0.1, your own machine (use the IP address you noted in step 4), your local router (use the IP address you noted in step 5), and a distant computer (if you're connected to the Internet, you can use an Internet-accessible site, such as www.linux.org). All of these ping tests should be successful. Note, however, that some systems are configured to ignore packets sent by ping. Thus, some of these tests may fail if you run into such systems. You can learn the configuration of local systems from their administrators, but for Internet sites, you may want to simply try another site if the first one you test fails.

7. Bring down the local Ethernet connection by typing **ifconfig eth0 down.**

8. Repeat steps 4–6. Note that the eth0 interface is no longer shown when you type ifconfig, all routes associated with it have been removed from the routing table, and pinging systems accessible from the interface no longer works. (Linux retains some information about its former Ethernet link, so you may still be able to ping the computer itself via its former eth0 address.)

9. Bring the local Ethernet connection back up by typing **ifconfig eth0 up** *address* **netmask** *mask*, where *address* is the original IP address and *mask* is the original netmask, both as identified in step 4.

10. Repeat steps 4–6. Note that the ifconfig command automatically added back your local network to the routing table but that the default route is still missing. As a result, you can't contact any systems that are located off the local network. If your DNS server is such a system, this means your ability to contact even local machines by name may be impaired as well.

11. Restore the default route by typing **route add default gw** *gateway*, where *gateway* is the router address you identified in step 5.

12. Repeat steps 4–6. If your network configuration is typical, all connectivity should be restored. (Some more exotic systems may still be lacking certain routes.)

Setting Additional Network Options

A typical desktop, laptop, or workstation, or even many servers, needs no more network configuration than described already. (An exception is firewall configuration, which is described in Chapter 7, "Advanced Network Configuration.") Some additional network options, though, are useful on many computers. These include advanced routing configurations and virtual private network (VPN) configurations. You should also be familiar with some basic network-monitoring tools.

Setting Advanced Router Options

As explained earlier, routers pass traffic from one network to another. You configure your Linux system to directly contact systems on the local network. You also give the computer a router's address, which your system uses as a gateway to the Internet at large. Any traffic that's not destined for the local network is directed at this router, which passes it on to its destination. In practice, there are likely to be a dozen or more routers between you and most Internet sites. Each router has at least two network interfaces and keeps a table of rules concerning where to send data based on the destination IP address. Your own Linux computer has such a table, but it's probably very simple compared to those on major Internet routers.

In addition to routing configuration, some routing-related commands are available that can help you understand network addressing on your network.

Configuring Linux as a Router

Linux can function as a router, which means it can link two or more networks together, directing traffic between them on the basis of its routing table. This task is handled, in part, by the route command. This command can be used to do much more than specify a single gateway system, though, as described earlier. A simplified version of the route syntax is as follows:

```
route {add | del} [-net | -host] target [netmask nm] [gw gw] ⏎
[reject] [[dev] interface]
```

You specify add or del along with a *target* (a computer or network address) and optionally other parameters. The -net and -host options force route to interpret the target as a network or computer address, respectively. The netmask option lets you set a netmask as you desire, and gw lets you specify a router through which packets to the specified *target* should go. (Some versions of route use gateway rather than gw.) The reject keyword installs a blocking route, which refuses all traffic destined for the specified network. (This is *not* a firewall, though.) Blocking routes appear in routing tables with an exclamation mark (!) under the Flags column. Finally, although route can usually figure out the interface device (for instance, eth0) on its own, you can force the issue with the dev option.

As an example, consider Figure 5.3, and particularly the two workstations in the 172.24.22.0/24 network. These computers both have a single network interface, but the network has two routers: The Linux computer in the center of Figure 5.3, which leads to the 192.168.5.0/24 network and the Internet; and the 172.24.22.1 router, which leads to the 10.10.10.0/24 network. Presumably these computers will have a default route set, as described earlier, to link to the Internet. You would then use the route command to add a second route to enable traffic to pass to the 10.10.10.0/24 network. You can set up this route with the following command:

```
# route add -net 10.10.10.0 netmask 255.255.255.0 gw 172.24.22.1
```

FIGURE 5.3 Some network configurations require unusual routing table configurations.

192.168.5.0/24 network   172.24.22.0/24 network

192.168.5.2 workstation   172.24.22.3 workstation

192.168.5.1 router   Linux Computer   172.24.22.1 router
                          172.24.22.4
              Switch   Switch
              192.168.5.4

192.168.5.3 workstation   172.24.22.2 workstation

Internet   10.10.10.0/24
                                                  network

A similar configuration is desirable for the computers on the 192.168.5.0/24 network. Setting multiple routes in this way is desirable, but it's not always absolutely necessary. If the subnet's main router knows about any secondary routers on the network, the main router will send packets directed to the relevant subnets back to the secondary router. For instance, suppose the 192.168.5.1 router knows that 192.168.5.4 (the Linux computer in the center of the figure) links to the 172.24.22.0/24 and 10.10.10.0/24 networks. If one of the workstations on the 192.168.5.0/24 network sends packets for the 10.10.10.0/24 subnet, the 192.168.5.1 router will redirect the packets appropriately. The problem is that this wastes bandwidth, since the same packets will traverse the 192.168.5.0/24 network twice: once from the workstation to the main router and again from the main router to the secondary router. Thus, setting the additional routing options on the relevant computers is desirable.

Incorrect routing tables can cause serious problems because some or all computers won't respond. You can examine your routing table by typing **route** alone and compare the results to what your routing table should be. (Consult a network administrator if you're not sure what your routing table should contain.) You can then delete incorrect routes and add new ones to replace them, if necessary. Ultimately, of course, changing your configuration files is the best solution, but typing a couple of route commands will do the trick in the short term.

Simply adding multiple routes can be useful if a computer has multiple network interfaces but should not function as a router. This might be true of a laptop computer that has both wired and wireless network connections, particularly if the wired and wireless networks don't connect in any other way.

A Linux computer that's connected to two networks, as in the Linux computer in the center of Figure 5.3, can communicate with both of them; however, this configuration does not automatically link the two networks together. That is, computers on the 192.168.5.0/24 and 172.24.22.0/24 networks will not be able to communicate with each other unless that central Linux computer is configured as a router. To enable this feature, you must modify a key file in the /proc filesystem:

```
# echo "1" > /proc/sys/net/ipv4/ip_forward
```

This command enables IP forwarding. Permanently setting this option requires modifying a configuration file. Some distributions set it in /etc/sysctl.conf:

```
net.ipv4.ip_forward = 1
```

Other distributions use other configuration files and options, such as /etc/sysconfig/ sysctl and its IP_FORWARD line. If you can't find it, try using grep to search for ip_forward or IP_FORWARD, or modify a local startup script to add the command to perform the change.

Checking Address Resolution

At a low level, TCP/IP relies on a protocol known as the Address Resolution Protocol (ARP). A Linux utility of the same name but in lowercase (arp) is used to monitor ARP activity on a single computer.

Network hardware devices, such as Ethernet cards, have built-in hardware addresses. You can determine a network interface's hardware address with ifconfig; it's on the first line of output, labeled HWaddr:

```
# ifconfig eth0
eth0   Link encap:Ethernet   HWaddr 00:A0:CC:24:BA:02
```

In this example, eth0's hardware address is 00:AD:CC:24:BA:02—a sequence of six bytes expressed in hexadecimal (base 16) and separated by colons (:). Other separator characters, such as dashes, are sometimes used. The first three bytes in an Ethernet hardware address represent the hardware's manufacturer, while the last three bytes are assigned by the manufacturer in a unique manner, much like a serial number.

Various Web sites, such as http://www.techzoom.net/tools/check-mac .en and http://telecom.tbi.net/ethercode.cgi, enable you to identify the manufacturer of an Ethernet device by its hardware address. This can sometimes be useful in tracking down hardware in the real world.

When two computers on the same network segment communicate, they do so by using each others' hardware addresses. When routers are involved, the sender sends the traffic to the router's hardware address; the router then repackages the data, using the next router's hardware address.

To communicate by hardware address, though, the IP address must be translated into a hardware address. This is ARP's job. A computer can send a broadcast message (that is, one that's received by all the local computers) asking the computer with a particular IP address to reply. When the target computer replies, ARP reads its hardware address, associates it with the requested IP address, and adds the two to the ARP cache.

The arp utility enables you to examine and modify the ARP cache. Typing **arp** alone displays the ARP cache:

```
$ arp
Address                 HWtype  HWaddress           Flags Mask   Iface
hindmost.example.com    ether   00:a0:c5:24:e1:4e   C            eth0
seeker.example.com      ether   00:1c:c0:b0:35:fc   C            eth0
```

Table 5.2 summarizes options to arp. The first two entries in Table 5.2 represent major operations to modify the ARP cache; the remaining entries can be used to tweak the output or interpretation of other options.

TABLE 5.2 Common arp options

Long option name	Short option name	Description
N/A	-d *address*	Deletes the specified address from the ARP cache. Only root may perform this action.
N/A	-s *address hw_address*	Associates the IP address or hostname *address* with the hardware address *hw_address*.
--verbose	-v	Produces additional output.
--numeric	-n	Displays IP addresses numerically rather than translated into hostnames.
--hw-type *type*	-t *type* or -H *type*	Sets the hardware type, such as ether for Ethernet (the default), arcnet for ARCnet, pronet for PROnet, or netrom for NET/ROM.
N/A	-a	Uses short (BSD-style) output.
--use-device	-D	Instead of interpreting *hw_address* as a hardware address, interpret it as a device.
--device *interface*	-i *interface*	Restricts output or operations to the specified *interface*, such as eth0 or eth1.
--file *filename*	-f *filename*	Obtains address information from the specified file.

Why would you want to view or modify the ARP cache? Sometimes the information can be necessary to configure servers or other tools. For instance, you might need computers' hardware addresses to configure a DHCP server (described in Chapter 7). Other times, you might want to clear a specific address, or even all addresses, because of changes to the network. For instance, if you replace an Ethernet card in a computer, its hardware address will change. In such a case, you might want to clear its entry from other computers' ARP caches to ensure that traffic to the altered computer will reach its destination.

 Linux keeps ARP cache entries for a limited period, so scenarios such as Ethernet card swaps will disrupt network communication only briefly even if you don't explicitly clear the ARP cache.

Using an All-In-One Networking Tool

An alternative to the ifconfig, route, and various other commands for many purposes is ip. This is a sort of Swiss Army knife of network commands. Its syntax is deceptively simple:

```
ip [ OPTIONS ] OBJECT { COMMAND | help }
```

To understand ip, you should begin with the *OBJECT*, which can take any of the values shown in Table 5.3. Each of these values has its own unique set of options and commands. The number of operations that can be performed with ip is dizzying. You should consult its man page for details.

TABLE 5.3 Possible ip *OBJECT* values

OBJECT name	Description
link	Performs actions on network hardware; similar to some ifconfig functions
addr	Associates or disassociates a device with an address; similar to some ifconfig functions
addrlabel	Displays or adjusts addresses in an IPv6 network
route	Displays or adjusts the routing table; similar to some route functions
rule	Displays or adjusts firewall table rules; similar to some iptables functions, as described in Chapter 7
neigh	Displays or adjusts ARP entries

TABLE 5.3   Possible ip *OBJECT* values *(continued)*

OBJECT name	Description
tunnel	Displays or adjusts tunneling features, which enables data to be transferred between networks by encapsulating many network protocols within just one protocol
maddr	Displays or adjusts multicast addresses, which are used to communicate with multiple computers simultaneously
mroute	Displays or adjusts multicast routes
monitor	Monitors network for activity

As an example of ip, consider its use to display the current routing table:

```
$ ip route list
172.24.21.0/24 dev eth1  proto kernel  scope link  src 172.24.21.2
192.168.1.0/24 dev eth0  proto kernel  scope link  src 192.168.1.2
127.0.0.0/8 dev lo  scope link
default via 192.168.1.1 dev eth0
```

This example reveals that the ip utility doesn't work exactly like the separate utilities that perform similar tasks—this output is different from the route output that can also reveal (or change) the routing table. As a practical matter, you might want to try ip and the many specific tools to determine which you prefer for particular tasks.

Configuring a VPN

Most networks rely, in part, on physical security to keep them safe. With an Ethernet local area network (LAN), for instance, traffic on the LAN itself cannot be intercepted without either physical access to the network wires or a compromise of a computer on the network. (Wireless access is more susceptible to attack, as described earlier.) When a network must span multiple locations using an untrusted intermediary carrier (such as the Internet), security becomes more of a problem. In these cases, a *virtual private network (VPN)* configuration is often employed. In a VPN, the two private network segments are linked via a router that encrypts data being sent to the remote location.

Naturally, Linux provides several VPN options. The LPIC-2 certification covers only one: OpenVPN (http://openvpn.net). This package ships with most Linux distributions, so you can probably install it using your package manager. That done, you should attend to some preliminary issues, generate keys, configure the VPN, and establish the VPN connection.

As with other network protocols, OpenVPN classifies one router as a client and another as a server. In some cases, which is which may seem obvious, because one (the server) will connect to many other OpenVPN routers (the clients). In other cases, which is which can be decided arbitrarily.

Preparing for VPN Use

The networks linked by the VPN are inherently private—they should have no or limited access to the Internet as a whole. Frequently, VPNs are used to link networks that use the private addresses summarized in Table 5.4, which are defined in the Internet standards document RFC-1918. These addresses can be used by anybody, but they shouldn't be routed to the Internet except through network address translation (NAT) routers or similar means. You can link as many such networks together as you like for your own purposes, though.

TABLE 5.4   RFC-1918 private address blocks

Class	Range	Prefix
A	10.0.0.0–10.255.255.255	10.0.0.0/8
B	172.16.0.0.0–172.31.255.255	172.16.0.0/12
C	192.168.0.0–192.168.255.255	192.168.0.0/16

You should ensure that the IP addresses used on all the networks linked by your VPN are unique. If two physically separate networks duplicate each others' IP addresses, problems will result. It's best to give each subnet its own unique set of addresses—for instance, 192.168.26.0/24 for one network and 192.168.27.0/24 for another. You can adjust the sizes of your subnets as necessary, keeping within the limits outlined in Table 5.4.

Managing VPN Keys

Like many encryption technologies, OpenVPN relies on *keys*—large numbers that can be used to encode or decode data. OpenVPN uses *public key cryptography*, which relies on *private keys* and *public keys* for encryption. As their names imply, private keys should be kept private (secret), whereas public keys can be distributed widely. Data encrypted by one key can be decrypted by the other. Thus, to communicate in a secure manner, two computers exchange their public keys. Each computer encrypts data using the other computer's public key; only the recipient can then decrypt the data using the matched private key.

Added to this system of public key cryptography is a certificate authority (CA), which is a computer that issues keys for other computers to use. The CA embeds identifying information in the keys and digitally signs them, thereby enabling both sides of the VPN connection to verify that the other side has obtained a key from the same CA and can therefore be trusted.

> For added security, the CA can be a computer that lacks network connections. This configuration guarantees that it can't be remotely compromised.

This system is fairly complex, which means you must take extra steps to implement it. In particular, you must first configure a system as a CA. OpenVPN ships with a set of scripts to help with this task. These scripts can usually be found in the /usr/share/openvpn/ easy-rsa, /usr/share/doc/packages/openvpn, or a similar directory. To prevent your customizations from being overwritten with package updates, you should copy the scripts to another location, such as /etc/openvpn.

With the scripts copied, edit the /etc/openvpn/vars file and edit the KEY_COUNTRY, KEY_ PROVINCE, KEY_CITY, KEY_ORG, and KEY_EMAIL parameters to reflect your organization. You should then type the following three commands while within /etc/openvpn to configure your CA:

```
# ./vars
# ./clean-all
# ./build-ca
```

After you type the final command, you'll be asked for various pieces of information (some of which default to the values you set in the vars file). With the CA keys generated, you can generate keys for an OpenVPN server and one or more clients:

```
# ./build-key-server server
# ./build-key client1
# ./build-key client2
```

After each of these commands, you'll be prompted to enter or verify information similar to that required when building the CA. The defaults for most values will work fine. Be sure to enter unique values for each system when prompted for a Common Name. One more step will finalize key generation:

```
# ./build-dh
```

This command computes a large prime number that's used in the encryption process. With this step done, you'll find all the OpenVPN keys and related files in the keys subdirectory. Table 5.5 summarizes these keys' purposes and characteristics. You should copy the files to the computers specified under the Copy To column of Table 5.5. This task must be done using a secure method—perhaps a hand-delivered removable medium such as a USB flash drive, or a copy using scp (SSH's file-copying command). Copy the files to /etc/openvpn or a subdirectory of that directory, being sure to copy *only* the files that should be copied to each computer.

TABLE 5.5 OpenVPN key files and purposes

Filename	Copy to	Purpose	Secret
`ca.crt`	Server and all clients	CA certificate	No
`ca.key`	Key signing machine only	CA key	Yes
`dh1024.pem`	Server only	Diffie Hellman parameters	No
`server.crt`	Server only	Server certificate	No
`server.key`	Server only	Server key	Yes
`client`*n*`.crt`	Client *n* only	Client *n* certificate	No
`client`*n*`.key`	Client *n* only	Client *n* key	Yes

Configuring the VPN

You must edit both client and server configuration files. You can find samples at `http://openvpn.net/index.php/open-source/documentation/howto.html#examples`, or you may find them in a directory such as `/usr/share/doc/packages/openvpn` or `/usr/share/doc/openvpn` on your computer. The client and server configuration files should be called `client.conf` and `server.conf`, respectively, and both should be copied to `/etc/openvpn`. You should then edit these files, paying particular attention to the following features:

- For both clients and server, edit the `ca`, `cert`, and `key` parameters to point to the key files you've copied to the system being configured. You must also set the `dh` parameter on the server.
- If client networks should be able to communicate with each other, uncomment the `client-to-client` directive on the *server's* configuration.
- Uncomment the `user nobody` and `group nobody` directives on the server to improve security.
- On the clients, edit the `remote` parameter to point to the server. This line includes both a hostname and a port number (1194 by default). Change the port number only if you change it on the server using its `port` directive or if the server is protected by a NAT router that forwards a different port to that number on the server.

The sample configuration files are well commented, so you can peruse them to locate other options you might want to adjust for your particular configuration.

Establishing the VPN Connection

With the server and clients configured, you can now test your VPN. To launch the VPN, type **openvpn** *config-file*, where *config-file* is the complete path to your VPN configuration file. This path will, of course, point to the server configuration for the server and the client configuration for each of your clients. You can check the output provided by the program for any error messages. The output should conclude with the message `Initialization Sequence Completed`. If all seems in order, you can test basic connectivity from the client to the server:

```
$ ping 10.8.0.1
```

The 10.8.0.1 address is given to the server in the default configuration files; change it if you altered this detail yourself. If this works, you can begin expanding the configuration to enable other computers on the client and/or server sides to communicate using the VPN. Suppose the server is on the 10.66.0.0/24 network. On the server configuration, add the following line to the configuration file to enable server-side systems to use the VPN:

```
push "route 10.66.0.0 255.255.255.0"
```

Change the addresses to match your network, of course. This enables links between machines on the local network and the remote (client) network. You must also adjust the server-side network's router to include an appropriate route, for the server's VPN subnet (10.8.0.0/24 by default). This change isn't necessary if the VPN router is also the network's conventional router. Note that you do *not* need to route traffic to the client's local subnet; as far as other systems on the server's network are concerned, an isolated VPN client will have an address in the 10.8.0.0/24 subnet.

If you want a client to function as a VPN router, rather than just as a single computer that connects for itself, you must make more changes. On the *server*, you must create a directory called /etc/openvpn/ccd and set the following directives in the server's configuration file:

```
client-config-dir ccd
route 192.168.4.0 255.255.255.0
```

Adjust the IP address and network mask on the `route` line for your client's network. In the /etc/openvpn/ccd directory, create a configuration file with the common name given to the OpenVPN client. This file should duplicate the `route` line in the main configuration file but using the keyword `iroute`:

```
iroute 192.168.4.0 255.255.255.0
```

If you want to enable the OpenVPN server to direct traffic between VPN client networks, add the following lines to the server's configuration file (again, changing the addresses as appropriate for your network):

```
client-to-client
```

```
push "route 192.168.4.0 255.255.255.0"
```

Finally, you must make changes to the default router configuration for both the server and client networks to direct traffic for the remote networks through their respective VPN systems.

With these changes in place, restart the client and server and test your connections using ping or other tools. If you have problems, consult the OpenVPN Web site, which contains extended instructions and troubleshooting information.

Many distributions ship with startup scripts that scan the /etc/openvpn directory for client and server configuration files and launch openvpn in the appropriate mode. If your system contains such files, you can shut down the program and restart it using these tools and configure the computer to start OpenVPN automatically when it boots.

Monitoring Network Traffic

Several network monitoring tools exist that can help you verify proper network functioning, check what programs are using the network, and monitor network traffic.

Using *nc*

The nc utility (also known as netcat) is a very powerful general-purpose networking tool. It can send arbitrary data, monitor network ports, and more. Its basic syntax is:

nc [*options*] [*hostname*] [*ports*]

Table 5.6 summarizes the most important of nc's many *options*. Consult its man page for more details. The nc program performs fairly low-level accesses and can be scripted, which enables you to create scripts using nc to scan for available servers on a network or perform other specialized tests.

TABLE 5.6   Common nc options

Option	Purpose
-d	Does not read from standard input.
-h	Displays help information.
-i *interval*	Inserts a delay between text sent and received.
-k	Keeps listening for a new connection after the current one terminates. Must be used in conjunction with -l.
-l	Listens for an incoming connection rather than establish an outgoing one.
-n	Does not perform DNS lookups.
-p *port*	Makes a connection using the specified outgoing port. May not be used with -l.
-r	Selects port numbers randomly.

TABLE 5.6   Common nc options *(continued)*

Option	Purpose
-s *ip-address*	Specifies the IP address of an outgoing connection. May not be used with -1.
-U	Uses Unix domain sockets.
-u	Uses UDP rather than TCP.
-v	Produces verbose output.
-w *timeout*	Terminates a connection if it has been inactive for *timeout* seconds.
-X *version*	Uses the specified proxy version; valid values are 4 (SOCKS v.4), 5 (SOCKS v.5; the default), and connect (HTTPS proxy). Used in conjunction with -x.
-x *address*[:*port*]	Makes a connection via the specified proxy server.
-z	Scans for a listening server without sending data to it.

Using *netstat*

Another useful diagnostic tool is netstat. This is something of a Swiss Army knife of network tools because it can be used in place of several others, depending on the parameters it's passed. It can also return information that's not easily obtained in other ways. Some examples include the following:

Interface Information   Pass netstat the --interface or -i parameter to obtain information about your network interfaces similar to what ifconfig returns. (Some versions of netstat return information in the same format, but others display the information differently.)

Routing Information   You can use the --route or -r parameter to obtain a routing table listing similar to what the route command displays.

Masquerade Information   Pass netstat the --masquerade or -M parameter to obtain information about connections mediated by Linux's NAT features, which often go by the name *IP masquerading*. NAT enables a Linux router to "hide" a network behind a single IP address. This can be a good way to stretch limited IPv4 addresses.

Program Use   Some versions of netstat support the --program (or -p) parameter, which attempts to provide information about the programs that are using network connections. This attempt isn't always successful, but it often is, so you can see what programs are making outside connections.

Open Ports   When used with various other parameters or without any parameters at all, netstat returns information about open ports and the systems to which they connect.

All Connections   The --all or -a option is used in conjunction with others. It causes netstat to display information about the ports that server programs open to listen for network connections, in addition to already-open connections.

Keep in mind that netstat is a powerful tool, and its options and output aren't entirely consistent from one distribution to another. You may want to peruse its man page and experiment with it to learn what it can do. As a basic example of netstat's use, consider the following:

```
# netstat -ap
Active Internet connections (servers and established)
Proto Recv-Q Send-Q Local Address           Foreign Address         State ➥
PID/Program name
tcp      0      0 *:ftp                      *:*                     LISTEN ➥
690/inetd
tcp      0      0 teela.example.com:ssh  nessus.example.co:39361 ESTABLISHED ➥
787/sshd
```

I've trimmed most of the entries from the preceding netstat output to make it manageable as an example.

The Local Address and Foreign Address columns specify the local and remote addresses, including both the hostname or IP address and the port number or associated name from /etc/services. The first of the two entries shown here isn't actively connected, so the local address, the foreign address, and the port number are all listed as asterisks (*). This entry does specify the local port, though—ftp. This line indicates that a server is running on the ftp port (TCP port 21). The State column specifies that the server is listening for a connection. The final column in this output, under the PID/Program name heading, indicates that the process with a process ID (PID) of 690 is using this port. In this case, it's inetd.

The second output line indicates that a connection has been established between teela .example.com and nessus.example.com (the second hostname is truncated). The local system (teela) is using the ssh port (TCP port 22), and port 39361 is used on the client (nessus). The process that's handling this connection on the local system is sshd, running as PID 787.

It may take some time to peruse the output of netstat, but doing so will leave you with a much-improved understanding of your system's network connections. If you spot servers listening for connections that you didn't realize were active, you should investigate the matter further. Some servers may be innocent or even necessary. Others may be pointless security risks.

When you use the -p option to obtain the name and PID of the process using a port, the netstat output is wider than 80 columns. You may want to open an extra-wide xterm window to handle this output, or you may want to redirect it to a file that you can study in a text editor capable of displaying more than 80 columns. (Redirecting the output can sometimes produce a file with extra formatting characters that may be confusing, though.)

To quickly spot servers listening for connections, pipe the output through a grep LISTEN command to filter on the listening state. The result will show all servers that are listening for connections, omitting client connections and specific server instances that are already connected to clients.

Using *tcpdump*

The tcpdump utility is a *packet sniffer*, which is a program that can intercept network packets and log them or display them on the screen. Packet sniffers can be useful diagnostic tools because they enable you to verify that a computer is actually receiving data from other computers. They also enable you to examine the data in its raw form, which can be useful if you understand enough of the protocol's implementation details to spot problems.

Although packet sniffers are useful diagnostic tools, they can also be abused. For instance, unscrupulous individuals can run packet sniffers to capture passwords that others send over the network. Depending on your network configuration, this trick can work even if the packet sniffer isn't running on either the sending or receiving computer. For this reason, many organizations have policies forbidding the use of packet sniffers except under limited circumstances. Thus, before running a packet sniffer, you should obtain written permission to use such a program from an individual who is authorized to grant such permission. Failure to do so can lead you into serious trouble, possibly up to losing your job or even being sued.

In its most basic form, you can use tcpdump by typing its name:

```
# tcpdump
tcpdump: verbose output suppressed, use -v or -vv for full protocol decode
listening on eth0, link-type EN10MB (Ethernet), capture size 96 bytes
19:31:55.503759 IP speaker.example.com.631 > 192.168.1.255.631: UDP, ↵
 length: 139
19:31:55.505400 IP nessus.example.com.33513 > speaker.example.com.domain: ↵
 46276+ PTR? 255.1.168.192.in-addr.arpa. (44)
19:31:55.506086 IP speaker.example.com.domain > nessus.example.com.33513: ↵
 46276 NXDomain* 0/1/0 (110)
```

The first thing to note about this command is that you must run it as root; ordinary users aren't allowed to monitor network traffic in this way. Once it's run, tcpdump summarizes what it's doing and then begins printing lines, one for each packet it monitors. (Some of these lines can be quite long and so may take more than one line on your display.) These lines include a time stamp, a stack identifier (IP in all of these examples), the origin system name or IP address and port, the destination system name or IP address and port, and packet-specific information. Ordinarily, tcpdump keeps displaying packets indefinitely, so you must terminate it by pressing Ctrl+C. Alternatively, you can pass it the -c *num* option to have it display *num* packets and then quit.

Even this basic output can be very helpful. For instance, consider the preceding example of three packets, which was captured on nessus.example.com. This computer successfully received one broadcast packet (addressed to 192.168.1.255) from speaker.example.com's UDP port 631, sent a packet to speaker.example.com, and received a packet from that system directed at nessus.example.com rather than sent as a broadcast. This sequence verifies that at least minimal communication exists between these two computers. If you were having problems establishing a connection, you could rule out a whole range of possibilities based on this evidence, such as faulty cables or a firewall that was blocking traffic.

If you need more information, tcpdump provides several options that enhance or modify its output. These include -A to display packet contents in ASCII, -D to display a list of interfaces to which tcpdump can listen, -n to display all addresses numerically, -v (and additional -v options, up to -vvv) to display additional packet information, and -w *file* to write the captured packets to the specified *file*. Consult tcpdump's man page for more details on these options and for additional options.

Using Wireshark

Wireshark (http://www.wireshark.org), formerly known as Ethereal, is another packet sniffer. It features deep analysis of network packets, meaning that the program can help you dig into network packets to discover the meanings they carry, thus enabling you to track down network problems—for instance, is a failure to authenticate due to a mismatched protocol version, a mistyped password, packets that are going missing, or some other problem?

 WARNING   Wireshark, just like tcpdump, can be abused. Before using it, obtain written permission from your superiors, lest you run afoul of policies forbidding the unauthorized use of packet sniffers.

The most basic use of Wireshark is via the tshark command, which by default displays raw packet data intercepted by the program:

```
# tshark
Running as user "root" and group "root". This could be dangerous.
Capturing on eth1
  0.000000 08:10:74:24:1b:d4 -> Broadcast    ARP Who has 192.168.1.1?  Tell ↵
192.168.1.254
```

```
0.308644   192.168.1.8 -> 192.168.1.2   SSH Encrypted response packet len=128
0.308721   192.168.1.8 -> 192.168.1.2   SSH Encrypted response packet len=48
```

This example (which is truncated; real output will continue indefinitely, or until you press Ctrl+C) shows an Address Resolution Protocol (ARP) broadcast followed by two SSH packets. If you want to restrict Wireshark's output, you can do so with a wide array of tshark options. Consult its man page for details.

You'll probably find it easier to use Wireshark with its GUI, which is often installed via a separate package from the main Wireshark package. On Fedora, for instance, you must install wireshark-gnome. You can then type **wireshark** to launch the main Wireshark GUI program. Selecting Capture ➤ Start then begins a capture of all traffic. (You can limit what's captured by using the Capture ➤ Capture Filters... option.) Selecting Capture ➤ Stop terminates the capture operation. The result resembles Figure 5.4. This window has three panes. The top pane presents a summary of each network packet, the middle pane presents protocol-specific analysis of the packet selected in the top pane, and the bottom pane shows the raw packet data.

FIGURE 5.4 Wireshark provides a GUI that enables a point-and-click study of captured network traffic.

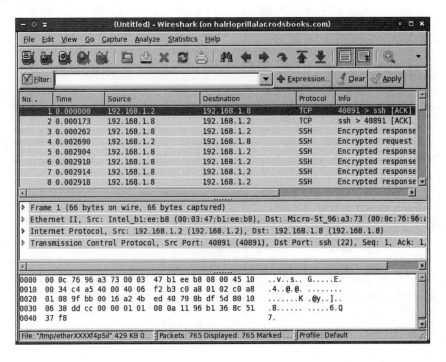

Using Nmap

Network scanners, such as Nmap (http://www.insecure.org/nmap/), can scan for open ports on the local computer or on other computers. This differs from a packet sniffer, such as tcpdump or Wireshark, in that a network scanner doesn't monitor traffic; it simply reports on ports that seem to accept incoming network packets.

WARNING   Network scanners are used by crackers for locating likely target systems, as well as by network administrators for legitimate purposes. Many organizations have policies forbidding the use of network scanners except under specific conditions. Therefore, you should check these policies and obtain explicit permission, signed and in writing, to perform a network scan. Failure to do so could cost you your job or even result in criminal charges, even if your intentions are honorable.

Nmap can perform a basic check for open ports. Pass the -sT parameter and the name of the target system to it, as shown here:

```
$ nmap -sT hindmost

Starting Nmap 5.21 ( http://nmap.org ) at 2010-10-15 10:39 EDT
Nmap scan report for hindmost (192.168.1.1)
Host is up (0.0054s latency).
rDNS record for 192.168.1.1: hindmost.example.com
Not shown: 997 filtered ports
PORT    STATE SERVICE
21/tcp open   ftp
23/tcp open   telnet
80/tcp open   http
```

NOTE   As with the output of netstat shown in "Using netstat," the preceding output for Nmap has been trimmed for brevity's sake.

This output shows three open ports—21, 23, and 80—used by ftp, telnet, and http, respectively. If you weren't aware that these ports were active, you should log into the scanned system and investigate further, using netstat or ps to locate the programs using these ports and, if desired, shut them down. The -sT option specifies a scan of TCP ports. A few servers, though, run on UDP ports, so you need to scan them by typing **nmap -sU** *hostname*. (This usage requires root privileges, unlike scanning TCP ports.)

Nmap is capable of more sophisticated scans, including "stealth" scans that aren't likely to be noticed by most types of firewalls, ping scans to detect which hosts are active, and more. The Nmap man page provides details.

Troubleshooting Network Issues

Much of this chapter has described an idealized world in which nothing ever goes wrong: Commands work as they should, network cables are perfect, computers never crash, and every child is above average. Unfortunately, the real world isn't like this. A great deal of the task of any Linux administrator is dealing with the cases in which things do *not* work as they should. Therefore, the rest of this chapter is devoted to the tools and skills required to help identify and resolve problems. Specific problem areas covered include hostname issues, connectivity difficulties, routing problems, and security-related issues.

Nothing can compete with real-world experience for learning about problem solving. If possible, you should set up a real network, preferably using computers that run different Linux distributions and non-Linux OSs; this will more or less guarantee you'll run into problems that you'll have to solve. If this isn't practical, try setting up a virtual network using virtualization software such as QEMU (http://wiki.qemu.org), VirtualBox (http://www.virtualbox.org), or VMware (http://www.vmware.com). Given enough RAM and disk space, you can run several virtual machines at once and link them in a virtual network, thus enabling you to run a variety of OSs and configurations.

Identifying Problem Spots

The first task in network problem solving is diagnosing the problem. This task can be a difficult one, because different problems can have similar symptoms. In the next few pages, I describe several tools, procedures, and rules of thumb that can help you narrow the scope of the problem to something manageable.

Localizing the Level of a Problem

Networks can be thought of as being built up in layers, from physical hardware (cables, network cards, and so on) at the lowest layers to high-level applications (Web browsers, SSH servers, and so on) at the highest layers. In-between layers include hardware drivers, kernel features that implement protocols like TCP and IP, and so on. These layers can be classified in several ways, such as the Open Systems Interconnection (OSI) model shown in Figure 5.5. TCP/IP networking is often described in a similar four-layer model consisting of the Link, Internet, Transport, and Application layers. Each layer is responsible for packing or unpacking data to or from the equivalent layer on the computer with which it's communicating, as well as communicating with the adjacent layers on its own system. In this way, data travels down the network stack from the sender and up the network stack on the recipient.

FIGURE 5.5   The OSI model describes a network stack in terms of several layers of hardware and software.

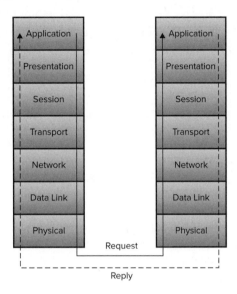

Thinking in terms of a network stack can help you isolate a problem. You needn't even know the details of what each layer does, although you do need to understand the roles of certain key subsystems, such as the hardware, drivers, network interface, name resolution, and applications. A break in a network cable, for instance, will interfere with *all* network traffic, whereas a failure of name resolution will affect only traffic that's addressed by hostname rather than by IP address. You can use this knowledge to perform some key tests when you discover a problem:

- Perform a test using a basic network access tool, such as `ping`. If the target system responds, you know that many of the lower layers work, since `ping` doesn't rely on servers to work. Be aware, however, that the ICMP packets used by `ping` are sometimes blocked by firewalls. You should try pinging several computers.

- Test both local computers (on the same physical network and using the same address block as the source system) and remote systems. If the local computers respond but the remote computers don't, the problem is likely a routing issue.

- Try accessing computers by both hostname and IP address. If hostname access fails but IP address access succeeds, chances are the problem is in name resolution.

- If possible, try using multiple high-level protocols. Sometimes a server computer will be properly configured for one protocol but not for another.

- Use the tools described earlier, in "Monitoring Network Traffic," to isolate the problem. Wireshark can be particularly helpful, since it can help you analyze individual network packets. You can see whether a server is replying at all to your requests; if it is, the problem is most likely in a high-level setting, such as an incorrect password or configuration file option. If a server doesn't reply at all, the server might be misconfigured, you might be attempting to reach it on the wrong port, or a firewall might be blocking access.

Subsequent sections of this chapter elaborate on several of these testing strategies.

Tracing a Route

The `ping` command, described earlier in "Checking Basic Connectivity," is a very useful tool in diagnosing network problems. A step up from `ping` is the `traceroute` command, which sends a series of three test packets to each computer between your system and a specified target system. The result looks something like this:

```
$ traceroute -n 10.1.0.43
traceroute to 10.1.0.43 (10.1.0.43), 30 hops max, 52 byte packets
 1   192.168.1.254   1.021 ms   36.519 ms   0.971 ms
 2   10.10.88.1   17.250 ms   9.959 ms   9.637 ms
 3   10.9.8.173   8.799 ms   19.501 ms   10.884 ms
 4   10.9.8.133   21.059 ms   9.231 ms   103.068 ms
 5   10.9.14.9   8.554 ms   12.982 ms   10.029 ms
 6   10.1.0.44   10.273 ms   9.987 ms   11.215 ms
 7   10.1.0.43   16.360 ms   *   8.102 ms
```

The -n option to this command tells it to display target computers' IP addresses rather than their hostnames. This can speed up the process a bit, particularly if you're having DNS problems, and it can sometimes make the output easier to read—but you may want to know the hostnames of problem systems because that can help you pinpoint who's responsible for a problem.

This sample output shows a great deal of variability in response times. The first hop, to 192.168.1.254, is purely local; this router responded in 1.021, 36.519, and 0.971 milliseconds (ms) to its three probes. (Presumably the second probe caught the system while it was busy with something else.) Probes of most subsequent systems are in the 8–20ms range, although one is at 103.068 ms. The final system has only two times; the middle probe never returned, as the asterisk (*) on this line indicates.

Using `traceroute`, you can localize problems in network connectivity. Highly variable times and missing times can indicate a router that's overloaded or that has an unreliable link to the previous system on the list. If you see a dramatic jump in times, it typically means that the physical distance between two routers is great. This is common in intercontinental links. Such jumps don't necessarily signify a problem unless the two systems are close enough that a huge jump isn't expected.

What can you do with the `traceroute` output? Most immediately, `traceroute` is helpful in determining whether a problem in network connectivity exists in a network for which you're responsible. For instance, the variability in the first hop of the preceding example could indicate a problem on the local network, but the lost packet associated with the final destination most likely is not a local problem. If the trouble link is within your jurisdiction, you can check the status of the problem system, nearby systems, and the network segment in general.

Some routers are configured in such a way that `traceroute` isn't a useful tool; these routers block all `traceroute` data, either to themselves only or for all packets that pass through them. If your `traceroute` output contains one or two lines of all asterisks but everything else seems OK, chances are you've run into such a system. If you see nothing but asterisks after a certain router but diagnostic tools such as `ping` still work, a router is probably blocking all `traceroute` operations.

Locating Running Processes

Many problems relate to the status of locally running programs. The `netstat` tool, described earlier in "Using `netstat`," can be useful in locating programs that are accessing the network, including identifying the ports they're using. If a server isn't responding to connection requests, you can use `netstat` to verify that it is in fact listening to the correct port. Because `netstat`'s output tends to be very long, you may want to pipe it through `less` or `grep` to enable browsing or to search for specific information. For instance, suppose you want to check for the presence of a Simple Mail Transport Protocol (SMTP) server, which should be active on port 25 (identified as `smtp`). You could do so as follows:

```
# netstat -ap | grep smtp
```

If an SMTP server is running, the fact should be apparent in the output. If `netstat` is run as `root`, the output will include the process ID (PID) number and process name of the server.

You can use the `watch` program to launch commands such as `netstat`. Doing so re-runs the program every two seconds and creates an updated display. This can be useful if you're looking for an intermittent connection.

Another tool that's useful in locating network-using programs is `lsof`. This program's main purpose is to list open files; however, the program's definition of "file" includes network sockets. Therefore, it's useful for some of the same purposes as `netstat`. Table 5.7 summarizes `lsof` options that are useful in this context. The program provides many more options that can fine-tune its output or that are relevant mostly for local file searches. Consult its man page for details.

TABLE 5.7 Common lsof options related to network diagnostics

Option	Purpose
-i [address]	Selects processes using network accesses, optionally restricted to those using the specified address. The address takes the form [46][protocol][@host name|hostaddr][:service|port], where 46 refers to the IP version, protocol is the protocol name (TCP or UDP), hostname is a hostname, hostaddr is an IP address, service is a service name, and port is a port number.
-l	Prevents conversion of user ID (UID) numbers to usernames.
+|-M	Enables (+) or disables (-) the reporting of port mapper registrations, which are used by Network File System (NFS) and some other servers. The default behavior is a compile-time option.
-n	Prevents conversion of IP addresses to hostnames in the output.
-P	Prevents conversion of port numbers to service names.
-t	Displays only process ID (PID) numbers; useful if you want to pipe the output to kill or some other program that operates on PID numbers.
-X	Skips display of information on TCP, UDP, and UDPLITE files. Essentially, this option restricts output to non-network information. As such, using it with -i is an error.

A basic use of lsof is to use it with its -i option:

```
# lsof -i
Password:
COMMAND     PID      USER    FD    TYPE   DEVICE SIZE/OFF NODE NAME
cupsd      7584      root    6u    IPv4   10405       0t0 TCP localhost:ipp ↩
  (LISTEN)
cupsd      7584      root    8u    IPv4   10408       0t0 UDP *:ipp
ntpd       7723      root    16u   IPv4   10619       0t0 UDP *:ntp
ntpd       7723      root    17u   IPv4   10623       0t0 UDP localhost:ntp
ntpd       7723      root    18u   IPv4   10624       0t0 UDP ↩
 nessus2.example.com:ntp
```

This output shows two processes using the network: cupsd and ntpd. Both processes are running as root and have multiple connections or are listening for incoming connections.

This output has been truncated for brevity. Be aware that lsof will display a limited list of network processes if run as an ordinary user; you must run it as root to obtain a complete list of network processes.

Examining Log Files

Log files can contain a wealth of information about networking issues. In practice, you may need to examine several log files and perhaps use tools such as grep to help you wade through the copious information stored in these files.

The first log file isn't really a file at all; it's the *kernel ring buffer*, which is a storage area for messages generated by the Linux kernel. You can access the kernel ring buffer by typing dmesg. The result will be a large number of messages, perhaps including some like this:

```
[ 14.335985] r8169 0000:02:00.0: eth0: RTL8168c/8111c at 0xffffc90011242000, ←
00:e0:4d:a3:24:a5, XID 1c2000c0 IRQ 40
[ 14.343594] udev: renamed network interface eth0 to eth1
```

Because the kernel ring buffer contains messages from the kernel, its information usually relates to drivers and other low-level activities. This example, for instance, shows a message displayed by the r8169 driver, which has been loaded to manage an Ethernet device for a Realtek (RTL) 8168c/8111c chipset. The first line indicates that the driver has been assigned the eth0 identifier. The second line, though, indicates that the udev subsystem has renamed eth0 to eth1. Such a detail can be critical; if you're expecting to find the network managed by the Realtek device on eth0, you'll have problems. In the face of such information, you should either adjust your network configuration to use eth1 rather than eth0 or adjust your udev configuration to *not* rename the network device. (Chapter 3, "Basic Filesystem Management," describes udev.)

The kernel ring buffer includes information on much more than network devices, so you may need to pipe the dmesg output through less or use grep to locate keywords. Furthermore, the kernel ring buffer has a limited size, and as messages accumulate, the earliest ones may be lost. For this reason, many distributions save a copy of the kernel ring buffer soon after the system boots in /var/log/dmesg. This file can be valuable because it can show you what happened when your hardware devices were first detected.

Several other files in /var/log can contain valuable debugging information. The /var/log/messages and /var/log/syslog files are particularly likely to be important. These files often contain messages from server programs that reflect normal server operations as well as faults, such as failed login attempts. Some servers create their own log files, or sometimes even several log files in a subdirectory. Samba and the Common Unix Printing System (CUPS), for instance, often create subdirectories called /var/log/samba and /var/log/cups, respectively.

You can use the tail program and its -f option to monitor changes in log files. Typing **tail -f /var/log/messages**, for instance, immediately shows you the last few lines of /var/log/messages. As new messages are added, they'll appear on the screen. This is useful if you want to check for new messages as you test a networking feature.

Resolving Hostname Problems

Hostname problems can take several forms, which in turn have several possible solutions. Previously in the section "Configuring Hostnames," hostname configuration was described. Recall that hostnames must be set both on the local computer and on a DNS server or other means of hostname resolution. The local hostname setting affects the hostname that the computer uses for itself, such as in bash prompts or embedded in network packets the computer sends to other computers. The hostname set in your network's DNS servers, on the other hand, affects how other computers contact your system.

If these two hostnames don't match, problems can result. If your computer claims that it has a particular hostname, but if that hostname isn't present in the DNS entries for your network or if that hostname is assigned to another computer, then some network protocols might not work correctly. For instance, if an email client, using local system calls, believes its hostname is franklin.luna.edu, it may embed that address in email messages sent from your computer. If this address doesn't exist in the DNS server, though, recipients of email sent from your computer won't be able to reply. If the address exists but is associated with another computer, email intended for you may be misdirected to another computer.

You can learn your own computer's hostname, as known locally, by typing **hostname**. This call returns the hostname portion only; if you want to know the FQDN, use the -f, --fqdn, or --long option, as in **hostname --fqdn**. You can verify that this name resolves to your machine by using the host command, which performs DNS lookups:

```
$ hostname -f
nessus.example.com
$ host nessus.example.com
nessus.example.com has address 192.168.1.2
```

You can combine the preceding two commands as **host `hostname -f`**. This command produces the same output as the second command, provided everything is set up correctly. Note that this command includes two back-ticks (`` ` ``), which appear to the left of the 1 key on most U.S. keyboards; these are not ordinary single-quote characters ('), which appear to the left of the Enter key on most U.S. keyboards.

If ifconfig shows that you have the IP address returned by host, your configuration is consistent. There are, however, some situations in which an inconsistency is normal. Examples include systems with multiple network interfaces, server farms that employ load balancing (directing traffic for one hostname to multiple servers), and different internal and external IP addresses or hostnames when a network uses NAT.

If your local DNS server handles lookups for a small private domain, you may want to verify that the *global* DNS network can find your hostname. To do this, pass the IP address of a remote DNS server after the hostname you want to look up with host:

```
$ host nessus.example.com 10.20.102.7
```

This example uses the DNS server at 10.20.102.7 to perform the name resolution, rather than whatever server is the currently configured default. You will have to obtain the IP address of a suitable name server, of course.

If your locally defined and DNS hostnames don't match, you have several possible recourses:

Adjust DNS or Other Network Name Resolution Systems   If you believe your DNS entries are wrong, you can try to adjust them or have them adjusted for you. Unless you control the DNS server, you'll have to contact somebody else—the DNS server administrator—to have this done. (Chapter 6, "DNS Server Configuration," covers DNS server administration.)

Adjust /etc/hosts   If your computer is part of a small local network, you can edit the /etc/hosts file. This file contains mappings of IP addresses to hostnames, typically for a small number of local computers. Note that editing this file adjusts name resolution for the computer that holds this file *only*. Thus, if you need to fix name resolution for a computer that's unreachable by its correct name, you must adjust the /etc/hosts files on all the computers that should be able to reach the computer in question.

Change the Local Hostname   You can change the computer's local hostname, typically by editing the /etc/hostname or /etc/HOSTNAME file.

Deeper DNS issues can be investigated using the dig utility. This utility queries DNS servers for information on individual hosts or entire domains. In its most basic form, it can be used much like host. To query a specific name server, add the server's IP address *before* the hostname, preceded by an at-sign (@):

```
$ dig @10.20.102.7 nessus.example.com
```

The output of dig is more verbose than that of host, and it's more useful when configuring or debugging DNS server configurations than for other purposes. Therefore, Chapter 6 describes dig in more detail.

If your computer doesn't seem to be resolving hostnames correctly, you can check the /etc/hosts file. If this file contains entries it shouldn't have, remove them; and if it lacks entries it should have, add them. You can also check the /etc/resolv.conf file. As described previously in "Adjusting Network Configuration Files," this file should contain a domain line that specifies a default domain name and up to three nameserver lines that specify the IP addresses of DNS servers:

```
domain example.com
nameserver 192.168.1.2
nameserver 10.9.16.30
nameserver 10.9.16.25
```

Verify that the DNS servers are working by querying each one directly with host or dig. If one isn't working, wait a while and try again, in case the problem is temporary. If a DNS server doesn't seem to respond at all for an extended period, perhaps its entry is in error. Setting the domain correctly is important for resolving hostnames that lack the domain component. You can search additional domains by adding a search line that lists additional domains, separated by spaces or tabs.

> If a computer uses DHCP for network configuration, the DHCP client will rewrite /etc/resolv.conf whenever it launches or renews its lease. If you find that incorrect information keeps creeping back into this file, you may need to adjust the configuration on your network's DHCP server or contact the person who maintains this server about the problem. Chapter 7 describes DHCP server configuration.

Resolving Connectivity Issues

Basic connectivity issues, in which a computer can't send or receive any network data, are usually caused by hardware problems (such as a disconnected cable) or incorrect basic configuration parameters. The previous sections "Connecting to a Network with DHCP" and "Connecting to a Network with a Static IP Address" describe how to configure your system using these methods.

If these methods aren't working, you should first verify that you're using the correct method—DHCP or static IP address assignment. If you're attempting to use DHCP but it's not working, you can try a few things to troubleshoot or correct the problem:

- Can other computers use the DHCP server? If not, perhaps the server is misconfigured. Consult Chapter 7 to learn about DHCP server configuration.

- Is the DHCP server configured to be selective about its clients? If the server only hands out IP addresses to computers with known hardware addresses or other characteristics, you may need to adjust the server's configuration so that it knows about your computer, or you may need to tweak your client configuration—say, by passing a particular name to the DHCP server.

- Are you on the same network segment as the DHCP server? Ordinarily, a DHCP server can only manage clients on its own physical network segment. Intervening routers usually don't pass DHCP traffic between segments.

- Try a different DHCP client. Sometimes changing clients is easier than tracking down an obscure incompatibility.

- Check your log files on both the client and the server. These files may contain clues about the problem.

Whether you're using DHCP or static IP address assignment, verify proper settings in /etc/network, /etc/sysconfig/network-scripts/, or other network configuration or script files, as described earlier in this chapter. A typo in an IP address, network mask, or other setting can prevent the system from working.

Don't overlook the possibility of hardware problems. A bad cable, a bad switch, or even a bad network card can cause untold grief. Although Linux's driver support for Ethernet devices is excellent, it's conceivable you have a card with poor support, so upgrading the driver or replacing the card with a better-supported one may be worthwhile. Unfortunately, Linux's support for Wi-Fi devices is spottier than its support for Ethernet. If you're having problems with unreliable Wi-Fi operation, you should check with the chipset manufacturer to see whether updated drivers are available. Perusing Internet forums may also lead you to updated drivers or workarounds for Wi-Fi woes.

Resolving Routing Problems

Routing problems can usually be diagnosed by `traceroute`, as described previously in "Tracing a Route." If the problem lies far from your computer, it may not be solvable by you. Unfortunately, routing problems crop up from time to time, and you may have no choice but to wait for the problem to be resolved by whomever is in charge of the affected router. You can try to fix problems that are closer to home, though:

- If the problem is with a router that you believe is under your ISP's control, you can contact your ISP about it.

- You can reboot your modem and any broadband router under your control. Sometimes this clears up routing problems in the first hop or so on a broadband Internet connection.

- Check your network mask (netmask) settings. If you have an incorrect network mask, your computer may be attempting to route packets that it shouldn't route or connect directly to computers for which this is impossible.

- Check that all the necessary routes are set. If your network has multiple routers, failure to set explicit routes for all of them can degrade network performance.

- If you've configured routers yourself, ensure that they're configured correctly. Check their routing tables, their network masks, and their settings in /proc/sys/net/ipv4/ ip_forward.

Resolving Security Problems

Some problems are related to security settings. One area that can cause mysterious problems is firewall settings. Chapter 7 describes firewalls in more detail; but for now, you can check your firewall settings by using the -L option to `iptables`:

```
# iptables -L
Chain INPUT (policy ACCEPT)
target     prot opt source              destination

Chain FORWARD (policy ACCEPT)
target     prot opt source              destination

Chain OUTPUT (policy ACCEPT)
target     prot opt source              destination
```

This example shows no firewall rules defined. If you see rules specified under the INPUT or OUTPUT chains, the ability of your computer to function as a client or server for particular protocols is impaired. Likewise if any of the chains sets a default policy of DROP instead of ACCEPT. Such a configuration isn't necessarily a bad thing; the whole point of a firewall is to prevent unwanted access to or from the computer. The firewall rules must be tailored to your use of the computer, though. For instance, you wouldn't want to block the incoming SMTP port on a mail server, except perhaps in a limited way—say, to prevent outside access to a server that exists only to handle outgoing mail from local computers. The FORWARD chain affects the forwarding of packets between network interfaces on routers, so this chain will only affect computers that are configured as routers.

Another security issue that can crop up is settings in the /etc/hosts.allow and /etc/hosts.deny files. These files are used mainly by the TCP Wrappers program, which is described in detail in Chapter 10, "Security." As with firewall rules, rules in these files can limit access to your computer; however, these files contain rules that affect servers that are configured to use TCP Wrappers. Thus, if a server isn't responding to connection requests, particularly if it's responding to some connection requests but not others, you can check these files for entries. If these files are empty except for comments, they shouldn't have any effect. If these files seem to be in use, consult Chapter 10 to learn about TCP Wrappers configuration, evaluate whether this configuration is appropriate, and change it if necessary.

Do not change either firewall or TCP Wrappers configurations unless you understand them. This is particularly true if you're new to administering a system or if you share administrative responsibility with another person. Firewall and TCP Wrappers rules are typically put in place for very good reasons, so changing them or, especially, disabling them should be done only after careful consideration. That said, such rules are sometimes enacted as part of an install-time option that you might have overlooked or accidentally set at too strict a level for your needs.

Summary

Network configuration is an extremely broad topic, ranging from setting hardware parameters to adjusting the options on dozens of different servers. This chapter covers some of the more basic network configuration topics, starting with activating the network interface. On Wi-Fi-equipped systems, this task begins with setting Wi-Fi options. On all systems, it includes using either DHCP or static IP address tools to bring up a basic configuration. Hostname configuration and checking connectivity round out this topic.

Some systems require more advanced network settings. One of these is router configuration (a topic that's revisited in Chapter 7). A secure router variant, VPN, requires even more configuration. You should also be familiar with a variety of tools, such as nmap, Wireshark, tcpdump, netstat, and nc, to display information on your network settings, on nearby computers, and on the data passing over your network ports.

Unfortunately, network configuration does not always proceed smoothly. Problems can crop up at any level, ranging from the cables connecting computers to esoteric details of server configuration. Being able to track down a problem is a skill best learned by experience, but knowing the tools and some basic rules of thumb will help you in this task.

Exam Essentials

Describe the wireless-specific tools needed to connect to a Wi-Fi network.   Prior to normal network configuration, you must link a computer to a Wi-Fi network using the iwconfig program, which takes a variety of parameters to specify the radio frequency, network password, and other features of the network. The iwlist command can be useful in helping to identify nearby networks, should you need details on them before connecting.

Describe the commands used to activate a network interface.   The ifconfig command does this job. Typically, you pass it an interface name, an IP address preceded by up, and a netmask preceded by netmask, as in **ifconfig eth0 up 192.168.29.39 netmask 255.255.255.0**. Most distributions provide a script called ifup that enables you to automatically bring up a network interface, once it's configured using distribution-specific configuration files.

Explain how routing tables are manipulated.   The route command is used to display or change routing tables. You can pass the add or del option, followed by additional options to specify the route to be added or deleted. For instance, **route add default gw 192.168.29.1** adds a default route using 192.168.29.1 as the gateway computer.

Summarize network address types.   At the lowest level, hardware addresses identify specific network devices, such as Ethernet ports. Hardware addresses are tied to Internet Protocol (IP) addresses via the Address Resolution Protocol (ARP). IP addresses are associated with hostnames via the Domain Name System (DNS) and /etc/hosts files.

Describe tools used for testing basic network connections.   The ping utility sends a series of simple packets from one computer to another; the recipient should then send a reply. This exchange can verify that basic connectivity exists. A more complex variant on ping is traceroute, which can test connection speed and reliability between all the computers that route traffic between two systems.

Explain the purpose and basic functions of a VPN.   A virtual private network (VPN) is a way to connect two networks across an untrusted network while maintaining the security of data transferred in the process. VPNs employ a series of cryptographic keys to encrypt data, and they tunnel a wide variety of network protocols over a single encrypted channel. When properly configured, a VPN link looks much like any other routed link to the bulk of the systems, but data cannot be easily interpreted by intervening routers, even if they've been compromised.

Summarize tools that can analyze network traffic and the capabilities of local computers.   The netstat utility can reveal what ports are open or in use on a local computer, while Nmap can scan remote computers for open ports. Wireshark and tcpdump are packet sniffers—they monitor traffic that passes over a computer's ports, which can be useful for diagnostic purposes. The nc (aka netcat) utility can send arbitrary network packets in order to test a remote system's capabilities. Many of these tools can be used legitimately or abused, so be cautious how you deploy them.

Describe how to study hostname resolution issues.   The host and dig commands can be used to perform hostname lookups, thus uncovering problems in a DNS configuration. You can learn your local hostname with the hostname command. If your local hostname doesn't match the computer's DNS hostname, some protocols may not work correctly.

Summarize how to use log files to diagnose network problems.   The kernel ring buffer, accessible via dmesg, contains low-level kernel messages concerning hardware devices. Several log files, most notable among them /var/log/messages and /var/log/syslog, contain information from higher-level utilities and server programs. Any of these logs may contain clues about problems, such as a failure to load a driver, a failure to obtain a network address via DHCP, or a network authentication failure.

Explain how incorrectly set security measures can interfere with networking.   Firewalls, TCP Wrappers, and other security measures are all meant to keep a system safe by denying access to or from particular network ports or computers. Used properly, these measures keep out miscreants; however, if the security measures are too broadly written, they deny access to legitimate users.

Review Questions

1. You try to set up a computer on a local network via a static TCP/IP configuration, but you lack a gateway address. Which of the following is true?

    A. Because the gateway address is necessary, no TCP/IP networking functions will work.

    B. TCP/IP networking will function, but you'll be unable to convert hostnames to IP addresses, or vice versa.

    C. You'll be able to communicate with machines on your local network segment but not with other systems.

    D. The computer won't be able to tell which other computers are local and which are remote.

2. Which of the following types of information is returned by typing `ifconfig eth0`? (Choose all that apply.)

    A. The names of programs that are using `eth0`

    B. The IP address assigned to `eth0`

    C. The hardware address of `eth0`

    D. The hostname associated with `eth0`

3. Under what circumstances might you use the `iwconfig` utility?

    A. You must diagnose problems on a Token Ring network.

    B. You need to bring up or shut down an Ethernet network link.

    C. You need to connect a Linux system to a new wireless network.

    D. You must diagnose the failure of a DHCP client on a PPP network.

4. Which of the following utilities can bring up a network connection? (Choose all that apply.)

    A. `ifconfig`

    B. `netstat`

    C. `ifup`

    D. `ping`

5. Which of the following commands should you use to add to host 192.168.0.10 a default gateway to 192.168.0.1?

    A. `route add default gw 192.168.0.10 192.168.0.1`

    B. `route add default gw 192.168.0.1`

    C. `route add 192.168.0.10 default 192.168.0.1`

    D. `route 192.168.0.10 gw 192.168.0.1`

6. You type **arp -n** at a command prompt. What type of output will you see?

    A. A summary of network packet errors

    B. Routing table information

    C. The IP address(es) of your name server(s)

    D. The mapping of IP addresses to MAC addresses

7. Which of the following commands might bring up an interface on **eth1**? (Select all that apply.)

    A. Type **dhclient eth1**.

    B. Type **ifup eth1**.

    C. Type **ifconfig eth1**.

    D. Type **network eth1**.

8. What is the purpose of the −n option to **route**?

    A. It causes no operation to be performed; **route** reports what it would do if −n were omitted.

    B. It precedes specification of a netmask when setting the route.

    C. It causes machines to be identified by IP address rather than hostname in output.

    D. It forces interpretation of a provided address as a network address rather than a host address.

9. Which of the following programs can monitor the network traffic coming into a computer, enabling you to analyze the packets' contents?

    A. OpenVPN

    B. arp

    C. netstat

    D. Wireshark

10. What does the following command accomplish, when typed as **root**?

    `# nmap -sU router.example.com`

    A. It adds a default route through `router.example.com` to the computer on which the command is typed.

    B. It watches for UDP network traffic to or from `router.example.com`, displaying each matching packet.

    C. It maps the Wi-Fi characteristics associated with the `router.example.com` wireless network.

    D. It scans `router.example.com` for open (listening) UDP ports and reports the results of this scan.

11. You know that your computer is running a Web server on port 80, but you don't know what Web server program you're using. How can you discover this information?

    A. Type `wget localhost` as an ordinary user.

    B. Type `lsof -i :80` as root.

    C. Type `ifconfig -p 80` as root.

    D. Type `ifconfig -q -s 80` as an ordinary user.

12. You want to link four branch offices' private networks to a company's central office's private network using OpenVPN. Which of the following conditions should you ensure is met to avoid problems?

    A. Each of the offices should use a different IP address range.

    B. Each of the offices should use a key from a different CA.

    C. Each of the offices should have approximately the same number of computers.

    D. Each of the offices should use DHCP on all its computers.

13. What files are used to configure TCP Wrappers?

    A. `/etc/hosts.allow` and `/etc/hosts.deny`

    B. Files in the `/etc/tcpd` directory tree

    C. `/etc/tcpwrap.conf` and `/var/spool/tcpwrap`

    D. Files in the `/etc/tcpw.d` directory tree

14. How can you learn what programs are currently accessing the network on a Linux system?

    A. Type `ifconfig -p eth0`.

    B. Examine `/proc/network/programs`.

    C. Examine `/etc/xinetd.conf`.

    D. Type `netstat -p`.

15. The `ping` utility responds normally when you use it with an IP address but not when you use it with a hostname that you're positive corresponds to this IP address. What might cause this problem? (Select all that apply.)

    A. The target computer may be configured to ignore packets from `ping`.

    B. Your computer's DNS configuration may be broken.

    C. The DNS configuration on the target system may be broken.

    D. The route between your computer and its DNS server may be incorrect.

16. What is the purpose of `/etc/hostname`, if it's present on the system?

    A. It holds the computer's default hostname.

    B. It holds a list of servers that resolve hostnames.

    C. It holds a list of IP addresses and associated hostnames.

    D. It holds the hostname of the local gateway computer.

17. Which of the following programs can be used to perform a DNS lookup?

    A. host

    B. dnslookup

    C. pump

    D. ifconfig

18. Your computer is in the example.com domain, but you want to be able to contact the neil
    .tranquility.luna.edu and buzz.tranquility.luna.edu servers by typing neil or buzz
    as the hostnames, respectively. How can you accomplish this goal? (Choose all that apply.)

    A. Add the lines host neil neil.tranquility.luna.edu and host buzz buzz
       .tranquility.luna.edu to your bash startup script.

    B. Add entries for neil and buzz, linking them to their IP addresses, to /etc/hosts.

    C. Add the line search tranquility.luna.edu to your /etc/resolv.conf file.

    D. Add the line nameserver tranquility.luna.edu to your /etc/resolv.conf file.

19. Which of the following entries are found in the /etc/hosts file?

    A. A list of hosts allowed to remotely access this one

    B. Mappings of IP addresses to hostnames

    C. A list of users allowed to remotely access this host

    D. Passwords for remote Web administration

20. Your computer has an IP address of 192.168.21.102, with a network mask of
    255.255.255.0. You're able to ping 192.168.21.7 and 192.168.21.98, but not 192.168.27.3
    or 10.78.21.102. If you know that all of these addresses are valid and the computers are
    turned on and connected to the network, which of the following is the most probable cause
    of this problem?

    A. The name server configuration is set incorrectly on 192.168.21.102.

    B. The default route is set incorrectly on 192.168.21.102.

    C. The DHCP servers must be activated on 192.168.27.3 and 10.78.21.102.

    D. The netmask is set incorrectly on 192.168.21.102.

Answers to Review Questions

1. C. The gateway computer is a router that transfers data between two or more network segments. As such, if a computer isn't configured to use a gateway, it won't be able to communicate beyond its local network segment. (If your DNS server is on a different network segment, name resolution via DNS won't work, although other types of name resolution, such as /etc/hosts file entries, will still work.)

2. B, C. When used to display information on an interface, ifconfig shows the hardware and IP addresses of the interface, the protocols (such as TCP/IP) bound to the interface, and statistics on transmitted and received packets. This command does *not* return information on programs using the interface or the hostname associated with the interface.

3. C. The iwconfig utility configures a Linux wireless (Wi-Fi) connection, so option C is correct. Options A, B, and D all refer to wired network hardware, for which iwconfig is useless.

4. A, C. The ifconfig command is Linux's basic tool for manually bringing up a network connection using options provided on the command line, while ifup is a utility that brings up a network connection based on the contents of the network configuration files. The netstat and ping commands are both useful network diagnostic tools, but they don't bring up network connections.

5. B. To add a default gateway of 192.168.0.1, the command would be **route add default gw 192.168.0.1**, as stated in option B. Specifying the IP address of the host system is not necessary and in fact will confuse the route command. Options A, C, and D are all distortions of the correct answer and will not work correctly.

6. D. The arp utility returns data from the Address Resolution Protocol (ARP) table, which holds mappings of IP addresses to hardware (MAC) addresses. The -n option displays IP addresses as such rather than converted into hostnames. Network packet error information, as stated in option A, can be obtained, along with other information, from ifconfig but not from arp. Routing table information, as stated in option B, is usually obtained from route or netstat -r. Your name server(s) IP address(es), as in option C, are most easily obtained by displaying the contents of /etc/resolv.conf.

7. A, B. The dhclient utility, if installed, attempts to configure and bring up the network(s) passed to it as options (or all networks if it's given no options) using a DHCP server for guidance. Thus, option A may work, although it won't work if no DHCP server is available. Option B applies whatever network options are configured using distribution-specific tools and brings up the network. Thus, options A and B both may work, although neither is guaranteed to work. Option C displays the network status of eth1, but it won't activate eth1 if it's not already active. There is no standard network utility in Linux. Thus, options C and D won't work.

8. C. The -n option is used when you want to use route to display the current routing table, and it does as option C specifies. There is no route parameter that behaves as option A specifies. Option B describes the purpose of the netmask parameter to route. Option D describes the purpose of the -net parameter to route.

9. D. Option D, Wireshark, is a packet sniffer, which means that it behaves as the question specifies. It includes sophisticated packet matching and analysis tools to help in this task. OpenVPN is a tool for connecting two networks in a secure way even over an insecure network. The arp utility enables inspection and alteration of a computer's Address Resolution Protocol (ARP) cache, which ties hardware addresses to IP addresses. The netstat utility is a general-purpose network utility that can display or change a wide variety of network data.

10. D. The Nmap utility performs network port scans, and the -sU option specifies a scan of UDP ports, so option D is correct. A default route is most likely to be created by using the route utility or by editing configuration files; Nmap can't do this job, so option A is incorrect. The task described in option B is best done by a packet sniffer, such as tcpdump or Wireshark; Nmap can't do this. The discovery of Wi-Fi characteristics is done by the iwlist utility, not by Nmap, so option C is incorrect.

11. B. The lsof program returns information on open files and the processes that are using them, "files" being defined in a way that includes network connections. Option B presents the correct syntax to obtain information on the process that's using port 80, including the command name of the process, so option B is correct. (You must run it as root to get the desired information.) Option A's wget command will retrieve the home page of the Web server, but it won't return information on what program is doing the serving, so this option is incorrect. The ifconfig command used in options C and D is used to inspect or manipulate a network interface, but it doesn't return information on processes using specific ports, so these options are both incorrect. (The -p and -q options to ifconfig are also both fictitious. The -s option alters the format of its display.)

12. A. Once connected, computers from the offices will be able to communicate with each other (or at least all of the branches will be able to communicate with the central office) via IP address. If the IP address ranges of any two offices were to overlap, routing confusion would ensue, so option A is correct. Option B is incorrect because the easiest way to configure keys for OpenVPN is to assign all the networks' keys from a single CA. The number of computers on each network is irrelevant to OpenVPN configuration, so option C is incorrect. OpenVPN does not require the use of DHCP, so option D is incorrect.

13. A. The /etc/hosts.allow and /etc/hosts.deny files are used by TCP Wrappers to control what clients may access servers that rely on TCP Wrappers; thus, option A is correct. Options B, C, and D all present fictitious filenames and directory names and so are incorrect.

14. D. The netstat program produces various network statistics, including the process IDs (PIDs) and names of programs currently accessing the network when passed the -p parameter. Thus, option D is correct. The ifconfig program can't produce this information, and the -p option to this program is fictitious, so option A is incorrect. Option B's /proc/network/programs file is also fictitious. Option C's /etc/xinetd.conf file is real and may provide some information about some servers that are using the network (as described in Chapter 10); but this file won't provide information about all servers, much less about clients that are accessing the network.

15. B, D. DNS problems can manifest as an ability to connect to computers using IP addresses but not using hostnames. Thus, options B and D (and various other DNS-related problems) could create the symptoms described. If the target system were configured to ignore `ping` packets, as described in option A, then it wouldn't respond when you identified it by IP address. The target system's DNS configuration (option C) doesn't enter into the equation, because it responds to the `ping` request via IP address alone.

16. A. Although not all systems use `/etc/hostname`, option A correctly describes it for those systems that use it. Option B describes the purpose of `/etc/resolv.conf`. Option C describes the purpose of `/etc/hosts`. Option D doesn't describe any standard Linux configuration file although the gateway computer's IP address is likely to appear in a distribution-specific configuration file.

17. A. The `host` program is a commonly used program to perform a DNS lookup. There is no standard `dnslookup` program, although the `nslookup` program is a deprecated program for performing DNS lookups. `pump` is a DHCP client, and `ifconfig` is used for configuration of networking parameters and cards.

18. B, C. The `/etc/hosts` file contains static mappings of hostnames to IP addresses, so adding entries as specified in option B will work (although these entries will need to be changed if these servers' IP addresses ever change). Option C's solution will also work, and it will continue to work if the servers' IP addresses change, provided that their DNS server is appropriately updated. Option A won't work because the `host` command is a DNS lookup tool; it doesn't create hostname aliases, as option A implies. Option D confuses the search and `nameserver` functions of `/etc/resolv.conf`. The `nameserver` line in this file specifies a DNS name server by IP address, so option D won't work.

19. B. The `/etc/hosts` file holds mappings of IP addresses to hostnames, on a one-line-per-mapping basis. It does not list the users or other hosts allowed to remotely access this one, nor does it affect remote administration through a Web browser.

20. B. The two reachable systems are on the same network block (192.168.21.0/24), so their network traffic would not pass through a router. The two unreachable systems are on different network blocks, which means their traffic must pass through a router. This pattern suggests that there's a routing problem, as in option B. (Another possibility is that the router itself is down or misconfigured.) Since all the computers in the question were specified by IP address, name server configuration, as in option A, isn't an issue. Option C implies that DHCP servers are required to respond to ping requests, but this isn't so; DHCP servers deliver IP addresses to DHCP clients. Although a change in the netmask might plausibly enable the first system to contact 192.168.27.3, if the two systems are connected to the same physical wires, the 10.78.21.102 system is much too different in IP address to make a misconfigured netmask a plausible explanation for this problem, as option D suggests.

Chapter

6

DNS Server Configuration

THE FOLLOWING LINUX PROFESSIONAL INSTITUTE OBJECTIVES ARE COVERED IN THIS CHAPTER:

- ✓ 207.1 Basic DNS Server Configuration (weight: 2)

- ✓ 207.2 Create and Maintain DNS Zones (weight: 2)

- ✓ 207.3 Securing a DNS Server (weight: 2)

As described in Chapter 5, "Network Configuration," three levels of network addresses are important: hardware addresses, Internet Protocol (IP) addresses, and hostnames. Converting between these address types is critical for the normal functioning of a network. The conversion between hardware addresses and IP addresses is accomplished by the Address Resolution Protocol (ARP), and this conversion needs no explicit configuration. (The arp utility, however, does provide the ability to monitor and change the automatic ARP activities.) The conversion between IP addresses and hostnames is most often handled by the Domain Name System (DNS), which is a worldwide distributed collection of servers. If your site is very large (and perhaps even if it's not), you may need to maintain a DNS server both for the benefit of outside sites and for internal use. This chapter therefore describes how to configure and maintain your own DNS server.

This chapter begins with a brief overview of what DNS is, including both the organization of the global DNS and an outline of how DNS configuration is split up on a Linux system. With these basics in mind, you can look at the nuts and bolts of setting up a Linux DNS server program to function in a simple caching-only mode. A more advanced configuration relies on configuration files defining multiple *zones*, which are collections of related computers managed by DNS. With suitable zone files enabled, a DNS server can manage name resolution for your domain. Finally, this chapter examines DNS security issues.

Understanding the Role of DNS

As described in Chapter 5, computer name resolution can be performed in a number of ways, including (but not limited to) an /etc/hosts file and DNS. An /etc/hosts file is a convenient way to manage name resolution for a small number of computers, such as a small home network with just two or three machines. Because /etc/hosts must be updated on every computer on a network whenever any machine's name or IP address changes or whenever a computer is added to or removed from the network, the viability of this approach drops rapidly as the number of computers increases.

In addition to /etc/hosts and DNS, several other name resolution systems exist, including Network Information Service (NIS), Windows Internet Name Service (WINS), and more. Such configurations are fairly exotic and are not covered on the LPIC-2 exam.

The DNS database is arranged in a hierarchical manner, as illustrated in Figure 6.1. The top of the hierarchy is referred to as the *root* and is written as a single dot (.). Below the root come the *top-level domains (TLDs)*, such as .com, .edu, .mil, .us, and .uk. Some TLDs are country code TLDs, such as .us (for the United States) and .uk (for the United Kingdom). As the United States originated the Internet, some TLDs are reserved for U.S. institutions, such as .mil for the U.S. military. The popular .com, .org, and .net TLDs are effectively international in scope. TLDs are further subdivided. Sometimes these refer to individual businesses, institutions, or even people, as in sybex.com or oberlin.edu. In other cases, another layer intervenes before individual registrants can claim a domain name. For instance, the .us TLD is divided into state-level domains, such as .ri.us for Rhode Island; and the .uk TLD is divided into academic (.ac.uk), commercial (.co.uk), and other groupings. Once a domain is registered, the domain's owner may choose to subdivide it further or assign computers names directly under the domain name. One popular name is www for a Web server, so www.oberlin.edu is Oberlin College's main Web server, to name just one example.

FIGURE 6.1   DNS is organized in a hierarchical way with each individual computer (the lowermost dots) having a name in a domain that itself has additional components, up to the root of the entire DNS hierarchy.

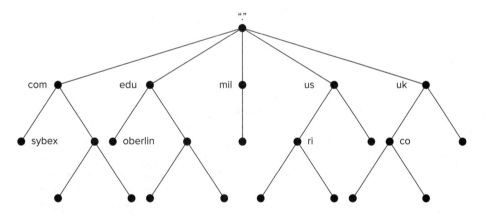

DNS servers are arranged in a way that's conceptually similar to the arrangement of domains. In particular, every domain and subdomain must have associated with it server computers that are *authoritative* for the domain—that is, these servers can be relied upon by the rest of the Internet to provide accurate information about the names and IP addresses of computers within the domain and to know the IP addresses of servers that are authoritative for its subdomains. For instance, the name server associated with the .edu domain must know the IP address of the name server responsible for the oberlin.edu domain, and this name server must know the IP address of the www.oberlin.edu computer. At the top of the hierarchy are the *root name servers*, which dole out the addresses of the TLD name servers. Because the root of the domain name hierarchy is a dot (.), domain names and hostnames must technically end in this character, as in `www.oberlin.edu.`; however, standard name resolution procedures add this feature automatically, so it's usually omitted.

Thus, to look up a hostname, the process begins with a query to the root name server, as in "what is the IP address of `www.oberlin.edu`?" The root name server is unlikely to know the answer and so replies with the address of the `.edu` server. The program doing the lookup then repeats the query with this server, which again most likely defers to another system. This process continues until a server knows the address of the target computer or until some error occurs, such as if an authoritative server for the domain doesn't have the answer.

This DNS lookup process may sound complicated, but given the speed of computers, it seldom takes very long. Furthermore, there are several simplifying factors. First, server programs and user programs such as Apache and Firefox are unlikely to need to do the full lookup; these programs ask the OS, which then passes the query on to one of the DNS servers specified in the basic network configuration, as described in Chapter 5. It's this DNS server, which probably resides on a different computer, that does the full recursive DNS lookup. Second, DNS servers can *cache* their results, meaning that they remember the lookup results for some period of time, typically hours to days. Thus, if you regularly access a favorite Web site, your local network's DNS server will be able to return the relevant IP address without performing a full recursive lookup most of the time; only when the cached data expires will a new full recursive lookup be necessary.

Given this arrangement, there are two reasons to run a DNS server:

- To deliver authoritative data for a domain you manage
- To perform full recursive DNS lookups for computers on your own network

In some cases, one server may perform both tasks. In other cases, you need only one function. In fact, if you need only the second function, name server configuration is simplified, because you don't need to deal with the details of domain management. This *caching-only* configuration constitutes the most basic DNS server configuration; adding support for custom zones enables your server to become authoritative for those zones.

This chapter, like the LPIC-2 certification, emphasizes configuration of the Berkeley Internet Name Daemon (BIND) server (`https://www.isc.org/software/bind`), which is a powerful and popular name server on Linux. Several other name servers exist, however, and in some cases may be preferable. The `dnsmasq` server (`http://freshmeat.net/projects/dnsmasq/`), for instance, is a small combination of DNS and Dynamic Host Configuration Protocol (DHCP) server that's particularly useful on small networks. The `djbdns` server (`http://cr.yp.to/djbdns.html`) is an alternative to BIND that bills itself as being particularly security-conscious. Although BIND is a fine server, you may want to consider such alternatives before deploying a real DNS configuration. In fact, using two different server programs on two different computers can sometimes be advantageous. If a security vulnerability or other bug takes down one server, the other is likely to remain unaffected, thus minimizing disruption to your site.

Real World Scenario

Obtaining a Domain

You may run a DNS server on a small local network without registering a domain name. Such a configuration normally uses a made-up domain name, ideally using a top-level domain (TLD, such as .com or .edu) that's not in use (such as .not); or you can configure the system as a forwarding-only server that doesn't handle any local hostnames.

You may also run a DNS server using a registered domain. The Internet Corporation for Assigned Names and Numbers (ICANN) maintains a list of accredited registrars (http://www.icann.org/en/registrars/accredited-list.html). Check this list to locate a registrar within the TLD you want to use. You may then register a domain name, which normally costs about $10 or $15 a year, and set up a DNS server to manage that domain. You can link your own DNS server to the global DNS network by entering your server's IP address in Web forms maintained by your domain registrar, or you can have your registrar maintain your public (Internet-accessible) DNS presence and set up your own DNS server for your private network's use only. Which approach is best depends on your needs and resources. If you run a lot of servers or want to provide your users with direct access to your network's systems from off-site, running your own publicly accessible DNS server makes sense, although doing so increases your security risks. Running a private DNS server is sensible if your network is protected behind a network address translation (NAT) router or if there's no need to provide direct outside access to most of your network's computers. (Note that your computers may still be accessible via IP address even if no hostnames point directly to them, so failing to provide DNS entries is an ineffective security measure.)

Running a Caching-Only Name Server

Suppose you're managing a network that connects to the Internet. Chances are your Internet service provider (ISP) provides a DNS server that your computers can use; however, this configuration can generate more network traffic than is necessary when multiple computers on your network make the same query for lookups of hostnames that your users commonly use. Configuring your own DNS server to manage these lookups, including caching the results, can save network bandwidth. Furthermore, it can speed up the DNS lookups, since the results can be pulled from your local computer's cache rather than directed over your Internet link to your ISP's DNS server. If the DNS server you configure is not authoritative for any domain, its configuration can be relatively simple. This is referred to as a *caching-only* name server.

To configure a caching-only name server, you must first edit the main BIND configuration file. Although the server won't manage its own zones, you must set some basic options in the server's zone configuration files. In some cases, you may need to update configuration files from older versions. Finally, with the changes in place, you can test the server's functioning.

> If you need to manage your own domain, you should still begin with a caching-only DNS configuration. Managing your own domain adds to the requirements of a caching-only name server; it doesn't significantly change the fundamentals of the caching-only configuration.

Modifying the Main BIND Configuration File

Before proceeding, be sure that BIND is installed on your computer. This program is usually installed in a package called bind. Use your package manager to install it, if necessary; or obtain it from its Web site (http://www.isc.org/software/bind) and compile it yourself.

> This chapter describes the configuration of BIND 9, which is the latest non-experimental version at press time as well as the version emphasized in the LPIC-2 objectives. An experimental BIND 10 is under development. If it has become current by the time you read this, you may need to research its configuration details yourself or use the older BIND 9.

The main BIND configuration file is /etc/named.conf. This file controls overall server operation, including global options (in a section that begins with the keyword options) and one or more zone sections that point to files that describe the domains the server manages. You can configure a caching-only server in one of three ways:

A Forwarding-Only Server   A server is said to be *forwarding-only* if it forwards all the name resolution requests it receives to one or more other servers. This configuration can be an effective one if you have an ISP that provides a conventional DNS server. A forwarding-only configuration can improve DNS lookup times because it takes advantage of the outside DNS server's cache, and that server is presumably closer to other servers than yours is. (This last point isn't always true, though, or it might be true but countered by other factors, such as a heavier load on your ISP's DNS server.)

A Server That Does Full Recursive Lookups Only   If your ISP doesn't provide DNS service or if that service is unreliable or slow, you can configure BIND to do a full recursive lookup for every query that can't be answered from its cache. Most DNS servers that belong to ISPs and large IT departments are configured this way. Performance can be worse than that of a forwarding-only server, but you won't be held hostage to your ISP's DNS server availability.

A Server That Does Both Forwarding and Full Recursive Lookups   You can configure BIND to attempt a forwarding lookup but fall back on a full recursive lookup if that initial attempt fails. This approach is a compromise that can work well if your ISP provides a DNS server but that server is unreliable.

The options section of named.conf, as shown in Listing 6.1, defines which of these three methods BIND uses. Most lines in this file end in a semicolon (;). (Omitting the semicolon is a common error in this file.) This punctuation denotes the end of a configuration option. Comments are indicated by two leading slashes (//). Some lines in Listing 6.1 are indented for readability, but BIND ignores this detail, so you can indent lines in whatever way you like.

Listing 6.1: Sample BIND /etc/named.conf configuration

```
options {
        directory "/var/named";
        forwarders {
                10.9.16.30;
                10.13.16.30;
                };
        listen-on {
                192.168.1.1;
                172.24.21.1;
        };
        allow-transfer {"none";};
        forward first;
};
logging {
        channel default_debug {
                file "data/named.run";
                severity dynamic;
        };
};
// Specify the root zone files
zone "." IN {
        type hint;
        file "named.ca";
};
include "/etc/named.rfc1912.zones";
```

The key parts of this definition are the forwarders lines and the forward first line in the options section. The forwarders definition specifies the DNS servers to which BIND should forward the lookup requests it receives. This example specifies two outside systems; BIND will try each of them in turn, stopping when it receives a reply. The forward first line tells BIND that it should function as a forwarding server if possible but that it should perform full recursive lookups if that fails. If you change this line to forward only, then BIND will *only* attempt to get an answer from the systems specified in the forwarders area. If you omit the forward only or forward first line and also omit the forwarders section, the server will perform full recursive lookups all the time.

Listing 6.1 has a listen-on section, which tells BIND on which IP addresses it should listen. This option is most useful on server computers that have multiple network interfaces;

you can have BIND respond to queries from some interfaces but not others. You can even configure BIND as a forwarding-only server for a single computer by having it listen only on the 127.0.0.1 address (the loopback address for the computer). You would then configure the computer to use this address for DNS resolution, as described in Chapter 5.

The `allow-transfer` section is a BIND security option. It's described in detail in "Securing Zone Transfers."

The `logging` and `zone` sections of Listing 6.1 set logging options and define one zone. If you simply want to configure a caching-only server, you can probably leave these options alone. (The upcoming sections "Modifying Zone Files" and "Creating and Maintaining DNS Zones" describe the zone section in more detail.)

BIND is a powerful and complex program, and it supports many other options in its /etc/named.conf configuration file. Chances are your BIND package came with a sample /etc/named.conf file that uses some of these options. In some cases, these configurations are designed to provide added security in case the package is installed accidentally. For instance, you might see lines like these:

```
listen-on port 53 { 127.0.0.1; };
listen-on-v6 port 53 { ::1; };
allow-query { localhost; };
```

These lines have the effect of limiting BIND so that it's useful only to the computer on which it runs. If you want to run a server for a network, these lines must be removed.

Modifying Zone Files

A DNS zone is a collection of related computers whose name/IP address mappings are managed by an authoritative server. In some cases, zones are more-or-less synonymous with domains. In other cases, though, they aren't, as described later in "Creating and Maintaining DNS Zones."

For a caching-only name server, chances are you'll make few or no zone file modifications. A forwarding-only server doesn't require zone file maintenance. If your system performs full recursive lookups, though, you must include a `zone "."` section for the DNS root zone, as shown in Listing 6.1. Chances are the default configuration provided by your distribution will work. You might, however, need to adjust it in some situations. The `file` line in the zone section refers to a file in the directory specified by the `directory` line in the `options` section—normally /var/named. This *zone file* defines the computers in a zone, as described in the upcoming section "Creating and Maintaining DNS Zones." You don't create or maintain the root zone, though; that's done by others. Nonetheless, your server must know the IP addresses of the root servers in order to perform a full recursive lookup. Thus, the root zone file must be kept up-to-date. Fortunately, the IP addresses of the root zone servers change rarely, so you won't need to update this file often.

If the root servers ever change, your existing configuration might not work. You can retrieve the current root zone file in various ways. One is to type the following command:

```
$ dig @a.root-servers.net . ns > db.cache
```

Alternatively, you can download `db.cache` from `ftp://ftp.internic.net/domain/`. (Note that this is an FTP site, not a Web site.) Once you've retrieved the latest zone file, you can replace the old one (`named.ca` in the preceding example; the filename you retrieve may not match what's used on your system) with the new file.

Updating from Older BIND Versions

BIND versions 8 and 9 both use more or less the same configuration file format, so you should have few problems if you encounter a system that runs BIND 8 but you need to update it to BIND 9.

If you happen to encounter a configuration file for the still older BIND 4, however, you'll have some challenges. (BIND numbering skipped from BIND 4 to BIND 8.) BIND 4 used the `/etc/named.boot` configuration file, which used a different syntax from that for BIND 8 and 9's `/etc/named.conf`. Most notably, in BIND 4 you can specify forwarding systems using a single punctuation-free line and forwarding options on another line:

```
forwarders 10.9.16.30 10.13.16.30
options forward-only
```

Omitting the `options` line but keeping the `forwarders` line implements a configuration similar to a BIND 9 `forward first` configuration. Omitting both these lines creates a full recursive lookup configuration.

Checking Changes

You can use standard SysV or Upstart utilities to start, restart, or reload your BIND configuration. Typically, the SysV keyword `reload` will be sufficient if you've made changes to an already-running server:

```
# /etc/init.d/named reload
```

This option causes BIND to reread its configuration and zone files and implement any changes it finds without discarding its cache or disrupting service. The `restart` option is more aggressive; it causes the server to shut down and start up again using the new configuration.

You can also pass the BIND server (which is typically called `named`) a `SIGHUP` signal to force it to reload its configuration files:

```
# killall -s SIGHUP named
```

You can, of course, locate the server's PID number and use `kill` instead:

```
# ps ax | grep named
2313 ?          Ssl     0:00 /usr/sbin/named -u named
2490 pts/0      R+      0:00 grep named
# kill -s SIGHUP 2313
```

Once it's running, you may control the named server using the rndc utility. You pass the utility any of several commands on the command line. For instance, typing **rndc reload** reloads the configuration files, **rndc stop** terminates the server, **rndc flush** flushes the server's caches, and **rndc status** displays the server's status information. Typing **rndc** alone presents a complete list of the commands it accepts.

Once you've implemented your changes, you can use tools such as host and dig to ascertain whether your server is working. Both programs are described briefly in Chapter 5, and dig is described in more detail later in this chapter in "Testing Your Configuration." Basic functionality can be tested by performing host lookups, specifying your server's IP address as the server to use:

```
$ host www.whitehouse.gov 192.168.1.8
Using domain server:
Name: 192.168.1.8
Address: 192.168.1.8#53
Aliases:

www.whitehouse.gov is an alias for www.whitehouse.gov.edgesuite.net.
www.whitehouse.gov.edgesuite.net is an alias for a1128.h.akamai.net.
a1128.h.akamai.net has address 72.215.224.35
a1128.h.akamai.net has address 72.215.224.75
```

This example illustrates a successful lookup using the server on 192.168.1.8. If you encounter error messages, it could be that your server's configuration is incorrect. You can try again, omitting the server's IP address or substituting another server's IP address, to compare the results. If necessary, review your configuration. You can also check /var/log/ messages after you reload or restart the server; this file may provide hints about what's not working in your configuration.

Creating and Maintaining DNS Zones

If your DNS server needs to be authoritative for any zones, you must configure your zone files. This task entails both adding new zone definitions to /etc/named.conf and creating a file defining each new zone. You must also test your configuration.

You can run an authoritative server either on the Internet at large or on a private network. In the latter case, your DNS server will be contacted only by local computers to handle name resolution on your own network.

Adding New Zones

A default /etc/named.conf file usually includes one or more zone file references, such as the one to the root zone presented earlier. These references begin with the keyword zone, include the name of the domain to be managed, and link to a zone file in another directory (normally /var/named).

To have your system deliver IP addresses for local computers, you must create both forward and reverse zone files (as described shortly) and point your main named.conf file to your new definitions. Modifying named.conf is fairly straightforward; your changes will look something like this:

```
zone "pangaea.edu" {
    type master;
    file "named.pangaea.edu";
};
zone "1.168.192.in-addr.arpa" {
    type master;
    file "named.192.168.1";
};
```

The first four lines point BIND to the *forward zone* file, which enables the server to return IP addresses when it's fed hostnames. The final four lines point BIND to the *reverse zone* file, which enables the server to return hostnames when it's fed IP addresses. Both definitions should include the type master option and specify a file (normally in /var/named) in which the definition will be created. (You can also specify other types, as in type slave. Slave DNS configurations are described later in "Running a Slave Server.") The forward zone is named after the domain name it defines—pangaea.edu in this example. The reverse zone is named after the IP address block it serves but with a couple of twists. First, the .in-addr.arpa string is added to the end of the IP address range. Second, the IP address range's numbers are reversed. For instance, if you're defining a reverse zone file for 192.168.1.0/24, you'd take the network portion of the address (192.168.1), reverse its numbers (1.168.192), and add .in-addr.arpa, resulting in 1.168.192.in-addr.arpa.

It's possible for a DNS server to be authoritative for a network's forward lookups but not for its reverse lookups, or vice versa. For instance, your DNS server might handle your own domain, but that domain could be a small network on an IP address block leased from a broadband ISP. In such a case, the broadband ISP might provide the reverse DNS lookup itself. If this is the case, you won't have to configure the reverse zone, but you will have to coordinate with your ISP to provide valid reverse DNS lookups from their DNS server.

Configuring Zone Files

Zone files are typically located in the /var/named directory, but this location is set in the /etc/named.conf file via the directory setting in the options section (see Listing 6.1). The names of the zone files are set via the file option in the relevant zone section, as just described. It's generally best to begin a new zone file by using an existing one as a template. The following pages present examples of both forward and reverse zone files, so you can use those as templates if necessary.

Configuring Forward Zones

A forward zone file creates the mapping of hostnames to IP addresses. Listing 6.2 shows an example. This file might be the named.pangaea.edu file referenced earlier.

Listing 6.2: Sample forward zone configuration file

```
$TTL 1D
pangaea.edu.        IN  SOA  dns1.pangaea.edu. admin.pangaea.edu. (
                    2011022003 ; serial
                    3600       ; refresh
                    600        ; retry
                    604800     ; expire
                    86400      ; default_ttl
                        )
dns1.pangaea.edu.          IN A     192.168.1.1
coelophysis.pangaea.edu.   IN A     192.168.1.2
peteinosaurus              IN A     192.168.1.3
                           IN A     192.168.1.4
pangaea.edu.               IN A     192.168.1.5
dns1.wegener.pangaea.edu.  IN A     172.24.25.2
www                        IN CNAME webhosting.example.com.
ftp                        IN CNAME plateosaurus
@                          IN MX    10 peteinosaurus
@                          IN MX    20 mail.example.com.
@                          IN NS    dns1.pangaea.edu.
wegener                    IN NS    dns1.wegener.pangaea.edu.
```

Most of the lines in a zone configuration file take the following form:

name IN *record-type record-contents*

The *name* is the name of the computer (or a name derived from the computer's address, in the case of reverse zone configuration files, as described shortly). You should pay careful attention to the trailing dot (.) in the fully qualified domain names (FQDNs) in Listing 6.2—the names that include both machine name and domain name portions. Technically, all DNS hostnames end in dots, although they can usually be omitted when you're using Web browsers, email clients, and most other tools. In the case of a zone file, though, the dots are mandatory when you specify a complete hostname. When a name does *not* end in a dot, BIND adds the current zone name—pangaea.edu. in the case of Listing 6.2. Thus, you can specify hostnames either completely (as in coelophysis.pangaea.edu.) or by host portion only (as in peteinosaurus). If you omit a name completely (as in 192.168.1.4 in Listing 6.2), the previous hostname (peteinosaurus in Listing 6.2) is linked to both IP addresses (192.168.1.3 and 192.168.1.4 in Listing 6.2). The DNS server delivers all the IP addresses that are so linked in a round-robin fashion. This can be used as a crude form of load balancing, enabling two server computers to share a load that neither alone could handle. The at-sign (@) is a stand-in for the domain itself; it's commonly used with NS and MX records, as shown in Listing 6.2.

Following the hostname comes the string IN, which stands for *Internet*. Next is a code for the resource record (RR) type. Several RR types are common and important:

A   An address (A) record links a hostname to an IPv4 address. You may specify the hostname as an FQDN or as a hostname without its domain portion, as described earlier. You may also assign an IP address to the domain name alone (as in pangaea.edu. in Listing 6.2).

AAAA   These records are the IPv6 equivalent of A records.

CNAME   A canonical name (CNAME) record links a hostname to another hostname. You may specify the *record-contents* either as a "bare" machine name or as an FQDN. In the latter case, the target system need not be in the same domain as the one specified by the SOA record. For instance, in Listing 6.2, www links to an outside system. You can create multiple records for the same CNAME, each linking to another computer, as a crude form of load balancing.

NS   A name server (NS) record provides the hostname of a DNS server for the domain. This record is used mainly by other DNS servers that are directed to yours by other systems when your DNS server functions on the Internet at large. NS records, like CNAME records, can point outside your own domain. An NS record can refer to a server for the main domain or for a subdomain if you provide the subdomain name, as in the case of the wegener.pangaea.edu. subdomain in Listing 6.2. This configuration *delegates* control of the subdomain to another server—dns1.wegener.pangaea.edu. in this example. One wrinkle of this configuration is that the delegated domain's DNS server computer's name must be known. To fulfill this requirement, this server has an A record in the parent domain, as in Listing 6.2.

MX   A mail exchanger (MX) record points to a mail server for the domain. Remote mail servers access this record to learn how to deliver mail that's addressed to your domain. The *record-contents* of these records includes both a priority code (10 or 20 in Listing 6.2) and a computer name. As with CNAME and NS records, MX records can point to systems in other domains. The mail server must be configured to accept mail for the domain, though.

PTR   Pointer (PTR) records are the opposite of A records; they link IP addresses to hostnames. As such, they don't exist in Listing 6.2. The upcoming section "Configuring Reverse Zones" covers this type of record in more detail.

SOA   The start of authority (SOA) record is the first one in Listing 6.2. This type of record is complex enough that I describe it in more detail shortly.

TXT   This record type enables you to set explanatory text associated with the domain.

Most BIND packages for Linux include one or more forward zone files, such as one for the localhost name and perhaps a rudimentary file (called named.empty or something similar) that you can use as a model for your own domain. You may also use Listing 6.2 as a model.

The SOA record is particularly complex. It provides various administrative details for the zone. The *name* is the domain name for the record, and this name is used as the default whenever a machine name without a trailing dot (.) appears in subsequent records. An at-sign (@) can function as a stand-in for the domain name; in that case, the zone name specified in the /etc/named.conf file is used instead.

The *record-contents* field of an SOA record is itself quite complex. It includes the primary name server (which should also have its own NS record), the email address of the domain's administrator but with a dot (.) instead of an at-sign (@; admin@pangaea .edu would be the email for Listing 6.2), and a set of numbers within parentheses. These numbers are:

Serial Number   This number is particularly important on networks that employ both master and slave DNS servers. Slave servers examine this value in zone files to determine whether to update their local versions of the zone file. If the serial number doesn't change, the slave server won't update its local file. This fact can cause confusion because if you forget to update your serial number, changes to your zone file may not propagate properly. You can use any system you like for creating serial numbers. Listing 6.2 uses a date with an appended revision number—2011022003 refers to the third change (03) on February 20, 2011. A simple incrementing number will work, too (1, then 2, then 3, and so on). Be sure your numbers increment in a strictly linear way—if you use the date, be sure to use *YYYYMMDD* format.

Refresh Time   This value tells slave servers how often to check back with the master server to update its records. The upcoming section "Running a Slave Server" describes slave server configuration.

Retry Time   This value tells slave servers how often to retry a connection to the master server in the event of a failure.

Expire Time   This value tells slaves how long to keep delivering data if the slave can't connect to the master server.

Minimum TTL   If a DNS client asks for information on a subdomain that doesn't exist, the server responds with a particular code (referred to as NXDOMAIN). This value tells clients how long to cache this response.

Times are specified in seconds, although you may append M, H, D, or W to specify times in minutes, hours, days, or weeks, respectively. Cache times for working domains are usually set in the range of hours to days; however, when testing a configuration, you might want to set cache times of just a minute or two. You might also want to lower the cache times on a working domain a few days prior to making major changes to your domain so that clients won't be delivering outdated information after you make your changes.

The $TTL 1D line in Listing 6.2 sets the time-to-live value for most responses. This is similar to the minimum TTL value in the SOA record, but it applies to most data delivered by the server. This option appeared in BIND 8.2 and became mandatory with BIND 9.

Configuring Reverse Zones

The utility of forward DNS lookups is obvious, but sometimes it's necessary to do the opposite: to find a hostname when given an IP address. This reverse lookup enables servers to record hostnames, rather than IP addresses, in log files. It's also used by tools such as traceroute to display routers' hostnames. In some cases, a reverse lookup can serve as a simple identity test: If a reverse lookup on the IP address followed by a forward lookup on the resulting hostname doesn't produce the client's IP address, then there's some suspicion about the client's identity. (Such problems can result from misconfiguration, though, not just from nefarious intent.) Similarly, some protocols, such as the Simple Mail Transfer Protocol (SMTP) embed hostnames in the transfers; if those don't match the reverse lookup on the client's IP address, then there's cause for suspicion. For all of these reasons, DNS supports reverse lookups.

Reverse zone files are conceptually similar to forward zone files; however, they use PTR records rather than A records, and they map IP addresses to hostnames using hostnames in the in-addr.arpa domain (or ip6.arpa in the case of IPv6 addresses) to hostnames. Reverse zone files also often lack some common features of forward zone files, such as MX listings. Listing 6.3 presents an example of a reverse DNS zone file. This listing might be used in conjunction with Listing 10.3.

Listing 6.3: Sample reverse zone configuration file

```
$TTL 1D
1.168.192.in-addr.arpa.    IN  SOA  dns1.pangaea.edu. admin.pangaea.edu. (
                2010022003 ; serial
                3600       ; refresh
                600        ; retry
                604800     ; expire
                86400      ; default_ttl
                    )
1.1.168.192.in-addr.arpa.  IN PTR    dns1.pangaea.edu.
2                          IN PTR    coelophysis.pangaea.edu.
3                          IN PTR    peteinosaurus.pangaea.edu.
4                          IN PTR    plateosaurus.pangaea.edu.
5                          IN PTR    pangaea.edu.
@                          IN NS     dns1.pangaea.edu.
```

The hostnames in reverse zone files (in the *name* fields of the files' entries) are based on the computers' IP addresses, as described earlier in "Adding New Zones." Listing 6.3 provides listings for the 192.168.1.0/24 domain, so its SOA field specifies 1.168.192.in-addr.arpa. as the domain name. As with forward entries, the *name* field may present either a complete hostname, including a trailing dot (.), or just the part of the hostname that comes to the left of the domain portion of the name. The latter is normally the final one to three numbers in the IP address but in reverse order. The domain name in PTR records ends in either in-addr.arpa (for IPv4 addresses) or ip6.arpa (for IPv6 addresses).

The *record-contents* portion of a reverse zone file's entries consists of DNS hostnames, complete with the domain portion and trailing dot (.), as illustrated in Listing 6.3. If you omit the DNS hostname, the record will be misinterpreted as being part of the domain defined by the reverse zone file—1.168.192.in-addr.arpa, in the case of Listing 6.3.

Testing Your Configuration

With the /etc/named.conf file and all the zone files configured, you can launch your DNS server or tell it to reread its configuration files. You normally do this via its SysV or Upstart startup script, as described in Chapter 1, "System Startup and Advanced System Management." This will launch the BIND server, which is normally called named. You may want to check your system log files at this point; it's not uncommon for a misconfiguration to cause the DNS server to fail to start or to misbehave in some other way. Such problems often leave traces in log files. If the server seems to be running, you can check its operation using host or dig, as described in Chapter 5 and in more detail shortly. The nslookup utility may also be used for this purpose. Be sure to test the system using the server computer itself, another computer on the local network that's configured to use your DNS server directly, and (if applicable) a remote system. Remote computers, though, may not immediately use your DNS server, since it can take minutes, hours, or sometimes even days for DNS changes to propagate through the entire DNS network.

Using *host*

Basic use of host, as described in Chapter 5, can reveal the A, CNAME, and PTR records on a server, as in these examples:

```
$ host coelophysis.pangaea.edu 192.168.1.1
Using domain server:
Name: 192.168.1.1
Address: 192.168.1.1#53
Aliases:

coelophysis.pangaea.edu has address 192.168.1.2
$ host www.pangaea.edu 192.168.1.1
Using domain server:
Name: 192.168.1.1
Address: 192.168.1.1#53
Aliases:
```

```
www.pangaea.edu is an alias for webhosting.example.com.
webhosting.example.com is an alias for example.com.
example.com has address 10.210.120.45
example.com mail is handled by 0 example.com.
$ host 192.168.1.2 192.168.1.1
Using domain server:
Name: 192.168.1.1
Address: 192.168.1.1#53
Aliases:

2.1.168.192.in-addr.arpa domain name pointer coelophysis.pangaea.edu.
```

The first two forward lookups take exactly the same form, and of course without foreknowledge of the zone's configuration, you can't know whether you'll get an A record reply (as in coelophysis.pangaea.edu) or a CNAME record reply (as in www.pangaea.edu). These example outputs reveal a domain configuration that is working correctly, for both forward and reverse lookups, at least for the tested hostnames and addresses; each query returns the expected results, as defined in Listings 6.2 and 6.3. (The ultimate IP address associated with webhosting.example.com is not specified in Listing 6.2, however, since this server is in a different domain from the one defined by that zone file.)

Table 6.1 summarizes additional host options. You must provide a hostname or IP address, but the server's hostname or IP address is optional. (The utility uses the computer's default name server if you omit the server's address.) Many of these options can be used to determine whether your name server is functioning correctly; for instance, you can use -t to check for specific record types, and you can use -l to verify that a server can deliver a zone file to its slaves. Table 6.1 is not complete; a few more options relate to highly specialized setups or IPv6 options. Consult the program's man page for details.

TABLE 6.1   Common host options

Option	Description
-C	Displays the SOA record for a domain.
-d or -v	Produces verbose output with additional information.
-l	Performs a zone transfer for a zone; useful only if the system you're using is authorized for such a transfer.
-N *num_dots*	Sets the number of dots in the name required for it to be considered implicitly absolute (with a trailing dot); if a name has fewer dots, it's searched in the domains listed in search or domain directives in /etc/resolv.conf.
-R *num_retries*	Sets the number of retries to be attempted.

TABLE 6.1   Common host options *(continued)*

Option	Description
-r	Performs a non-recursive query; the server will respond as it would to another name server.
-T	Performs a query using TCP rather than UDP.
-t *type*	Requests data on the specific record *type*, such as SOA, CNAME, PTR, and so on.
-W *seconds*	Waits the specified time for a reply before timing out.
-w	Waits forever; queries never time out.
-s	Causes host to *not* query another name server if the first one responds with a SERVFAIL message.
-a	Equivalent to using -v and -t ALL.
-4	Performs IPv4 lookups only.
-6	Performs IPv6 lookups only.

Using *nslookup*

The nslookup utility has been deprecated, meaning that it's no longer officially supported and may be removed from distributions at any time. It's conceptually similar to host, but its syntax is different and it includes an interactive mode. In its most basic use, nslookup can work much like host:

```
$ nslookup coelophysis.pangaea.edu 192.168.1.1
Server:        192.168.1.1
Address:       192.168.1.1#53

Name: coelophysis.pangaea.edu
Address: 192.168.1.2
```

Options, which are summarized in Table 6.2, may be preceded by a dash (-) on the command line or entered using the keyword set in interactive mode, as in set debug to activate debugging mode. Many of these option names may be preceded by no to reverse their meaning, as in nodebug to deactivate debugging mode. (Options that take arguments are exceptions to this rule.) Unless otherwise stated, the options specified in Table 6.2 are the defaults; you should precede these names by no to change the program's behavior.

TABLE 6.2 Common nslookup options

Option	Description
debug	Displays timeouts and additional debugging information. Debugging mode is disabled by default.
d2	Displays an additional layer of debugging information, above and beyond that displayed by debug. This option is disabled by default.
defname	Adds the default domain name if a name does not end in a dot (.).
search	Searches each of the domains specified by the search parameter in /etc/resolv.conf if a name does not end in a dot (.).
recurse	Asks the server to perform a recursive search, similar to the way most clients work. Using norecurse causes nslookup to act more like a DNS server doing its own recursive search.
vc	Performs queries using TCP. The default behavior is to use UDP.
ignoretc	Causes named to ignore truncated packets rather than retry the operation using TCP.
port=*num*	Changes the port number on which named queries the server.
querytype=*type*	Sets the type of the query (A, CNAME, and so on).
timeout=*seconds*	Sets the timeout period; if the server hasn't responded in the specified time, nslookup resends the query and doubles the timeout period.
retry=*num*	Specifies the number of tries before nslookup gives up on the query.
root=*root-server*	Sets the root server used for recursive lookups.
domain=*domain*	Sets the domain used in lookups when defname is set.
srchlist=*domains*	Sets one or more domains used in lookups when search is set.

Using *dig*

The dig utility, also briefly described in Chapter 5, provides greater flexibility than host, and so dig can be used to more thoroughly test a name server's configuration. Its basic syntax is:

```
dig [@server] [options] [name] [type] [queryopt...]
```

Table 6.3 summarizes common dig options. Some of these options are designed to enable dig to read lookup requests from a file, which can enable you to perform a series of tests with a single command. The *type* is the query type (A, MX, PTR, and so on), and *queryopt* is one of numerous options that fine-tunes the way the program performs its work. Consult dig's man page for details on the *queryopt*.

TABLE 6.3 Common dig options

Option	Description
-b *address*	Sets the address used to make a query. Useful mainly on hosts with multiple IP addresses.
-f *filename*	Performs batch queries, reading lookup requests from *filename*. Each line of this file should contain one query.
-p *port*	Accesses the specified *port* on the server rather than the default (53).
-t *type*	Sets the query type. Note that the -t string can often be omitted; however, it is necessary to avoid ambiguity in case of lookups of certain TLDs, which can be misinterpreted as dig option names.
-q *name*	Sets the host or domain name to be looked up. Normally, the -q portion may be omitted, but it's sometimes necessary to distinguish the name from other options.
-x *addr*	Performs a reverse lookup on the specified IP address.
-4	Performs only IPv4 lookups.
-6	Performs only IPv6 lookups.

The basic dig output on a simple query of a single computer tends to be rather verbose, as illustrated by this output (with interspersed explanations):

```
$ dig @192.168.1.1 coelophysis.pangaea.edu

; <<>> DiG 9.4.3-P3 <<>> @192.168.1.1 coelophysis.pangaea.edu
; (1 server found)
;; global options:  printcmd
```

These lines display the version of the dig program, repeat back the command, and summarize global options (printcmd in this example; this option is set by default).

```
;; Got answer:
;; ->>HEADER<<- opcode: QUERY, status: NOERROR, id: 4865
;; flags: qr rd ra; QUERY: 1, ANSWER: 1, AUTHORITY: 0, ADDITIONAL: 0
```

These lines provide technical details about the output. You can disable it by including the +nocomments option; however, this also disables several other comment headers.

```
;; QUESTION SECTION:
; coelophysis.pangaea.edu.          IN    A
```

This section summarizes the query—in this case, it's telling you that you searched for an A record corresponding to coelophysis.pangaea.edu. You can disable this output by using the +noquestion option.

```
;; ANSWER SECTION:
coelophysis.pangaea.edu.    15    IN    A    192.168.1.2
```

The answer to your query appears here. The output resembles the line that defines the computer in question in the DNS zone file. You can disable this output by using the +noanswer option, although this defeats the usual purpose for running dig.

```
;; AUTHORITY SECTION:
pangaea.edu.                27    IN    NS    dns1.pangaea.edu.
```

In addition to the main information requested (an A record, by default), dig returns information on the name servers that are authoritative for the domain. You might use this information to query these servers directly. You can disable this output by including the +noauthority option.

```
;; ADDITIONAL SECTION:
dns1.pangaea.edu.           27    IN    A    192.168.1.1
```

This section includes the IP addresses of the name servers listed in the authority section. You can disable this section by including the +noadditional option.

```
;; Query time: 114 msec
;; SERVER: 192.168.1.1#53(192.168.1.1)
;; WHEN: Fri Dec 17 12:38:39 2010
;; MSG SIZE  rcvd: 154
```

Finally, dig returns some statistics on the query itself, including the time it took, the server name, the date, and the size of the returned data packet. You can disable this information by including the +nostats option.

If a query doesn't return a section you're interested in, you might be able to get it to appear by including the option used to disable it but minus the no part—for instance +additional to make the additional section appear. As noted earlier, you can specify the query type to obtain special record types—MX for a domain's MX records, for instance.

Running a Slave Server

Many sites run multiple DNS servers. This practice helps spread the load and provides redundancy—if one server goes down, the other can still handle the critical task of managing name resolution. If the two servers are connected to the Internet via different routes, the domain's name resolution can continue to function even if one route goes down entirely.

The problem with running multiple DNS servers is keeping them synchronized—it's a nuisance, at best, to have to reconfigure zone files on multiple servers. Therefore, the DNS protocols provide a way to handle this task automatically. One server, known as the *master*, holds the zone files that you edit whenever you need to make changes. One or more additional servers, known as *slaves*, periodically check with the master and transfer the master's zone files, should that be necessary. To implement this configuration, you must configure the slave server. You may also need to tweak the configuration to improve the security of your DNS servers.

Configuring a Slave Server

To configure a slave server, you set up its /etc/named.conf file much like a master server; however, you change the zone section to identify it as a slave:

```
zone "pangaea.edu" {
        type slave;
        file "named.pangaea.edu";
        masters { 192.168.1.1; }
};
```

This configuration tells BIND that it's to function as a slave server for the pangaea.edu zone and that it's to retrieve the zone file from 192.168.1.1. You can specify several servers, separated by semicolons (;), to which the slave will synchronize; in fact, one slave can synchronize against another (the masters keyword is still used in this case). The zone file will be retrieved and placed in the directory specified by the directory directive (see Listing 6.1).

If the server is to function as a slave for multiple zones, you must include separate zone definitions for each zone. Each zone can synchronize against a different master.

If you administer your own reverse DNS zones, remember to include them in your slave configuration. You should *not*, however, set up a slave configuration for the DNS root zones or for localhost reverse lookups (which are usually included in default BIND configurations).

A BIND server may function as a master for some zones and a slave for others. This type of configuration is sometimes employed by small sites that agree to serve as slaves for each others' domains. Such arrangements can satisfy the need to have two or more DNS servers for a domain, with the added benefit of placing the DNS servers on different networks for improved reliability.

Securing Zone Transfers

Security is an issue for DNS zone transfers. Suppose a master server accepts zone transfer requests from any computer. A would-be attacker could then request such a transfer and obtain the hostnames and IP addresses of all the computers in the zone. This information could make the attacker's job easier, or it might be used in other nefarious endeavors, such as social engineering attacks—the miscreant could call somebody in your organization and claim to need information on the network. Knowledge of the computer names could help trick the victim into believing the attacker.

For this reason, BIND provides the `allow-transfers` directive, which was used in Listing 6.1 to deny all zone transfers:

```
allow-transfer {"none";};
```

If you want your DNS server to transfer data to slaves, you can change this option to something less restrictive by specifying the IP addresses to which the server will deliver its zone files:

```
allow-transfer {192.168.23.1; 172.24.21.1;);
```

This configuration allows the specified computers to retrieve zone files. You can include this directive in a `zone` section, in which case it applies only to that zone and overrides the global setting.

Restricting zone transfers in this way is a good policy; however, for still better security, you can employ DNS Security Extensions (DNSSEC). This technology defends against DNS *cache poisoning*, in which fake data can be inserted into a DNS server's cache of other domains' IP addresses. Using cache poisoning, a miscreant can redirect traffic intended for one domain to another one, enabling the attacker to impersonate a Web merchant, bank, or other site that users trust with sensitive data.

To create a zone configuration using DNSSEC, you must first change into the directory in which the original zone files exist (typically /var/named). You can then generate a key and sign your zone files with that key. The key generation is accomplished with the `dnssec-keygen` command, as in:

```
$ dnssec-keygen -a RSASHA1 -b 768 -n ZONE pangaea.edu.
```

This command generates two files, Kpangaea.edu.+005+*nnnnn*.key and Kpangaea .edu.+005+*nnnnn*.private, where *nnnnn* is a numerical value. The first file is a public key that can (and must) be distributed to other servers, while the second file is a private key file that's used to sign your zone files using the `dnssec-signzone` program:

```
$ dnssec-signzone -o pangaea.edu named.pangaea.edu ↵
Kpangaea.edu.+005+nnnnn.private
```

The output is a single file, called zone.pangaea.edu.signed, based on the original named.pangaea.edu zone file. You should use this file as the zone file for the domain, rather than the original zone file.

Making Additional Security Improvements

A couple of miscellaneous security features deserve attention. These are running BIND in a *chroot jail*, which can help keep a buggy or compromised server from damaging the rest of your system, and using a *split DNS* configuration, in which DNS resolution can vary depending on the client's location in the network.

Running BIND in a Jail

A security feature that's often employed with BIND is to run it in a chroot jail. The chroot command's name stands for *change root*, and the idea is to run the program so that it believes the computer's root directory (/) is something other than what the root directory really is. The result is that the server can only access files in this alternate directory tree, reducing the risk that a compromised server can be used to modify files that aren't related to the server itself.

 Some distributions ship with BIND startup scripts that automatically or optionally run the server in a chroot jail. If you're using such a distribution, you should consult its documentation; chances are you can run the server in a chroot jail with less effort than is described here.

To begin with this configuration, you should first ensure that a suitable account exists on your system. Check your /etc/passwd file for an entry for named. If one doesn't exist, create it. It should look something like this:

```
named:x:200:200:Nameserver:/chroot/named:/bin/false
```

The key point for this account is that it's specific to the named server and that it's a system account. User accounts should not be used; nor should the nobody account, which runs many other miscellaneous programs. Ensure that the user ID (UID) and group ID (GID) values are unique. The user directory (/chroot/named in this example) must exist; it will become the chroot jail environment. Finally, the default shell must be something that provides no access to the system—/bin/false is used in this example.

To prepare the chroot directory (such as /chroot/named), you must create several subdirectories and files that mirror part of the structure of the standard Linux filesystem, but within the jail directory. To begin, you should create the chroot environment, including the etc/namedb/slave and var/run subdirectories within it:

```
# mkdir -p /chroot/named
# cd /chroot/named
# mkdir -p dev etc/namedb/slave var/run
```

Note that you do *not* include leading slashes (/) in the final command's directory specifications, since you want to create these directories within the chroot environment. You must then copy a few configuration files to the new environment and adjust their ownership for the new account you've created:

```
# cp -p /etc/named.conf /chroot/named/etc/
# cp -a /var/named/* /chroot/named/etc/namedb/
# cp /etc/localtime /chroot/named/etc/
# chown -R named:named /chroot/named/etc/namedb/slave
# chown named:named /chroot/named/var/run
```

Finally, BIND uses the /dev/null and /dev/random device nodes, so you need to create duplicates of these nodes in the chroot environment and give them appropriate permissions:

```
# mknod /chroot/named/dev/null c 1 3
# mknod /chroot/named/dev/random c 1 8
# chmod 666 /chroot/named/dev/{null,random}
```

You must now modify the configuration file to launch named with the -t /chroot/named option; this will cause it to lock itself into its jail as soon as it's launched. You should be able to modify your SysV or Upstart startup scripts to perform this task.

Configuring Split DNS

A split DNS (also known as *split horizon* or *dual horizon* DNS) configuration is often used on networks with separate heavily protected and public sections. In some cases, both parts of the network use the same global IP address space, and the goal is to prevent information on the internal names and IP addresses from becoming widely known. In other cases, the internal network might be part of a private address space and might either have no direct connection to the Internet or be linked via a Network Address Translation (NAT) configuration.

In either case, a split DNS configuration involves setting up two DNS servers. One server, on the external network, is configured as a normal authoritative server for the domain. Despite its being an authoritative server, however, this system has information on the publicly-accessible computers only; its zone files omit the names and IP addresses of the computers on the private network.

WARNING   Delivering IP addresses from the reserved private address spaces on the Internet at large can have negative and confusing consequences. If a remote client happens to be behind a NAT firewall on *another* private network that uses the same address space as your own network, your hostnames will resolve into IP addresses that, to the remote client, are on the local network. This will be confusing at best.

The internal server's configuration will typically point to the external server as a forwarder, as described earlier in "Running a Caching-Only Name Server"; however, the internal server will *also* claim to be authoritative for the domain, or at least for whatever subdomains you use internally. Internal clients using the internal server will therefore be able to resolve regular Internet hostnames, and they will be able to resolve the names of those internal systems that aren't resolvable from outside.

Summary

DNS is one of the most fundamental protocols upon which the Internet is based, and Linux is an excellent platform for running DNS servers. One of the most popular and influential of these is BIND. This server can be configured as a caching-only server, in which the server is not authoritative for its own domains but only caches DNS accesses from your local network in order to improve performance. Adding to this role, BIND can become authoritative for one or more zones, meaning that other servers (as well as clients) refer to your server as the final arbiter of information on the zones for which it is authoritative.

If BIND (or any other DNS server) functions as an authoritative server for a domain, you must maintain the appropriate zone files. These files come in two varieties: forward and reverse. Forward zone files enable the server to deliver IP addresses when a client asks about names, while reverse zone files provide data about the opposite relationship.

Like any server, BIND poses security challenges, and special configurations can be used to reduce BIND's risks. One of the challenges relates to slave configuration; you can restrict BIND to deliver full zone data only to authorized slave computers. A second challenge is that of DNS cache poisoning, which can be countered by implementing DNSSEC encryption and authentication. Finally, you can minimize the risks posed by a compromised server by running it in a `chroot` jail.

Exam Essentials

Summarize the main BIND configuration files.   The `/etc/named.conf` file controls the overall BIND configuration. Typically, files in `/var/named` hold zone files; however, this location can be altered by changing the `directory` option in `/etc/named.conf`.

Describe methods of reloading altered zone files.   Most SysV startup scripts enable reloading zone files by passing the `reload` option. The `restart` option will also work but is more disruptive. The `rndc` utility can also be used for this function; typing **rndc reload** does the job. Passing the `SIGHUP` signal via `kill` or `killall` can also reload zone files.

Explain DNS forwarding options.   DNS forwarding refers to BIND's ability to query another DNS server as if BIND were an ordinary client program, rather than perform a full recursive lookup of its own. BIND may perform full recursive lookups (no forwarding), it may attempt to forward a query and then perform a full recursive lookup if that fails (`forward first`), or it may function as a forwarding server only (`forward only`).

Explain the difference between forward and reverse zones.   Forward zones enable a server to return IP addresses when fed hostnames; reverse zones enable a server to return hostnames when fed IP addresses. Both zone types are critical to normal functioning of the Internet, although any given server might not handle both forward and reverse zones for a given set of computers.

Summarize common zone file resource record types.   A records provide hostname-to-IPv4-address lookups, AAAA records provide hostname-to-IPv6-address lookups, MX records return mail server information for a domain, PTR records provide IP address to hostname lookups, CNAME records define hostname "aliases"—duplicate names for a computer, NS records point to a domain's name servers, TXT records provide miscellaneous information, and SOA records define the zone as a whole.

Describe three tools for performing DNS queries.   The host, nslookup, and dig utilities can all perform DNS queries. The host utility is commonly used to perform simple lookups, but it has some advanced features. The nslookup utility is deprecated but has some unique features that keep it in service, such as an interactive mode. The dig utility can perform more advanced DNS lookups.

Explain the function of a chroot jail.   A chroot jail can isolate a server from most of the computer's filesystem, minimizing the risk that a buggy or compromised server will be able to damage anything but its own configuration. BIND can be run in a chroot jail.

Describe the purpose of DNSSEC.   The DNS Security Extensions (DNSSEC) provides protocols designed to enhance the security of the worldwide DNS network as a whole. They employ cryptographic keys to reduce the risk of miscreants injecting forged data into servers' DNS caches, a practice that can enable the miscreants to impersonate sites they don't control.

Review Questions

1. A Linux system administrator types **rndc flush** at a `root` command prompt on a computer that's running a DNS server. What will be the effect?

    A. The DNS server program will restart.

    B. All the DNS server's zone files will be emptied.

    C. The DNS server's caches will be cleared.

    D. The DNS server computer will restart.

2. In which directory are DNS zone files typically stored on a system that runs the popular Linux DNS server, named?

    A. `/etc/dns`

    B. `/var/dns`

    C. `/etc/named`

    D. `/var/named`

3. Which of the following is an advantage of a forwarding-only DNS server configuration vs. a full recursive lookup configuration?

    A. A forwarding-only configuration will operate even if your ISP's DNS server becomes unresponsive.

    B. A forwarding-only configuration can cache DNS data for local access.

    C. A forwarding-only configuration eliminates the need for an ISP.

    D. A forwarding-only configuration is often faster than a full-recursive configuration.

4. What is the effect of the following line, found within the `options` section of a `/etc/named.conf` file?

    `directory "/home/sam/bind";`

    A. It tells BIND to look in the `/home/sam/bind` directory for its zone files.

    B. It guarantees that the user `sam` will be able to edit the BIND configuration.

    C. It configures BIND to run as the user `sam`, thus improving the server's security.

    D. It locks BIND in a `chroot` jail located at `/home/sam/bind`.

5. How can you use the `kill` command to cause BIND to reload its configuration files? Assume the server's PID is 2798.

    A. `kill 2798`

    B. `kill -9 2798`

    C. `kill -s SIGHUP 2798`

    D. `kill -s SIGTERM 2798`

6. What is the effect of the following /etc/named.conf lines?

```
listen-on port 53 { 127.0.0.1; };
listen-on-v6 port 53 { ::1; };
```

   A. The server can be accessed only from the computer on which it's running.

   B. The server will run using a firewall on port 53.

   C. The server will be available to remote computers via both IPv4 and IPv6.

   D. The server will be available to remote computers via IPv6 only.

7. Which of the following is a problem that a caching-only DNS server can help solve?

   A. Your ISP's DNS server is reliable but sluggish.

   B. You need to manage the hostnames of 150 computers.

   C. You need to provide a second DNS server for your domain.

   D. Your entire network connection frequently goes down.

8. What is the purpose of the following lines in /etc/named.conf?

```
zone "1.168.192.in-addr.arpa" {
    type master;
    file "named.192.168.1";
};
```

   A. It tells the DNS server to use the file named.192.168.1 to look up IP addresses for names in the in-addr.arpa domain.

   B. It tells the DNS server to use the file named.192.168.1 to look up hostnames when given IP addresses.

   C. It tells the DNS server to ignore ("zone out") requests in the 192.168.1.x IP address block.

   D. It tells the DNS server to retrieve the file named.192.168.1 from the master server for the domain in question.

9. Which of the following tools provides an interactive mode for performing DNS lookups?

   A. named

   B. nslookup

   C. dig

   D. host

10. Which of the following are legal record types in a DNS zone file? (Choose all that apply.)

   A. MX

   B. DNS

   C. ZF

   D. CNAME

11. Which of the following options is true of the following DNS zone file entry?

```
example.net.    IN  SOA  dns.pangaea.edu. fred.example.com. (
                7           ; serial
                3600        ; refresh
                600         ; retry
                604800      ; expire
                86400       ; default_ttl
                        )
```

A. The serial number (7) is invalid; this number must be a date-based code, such as 2011071101.

B. The primary DNS server entry (dns.pangaea.edu) is invalid; this server must exist within the main (example.net) domain.

C. You should send email to fred@example.com concerning any DNS-related problems with the example.net domain.

D. This domain has precisely two DNS servers: dns.pangaea.edu and fred.example.com.

12. You want to enable users to access the computer with the IP address of 192.168.17.198 as linus.example.com. What line would you place in the zone file for example.com to accomplish this task?

A. linus   IN A   192.168.17.198

B. linus   IN MX   192.168.17.198

C. 198   IN TXT linus.example.com.

D. 198   IN PTR linus.example.com.

13. What is the effect of the following two DNS zone file entries?

```
tycho.luna.edu.      IN A      192.168.23.5
www                  IN CNAME  tycho
```

A. The same computer (192.168.23.5) may be accessed as either tycho.luna.edu or www.tycho.luna.edu.

B. The same computer (192.168.23.5) may be accessed as either tycho.luna.edu or www.luna.edu.

C. Email sent to the www.luna.edu domain is delivered to tycho.luna.edu.

D. The server will fail to start, since a stray dot (.) appears at the end of the hostname tycho.luna.edu.

14. The zone file for the `luna.edu` domain includes the following line:

    ```
    imbrium     IN NS     dns1.imbrium.luna.edu.
    ```

    What other information must also appear in this zone file to make this line legal?

    A. A CNAME record for `dns1.imbrium.luna.edu.`

    B. An MX record for `imbrium.luna.edu.`

    C. A PTR record for `imbium.luna.edu.`

    D. An A record for `dns1.imbrium.luna.edu.`

15. What is the safest account to use for running BIND?

    A. The `nobody` account

    B. An ordinary login user account

    C. A server-specific system account

    D. The `root` account

16. Which of the following security problems does DNSSEC most directly address?

    A. Intruders on the server

    B. Unauthorized zone transfers

    C. Cache poisoning

    D. Social engineering

17. What is a characteristic of a split DNS configuration?

    A. Name resolution can be different for computers depending on their locations.

    B. Full recursive lookups occur only if a forwarding lookup fails.

    C. Hostname-to-IP address and IP address-to-hostname lookups occur on different servers.

    D. Hostnames can resolve to IP addresses, but not the other way around.

18. Which of the following is an advantage of running BIND in a `chroot` jail?

    A. BIND encrypts the transfer of data to and from all its clients.

    B. If BIND malfunctions or is compromised, it is less likely to damage other parts of the computer.

    C. BIND can authenticate itself to other servers, reducing the chances of cache poisoning.

    D. The server refuses to transfer complete zone files except to slaves on a short list.

19. What program must you run to create a key for DNSSEC purposes?

   A. keygen-dnssec

   B. genkey-dnssec

   C. dnssec-keygen

   D. dnssec-genkey

20. Assuming it's properly configured, what can you say about a BIND server that has the following line in its /etc/named.conf file?

`allow-transfer {10.23.98.102; 10.202.79.121;);`

   A. It's a slave that transfers data from two other computers.

   B. It's a master or slave that allows zone transfers to two other computers.

   C. It's a slave that transfers data to two other computers.

   D. It's a master that transfers data on two Ethernet interfaces.

Answers to Review Questions

1. C. The `rndc` program provides a control interface for the DNS server program, `named`. The `flush` option to `rndc` clears (flushes) the cache of recent DNS lookups, so option C is correct. None of the remaining options describes anything that `rndc` can do, although the `reload` option will cause `named` to reload its zone files, which is partway to option A.

2. D. The `/var/named` directory holds DNS zone files on a typical Linux DNS server that runs `named`. Options A, B, and C are all fictitious; these locations don't normally exist.

3. D. By pushing the full recursive lookup's activities to your (usually better-connected) ISP's DNS server, overall speed is usually improved by using a forwarding-only configuration, so option D is correct. Option A has it backward; by relying on your ISP's DNS server, a forwarding-only configuration ensures that DNS lookups will fail if your ISP's DNS server becomes unresponsive. Both forwarding-only and full recursive configurations can cache DNS data, so option B is incorrect. Neither type of configuration eliminates the need for an Internet service provider (ISP), so option C is incorrect.

4. A. The `directory` option tells BIND where to look for its zone files, so option A is correct. (This is, of course, a highly unusual location for BIND's zone files and is probably a poor choice for this location.) Option B is incorrect because the `/home/sam/bind` directory, and the files it contains, might or might not be owned, and therefore be editable, by `sam`. Although running BIND as a non-`root` user is a useful security option, a normal user account is normally not used for this purpose, and the specified line does not tell BIND to run as `sam`, making option C incorrect. This line does not lock BIND in a `chroot` jail, so option D is incorrect.

5. C. Passing a SIGHUP signal to BIND causes it to reread its configuration files, making option C correct. None of the other options passes a SIGHUP signal to the server, so they're all wrong.

6. A. These two lines tell the server to listen for connections only via the IPv4 and IPv6 `localhost` addresses, effectively limiting access to the local computer only, as option A describes. These options do not create a firewall on any port, so option B is incorrect. Options C and D are both incorrect because the lines ensure that remote computers will not be able to access the server, whether by IPv4 or IPv6.

7. A. A caching-only DNS server can help speed up DNS lookups by storing previous lookup requests for a period and optionally bypassing an ISP's DNS server to perform its own recursive lookups. Both features can help overcome the problem described in option A. Option B describes a problem that can be solved by a DNS server that's authoritative for one or more domains, not a caching-only server. Option C requires a second authoritative server, possibly configured as a slave, not a caching-only server. Although a caching-only server can work around a sluggish or unreliable ISP-provided DNS server, it won't help much if the entire network goes down, since real Internet accesses rely on protocols not cached by a DNS server, so option D is incorrect.

8. B. Zone file definitions in /etc/named.conf tell the DNS server where to look to find mappings of IP addresses to hostnames, or vice versa. The in-addr.arpa pseudo-domain is reserved for reverse DNS lookups—the server returns hostnames when given IP addresses. The file directive points the server to the file that holds the mappings. Thus, option B is correct. Option A is incorrect because reverse DNS lookups return hostnames, not IP addresses. A zone directive is not an instruction to ignore a domain or address block, contrary to option C. The type master line in the example tells the server that it is the master DNS server for this zone, not to retrieve a file from another master server, so option D is incorrect.

9. B. The nslookup tool, although deprecated, provides a flexible interactive mode. The BIND server's executable is called named; this is a DNS server, not a user DNS client. The dig utility can perform complex DNS lookup tasks, but it lacks an interactive mode. The host utility is generally considered the successor to nslookup, but it lacks an interactive mode.

10. A, D. Mail exchanger (MX) and canonical name (CNAME) records are common in forward zone files. There are no such thing as DNS and ZF records. Other common record types include Address (A), Name Server (NS), Pointer (PTR), and Start of Authority (SOA) records. (PTR records are used in reverse zone files.)

11. C. Option C is correct; an administrative contact email address is embedded in the SOA record, but with the at-sign (@) replaced by a dot (.). Option A is incorrect because the serial number need not be date-based, although date-based serial numbers are common. Option B is incorrect because the primary DNS server for a domain need not be part of the domain it serves. Option D is incorrect because the SOA record identifies only one DNS server; others may be specified via separate NS records.

12. A. The question is asking for an address (A) record entry for the forward zone file, and option A presents such an entry. Option B presents a valid mail exchanger (MX) record, but that's not what the question asked for. Option C presents a text (TXT) record that might appear in a reverse zone file, but it's a somewhat odd one. Option D presents a correct pointer (PTR) record for the reverse zone file, but that's not what the question asked for.

13. B. A canonical name (CNAME) record creates a sort of alias, enabling a second name to access a computer that already has a hostname. Option B correctly describes the effect of the CNAME record in this example, given the address (A) record that also appears in this example. The CNAME entry shown does *not* create a name of www.tycho.luna.edu, contrary to option A. Email delivery to a domain can be adjusted via an MX record, but the example includes no such record; and even if the second record were an MX record rather than a CNAME record, option C would not describe its effect. The dot at the end of tycho.luna.edu in the first entry identifies a complete hostname; either it's required or the domain name portion of the name must be omitted (as in www on the second line), contrary to option D.

14. D. The specific configuration is part of a domain delegation; `dns1.imbrium.luna`
`.edu` handles DNS lookups for the `imbrium` subdomain of `luna.edu`. For this line to be
meaningful, though, the `luna.edu` DNS server must have the IP address for `dns1.imbrium`
`.luna.edu`, and this requires an A record for that FQDN to appear in the `luna.edu` zone file,
as option D specifies. A CNAME record for this hostname would be useless, an MX record
for the subdomain is not required, and a PTR record for the subdomain makes no sense.

15. C. BIND is best run using a system account that's used only by BIND; thus, option C is
correct. Although the `nobody` account is low in privilege, many other programs use it,
making security breaches possible when using it. Ordinary login users should not run BIND,
for similar reasons. Running BIND as `root` is extremely dangerous, given `root`'s power.

16. C. DNSSEC provides a way for servers to authenticate themselves, thus reducing the
risk of cache poisoning, in which an attacker inserts false data into the DNS cache of
non-authoritative servers. Thus, option C is correct. DNSSEC doesn't directly prevent
intruders from breaking into the computer, so option A is incorrect. Zone transfers are
usually restricted by means of IP address restrictions on who may transfer zone data, not
by DNSSEC; thus, option B is incorrect. Social engineering is a technique in which an
attacker assumes a false identity or otherwise tricks a human being into giving up critical
information. DNSSEC does little or nothing to address social engineering attacks.

17. A. Option A correctly summarizes the meaning of a split DNS configuration. Option B
describes the effect of a forward-first policy on a name server configured to use forwarding, but
this is not called *split DNS*. Option C describes a common way for DNS to be organized,
but this system is not known as *split DNS*. Option D describes what happens if only forward
zones are defined but no matching reverse zone exists, but this is not called *split DNS*.

18. B. Option B correctly summarizes one of the advantages of running BIND (or any
server) in a `chroot` jail. Option B is essentially fictitious. Option C describes the action
of DNSSEC. Option D describes the effect of restricting zone file transfers using the
`allow-transfer` option.

19. B. Option B is the correct program; the other options are scramblings of this program's
name.

20. B. The `allow-transfer` option tells BIND which other computers may access its zone
files. Although masters typically transfer data to slaves, slaves can exchange data between
themselves, so this line could appear in either a master or a slave computer. Thus, option
B is correct. Option A is incorrect because slaves use the `masters` option, not `allow-
transfer`, to specify the computers from which they retrieve data. Although the computer
could be a slave, this isn't certain so option C is correct. Option D is incorrect because the
`listen-on` option, not the `allow-transfer` option, specifies the Ethernet ports on which
BIND listens.

The LPI 202 Exam (60 Weights)

PART II

Chapter

7

Advanced Network Configuration

THE FOLLOWING LINUX PROFESSIONAL INSTITUTE OBJECTIVES ARE COVERED IN THIS CHAPTER:

- ✓ **210.1 DHCP configuration (weight: 2)**
- ✓ **210.3 LDAP client usage (weight: 2)**
- ✓ **212.1 Configuring a router (weight: 3)**
- ✓ **212.3 Secure shell (weight: 4)**

Previous chapters have touched upon Linux's role as a network server platform; in fact, Chapter 6, "DNS Server Configuration," is devoted to one important network server package that Linux can run. This chapter begins an examination of other advanced networking tasks that Linux can perform. One of these, running Dynamic Host Configuration Protocol (DHCP) server software, is often paired with the Domain Name Service (DNS) role described in Chapter 6. The Lightweight Directory Access Protocol (LDAP) is a network-enabled tool for managing data, and Linux can access an LDAP server to manage its users, so that topic is next. As touched upon in Chapter 5, "Networking Configuration," Linux can function as a router, and this chapter expands on this topic by examining Linux router configuration in more detail. Finally, this chapter looks at the Secure Shell (SSH) server, which is a text-mode login protocol that includes encryption capabilities and the ability to tunnel other protocols.

Configuring a DHCP Server

Chapter 5 describes the use of DHCP to configure a Linux system's networking options. If you want to use DHCP in this way, consult that chapter. This section is devoted to the other side of the coin—configuring Linux to deliver IP addresses to other computers.

Before embarking on setting up a DHCP server, you should know when it is and is not appropriate to use one. If you've decided to use the server, you must know where to find it and how to install it. You can then set general network-wide options. You must also tell the server what IP addresses it can deliver. The easiest configuration is to deliver *dynamic* IP addresses, meaning that clients aren't guaranteed the same IP address time after time. If necessary, you can also configure your DHCP server to deliver *fixed* IP addresses, meaning that any given client receives the same IP address whenever it asks for one. (This contrasts with *static* assignment, which is done without DHCP. If a computer can function with either a truly static address or a fixed address assigned via DHCP, I use the term *fixed*. Be aware that these terms are not entirely standardized.) If your network spans multiple network segments, you may need to take extra steps to ensure that DHCP works on all those segments.

Small office and home networks often use broadband routers. These devices are small boxes that include simple Network Address Translation (NAT) routers, switches, and often additional functionality in small and easy-to-configure packages. These devices can usually function as DHCP servers. Using them for this purpose can result in easier DHCP administration than is possible with a Linux DHCP server. On the other hand, a Linux DHCP server is far more flexible than the DHCP servers that come with small broadband routers.

When to Use DHCP

Chapter 5's description of DHCP advised using that protocol for configuring computers' network settings if your network uses DHCP—that is, if a DHCP server is available. In turn, the question of whether to run a DHCP server is answered by whether you want to use DHCP to configure most of your computers' networking features. This logic is somewhat circular, though, and the way to break out of the cycle is to consider the network as a whole. Which is better, configuring each computer's IP address and related information individually or setting up an extra server to handle the job?

One of the considerations in determining DHCP's value is the amount of effort invested in administering systems. All other things being equal, the break-even point for setting up a DHCP server is somewhere between half a dozen and a dozen computers. Less than that number, it's generally simpler to use static IP addresses. More than that number, the effort invested in DHCP configuration is less than the extra effort of maintaining static IP addresses. Of course, other issues can intervene. Factors that tend to favor DHCP include ordinary users maintaining their computers' network settings, high turnover rates in computers or the OSs installed on them (such as networks with lots of laptops or OS reinstallations), the presence of multiboot systems, a network with odd or tricky configurations, and a network dominated by clients that don't need fixed IP addresses. Static IP address assignment is most useful when your network includes many servers that operate best on fixed IP addresses. Some factors can swing either way. For instance, consider a network with a diverse population of OSs. Maintaining such a system with static IP addresses can be tricky because you must know how to assign static IP addresses to each OS, including any quirks each OS has in this respect. DHCP can help simplify this configuration, although perhaps not dramatically—you must still know how to tell each OS to use DHCP, after all. On the downside, specific DHCP clients and servers may have interactive quirks, so you might run into problems configuring some of the more exotic OSs using DHCP. (In my experience, though, Linux's standard DHCP server works without problems with every client OS I've used.)

If your network includes some systems that must operate with fixed IP addresses and some that don't need fixed addresses, you have three choices. You can assign all IP addresses statically, you can assign some addresses via DHCP and assign others statically, or you can use DHCP for all computers and configure the DHCP server to provide fixed addresses to at least some clients. Mixing DHCP and static IP addresses isn't a problem; you must simply use a range of addresses for static IP addresses that DHCP won't try to assign. In fact, the DHCP server itself is likely to be assigned a static IP address.

Basic DHCP Installation

The main DHCP server package for Linux is written by the Internet Software Consortium (ISC; http://www.isc.org/software/dhcp). This server usually ships in a package called dhcp, dhcp-server, or dhcp3-server. (At press time, the latest DHCP server version is 4.2.0; however, most Linux distributions still ship with 3.*x* versions of the server.) ISC also makes available a DHCP client, dhcpcd, which ships with many Linux distributions. The client, though, doesn't have the dominant position in the Linux world that the ISC dhcpd server holds. Other DHCP clients, most notably dhclient, run on many systems. The ISC dhcpd server works with these non–ISC DHCP clients, as well as with DHCP clients on other OSs.

ISC's DHCP server is not the only one available. One notable alternative is Dnsmasq (http://freshmeat.net/projects/dnsmasq/), which combines DHCP and DNS functionality in one package. Dnsmasq isn't as full-featured as either the ISC DHCP server or the BIND DNS server described in Chapter 6; however, it is easier to configure and is a good choice for a small network with simple needs.

In addition to handling DHCP clients, the ISC DHCP server handles the older Bootstrap Protocol (BOOTP). No additional configuration is required to handle BOOTP, although some options are relevant only for DHCP.

Typically, a DHCP server has a static IP address itself. When it comes time to declare a range of IP addresses the server should deliver, you must be careful to exclude the server's own IP address from this range.

If you compile your own kernel, as described in Chapter 2, "Linux Kernel Configuration," you should be aware of one kernel feature required by the DHCP server: the Packet Socket option, which is accessible from the Networking Options submenu when configuring the kernel. This submenu is accessed from the Networking Support menu, as shown in Figure 7.1 for a 2.6.35.4 kernel.

FIGURE 7.1   You must enable certain kernel options to run a recent DHCP server

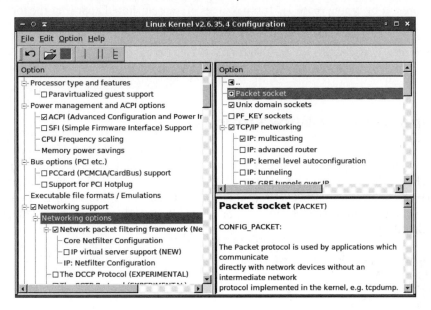

The DHCP server configuration file is dhcpd.conf, which is likely to be in /etc or /etc/dhcp3. This file can contain comments, denoted by a leading hash mark (#). Lines that aren't comments are either *parameters*, which describe general configuration features, or *declarations*, which describe the network's computers and the IP addresses the server can deliver to those computers. The upcoming section "Setting Network-Wide Options" describes parameters in more detail. The following two sections, "Configuring Delivery of Dynamic Addresses" and "Configuring Delivery of Fixed Addresses," describe declarations in more detail. Some declarations are fairly complex and include parameters within them. These declarations indicate their multiline nature by using curly braces ({ }) to surround the multiline material.

Some DHCP clients (particularly some Windows systems) require responses from the DHCP server to be addressed to 255.255.255.255. Unfortunately, Linux sometimes changes such replies to have a return address corresponding to your network's broadcast address, such as 172.27.255.255 for the 172.27.0.0/16 network. If some of your clients don't seem to pick up network configurations when you use DHCP, you can change the Linux server's behavior by adding an appropriate route for the 255.255.255.255 address:

```
# route add -host 255.255.255.255 dev eth0
```

Of course, you should adjust this command if the device isn't eth0. This problem is particularly likely to occur if your DHCP server has multiple network interfaces. Some DHCP configurations add this route by default. If yours doesn't, you can modify the DHCP startup script or add the command to a local startup script. You can verify whether this route is present by typing **route -n**. If the route is present, it should appear at the top of the output, as follows:

```
Destination     Gateway        Genmask          Flags Metric Ref    Use Iface
255.255.255.255 0.0.0.0        255.255.255.255 UH     0     0        0 eth0
```

Setting Network-Wide Options

Most DHCP configuration files begin with a series of parameters that set global options. Listing 7.1 shows a typical small dhcpd.conf file, including many of the global options you might use. Many, but not all, of these global options begin with the keyword option. Whether or not a parameter begins with this keyword, most are followed by a value. This value may be an IP address, a hostname, a number, a Boolean keyword (true or false), or some other data.

Listing 7.1: Sample dhcpd.conf file

```
default-lease-time 86400;
max-lease-time 172800;
option subnet-mask 255.255.255.0;
option routers 172.27.15.1;
option domain-name-servers 172.27.15.2,10.72.81.2;
option domain-name "example.com";
option netbios-name-servers 172.27.15.2;
option netbios-node-type 8;
get-lease-hostnames true;

subnet 172.27.15.0 netmask 255.255.255.0 {
    range 172.27.15.50 172.27.15.254;
}
```

Table 7.1 summarizes some of the more common global options you might want to set. Many of these options are demonstrated in Listing 7.1. All parameter lines end with semicolons (;). Some parameters take more than one value. For instance, the option domain-name-servers line in Listing 7.1 provides two IP addresses, separated by a comma. In most cases, you can substitute hostnames for IP addresses. Doing so puts your server at the mercy of the DNS server, though; if it goes down or is compromised, your DHCP server may be unable to provide the information, or it may provide incorrect information.

TABLE 7.1 Common global DHCP server parameters

Parameter	Value	Description
default-lease-time	Integer	Sets the default lease time in seconds. Clients may request a specific lease time that can override this value. Typical lease times are between a couple of hours and several days—tens or hundreds of thousands of seconds. Shorter lease times are in order if you're planning major network changes in the near future or if the network sees a lot of changes—for example, if laptop computers are being connected for an hour or two and then disconnected.
max-lease-time	Integer	Sets the maximum lease time, in seconds, the server will grant. If a client asks for a lease time longer than this value, the server grants a lease of this value. This value is ignored if the server is responding to a BOOTP request.
min-lease-time	Integer	Sets the minimum lease time, in seconds, the server will grant. If a client asks for a lease time shorter than this value, the server grants a lease of this value.
get-lease-hostnames	Boolean	If true, the server looks up the hostname associated with an IP address and returns that hostname to the client, which may use this value in setting its own hostname. By default or if this parameter is false, the server doesn't do this lookup.
use-host-decl-names	Boolean	If true, the server returns the hostname provided by the client as the client's assigned hostname.
ping-check	Boolean	If true, the server pings an address before assigning a lease on that address to a client. If the server receives a response, the server doesn't assign that address. This may be used to ensure that the server doesn't assign addresses that are already in use (say, by systems misconfigured with static IP addresses they should not be using). If the pinged system is also configured to ignore pings, this check won't work as intended.

TABLE 7.1 Common global DHCP server parameters *(continued)*

Parameter	Value	Description
`option subnet-mask`	Subnet mask (dotted quad format)	Sets the subnet mask to be assigned to clients.
`option routers`	IP addresses	The IP address or addresses for the subnet's router or routers.
`option domain-name-servers`	IP addresses	The IP address or addresses of DNS servers the clients may use.
`option domain-name`	Domain name	The name of the domain in which the clients reside.
`option netbios-name-servers`	IP addresses	The IP address or addresses of NetBIOS Name Service (NBNS) servers, aka Windows Internet Name Service (WINS) servers. These servers can be an important part of Server Message Block/Common Internet File System (SMB/CIFS) file sharing on Windows-dominated networks.
`option netbios-node-type`	Binary code	A code for how NetBIOS clients should attempt name resolution. Values are 1 to use broadcasts, 2 to use a WINS server, 4 to try broadcasts first followed by a WINS server, and 8 to try a WINS server first followed by a broadcast. The best option is 8 if you provide a WINS server with the `option netbios-name-servers` parameter and, of course, configure the specified system as a WINS server.

Table 7.1 is far from complete, but it describes the most common options. For information on more options, consult the `dhcp-options` and `dhcp-eval` man pages. Some of the options, such as the NetBIOS options in Table 7.1, set values that many DHCP clients ignore.

Notably absent from Table 7.1 is any method of setting the IP address that clients are to receive. This option does appear in Listing 7.1, though, as part of the **subnet** declaration. The next two sections cover options for assigning IP addresses in more detail.

Configuring Delivery of Dynamic Addresses

Listing 7.1 is adequate for assigning dynamic IP addresses to no more than 205 computers. The lines that accomplish this task are the final three lines of the listing:

```
subnet 172.27.15.0 netmask 255.255.255.0 {
   range 172.27.15.50 172.27.15.254;
}
```

These lines make up a declaration. In this case, the declaration applies to the 172.27.15.0/24 network, as defined on the first line of the declaration. The parameters that appear between the curly braces apply only to machines in that block of addresses. You can create multiple subnet declarations if you like, and in some cases you might need to do this. For instance, the server might have multiple network interfaces and need to assign different IP addresses to machines on different physical subnets. For a network with a single physical subnet, a declaration similar to the one in Listing 7.1 should work just fine. This declaration's second line, consisting of a range parameter, defines the IP address range that the server delivers: 172.27.15.50 to 172.27.15.254. When you boot a DHCP client computer, it might receive any address in this range, depending on which addresses the server has already assigned. If you have more computers than this range permits, then you should expand it (if possible) or create another subnet declaration that provides additional addresses. If you need significantly more than 205 addresses, expanding the declaration will probably require changing the netmask. For instance, using a netmask of 255.255.240.0 enables you to assign addresses ranging from 172.27.0.1 through 172.27.15.254. (You'd specify a subnet of 172.27.0.0 rather than 172.27.15.0 in this case.) Of course, you must have the right to use whatever addresses you pick.

> If possible, define a range that's substantially larger than the number of computers on your network. Doing so will give your network room to grow, and it will provide a buffer against addresses being claimed and not released, thereby consuming a lease unnecessarily.

Given the 172.27.15.0/24 network block, Listing 7.1's reservation of only 205 IP addresses means that the first 49 addresses are available for static assignment. Typically, at least one of these addresses will be assigned to the network's router (172.27.15.1 in Listing 7.1), and one will go to the DHCP server itself. Others might go to a name server, mail server, or other servers that are best run with static IP addresses. Alternatively, you can run some of these servers using DHCP and assign them fixed addresses, as described in the next section.

> An address with a machine portion, in binary, of all 0s or all 1s has special meaning in TCP/IP addressing. All-0 addresses refer to the network itself, and all-1 addresses are used for broadcasts. You should never attempt to assign such an address using DHCP, nor should you attempt to assign it statically for that matter.

Configuring Delivery of Fixed Addresses

If you want to run servers but configure them to acquire their IP addresses and other information via DHCP, you can do so. This practice normally requires that you do one of two things, though:

- Link your network's DHCP and DNS servers so that the DNS server delivers the correct IP address for a given hostname. This practice may be reasonably reliable on a local network, but it may not be reliable if your systems should be accessible from the outside world, because your DNS server's entries will be cached by clients' DNS servers. Clients may, therefore, end up using an out-of-date DNS entry. Even if you configure the DNS server with a short lifetime for these entries, some DNS servers may ignore this information, possibly resulting in mismatched hostnames and IP addresses. This configuration also requires making intricate changes to both the DHCP and DNS servers' configurations. For these reasons, I don't describe this approach in this book.

- Configure your DHCP server to assign an unchanging IP address to the server computers. This goal can be achieved in several ways. The method I describe in this section involves using the *Media Access Control (MAC) address*, aka the *hardware address*, of the DHCP client computer to identify that system and enable the DHCP server to assign a fixed IP address to that system each time it boots. This is also sometimes called a *reserved* address.

Locating the MAC Address

The first step in providing a fixed address, at least when using the MAC address approach described here, is to locate the DHCP client's MAC address. For Ethernet devices, this address is a 6-byte number that's usually expressed in hexadecimal (base 16), typically with colons, dashes, or some other punctuation separating bytes. You can locate the MAC address in several ways:

Hardware Stickers   Some network interface cards (NICs) have stickers affixed to them with MAC addresses. Similar stickers may exist on the external case of computers that ship with built-in Ethernet interfaces. Locating the MAC address in this way is straightforward if you haven't yet installed the NIC, but it may not be convenient if it's already buried inside a computer. Many NICs also lack this sticker.

Linux DHCP Clients   On a Linux client, you can type `ifconfig eth0` (changing eth0 to another interface name, if appropriate). This command produces information on the network interface, including the hardware address (labeled `HWaddr`) on the first line of the output. This command requires that the interface be activated, although it need not be assigned an IP address.

Windows DHCP Clients   Windows provides a tool similar to Linux's `ifconfig` for displaying information about the network interface. Type `IPCONFIG /ALL` in a Command Prompt window to learn about your interfaces. A line labeled `Physical Address` should reveal the MAC address.

Mac OS DHCP Clients   Mac OS X provides an `ifconfig` command that's similar to Linux's command of this name, although it's not identical. Nonetheless, you can open an OS X Terminal application and type `ifconfig`. The hardware address will probably appear in the section for en0 and will be labeled `ether`; however, this might not always be the case, particularly for WiFi hardware.

Using GUI Tools   Most modern OSs provide a way to find the hardware address via their GUI configuration tools. The exact method varies with the OS. As an example, in Windows 7, go to Control Panel ➢ Network And Internet ➢ Network And Sharing Center, and then click the name of your connection near the right side of the window. The result is a dialog box showing the status of a network connection. Click the Details button to obtain a Network Connection Details dialog box, similar to the one in Figure 7.2. The MAC address appears as the Physical Address line in this dialog box.

FIGURE 7.2   Most OSs provide GUI tools that can display a computer's hardware address

Locating the Address from the DHCP Server   No matter what OS the client uses, you can locate the MAC address from the DHCP server in several ways. One method is to configure the DHCP client to use DHCP and then activate its network interface. Assuming the server is configured to deliver addresses as described in the earlier section "Configuring Delivery of Dynamic Addresses," the DHCP client should pick up an address. You can then examine the DHCP server's logs for evidence of a lease granted for that address. The DHCP leases file (typically `/var/lib/dhcp/dhcpd.leases`) should include a multiline entry identifying the IP address and MAC address. Typing **grep dhcpd /var/log/messages | tail -n 1** or **grep dhcpd /var/log/daemon.log | tail -n 1** as root should also reveal an entry with the IP address and MAC address in question. (If some other DHCP activity occurs between the target system's lease being granted and you typing this command, though, that activity will show up instead. Increase the number from 1 to 2 or higher to reveal earlier entries.) Finally, you can type **ping -c 1 *ip.addr*; /sbin/arp *ip.addr***, where *ip.addr* is the IP address, to learn the MAC address of the computer. This last approach will also work if you temporarily configure the future DHCP client with a static IP address.

DHCP Server Fixed Address Options

Once you have the MAC address of a DHCP client, you can add an entry to the DHCP server's dhcpd.conf file for that client. This entry can go within the subnet declaration, as shown in Listing 7.1, or the entry can go after the subnet declaration. Either way, the entry looks like this:

```
host calvin.example.com {
    hardware ethernet 00:80:C6:F9:3B:BA;
    fixed-address 172.27.15.2;
}
```

The host declaration tells the server that you're defining parameters for a specific computer. Place the computer's hostname after the keyword host, and end the line with an open curly brace. Lines between this one and the closing curly brace that defines the end of the declaration apply only to this host.

The hardware parameter provides a means for the server to identify the host. This parameter is followed by a keyword for the hardware type (ethernet in this example, but token-ring is also valid) and the MAC address, using colons (:) to separate bytes of the address. The fixed-address line, of course, defines the IP address that's to be given to this host. Be sure that the address is not also specified in the range line for any subnet declaration!

Wireless clients are typically linked to a network by a wireless access point (WAP) or router and appear to be Ethernet devices from the DHCP server's point of view. Broadband routers invariably include their own DHCP servers, so you have a choice of using your broadband router's server or disabling it and configuring a Linux DHCP server.

After you add this entry and restart the server, it should begin delivering the fixed IP address you specify with the fixed-address parameter to that client. Of course, this will work only as long as the hardware address remains unchanged. If you replace a computer's NIC, you must update the hardware line to reflect the change.

Configuring a DHCP Relay Agent

If your network spans multiple network segments with routers in between the segments, you must make suitable adjustments to your DHCP configuration. Possibilities include:

Run Multiple DHCP Servers   You can run a different DHCP server on each subnet. Of course, this approach increases your configuration effort; however, it might be acceptable if you can rely on an easy-to-configure DHCP server, such as one built into a broadband router, for one of the network segments.

Run the DHCP Server on the Router   A DHCP server run on a router, or some other computer with interfaces on multiple networks, can serve all the networks to which the computer is connected. This solution can be fairly straightforward; however, you might not want to run a DHCP server on a router for security reasons.

Configure the Router to Route DHCP Broadcasts   Some routers provide options to relay DHCP requests from one subnet to another. Cisco's `ip-helper address` option, for instance, does this. Consult your router's documentation for information on this approach.

Run a DHCP Relay Agent   The ISC's DHCP server software includes a program, `dhcrelay` or `dhcrelay3`, that can relay DHCP broadcasts from one subnet to another one. This program must be installed on one computer on each subnet that does not have its own DHCP server computer. Note that the `dhcrelay` program does *not* need to run on a router or other computer connected to both networks.

The `dhcrelay` program may be included in the main DHCP package or in another one, such as `dhcp3-relay`. The most basic use of `dhcrelay` launches it using just the name or IP address of the DHCP server on a remote network:

```
# dhcrelay 172.27.15.2
```

The relay agent will then relay all the DHCP requests it receives to the specified name or IP address. You can fine-tune the software's behavior by using various options, such as `-i` *interface* to specify one or more interfaces on which to listen. (You must include both the interface on which DHCP clients exist and the interface with the DHCP server or the router to the DHCP server if the system has multiple interfaces.) Consult `dhcrelay`'s man page for more information on its options, most of which are highly technical.

In practice, you'll probably want to have `dhcrelay` start automatically. To do that, you must enter the DHCP server's name or IP address, along with any other options, in a distribution-specific configuration file. In Debian and Ubuntu, for instance, the file is `/etc/default/dhcp3-relay`, and you edit the SERVERS option to specify the DHCP server's address; on a Fedora system, the file is `/etc/sysconfig/dhcrelay`, and you edit the DHCPSERVERS option. Alternatively, you can create a suitable line in a local startup script.

Managing LDAP Accounts

You should already be familiar with the concepts of Linux accounts and account management using tools such as `useradd`, `usermod`, and `passwd`, along with files such as `/etc/passwd` and `/etc/shadow`. These concepts, tools, and files are all part of the LPIC-1 certification. Such configurations are adequate for Linux computers with few accounts or with accounts that aren't shared with other computers on a network. In many networked environments, though, it's desirable to give a large number of users accounts on a large number of Linux (or even non-Linux) computers. Managing such environments can quickly become a challenge; any change requires replication on all the computers, which can be a logistical nightmare. The solution to this problem is to deploy a network login protocol. Several such protocols exist, LDAP being one of them. The following pages describe some fundamental LDAP principles and common LDAP account management tools.

Completely configuring LDAP is not covered in the LPIC-2 objectives and is beyond the scope of this book. To completely configure LDAP, you must configure an LDAP server and adjust the configuration of every client that must use the LDAP server. A short (chapter-length) description of how to do this appears in my *Linux in a Windows World* (O'Reilly, 2005). You can find more thorough coverage of LDAP in LDAP-specific books, such as Matt Butcher's *Mastering OpenLDAP: Configuring, Securing, and Integrating Directory Services* (Packt, 2007).

What Does LDAP Do?

In a network authentication scheme, one computer holds a database of account information and other computers are configured as clients of that authentication server. (Backups of the authentication server can also exist in case the main server goes down.) When a user attempts to log in to a client, that computer sends the username and password (possibly encrypted) to the server, which then tells the client whether the user is authorized. The server can also provide additional information, such as the location of the user's home directory.

Several network authentication protocols exist. These include LDAP (described here), Kerberos, Windows NT domains, and Network Information Service (NIS). The Windows Active Directory (AD) system merges features of both LDAP and Kerberos.

LDAP is a *directory* system, which requires elaboration. In LDAP terms, a directory is not the same as a filesystem directory, although the two concepts are similar. An LDAP directory is essentially a database, but it's a database that's organized in a hierarchical fashion and that's designed to be read more often than it is written. Like filesystem directories, LDAP directories have a root (referred to as a *base* in LDAP parlance), and information is stored relative to that base. In the following pages, the meaning of the word *directory* should be clear by context whether it refers to a filesystem directory or an LDAP directory.

When using LDAP, user accounts must be managed in a different way than on a computer with a local account database. Several utilities, which are included with the popular OpenLDAP server (http://www.openldap.org), provide substitutes for Linux account maintenance tools such as useradd, userdel, and passwd.

Preparing a System to Use LDAP Tools

You may use the LDAP account maintenance tools on any computer that's properly configured as an LDAP client. To do this, you must install the OpenLDAP software, or at least its clients, and edit the /etc/openldap/ldap.conf file. This file specifies the base of the LDAP directory, the location of the LDAP server, and an encryption key if your LDAP server uses one:

```
BASE       dc=pangaea,dc=edu
URI        ldaps://ldap.pangaea.edu
TLS_CACERT /etc/openldap/ssl/certs/slapd-cert.crt
```

The BASE line specifies the base of the LDAP directory. It's normally derived from your Internet domain name (pangaea.edu in this example), but it can be something else. The URI line specifies the LDAP server's hostname, typically preceded by ldap:// or ldaps://, the latter denoting a server that employs encryption. If the LDAP server supports encryption, you should specify a certificate file with the TLS_CACERT line. (Alternatively, the TLS_CACERTDIR line specifies a directory in which a certificate can be found.) You must copy the certificate file from the LDAP server.

Working with LDIF Files

LDAP uses the LDAP Data Interchange Format (LDIF) as a way of transferring data, and a basic understanding of LDIF is necessary for LDAP account maintenance. An LDIF file consists of a series of attribute names and values, separated by colons. For account maintenance, these files must contain data equivalent to the entries in /etc/passwd and /etc/shadow. To maintain Linux group data, LDIF files with the equivalent of /etc/group must be available. Listings 7.2 and 7.3 show samples of password and group LDIF files, holding data on a single user and a single group, respectively.

Listing 7.2: Sample LDIF file holding user data

```
dn: uid=maryann,ou=People,dc=pangaea,dc=edu
uid: maryann
cn: maryann
objectClass: account
objectClass: posixAccount
objectClass: top
objectClass: shadowAccount
userPassword: {SSHA}dUR1zOPZslHC6AGhGxAhcIYHpa7lqRGn
shadowLastChange: 14262
shadowMax: 99999
shadowWarning: 7
loginShell: /bin/bash
gecos: Maryann
uidNumber: 1010
gidNumber: 100
homeDirectory: /home/maryann
```

> The uid value in Listing 7.2 corresponds to a Linux username; the Linux
> UID value appears on the uidNumber line.

Listing 7.3: Sample LDIF file holding group data

```
dn: cn=users,ou=Group,dc=pangaea,dc=edu
objectClass: posixGroup
objectClass: top
cn: users
userPassword: {crypt}x
gidNumber: 100
memberUid: maryann
```

To add or modify accounts or groups, you should have suitable LDIF files. (Alternatively, you can type the information directly, but it's usually easier to have the data in a file.) Each file can hold multiple entries, so you can add several users at once by creating a single file that defines several users. Ensure that a blank line separates entries for different accounts.

Special attention is required for the userPassword entry in the user data file. This entry is typically encrypted using any of several encryption schemes. In Listing 7.2, SSHA encryption was used. You can create an encrypted password by typing **slappasswd**, which prompts you for a password (you must enter it twice) and displays a string that you can then cut and paste into the LDIF file. Additional `slappasswd` options are described shortly, in "Modifying Accounts."

If the account directory is new, you must initialize it by using two special entries:

```
dn: dc=pangaea,dc=edu
objectClass: domain
dc: pangaea

dn: ou=People,dc=pangaea,dc=edu
objectClass: organizationalUnit
ou: People
```

You can place these two entries at the start of the first LDIF file you use to create accounts, or you can enter them in their own separate file. Of course, you should modify them to reflect your own configuration by changing references to pangaea and edu to your own site's equivalents. A similar entry is required to initialize the groups directory:

```
dn: ou=Group,dc=pangaea,dc=edu
objectClass: organizationalUnit
ou: Group
```

 Real World Scenario

Migrating a User Database to LDAP

If you have a computer with an existing user database and you want to migrate it to LDAP, a set of scripts to convert the standard Linux files to LDIF format can help. Such scripts exist at `http://www.padl.com/OSS/MigrationTools.html`. The bulk of that Web page describes the meanings of various variables used by the scripts. Download links appear at the end of the page; scroll down and click to download a tarball containing the scripts.

After you've downloaded and extracted the scripts, you must edit the `migrate_common.ph` file for your site. Change the $DEFAULT_MAIL_DOMAIN and $DEFAULT_BASE variables to refer to your DNS mail domain name and LDAP base, respectively.

With suitable customization in place, you can type the following commands, from within the script directory, to create LDIF files for accounts and groups:

```
# ./migrate_passwd.pl /etc/passwd passwd.ldif
# ./migrate_group.pl /etc/group group.ldif
```

The resulting passwd.ldif and group.ldif files contain LDIF equivalents of your /etc/passwd and /etc/group files. You should edit these files to remove non-login system accounts and groups, as well as any users you don't want to authenticate via LDAP. With your final edited files in hand, you can add them to the LDAP directory, as described next.

Adding Accounts

With basic configuration out of the way, you can begin account maintenance tasks. If the LDAP directory is empty, a good place to start is with adding users. Prepare one or more LDIF files for users and groups, and then add each one using ldapadd:

```
$ ldapadd -D cn=manager,dc=pangaea,dc=edu -W -f acct.ldif
```

Ordinary users may run ldapadd and other LDAP administrative tools; LDAP relies on its own authentication, rather than the local login security, to provide proper security.

This example adds the accounts specified in acct.ldif to the LDAP server specified in the /etc/openldap/ldap.conf file. The option to -D is a distinguished name (DN) that refers to an administrative account on the LDAP server; you must know this DN and its associated password to be able to add accounts. Several other options passed to ldapadd are important, as summarized in Table 7.2. Consult ldapadd's man page for additional options.

TABLE 7.2   Important ldapadd options

Option	Description
-c	Continues processing the input file even if errors are detected.
-S *file*	Problem records are written to *file*, with error messages added as comments.
-n	Doesn't modify the directory but does show what would be done.
-v	Creates verbose output.
-d *level*	Sets a numeric debugging level. Requires a binary compiled with LDAP_DEBUG set.
-f *file*	Reads LDIF records from the specified *file*.
-x	Uses a simpler authentication method rather than the default of Simple Authentication and Security Layer (SASL).
-D *binddn*	Binds to the directory using the specified distinguished name (DN).
-W	Prompts for authentication.

Option	Description
-w *password*	Uses the specified password to authenticate. (Delivering a password in this way is risky, since it can be retrieved from your shell's history.)
-y *password_file*	Reads the password from *password_file*.
-H *ldapuri*	Accesses the LDAP server at the specified uniform resource identifier (URI). Old versions used –h rather than –H.
-P *version*	Uses the specified LDAP version (2 or 3).
-Z[Z]	Attempts to use StartTLS (Transport Layer Security) authentication. Using –ZZ requires this operation to succeed.

Modifying Accounts

To modify an account, you use the ldapmodify command, which works much like ldapadd. (In fact, one command is a symbolic link to the other on many systems.) Thus, the options to Table 7.2 apply to ldapmodify as well. Ordinarily, though, you use ldapmodify to modify an existing account. You can edit an existing LDIF file and then pass it back via ldapmodify to change the account.

One important account setting you're likely to need to change from time to time is the password. If you want to store passwords in a hashed (one-way encrypted) form, you'll need to encrypt them in some way when you modify the LDIF file. As noted earlier, the slappasswd utility can do this job. Type its name, and you'll be prompted to enter a password twice (it doesn't echo), whereupon the utility prints the hashed password:

```
$ slappasswd
New password:
Re-enter new password:
{SSHA}2UtAPbD+/juSg5k2vK3mY3ECtqsDRkkT
```

Cut and paste the displayed password value into the LDIF file and then run it through ldapmodify to change the password.

Various options to slappasswd modify its operation, as summarized in Table 7.3. A few more obscure options exist, as well; consult the program's man page for details.

TABLE 7.3 Important slappasswd options

Option	Description
-v	Displays verbose output.
-s *password*	Creates a hash of the specified *password*.
-T *file*	Creates a hash from the contents of *file*.
-h *scheme*	Uses the specified *scheme* to hash the password. Valid options for *scheme* are {CRYPT}, {MD5}, {SMD5}, {SSHA}, and {SHA}, with {SSHA} being the default.

Although you can change a user's password with slappasswd and ldapmodify, a simplified approach is to use ldappasswd, which effectively combines both commands in one, obviating the need to deal with an intermediary LDIF file:

```
$ ldappasswd -D cn=manager,dc=pangaea,dc=edu -W -S ↵
    uid=maryann,ou=People,dc=pangaea,dc=edu
New password:
Re-enter new password:
Enter LDAP Password:
Result: Success (0)
```

This example changes the password for maryann. A quirk is that the user must enter the manager's password *after* entering the user's new password. Many variants of this command are possible; for instance, by substituting the user's DN for the manager's DN, users may change their own passwords.

With the exception of -C, -S, -f, and -P, the options in Table 7.2 apply to ldappasswd. In addition, Table 7.4 summarizes options unique to ldappasswd. Consult the program's man page for still more options.

TABLE 7.4 Important ldappasswd options (see also Table 7.2)

Option	Description
-A	Prompts for the old password.
-a *password*	Uses the specified *password* as the old password.
-t *file*	Reads the old password from *file*.

Option	Description
-n	Does not set the password (used in conjunction with -v or -d).
-S	Prompts for the new password. (Note that -S has a different meaning with most related utilities.)
-s *new_password*	Sets the new password to *new_password*.
-T *file*	Reads the new password from *file*.

In most cases, users can change their own passwords using passwd on an LDAP client system, just as if the account database were local. This ability depends on the configuration of the Pluggable Authentication Modules (PAM) system on the client, though. Given the simplicity of passwd compared to ldappasswd, using passwd is preferable for most users.

Deleting Accounts

Of course, from time to time you may need to delete accounts. You can do so with the ldapdelete command, which can be used to delete a single account like this:

```
$ ldapdelete -D cn=manager,dc=pangaea,dc=edu -W cn=nemo,dc=pangaea,dc=edu
```

This command will delete the nemo user (or, more precisely, the account with the canonical name that matches cn=nemo,dc=pangaea,dc=edu) from the directory, providing of course that the user typing this command has the correct password!

The ldapdelete command works with all the same options described in Table 7.2 except for -S and -C. The meaning of -f is slightly different, as well; the file specified by -f contains a list of DNs that are to be deleted. Consult the man page for ldapdelete for information on additional options.

Querying a Server About Accounts

Several tools can provide information about LDAP accounts. One very convenient tool is getent. You pass the string passwd or group to getent to see a list of accounts or groups, respectively. You can also add the account or group name to obtain information on a particular account or group:

```
$ getent passwd maryann
maryann:x:1010:100:Maryann:/home/maryann:/bin/bash
```

This output verifies that the maryann account exists, and it displays various information about the account in the same format that the /etc/passwd file uses. The getent utility returns information from various sources, though, including local account databases; and it works only if the client is properly configured to use LDAP for account management. Using the -s ldap option restricts the search to LDAP sources.

An LDAP-specific tool is ldapsearch. Using this utility, you can search for data using any field in the database. Typically, you don't need much in the way of authentication to use it, either. For instance, you can search for data on the user maryann by typing this:

```
$ ldapsearch uid=maryann
```

The program will display any matching directory entries one after another. Of course, in this case there will probably be just one matching entry; however, you could search for members of a particular group, users who use a particular shell, or other non-unique features to obtain information on all such users.

The ldapsearch utility searches on criteria, or *filters*, defined in the Request For Comments (RFC) 4515 document (http://www.rfc-editor.org/rfc/rfc4515.txt, among other locations). The RFC 4515 filters can be quite complex. They're conceptually similar to regular expressions, which are used by several other Linux tools; but the syntax of RFC 4515 filters is quite different. For instance, consider the following filter:

```
(&(uid=maryann)(!(ou=Accounting)))
```

The filter will find users with an account name of maryann who are *not* members of the Accounting department (the exclamation mark serves a negation function). Such a search might be useful if your LDAP server hosts separate account databases for different departments or other groups. In such a configuration, the same username might be used by two people, much like two files can have the same name in two filesystem directories and yet be distinct. In most cases a much simpler search filter will suffice, though. If you need to use more complex search filters, you should consult RFC 4515.

As with other LDAP maintenance tools, various options are available in ldapsearch. The options listed in Table 7.2 are all supported; in addition, Table 7.5 summarizes some additional options. The -f option specifies a file in which a series of search criteria appear. Still more options are available; consult the program's man page for details.

TABLE 7.5   Important ldapsearch options (see also Table 7.2)

Option	Description
-A	Retrieves the attribute but not its value
-L	Displays results as LDIF records
-S *attribute*	Sorts the results based on the specified *attribute*
-b *base*	Searches the directory from the specified *base* rather than from the default
-z *number*	Retrieves at most *number* entries, with 0 meaning no limit

Configuring a Router

Chapter 5 describes basic network configuration, including the use of the route command and the most basic router configuration options. This chapter expands on this topic, focusing on Network Address Translation (NAT), firewall configurations, and automatic routing maintenance. These tools can help keep your network safe from unwanted attack—and just as importantly, they can keep your own network from becoming a source of unwanted attacks on others!

Understanding Types of Routing

Small computer networks enable computers to communicate more or less directly with one another. On such networks, computers can address each others' hardware using media access control (MAC) addresses, aka hardware addresses, as described in Chapter 5. This approach works fine for a small office network; however, such a configuration doesn't scale well to the sizes needed for large organizations, much less for the globe-spanning Internet. At such scales, it's necessary to link multiple small networks, each of which is known as a network segment, using special computers—routers.

At its core, a router is simply a computer that can transfer network data packets between two or more network segments. Depending upon the router's configuration, though, it may perform additional tasks, some of which are described in other chapters of this book:

VPN   A *virtual private network (VPN) router* encapsulates packets for transmission over an encrypted network link over an untrusted network. VPN configuration is described in Chapter 5.

Firewall   A *firewall* is a computer or software configuration that selectively rejects certain types of network traffic. Firewalls can block traffic based on a variety of criteria, including source IP address, destination IP address, source port number, and destination port number. Not all firewalls are routers, though; firewalls can protect isolated computers. Likewise, not all routers run firewalls. Many routers do run firewall software, though. Such routers typically employ *packet-filter* firewall configurations, meaning that the firewall uses low-level packet-based rules to determine what data to pass, as opposed to higher-level protocol-based rules. The upcoming section "Configuring Firewall Rules" describes Linux packet-filter firewall configuration.

NAT   *Network Address Translation (NAT)*, aka *IP masquerading*, enables a router to "hide" one network from another while still enabling the hidden network to access the other one. This is a very useful security tool for small private networks that can run with new or no externally accessible servers; the protected network can run internal servers with little risk that an outsider can access those servers. NAT can also stretch the limited supply of IPv4 addresses; an organization can give a dozen, a hundred, or more computers access to the Internet while consuming just one IP address. The upcoming section "Configuring NAT" describes Linux's NAT capabilities.

It's important to realize that not every computer that links two networks is a router. Some computers have two network interfaces and can even run the same server on both networks, but by itself, such a configuration does not transfer data between the networks, except perhaps in a limited way, depending on the server's configuration. Some setups can employ a *proxy server*, which is a way for the system to relay data for a limited number of protocols, but a proxy server is not a router because a router relays packets for a wide variety of protocols.

Activating Routing

To use a computer as a router, you must first configure it to use two or more network interfaces, as described in Chapter 5. You must then link those interfaces by placing the value 1 in the /proc/sys/net/ipv4/ip_forward pseudo-file:

```
# echo "1" > /proc/sys/net/ipv4/ip_forward
```

The /proc/sys/net/ipv4 pseudo-directory contains a large number of pseudo-files that control many low-level features of your IPv4 network connections. Most of these pseudo-files should not be adjusted unless you fully understand their purpose and function. On rare occasion, adjusting one can be helpful to improve performance or enable a feature. Placing a 1 value in the ip_forward pseudo-file on a router is one such occasion.

With this change in place, the computer is configured as a router. Of course, computers on both of its networks must know of its router status—that is, the Linux router must be listed as a gateway in the routing tables of at least one computer on each network interface.

Configuring Firewall Rules

Linux's packet-filter firewall rules are implemented using a tool known as iptables. This program enables you to describe criteria that can match packets based on addresses, port numbers, and so on. Packets that match the criteria you specify are passed, and others are rejected, or vice versa, depending on your defaults. In the following pages, I describe basic iptables principles, summarize how to check the existing configuration, explain the syntax of the iptables utility, and present a sample configuration.

Linux kernel versions 2.4.*x* and 2.6.*x* use iptables. The earlier 2.0.*x* and 2.2.*x* kernel series used tools known as ipfwadm and ipchains, respectively. If your system uses IPv6, you must use the ip6tables tool. These programs are similar in principle to iptables, but they differ in many details. The ipfwadm and ipchains tools, in particular, are less powerful than iptables.

Basics of *iptables*

The Linux kernel uses a series of rules to determine what to do with any given packet it receives or that's generated by local processes. These rules are arranged in *chains*, which provide a series of patterns and actions to be taken should a packet match the pattern. The first rule to match a pattern determines what the system does with the packet—accept it, reject it, or pass it to another chain. The chains are in turn organized into *tables*, with relationships between them. The most important table is the filter table, which is illustrated in Figure 7.3. In this table, the INPUT chain processes packets destined for local programs, the FORWARD chain processes packets that the system is to forward (as in a router), and the OUTPUT chain processes packets that originate locally and are destined for outside systems. Any given packet passes through just one of these chains. Other standard tables include the nat table, which handles Network Address Translation (NAT), and the mangle table, which modifies packets in specialized ways.

FIGURE 7.3 Linux uses a series of rules, which are defined in chains that are called at various points during processing, to determine the fate of network packets

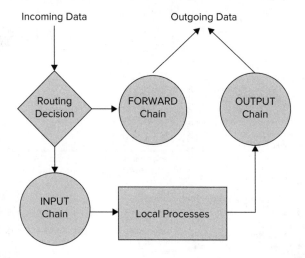

To create a packet-filter firewall, you must design a series of rules for specific tables and chains. For instance, you might tell the INPUT chain to discard any packets directed at port 80 (the Web server port) that don't originate from the local network. Another set of rules might tell the OUTPUT chain to block all outgoing packets from local processes destined for port 25 (the SMTP mail server) except for those directed at your network's mail server computer. A router is likely to include a number of special rules for the FORWARD chain, as well, in order to control routing features independently of local programs' accesses.

Linux provides the iptables utility for manipulating firewall rules. This program relies on the presence of assorted options in the Linux kernel. Most importantly, you must enable the Networking Support ➢ Networking Options ➢ Network Packet Filtering Framework (Netfilter) option. Once you've done this, you can activate various options in the IP: Netfilter Configuration submenu, most notably the IP Tables Support option, as shown in Figure 7.4. I recommend you build just about everything else, as well, at least as modules. Most Linux distributions ship with most of these options compiled as modules.

FIGURE 7.4 Linux kernel options must be enabled before a packet filter firewall can be built

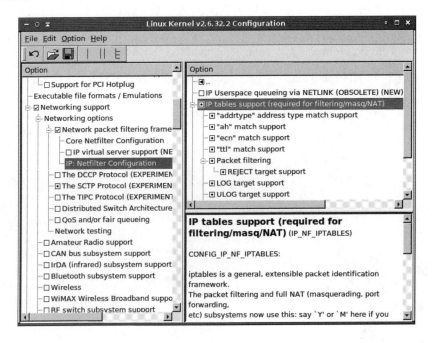

The iptables tool accepts a number of table and command options, the most important of which are summarized in Table 7.6. (Options related to rules are described later in "Using iptables.") Additional options are described in the man page for iptables.

TABLE 7.6   Common iptables table and command options

Long option name	Short option name	Description
--table *table*	-t *table*	Specifies the table to be operated upon. For firewalls, this will most often be filter, which is the default. For NAT configurations, the table name is nat.
--list [*chain*]	-L [*chain*]	Displays the current configuration for the specified chain or for all chains if *chain* is omitted.
--list-rules [*chain*]	-S [*chain*]	Displays the rules in the current chain or for all chains if *chain* is omitted. Produces more terse output than -L.
--flush [*chain*]	-F [*chain*]	Removes all rules for the specified chain or for all chains if *chain* is omitted.
--policy *chain* *target*	-P *chain* *target*	Sets the default policy (described in detail in "Setting the Default Policy") for the specified chain.
--append *chain* *rule*	-A *chain* *rule*	Adds a new rule to the specified chain.
--delete *chain* *rule*	-D *chain* *rule*	Deletes an existing rule from a chain. The rule may be specified either as a number or as a description.
--insert *chain* [*number*] *rule*	-I *chain* [*number*] *rule*	Inserts a new rule into a chain at the specified position (*number*). If *number* is omitted, the rule is inserted at the head of the chain.
--replace *chain* *number* *rule*	-R *chain* *number* *rule*	Replaces an existing rule (specified by *number*) with a new one.

Checking the Configuration

The iptables program responds to the -L parameter by displaying a list of the rules that make up a given table. You may optionally pass a table name by using the -t parameter. For instance, Listing 7.4 shows how to view the current filter table.

Listing 7.4: Sample use of `iptables` to view firewall configuration

```
# iptables -L -t filter
Chain INPUT (policy ACCEPT)
target     prot opt source              destination
DROP       all  --  172.24.0.0/16       anywhere

Chain FORWARD (policy DROP)
target     prot opt source              destination

Chain OUTPUT (policy ACCEPT)
target     prot opt source              destination
```

The default table is `filter`, so omitting `-t filter` from this command produces the same output. The table summarized by this output is nearly empty; the `FORWARD` and `OUTPUT` chains have no rules, and the `INPUT` chain has just one rule—it drops all input from the `172.24.0.0/16` network. Although the format of information presented by `iptables -L` isn't exactly equivalent to what you use when you create a rule, the similarities are strong enough that you should be able to interpret the output once you know how to create rules.

Setting the Default Policy

One critically important consideration when designing a firewall is the *default policy*, which is what the firewall does with packets that don't match any rules in a chain. In fact, in the standard `filter` table, there are three default policies, one each for the `INPUT`, `FORWARD`, and `OUTPUT` chains. The default policy corresponds to an action that the system can take. Three options are common, as described in Table 7.7, although only two may be used as a default rule.

TABLE 7.7 Common firewall policies

Policy	Description
ACCEPT	An ACCEPT action causes the system to accept the packet and pass it on to the next chain or system. For instance, if the INPUT chain's default policy is ACCEPT, any packet that doesn't match a rule is passed to the target program (assuming one is using the specified port).
DROP	This action causes the system to ignore the packet—to "drop it on the floor," as it were. To the system that sends the packet (which could be a remote computer or a local program, depending on the chain involved), it appears that the packet was lost due to a routing error or the like.
REJECT	This action is much like DROP, except that the kernel returns a code to the calling computer or program indicating that the packet has been rejected. This behavior is similar to what would happen if no program were using the target port. This action requires that you compile explicit support for it into the kernel, either in the main kernel file or as a module. Unfortunately, REJECT doesn't work as a default policy, but you can use it as a target for more specific rules.

Typing `iptables -L` reveals the default policy, as shown in Listing 7.4—in that example, the INPUT and OUTPUT chains have a default policy of ACCEPT, whereas the FORWARD chain has a default policy of DROP. To change the default policy, you should first flush the chain of all its rules by passing the -F parameter and the chain name to `iptables`. You can then pass the -P parameter to `iptables`, along with the policy name. In both cases, you can optionally include -t and the table name:

```
# iptables -t filter -F FORWARD
# iptables -F INPUT
# iptables -P FORWARD DROP
# iptables -t filter -P INPUT DROP
```

As a general rule, the safest default policy is a closed one—that is, to use DROP. When you use such a default policy, you must explicitly open ports with firewall rules. This means that if a server is running on your computer without your knowledge, it doesn't pose a security risk because packets can't reach it and it can't send packets. Likewise, if you close outgoing ports, malicious software or individuals may not be able to launch attacks on others unless they use the protocols you've approved for use. Using DROP as a default policy for the FORWARD chain on a router means your network will be very well protected and will be unable to serve as a base for outgoing attacks, as well. On the other hand, a default closed policy means you must design your firewall rules very carefully; an oversight can cause an important client or server to stop working.

Although you cannot set the default policy to REJECT, you can achieve much the same end by other means. Specifically, you can insert a rule at the end of the chain that uses REJECT on all packets not matched by previous rules. If you do this, the default policy as set via the -P option to `iptables` becomes irrelevant. The next section, "Using `iptables`," describes how to create individual rules.

If you want a default closed policy, you must decide between using DROP (directly) and REJECT (via a workaround as described in the previous tip). There are good arguments to be made in favor of both rules. DROP is the "stealthy" option. If you were to use DROP on every port and protocol, many network scanners would fail to detect your computer at all; it would appear not to exist. Of course, such an extreme policy would make the network useless; in practice, you must let *some* traffic through, and this frequently gives information to crackers. For instance, if a system drops everything but port-80 accesses, the cracker knows you're running a Web server (or something else) on port 80. Because computers don't normally drop packets, though, the cracker also knows you're running a firewall with a default DROP policy. By contrast, REJECT does a poorer job of hiding your system's presence from casual scans, but once a cracker has found your system, it's less obvious that you're running a firewall.

On occasion, these different policies can have an effect on protocols. Specifically, many protocols are designed to keep trying to make connections if packets are lost. This behavior can sometimes result in connection delays for related protocols if you use a default DROP policy. For instance, a server might try contacting your computer's port 113, which is used by the ident (aka auth) server. This server provides information about who on your system is making connection requests to servers, the goal being to provide a trail in log files to help track abuse back to its source. (TCP Wrappers can also use an ident server as an authorization tool.) If your system uses an INPUT chain DROP rule on port 113, the result can be connection delays if a remote server tries to use your ident server. Of course, you can overcome such problems on a case-by-case basis by adding ordinary rules to the offending chain, overriding the default DROP rule with a REJECT rule, or perhaps even overriding an ACCEPT rule.

If your computer has two network interfaces but it should not function as a router, use a DROP default policy on the FORWARD chain. Doing so will prevent the computer from functioning as a router, even if you inadvertently configure it to forward packets in another way.

Using *iptables*

To add a rule to a chain, you call iptables with a command such as this:

```
# iptables -A CHAIN selection-criteria  -j TARGET
```

The *CHAIN* in this command is the chain name—INPUT, OUTPUT, or FORWARD for the filter table. The *TARGET* is the firewall target that's to process the packet, such as ACCEPT, REJECT, or DROP. You can also specify a LOG target, which logs information about the packet and then tries to match the next rule. Various other targets are also available; consult the iptables documentation for details.

The tricky part of this command is in the *selection-criteria* component. You can specify many different criteria to match different features of a packet. If you specify more than one criterion, all of them must match in order for a rule to apply. Some of the possible criteria are summarized in Table 7.8. Many additional matching rules are available; consult the man page for iptables for more information.

TABLE 7.8 Common iptables matching criteria

Long option name	Short option name	Description
--match *name*	-m *name*	Adds extended matching rules provided by the named module.
--protocol *protocol*	-p *protocol*	Sets the protocol in a rule (tcp, udp, udplite, icmp, esp, ah, sctp, or all, with all matching any protocol type).

Long option name	Short option name	Description
--source-port *port*[:*port*]	--sport *port*[:*port*]	Specifies the originating port in a rule. You may specify a single port or a range by separating the port numbers by a colon, as in --sport 1024:65535 to match any ports between 1024 and 65,535, inclusive.
--destination-port *port*[:*port*]	--dport *port*[:*port*]	Specifies the destination port in a rule. This option works just like the --source-port option but for destination ports.
--source *address*[/*mask*]	-s *address*[/*mask*]	Specifies the source address in a rule. You can provide either a single IP address or a network block by including the /*mask* value.
--destination *address*[/*mask*]	-d *address*[/*mask*]	Specifies the destination address in a rule. This option works just like the --source option but for the destination address.
--in-interface *name*	-i *name*	Specifies the input interface in a rule. This option is meaningless for the OUTPUT chain.
--out-interface *name*	-o *name*	Specifies the output interface in a rule. This option is meaningless with the INPUT chain.
--state *state*	N/A	Specifies the connection state in a rule—that is, whether the packet is establishing a new connection, continuing an existing connection, or what have you. Legal *state* values are INVALID, NEW, ESTABLISHED, or RELATED. You may need to precede this option with -m state.
--jump *target*	-j *target*	Tells iptables what to do if a packet matches a rule.
--goto *chain*	-g *chain*	Tells iptables to continue processing in a new chain.

All Linux computers use a *loopback* or *localhost* interface, identified as lo, for certain local network activity. You can create a filter using the -i or -o option and this interface name to enable your system to talk to itself, which is necessary for certain tools, such as X servers and print queues, to work.

Many of these options are used in pairs that match packets traveling in opposite directions. You must remember that most networking connections involve two-way communications. One side sends a packet or a stream of packets to the other side, and the second side replies. Therefore, with a default DENY policy, it's not enough to simply unblock, say, packets directed at your Web server (with the `--destination-port` and possibly other options) on your INPUT chain. You must also unblock packets coming from the Web server (with the `--source-port` and possibly other options) on the OUTPUT chain. If you reverse the chains with which these rules are associated, you affect the ability of clients to communicate.

A Sample Configuration

The options described in the preceding section may seem complex, and indeed they enable you to create a sophisticated set of firewall rules. To better understand these rules, consider Listing 7.5, which shows a simple firewall rule set as a bash script. This script is a minimal one that might be run on a workstation or server. Aside from flushing and setting the default policy, this script doesn't touch the FORWARD chain. To configure a router as a firewall, you'd have to create rules for the FORWARD chain reflecting the types of traffic you want to pass between networks.

Listing 7.5: A sample iptables firewall script

```
#!/bin/bash

iptables -F INPUT
iptables -F FORWARD
iptables -F OUTPUT

iptables -P INPUT DROP
iptables -P FORWARD DROP
iptables -P OUTPUT DROP

# Let traffic on the loopback interface pass
iptables -A OUTPUT -d 127.0.0.1 -o lo -j ACCEPT
iptables -A INPUT -s 127.0.0.1 -i lo -j ACCEPT

# Let DNS traffic pass
iptables -A OUTPUT -p udp --dport 53 -j ACCEPT
iptables -A INPUT -p udp --sport 53 -j ACCEPT

# Let clients' TCP traffic pass
iptables -A OUTPUT -p tcp --sport 1024:65535 -m state \
        --state NEW,ESTABLISHED,RELATED -j ACCEPT
```

```
iptables -A INPUT -p tcp --dport 1024:65535 -m state \
        --state ESTABLISHED,RELATED -j ACCEPT

# Let local connections to local SSH server pass
iptables -A OUTPUT -p tcp --sport 22 -d 172.24.1.0/24 -m state \
        --state ESTABLISHED,RELATED -j ACCEPT
iptables -A INPUT -p tcp --dport 22 -s 172.24.1.0/24 -m state \
        --state NEW,ESTABLISHED,RELATED -j ACCEPT
```

Listing 7.5 begins with a series of six calls to `iptables` that flush the firewall rule chain and set the default policy. These lines ensure that when you run this script, you won't add to an existing rule set, which could bloat the chains, thereby degrading performance and causing unexpected effects. The remaining lines are broken into four parts, each of which has two `iptables` calls. These parts set rules relating to specific types of traffic:

Loopback Interface Traffic   The two lines that refer to 127.0.0.1 allow the computer to communicate with itself over the loopback interface (`lo`). The references to 127.0.0.1 and the associated `-d` and `-s` parameters are arguably a bit paranoid; anything coming over the `lo` interface should come from this address.

DNS Queries   Most systems rely on a DNS server to translate hostnames to IP addresses. To keep this system working, you must enable access to and from remote DNS servers, which run on UDP port 53. The DNS rules in Listing 7.5 are actually rather permissive, because they enable traffic to or from *any* DNS server to pass. In theory, a miscreant could run something other than a DNS server on UDP port 53 to use this rule to bypass your security. In practice, though, such abuse would be unlikely to work, because it would require something other than DNS on the local system to use the oddly configured external client or server. If you like, you could add IP address restrictions to these lines to improve the security.

Client Traffic   The next two calls to `iptables` create a broad set of acceptance conditions. Network clients generally use high TCP ports—those numbered between 1024 and 65535. These rules, therefore, open those ports to access in both directions but with a twist: These rules use stateful packet inspection to ensure that NEW packets are allowed only on *outgoing* connections. The omission of the NEW state from the INPUT chain means that a server run on a high port (as an ordinary user might try in an attempt to get around your system's security) won't be able to accept connections. Both rules also omit the INVALID state, which can reduce the chance of a miscreant intercepting and "hijacking" an established connection.

Local SSH Server Traffic   The final two calls to `iptables` open a hole in the firewall to enable local computers to make connections to the SSH server. This server runs on port 22, so traffic to and from that port and originating from or destined to the local (172.24.1.0/24) network is accepted. As with the client traffic rules, these rules employ stateful inspection as an added precaution. INVALID packets are rejected in both directions, and NEW packets are accepted only on input packets.

Many firewall scripts define variables that contain the host machine's IP address and the address for the local network, and then they refer to these variables, rather than using them directly, as Listing 7.5 does. This practice greatly simplifies changing the script if your IP address changes or if the script is to run on multiple computers.

Configuring NAT

As described earlier, NAT is a useful tool for protecting a network and for stretching a limited budget of IP addresses. Once you've decided to use NAT, you can enable NAT features using `iptables`. That done, you may want to investigate port redirection options, which enable you to overcome some of NAT's limitations.

Enabling NAT Features

NAT configuration is surprisingly simple. A single `iptables` command enables NAT features:

```
# iptables -t nat -A POSTROUTING -o eth0 -j MASQUERADE
```

This line tells the kernel to route traffic such that data passed through `eth0` is masqueraded. That is, `eth0` should normally be connected to the Internet, whereas `eth1` (or other interfaces) should be connected to the private network you want to protect. Of course, you can change the network specification in this command, if necessary.

To be useful, NAT also requires normal router configuration—that is, you must store the value 1 in `/proc/sys/net/ipv4/ip_forward`, as described earlier in "Activating Routing."

Redirecting Ports

Ordinarily, one of the big advantages of NAT is that computers on the Internet cannot initiate contact with computers protected by the NAT router. Sometimes, though, this advantage can be a problem. Suppose, for instance, that you need to access just one computer on your network. The NAT router now becomes an obstacle to be overcome.

One solution to this problem is to use the NAT router as an intermediary system. For instance, you could use SSH to log into the NAT router and then access the target computer from the NAT router. This approach can be acceptable in some situations, but it may be awkward or downright unacceptable in others. In such cases, a solution known as *port forwarding* is available. This technique enables traffic directed at one port to be forwarded to another port, another computer, or another port on another computer. Port forwarding is accomplished with the `--jump` (`-j`) `iptables` rule, using the `DNAT` target, as in this example:

```
# iptables -t nat -A PREROUTING -p tcp -i eth0 --dport 22 -j DNAT ↵
   --to-destination 192.168.107.64:22
```

To understand this command, try breaking it down piece by piece:

- The -t nat directive tells the program to work on the nat table. Although port forwarding can be done on computers that don't function as NAT routers, it uses the nat table.

- Although most NAT operations occur after routing in the kernel, port forwarding occurs before routing, which is the reason for the -A PREROUTING option.

- This particular example forwards a TCP port (-p tcp); however, port forwarding can be done on other port types.

- Packets directed at eth0 (-i eth0) are to be forwarded. If this computer were the same one configured in "Enabling NAT Features," this rule would redirect traffic directed at the NAT router's external interface.

- Ports directed at port 22 (--dport 22), the SSH port, will be redirected.

- The -j DNAT option tells the kernel to perform NAT on the destination (DNAT) rather than the source (SNAT) address. The NAT operations are then restricted according to the other rules.

- The --to-destination option specifies where packets that meet the other criteria are to be redirected—in this case, to port 22 on 192.168.107.64.

The net effect of this example is that any attempt to reach the NAT router by SSH from its external address will instead reach 192.168.107.64's SSH port. You can write several such rules, effectively enabling as many internal computers as you like to function as servers on the Internet at large. One important limitation, though, is that you can still have only one server on each external port. (Advanced load balancing tools can provide some relief from this limitation but are beyond the scope of this book.) If you need to access, say, two different computers' SSH servers, you must forward data for one from a non-standard external port number.

Automatic Routing Configuration

The preceding descriptions rely on one-time commands or, in the case of Listing 7.5, a single script to implement firewall and other router features. This isn't always convenient, though. In particular, it's usually desirable to have a computer set up its firewall rules automatically whenever it boots. This can be done by implementing your firewall rules as a startup script, and many distributions have facilities to do this by default. You may also want to investigate a tool called routed, which helps automate the maintenance of routing tables on a full-fledged Internet router.

Restoring Routing Rules Automatically

The iptables utility is a flexible tool for creating packet-filter firewalls, NAT configurations, and port forwarding; however, individual iptables commands typically do just a small fraction of the entire job you want done. Therefore, it's usually best to create a script to set up your desired configuration. (You might even create two or three scripts, each one handling part of the job, such as separating port forwarding from firewall configurations.) Listing 7.5 is an example of such a script, albeit a simple one.

The simplest way to have your firewall scripts run automatically is usually to call them from system startup scripts. Common names for these local startup scripts include /etc/rc.local (used by Debian, Ubuntu, and related distributions), /etc/rc.d/rc.local (used by Red Hat, Fedora, and related distributions), /etc/init.d/boot.local (used by OpenSUSE), and /etc/conf.d/local.start (used by Gentoo). Place a call to your firewall script in the local startup script for your distribution, and it will run automatically whenever you start the computer.

Another method of launching your firewall script is to create a custom SysV or Upstart script for it. These scripts are described in Chapter 1; however, creating a new script is more difficult than modifying an existing one. The main advantage to doing it this way rather than calling your firewall script in a local startup script is that you gain flexibility; you can add support for start, stop, restart, or other options (each of which may require its own supporting firewall script), and you can have the firewall start in only some runlevels. You can also have the firewall start up immediately after the network, thus reducing the narrow window of vulnerability between the time when the network becomes active and the firewall begins protecting the computer.

Many distributions provide their own firewall scripts and typically configuration tools to go with them. For instance, typing **system-config-firewall** in a Fedora system launches its GUI firewall configuration utility. Enabling the firewall activates it when you reboot. Tools such as this can be convenient shortcuts and are often adequate; however, writing your own rules with iptables is almost certain to be more flexible and may be necessary if you need to use exotic features or create an unusual configuration.

WARNING   Distributions' firewall tools and your own custom iptables scripts can conflict with one another. If you write your own iptables script and find that a completely different firewall configuration is active when you reboot, it's likely that the distribution's firewall tool has replaced your custom script's settings. Try to track down your distribution's tool and either disable it or use it to create your desired configuration. If you do the latter, be sure to disable your original script to avoid confusion in the future.

Using *routed*

Most of this chapter's router information is concerned with firewalls, NAT, port forwarding, and related topics; however, one other routing topic requires mention: routing path determination. Consider Figure 7.5, which depicts a network at a mid-sized company. This network contains five departments, each with its own subnet and a router that connects to two other networks in a ring arrangement. Suppose that a user on the R&D network needs to access a computer on the Personnel network. Assuming equally good connections between the routers, the optimum route traverses the Marketing router; however, if that router goes down, the connection can still be made via the Manufacturing and Customer Support routers. The trouble, however, is that the R&D router is likely to specify only one route to Personnel—probably via Marketing. Thus, when the Marketing router goes down, so will the connection to Personnel, even though another route does exist.

FIGURE 7.5 In a mid-sized network, multiple paths between two subnets are often possible

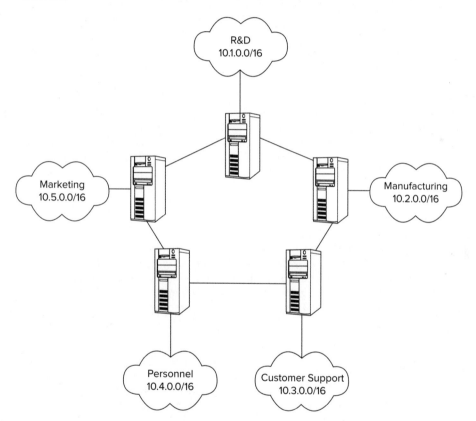

The solution to this problem lies in a routing protocol, which enables routers to communicate among themselves to discover the optimum route and to adjust routing tables appropriately. Several routing protocols exist, but the one described here is the *Routing Information Protocol (RIP)*, which detects the number of routers between a source and a destination and adjusts the routing table to minimize this number for any given destination. RIP is a fairly simple routing protocol that's most often used on small and mid-sized networks, such as those in corporations and universities; its technical limitations make it unsuitable for use on the Internet as a whole.

In Linux, RIP is implemented via the routed daemon, which can be installed via a package of the same name. This program normally requires no configuration; it can be launched by a system startup script, and thereafter it adjusts network routing tables on all interfaces automatically. It does this by using RIP broadcasts and adjusting the computer's routing table according to the replies it receives.

Keep in mind that routed relies on the presence of other RIP servers on the routers to which it connects. In Figure 7.5, all five of the routers depicted must be running routed (or some other RIP server) to obtain the full benefit of this protocol.

Configuring SSH

In the past, Telnet has been the remote text-mode login protocol of choice on Linux and Unix systems. Unfortunately, Telnet is severely lacking in security features. Thus, in recent years SSH has grown in popularity, and it is in fact the preferred remote login tool. SSH can also handle file transfer tasks similar to those of the File Transfer Protocol (FTP). For these reasons, knowing how to configure SSH can be helpful. This task requires knowing a bit about SSH generally and about the SSH configuration file under Linux. I conclude the look at SSH with information about the security implications of running the server.

 SSH is complex enough that I can't cover more than its basics in this chapter. Consult OpenSSH's documentation or a book on the topic, such as *SSH, The Secure Shell: The Definitive Guide, Second Edition*, by Daniel J. Barrett, Richard Silverman, and Robert G. Byrnes (O'Reilly, 2005), or *Implementing SSH: Strategies for Optimizing the Secure Shell*, by Himanshu Dwivedi (Wiley, 2003), for more details.

SSH Basics

Linux supports remote login access through several different servers, including Telnet, Virtual Network Computing (VNC), and even X. Unfortunately, most of these methods suffer from a major drawback: They transfer most or all data over the network in unencrypted form. This fact means anybody who can monitor network traffic can easily snatch sensitive data, often including passwords. (VNC and a few other protocols encrypt passwords but not other data.) This limitation puts a serious dent in the utility of these remote login tools; after all, if using a remote access protocol means you'll be giving away sensitive data or compromising your entire computer, it's not a very useful protocol.

WARNING   Non-encrypting remote access tools are particularly risky for performing work as root, either by logging in directly as root or by logging in as an ordinary user and then using su, sudo, or other tools to acquire root privileges.

SSH was designed to close this potentially major security hole by employing strong encryption techniques for all parts of the network connection. SSH encrypts the password exchange and all subsequent data transfers, making it a much safer protocol for remote access.

In addition to encryption, SSH provides file transfer features and the ability to *tunnel* other network protocols—that is, to enable non-encrypted protocols to piggyback their data over an SSH connection, thus delivering SSH's encryption advantages to other protocols. This feature is frequently employed in conjunction with X, enabling encrypted remote GUI access, but it can be used with other protocols, as well.

Of course, SSH's advantages don't come without a price. The main drawback of SSH is that the encryption and decryption consume CPU time. This fact slows down SSH connections compared to those of direct connections and can degrade overall system performance. This effect is modest, though, particularly for plain text-mode connections. If you tunnel a protocol that transfers much more data, such as X, you may see a greater performance drop when using SSH. Even in this case, the improved security is generally worth the slight speed cost.

Several SSH servers are available for Linux, but the most popular by far is the OpenSSH server (http://www.openssh.org). This program was one of the first open source implementations of the SSH protocol, which was developed by the commercial SSH Communications Security, now known as Tectia (http://www.tectia.com), whose server is sold under the name SSH Tectia. OpenSSH, SSH Tectia, and other SSH products can interoperate with one another, assuming they're all configured to support at least one common level of the SSH protocol. OpenSSH 5.6, the latest version as I write, supports SSH levels 1.3, 1.5, and 2.0, with 2.0 being the preferred level because of known vulnerabilities in the earlier versions.

OpenSSH may be launched via either a super server (inetd or xinetd) or a system startup script (SysV or Upstart). The latter method is preferred, because the server may need to perform CPU-intensive tasks upon starting, so if it's started from a super server, OpenSSH may be sluggish to respond to connection requests, particularly on systems with weaker CPUs. Most distributions deliver SysV startup scripts with their SSH packages. If you make changes to your SSH configuration, you may need to pass the reload or restart option to the startup script, as in **/etc/init.d/sshd reload**. (Chapter 1 covers startup scripts in more detail.) However it's launched, the OpenSSH server binary name is sshd—the same as the binary name for SSH Tectia.

Setting SSH Options for Your System

For the most part, SSH works reasonably well when it's first installed, so you may not need to make any changes to its configuration. If you do need to make changes, though, these are mostly handled through the main SSH configuration file, /etc/ssh/sshd_config. You can also edit some additional files to limit access to the SSH server or to change how SSH manages the login process.

Configuring Basic SSH Features

The /etc/ssh/sshd_config file consists mainly of option lines that take the following form:

Option value

> Don't confuse the sshd_config file with the ssh_config file. The former controls the OpenSSH server, whereas the latter controls the SSH client program, ssh.

In addition to configuration lines, the sshd_config file holds comments, which are denoted by hash marks (#) or semicolons (;). Most sample configuration files include a large number of SSH options that are commented out; these lines specify the default values, so uncommenting the lines by removing the comment character without otherwise changing them will have no effect. If you want to change an option, uncomment the line and change it. Most options' default values are suitable for most systems. Table 7.9 includes some that you may want to check and, perhaps, change.

TABLE 7.9   Important sshd_config options

Option	Description
Protocol	This option specifies the protocol levels OpenSSH understands. Possible values are 1 and 2. You can configure OpenSSH to support both protocols by separating them by a comma, as in 1,2 or 2,1, which are equivalent. Given that OpenSSH protocol level 1 has been compromised, the safest configuration is to set Protocol 2. This limits the server's ability to communicate with older clients, though.
PasswordAuthentication	This option specifies whether authentication via passwords is supported. The default value is yes.

Option	Description
PubkeyAuthentication	This option, which is meaningful only for SSH level 2, specifies whether public key authentication is supported. This authentication type is important when configuring the system to permit logins without passwords, as described in "Configuring Logins Without Passwords." The default value is yes.
UsePAM	If set to yes (the default is no), this option enables sshd to authenticate users via the standard Linux Pluggable Authentication Modules (PAM) system, which may be desirable if you've enabled unusual authentication tools such as LDAP.
AllowUsers	You can specify a set of users, whose names are separated by spaces, who are allowed to log in via SSH with this option. By default, any user with a valid account and authentication method may log in.
DenyUsers	This option works much like AllowUsers but in reverse; users listed with this option are denied the ability to log in.
PermitRootLogin	By default, this option is set to yes, which enables OpenSSH to accept direct logins by root. This is safer than a similar configuration under Telnet, but for a bit of added security, set this value to no. The result will be that anybody wanting to perform remote work as root will need to first log in as an ordinary user, which means that an intruder who has somehow acquired the root password will also need a regular username and its password.
X11Forwarding	This option specifies whether OpenSSH's X tunneling features should be active. If you want to enable remote users to run X programs via SSH, you must set this option to yes. Doing so can degrade security of the client's X display, though, depending on certain other options; that's the reason for the conservative default value of no.
AllowTcpForwarding	When set to yes (the default), the server will accept tunneled protocols, as described in "Tunneling Arbitrary Protocols."

For information about additional options, consult the man page for sshd_config. If you make changes to the SSH configuration, remember to restart it using the server's SysV startup script.

Generating SSH Keys

Part of SSH's security involves *encryption keys*. Each server system and each user has a unique number, or key, for identification purposes. In fact, SSH uses a security system that involves two keys: a *public key* and a *private key*. These two keys are mathematically linked in such a way that data encrypted with a particular public key may be decrypted only with the matching private key. When establishing a connection, each side sends its public key to the other. Thereafter, each side encrypts data with the other side's public key, ensuring that the data can be decrypted only by the intended recipient. In practice, this is just the first step of the process, but it's critical. What's more, SSH clients typically retain the public keys of servers they've contacted. This enables them to spot changes to the public key. Such changes can be signs of tampering.

Most OpenSSH server startup scripts include code that looks for stored public and private keys and, if they're not present, generates them. In total, four to six keys are needed: public and private keys for two or three encryption tools SSH supports. These keys are normally stored in /etc/ssh and are called ssh_host_rsa_key and ssh_host_dsa_key for private keys, with .pub filename extensions added for public keys. Some systems add ssh_host_rsa1_key and its associated public key to support SSH level 1.*x*. If your system doesn't have these keys and you can't get the SSH server to start up, you can generate the keys with the ssh-keygen command:

```
# ssh-keygen -q -t rsa1 -f /etc/ssh/ssh_host_rsa1_key -C '' -N ''
# ssh-keygen -q -t rsa -f /etc/ssh/ssh_host_rsa_key -C '' -N ''
# ssh-keygen -q -t dsa -f /etc/ssh/ssh_host_dsa_key -C '' -N ''
```

Each of these commands generates both a private key (named in the -f parameter) and a public key (with the same name but with .pub appended).

Don't run these ssh-keygen commands if the SSH key files already exist. Replacing the working files will cause clients who've already connected to the SSH server to complain about the changed keys and possibly refuse to establish a connection.

WARNING   Be sure the private keys are suitably protected; if an intruder obtains one of these keys, the intruder can impersonate your system. Typically, these files should have 0600 (-rw-------) permissions and be owned by root. The public key files (with .pub filename extensions) should be readable by all users, though—typically, ownership by root and permissions of 0644 (-rw-r--r--) are appropriate.

When you configure a client system, you may want to consider creating a global cache of host keys. As already noted, the ssh program records host keys for each individual user. (It stores these in the ~/.ssh/known_hosts file.) When you set up the client, you can populate the global ssh_known_hosts file, which is normally stored in /etc or /etc/ssh. Doing so ensures that the public key list is as accurate as the sources you use to populate the global file. It also eliminates confirmation messages when users connect to the hosts whose keys you've selected to include in the global file.

How do you create this file? One simple way is to copy the file from a user account that's been used to connect to the servers you want to include. For instance, you can type **cp /home/ecernan/.ssh/known_hosts /etc/ssh/ssh_known_hosts** to use ecernan's file. You may want to manually review this file before copying it. It consists of one line per host. Each line begins with a hostname, IP address, or both, and continues with the key type and the key. You can ignore most of this information, but pay attention to the hostnames and IP addresses. Ensure that the list includes all the SSH servers your client is likely to want to use and that it does *not* include inappropriate or unnecessary servers. You can remove lines in your text editor, if necessary. To add entries, use the account whose file you're copying to connect to the system you want to add. Chances are, ssh will display a warning about connecting to an unknown system. Confirm that you want to do so. Once you do this and reload the file, you should see an entry for the server.

OpenSSH 4.0 and later support hashing of hostnames in the known hosts file; this is done by setting HashKnownHosts yes in the /etc/ssh/ ssh_config file. When this feature is enabled, the hostname is encrypted using a one-way encryption algorithm and stored in this form. The idea is that you'll still be able to authenticate SSH servers to which you connect, because a hash of the typed hostname will match a hash of the stored hostname, but if an intruder steals your known hosts file, the intruder will be unable to determine the identities of the computers to which you've been connecting. One drawback to this feature is that it complicates legitimate manual editing of the known_hosts file.

Copying Files Using SSH

Most users employ the ssh client program, which provides remote login access—type **ssh** *othersystem* to log into *othersystem* using the same username you're using on the client system; or add a username, as in **ssh** *user@othersystem*, to log in using another username.

SSH includes a file-copying command, too: scp. This command works much like the cp command for copying files locally; however, you must specify the target computer, and optionally the username, just before the target filename. For instance, to copy the file masterpiece.c to the lisa account on leonardo.example.com, you would type

```
$ scp masterpiece.c lisa@leonardo.example.com:
```

The colon (:) that terminates this command is extremely important; if you omit it, you'll find that scp works like cp, and you'll end up with a file called lisa@leonardo.example.com on the client computer. If you want to rename the file, you can do so by including the new name following the colon.

Logging In Without a Password

If you use SSH a lot or if you use it in automated tools, you'll no doubt become annoyed by the need to type a password with every connection. There is a way around this requirement: You can set up the SSH client with keys and give the public key to the server computer. With this configuration, the SSH client computer can identify itself, possibly obviating the need for you to type a password.

WARNING Configuring SSH to operate without the use of passwords is convenient, but it does increase security risks. If somebody you don't trust ever gains access to your account on the SSH client system, that person will be able to log into the SSH server system as you without the benefit of your password. Thus, you should create a password-less login only from a client that's very well protected, if at all. Configuring access to the root account in this way is particularly risky.

To configure SSH to not require a password, you must generate your own SSH key on the client system using ssh-keygen, copy that key file to the server, and add it to the ~/.ssh/authorized_keys or ~/.ssh/authorized_keys2 file. Thereafter, logins from the client to the server will require no password. Exercise 7.1 walks you through this procedure in more detail.

EXERCISE 7.1

Configuring Logins Without Passwords

This exercise guides you through the process of enabling SSH logins without passwords. You will require access to two computers, an SSH client and an SSH server. (In a pinch, you can use one computer in both roles, but this will obscure which files originate on or end up on which computer.) The SSH server must already be configured to accept logins.

1. Log into the SSH client system as the user who will be performing remote access.

2. Type the following command to generate a version 2 SSH key:

    ```
    $ ssh-keygen -q -t rsa -f ~/.ssh/id_rsa -C '' -N ''
    ```

3. Step 2 generates two files: id_rsa and id_rsa.pub. Transfer the second of these files to the SSH server computer in any way that's convenient—via a USB flash drive, by using scp, or by any other means. Copy the file under a temporary name, such as temp.rsa, to ensure you don't accidentally overwrite a like-named file on the server.

4. Log into the SSH server system. If you use SSH, you'll need to type your password.

5. Add the contents of the file you've just transferred to the end of the ~/.ssh/ authorized_keys file. (This file is sometimes called ~/.ssh/authorized_keys2, so you should check to see which is present. If neither is present, you may need to experiment.) Typing **cat ~/temp.rsa >> ~/.ssh/authorized_keys** should do this job, if you stored the original file as ~/temp.rsa.

If you omit the -N '' parameter in step 2, ssh-keygen will prompt for a passphrase. You will then need to enter this passphrase to log into the remote system; this effectively trades a client-based passphrase and SSH key exchange for a server-based password.

If you now log out of the SSH server system and try to log in again via SSH from the client, you shouldn't be prompted for a password; the two computers handle the authentication automatically. If this doesn't work, chances are the ~/.ssh/authorized_keys file needs another name, as described earlier. You may also want to check that the file includes a line matching the contents of the original public-key file on the client. Some older clients may require you to specify that you use version 2 of the SSH protocol by including the -2 option:

```
$ ssh -2 server
```

Using *ssh-agent*

Another SSH authentication option is to use the ssh-agent program. This program requires a password to initiate connections, so it's more secure than configuring logins without passwords; however, ssh-agent remembers your password, so you need to type it only once per local session. To use ssh-agent, follow these steps:

1. Follow the procedure for enabling no-password logins described in Exercise 7.1 but with one change: Omit the -N '' option from the ssh-keygen command in step 2. You'll be asked for a passphrase at this step. This passphrase will be your key for all SSH logins managed via ssh-agent.

2. On the SSH client system, type **ssh-agent /bin/bash**. This launches ssh-agent, which in turn launches bash. You'll use this bash session for subsequent SSH logins.

3. In your new shell, type **ssh-add ~/.ssh/id_rsa**. This adds your RSA key to the set that's managed by ssh-agent. You'll be asked to type your SSH passphrase at this time.

From this point on, whenever you use SSH to connect to a remote system to which you've given your public key, you won't need to type a password. You *will*, however, have to repeat steps 2 and 3 whenever you log into your computer, and the benefits will accrue only to the shell launched in step 2 or any shells you launch from that one.

If you make heavy use of this facility, you can insert ssh-agent into your normal login procedure. For instance, you can edit /etc/passwd so that ssh-agent /bin/bash is your login shell. For a GUI login, you can rename your normal GUI login script (for instance, change ~/.xsession to ~/.xsession-nossh) and create a new GUI login script that calls ssh-agent with the renamed script as its parameter. Either action inserts ssh-agent at the root of your user process tree so that any call to SSH uses ssh-agent.

Using SSH Login Scripts

Ordinarily, an SSH text-mode login session runs the user's configured shell, which runs the shell's defined login scripts. The OpenSSH server also supports its own login script, `sshrc` (normally stored in /etc or /etc/ssh). The OpenSSH server runs this script using /bin/sh, which is normally a symbolic link to bash, so you can treat it as an ordinary bash script.

Setting Up SSH Port Tunnels

SSH has the ability to extend its encryption capabilities to other protocols, but doing so requires extra configuration. The way this is done is known as *tunneling.* You can tunnel just about any protocol, but tunneling X is particularly common.

> SSH port tunnels are conceptually similar to VPN configurations, as described in Chapter 5. VPNs encrypt all the traffic between two computers or networks, whereas SSH is generally used to encrypt just one protocol or perhaps a small number of them. SSH's tunneling features can be stretched to create a true VPN, though, if you're so motivated. Many sites, including `http://tldp.org/HOWTO/ppp-ssh/`, describe ways to do this.

Tunneling Arbitrary Protocols

Figure 7.6 illustrates the basic idea behind an SSH tunnel. The server computer runs two server programs: a server for the tunneled protocol (Figure 7.6 uses the Internet Mail Access Protocol [IMAP] as an example) and an SSH server. The client computer also runs two clients: one for the tunneled protocol and one for SSH. The SSH client also listens for connections for the tunneled protocol; it's effectively both a client and a server. When the SSH client receives a connection from the tunneled protocol's client, the result is that the tunneled protocol's connection is encrypted using SSH, tunneled to the SSH server, and then directed to the target server. Thus, data pass over the network in encrypted form, even if the target protocol doesn't support encryption.

FIGURE 7.6   An SSH tunnel extends SSH's encryption benefits to other protocols

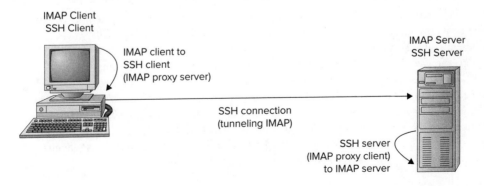

IMAP Client
SSH Client

IMAP client to
SSH client
(IMAP proxy server)

IMAP Server
SSH Server

SSH connection
(tunneling IMAP)

SSH server
(IMAP proxy client)
to IMAP server

Of course, all of this requires special configuration. The default configuration on the server enables tunneling; but to be sure, check the `/etc/ssh/sshd_config` file on the server for the following option:

```
AllowTcpForwarding no
```

If this line is present, change `no` to `yes`. If it's not present or if it's already set to `yes`, you shouldn't need to change your SSH server configuration.

On the client side, you must establish a special SSH connection to the server computer. You do this with the normal `ssh` client program, but you must pass it several parameters. An example will help illustrate this use of `ssh`:

```
# ssh -N -f -L 142:mail.luna.edu:143 benf@mail.luna.edu
```

The `-N` and `-f` options tell `ssh` to not execute a remote command and to execute in the background after asking for a password, respectively. These options are necessary to create a tunnel. The `-L` option specifies the local port on which to listen, the remote computer to which to connect, and the port on the remote computer to which to connect. This example listens on the local port 142 and connects to port 143 on `mail.luna.edu`. (You're likely to use the same port number on both ends; I changed the local port number in this example to more clearly distinguish between the local and remote port numbers.) The final parameter (`benf@mail.luna.edu` in this example) is the remote username and computer to which the tunnel goes. Note that this computer need not be the same as the target system specified via `-L`.

> If you want SSH on the client system to listen to a privileged port (that is, one numbered below 1024), you must execute the `ssh` program as root, as shown in the preceding example. If listening to a non-privileged port is acceptable, you can run the `ssh` client as a normal user.

With the tunnel established, you can use the client program to connect to the local port specified by the first number in the `-L` parameter (port 142 in the preceding example). For instance, this example is intended to forward IMAP traffic, so you'd configure a mail reader on the client to retrieve IMAP email from port 142 on `localhost`. When the email reader does this, SSH kicks in and forwards traffic to the SSH server, which then passes the data on to the local port 143, which is presumably running the real IMAP server. All of this is hidden from the email reader program; as far as it's concerned, it is retrieving email from a local IMAP server.

Tunneling X

Because an X server runs on the computer at which a user sits rather than on a remote computer, tunneling X works differently from tunneling other protocols. To tunnel X, the SSH server has to pretend to be an X server for the benefit of its X-based programs. The SSH server can then forward the X data it receives to the SSH client, which is presumably running on the same computer as the user's X server. (In fact, though, it's possible to relay X through an arbitrary number of SSH connections.)

This configuration is much simpler to manage than is tunneling most other protocols. In terms of configuration, you must ensure that the server's /etc/ssh/sshd_config file includes the following line:

X11Forwarding yes

If this line reads no rather than yes, change it to read yes.

On the client side, the /etc/ssh/ssh_config file should have the following option set:

ForwardX11 yes

This feature is less critical, though; it can be overridden on a case-by-case basis by using the -X or -x options to ssh to enable or disable, respectively, X tunneling. Setting the default in the global client configuration file is merely a convenience.

With these options set or with forwarding enabled on the server and -X used on the client, users will be able to launch X-based programs hosted on the SSH server computer from the SSH client computer, much as they would local programs.

SSH can compress data, which can improve the performance of tunneled sessions. On the client side, compression is enabled by adding a -C option to the ssh command. Adding compression to the mix can greatly enhance performance when tunneling X or other data-heavy protocols. I've found speed improvements on the order of 7x when using -C with graphics-heavy X applications tunneled through SSH over the Internet. The exact amount of benefit varies with the speed of the network connection, the nature of the data being transferred, the CPU speeds of both systems, and the CPU load on both systems.

SSH Security Considerations

SSH is intended to solve security problems rather than create them. Indeed, on the whole using SSH is superior to using Telnet for remote logins, and SSH can also take over FTP-like functions and tunnel other protocols. Thus, SSH is a big security plus compared to using less-secure tools.

Like all servers, though, SSH can be a security liability if it's run unnecessarily or inappropriately. Ideally, you should configure SSH to accept only protocol level 2 connections and to refuse direct root logins. If X forwarding is unnecessary, you should disable this feature. If possible, use TCP Wrappers or a firewall to limit the machines that can contact an SSH server. As with all servers, you should keep SSH up to date; there's always the possibility of a bug causing problems.

You should consider whether you really need a remote text-mode login server. Such a server can be a great convenience—often enough to justify the modest risk involved. For extremely high-security systems, though, using the computer exclusively from the console may be an appropriate approach to security.

One unusual security issue with SSH is its keys. As noted earlier, the private-key files are extremely sensitive and should be protected from prying eyes. Remember to protect the backups of these files, as well—don't leave a system backup tape lying around where it can be easily stolen.

Summary

One of Linux's biggest strengths is in its excellent tools for networking. This chapter introduced several of these tools, starting with the ISC DHCP server, which is commonly used to configure other computers' basic network settings. Although configuring this server takes some effort, doing so can save much more effort in configuring a wide range of Linux and non-Linux computers on your network.

Linux can also function as a network login server by using LDAP or various other tools. Although a full description of LDAP configuration is beyond the scope of this chapter, several LDAP account maintenance tools were described, providing you with the knowledge to add, delete, and modify user accounts on an LDAP server. Such tools can supplement, to the point of mostly replacing, the standard Linux account maintenance tools.

Routing is another area where Linux excels; you can configure Linux as a router for a small or large network. When you do this, you may want to configure firewall rules to protect both the router computer itself and the computers on one or both sides of the connection. These rules are implemented with the `iptables` utility, which fine-tunes how Linux routes packets. Another routing configuration is that of a NAT router, which is commonly employed to connect a small network to the Internet as a whole, keeping that network hidden from prying eyes on the Internet as a security measure. Finally, the RIP routing protocol, implemented in Linux by the routed daemon, helps you keep your routing tables up-to-date, should your system be part of a moderately complex collection of networks.

The final miscellaneous network topic covered in this chapter was the SSH server, which is the preferred remote login protocol for most purposes today. SSH is basically a text-mode protocol that supports strong encryption. Several variant configurations, such as options to support logins without using a password, can enhance its utility. SSH can also be used to tunnel other protocols, providing SSH's security benefits to whatever protocols need it.

Exam Essentials

Provide an overview of DHCP operation.   When a DHCP client boots or starts its network, it sends a broadcast to its local network segment seeking a DHCP server. If a server is present, it replies to the client, using the client's hardware address. The two computers can then communicate to negotiate a DHCP lease, which is a time-limited right to use an IP address. Before the lease expires, the client contacts the server to extend the lease. In addition to client IP address information, DHCP servers tell clients about the netmask, gateways, DNS servers, and other common network features.

Distinguish between dynamic and static DHCP leases.   Dynamic DHCP leases are assigned on a first-come, first-served basis from a pool of IP addresses. DHCP clients assigned a dynamic IP address can receive a different IP address each time they boot. Static DHCP leases, by contrast, are reserved for particular computers (identified by means of a hardware address or a claimed name); recipients of such addresses should seldom or never see their IP addresses change. Such leases are often reserved for server computers to simplify name resolution.

Describe where LDAP is best deployed for account management.   Networks on which many users need accounts on many computers are good candidates for LDAP account management. LDAP can centralize account management, enabling an administrator to make one change to add, delete, or modify an account on all the network's computers. Such changes can become a nightmare without LDAP when the number of computers grows too large, or even when the number of account changes grows large with just a few computers.

Summarize the important LDAP account management commands.   The `ldapadd` command adds an account, `ldapdelete` deletes an account, `ldapsearch` searches for account information, `ldapmodify` modifies an existing account, and `ldappasswd` changes a password. The `ldapadd` and `ldapmodify` commands both operate on LDIF files, which summarize the account information in a standardized format.

Explain the significance of NAT.   Network Address Translation (NAT) is a technique that enables a router to pretend to be the originating source of outgoing network traffic for an entire network, effectively "hiding" that network from the outside world. NAT is a useful security tool, since it makes it very difficult for an outsider to detect, much less attack, servers on the protected network. NAT can also stretch a limited number of IP addresses, since the protected network can exist in a private IP address space that's not officially part of the Internet.

Describe the conceptual framework behind `iptables`.   Linux uses a series of *chains* to determine how to direct network traffic. The INPUT chain handles incoming traffic, the OUTPUT chain handles outgoing traffic, and the FORWARD chain handles forwarded traffic (in a router). You can use `iptables` to associate rules with these chains that alter the way packets with specific criteria (such as a source port number or a destination IP address) are handled; they can be blocked or modified in various ways.

Summarize how a firewall is implemented in Linux.   Linux firewalls are generated by scripts that make repeated calls to `iptables`. Most of these calls set up one new rule to match one type of packet and alter how the system handles it. (A few calls can clear a chain of all rules, set a default policy, or otherwise act on more than one rule.) When the finished script is executed, it implements a new firewall configuration, which is retained by the kernel and used until it is altered again or the system reboots.

Explain the purpose of SSH.   The Secure Shell (SSH) is fundamentally a text-mode remote login protocol that provides encryption of all data transferred. SSH's encryption makes it the preferred remote-login protocol in Linux. SSH also offers tunneling of other protocols, which can turn an insecure unencrypted protocol into a much more secure encrypted one.

Describe the SSH configuration files.   The main SSH server configuration file is `/etc/ssh/sshd_config`. This file should not be confused with the SSH client configuration file, `/etc/ssh/ssh_config`. Both files consist of lines with option/value pairs that set SSH options.

Explain SSH's encryption keys.   An SSH server uses a number of encryption keys, which come in private and public pairs. Private keys are secret and must be stored with limited access on the server in `/etc/ssh`. Public keys have the same filename as their matching private keys, but with the filename extension `.pub`. These keys must be readable to any SSH user, and they are distributed to SSH client systems. Similar key pairs can be generated by users to enable logins without passwords or session-based logins using `ssh-agent`.

Summarize SSH protocol levels.   SSH levels 1.3 and 1.5 (collectively known as SSH 1.*x* or SSH 1) have known security problems and should be avoided whenever possible. The current version, SSH 2.0 or SSH 2, is much more secure. If your SSH server communicates only with reasonably modern clients, you can set the `Protocol 2` option in `/etc/ssh/sshd_config` to restrict support to SSH level 2 clients, ensuring that the insecure SSH 1 is not used on your system.

Review Questions

1. What is wrong with the following subnet declaration in an ISC DHCP server's `/etc/dhcpd.conf` file?

    ```
    subnet 10.107.5.0 {
        range 10.107.5.1 10.107.5.200;
    }
    ```

    A. It lacks domain name data.

    B. It lacks network mask data.

    C. It lacks a DNS server IP address.

    D. It lacks a gateway IP address.

2. Where does the ISC DHCP server store data on the leases it has issued?

    A. `leases.conf`, typically in `/var/dhcp`

    B. `leases.log`, typically in `/var/log/dhcp`

    C. `dhcpd.log`, typically in `/var/dhcp/leases`

    D. `dhcpd.leases`, typically in `/var/lib/dhcp`

3. You set a global `max-lease-time 3600` option in the DHCP configuration file. What is the effect of this configuration?

    A. DHCP clients will receive leases of at most 1 hour (3,600 seconds), even if they ask for longer leases.

    B. DHCP clients will receive leases of 1 hour (3,600 seconds) unless they ask for longer or shorter leases.

    C. DHCP clients will receive leases of at least 1 hour (3,600 seconds), even if they ask for shorter leases.

    D. DHCP clients will receive leases at most 1 hour (3,600 seconds) unless they're configured for fixed IP addresses.

4. On which of the following computers might you most plausibly run the `dhcrelay` program? (Select two.)

    A. A computer that runs `dhcpd` on a subnet that links to the Internet via a NAT router

    B. A computer on a completely isolated network that has no router and no DHCP server of its own

    C. A router between two subnets, one of which has a DHCP server and the other of which does not

    D. A computer on a subnet with no DHCP server of its own, with a DHCP server configured to serve the first subnet on a nearby subnet

5. What is wrong with the following entry in an LDIF file intended for use in managing Linux accounts?

`uid: tsparker`

A. This entry should use the `username` attribute name, not `uid`.

B. The `uid` attribute name requires a full distinguished name.

C. The `uid` attribute requires a numeric Linux user ID (UID) value.

D. Nothing is wrong with this entry.

6. You've prepared an LDIF file (`newusers.ldif`) with several new user definitions, and you want to add these new users to your LDAP-based account directory for `example.com`, using the administrative account called `manager`. How can you do so, assuming your system is properly configured to enable such modifications?

A. `ldapadd -D manager@example.com newusers.ldif`

B. `ldapadd cn=manager,dc=example,dc=com newusers.ldif`

C. `ldapadd -D manager@example.com -W -f newusers.ldif`

D. `ldapadd -D cn=manager,dc=example,dc=com -W -f newusers.ldif`

7. You want to remove the Z shell (`zsh`) from a computer whose users are all defined via an LDAP server. Before doing so, though, you want to check that none of these users relies on `zsh` as the default shell. How can you check to see whether any users do so?

A. `ldapmodify --search loginShell=/bin/zsh`

B. `ldappasswd --search loginShell=/bin/zsh`

C. `ldap --search loginShell=/bin/zsh`

D. `ldapsearch loginShell=/bin/zsh`

8. What is the default method of encrypting passwords in LDAP?

A. Cleartext

B. MD5

C. SSHA

D. CRYPT

9. Which of the following is a *disadvantage* of using NAT to connect a small business's network to the Internet?

A. The business can acquire a smaller block of Internet-accessible IP addresses than might be required without NAT.

B. A buggy Web server that's accidentally left running on the internal network will be protected from miscreants on the Internet.

C. It will be difficult to run file and printer sharing servers on the internal network for use by clients on the internal network.

D. Additional configuration will be required if servers on the internal network should be accessible to the Internet.

10. You want to configure a router for a small network so that external sites cannot connect to the SSH port on internal computers, but you want no such restriction for the router itself. What is the *best* chain to modify to accomplish this goal?

    A. INPUT

    B. OUTPUT

    C. FORWARD

    D. ACCEPT

11. Which of the following is true of the DROP policy for `iptables`?

    A. It replies as if the computer was available but running no software on the target port.

    B. It ignores packets, providing the illusion of a network error between the sender and recipient.

    C. It may be used only on ports that are opened by servers, not clients.

    D. It may be applied as a default policy but not on a port-by-port basis.

12. A firewall script includes the following two lines. What is their purpose?

    ```
    iptables -A OUTPUT -d 127.0.0.1 -o lo -j ACCEPT
    iptables -A INPUT -s 127.0.0.1 -i lo -j ACCEPT
    ```

    A. To set the default policy for all chains to ACCEPT; subsequent rules will use DROP or REJECT

    B. To enable routing of localhost traffic on a computer configured as a router

    C. To enable communications over the localhost interface for local programs

    D. To set the default policy for the OUTPUT and INPUT chains to ACCEPT, leaving the FORWARD chain unaffected

13. Broadly speaking, how will use of `iptables` on a router with firewall features differ from its use on a workstation?

    A. A router's `iptables` rules will emphasize the FORWARD chain; a workstation's will emphasize the INPUT and OUTPUT chains.

    B. A router's `iptables` rules will most likely use a default DROP policy, whereas a workstation's will probably use a default ACCEPT policy.

    C. A router's `iptables` rules will be activated by a script, whereas a workstation's will be configured using a GUI tool.

    D. A router's `iptables` rules will emphasize privileged port numbers, whereas a workstation's will emphasize unprivileged port numbers.

14. What program can you use to generate a key that will enable logins to remote SSH servers without using a password?

    A. authorized_keys

    B. ssh-keygen

    C. sshpasswd

    D. id_rsa

15. To whom should you distribute your server's main SSH private key?

    A. Only to servers with which you want to communicate

    B. Only to servers that have already provided their own public keys

    C. To anybody who can provide a matching SSH public key

    D. None of the above

16. Which of the following commands creates an encrypted login to a remote computer (neptune), definitely enabling use of X-based programs run on the remote computer and using the local computer's X server? (Assume that neptune is configured to enable X forwarding.)

    A. ssh -XC neptune

    B. ssh neptune

    C. ssh --ForwardX11 neptune

    D. ssh -x neptune

17. Which two of the following servers might you consider retiring after activating an SSH server? (Select two.)

    A. SMTP

    B. Telnet

    C. FTP

    D. NFS

18. You find that the ssh_host_dsa_key file in /etc/ssh has 0666 (-rw-rw-rw-) permissions. Your SSH server has been in operation for several months. Should you be concerned?

    A. Yes

    B. No

    C. Only if the ssh_host_dsa_key.pub file is also world-readable

    D. Only if you're launching SSH from a super server

19. For best SSH server security, how should you set the `Protocol` option in `/etc/ssh/sshd_config`?

   A. `Protocol 1`

   B. `Protocol 2`

   C. `Protocol 1,2`

   D. `Protocol 2,1`

20. Why is it unwise to allow `root` to log on directly using SSH?

   A. Somebody with the `root` password but no other password can then break into the computer.

   B. The `root` password should never be sent over a network connection; allowing `root` logins in this way is inviting disaster.

   C. SSH stores all login information, including passwords, in a publicly readable file.

   D. When logged on using SSH, `root`'s commands can be easily intercepted and duplicated by undesirable elements.

Answers to Review Questions

1. B. A `subnet` declaration begins with that keyword followed by a subnet number, the `netmask` keyword, and a network mask value. Thus, option B is correct; the network mask data should be present. Options A, C, and D are all correct observations but incorrect answers because these pieces of information may all be declared elsewhere and in fact aren't strictly necessary.

2. D. DHCP lease information is stored in a file called `dhcpd.leases`. This file is often, but not always, stored in `/var/lib/dhcp`, making option D correct. Although the locations specified in options A, B, and D are all theoretically plausible, they all specify incorrect filenames and so are incorrect.

3. A. Option A correctly describes the meaning of this option. (Note, however, that this option is ignored for clients that use BOOTP rather than DHCP.) Option B describes the effect of the `default-lease-time` option, and option C describes the effect of the `min-lease-time` option. Option D is incorrect because a fixed IP address configuration does not automatically override the lease time options. (A fixed IP address block could include its own `max-lease-time` option to override the global option, though.)

4. Answers: C, D. The `dhcrelay` program acts as a proxy server for a DHCP server located elsewhere; `dhcrelay` responds to DHCP clients, but it relays the client's requests to another subnet's DHCP server and then delivers the server's responses back to the client. The `dhcrelay` program does not need to be on the same subnet as the DHCP server, but if it is (as, for instance, in the case of a router), it will work fine. Thus, options C and D are both valid locations for a computer running `dhcrelay`. Option A is incorrect because the specified computer runs a full DHCP server (`dhcpd`), so `dhcrelay` isn't likely to do any good; even if it were being used as a backup or to handle a few computers in an exotic configuration, the only computers to which it could relay traffic are isolated from the target network by a NAT router. Thus, this configuration would be bizarre at best and dangerous at worst. Option B is incorrect because `dhcrelay` would have no way to contact a DHCP server. If option B's network is functional, it's presumably configured using static IP addresses rather than DHCP, making `dhcrelay` pointless.

5. D. The LDIF `uid` attribute name identifies a Linux username, so it can take the value of any legal Linux username. As `tsparker` is a legal Linux username, there is nothing wrong with this entry, making option D correct. There is no `username` attribute name in a Linux account management LDIF file, so option A is incorrect. Because the `uid` attribute is a Linux username, not a distinguished name (DN), option B is incorrect. Confusingly, the `uid` attribute name refers to a Linux username; Linux UID values are specified with the `uidNumber` attribute name, making option C incorrect.

6. D. Option D presents the correct syntax for performing the task specified in the question. Options A and C both incorrectly express the distinguished name (DN) for the account used to perform administrative tasks, and options A and B both omit the `-W` (prompt for authentication) and `-f` (to pass a filename) options.

7. D. The `ldapsearch` utility searches an LDAP directory for records matching the specified field. Option D presents the correct syntax to perform a search for accounts using `/bin/zsh` as the default shell. The `ldapmodify` and `ldappasswd` commands are used to submit a modified LDIF file and change a password, respectively; neither is used to search records. There is no standard utility called `ldap`.

8. C. By default, LDAP uses SSHA for password encryption. Cleartext, MD5, and CRYPT are all valid alternatives, but none of them is the default. (Cleartext is also very inadvisable, since this refers to no encryption at all.)

9. D. By its nature, NAT blocks access to the protected network's servers. This feature can be overcome by port redirection, but doing so requires extra configuration effort; thus, option D is correct. Options A and B both describe features of NAT, but these features are advantages, not disadvantages, of NAT. Option C is incorrect because NAT does not affect the ability to run servers on an internal network for use by clients on that same network; only outside access to those servers is affected.

10. C. The FORWARD chain controls packets that a router forwards between networks, which is the type of action the question describes; thus, option C is correct. The INPUT and OUTPUT chains affect packets accepted by or sent by the computer, respectively, so modifying those chains would affect the router itself. (You could add rules based on IP addresses or other criteria to accomplish the stated goals using these chains, but that adds complexity, making these chains less desirable choices at best.) There is no standard ACCEPT chain, although this is a common action, meaning that a packet is to be passed.

11. B. The DROP policy causes the computer to respond as described in option B. Option A describes the REJECT policy, not the DROP policy. Contrary to option C, DROP may be used on any port, whether it's used by clients or servers. Contrary to option D, DROP may be used either as a default policy or on a port-by-port basis.

12. C. Linux uses the localhost (127.0.0.1) IP address for local communications; network-enabled programs use this address for communications even on one system. If your default `iptables` policy is DROP or REJECT, this interface will be blocked, so it's necessary to unblock it using lines like those shown in the question, making option C correct. The default policy, referenced in options A and D, is set using the `-P` option, as in `iptables -t filter -P FORWARD DROP`, so these options are incorrect. Routing of localhost traffic makes no logical sense—localhost traffic is, by definition, local and therefore is not routed—so option B is incorrect.

13. A. The FORWARD chain is used for forwarding traffic, as in a router, so a router's firewall will include rules that affect the way the router forwards network traffic. A workstation doesn't normally forward traffic, so there will be few or no rules affecting the FORWARD chain on a workstation, making option A correct. Contrary to option B, both workstations and routers may use either the DROP policy or the ACCEPT policy (or the REJECT policy) as a default, although ACCEPT is the least-preferred policy. Although both scripts and GUI tools can be used to create a firewall, there is no necessary link between these tools and the type of computer, as option C suggests, so that option is incorrect. Option D is incorrect because, although the distinction between privileged and unprivileged port numbers is an important one, only the server's port numbers (which are, by and large, privileged) are fixed, so even a workstation's `iptables` rules will emphasize these port numbers.

14. B. The ssh_keygen utility generates SSH keys, including private keys for individuals, that can be used instead of passwords for remote logins to SSH servers. (These keys must be transferred and added to appropriate files on the server; using ssh-keygen alone isn't enough to accomplish the goal.) Option A's authorized_keys is a file in which keys are stored on a server; it's not a program to generate them. Option C's sshpasswd is fictitious. Option D's id_rsa is the file in which private keys are stored on the client; it's not a program to generate them.

15. D. SSH private keys are extremely sensitive, and they should not normally be distributed to anybody, since possession of another system's private key will make it easier for a miscreant to pretend to be you. Thus, option D is correct. It's safe to distribute *public* keys widely, as in any of the other options, and in fact SSH does this automatically; but *private* keys should remain just that: *private*.

16. A. The -X option to ssh enables X forwarding on the SSH client side, and -C enables compression. Thus, option A does as the question asks. (Compression was not specified as required in the question but was also not forbidden.) Option B might work, but only if the system is configured to forward X connections by default; since the question specifies that X forwarding is definitely required, option B is not correct. Option C is incorrect because there is no --ForwardX11 option to ssh; however, ForwardX11 is a valid option in the ssh configuration file, /etc/ssh_config. A lowercase -x, as in option D, *disables* X forwarding, so this option is incorrect.

17. Answers: B, C. SSH is most directly a replacement for Telnet, but SSH also includes file-transfer features that enable it to replace FTP in many situations. SSH is not a direct replacement for either SMTP or NFS.

18. A. The ssh_host_dsa_key file holds one of three critical private keys for SSH. The fact that this key is readable (and writeable!) to the entire world is disturbing. In principle, a miscreant who has acquired this file might be able to redirect traffic and masquerade as your system, duping users into delivering passwords and other sensitive data.

19. B. SSH protocol level 2 is more secure than protocol level 1; thus, option B (specifying acceptance of level 2 only) is the safest approach. Option A is the *least* safe approach because it precludes the use of the safer level 2. Options C and D are exactly equivalent in practice; both support both protocol levels.

20. A. Allowing only normal users to log in via SSH effectively requires two passwords for any remote root maintenance, improving security. SSH encrypts all connections, so it's unlikely that the password, or commands issued during an SSH session, will be intercepted. (Nonetheless, some administrators prefer not to take even this small risk.) SSH doesn't store passwords in a file.

Chapter

8

Configuring File Servers

THE FOLLOWING LINUX PROFESSIONAL INSTITUTE OBJECTIVES ARE COVERED IN THIS CHAPTER:

- ✓ 209.1 SAMBA Server Configuration (weight: 4)
- ✓ 209.2 NFS Server Configuration (weight: 4)
- ✓ 212.2 Securing FTP Servers (weight: 2)

In many offices, one of Linux's major roles is as a *file server*—a computer that holds files that are read, modified, and written by client computers. A file server can help centralize data storage for administrative and backup purposes, and it can facilitate collaboration by enabling users to share or exchange documents.

Linux is well suited to the role of a file server because it has excellent server programs for the most common protocols: The Samba Suite (`http://www.samba.org`) is a powerful and highly configurable package that manages the Server Message Block/Common Internet File System (SMB/CIFS) protocol used on many Windows-dominated networks; the Network File System (NFS) protocol, which is Unix's dominant file sharing protocol, is handled by a server of the same name; and several Linux server programs exist to handle the File Transfer Protocol (FTP), which is a popular means of cross-platform file sharing, particularly on the Internet.

Understanding the Role of a File Server

In some sense, many servers are file servers; for instance, email messages and Web pages can be thought of as files and indeed are stored as such on disks. A file server as typically defined, though, gives users access to files as such. Some file server protocols, including SMB/CIFS and NFS, are designed to provide common filesystem features to clients. This enables clients to treat the file server as if it were a hard disk, mounting it and giving users access to files on the server as if they were local files. (In SMB/CIFS, the directories shared in this way are referred to as *shares*; in NFS, they're referred to as *exports*.) This model for a file server is extremely powerful, since it simplifies the user experience; users can double-click network share icons on their desktops and then double-click file icons to launch applications associated with the file types, such as a word processor or a graphics editor.

SMB/CIFS was designed with DOS, Windows, and OS/2 in mind, and so it supports the filesystem features that are common to these OSs. This fact presents certain challenges for Samba, since Samba must map the Microsoft-style filesystem features onto the nearest Linux equivalents. Much of Samba's complexity derives from the need to make these mappings. In most cases, this works well, and users can be blissfully unaware that their files are stored on a Linux computer. Samba also supports extensions, implemented in the CIFS portion of the SMB/CIFS protocols, that enable it to store Unix-style filesystem metadata so that Samba can act as a server for Unix and Linux clients while retaining their native filesystem metadata. Since it originated in the Unix world, NFS is even better suited to act as a server for Unix and Linux clients; NFS more directly maps Unix-style filesystem metadata onto the underlying filesystem.

 SMB/CIFS was originally implemented over a protocol stack known as NetBIOS Extended User Interface (NetBEUI). The standard Linux kernel doesn't support NetBEUI, though, and SMB/CIFS today is usually run over the same Transmission Control Protocol/Internet Protocol (TCP/IP) stack that handles most other network protocols. A few NetBEUI remnants remain in SMB/CIFS, though; for instance, computers using SMB/CIFS can optionally use a NetBIOS name instead of a TCP/IP hostname.

FTP is typically used in a different way; this protocol doesn't support all the filesystem features normally needed to mount a filesystem. Instead, FTP servers are typically accessed via FTP client programs, such as the text-mode `ftp` or `ncftp` or the GUI gFTP. Linux provides FTP clients, as part of the Filesystems in Userspace (FUSE; `http://fuse.sourceforge.net`) project, that enable FTP sites to be mounted like filesystems, but for the most part, FTP involves dedicated user-mode clients rather than the filesystem mounts that are common with SMB/CIFS and NFS.

 Real World Scenario

Alternatives to SMB/CIFS, NFS, and FTP

In some cases, you may need to use a file server protocol other than SMB/CIFS, NFS, and FTP. One alternative is the Hypertext Transfer Protocol (HTTP), which is the protocol used for the World Wide Web (WWW or Web for short). Chapter 9, "Configuring Web and Email Servers" describes the configuration of the popular Apache Web server. Although HTTP is a useful protocol, it's mainly intended for one-way access—users retrieve Web pages, but the ability to upload documents to Web sites is more limited. HTTP also requires most transfers to be self-contained, including any required authentication, whereas SMB/CIFS, NFS, and FTP establish a connection that can then be used more simply over an extended period.

Another alternative to the main protocols described in this chapter is AppleShare (also known as AppleShare File Protocol, or AFP), which is part of the AppleTalk protocol suite. AppleShare was once a very common protocol on networks dominated by Apple computers, and Mac OS X still supports it. In Linux, the Netatalk package (`http://netatalk.sourceforge.net`) supports AppleShare IP, which is a variant of AppleShare that works over TCP/IP rather than the largely obsolete AppleTalk protocol stack. Because OS X supports both SMB/CIFS and NFS, there's usually no need to deploy Netatalk on a Linux computer; however, if you have very old Mac clients, using Netatalk may be beneficial.

A protocol that competes with SMB/CIFS is Novell's NetWare (or the NetWare Core Protocol, or NCP), which typically runs over its Internet Packet Exchange/Sequenced Packet Exchange (IPX/SPX) protocol stack. The Linux kernel includes IPX/SPX support, and NCP is implemented in Mars_nwe (http://www.compu-art.de/mars_nwe/). Novell has also released official Linux NCP support, currently available as Open Enterprise Server (OES). Chances are SMB/CIFS is a better option unless you have a network that relies heavily on legacy NetWare protocols. A Linux server could function as a transitional platform, enabling the same files to be served via both NCP and SMB/CIFS while you phase out the NetWare clients.

Configuring a Samba Server

The Samba server suite, which is usually installed via a package called samba or samba-server, handles the SMB/CIFS protocol that's common on Windows networks. To configure Samba, you must first set some critical global options. You may also need to adjust the mapping of Windows to Linux usernames and passwords. You can then define file and printer shares, which enable sharing of files and printers. You can also configure Linux as an SMB/CIFS client, using Samba, Windows, or even more exotic SMB/CIFS servers.

Setting Global Samba Options

Samba's main configuration file is called smb.conf, and it's stored in the /etc/samba directory on all major Linux distributions. Some older or obscure distributions may store this file in another directory, such as /etc/samba.d or /etc/smb. The smb.conf file is broken down into sections, each of which is led by a name in square brackets, such as [global] or [home]. Subsequent lines, up until the next section name, belong to the specified section.

Understanding Samba Configuration File Sections

Three types of sections exist:

The Global Section The first section in most smb.conf files is the [global] section. This section defines global defaults and sets options that affect the overall performance of the server, such as its NetBIOS name.

File Shares File shares enable Samba to deliver files to clients and to accept files from clients.

Printer Shares Printer shares are very similar to file shares in many respects, but Samba sends the files that a printer share accepts into Linux's local print queue, so they end up being printed.

Within each section, options are assigned using lines of the following form:

`option = value`

Options and most values are case-insensitive. (Some values are Linux pathnames or other inherently case-sensitive strings, though.) Boolean values of 1, True, and Yes are equivalent, as are 0, False, and No. Hash marks (#) and semicolons (;) are both comment characters; lines beginning with these characters are ignored.

Setting Basic Global Options

The [global] section is particularly important to Samba's functioning. In fact, your Samba server probably won't be useable by your Windows clients until you've made one or two changes to this section. Table 8.1 summarizes some of the features you might want to change in this section. As with similar tables throughout this chapter, Table 8.1 is far from complete. You may need to consult the Samba documentation or a book on the server to learn about additional options if you have problems. The man page for smb.conf is unusually complete—but for this very reason, it can take a while to read it or even to search it for relevant information.

TABLE 8.1   Common global Samba options

Option	Type of value	Meaning
workgroup	String	NetBIOS workgroup or NetBIOS domain name. Often, but not always, related to the network's TCP/IP domain name.
netbios name	String	Computer's NetBIOS name. Often, but not always, the same as the computer's TCP/IP hostname without the domain portion. This is also the default value.
printing	String	Name of the printing system, such as LPRng or CUPS. Samba adjusts its printing command to suit the printing system.
printcap name	Filename	Name of the /etc/printcap file or a stand-in for it (such as cups). This option is necessary for the [printers] share to operate correctly.
load printers	Boolean	Whether to make all your locally defined printers available when a [printers] share is present. The default value is Yes.
hosts allow and hosts deny	Host names or IP addresses	Host-based access controls, similar to those provided by TCP Wrappers or xinetd.

TABLE 8.1   Common global Samba options *(continued)*

Option	Type of value	Meaning
security	Share, User, Server, Domain, or ADS	Specifies how Samba authenticates local users—by mimicking the method used by Windows 9x/Me (Share) on a share-by-share basis, by using usernames and passwords (User), by sending an authentication request to another computer (Server), by deferring to an NT domain controller (Domain), or by deferring to an Active Directory (AD) domain controller (ADS).
encrypt passwords	Boolean	Specifies whether to require encrypted passwords.
smb passwd file	Filename	Encrypted password file.
password server	Hostname or IP address	Identifies the network's domain controller, as described shortly.
username map	Filename	File that holds mappings of Windows-style and Linux-style usernames.
name resolve order	One or more of lmhosts, host, wins, or bcast	Tells Samba how to resolve names: lmhosts uses a file called /etc/samba/lmhosts (similar to the /etc/hosts file); host means to use normal DNS name resolution; wins means to use a Windows Internet Name Service (WINS) server specified via the wins server option; and bcast means to use NetBIOS name broadcasts. Multiple values may be separated by spaces.

NetBIOS domains and TCP/IP domains are conceptually similar, but they aren't identical. For simplicity, you may want to configure your networks in such a way that you use a single name for both domain types; but if you're using a pre-existing network, you may find that a computer is on a NetBIOS domain with one name and a TCP/IP domain with another name.

Setting Password Options

Two of the options in Table 8.1 are very important for most systems. The first of these options is encrypt passwords. All versions of Windows since Windows 95 OEM Service Release 2 (OSR2) and Windows NT 4.0 Service Pack 3 use encrypted passwords by default. If encrypt passwords is set to No, Samba uses the Linux username and password database.

In this case, recent Windows clients won't connect to Samba unless the Samba or Windows client configuration is changed. When `encrypt passwords` is set to `Yes`, Samba requires its own password database, which is independent of the standard Linux password database. In this case, recent Windows clients will connect to the Samba server. In practice, it's usually easiest and safest to use encrypted passwords. To do so, follow these steps:

1. If necessary, set `encrypt passwords` to Yes.

2. As root, type **smbpasswd -a *username*** at a command prompt, where *username* is a username for a user who should have access to the Samba server. The program will prompt for a new password, and then it will prompt you to type it again. The first time you issue this command, it will complain that the `passdb` database doesn't exist. You can ignore this complaint.

3. Repeat step 2 for all the users who should have Samba access.

If you have many users, the process of adding them all to Samba's encrypted password database can be tedious, but it's necessary. Many distributions include a script called `mksmbpasswd` or `mksmbpasswd.sh` that can create a Samba password file from a Linux /etc/passwd file. Unfortunately, Linux and Samba use different methods of encrypting passwords, so it's not possible to convert actual passwords. The resulting Samba password file includes usernames but no passwords. As a result, `mksmbpasswd` saves little or no effort. If you can run with unencrypted passwords for a time, though, you could use this script and use the `update encrypted = Yes` option. Samba will then add passwords to its encrypted database as users log on using unencrypted passwords. (You must run with `encrypt passwords = No` for this process to work.) This practice might be useful if you were migrating a network from unencrypted to encrypted passwords, but for most existing installations, it's not an option.

As just described, local Samba passwords rely on a setting of the `security` option to `User`. This option causes Samba to maintain its own list of users and passwords or to rely on the regular Linux account database, as just described. Another approach, described shortly, employs a domain controller for account maintenance. A third approach, exemplified by `security = Share`, attempts to mimic the way that old Windows 9*x*/Me servers authenticated users: No username is used, and instead a unique password is used with each share. When set to use this method, Samba runs through a series of accounts for authentication, including any username that the client might send even though it's not required to do so, the name of the share, the client's NetBIOS name, and any usernames explicitly provided by the `username` parameter (if present) in the share. This is an awkward system of checks, so in most cases, user-level security or one of the options that relies on a domain controller is used.

The smbpasswd utility is Samba's equivalent to the standard Linux passwd utility. When Samba is configured to use local accounts (that is, `security = User`), users can type **smbpasswd** to change their local passwords. When you join a domain, as described later, users can use the `-r` option to specify a remote domain controller, as in **smbpasswd -r central** to change the password on the computer called `central`.

Setting Workgroup or Domain Options

The second option you'll most likely have to adjust from Table 8.1 is workgroup. SMB/CIFS networks are built atop NetBIOS workgroups or domains. If your Samba server's workgroup name isn't set correctly, your Windows clients won't be able to find it—at least, not easily. If you don't know what your workgroup name is, try typing the following command (note the trailing dash in the command):

```
$ nmblookup -MS -
querying __MSBROWSE__ on 192.168.1.255
192.168.1.1 __MSBROWSE__<01>
Looking up status of 192.168.1.1
        SPEAKER         <00> -          M <ACTIVE>
        SPEAKER         <03> -          M <ACTIVE>
        SPEAKER         <20> -          M <ACTIVE>
        ..__MSBROWSE__. <01> - <GROUP> M <ACTIVE>
        RINGWORLD       <00> - <GROUP> M <ACTIVE>
        RINGWORLD       <1b> -          M <ACTIVE>
        RINGWORLD       <1c> - <GROUP> M <ACTIVE>
        RINGWORLD       <1d> -          M <ACTIVE>
        RINGWORLD       <1e> - <GROUP> M <ACTIVE>
```

The output includes information on both the *master browser* computer (which manages lists of computers for browsing with GUI server-locating tools) and on the workgroup. In this case, SPEAKER is the master browser for the RINGWORLD workgroup.

Many Windows networks today use a domain configuration rather than a workgroup configuration. Domains may be either NT domains or Active Directory (AD) domains. A domain is basically a workgroup with some additional features, most of which relate to user authentication. You specify the domain name using the same workgroup option used to specify the workgroup; however, to use a domain controller for authentication, you must also set three additional options:

- You must set the name of the domain controller with the password server option.

- You must set encrypt passwords to Yes.

- You must set the security option to Server, Domain, or ADS.

Using security = Server is the simplest method to use, but in this configuration, the Samba server isn't a full member of the domain. Setting security = Domain causes Samba to fully join a domain using the older NT protocols, and using security = ADS causes Samba to fully join the domain using the newer AD protocols.

If you use either domain- or AD-level security, you must explicitly join the domain using the following command:

```
$ net join member -U adminuser
```

In this command, *adminuser* is the domain's administrative user, as defined on the domain controller. The domain controller may need to be configured to permit the Samba server to join the domain. If all goes well, you'll be prompted for a password, and Samba will store the necessary information locally so that you won't need to join the domain again; this command need be typed only once. In practice, using domain- or AD-level security can be tricky; a number of finicky details can cause the `net join` command to fail. The Samba developers encourage use of full domain membership over server-level security, though.

Any of these approaches to security (server, domain, or ADS) have the advantage that you needn't maintain a full Samba account database on the server computer. You must, however, maintain a conventional Linux account database for the computer's users. On a network with few users, you can probably do this manually. On a larger network, though, you might want to use tools to help automate this task. Some possibilities include:

Use a Local Script   The `add user script` option in Samba can run a script when a user is authenticated. If you write a simple script to add a local account, you can ensure that you'll have local accounts for all your users. This approach will *not*, however, automatically remove accounts when they're removed from the domain controller.

Use LDAP   A Lightweight Directory Access Protocol (LDAP) server, as described briefly in Chapter 7, "Advanced Network Configuration," can manage accounts. If you're using an AD server for Windows, you can extend it to fill this role.

Use Winbind   Samba includes an ancillary package called Winbind, which enables Linux to use a domain controller much like it can use an LDAP server. Using Winbind can be convenient on a Windows-dominated network, but it requires generating and storing some Linux-specific information locally, since a Windows server knows nothing about features like Linux user ID (UID) numbers and home directories.

Full descriptions of these options are beyond the scope of this book; I mention them here only so that you can explore them yourself should the need arise.

Mapping Linux and Windows Usernames

Linux usernames are generally short single words, such as `tgilliam` or `samlowry`. Windows networks often favor using fuller mixed-case names with spaces, such as `T Gilliam` or `Sam Lowry`. You can use either type of name in either OS (although some Linux utilities, such as `useradd`, impose more stringent rules); however, it's sometimes necessary to create a way to "translate" usernames between the two systems. This is done via the file specified via the `username map` option in `smb.conf` (the filename `username.map` is often used for this purpose, but you can use any filename you like). Each line in this file begins with a single Linux username and continues with an equal sign (=) and a space-delimited list of usernames that will be accepted in its place. Listing 8.1 provides an example.

Listing 8.1: An example `username.map` file

```
!tgilliam = "T Gilliam" Terry
!samlowry = slowry "Sam Lowry" Sam
!jlayton = Jill
!tuttle = @heating
nobody = *
```

Listing 8.1 illustrates several features of the username map file:

- Because spaces are used to separate usernames on the right side of each entry, quotes (") must be used to specify a username that includes a space.

- Usernames on the right side may be unusual by typical Linux standards, as in Sam Lowry; or they can be ordinary by Linux standards, as in slowry.

- An ampersand (@) leading a right-side name means to decode the name into all the members of that local or Network Information System (NIS) group. Thus, Listing 8.1 converts all members of the heating group into the local username tuttle.

- An asterisk (*) is a wildcard that matches any name, which may be used to map unknown names to a known local user.

- Ordinarily, processing continues after a match has been made. An exclamation mark (!) at the start of an entry means to stop processing at that point if it matches a name. This is particularly important on the lines *before* using wildcards, lest all usernames be converted to the default name (nobody in Listing 8.1). Protecting groups specified via an ampersand can be important, too.

When using share- or user-level security, the username map is applied *before* authentication, so Windows-style usernames are mapped to Linux-style usernames before the password is authenticated. When using server-, domain-, or ADS-level security, though, the username map file is applied *after* authentication. This enables the domain controller to store the Windows-style username, while the Samba server can rely on its local Linux username internally.

Configuring File Shares

File shares begin with the share name in square brackets and continue until the next share definition or until the end of the file. Typically, lines after the share name line are indented, although this isn't required. A fairly basic file share looks like this:

```
[test]
    comment = Test share on %L
    path = /exports/shared
    writeable = Yes
```

This share delivers the contents of /exports/shared under the share name `test`. Most of these options aren't actually required; they provide extra information to clients (the `comment` option) or set features of the share (the `writeable` option). Even the `path` option can be omitted—the default value is /tmp, except in one special case, described shortly. Table 8.2 summarizes some of the most common file share options.

TABLE 8.2 Common file share Samba options

Option	Type of value	Meaning
comment	String	A one-line description of the share, which appears in some views of the share from the client.
path or directory	Directory name	The directory to be shared.
browseable or browsable	Boolean	Whether the share appears in browsers. The default value is Yes.
writeable, writable, or write ok	Boolean	Whether users can write to the share, given the appropriate permissions. The default value is No.
create mask	Octal permission string	The Linux permissions assigned to new files created by clients. (Execute permission bits may be modified by other options, though.)
directory mask	Octal permission string	The Linux permissions assigned to new directories created by clients. (Execute permission bits may be modified by other options, though.)
nt acl support	Boolean	Whether to map Linux file ownership and permissions onto Windows NT-style ACLs. The default value is Yes.
force user	Username	An override to the username assigned to new files created by users. Also affects the files the user can read or write.
available	Boolean	Whether the share is active; setting this option to No effectively disables the share. (Note that valid is similar, but more extreme. Samba's developers encourage use of available = No rather than valid = No to disable a share.)
valid users	Username list	Specifies users who are authorized to access the share.

Many Samba options are available with alternative spellings or synonyms. For instance, `writeable`, `writable`, and `write ok` are all synonymous. An antonym for all of these is `read only`; `read only = True` is the same as `writeable = False`.

Many Samba file share options affect how Samba handles the translation between Linux ownership, permissions, filenames, and other filesystem details and features that DOS and Windows expect on their filesystems. DOS and Windows 9x/Me don't support Linux ownership and permissions, so Samba uses `create mask` and `directory mask` to set default permissions. Samba uses the username of the individual who mounted the share to set the owner of new files, unless `force user` overrides that setting. Modern versions of Windows support ownership and access control lists (ACLs). When such a client connects to Samba, the server maps Linux ownership and permissions onto limited ACLs. If you use an ACL-enabled filesystem with a recent Samba package, you get better ACL support for your clients.

One special Samba file share comes predefined in many distributions' `smb.conf` files: `[homes]`. This share is unusual because it maps to the user's home directory. For instance, if the user `jill` has a home directory of `/home/jill` and if this user opens a browser onto the server from a Windows machine, a `[homes]` share will appear under the name `jill`. If this user opens this share, she'll find files from her home directory available in the share.

To display a `[homes]` share with the user's username, the user must have logged into the server. A few non-Windows SMB/CIFS browsers don't prompt for a password, and hence aren't fully logged in, until after the user selects the share to open. In these browsers, the `[homes]` share appears by that name, but when the user accesses the share, it opens on the user's home directory.

The `[homes]` share is unusual in a couple of configuration details. First, it normally includes a `browseable = No` option, which would ordinarily make the share disappear from browse lists. In the case of `[homes]`, this option makes the share name `homes` disappear from browse lists, but a share named after the user remains in the browse list. Second, `[homes]` shares usually lack a `path` option. Samba knows to map this share to the users' home directories rather than to a fixed location.

Configuring Printer Shares

Samba printer shares are similar to file shares. The primary distinguishing characteristic is the `printable = Yes` option, which tells Samba to treat the share as a printer share. If this option is set, Samba tries to send files destined for the printer to a local print queue of the same name as the Samba printer share. (If you want to use another print queue name, you can set it with the `printer` option.)

Rather than define printers one by one, many Samba configurations rely on a special printer share name that's akin to the [homes] share for file shares: [printers]. This share might look something like this:

```
[printers]
    comment = All Printers
    browseable = no
    path = /tmp
    printable = yes
    create mode = 0700
```

If this share is present and if the [global] section does *not* include a load printers = No option, Samba scans your available printers and creates a printer share for every print queue on the system. This feature can be a convenient way to share all of your printers at once.

Samba delivers the print job via the local printing system—BSD LPD, LPRng, CUPS, or something more exotic if that's what you use. The global printing option defines how Samba submits print jobs, so be sure this option is set correctly. In all cases, the format of the job Samba submits must be something that the print queue can handle. Because Samba simply passes a file it receives from the client on to the server's printing system, this means the client must have a print driver that generates output the Linux print queue can process. In most cases, Linux print queues are designed to handle PostScript input, so using a generic PostScript driver on the client is in order. As a general rule, drivers for Apple LaserWriter models work well for monochrome printers, and QMS magicolor PostScript drivers work well for color printers. If your printer is a PostScript model, you can try using the driver provided by the manufacturer. On occasion, though, these drivers create output that includes mode-switching codes that confuse Linux print queues, so you may need to use another driver. Alternatively, you can include the postscript = Yes option; this tells Samba to tack a PostScript identifier onto the start of the file, causing the Linux print queue to correctly identify the output as PostScript.

If your printer is a non-PostScript model, you can try using its native driver. This practice will work only if the Linux print queue recognizes the format and passes print jobs unmodified to the printer, though. If necessary, you can create a "raw" print queue to pass data through without changes.

Many, but not all, printers that can't be made to work from Linux can still be served to Linux clients using Samba and a raw print queue. A few such printers rely on two-way communication between the printer and Windows printer driver. Such printers won't work via Samba unless they're supported in Linux.

In practice, it's hard to say which is better—to use Windows PostScript drivers with a Linux print queue that interprets PostScript using Ghostscript, or the printer's native drivers in Windows and a raw queue. The PostScript approach is likely to reduce network traffic when printing text, but it imposes a greater CPU load on the print server. The native driver approach is likely to increase network traffic when printing text and shifts the CPU load onto the clients. The PostScript approach may be desirable if you use applications that work best with PostScript printers, such as some desktop publishing and graphics tools. Native drivers often give more convenient access to printer features such as resolution adjustments. Either approach could produce superior output; the best approach depends on the drivers in question and the type of printing. I recommend you try both approaches. You may want to create two queues, one for each method. (If your Linux queue is smart enough to recognize the file type, you'll need only one Samba printer share; you can create multiple queues on the clients that print to the same Samba share.)

Checking Your Configuration and Running Samba

Once you've made changes to your smb.conf file, you can restart or reload the Samba server by using your SysV or Upstart startup script. Before you do this, though, you might want to use the testparm utility, which scans your smb.conf file and flags any errors it finds:

```
# testparm
Load smb config files from /etc/samba/smb.conf
WARNING: The "printer admin" option is deprecated
Processing section "[homes]"
Processing section "[netlogon]"
Processing section "[profiles]"
Processing section "[smbpdf]"
Processing section "[printers]"
Processing section "[print$]"
Loaded services file OK.
Warning: Service smbpdf defines a print command, but rameter is ignored ↩
 when using CUPS libraries.
Server role: ROLE_DOMAIN_PDC
Press enter to see a dump of your service definitions
```

Most of these example output lines are simply informative, such as the Processing lines and the Server role line. This example produced two warnings, though. The first identified a deprecated option (printer admin), which is still honored but is flagged for removal in the future. The second identifies a problem with a parameter that's ignored in the smbpdf share. (This chapter doesn't present the smb.conf file that produced this testparm output, so I don't describe correcting these specific errors. You should research any warnings or errors that crop up on your own system, since they're likely to be highly idiosyncratic to *your* configuration.)

Once Samba is running, it consists of two main server programs: smbd and nmbd. The smbd daemon handles the bulk of the file-sharing duties; it responds to connection attempts related to file and printer sharing. The nmbd daemon handles the behind-the-scenes NetBIOS "glue" functions, such as name resolution. (NetBIOS over TCP/IP implements its own name resolution system independent of TCP/IP hostnames, and it implements features such as file browsing. These duties are handled by nmbd.)

You can use the nmblookup utility to query servers about their names and related NetBIOS features. The preceding section "Setting Workgroup or Domain Options" showed an example of using this utility to locate your local workgroup or domain name. It's more often used much like the host utility, as a means of locating the IP address associated with a NetBIOS name:

```
$ nmblookup nessus
querying nessus on 192.168.1.255
192.168.1.2 nessus<00>
```

This output reveals that the IP address of the nessus computer is 192.168.1.2. You can pass additional options to nmblookup to perform more advanced queries. Consult the program's man page for details.

The smbstatus utility tells you about the current status of your Samba server, including the clients that are connected to it and the files that are currently open:

```
$ smbstatus
Processing section "[homes]"
Processing section "[netlogon]"
Processing section "[smbpdf]"
Processing section "[printers]"
Processing section "[print$]"

Samba version 3.4.9
PID      Username     Group         Machine
-------------------------------------------------------------------
20225    samlowry     users          172.24.21.5  (172.24.21.5)
20209    jill         users          helpman       (172.24.21.9)


Service      pid      machine       Connected at
--------------------------------------------------------
jill         20209    helpman       Sat Nov 13 13:24:22 2010
samlowry     20225    172.24.21.5   Sat Nov 13 13:26:30 2010


Locked files:
Pid          Uid       DenyMode      Access      R/W       Oplock
SharePath    Name      Time
-------------------------------------------------------------------
20209        500           DENY_NONE 0x100081    RDONLY    NONE
/home/jill        .   Sat Nov 13 13:24:23 2010
```

This example shows connections from two computers (172.24.21.5 and helpman), which have opened the jill and samlowry shares (two user home shares on the server). One client has opened the /home/jill directory on the server, but no files are currently open.

Some programs open and then close files and then open and close the files again to save changes. Thus, you can't conclude from the absence of open files that a client is not using the server; it could simply be that the user is editing files and will require the server to be available in the future.

The smbstatus utility supports many options that can fine-tune the output it produces. Consult the program's man page for details.

Checking Samba Log Files

The /var/log/samba directory holds Samba's log files. Several such files exist. Most commonly, the nmbd and smbd servers create the log.nmbd and log.smbd files, respectively. These files hold information on these servers generally. In addition, files named after the names or IP addresses associated with specific clients, such as log.central or log.10.27.107.24, hold information on connection attempts for these clients.

Log files can be a treasure trove of information if you run into problems with Samba. If a client can't connect, you can examine the log.nmbd and log.smbd files, along with any files for that particular client. (Check using both its name and its IP address.) Look for obvious error messages soon after you attempt to connect. You may also want to compare what happens with the problem client to equivalent log entries from a client that has no problems—assuming of course that a problem is isolated to just one or a few clients!

You can also check log files on the client side; however, such logs are unlikely to appear in /var/log/samba. Instead, check /var/log/messages, /var/log/syslog, or other log files for problems related to mounting an SMB/CIFS share.

Using Linux as an SMB/CIFS Client

Linux includes tools that provide the ability to interact with Windows systems or Samba servers as an SMB/CIFS client, rather than a server. Samba includes a major client program called smbclient. In addition, you can use the smbfs or cifs filesystem type code with the regular Linux mount command.

Using a Dedicated Client Program

The smbclient program provides an FTP-like access to remote shares. Specifically, smbclient mimics the behavior of the standard text-mode ftp program, so if you're familiar with ftp, you should feel at home with smbclient. Even though SMB/CIFS is generally used by an OS client that mounts the shares locally, using smbclient can be a useful tool because it can provide convenient access to a server that you don't use on a regular basis with minimal setup configuration. You may also find that smbclient can provide useful debugging information that can be harder to obtain when you use a more conventional share-mounting approach to using the server.

The basic syntax for smbclient is:

```
smbclient [//SERVER/SHARE] [password] [options]
```

> In Linux, SMB/CIFS shares are usually referred to as //SERVER/SHARE. In Windows, the slash (/) characters become backslash (\) characters, in keeping with Windows conventions. Thus, the Windows reference would be to \\SERVER\SHARE. In both OSs, the case of the server and share names is irrelevant, although uppercase is more commonly used for NetBIOS server names.

Table 8.3 summarizes the most common and useful *options*, but you should consult the program's man page for additional options and operational details. Most of your interactions with smbclient will take place at its own internal smb: \> prompt, at which you can type commands such as help, ls, cd, rename, get, put, and exit. Many of these commands function just like their ftp equivalents, many of which are in turn similar to regular Linux shell commands. Type **help** *command* or consult the man page for smbclient to learn more about these commands.

TABLE 8.3 Common smbclient options

Short option name	Long option name	Meaning
-I *ip-address*	N/A	Connects to the specified IP address rather than to the computer with the NetBIOS name of *SERVER*.
-L *HOST*	N/A	Lists shares available on *HOST*.
-s *filename*	N/A	Uses *filename* as the configuration file rather than smb.conf in whatever directory your build uses (generally /etc/samba).
-N	N/A	Suppresses the normal prompt for a password. If the type of access you're invoking would normally require a password, this option will cause the operation to fail.
-A *filename*	--authentication-file *filename*	Obtains the username and password from the specified *filename*.

TABLE 8.3 Common smbclient options *(continued)*

Short option name	Long option name	Meaning
-U *username* [*%password*]	--user=*username* [*%password*]	Uses the specified *username* and, optionally, *password* when connecting to the server. If this option is omitted, your current login username is used, and the program prompts you for a password or uses the password specified on the command line, if you include one.
-n *NAME*	N/A	Passes *NAME* as the computer's NetBIOS name when connecting.
-W *WORKGROUP*	--workgroup=*WORKGROUP*	Passes *WORKGROUP* as the computer's workgroup or domain name.
-c *commands*	N/A	Accepts *commands* as commands that smbclient should run. (Multiple commands should be separated by semicolons.) You can use this feature to create scripts that interact with SMB/CIFS servers.

As an example, consider the following interactions:

```
$ smbclient //SERVICES/jill -U jill
Enter jill's password:
Domain=[CENTRAL] OS=[Unix] Server=[Samba 3.4.9]
smb: \> ls
  .                                  D        0  Sat Nov 13 17:07:04 2010
  ..                                 D        0  Sun Nov 29 00:34:30 2009
  EFI                                D        0  Fri Oct 16 16:00:55 2009
  linux-2.6.36.tar.bz2                  70277083  Tue Nov  9 09:34:47 2010
  Form27b-6.pdf                            79081  Sun Oct 31 23:25:38 2010
smb: \> get Form26b-6.pdf
getting file \Form26b-6.pdf of size 79081 as Form26b-6.pdf (4542.8 ↵
 KiloBytes/sec) (average 4542.8 KiloBytes/sec)
smb: \> exit
```

This sequence logs into the SERVICES server as jill, obtains a file listing, and retrieves one file (Form27b-6.pdf).

The -A option enables you to store your authentication credentials in a file, which is often useful for scripts. If you use this option, ensure that the file you create has the minimum necessary permissions (generally 0600 or even 0400). It contains three lines:

```
username = user
password = pass
domain = dom
```

Mounting SMB/CIFS Shares

The usual way to mount SMB/CIFS shares is via the standard Linux mount command. This requires you to pass a filesystem type of either smbfs or cifs with the -t parameter, along with the server and share name rather than a local Linux device filename:

```
# mount -t cifs //services/jill /mnt/services
```

> **WARNING**   Support for smbfs has been removed from the 2.6.37 and later kernels. Thus, on recent Linux installations, you must use cifs rather than smbfs. If you're upgrading an old system, you may need to make changes to /etc/fstab or any other file that references the smbfs type code.

Typing this command will ordinarily result in a password prompt. The program uses the value of the USER environment variable as the username unless you use the user=*username* option to set another username. This and other options may be specified via the -o option to mount, as in **mount -t cifs -o user=jill //services/jill /mnt/services**. Table 8.4 summarizes some of the more useful mount options. Consult the man pages for mount.cifs and mount.smbfs for more details. The credentials option is particularly important, since it enables you to automatically mount a share without placing the sensitive password information in /etc/fstab. The format of the credentials file is similar to that described earlier, with reference to smbclient; however, if you include a workgroup/domain name, it should be identified by the workgroup keyword rather than domain.

TABLE 8.4   Important smbfs and cifs mount options

Mount Option	Meaning
user=*name* or username=*name*	Passes *name* as the username for access to the server.
password=*pass*	Uses *pass* as the password for access to the server.

TABLE 8.4 Important smbfs and cifs mount options *(continued)*

Mount Option	Meaning
credentials=*filename*	Obtains the username and password from the specified file.
uid=*UID*	Sets the default UID for files stored on the server. Should not be used for most servers that support the CIFS Unix extensions, such as Samba servers.
gid=*GID*	Sets the default GID for files stored on the server. Should not be used for most servers that support the CIFS Unix extensions, such as Samba servers.
file_mode=*mode*	Sets the default file mode for files stored on the server. Should not be used for most servers that support the CIFS Unix extensions, such as Samba servers.
dir_mode=*mode*	Sets the default mode for directories stored on the server. Should not be used for most servers that support the CIFS Unix extensions, such as Samba servers.

You can mount a share automatically when the computer boots, or enable ordinary users to mount shares, by including entries in /etc/fstab, such as this one:

```
//SERVICES/jill  /mnt/jill-serv  cifs  credentials=/etc/samba/jill  0 0
```

This example mounts the jill share on the SERVICES server to the /mnt/jill-serv mount point using credentials in /etc/samba/jill whenever the computer boots. You can of course change the mount options, many of which are the same as the options for local filesystems described in Chapter 3, "Basic Filesystem Management."

Once an SMB/CIFS share is mounted, you can access it much as you would an ordinary filesystem. You should be aware, however, that you may have to deal with strange or limiting ownership and permissions rules, since Windows SMB/CIFS servers don't support the Unix-style ownership and permissions that Linux uses. If the server is a Unix or Linux system running Samba, matters may improve, but supporting two sets of conflicting rules sometimes creates a tangled mess of rules that can be hard to overcome. In such cases, you may prefer to simplify by implementing NFS for file sharing between these similar OSs.

Configuring an NFS Server

If your network hosts more than a handful of Linux or Unix file-sharing clients, you may want to use NFS instead of or in addition to Samba. Because NFS was designed with Unix ownership and permissions in mind, it's a more natural fit between a Linux server and Linux or Unix clients than is SMB/CIFS, which was designed with DOS, Windows, and OS/2 clients in mind. (NFS clients for Windows and other non-Linux/Unix OSs are available, but it's generally better to use Samba when serving such clients.)

To configure NFS, you should first look at NFS prerequisites, such as kernel and package options. You can then move on to setting up the NFS exports by editing the /etc/ fstab file. (Recall that an export is the NFS equivalent of an SMB/CIFS share.) You should also know how to make temporary changes to the NFS configuration and adjust options that affect NFS security. Finally, you should know how to mount NFS exports on a client system.

Setting NFS Prerequisites

Every major Linux distribution ships with an NFS server called rpc.nfsd. In most distributions, this server is part of the nfs-utils package, but Debian, Ubuntu, and related distributions place it in the nfs-kernel-server package. These standard servers rely on NFS server support that's built into the kernel, as described shortly. Older NFS servers did not rely on this support, and such servers are still available on some distributions. For instance, Debian's nfs-user-server runs entirely in user space without taking advantage of the kernel NFS server support.

Many distributions present options to activate the NFS server at system installation or when you install the NFS server package. For others, you may need to create or activate a SysV, Upstart, or local startup script, as described in Chapter 1, "System Startup and Advanced System Management." The startup script is called nfs-kernel-server (or nfs-user-server for the user-mode server) in Debian and Ubuntu, nfs in Mandriva and Red Hat, and nfsserver in OpenSUSE.

To use a kernel-based server, your kernel must include the appropriate options to support NFS features. Other kernel features are required to mount another computer's NFS exports. Both sets of options are accessible from the File Systems ➢ Network File Systems kernel configuration menu, as shown in Figure 8.1 for a 2.6.37 kernel. (Chapter 2, "Linux Kernel Configuration," describes configuring a kernel in more detail.) The NFS Client Support option enables support for NFS *client* functionality, and the NFS Server Support option activates NFS server functionality.

FIGURE 8.1 The Linux kernel provides NFS support options in its configuration tool

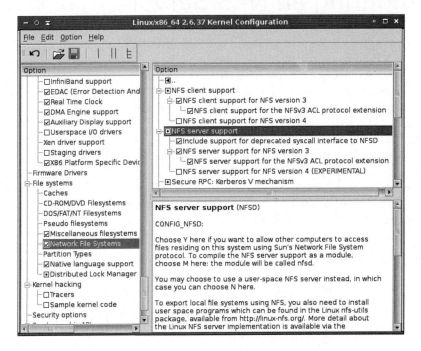

NFS has undergone several revisions over the years. These NFS version numbers are often appended to the *NFS* acronym, as in *NFSv2* for NFS version 2. This level is the default in the Linux kernel options; to use NFSv3 or NFSv4, you must activate extra features, which are visible in Figure 8.1's menu. As of the 2.6.*x* kernels, NFS support through NFSv3 is reasonably stable and complete. NFSv4 server support is still considered experimental as of the 2.6.37 kernel (the latest as I write). I recommend avoiding the use of an experimental NFS driver; it may result in poor performance, lost files, or other problems.

All Linux distributions' default kernels support NFS, although it's sometimes compiled as separate modules—nfs.o for the NFS client and nfsd.o for the NFS server. The appropriate module should load automatically when you try to mount a remote export or start the NFS server. Although the NFS support modules aren't hardware drivers, loading them is done using the same tools you use to load hardware driver modules. Some distributions ship with this support compiled into the main kernel file rather than as a module.

Linux's NFS implementation relies on several additional programs. These programs should be installed automatically with the NFS server. For the most part, these programs operate behind the scenes and require no special configuration, but you should be aware of their existence. Table 8.5 summarizes these programs. These programs relate to the *Remote Procedure Call (RPC)* mechanism, which is a method of enabling one computer to trigger the activation of a function on another computer. NFS relies on RPC, and so requires various RPC helper programs to be running.

TABLE 8.5 NFS's RPC support programs

Mount option	Meaning
rpc.idmapd	This program, which works only with NFSv4 and later, maps usernames and UIDs between systems. This feature can be important if two computers both support the same users but use different UID numbers for those users.
rpc.mountd	This program, which runs on the server, helps manage mount requests from NFS clients. It communicates with clients and sends them information on the export and keeps track of which clients are connected to the server. This program is sometimes referred to as mountd.
rpc.nfsd	This program is the user-space front-end to the kernel-space nfsd process, which does the bulk of the NFS server work.
rpc.statd	This program tells NFS clients when the NFS server is about to reboot, which helps clients manage this event.
portmap	This program (also known as the *portmapper*) runs on the server and tells clients what port number they should contact to use the NFS server or certain other servers.

Setting Basic Export Options

Linux uses the /etc/exports file to describe the directories that an NFS server exports. Lines in this file may be comments, which begin with hash marks (#), or they may be export definitions. Each export definition takes the following form:

/directory client(*options*) [*client*(*options*)[...]]

The */directory* is the directory that's to be made available, such as /home or /opt/ OpenOffice.org. Following the directory are one or more client specifications. You can list clients in any of several ways:

Hostnames   You can provide a computer's hostname, such as services.luna.edu or services. If you omit the domain name, the server assumes you're referring to a computer in its own domain.

Wildcards   If you want to export a directory to all the computers in a domain or to certain subsets of them, you might be able to use the asterisk (*) and question mark (?) wildcards. These features work much like their equivalents in shells when used to specify filenames. They don't match dots in hostnames, though. For instance, `*.luna.edu` matches `central.luna.edu` and `services.luna.edu` but not `helpman.info.luna.edu`.

IP Addresses   You can specify a computer by IP address, as in `172.24.202.7`. This method is harder for humans to interpret than hostnames, but it has a security advantage because it doesn't rely on a Domain Name System (DNS) server to convert the hostname to an IP address. If you use hostnames, an attacker could conceivably gain access to your NFS server by first taking over a DNS server.

Network Addresses   You can specify a network by IP address range by providing the IP address, a slash, and a netmask. The netmask can be specified either in dotted-decimal form or as the number of bits in the network portion of the address. For instance, `172.24.0.0/255.255.0.0` and `172.24.0.0/16` are equivalent.

NIS Netgroups   Although it's seldom used today, the Network Information System (NIS) enables you to specify an NIS netgroup by preceding its name with an at sign, as in `@tranquility`.

Following each client specification is a comma-separated list of options. Table 8.6 summarizes the most common of these options. You can find additional options in the exports man page.

TABLE 8.6   Common NFS export options

Option	Meaning
secure or insecure	Specifies that the client must connect (secure) or need not connect (insecure) from a secure port (one numbered below 1024). The default value is secure.
rw or ro	Specifies read/write (rw) or read-only (ro) client access to the export. The default in recent Linux NFS servers is ro, but some versions have used rw. I recommend making your choice explicit to avoid the possibility of confusion.
sync or async	The async option can improve performance at the cost of a risk of data corruption in the event of a system crash. In kernel NFS servers up to and including version 1.0.0, async was the default, but more recent versions use sync as the default.

Option	Meaning
hide or nohide	Ordinarily or when you use the hide option, the NFS server "hides" filesystems mounted inside an exported directory. For instance, if you export /usr and if /usr/local is a separate partition, clients won't see /usr/local's contents. If you specify nohide, clients will see files and subdirectories in /usr/local. The nohide option can confuse some clients and works only with single-host specifications (hostnames and IP addresses). Instead of using nohide, you can export each partition individually and mount each export on the NFS clients.
root_squash or no_root_squash	For security reasons, the NFS server normally "squashes" access from root on the client, substituting a low-privilege user ID for the root user ID. You can grant the remote root user full root access to the exported directory by using the no_root_squash option. This option is potentially very dangerous, although it's sometimes necessary, as when an NFS client is used to back up other computers.
all_squash or no_all_squash	This option specifies whether to apply "squashing" to accesses from ordinary users. Squashing such accesses can be desirable as a means of providing a modest security increase on read-only exports.
acl or no_acl	Ordinarily or when acl is specified, NFS shares ACL information with clients. With no_acl, the server will not do so, which can change who may access files and in what ways; however, using no_acl requires a kernel patched to support this option.
fsid=[num|root|uuid]	Many filesystems have identifying serial numbers, some of which take the form of a Universally Unique Identifier (UUID). Ordinarily, NFS shares this information with clients; however, you can override the identifier by specifying a short integer (num), by specifying a full UUID (uuid), or by identifying the filesystem as the root of all those exported by the NFS server.

The options available in the NFS server have changed between NFS server versions in the past, and they may change in the future. Consult the man page for exports for details if you have problems with any of these options.

As an example of an NFS /etc/exports file, consider Listing 8.2. This file defines three exports—for /home, /opt, and /exports. The /home export is fairly straightforward. The clients of this export (helpman, kurtzmann, and ida) are defined using hostnames without domain names. All of these clients have read/write access to the share. All except kurtzmann must connect from a secure port, but kurtzmann is granted an exception to this rule. Perhaps kurtzmann is running a non-Unix OS that uses a high-numbered port for NFS access. The /opt export is made available to two clients, helpman.luna.edu and ida.luna.edu. The first of these clients has full read/write access to the share, and root access from this client is not squashed. You might use this configuration if the client's administrator needs to be able to add software to the /opt export, but this configuration is risky—a security problem could allow a miscreant to change files in this potentially sensitive directory. Finally, the /exports directory is exported to all computers in the info.luna.edu domain (but not its subdomains) and to all computers in the 172.24.0.0/16 network. In the case of the info.luna.edu domain, all user accesses are squashed. In both cases, no client can write to the export.

Listing 8.2: Example /etc/exports file

```
/home helpman(rw) kurtzmann(rw,insecure) ida(rw)
/opt helpman.luna.edu(rw,no_root_squash) ida.luna.edu(ro,nohide)
/exports *.info.luna.edu(ro,all_squash) 172.24.0.0/16(ro)
```

If you make changes to your /etc/exports file, you can tell the NFS server about those changes with the exportfs program. Specifically, type **exportfs -r** as root to update the server's list of available exports to match the exports file. You can also use this utility's -u option to make a specific export unavailable or use various other options to have other effects. The upcoming section "Adjusting a Running NFS Server" describes additional exportfs options.

Managing Exports on the Fly

It's frequently necessary to monitor the operation of an NFS server and to implement changes in the configuration without bringing the server down. Several tools exist for this purpose: exportfs, showmount, and nfsstat. The /proc/mounts file, described in Chapter 3, can also be useful in this regard.

Adjusting a Running NFS Server

In addition to /etc/exports, NFS enables nonpermanent changes to its exports via the exportfs command. Used without any options, exportfs displays a list of active NFS exports, similar to the contents of /etc/exports, but with one line per export (so if you list a directory as being exported to three systems or networks, three lines will appear in the exportfs output for that directory). Adding options enables you to modify your system's

NFS exports. Table 8.7 summarizes the most important of these options. The man page for exportfs provides details on more obscure options.

TABLE 8.7 Common exportfs options

Option	Explanation
-a	Reads /etc/exports and exports all the directories listed there. (When used with -u, unexports all directories.)
-r	Reexports all directories. This has the effect of unexporting directories that are not listed in /etc/exports.
-o *options*	Implements the specified *options*, which take the same form as those in /etc/exports.
-u	Unexports one or more directories.
-f	Flushes and rebuilds the exports table.
-v	Adds verbose messages to the program's output.

When using exportfs to add or delete exports, you specify a client and directory in the form *client:/export/directory*. You don't need to specify any of the options from Table 8.7 when exporting a new directory, but you must use the -u option to unexport a directory. For instance, suppose your NFS server is currently exporting /var/www to 192.168.23.0/24 as a means to enable local users to edit a Web server's files. You want to move this directory to /var/apache/webfiles. You could implement these changes by typing the following commands:

```
# exportfs -u 192.168.23.0/24:/var/www
# exportfs 192.168.23.0/24:/var/apache/webfiles
```

This change will be temporary, however; you should also edit /etc/exports. In fact, you might prefer to edit /etc/exports first and then type **exportfs -r**, thus implementing your changes.

Identifying Mounted Exports

A second tool for managing NFS is showmount, which displays information on current NFS activity. Used without options, this tool reveals the IP addresses of the computers that are currently using the server. Table 8.8 summarizes showmount's most common options.

TABLE 8.8 Common showmount options

Option	Option abbreviation	Explanation
--all	-a	Displays both the IP addresses of clients and the directories they're using.
--directories	-d	Displays the directories currently being shared by the server but not the identities of clients.
--exports	-e	Displays the current available exports (similar to the default output of exportfs, but each export uses just one line of output).
--help	-h	Presents basic help information.
--version	-v	Prints the program's version number.
--no-headers	None	Suppresses explanatory headers in the output.

You can use showmount to display information on the server running on any computer, network firewall and other security options permitting. By default, the program displays information on the local computer's NFS server, but if you add a computer hostname, the result is information on that computer:

```
$ showmount -a central
All mount points on central:
172.24.21.5:/home
172.24.21.5:/home/jill/photos
192.168.1.4:/home
192.168.1.4:/home/tuttle
```

In this example, 172.24.21.5 is accessing /home/jill/photos (part of the /home export), and 192.168.1.4 is accessing /home/tuttle (also part of the /home export).

Measuring NFS Activity

The nfsstat utility provides statistics related to NFS and RPC client and server activity. Table 8.9 summarizes some important nfsstat options. It should be emphasized that nfsstat provides both client and server information, so you can use it from either side of an NFS connection, although of course the information provided on each side won't be identical.

TABLE 8.9   Common nfsstat options

Short option name	Long option name	Meaning
-s	--server	Displays only server statistics.
-c	--client	Displays only client statistics.
-n	--nfs	Displays only NFS statistics.
-r	--rpc	Displays only RPC statistics.
-2, -3, or -4	N/A	Displays statistics on the specified NFS version.
-m	--mounts	Displays information on mounted NFS exports, including their names and current mount options (whether specified implicitly or explicitly).
-o *facility*	N/A	Displays information on the specified *facility*, which must be one of nfs, rpc, net, fh, rc, or all.
-Z	--sleep	Takes a snapshot of the current statistics, pauses, and then displays the differences between the snapshot and the state of the system when it receives a SIGINT signal (as when the user presses Ctrl+C).

Much of nfsstat's output is cryptic, but you can glean some useful information from the entries you understand. For instance, columns labeled read, write, create, and mkdir specify bytes read and written and the number of files and directories created, respectively. The output of the -m (--mounts) option can be particularly useful on an NFS client, since you can learn how an export is mounted. This information can provide clues to problems, such as if a user can't create new files. (For instance, is the share mounted read-only?)

Checking on RPC Activity

The rpcinfo utility provides access to RPC data. This program can be useful for identifying what RPC-enabled servers are running on a computer or network. The most useful option is probably -p, which should include lines such as the following, which denote NFS versions 2 and 3 running on both TCP and UDP:

```
$ rpcinfo -p
    100003    2    udp    2049    nfs
    100003    3    udp    2049    nfs
    100003    2    tcp    2049    nfs
    100003    3    tcp    2049    nfs
```

Additional output has been removed from this example output for brevity. Table 8.10 summarizes other rpcinfo options. Some of these are fairly obscure.

TABLE 8.10   Common rpcinfo options

Option name	Meaning
-p [host]	Probes host (or the local computer) and displays all registered RPC programs
-u host program	Using UDP, tells program on host to run procedure 0 and reports the results
-t host program	Using TCP, tells program on host to run procedure 0 and reports the results
-n portnum	Uses portnum as the port number (used with the -u and -t options)
-b program version	Broadcasts to the local network a request to run procedure 0 using the specified program and version and reports the result
-d program version	Enables the superuser to delete the registration of the specified program and version on the local computer

EXERCISE 8.1

Managing an NFS Server

This activity illustrates how to manage an NFS server. This exercise assumes you have access to just one Linux computer, so it uses one computer as both client and server; however, you can split up the roles across two computers if you have appropriate access. To perform this exercise, follow these steps:

1. Log into your Linux computer. You'll need root access to perform some of these actions, so you may want to log in as root or use su to acquire root privileges in one window.

2. Use your distribution's package management tools to install the NFS server and client programs. The package names vary from one distribution to another; for instance, in Ubuntu, you must install the nfs-common and nfs-kernel-server packages, but in Fedora, you must install the nfs-utils package.

3. If it's not already running, launch your NFS server. This can usually be done by typing /etc/init.d/nfs start or /etc/init.d/nfs-kernel-server start as root.

4. Type `rpcinfo -p`. You will see a list of RPC-enabled servers that are running. This list should include entries for your NFS server. Note which versions are supported and whether they support TCP, UDP, or both.

5. Load /etc/exports into a text editor.

6. Create an export by typing its entry in your text editor. For instance, you might create an export to share the /home directory:

    /home 127.0.0.1(rw)

    If you have access to a second computer to use as a client, you can substitute its hostname or IP address for 127.0.0.1 in this example.

7. On your client, attempt to mount the share by typing `mount localhost:/home /mnt` as root. (Change `localhost`, /home, and /mnt as needed for the server you're using, the export you've defined, and the mount point you want to use locally.) This attempt will fail.

8. Type `exportfs -r` as root to tell the server to reload /etc/exports.

9. Repeat step #7. This time it should succeed. Verify that /mnt provides access to the files in the exported directory on the server.

10. Type `showmount -a` to see what clients are using the server, as well as what directories they're accessing. You should see your one exported share associated with your client's IP address. If your computer had previously been configured for NFS duty, you may see additional exports and clients, as well.

11. Type `nfsstat -s` to see statistics on the requests the NFS server has handled.

12. Use the client to perform some harmless actions in the mounted export, such as reading a text file.

13. Repeat step #11. Compare the two nfsstat outputs. You should see that some of the values have changed. For instance, if you read a text file, the read value should increase.

14. Type `umount /mnt` as root on the client (changing /mnt, if necessary) to unmount the exported directory.

15. In the editor that's open on /etc/exports, remove the entry you created.

16. Type `exportfs -u 127.0.0.1:/home` as root to tell the server to stop serving the /home export. (Change the IP address or hostname and export directory as necessary for your system.) Note that typing `exportfs -r` would work as well at this point; this exercise calls for you to use -u to see how it works.

You can of course experiment further with the NFS utilities, perhaps before performing steps 15 and 16. If the computer should not be running an NFS server, it would be prudent to uninstall it using your package manager when you're done with this exercise.

Improving NFS Security

Most servers use passwords or some other authentication tool to control access to files. NFS works differently; an NFS server trusts the client system to control access to files. Once a directory is exported via NFS, any client computer that's authorized to access the directory in /etc/exports may do so in any way the /etc/exports definition permits. The idea is that the client computer will have a user base that's compatible with the user base on the server and that the client computer is trustworthy.

These assumptions weren't unreasonable when NFS was created, but in today's computing environment, they're a bit risky. Somebody with a notebook computer and wireless networking hardware may be able to access your server and masquerade as another computer if you use a wireless network. Even with a wired network, a compromised system or physical access can enable an attacker to pretend to be a trusted system. An attacker can control the user database on the attacking computer or use a custom NFS client program that doesn't play by the usual security rules, thus bypassing the intent of the NFS security scheme. Therefore, you should be cautious about NFS security. Don't add a computer to /etc/exports unless it's really necessary, and don't give clients read/write access unless they really need it. The no_root_squash option is particularly risky. You might also want to use IP addresses rather than hostnames to specify computers in /etc/exports; this practice makes masquerading as a trusted system a little more difficult.

An additional security precaution is to protect the port mapper or NFS server ports using firewall rules (as described in Chapter 7) or TCP Wrappers (as described in Chapter 10, "Security"). Either approach will prevent unauthorized computers from accessing the NFS server. (The same can and should be done with Samba and other servers, of course.)

Using Linux as an NFS Client

Linux's NFS client is, essentially, the Linux kernel itself. The kernel treats another computer's NFS export as a filesystem that can be mounted via the mount command or an entry in /etc/fstab. Chapter 3 describes these tools in detail. The rules for using NFS exports are similar to those for using regular filesystems on partitions, although some details differ. To mount an NFS export, you specify the nfs filesystem type. (Use nfs4 to force use of NFSv4, if both client and server support it.) In some cases, Linux can determine from context that you mean nfs, so you can sometimes omit this option. Instead of specifying a Linux device filename, you specify the host and export name. (For protection against a DNS server compromise or as a matter of preference, you can use an IP address rather than a hostname.) For instance, to mount /home from central.luna.edu at /mnt/morehome, you might type the following command:

```
# mount -t nfs central.luna.edu:/home /mnt/morehome
```

 If you don't know what exports a server makes available, you can type showmount -e *servername*. The result is a list of exports available on *servername*, along with the clients that can connect to each export.

In the case of the preceding example, you can omit the -t nfs specification, and if your client is in luna.edu or is configured to search that domain via a search line in /etc/resolv.conf, you can specify the export as central:/home rather than central.luna.edu:/home. If you want to mount an export whenever the computer boots or give ordinary users the power to mount an export, you can do so by adding an entry to /etc/fstab. For instance, the following line mounts this export at boot time:

```
central.luna.edu:/home  /mnt/morehome  nfs  defaults  0  0
```

You can add many standard mount options, as well; for instance, specifying an option of ro causes a read-only mount, even if the server has granted your system read/write access. (You cannot use rw to gain read/write access if the server gives you only read-only access, though.) There are also a few NFS-specific mount options. The most important of these may be hard and soft. Ordinarily or if you explicitly specify hard, a program trying to access an NFS server will block (become unresponsive while waiting for input) if the server doesn't respond. When the server becomes available, the program will continue where it left off. If you specify soft, though, the kernel's NFS client will eventually time out and deliver an error message to the client. If your network or NFS server is flaky, you may prefer soft, because you'll be better able to kill processes that hang because of an inability to access NFS exports. If your network is functioning normally, though, hard is the preferred behavior, because specifying soft can cause occasional problems on a well-behaved network.

Another NFS-specific mount option you may want to use is proto=*transport*, where *transport* is either tcp or udp. (Alternatively, you may use tcp or udp as options, without the proto= part.) NFS was originally a UDP-based protocol, which works well on reliable local networks. Using TCP adds features that can improve reliability if the network is unreliable, but these features also add overhead you might prefer to avoid. You may want to experiment with both settings to see which works best on your network.

Once an export is mounted, all ordinary users can access that export, within limits imposed by file ownership and permissions. One potential caveat is that NFS uses user ID (UID) and group ID (GID) numbers in handling ownership and permissions. If users have accounts on both the client and the server computer, the users' UIDs and GIDs on those two systems must match, or the users won't be able to access their own files. A similar problem can arise if users have accounts on two or more clients that access the same server. Various workarounds have been deployed to fix this problem, some of which aren't current. Three approaches are best today:

Manually Synchronize Usernames   On a small network with few users, you can manually maintain your accounts so that the same user has the same UID on all systems, and likewise for GID values. This approach becomes quite tedious on larger networks with many users, though.

Use an ID Mapper   You can use the rpc.idmap server, described previously, which can automatically map usernames and UID values. This server must be run on both the NFS server and the NFS client.

Use a Central Login Server If you use LDAP or some other centralized login server, the problem can go away, since users managed by the login server will have the same UID values on all the network's computers.

Note that UID synchronization isn't required for fundamentally public read-only exports, such as exports of directories holding software or shared read-only templates, unless some users should be restricted from accessing these files. Also, if an NFS server holds home directories but users don't need to log into that computer directly, you don't need to synchronize UIDs and GIDs because the users don't need accounts on the server. (You do still need to synchronize UIDs and GIDs across multiple clients in this case, though.) If the server doesn't have accounts for its NFS users, be sure any directory to which users should be able to write has permissions to enable world writing, or at least writing by the appropriate group, which in this case must be mapped appropriately.

Configuring an FTP Server

FTP has long been a popular server. The protocol has some peculiarities, but every OS that has a serious TCP/IP stack has an FTP client. FTP is typically used in one or both of two ways:

- Users must authenticate themselves to the server by providing a username and password. They can then read, and often write, files to their home directory or to common areas on the computer.

- Users provide a username of anonymous and any password (conventionally their email addresses). They can then read, but usually not write, data stored in public directories. This *anonymous FTP access* is a popular means of delivering public files such as software upgrades, multimedia files, and so on.

Both configurations share many features, but certain details differ. How you set up an FTP server to use either system depends on the server you choose. Several such servers exist for Linux. The next section describes your choices and then covers two popular FTP servers, Pure-FTPd and vsftpd, in more detail.

 One of FTP's major problems when used for authenticated user access is that FTP sends all data, including passwords, in an unencrypted form. This fact means that miscreants on the server's network, the client's network, or intervening networks may be able to use packet sniffers to steal users' passwords. This issue isn't as much of a problem for anonymous access, which is supposed to be public.

Although anonymous access is often necessary on public FTP servers, it should be avoided if only authenticated users should have access to the server. Also, anonymous access is best restricted to downloads only; if a site enables anonymous uploads, then anybody on the Internet can upload files to your server, including illegal content. If others can anonymously retrieve those files, then your site can quickly become an unwitting hosting site for piracy.

If you really do need to enable anonymous uploads (say, to permit customers to submit files in support of bug reports), you can minimize the risks by giving the anonymous upload directory permissions of 733 (rwx-wx-wx) or 773 (rwxrwx-wx) and ownership by root. If you use 773 permissions, give group ownership to a group that contains users who should be able to read the directory, but ensure that the account used for anonymous access by the FTP server is *not* in this group! This configuration will enable anonymous users to upload files to this directory but not download files from it. If you use an existing directory, type `chmod -R u-r /path/to/incoming/dir` to ensure that no files within it can be read by random users before you put this configuration in place.

Selecting an FTP Server

FTP is an old protocol, and numerous implementations of it have sprung up over the years. These servers vary in many details; however, they all serve the same protocol, and they all look very much alike to their users. FTP server options for Linux include the following:

Pure-FTPd   This server, headquartered at `http://www.pureftpd.org`, is an FTP server that emphasizes security. Many distributions ship with it, typically under the package name `pure-ftpd`.

vsftpd   This server aims to excel at security, stability, and speed. In doing so, its developers have chosen to eschew some of the more advanced features of servers such as ProFTPd. If you don't need those features, this trade-off may be more than acceptable. You can learn more from its Web site, `http://vsftpd.beasts.org`. It's available with a growing number of Linux distributions, usually with the package name `vsftpd`.

ProFTPd   This server, headquartered at `http://proftpd.org`, is one of the more popular of the very complex FTP servers. It ships with most major Linux distributions. Its configuration file is modeled after that of Apache, and the server supports many advanced features. It is accordingly much harder to configure.

This list of FTP servers is far from complete. Gentoo Linux, which has a fairly complete software repository, has at least seven distinct FTP servers. Many more very obscure servers are available. If you have special needs, you might want to investigate some of these alternatives.

Because FTP can potentially provide users with substantial access to the system—the ability to read or write any file, within limits imposed by Linux file ownership and permissions—FTP servers are unusually sensitive from a security point of view. As a result, the Web pages for many FTP servers emphasize their developers' attention to security. Most

FTP servers provide explicit support for locking themselves in chroot jails, as described with reference to DNS servers in Chapter 6, "DNS Server Configuration."

For a small FTP site, chances are any of the servers in the preceding list will work well. Because they both ship with multiple Linux distributions, the next two sections focus on Pure-FTPd and vsftpd.

Understanding FTP Basics

FTP is an old and quirky protocol, and it presents a couple of pitfalls that are unique to FTP. These are largely client-side problems, so users should be aware of them; however, if you configure a firewall, as described in Chapter 7, you may need to take the first of these issues into account.

The first FTP quirk is in the way it manages ports. Two ports (TCP ports 20 and 21) are registered to FTP. Port 20 is the data port, which is used for data transfers; and port 21 is the command port, which is used for issuing commands. The big problem with this configuration is that in the conventional *FTP active mode*, the client initiates the connection to the command port, and then the server initiates a reverse connection to the client from the server's command port. This server-to-client connection is blocked by some firewalls, so FTP often fails on firewalls that aren't explicitly configured to permit this connection. A client-side workaround to this problem is to use *FTP passive mode* (by typing **passive** in the ftp program or by selecting equivalent options in GUI or other FTP clients). In passive mode, the FTP client initiates both connections, which overcomes the problem of firewalls that block all incoming connections. Passive mode uses an unprivileged port on the server for its data transfers, though, which can sometimes run afoul of firewalls. Thus, you may need to try both active and passive modes to determine which one works best. You should check your FTP client's documentation to learn which mode it uses by default.

The second FTP quirk relates to transfer mode. FTP clients often default to ASCII (plain-text) transfer mode, in which the files are transferred in such a way as to dynamically alter the character encoding to account for the different ways that different OSs store plain-text files. (Linux/Unix, Windows, and the original Mac OS all used different line-ending conventions, and some even more exotic systems use non ASCII encoding methods.) Using ASCII mode works well for plain-text files, but this mode will almost always corrupt binary files, such as tarballs, graphics files, word processing documents, and so on. You can use the ascii and binary options in ftp, or similar options in other FTP clients, to set the transfer mode. If in doubt, use binary mode; most text editors today can handle any of the common line-ending types, so retrieving a text file in the wrong format will cause minimal or no problems. Some Linux configuration files must use Unix-style line endings, though, so you may need to pay attention to this detail if you transfer such files.

You should also be aware of the way in which the FTP server launches. Some FTP servers favor being launched via SysV, Upstart, or local startup scripts; but others work better when launched via a super server, such as inetd or xinetd. Chances are your distribution's package includes the necessary startup scripts and configuration files, but you may need to reconfigure your system to launch the server in your runlevel. (Sometimes the default configuration is to *not* launch the server, as a safety measure in case it's installed accidentally.)

Configuring Pure-FTPd

The Pure-FTPd server is designed to be controlled mostly through command-line arguments rather than a configuration file. Thus, if you want to adjust its main options, you must track down the distribution-specific file in which these options are stored and modify it. For instance, in Ubuntu you can edit /etc/default/pure-ftpd-common and files in /etc/pure-ftpd/conf, in Fedora you can edit /etc/pure-ftpd/pure-ftpd.conf, and in Gentoo you can edit /etc/conf.d/pure-ftpd. Table 8.11 summarizes the most important Pure-FTPd options; however, many more are available—consult the server's man page for details.

TABLE 8.11   Common pure-ftpd options

Short option name	Long option name	Meaning
-4	--ipv4only	Accepts only IPv4 connections.
-6	--ipv6only	Accepts only IPv6 connections.
-a *gid*	--trustedgid *gid*	Causes users in the specified group to *not* be chrooted to their home directories; others (except for root) are chrooted. Without this option, only anonymous access is chrooted.
-A	--chrooteveryone	Causes all accesses except for root to be chrooted to their home directories.
-B	--daemonize	Starts the server in the background.
-c *num*	--maxclientsnumber *num*	Accepts at most *num* simultaneous client connections. The default value is 50.
-C *num*	--maxclientsperip *num*	Accepts at most *num* simultaneous connections per client IP address. This option works only in stand-alone mode (super servers provide similar functionality).
-e	--anonymousonly	Supports only anonymous access.

TABLE 8.11 Common pure-ftpd options *(continued)*

Short option name	Long option name	Meaning
-E	--noanonymous	Supports only non-anonymous (normal user) access.
-i	--anonymous cantupload	Disables upload support for anonymous users.
-M	--anonymous cancreatedirs	Allows anonymous users to create directories.
-N	--natmode	Uses active mode by default; useful behind some NAT routers.
-u *uid*	--minuid *uid*	Disallows access to users with UID numbers below *uid*.

When used for anonymous access, Pure-FTPd requires that the computer have an account called ftp, and it enables anonymous users to download from and (if so configured via command-line options) upload to the anonymous directory. Scripts included with the pure-ftpd package might or might not set up the necessary account and home directory, so you should check for their presence. Also, some distributions' Pure-FTPd packages disallow anonymous access by default; thus, you may need to track down your distribution-specific configuration files and modify them appropriately. Because Pure-FTPd has no standard configuration file, the details of this task will vary greatly from one distribution to another.

Configuring *vsftpd*

A second FTP server that's popular on modern Linux systems is vsftpd. Ordinarily, vsftpd is run from a super server; however, it can be run from a SysV or local startup script if you prefer. The vsftpd configuration file is /etc/vsftpd.conf or /etc/vsftpd/vsftpd.conf. This file contains comment lines, which begin with hash marks (#), and directive lines that take this form:

option=value

There must be no stray spaces surrounding the equal sign in vsftpd directives. Table 8.12 summarizes some of the most important vsftpd directives. This table doesn't cover all of the available directives; check the man page for vsftpd.conf for information on additional directives.

TABLE 8.12 Important `vsftpd.conf` directives

Directive	Value	Meaning
listen	YES or NO	If YES, vsftpd binds itself to the FTP port to listen for IPv4 connections. Set this value to YES if vsftpd is run from a SysV or local startup script; leave it at its default value (NO) if it's run from a super server.
listen_ipv6	YES or NO	This option works much like listen, but it applies to IPv6 connections rather than IPv4 connections.
ftpd_banner	String	Sets a welcome message that appears in the user's FTP client program when connecting.
nopriv_user	Username	The username vsftpd uses for unprivileged operations.
ftp_username	Username	The username vsftpd uses for anonymous access. The default is ftp.
local_enable	YES or NO	Whether to accept authenticated local user logins.
anonymous_enable	YES or NO	Whether to accept anonymous logins.
anon_root	Directory name	Sets the directory to be used as the root directory for anonymous access. This directory must normally not be writeable to the anonymous user, unless anon_upload_enable is YES. The default is the anonymous user's home directory, as specified in /etc/passwd.
chroot_local_user	YES or NO	Tells vsftpd whether to use chroot when accepting local user logins.
userlist_enable	YES or NO	If YES, vsftpd checks the file specified by userlist_file and denies logins to these users before asking for a password.
write_enable	YES or NO	Grants or denies the ability to write files—that is, for users to upload files as well as download them.
anon_upload_enable	YES or NO	Grants or denies anonymous users the ability to upload files. If YES, write_enable must also be YES.

The default vsftpd configuration file often supports both authenticated local user logins and anonymous logins. Typically, vsftpd performs a chroot for anonymous users, but it does not do so for authenticated local users. If you want to verify or change these features, check the configuration file for the following lines, and change them as necessary:

```
anonymous_enable=YES
local_enable=YES
```

You can also change additional options related to these, such as the location of the anonymous root directory (anon_root) and whether to chroot into authenticated users' home directories when they log in (chroot_local_user).

Summary

File servers are a critical component of many networks, and Linux supports a wide variety of software to handle this task. This chapter describes servers used to handle three specific protocols. The Samba server handles the SMB/CIFS protocol, which is the dominant file-sharing protocol on Windows networks. Samba has to "translate" certain features to make Windows clients happy, and it does this job very well. To satisfy Linux and Unix clients, Samba adds more features, but for these clients, the NFS protocol is generally a better choice. Unlike Samba, NFS can present a more truthful view of the underlying filesystem to its clients, which streamlines and simplifies the file-sharing process. The final protocol described in this chapter is FTP, which is intended for use by dedicated client programs, rather than OSs that treat the server as if it were a filesystem to be mounted. Quite a few FTP servers are available for Linux, but this chapter covers just two of the most popular ones, Pure-FTPd and vsftpd. Both servers provide a variety of options to enable logins by username and password or for anonymous users. Because FTP is often used to deliver files on the Internet at large (as opposed to the local use that's more common for SMB/CIFS and NFS), FTP security is particularly important, and you should be sure to configure your FTP server in as secure a manner as possible.

Exam Essentials

Explain the difference between user- and share-level security in Samba. Share-level security emulates the old Windows 9x/Me security model, in which passwords are associated with shares rather than accounts. User-level security employs a security model similar to that of Linux, in which accounts have passwords and clients must send a username to the server, along with the password.

Describe the two major Samba daemons. The nmbd daemon handles name resolution and similar background and support tasks for a Samba server. The smbd daemon handles the bulk of the Samba file- and printer-sharing work. Both daemons are necessary for a fully functional Samba installation.

Summarize two methods of using a Linux computer as an SMB/CIFS client.   The smbclient program connects to an SMB/CIFS server and presents a user interface similar to that of the text-mode ftp program. Users can transfer files, delete files, rename files, and so on. The Linux mount command, in conjunction with suitable kernel filesystem support and helper programs, enables the system administrator (or users, if appropriate /etc/fstab entries exist) to mount SMB/CIFS shares as if they were local filesystems. Users can then do anything they could do with files stored on a local filesystem, using normal file-maintenance tools (cp, mv, and so on) or applications.

Describe the smb.conf file's structure.   Samba's configuration file, smb.conf, is broken into sections, each of which begins with a name in square brackets. The [global] section sets global options, and most subsequent sections set options for a single file or printer share. (The [homes] and [printers] share definitions both create multiple shares based on all users and all printers, respectively.) Within each section, options take the form *option* = *Value*, where *option* is an option name and *Value* is its value. All options and most values are case-insensitive.

Describe the /etc/exports file structure.   The NFS server's main configuration file, /etc/exports, consists of a series of lines, one per export. Each line begins with the directory that's to be exported and begins with a series of space-delimited server or server group definitions. Each of these definitions consists of a hostname, network name, IP address, or IP address range followed by a series of options in parentheses. These options are comma-separated.

Explain why proper access restrictions are so important for NFS.   Unlike many servers, NFS requires no password to gain entry. Thus, an NFS server that does not restrict access based on IP addresses can be easily invaded by anybody with physical access to the local network (or by anybody on the Internet, if the server is exposed to it). For this reason, specifying clients in a limited way in /etc/exports is very important for NFS.

Summarize how NFS exports may be modified without restarting the server.   The exportfs command can modify an NFS server's exports on the fly, enabling changes without modifying /etc/exports or restarting the server. The -o option enables you to set new options using the same format as the entries in /etc/exports; -u unexports a single directory; -r re-implements the /etc/exports file; and so on.

Describe how NFS exports may be mounted on a client.   NFS clients use the mount command or /etc/fstab entries much as they would for local filesystems. You should use the filesystem type code of nfs (or nfs4 for NFSv4 servers), and instead of a device filename, you specify the server and export in the form *server:/export*.

Explain the difference between active and passive FTP.   FTP traditionally employs active mode, in which the client initiates a connection with the server and the server then implements a reverse connection with the client. This unusual connection approach causes problems with some firewalls. In FTP passive mode, the client initiates two separate connections with the server, which works better with some firewalls. (Some clients now use passive mode by default.)

Name some of the popular FTP servers for Linux.   The Pure-FTPd and vsftpd servers both provide full-featured FTP server features but are configured in very different ways from one another. The ProFTPd server is another popular FTP server for Linux. It provides extra functionality but is much harder to configure.

Review Questions

1. A Samba server (dance) includes a [homes] share definition but no [sammy] share definition. Assuming the relevant account exists, what will then happen when the user sammy on a client attempts to access \\dance\sammy?

    A. An error message will appear because the [sammy] share doesn't exist.

    B. If the user enters the correct password, he'll be given access to the /home directory on the server.

    C. The user will be given access to the /tmp directory whether or not a correct password is entered.

    D. If the user enters the correct password, he'll be given access to his home directory's files on the server.

2. You're configuring a Samba server to participate in an existing Windows domain that's managed by a Windows 7 domain controller. You want users to be able to authenticate using the Windows controller's account database. How would you set the security option in smb.conf to achieve this result? (Choose all that apply.)

    A. security = User

    B. security = Server

    C. security = Domain

    D. security = ADS

3. What does the following line in an smb.conf file mean?

    ```
    name resolve order = lmhosts
    ```

    A. Samba uses the lmhosts file preferentially for name resolution but will use other methods if necessary.

    B. Samba uses the lmhosts file exclusively for name resolution and does not fall back on other methods.

    C. Samba uses the lmhosts file as source material when it functions as a NetBIOS name server.

    D. Samba uses the lmhosts file's contents to determine the priority given to different clients' name-resolution requests.

4. What is wrong with the following Samba share definition?

    ```
    [themes]
    comment: Themes for all users
    writable: 0
    path: /usr/share/themes
    public: 1
    ```

A. Lines within a share definition require an equal sign (=), not a colon (:), to separate the option from the value.

B. Lines following the share definition line must be indented at least one space.

C. The Boolean options (`writable` and `public`) require No or Yes values, not 0 or 1 values.

D. Nothing is wrong with it.

5. Which of the following things can you do when you access a file on an SMB/CIFS share using `mount` that you can't do when accessing it via `smbclient`?

A. Delete the file from the server.

B. Use Emacs to edit the file while it's on the server.

C. Copy the file from the server to the client.

D. Rename the file while it's on the server.

6. You want to add a Samba server to an existing Windows network, on which users are used to using their full names, including spaces, as usernames. What file would you edit to enable users to continue using those usernames, while converting them to more conventional and shorter Linux usernames?

A. The file pointed to by the `username map` option in `smb.conf`

B. The `/etc/samba/username.map` file

C. The file pointed to by the `smb passwd file` option in `smb.conf`

D. The `/etc/samba/smbpasswd` file

7. How can you verify that your `smb.conf` file contains no serious syntax errors before launching a Samba server?

A. Type **check-samba**.

B. Type **smbchkconfig**.

C. Type **smbd --check smb.conf**.

D. Type **testparm**.

8. What does it mean when a Samba server's `security` option is set to Share?

A. Samba attempts to emulate Windows 9x/Me-style authentication.

B. Samba enables access to files and printers, rather than being offline.

C. Samba uses SMB/CIFS style file-sharing rather than the Export style used by NFS.

D. Samba functions as both a client and a server on the network.

9. How does an NFS server determine who may access files it's exporting?

A. It uses the local file ownership and permission in conjunction with the client's user authentication and a list of trusted client computers.

B. It uses a password that's sent in unencrypted form across the network.

C. It uses a password that's sent in encrypted form across the network.

D. It uses the contents of individual users' `.rlogin` files to determine which client computers may access a share.

10. You want to export the /home directory to two computers via NFS: `remington` should have full read/write access, while `gentle` should have read-only access. How would you configure this in /etc/exports?

    A. `remington(/home,rw) gentle(/home,ro)`

    B. `[homes] remington(readwrite) gentle(readonly)`

    C. `/home remington(rw) gentle(ro)`

    D. `remington(/home,readwrite) gentle(/home,readonly)`

11. You want to temporarily export the /mnt/cdrom directory using NFS so that `reader` `.example.org` may read but not write the export. Assuming an NFS server is already running, what would you type at a shell prompt to accomplish this goal?

    A. `exports -o ro reader.example.org:/mnt/cdrom`

    B. `showmount -o ro reader.example.org:/mnt/cdrom`

    C. `exportfs -o ro reader.example.org:/mnt/cdrom`

    D. `mount -o ro reader.example.org:/mnt/cdrom`

12. In what way is Linux's most popular NFS server unusual, compared to most other Linux servers?

    A. The Linux NFS server requires execute permissions to be present on all served files.

    B. The Linux NFS server cannot serve Windows or Mac OS X clients.

    C. The Linux NFS server includes a kernel-based component.

    D. The Linux NFS server must be run from a super server such as `inetd` or `xinetd`.

13. What is the function of the portmapper with respect to NFS?

    A. It listens to the NFS port and hands off connections to the NFS server.

    B. It creates a map of NFS clients to help the server optimize its speed.

    C. It tells clients on which port the NFS server is running.

    D. It maintains information on local filesystems and their relationship to NFS exports.

14. What is wrong with the following /etc/fstab entry to mount an NFS export?

    `//central/jill  /mnt/jill  nfs  users  0  0`

    A. It uses an SMB/CIFS-style, not NFS-style, server/export description.

    B. The `users` option is not valid with an NFS entry in /etc/fstab.

    C. An NFS server should not be exporting /jill, but /home/jill.

    D. The dump code for an NFS mount should be 1, not 0.

15. Why should you use the `no_root_squash` option with caution on NFS exports?

A. This option gives `root` on client systems `root` privileges within exported directories on the server, which is dangerous if the client is compromised.

B. This option causes the NFS server to run outside of its `chroot` jail, which gives it access to user and system files it should not be able to access.

C. This option gives `root` full shell login privileges on the server without going through a regular account, thus making it easier for an intruder who lacks a user password.

D. This option enables ordinary users to log into the NFS server as `root`, which can quickly lead to security compromises if your users are untrustworthy.

16. You know that the computer `hereville` has an NFS export you want to use, but you can't recall its name. How can you discover this information?

A. `smbclient //hereville`

B. `showmount -e hereville`

C. `nfsclient --show hereville`

D. `nfsstat --server hereville`

17. What configuration file should you edit to enable anonymous access to a Pure-FTPd server?

A. `/etc/pure-ftpd/conf/NoAnonymous`

B. `/etc/pure-ftpd/pure-ftpd.conf`

C. `/etc/conf.d/pure-ftpd`

D. More information is required to answer this question.

18. What `vsftpd.conf` option would you set to allow anonymous users to access the FTP server?

A. `anon=YES`

B. `anonymous_enable=YES`

C. `anonymous=YES`

D. `noanonymous=NO`

19. Which is the *best* way to launch an FTP server?

A. From a SysV startup script.

B. From a super server.

C. From a local startup script.

D. It's impossible to say without more information.

20. A small network is protected by a very strict firewall. This firewall prevents all outside systems from initiating connections to any computer inside the firewall; only connections initiated from within the local network are permitted. How will this firewall impact users on the local network who need to download files from external FTP sites?

A. The users will have to use ASCII FTP transfers.

B. The users will have to use binary FTP transfers.

C. The users will have to use passive FTP transfers.

D. The users will have to use active FTP transfers.

Answers to Review Questions

1. D. The [homes] share in Samba is special; it gives access to users' home directories, with each user being given access to his or her own home directory, as option D describes. Option A is incorrect because the point of the [homes] share is to enable access to home directories without having to explicitly define a new share for each user. Option B is incorrect because the [homes] share gives access to users' individual home directories, not to the Linux /home directory, which is typically the directory in which all users' home directories reside. Option C is incorrect because a correct password is still normally required to access [homes] and because this share doesn't give access to /tmp unless options are set strangely. (The default directory for most Samba shares is /tmp, but this isn't true of [homes].)

2. B, C, D. The Server setting tells Samba to authenticate against the domain controller without fully joining the domain. The Domain setting tells Samba to fully join the domain using Windows NT 4 protocols. The ADS setting tells Samba to fully join the domain using Active Directory (AD) protocols. Any of these options will work, if properly configured. The User setting tells Samba to use its local account database, so this setting won't do as the question specifies.

3. B. The name resolve order option in Samba determines what tools Samba uses to resolve hostnames into IP addresses. Since only one option (lmhosts) appears in this example, this is the only tool that's used, as stated by option B. Option A is incorrect because no other methods will be used. Options C and D are incorrect because the name resolve order option controls Samba's own name resolution, not how it functions as a NetBIOS name server or how it delivers names to clients.

4. A. As specified in option A, Samba's smb.conf file separates options from values with an equal sign (=), not a colon (:). Option B is incorrect because, although the lines containing a share's option/value pairs are often indented, this is not a requirement. Option C is incorrect because 0, No, and False are all synonymous in Boolean options, as are 1, Yes, and True.

5. B. The single most important ability that mounting an SMB/CIFS share gives you, compared to accessing it with the ftp-like smbclient, is that mounting the share enables ordinary programs to treat the file as if it were a local file. Emacs, being an ordinary program, can therefore edit the file on the SMB/CIFS server, as option B describes. Options A, C, and D are all things that can be done using both smbclient and normal file-manipulation tools on a mounted file share.

6. A. The username map option in smb.conf specifies where a mapping of Windows to Linux usernames can be found, so option A is correct. Although /etc/samba/username.map is a common filename to specify via the username map option, it's not the only possibility, so option B is incorrect. The smb passwd file option tells Samba where to find its user password file, but this file doesn't include mapping of Windows to Linux usernames, so option C is incorrect. A common name for the Samba password file is /etc/samba/smbpasswd, but this filename does not conventionally hold mappings of Windows to Linux usernames, so option D is incorrect.

7. D. The `testparm` program checks your `smb.conf` file for various simple types of errors. (It cannot check for all errors, though.) Thus, option D is correct. The `check-samba` and `smbchkconfig` programs are fictitious, so options A and B are incorrect. The `smbd` program is one of the major Samba server programs, but it has no `--check` option, so option C is incorrect.

8. A. Share-level security refers to the authentication method used: Samba emulates, as best it can, Windows 9*x*/Me-style authentication, in which passwords are associated with shares rather than users. Thus, option A is correct. Although various Samba options can temporarily disable file and printer access, that is not true of `security = Share`, so option B is incorrect. The terms *share* and *export* have similar meanings but are used in reference to SMB/CIFS and NFS, respectively; but `Export` is not a valid value for Samba's `security` parameter, so option C is incorrect. Samba is fundamentally a server, although the Linux kernel and some ancillary Samba programs (such as `smbclient`) can function as clients. The `security` option in `smb.conf` doesn't directly affect the status of the computer as an SMB/CIFS client, though, so option D is incorrect.

9. A. NFS uses a "trusted host" policy to let clients police their own users, including access to the NFS server's files, which is what option A describes. NFS does not use a password, so options B and C are incorrect; nor does it use the `.rlogin` file in users' home directories, so option D is incorrect.

10. C. Option C presents the correct syntax for achieving the specified goal in `/etc/exports`. Options A and D incorrectly place the exported directory name in the option list for each client. Option B uses `[homes]` (a Samba name for users' home directories) rather than `/homes`. Options B and D incorrectly expand the `ro` and `rw` codes into `readonly` and `readwrite`.

11. C. The `exportfs` program controls the NFS server; it adds or removes directories and clients from the list the server maintains, thus temporarily extending or restricting the list that's normally maintained in `/etc/exports`. Option C presents the correct syntax for this program to achieve the stated goal. There is no standard `exports` command, so option A is incorrect. Option B's `showmount` command displays information on the clients that are using the server, but it doesn't change the export list. The `mount` command mounts a remote export; it doesn't affect what's exported, so option D is incorrect.

12. C. Linux's kernel-based NFS server features help improve its performance. Most other servers do not include such kernel-based help, so option C is correct. Option A describes a fictitious requirement of the NFS server. Although few Windows computers have NFS clients, NFS clients for Windows are available; and OS X includes an NFS client. Thus, option B is incorrect. Contrary to option D, Linux's NFS server is run directly, not from a super server.

13. C. Option C correctly summarizes the role of the portmapper. Option A describes the function of a super server, such as `inetd` or `xinetd`, except that super servers aren't commonly used with NFS servers. Options B and D are made-up descriptions of solutions to nonexistent problems.

14. A. The correct form for an NFS export definition in /etc/fstab is *server:/share*, so this entry should probably begin central:/jill or central:/home/jill. The entry instead uses the SMB/CIFS-style share definition, as option A states. Contrary to option B, the users option is perfectly valid for NFS entries in /etc/fstab. Although exporting a directory called /jill is indeed unusual, it is not illegal, and because a more serious problem is correct in the form of option A, option C is incorrect. The dump utility is used for backing up local ext2, ext3, and ext4 filesystems, not NFS exports, so the dump code should be 0 on NFS entries in /etc/fstab, contrary to option D.

15. A. The no_root_squash option does as option A specifies, which is useful if a client needs access to restricted files on the server, but it also poses the risk specified in option A. The no_root_squash option has nothing to do with chroot jails, so option B is incorrect. Option C describes a Secure Shell (SSH) login option and its risks, but because NFS does not provide login shell access or use passwords, it is an incorrect answer to this question. NFS doesn't allow users to "log into" a server in the sense suggested by option D, making that option incorrect.

16. B. The showmount utility displays information about the server you specify. Details vary with the options you pass it, but -e produces a list of the server's exports, making option B correct. The smbclient program is used for accessing SMB/CIFS servers, not NFS servers, and option A's syntax is incorrect even for discovering SMB/CIFS shares. The nfsclient program is fictitious. The nfsstat program displays statistics related to NFS use, and although option D is a valid command for producing such information, it won't display information on available exports on the server, as the question requires.

17. D. Pure-FTPd has no standard configuration file; instead, it relies on command-line arguments to change its behavior. Unfortunately, different distributions handle passing these arguments to the server in different ways, so you need to know the distribution to answer the question, making option D correct. Options A, B, and C are each correct, but only for specific distributions: Ubuntu, Fedora, and Gentoo.

18. B. Option B is correct. Options A and C are fictitious; neither anon nor anonymous is a valid vsftpd.conf option. Option D is also not a valid vsftpd.conf option, but passing --noanonymous to the pure-ftpd server is one way to *disable* anonymous access with that server.

19. D. FTP server programs vary in design; some are intended to be run from a local or SysV startup script, others are intended to be run from super servers, and others can be launched in either way. The needs of the site must also be considered; for instance, a lightly used FTP server might best be launched from a super server, whereas an FTP server that's in constant use might better be launched from a startup script. Thus, option D is correct. Because there is no single best way, options A, B, and C are all incorrect answers.

20. C. Passive FTP transfers involve the FTP client initiating two connections to the FTP server, which should not run afoul of the firewall configuration described in the question, so option C is correct. The alternative to passive FTP transfers is active FTP transfers, in which the client initiates one connection to the server and the server then initiates a return connection to the client. Since the firewall blocks incoming connections, an active FTP transfer will be blocked by the described firewall, making option D incorrect. The issue of ASCII vs. binary transfers is independent of the issue of passive vs. active transfers and is irrelevant to firewall configuration, so options A and B are both incorrect.

Chapter
9

Configuring Web and Email Servers

THE FOLLOWING LINUX PROFESSIONAL INSTITUTE OBJECTIVES ARE COVERED IN THIS CHAPTER:

- ✓ 208.1 Implementing a Web server (weight: 3)
- ✓ 208.2 Maintaining a Web server (weight: 2)
- ✓ 208.3 Implementing a proxy server (weight: 1)
- ✓ 211.1 Using email servers (weight: 3)
- ✓ 211.2 Managing local email delivery (weight: 2)
- ✓ 211.3 Managing remote email delivery (weight: 2)

Two of the most important parts of the Internet are email and the World Wide Web (WWW or Web for short). In fact, Linux plays a role in both of these Internet subsystems; email and Web server software exists for Linux, and both Linux and the common Linux server programs are important in today's implementation of these tools.

Web server configuration can involve multiple protocols and programs, sometimes on multiple computers. You may be asked to set up a Web server and help maintain the documents on that server. You should also be aware of proxy servers, which sit between users and outside Web servers in order to filter content or improve performance.

Email is delivered through several protocols, as described later in "Understanding Email," so configuring Linux as a mail server computer may require you to set up several different server programs. Additional programs help to "glue" everything together, enabling local delivery, access to junk mail filters, and so on. It's critical that you understand how these protocols and software interact, as well as the basics of how to configure the individual programs.

Understanding Web Servers

Web servers implement the *Hypertext Transfer Protocol (HTTP)* and are extremely important to today's Internet. Even local networks often employ Web servers for purely local purposes. Web servers are similar to file servers (described in Chapter 8, "Configuring File Servers") in that they provide more or less direct access to files stored on the server computer; but Web servers are designed to quickly deliver one or a few files at a time, typically without requiring authentication, and then terminate a connection. Although uploading files to a Web site is possible, a simple configuration typically disallows such access; such simple Web sites are read-only in nature.

These features are ideal for the Web, which enables users to read information on a wide variety of Web sites from around the globe with minimal fuss. Some critical features of Web sites, such as the hyperlinks that enable moving from one site to another by clicking a link, are implemented in the main type of document delivered by Web servers. This document type is known as the *Hypertext Markup Language (HTML)*. It provides document formatting features to enable setting fonts, creating lists, and so on; embedding certain related files, such as graphics, in the Web page; and linking to other documents on the same or other sites. HTTP and HTML are distinct; it's possible to run a Web site (using HTTP) that hosts no HTML files, and it's possible to use HTML files without a Web server. As a practical matter, though, the two are usually linked; a Web server exists to deliver HTML files to clients, and those files are created with a Web server as delivery mechanism in mind. Neither the LPIC-2 exam nor this chapter covers HTML in any detail; you should merely be aware of how HTML fits in with HTTP.

Web sites today often employ more complex document types, such as scripts and other dynamic content. Web sites built on such documents can be much more interactive than the traditional static HTML files that dominated the Web a decade ago. Several types of dynamic content exist, and each has its own configuration options. This chapter covers the basics of *PHP: Hypertext Preprocessor (PHP)* and Perl scripts on Web sites in the "Configuring Scripts" section.

In principle, any computer can run a Web server. On the Internet at large, most Web server computers have the hostname www in their respective domains or subdomains. This is only a convention, though; many sites employ other names or run multiple Web servers on a single domain for one reason or another.

Many Web server programs are available, both for Linux and for other platforms. The most popular, however, is Apache (`http://httpd.apache.org`). This chapter describes how to configure this software for common Web server duties. If you need to run another server, you should consult its documentation.

 Apache 2.2.17 is the newest version available as I write. Some configuration options changed between the 1.3.*x* series and the 2.*x* series. This chapter emphasizes the more recent software. If you're using an older 1.3.*x* version, you may need to deviate from the descriptions in this chapter. (The 1.3.*x* series is still being maintained, but most new installations should use a 2.2.*x* version.)

Setting Basic Apache Options

The primary Apache configuration file is called `apache.conf`, `httpd.conf`, or (for Apache 2.*x* on some Linux distributions) `apache2.conf` or `httpd2.conf`. This file is usually located in `/etc/apache`, `/etc/apache2`, `/etc/httpd`, or `/etc/httpd/conf`. Whatever the filename or location, most of the lines in this file are either comments that begin with hash marks (#) or option lines that take the following form:

Directive Value

The *Directive* is the name of a parameter you want to adjust, and the *Value* is the value given to the parameter. The *Value* may be a number, a filename, or an arbitrary string.

Some directives appear in named blocks that begin and end with codes enclosed in angle brackets, such as this:

```
<IfDefine APACHEPROXIED>
    Listen 8080
</IfDefine>
```

This particular example sets the `Listen` directive to 8080 if the `APACHEPROXIED` variable is defined. Note that the final line uses the name specified in the first line but is preceded by a slash (/). This arrangement signifies the start and end of a block of options albeit one that contains just one option in this example.

Apache is designed in a modular way—many of its features can be compiled as separate modules that can be loaded at run time or left unloaded. Precisely which features are compiled as modules and which are compiled into the main Apache executable (typically called `apache`, `apache2`, `httpd`, or `httpd2`) varies from one distribution to another. To load a module, you use the `LoadModule` directive, and many Apache configuration files have a large number of these directives early in the file. With Apache 1.3.*x* (but not for Apache 2.*x*), you may need to use the `AddModule` directive to activate the features of a module that's compiled into the main binary. You may want to peruse these modules to see what features are enabled by default.

 Commenting out the LoadModule directives for unused features can be a good security measure. For instance, if you have no need to deliver dynamic content, commenting out the cgi_module can reduce the chance that an accidental misconfiguration or intentional cracking will cause damage. Unfortunately, it's hard to know what each module does, so I recommend caution in commenting out module definitions.

The `Include` directive loads additional files as if they were part of the main configuration file. Some distributions take advantage of this feature to place module support in separate files, typically in the `mods-available` and `mods-enabled` subdirectories. The files in `mods-enabled` are loaded via an `Include` statement. These files are actually symbolic links to equivalent files in `mods-available` The result is that system configuration scripts can enable or disable modules by creating or removing appropriate symbolic links in these directories.

In addition to the main configuration file, a handful of additional files are important:

access.conf Not all Apache configurations use this file, which is essentially a supplemental file that tells Apache how to treat specific directories. Many systems roll this information into the main configuration file. For those that don't, an `AccessConfig` directive in the main file points to the `access.conf` file.

mime.types or **apache-mime.types** This file defines assorted *Multipurpose Internet Mail Extension (MIME)* types, which are codes that help identify the type of a file. HTTP transfers identify files by MIME type, but Linux filesystems don't store MIME type information natively. Therefore, Apache uses this file to map filename extensions (such as `.html` or `.txt`) to MIME types. The default file handles most common files you're likely to deliver on your Web server, but you may need to add MIME types if you place exotic file types on the server.

magic This file exists in support of a second method of determining a file's MIME type. Rather than rely on filename extensions, this file includes "fingerprints" for many file types based on the files' contents. You shouldn't try to adjust this file unless you have precise instructions on doing so for a particular file type or if you possess a deep understanding of the file's internal format.

These files typically reside in the same directory that holds the main Apache configuration file. You're most likely to need to adjust `access.conf`, but only on systems that use it by default or if you choose to use this configuration option. If you deliver unusual file types, the best way to associate MIME types with those files is usually by adjusting the `mime.types` or `apache-mime.types` file; modifying the `magic` file is much trickier.

Users or Web site maintainers can override some Apache configuration options using the `.htaccess` files in the directories that Apache serves. The format of the `.htaccess` file is just like that of the main Apache configuration file, but the options set in this file affect only the directory tree in which the `.htaccess` file resides. Normally, this file is used only by users whose personal Web pages are shared with a global `UserDir` directive or by Web site maintainers who may edit one or more subdirectories of the server's main Web space directory but who don't have full administrative access to edit the main Apache configuration file.

Configuring Apache to Host Your Site

A default Apache configuration file usually works at least minimally. You can test your installation after installing it by entering **http://localhost** as the location in a Web browser running on the same computer. You should see a generic page appear, as shown in Figure 9.1, which depicts the default page on an Ubuntu 10.10 system. Details vary from one distribution to another, so don't be surprised if your default page looks different from Figure 9.1. You should also test access to the server from other computers to be sure firewall rules (described in Chapter 7, "Advanced Network Configuration") or other problems aren't blocking access to the server. If you can't access the server, check that it's running. It should appear as `apache`, `apache2`, `httpd`, or `httpd2` in a `ps` listing. Apache 1.3 can also be run from a super server, although this configuration is not common.

FIGURE 9.1 Once installed and run, a default Apache configuration displays a generic Apache Web page or a page for your distribution.

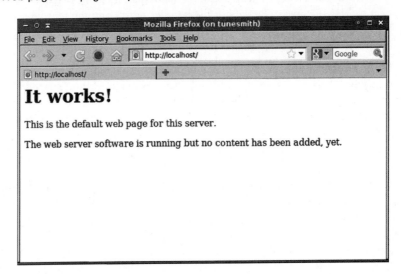

Once the server is running, you may want to adjust some of its defaults. Some common features you might want to change include the server's user and group, the location of Web pages the server delivers, and virtual domains. Two still more advanced options—delivering secure Web pages and serving dynamic content—may also need adjustment.

Setting the Apache User and Group

Like most servers that start with SysV, Upstart, or local startup scripts, Apache starts running as root. Apache supports two directives that adjust the username and group name under which the server runs after it's started. These directives are User and Group. For instance, you might include the following lines to have Apache run as the user apache in the group called agroup:

```
User apache
Group agroup
```

After you've set these options, a check of these features using ps (as in **ps aux | grep apache** or **ps aux | grep httpd**) should reveal that most instances of Apache are running as the specified user and group. The first instance, though, will continue to run as root. This instance doesn't directly respond to incoming requests, though.

Real World Scenario

Running Apache in a chroot Jail

Ensuring that Apache runs in a low-privilege account is a good security measure; however, you can go further. As with the Berkeley Internet Name Domain (BIND) server described in Chapter 6, "DNS Server Configuration," you can run Apache in a chroot jail. Doing so limits the damage that Apache can do should it be compromised or should poorly written scripts run amok. You'll need to take some extra configuration to do this, though.

Much of the task of running Apache in a chroot jail is similar to that described in Chapter 6 for BIND. Broadly speaking, you must create a directory tree to house Apache, copy configuration files and support libraries to that directory tree, and modify your Apache startup script to launch the server using the chroot command. (Unlike BIND, Apache doesn't have an option to do this itself.)

If you need more information, numerous Web pages describe this configuration in more detail; doing a Web search on **Apache chroot** will find them. You may want to check your distribution's documentation first, though; it may provide a streamlined setup method.

Changing Web Page Locations

As a general rule, Apache supports two types of static Web pages: a site's Web pages and individual users' Web pages. A site's Web pages are maintained by the system administrator or a designated Web master; most ordinary users can't modify these pages. Multiuser systems sometimes provide users with Web space. These pages are typically served from subdirectories of the users' home directories. Naturally, Apache provides tools for changing the locations of both site Web pages and individuals' Web pages.

Understanding Web Addresses

To understand how Apache returns Web pages, it's helpful to look at how an HTTP request is structured. The usual form of this request, as typed by a person in the Address or Location field of a Web browser, is as a *Uniform Resource Identifier (URI)*, which looks like this:

```
http://www.example.com/products/biggie.html#orig
```

    The *URI* acronym is the official replacement for another acronym, *Uniform Resource Locator (URL)*. Although *URL* is still in common use, it's officially an "informal" term.

This URI consists of four components:

The Protocol   The first few characters of a URI specify the protocol—http in this case. The protocol is terminated by a colon (:), and in many cases (including URIs for HTTP transfers) two slashes follow it. Other common protocols in URIs include https (secure HTTP), ftp, and email.

The Hostname   The hostname follows the protocol name in HTTP URIs, as well as some other types of URIs, such as FTP URIs. In this example, the hostname is www.example.com.

The Filename   After the hostname in HTTP URIs comes the filename that's to be retrieved—/products/biggie.html in this example. The filename can be a single file or a complete path to a file, as in this example. Normally, the filename is specified relative to the server's document root, as described next, in "Changing the Site's Web Page." If a tilde (~) leads the filename, though, it's relative to a specified user's Web storage area, as described in the upcoming section "Enabling User Web Pages."

Additional Information   Some URIs include additional information. The preceding example specifies #orig after the filename, meaning that the browser should locate a tag called orig within the page and display the text at that point. Dynamic content uses this part of the URI to enable browsers to pass data to the Web server for processing.

Many of these components can be omitted or abbreviated. For instance, most Web browsers assume an HTTP transfer if you start the URI with the hostname. If you omit the filename, the Web server assumes a default filename. In Apache, you can set this default with the DirectoryIndex directive. If you provide more than one value for this directive, Apache searches for them all. Most installations create a default that searches for one or more of index.htm, index.html, or index.shtml. If you're moving an existing set of Web pages to Apache and that set includes a different default index filename, you may want to change the default.

Changing the Site's Web Page

One of the earliest directives in the Apache configuration file is probably a DocumentRoot directive, which tells Apache where to look for the Web pages it delivers. You'll find the default Web pages, such as the one displayed in Figure 9.1, in this location. To use Apache to deliver your own site's pages, you can do one of two things:

■   Change the DocumentRoot directive to point to another directory in which you've stored your Web site's pages.

■   Replace the files in the default DocumentRoot directory with ones you create.

As with module configurations, some Apache installations place Web site configuration data, including DocumentRoot, in a separate configuration file, typically in the sites-available/default file (with a symbolic link in sites-enabled/default).

Changing the `DocumentRoot` directive is slightly preferable because it reduces the odds that your Web pages will be accidentally overwritten when you upgrade your Web server installation. Using an unusual location for the server's home page can also reduce the risk of a scripted attack that uses some other system vulnerability to overwrite your site's files; if the attacker doesn't know where your files reside, they can't be overwritten. When you create a new directory to house your site, you should be sure that it's readable to the user under whose name Apache runs. This username is often specified with the `User` directive in the main Apache configuration file. The group may also be important; that's set via the `Group` directive. Because public Web sites seldom contain sensitive data, it's not uncommon to make the directories and the files within them readable to the world.

Typically, the *Web master* is responsible for maintaining the Web site. The Web master may also be the system administrator, but this isn't always the case. The Web master normally has full write access to the site's Web page directory, and the Web master may in fact be the owner of this directory tree and all the files within it. The default document root directory isn't normally the Web master's home directory, though; configuring the system in this way would enable anybody to download files such as the Web master's `.bashrc` file.

Enabling User Web Pages

In addition to a site's main Web pages, Apache can deliver Web pages belonging to individual users. To activate this feature, you must set the `UserDir` directive, which takes the name of a directory within a user's home directory as an argument. (This directive may appear in the `mods-available/userdir.conf` file, which must be activated by symbolically linking it to a file in the `mods-enabled` directory.) For instance, you might use the following definition:

```
UserDir public_html
```

Once this directive is set, users can create subdirectories called `public_html` and store their personal Web pages in that directory. For instance, suppose a remote user enters **http://www.example.com/~charlotte/apage.html** as a URI. If the server is configured with `UserDir` set to `public_html` and if the user `charlotte` has a home directory of `/home/charlotte`, then Apache will attempt to return `/home/charlotte/public_html/apage.html` to the client.

The directories leading to the one specified by `UserDir`, including that directory, must be accessible to the account used to run Apache. This includes both the read bit and the execute bit (which in the case of directories means the ability to traverse the directory tree). Typically, setting world permissions on these directories is appropriate; however, setting group permissions is adequate if the Apache process is run using a suitable group.

WARNING   Be sure when you set up the `UserDir` directive and the root user's home directory (typically `/root`), that outsiders can't retrieve files from root's home directory. Such a configuration is a potential security threat.

The delivery of user Web pages relies on the userdir_module module. If your site shouldn't deliver user Web pages, you may want to remove the LoadModule directive that loads this module. If you remove this directive, an attempt to use the UserDir directive will cause Apache to fail at startup, unless it's surrounded by an <IfModule mod_userdir.c> directive to test for the module's presence. If your installation uses separate directories with per-module configuration files, enabling or disabling the relevant file will automatically enable or disable both the module and the UserDir directive.

Serving Virtual Domains

A single Apache Web server can deliver pages for multiple domains. This configuration is extremely important for Web-hosting ISPs, which run Web servers that respond differently to requests for each client. For instance, one ISP might deliver Web pages for www.example.com, www.pangaea.edu, and many more. To do this without devoting an entire computer and IP address to each domain, the ISP must configure the Web server to respond differently depending on the hostname part of the URI. This practice is known as configuring *virtual domains*. Of course, if you're an ISP hosting virtual domains, this chapter is inadequate for your job; you should read several books on Apache or hire a system administrator with substantial experience running Apache or some other Web server. Nonetheless, virtual domains can be useful even on some smaller sites. For instance, a small company might change its name and want its Web server to respond differently to two hostnames. An individual or small business might also partner with another individual or small business to set up Web sites on a broadband connection, minimizing the costs associated with running their Web sites in this way. Two methods of delivering virtual domains are common: VirtualDocumentRoot and VirtualHost.

Using *VirtualDocumentRoot*

The idea behind the VirtualDocumentRoot directive is to tell Apache which directory to use as the document root directory based on the hostname used by the client. VirtualDocumentRoot works much like the standard DocumentRoot directive, except that you include variables, as specified in Table 9.1, in the directive's value.

TABLE 9.1 Variables used in conjunction with VirtualDocumentRoot

Variable	Meaning
%%	A single % in the directory name.
%N.M	Parts of the name. N is a number that refers to the dot-separated name component. For instance, if the name is www.example.com, %1 means www, %2 means example, and so on. Negative numbers count from the end; 1 means com, %-2 is example, and so on. An N of 0 refers to the entire hostname. The optional M refers to the number of characters within the name. For instance, %2.4 would be exam. Negative M values count from the end of the component, so %2.-4 would be mple.

If you want to set up virtual domains based on the IP address of the server (for servers with multiple IP addresses), you can use `VirtualDocumentRootIP`, which works much like `VirtualDocumentRoot` but uses IP addresses rather than hostnames.

The `VirtualDocumentRoot` directive is most useful when you want to host a large number of domains or when the domains change frequently. You can set up a domain merely by creating a new subdirectory. For instance, suppose you want to create a directory structure of the form */home/httpd/tld/domain*, as in */home/httpd/com/example* as the document root directory for `www.example.com`. A configuration accommodating this layout would look like this:

```
VirtualDocumentRoot /home/httpd/%-1/%-2
```

Alternatively, suppose you want to alphabetize your domains so that `www.example.com`'s document root directory would be in */home/httpd/e/example*. This arrangement could be achieved using the following entry:

```
VirtualDocumentRoot /home/httpd/%-2.1/%-2
```

Some configurations could create duplicate entries. For instance, the preceding entry will try to place both example.com's and example.org's document roots in the same directory. To avoid the problem, use the %0 variable in the path, which uses the entire hostname.

Whenever you use `VirtualDocumentRoot`, you should set the following line in your Apache configuration file:

```
UseCanonicalNames Off
```

Ordinarily (or when `UseCanonicalNames` is set to `On`), Apache tries to use the hostname of the machine on which it runs when performing relative accesses within a Web site—that is, when a Web page omits the protocol and hostname portions of a URI in a link and provides only the document filename. This practice is likely to lead to "file not found" errors or incorrect pages returned, because Apache will look up the wrong site's documents. Setting `UseCanonicalNames` to `Off`, though, tells Apache to instead use the hostname provided by the client with the original access, which results in a correct lookup.

Using *VirtualHost*

Another approach to defining virtual domains is to create `VirtualHost` directive blocks. These blocks must be preceded in the file with a line that defines the interfaces on which you want to define virtual hosts:

```
NameVirtualHost *
```

This example tells the system to create virtual hosts on all interfaces. If the system has multiple interfaces and you only want to create virtual hosts on one interface, you can specify the IP address rather than an asterisk as the value of this directive. At some point after the `NameVirtualHost` directive in the Apache configuration file are `VirtualHost` directive blocks for each hostname:

```
<VirtualHost *>
   ServerName www.example.com
   DocumentRoot /home/httpd/business
</VirtualHost>

<VirtualHost *>
   ServerName www.luna.edu
   DocumentRoot /home/httpd/loonie/html
   ScriptAlias /cgi-bin/ "/home/httpd/loonie/cgi-bin/"
</VirtualHost>
```

As with a `VirtualDocumentRoot` configuration, you should be sure to set `UseCanonicalNames` to `Off` in the main Apache configuration file. Failure to do so is likely to result in spurious "document not found" errors and possibly failures to retrieve documents when Web pages use relative document references in URIs.

One of the big advantages of `VirtualHost` definitions over `VirtualDocumentRoot` is that you can customize each server to respond differently. For instance, the preceding example uses document root filenames that are unique but that aren't systematically related to the hostnames. The definition for `www.luna.edu` also activates a dynamic content directory via the `ScriptAlias` directive, which is described in more detail in the upcoming section "Serving Dynamic Content with CGI Scripts." These advantages can be very important for many servers that handle just a few domains. The drawback to this approach is that you must change the configuration file every time you add or delete a domain, which can be a hassle if you change the domains you handle on a regular basis.

Configuring Scripts

Many sites run a Web server merely to deliver static content—that is, pages whose content doesn't change. Web servers can also run dynamic content, though, such as Common Gateway Interface (CGI) scripts, PHP: Hypertext Preprocessor (PHP; a recursive acronym, formerly expanded as *Personal Home Page*) scripts, or mod_perl scripts. These scripts can extend the functionality of a Web server, enabling it to provide dynamic content or perform computing functions on behalf of clients. Each of these technologies is extremely complex, and this section provides only enough information for you to activate support for it in Apache. If you need to maintain a site that relies on scripting technology, you should consult additional documentation on the topic.

WARNING Enabling scripting features on a Web server can be risky, because an incorrect configuration with buggy scripts can give an attacker a way to compromise the computer's security as a whole. Thus, I strongly recommend you not attempt this unless you learn far more about Web servers and their scripting capabilities than I can present in this brief introduction to this topic.

CGI scripts are scripts or programs that run on the Web server at the request of a client. CGI scripts can be written in any language—C, C++, Perl, Bash, Python, or others. CGI scripts may be actual scripts or compiled programs, but because they're usually true scripts, the term *CGI script* applies to any sort of CGI program, even if it's compiled. The script must be written in such a way that it generates a valid Web page for users, but that topic is far too complex to cover here.

To activate CGI script support in Apache, you typically point to a special CGI directory using the `ScriptAlias` directive:

```
ScriptAlias /cgi-bin /usr/www/cgi-bin
```

This line tells Apache to look in `/usr/www/cgi-bin` for scripts. This directory may be a subdirectory of the parent of the `DocumentRoot` directory, but their locations can be quite different if you prefer.

PHP, by contrast, is a scripting language that's designed explicitly for building Web pages. As with CGI scripts, writing PHP scripts is a complex topic that's not covered on the LPIC-2 exams. You should, however, know how to activate PHP support in Apache. To begin this task, ensure that you've installed the necessary PHP packages. Chances are you'll need one called `php`, and perhaps various support or ancillary packages, too.

With PHP installed, you can configure Apache to support it. This is done via Apache configuration lines like the following:

```
# Use for PHP 5.x:
LoadModule php5_module          modules/libphp5.so
AddHandler php5-script php

# Add index.php to your DirectoryIndex line:
DirectoryIndex index.html index.php
AddType text/html       php
```

NOTE The preceding configuration works for PHP version 5. If you're using another PHP version, you may need to change the filenames.

The first couple of lines in this configuration simply load the PHP module and handler. The `DirectoryIndex` and `AddType` lines help Apache manage the PHP files. The `DirectoryIndex` line will replace existing lines in your configuration—or more precisely, you should ensure that index.php appears on the DirectoryIndex line along with any other filenames you use for index files.

In addition to these global options, directories that hold PHP scripts may include files called php.ini, which set various PHP interpreter options. There are quite a few options, such as user_dir, include_path, and extension. If you need to tweak your PHP settings, I recommend starting from a sample file, such as the global php.ini file in /etc.

The mod_perl scripting solution enables Apache to run Perl scripts directly, rather than relying on the normal CGI tools to do so. You may need to install a package called apache-mod_perl, libapache2-mod-perl2, or something similar to enable this support.

With the mod_perl support installed, you must activate it. In most cases, this is done by including a configuration file that ships with the package, such as mods-available/perl .load or modules.d/75_mod_perl.conf. If such a file isn't available, the following line, added to your main Apache configuration file, will do the job:

```
LoadModule perl_module /usr/lib/apache2/modules/mod_perl.so
```

You may need to modify the path to the mod_perl.so file for your installation. You will also need to define a directory to hold the site's Perl scripts:

```
<Directory /var/www/perl>
    AllowOverride All
    SetHandler perl-script
    PerlResponseHandler ModPerl::Registry
    PerlOptions +ParseHeaders
    Options -Indexes FollowSymLinks MultiViews ExecCGI
    Order allow,deny
    Allow from all
</Directory>
```

Typically, this directory will be a subdirectory of the main site's directory (/var/www in this example). When a user accesses a Perl script file, the result will then be that the script runs. Normally, the script will generate dynamic content.

Whatever scripting tool you use, you can restart Apache via its SysV startup script to have it enable scripting support. It's then up to you or your Web developers to create appropriate scripts to manage dynamic content on your site. This is a complex topic that's not covered on the LPIC-2 exams.

Enabling Encryption

Secure HTTP is denoted by an https:// header in the URI. This protocol is an HTTP variant that uses encryption to keep data transfers private. Apache supports secure HTTP transfers, but configuring it to do so is a three-step process:

1. You must install a special version of Apache or add-on package that enables encryption.

2. You must obtain or create a *certificate*, which is an encryption key.

3. You must configure Apache to listen on the secure HTTP port and respond to requests on that port using encryption.

Installing Secure Apache

Secure HTTP relies on an encryption protocol known as the *Secure Sockets Layer (SSL)*. To implement SSL, your system needs an SSL library. Today, OpenSSL (http://www .openssl.org) is the most common choice for this job. OpenSSL ships with many Linux distributions, so you can probably install it from your main installation medium.

In addition to SSL, you must install an SSL-enabled version of Apache or an SSL module for Apache. Modern distributions typically ship with a suitable module package for Apache 2.*x*, with a name such as apache-mod_ssl. Sometimes the appropriate module is installed along with the main Apache package or in a generic support package. If you're using an older Apache 1.3 installation, you may need to use a special version of Apache, such as Apache-SSL (http://www.apache-ssl.org).

Obtaining or Creating a Certificate

Just as with a virtual private network (VPN), as described in Chapter 5, "Networking Configuration," HTTPS relies on keys and certificates to authenticate each side to the other. In the case of HTTPS, though, it's typically important that the server be able to prove its identity to the client, with no previous contact between the two systems. Consider a Web merchant who asks for a credit card number, for instance; the user wants to be sure that the server belongs to a legitimate merchant and not an imposter. The true identity of the client is typically less important in this situation.

 If you do need to establish two-way trust between the Web server and the Web client, you can do so. You must acquire keys for both systems (you may be able to generate the client's key yourself) and use the SSLRequire directive to point the server to the public keys for the clients who should be allowed to connect. Consult the Apache documentation for more details about this type of configuration.

To provide this level of trust, HTTPS relies on certificates and keys that are signed by any of a handful of publicly known certificate authorities (CAs). Every modern Web browser has a list of CA signatures and so can verify that a Web site's keys have been signed by an appropriate CA and that the Web site is, therefore, what it claims to be. This system isn't absolutely perfect, but it's reasonably reliable.

To deliver secure content, you need a certificate. For many purposes, the best way to do this is to buy one from a CA. A list of about two dozen CAs is available at http://www .apache-ssl.org/#Digital_Certificates. Before obtaining a certificate from a CA, you should research the companies' policies and determine how widely recognized their certificate signatures are. There's no point in buying a cut-rate certificate if your users' browsers generate alerts about unknown signatures. You could create your own certificate that would produce the same result.

Creating your own certificate makes sense if you don't care about authenticating the identity of the server or if this authentication is required on only a few systems. For instance, if you want to encrypt certain Web server accesses on a small local network, or even between offices that are geographically separated, you don't need to go to a CA. You can tell your Web browsers to accept your own locally generated certificate. Of course, telling your users to accept your personal certificate but not to accept suspicious certificates from other sites may be confusing.

Whether you obtain your certificate from a CA or generate it locally, you must make it available to Apache. Typically, this is done by copying the certificate to a special certificate directory somewhere in /etc, such as /etc/ssl/apache. If you use a script to generate a certificate, the script may do this automatically, or it may place the certificate in another directory, such as the main Apache configuration directory. The certificate consists of two files: a certificate file (which often has a .crt extension) and a key (which often has a .key extension).

Be sure you protect the certificate and key from prying eyes. The default configuration when utilities create these files uses root ownership and 0600 permissions to accomplish this task. If you copy the files, be sure these features are preserved. A miscreant who copies these files can impersonate your (formerly) secure web server!

Configuring Apache to Use Encryption

Apache 2.*x* systems tend to need only very minimal configuration file changes to support SSL. With these systems, you may only need to load the SSL module with a line like this:

```
LoadModule ssl_module /usr/lib/apache2/modules/mod_ssl.so
```

You may need to adjust the location of the SSL module for your system. If your installation uses module loading and configuration files, you should be able to activate SSL support by creating an appropriate symbolic link to use the SSL file. Once activated in this way, an Apache 2.*x* system will respond both to ordinary HTTP and secure HTTP requests. Table 9.2 summarizes some of the Apache configuration options that affect SSL operation. The SSLRequireSSL directive is particularly noteworthy, because it can help keep your Web server from inadvertently delivering sensitive data over an unencrypted link.

TABLE 9.2 Directives that affect SSL operation

Directive	Meaning
Listen	This option binds the server to a particular port. The secure HTTP port is 443.
SSLEngine	You can set this option to on or off to enable or disable SSL.

Directive	Meaning
`SSLRequireSSL`	Ordinarily, Apache will deliver files to both ordinary HTTP and secure HTTP clients. Using this option tells Apache to deliver files only to clients that have made secure connections. This directive takes no value, and it is normally placed within a `<Directory>` directive block.
`SSLCACertificatePath`	This directive points to the directory in which the SSL certificate resides, such as `/etc/ssl/apache`.
`SSLCertificateFile`	This directive identifies the SSL certificate file, such as `/etc/ssl/apache/server.crt`.

Limiting Access to Apache

Web servers are frequently targets of attack. Several Apache features are designed to address this problem. Most notably, you can limit the number and types of connections that Apache will accept, and you can configure Apache to require user authentication.

Limiting Connections to Apache

Apache enables you to limit the absolute number of connections handled by the server. This is typically done through a block of options like this:

```
<IfModule mpm_prefork_module>
    StartServers          5
    MinSpareServers       5
    MaxSpareServers      10
    MaxClients          150
    MaxRequestsPerChild   0
</IfModule>
```

These options tell Apache to launch five servers initially (`StartServers`), to keep between 5 and 10 servers available to respond to requests at all times (`MinSpareServers` and `MaxSpareServers`), to launch at most 150 server instances (`MaxClients`), and to impose no limit on the number of requests the server handles (`MaxRequestsPerChild`; a value of 0 means no limit). Setting these options appropriately can limit the potential for abuse. The `MaxClients` value is particularly important; without such a restriction, an attacker need only orchestrate a huge number of requests on the server to force it to launch enough processes to bring the server computer to its knees. Under the weight of such an attack, you might find it difficult to shut down Apache, much less deal with the attack in a more targeted way. By using MaxClients, you at least stand a chance of retaining control of the computer, which will enable you to read log files and track the attack as it proceeds.

Unfortunately, suitable values for MaxClients and the other options can be hard to ascertain; they depend on factors such as the normal load on the server, the quality of your network connection, the amount of RAM in the computer, and the speed of your hard disk. You may need to monitor the Apache log files and perform experiments to determine how to set these options.

Setting User Authentication Options

Although many Web sites are intended for free access without an account or password, some sites require authentication. Web forums, for instance, typically require you to enter a username and password before you can post. Such logins are handled by Apache user authentication tools. To begin using these tools, you must first load the mod_auth module. You can do this directly in the main configuration file:

```
LoadModule auth_module /usr/lib/apache2/modules/mod_auth.so
```

The mod_auth module is available in Apache versions prior to 2.1. More recent versions employ similar functionality via more specialized modules, such as mod_auth_basic (which is similar to the earlier mod_auth), mod_auth_pam (which works via the Pluggable Authentication Modules system), and mod_auth_ldap (which uses an LDAP server for authentication).

Alternatively, if your installation loads modules using a separate directory with module configuration files, you can create appropriate links to load the relevant module.

With the appropriate module loaded, you can then generate a password file. Be sure that the file you generate resides outside of the directories that the Web server makes available to clients; you don't want users to be able to retrieve the password file. To create the file, use htpasswd, telling it to create a new file via its -c option, specifying the password file, and terminating the command with the name of the user with which to associate the password:

```
# htpasswd -c /etc/apache/passwd/passwords charlotte
New password:
Re-type new password:
Adding password for user charlotte
```

To require a password, you must specify several options in your Apache configuration file. These options can reside in a suitable directory definition within the main configuration file, or they can go in a .htaccess file within the directory you want to protect:

```
AuthType Basic
AuthName "Restricted Files"
```

```
# (Following line optional)
AuthBasicProvider file
AuthUserFile /etc/apache/passwd/passwords
Require user charlotte
```

If you want to enable more than one user to access files in the password-protected directory, you must modify your configuration. One way of doing this is by specifying a group. This is done in a group definition file (say, /etc/apache/passwd/group), which contains just one line that holds the relevant usernames:

```
GroupName: charlotte wilbur fern
```

You can then add the additional users to the password file by repeating the same htpasswd command, but be sure to omit the -c option, since this option creates a new password file; and change the username for each user. You then modify the Apache configuration for the directory to:

```
AuthType Basic
AuthName "Restricted Files"
# (Following line optional)
AuthBasicProvider file
AuthUserFile /etc/apache/passwd/passwords
AuthGroupFile /etc/apache/passwd/groups
Require group GroupName
```

A somewhat simpler way to accomplish this goal is to add users to your password file and then change the Require line:

```
Require valid-user
```

This configuration bypasses the need to create a group; instead, any user listed in the password file may access the restricted files.

Controlling Apache

You can start, stop, and restart Apache via its SysV or Upstart startup script, just as you can control many other services. Another tool, apachectl or apache2ctl, provides similar capabilities, plus some more. In fact, Apache startup scripts often work by invoking apache2ctl. With Apache running, you may need to check its log files for information on how it's working.

Using *apache2ctl*

Typically, you'll call apache2ctl by typing **apachectl** or **apache2ctl** along with an option, the most common of which are summarized in Table 9.3.

TABLE 9.3 Common apache2ctl commands

Command name	Effect
start	Launches Apache.
stop	Terminates Apache.
graceful-stop	Similar to stop, but requests that are currently being serviced are permitted to complete.
restart	Restarts Apache. If it's not running, restart is identical to start.
graceful	Similar to restart, but requests that are currently being serviced are permitted to complete.
fullstatus	Displays a status report, including a list of requests being serviced. This option requires the mod_status module be enabled.
status	Similar to fullstatus but omits the list of requests being serviced.
configtest	Performs a test of the configuration file syntax and reports any errors.

You might use apache2ctl rather than the Apache SysV startup script if you need to get a status report or check the syntax of your configuration file. You may want to check your SysV startup script to see whether it uses the normal or graceful options for stopping and restarting.

In Exercise 9.1, you will set up and test a basic Apache server.

EXERCISE 9.1

Configuring Apache

This exercise guides you through the process of configuring an Apache server, including making a minor change to its configuration file and controlling the running server. Before beginning, you should use your distribution's package manager to install Apache. The package is likely to be called apache, apache2, httpd, or httpd2. Be aware that your configuration file and default Web site names and locations may vary from those described in this exercise. (This exercise is based on an Ubuntu 10.10 installation.)

Once you've installed Apache, follow these steps:

1. Log in as root, acquire root privileges via su, or be prepared to use sudo to perform most of the remaining steps in this exercise.

2. Load the main Apache configuration file (/etc/apache2/apache2.conf for Ubuntu) into your favorite text editor.

3. If the main Apache configuration file doesn't include a DocumentRoot option, use grep to locate the file that does, as in **grep -r DocumentRoot /etc/apache2/***. Load the file you find into a text editor. (If multiple files contain this directive, you'll need to scan the main configuration file to determine which file to load.) In the case of Ubuntu 10.10, you should load the /etc/apache2/sites-available/default file.

4. Locate the DocumentRoot directive, and change it to point to a new location, such as /var/mywww.

5. At your bash shell, type **apache2ctl configtest**. The program should respond with Syntax OK. If it doesn't, review your Apache configuration file changes; chances are you accidentally changed something you should not have changed.

6. Create the directory you specified in step 4.

7. Ensure that the permissions on the directory you created in step 6 grant write access to just one user (you can use root for the moment, but in the long run a Web master account might be more appropriate) but that all users, or at least the account used to run Apache, can read the directory.

8. Type **cp /var/www/index.html /var/mywww** to copy the server's default home page to the new location. Alternatively, obtain a valid HTML file that doesn't rely too heavily on other files, and copy it to /var/mywww.

9. Load /var/mywww/index.html into a text editor.

10. Make changes to /var/mywww/index.html so you can easily identify it. You don't need much understanding of HTML to do this; just locate something that's clearly English text rather than HTML control tags and change it.

11. Type **apache2ctl restart**. This will start the server, or restart it if it was already running.

12. As a non-root user, launch a Web browser.

13. Type **http://localhost** into the Web browser's URI field. You should see your modified Web page appear. If it doesn't, you'll have to debug the configuration to determine whether the server is running, is running but isn't responding to a localhost connection, is pointing to the wrong directory, or has some other problem.

14. If your computer is on a network, try accessing it from another computer by typing `http://`*servername* in the URI field of a Web browser on another computer, where *servername* is the hostname or IP address of the computer you're configuring. If you see your modified Web page, everything is fine. If not, you'll have to debug the problem.

15. Type `apache2ctl stop`. Verify that the server has stopped by refreshing your Web browser's page. (If you're using a proxy server, as described in the upcoming section "Implementing a Proxy Server," your browser may continue to show the page even though the Apache server has stopped.)

At this point, you could continue adding HTML files to the /var/mywww directory to create a full Web site; however, because running a Web server unnecessarily is a security risk, it's best to completely uninstall Apache from your computer, or at least ensure that it doesn't run when you reboot your computer. You can do this by checking and, if necessary, changing your SysV or Upstart configuration, as described in Chapter 1.

Managing Apache Log Files

Many Apache installations create a log directory, called /var/log/apache2, /var/log/httpd, or something similar, to hold Apache's log files. Typically, `error.log` holds both error messages and notifications of routine server start and stop actions, `access.log` holds information on Web page accesses, and `other_vhosts_access.log` holds virtual host access information. There are variants on the filenames, though, so check your server to see what the files are called. Also, log files are likely to be automatically rotated and archived, so if the server has been running for a while, you're likely to see old log files as well as the current ones.

You can use `error.log` to help diagnose problems with the server that prevent it from starting or that negatively impact it in a less drastic manner. You should treat this file much as you would entries from any other server in their server-specific or general-purpose log files.

The `access.log` file, by contrast, details routine server accesses. Its entries resemble the following:

```
127.0.0.1 - - [29/Nov/2010:15:57:41 -0500] "HEAD / HTTP/1.1" 200 338 "-" ↵
 "Mozilla/5.0 (X11; U; Linux i686; en-US) AppleWebKit/534.7 (KHTML, like ↵
Gecko) Ubuntu/10.10 Chromium/7.0.517.44 Chrome/7.0.517.44 Safari/534.7"
```

This entry is loaded with information, much of which (such as the date) is self-explanatory. Some information is less clear, though. Each entry begins with an IP address or hostname, enabling you to identify the server's clients. In the preceding example,

HEAD / specifies the retrieved document—in this case, the root of the Web site was requested. The last two lines in this example contain information identifying the browser, OS, and platform used to access the server—Chromium running on an i686 Ubuntu installation in this example.

You can peruse the log files manually if you like, and if you're looking for some specific piece of information, direct examination can make a great deal of sense. Frequently, though, you'll want to rely on a log file analysis tool, such as Webalizer (`http://www .webalizer.org`) or AWStats (`http://awstats.sourceforge.net/`). Such tools can summarize how many visitors a site has had over given periods of time, identify when the server is busiest, locate the most popular files served, and so on. Most such tools can generate graphs to help you visualize the data.

Implementing a Proxy Server

A *proxy server* is a program that accepts network access requests on behalf of a client, accesses the target server, and relays the results back to the client. In some respects, a proxy server is similar to a firewall computer; however, a proxy processes access requests at a higher level. For instance, a Web proxy server parses the URIs sent by clients and can fully assemble the Web pages sent in response. This enables a proxy server to use high-level rules to block undesirable Web pages, to cache data for quicker subsequent accesses, or to perform other high-level tasks.

Selecting a Proxy Server

Proxy servers exist for many purposes, and different proxy servers exist to meet a variety of needs:

Squid   This proxy server, which is described in more detail shortly, exists mainly to cache data for speedy access. If you have an office with users who tend to access the same Web sites, Squid can cache recent accesses, thus improving browsing speeds for your entire office. You can learn more at `http://www.squid-cache.org`.

Privoxy   Instead of improving speed, this server aims to filter ads and improve privacy by removing some types of Web browser tracking features from some Web sites. It's headquartered at `http://www.privoxy.org`.

Tinyproxy   This proxy, based at `https://banu.com/tinyproxy/`, is intended to be a lightweight proxy server that performs some minimal filtering operations.

A Web search will turn up many more proxy servers for Linux. Many of these are actually implemented using Squid, since Squid is an extremely flexible tool. The following pages describe Squid in greater detail, because it's unusually flexible and is covered on the LPIC 202 exam.

Real World Scenario

Using an Anonymizing or Tunneling Proxy Server

An *anonymizing proxy server* is a proxy server whose purpose is to keep your identity confidential. A similar service is a *tunneling proxy server*, which exists to help users work around blocks imposed by Web sites, ISPs, or national censors. Whether a proxy server is called *anonymizing* or *tunneling* depends largely on its purpose; the two work in a very similar fashion.

You don't run such a proxy server locally (unless you intend to make the anonymizing or tunneling service available to others); instead, you configure your Web browser to access a server run by somebody else. When you do this, the ultimate Web server sees your Web accesses as coming from the anonymizing or tunneling server, rather than from your own IP address; and your accesses can be directed to an IP address other than the ultimate destination (namely, the proxy server), thus working around blocks that might otherwise prevent you from accessing the site.

Anonymizing and tunneling proxy servers are sometimes abused to aid in piracy; however, they can also be used simply to help protect your privacy or to work around intentional or unintentional network problems or censorship.

Configuring Squid

Squid's emphasis is on caching data for speed, rather than providing security or other features. If you install Squid and then immediately launch it, the program will work in this capacity immediately; however, its configuration file, /etc/squid/squid.conf, provides a dizzying array of options. If you need to adjust Squid's configuration, you can peruse this configuration file, preferably in conjunction with Squid's documentation.

You can install Squid on an individual client computer to gain some benefits; however, Squid works best when it runs on a central server computer and caches requests from multiple clients. For instance, if Fred accesses a Web page from his desktop system, a Squid proxy running on a different but nearby system can cache that page locally. If Mary then accesses the same page from her computer, Squid can deliver the cached page. If Squid were installed separately on Fred's and Mary's computers, it wouldn't be able to deliver the cached copy to Mary, thus eliminating Squid's benefits.

Squid is a proxy server, and as a server it must be run in one of the ways appropriate to servers. Typically, this means that Squid is run from a SysV startup script. If you've just installed Squid, you should be sure to launch it manually the first time and ensure that it's configured to run automatically when you reboot the computer.

Adjusting Access Rules

Squid implements optional security rules that enable setting access control policies based on the client's IP address, port number, number of connections, username and password, or many other features. These *access control lists (ACLs)* can be used to fine-tune proxy access. For instance, you could use firewall rules to block outgoing Web access except via Squid and then use Squid's rules to enable only certain computers or users to access the Web. To implement such a configuration, you use three commands in the Squid configuration file: auth_param, acl, and http_access. You're likely to call each of these commands multiple times to set various options.

WARNING   Squid's authentication mechanism causes passwords to be relayed in unencrypted form. This might be acceptable on a local network, but you should be aware of the risks. Disgruntled local users or intruders who gain access to a local machine might be able to intercept passwords and wreak havoc. Wi-Fi users' data can be easily intercepted unless it's properly encrypted. For best safety, use different passwords on the proxy server than on other computers on the network.

The auth_param command tells Squid what mechanism to use for authenticating users—local Pluggable Authentication Modules (PAM), a Samba or Windows domain controller, a Lightweight Directory Access Protocol (LDAP) server, or what have you. A typical configuration might resemble the following:

```
auth_param basic program /usr/lib/squid/pam_auth
auth_param basic children 5
auth_param basic realm Squid proxy-caching Web server
auth_param basic credentialsttl 2 hours
```

This example tells Squid to use the /usr/lib/squid/pam_auth program as a helper for authentication, to spawn five authentication processes to handle initial authentication requests, to deliver Squid proxy-caching Web server as part of the authentication prompt, and to retain users' credentials for two hours. Many other options to auth_param are available; consult the Squid documentation (including extensive comments in its configuration file) for further information.

With auth_param set up, you must now use the acl command to define an ACL:

```
acl myacl proxy_auth REQUIRED
```

This ACL is called myacl, it is required, and it's defined as a proxy_auth ACL, meaning that it relies on the authentication mechanisms defined with auth_param. You can further adjust this configuration; again, consult the Squid documentation for details.

Finally, you must use `http_access` to define access rules that use `myacl` (or other rules):

```
http_access deny !myacl
http_access allow localnet
http_access deny all
```

This configuration tells Squid to deny any user that does not pass the `myacl` test (the exclamation mark, !, serves as a negation symbol), to allow access to any user who passes the first test and who is on the local network, and to deny all other users. Once again, many variants on this configuration are possible; consult the Squid documentation for details.

> If your current configuration file has existing `auth_param` or `http_access` options, you should comment them out to be sure that your new ones are applied correctly. Existing `acl` commands can coexist with your new ones provided you use a unique name for your new ACL (`myacl` in these examples).

Configuring Clients to Use a Proxy Server

In addition to installing and running Squid (or any other proxy server) on its host system, you must configure clients to use it. This is typically done by selecting appropriate options in your clients' Web servers. For instance, in Mozilla Firefox on Linux, you should select Edit ➢ Preferences to reveal the Firefox Preferences dialog box. Select the Advanced option, click the Network tab, and click the Settings button. The result will be the Connection Settings dialog box, shown in Figure 9.2 along with the Firefox Preferences dialog box. Select Manual Proxy Configuration, and enter the hostname or IP address of the proxy server computer, along with the port number it's using. (Squid defaults to port 3128.)

FIGURE 9.2 You must configure Web browsers to use a proxy server such as Squid

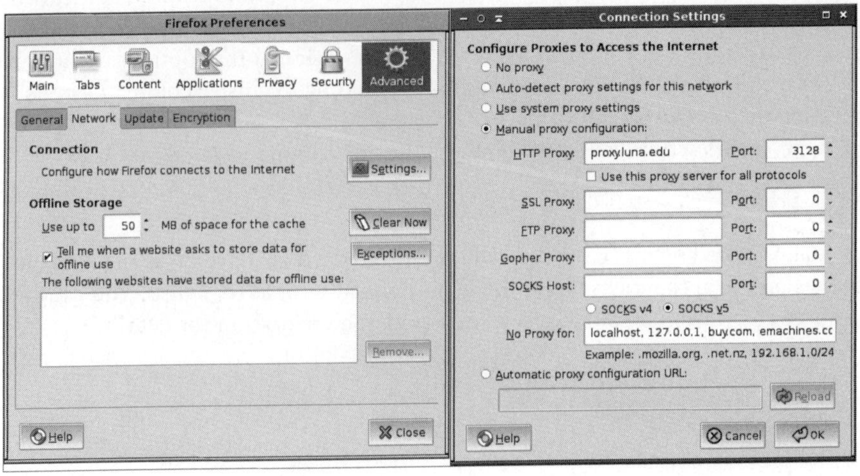

If you configure Squid to require authentication, your next attempt to access the Internet after configuring your browser to use Squid will produce an authentication dialog box, such as the one shown in Figure 9.3, which shows the dialog box produced by Konqueror. Once you enter a username and password, you'll be able to browse the Internet normally until the password expires (as determined by the `credentialsttl` option set via `auth_param`).

FIGURE 9.3   When Squid is configured to require authentication, it causes the browser to display an authentication dialog box

Another way to use a proxy server is to use an `iptables` firewall configuration on your network's router to redirect all outgoing Web traffic to the proxy server. (Chapter 7 describes `iptables`.) This configuration obviates the need to configure each client individually; however, it also means that if the proxy server corrupts data, your users will have no recourse. Authentication may not work via this mechanism, either. If you attempt such a configuration, be sure to exempt the proxy server computer from the rule, lest you set up an infinite loop in which the proxy server's traffic is redirected to itself!

Understanding Email

Internet mail delivery today is dominated by a protocol known as the *Simple Mail Transfer Protocol (SMTP)*. This protocol is an example of a *push protocol*, meaning that the sending system initiates the transfer. A user writes a message using a mail reader and then tells the mail reader to send the mail. The mail reader contacts a local SMTP server, which may run on the same or another computer. The SMTP server accepts the message for delivery, looks up the recipient address, and delivers the message to the recipient system. In some cases, the recipient system may forward the mail to another system, which handles the mail account for the addressee. Depending on how the recipient reads mail, that person may use the destination mail server computer directly or run a mail client on another computer. In the latter case, the mail client uses a protocol such as the *Post Office Protocol (POP)* or the *Internet Message Access Protocol (IMAP)* to retrieve the mail from the local mail server. POP and IMAP are both examples of *pull protocols*, in which the recipient, rather than the sender, initiates the data transfer. Figure 9.4 outlines this configuration. The Internet's mail system is flexible enough that the total number of links between the sender and recipient may be more or less than the number depicted in Figure 9.4, though.

FIGURE 9.4 Email typically traverses several links between sender and recipient

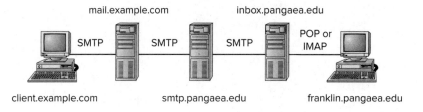

 Although POP and IMAP are often used as the final link in the email delivery chain, as depicted in Figure 9.4, this doesn't need to be the case. The Fetchmail program (http://fetchmail.berlios.de) functions as a POP or IMAP client and then injects the retrieved messages into a local mail queue, effectively enabling these protocols to function at other points in the chain. Fetchmail is handy if you rely on an outside ISP to manage your Internet domain, including its Internet-accessible email addresses, but want to run your own mail system (perhaps even including your own POP or IMAP server) internally.

Three of the computers in Figure 9.4—mail.example.com, smtp.pangaea.edu, and inbox.pangaea.edu—must run SMTP servers. These servers can be entirely different products running on different platforms. In addition to running an SMTP server, Figure 9.4's inbox.pangaea.edu must run a POP or IMAP server. The two end-point computers—client.example.com and franklin.pangaea.edu—need not run mail servers. Instead, client.example.com connects to the SMTP server on mail.example.com to send mail, and franklin.pangaea.edu connects to the POP or IMAP server on inbox .pangaea.edu to retrieve mail.

Configuring a Push Mail Server

SMTP's importance in the email delivery chain means that the vast majority of email server computers will run an SMTP server (also known as a *mail transfer agent*, or *MTA*). Before you begin installing software, though, you must understand email addressing and domain email issues. With this task in hand, you must decide which email server program to run, since several are available for Linux. This chapter covers two SMTP servers, sendmail and Postfix, in the sections "Running Sendmail" and "Running Postfix," in enough detail to enable you to perform basic mail server configuration tasks.

Email servers are complex enough that entire books have been written about the major servers. You should consult a title such as Costales, Assmann, Jansen, and Shapiro's *sendmail, 4th Edition* (O'Reilly, 2007) or Dent's *Postfix: The Definitive Guide* (O'Reilly, 2003) if you need to do more than basic mail server configuration.

Configuring a Domain to Accept Mail

Internet email addresses can take one of two forms:

- *username@host.name*, where *username* is the recipient's username and *host.name* is a computer's hostname. (The address can also use an IP address, typically surrounded by square brackets, in place of a hostname.) For instance, mail might be addressed to ben@smtp.pangaea.edu. This form of addressing is likely to work so long as the target computer is configured to accept mail addressed to it.

- *username@domain.name*, where *username* is the recipient's username and *domain.name* is the domain name. For instance, mail might be addressed to ben@pangaea.edu. Such addressing is usually shorter than an address that includes the mail server computer's full hostname, and it can be more reliable, depending on the domain's configuration.

For the second sort of address to work, the domain requires a special Domain Name System (DNS) entry. This entry is known as a *mail exchanger (MX) record*, and it points sending mail servers to a specific mail server computer. For instance, the MX record for pangaea.edu might point to smtp.pangaea.edu. Therefore, mail addressed to ben@pangaea.edu is delivered to the smtp.pangaea.edu server, which may process it locally or forward it to another computer.

Chapter 6, "DNS Server Configuration," describes configuring the Berkeley Internet Name Domain (BIND) DNS server. In brief, an MX record belongs in the domain's control file, which is usually in /var/named and is usually named after the domain, such as named .pangaea.edu for pangaea.edu. (The exact name is arbitrary, though.) An MX record for `pangaea.edu`, pointing external SMTP servers to `smtp.pangaea.edu` for mail delivery, would look like this:

```
@   IN   MX   5   smtp.pangaea.edu.
```

If another system administrator runs your domain's DNS server, consult that individual about MX record administration. If you use an outside provider, such as a domain registrar's DNS server, you may need to enter the MX record information in a Web-based form. These forms may attempt to mirror the layout of information you'd find in a DNS server's configuration, as just described, but they may not allow you to change fixed information. Alternatively, the form may present simplified data entry fields, such as fields for the server priority code and hostname alone.

It's possible for a computer on one domain to function as a mail server for an entirely different domain. For instance, `mail.example.com` could be the mail server for `pangaea.edu`. This configuration requires setting up the server to accept mail addressed to the domain in question and of course entering the full path to the mail server in the target domain's MX record.

Choosing an Email Server

A wide variety of SMTP servers can run on Linux. The most popular Linux mail servers are all very powerful programs that are capable of handling large domains' mail needs, when paired with sufficiently powerful hardware. The most popular servers are:

Sendmail   This server, headquartered at `http://www.sendmail.org`, has long dominated Internet mail delivery. Although not as dominant as it once was, surveys suggest that sendmail remains the most popular open source mail server. Unfortunately, sendmail has also earned a reputation for a difficult-to-master configuration file format. Fortunately, tools to create a configuration file from a simpler file are common.

Postfix   This server is comparable to sendmail in popularity. Postfix uses a series of small programs to handle mail delivery tasks, as opposed to the monolithic approach used by sendmail. The result is greater speed and, at least in theory, less chance of serious security flaws. (In practice, Postfix has a good security record.) Its configuration is much easier to handle than is sendmail's. You can learn more at `http://www.postfix.org`.

Exim   This mail server, described at `http://www.exim.org`, is not quite as popular as sendmail or Postfix, but it is still a popular Linux mail server. Like sendmail, Exim uses a monolithic design, but Exim's configuration file is much more intelligible. This server includes extensive pattern-matching tools that are very useful in fighting spam.

qmail   This server's popularity is roughly equal to or a bit lower than Exim's, depending on the survey. Most major distributions don't ship with qmail because its license terms are peculiar—they don't permit distribution of binaries except under limited conditions. Like Postfix, qmail uses a modular design that emphasizes speed and security. Check `http://www.qmail.org` for more information.

For light duty—say, for a small business or personal mail server—any of these programs will work quite well. For such cases, I recommend sticking with whatever software is the standard for your distribution. For larger installations or if you need advanced features, you may want to investigate alternatives to your distribution's default server more closely. You may find particular features, such as Exim's pattern-matching tools or the modular design of Postfix and qmail, appealing. All of these servers are capable of handling large or busy domains, although sendmail may require speedier hardware than the others to handle a given volume of mail. For small sites, even sendmail won't stress any but the weakest computers.

The following sections describe the configuration of sendmail and Postfix in more detail. I've not included sections on Exim and qmail because they're less popular and aren't included in the LPI objectives, except for a brief mention of Exim, but they're certainly worth considering if you want to change your mail server.

Running Sendmail

Most Linux distributions provide a sendmail package, although many install Postfix or Exim as the default mail server. If you want to run sendmail with a distribution that normally uses another mail server, you must remove the standard mail server and install sendmail. Unfortunately, sendmail configuration file locations and names vary somewhat from one distribution to another, so you must know where to look to find these files. Once found, you can change many sendmail options, such as the addresses the server considers local and relay options.

Many programs rely on the presence of an executable file called sendmail. For this reason, mail servers other than sendmail usually include an executable called sendmail, which is often a link to the equivalent program file for the other mail server.

Using Sendmail Configuration Files

The main sendmail configuration file is called sendmail.cf, and it's typically located in /etc/mail. Unfortunately, this file is both very long and difficult to understand. You should *not* attempt to edit this file directly; instead, you should edit a configuration file that can be used to generate a sendmail.cf file. This source configuration file is written using the m4 macro processing language, which is more intelligible than the raw sendmail configuration file format. To edit and compile an m4 configuration file for sendmail, you might need to install additional packages:

The m4 Macro Language   You must install the m4 macro language. This software usually comes in a package called m4. Look for a program file called m4 (often stored in /usr/bin) to ascertain whether it's already installed on your system. If it isn't, look for and install the package that came with your Linux distribution.

Sendmail m4 Configuration Files   You need a set of m4 configuration files for sendmail in order to modify your configuration. These files are usually installed from the sendmail-cf package.

Most distributions ship with default m4 configuration files that can be used to rebuild the standard sendmail.cf file that ships with the distribution. (If you rebuild the default file, a few comments differ, but the rebuilt file is functionally identical to the original.) The default configuration file's name varies, but it could be called sendmail.mc, linux.smtp.mc, or something else. It might reside in /etc/mail, /usr/share/sendmail/cf, or elsewhere. For Red Hat, the default file is /etc/mail/sendmail.mc. (This file actually ships with the sendmail package rather than sendmail-cf.) Slackware's default file is /usr/share/sendmail/cf/cf/linux.smtp.mc.

To make changes to your configuration, follow these steps as root:

1. Back up your default /etc/mail/sendmail.cf file.

2. Change to the directory in which the original m4 configuration file resides.

3. Copy the original file to a new name; for instance, you might call it myconfig.mc.

4. Edit the configuration file as described in the next few sections or to achieve other ends.

5. Type the following command to create a new /etc/mail/sendmail.cf file:

```
# m4 < myconfig.mc > /etc/mail/sendmail.cf
```

If all goes well, the m4 command won't display any messages in your command shell, but if you check, you should find that the /etc/mail/sendmail.cf file is new. You can then tell sendmail to read the new configuration file:

```
# killall -HUP sendmail
```

This command tells all running sendmail instances to reread their configuration files and implement any changes. You can then test those changes in whatever way is appropriate—by sending or receiving mail and checking whether the changes you set are implemented.

In addition to the main sendmail.cf file, several other files are important in sendmail's configuration. Most of these files reside in /etc/mail, but some may reside in /etc. Two of the most important of these files are:

access.db   This file, which usually resides in /etc/mail, controls access to the sendmail server. By listing or not listing particular systems in this file in specific ways, you can adjust which systems can use sendmail to relay mail to other systems. This file is a binary database built from the plain-text access file using the makemap program.

aliases.db   Like access.db, this file is a binary database file built from a plain-text file (aliases) using newaliases. This file appears in /etc or /etc/mail, depending on your distribution. This file lists *aliases* for particular usernames or addresses. For instance, if you set up an alias linking the name postmaster to root, all mail addressed to postmaster is delivered to root. Aliases are described in more detail later in "Setting Up Aliases and Forwarding."

Configuring the Hostname in Sendmail

Email messages have names embedded in them. These names identify the computer, so in theory they should be the same as the computer's hostname. Sometimes, though, the names in the header may need to be changed. For instance, you might want outgoing mail to be associated with your domain name rather than with the mail server name. Configuring your mail server in this way can head off problems down the road—say, if you change your mail server system. If your outgoing mail had used the mail server's true hostname, replies to old messages might continue to be addressed to this system and, therefore, bounce. To set the name that's used in the From: headers in mail messages, you should add lines such as the following to the m4 configuration file and rebuild your main configuration file:

```
MASQUERADE_AS(`target-address')
FEATURE(masquerade_envelope)
```

> The MASQUERADE_AS line includes two types of single quote characters. The lead character is a back-tick, accessible on most keyboards on the key to the left of the 1 key. The close quote is an ordinary single quote character, which is on the key to the left of the Enter key on most keyboards. If you use the wrong characters, these lines won't work.

Of course, you should change the *target-address* in the first of these sample lines to the address you want to use, such as pangaea.edu. The MASQUERADE_AS line changes only the address displayed in the From: mail header line. It also changes this configuration only if the mail reader doesn't specify a different address. Many clients enable users to set arbitrary return addresses, and these values override whatever option you set in sendmail. The FEATURE(masquerade_envelope) line goes further; it overrides the settings users enter in their mail clients. You might use this option if you want to limit users' ability to set bogus return addresses in their mail readers.

Configuring Sendmail to Accept Incoming Mail

To accept incoming mail, sendmail must be configured to accept incoming network connections. Many distributions ship with configurations that block connections from anything but the local computer. This configuration is good for workstations that may need to send outgoing mail or send mail between local users but that shouldn't receive mail from outside systems. If you want to receive mail from other computers, you must modify this configuration. To do so, edit the m4 configuration file (such as /etc/mail/sendmail.mc). Look for the following line:

```
DAEMON_OPTIONS(`Port=smtp,Addr=127.0.0.1, Name=MTA')dnl
```

Comment out this line by adding the string dnl and a space to the start of the line. (Unlike most configuration files, sendmail m4 files use dnl as a comment indicator.) You can then create a new sendmail.cf file, as described in the earlier section "Using Sendmail Configuration Files." Restart the server by typing **killall -HUP sendmail** or by passing restart to the server's SysV startup script, and the server should accept connections from remote systems.

Another aspect of accepting remote connections is telling sendmail what hostnames to recognize as local. For instance, consider Figure 9.4. If smtp.pangaea.edu is the computer to which the pangaea.edu domain's MX record points, then smtp.pangaea.edu must know to accept mail addressed to *user*@pangaea.edu. Ordinarily, sendmail rejects messages addressed to anything but the computer's own hostname. You can change this behavior by adding any aliases for the mail server computer itself to a special configuration file. This file is called /etc/mail/local-host-names, and its use is enabled by default in some distributions' sendmail configurations. In others, you must first add a line to the sendmail m4 configuration file and create a new sendmail.cf file, as described previously in "Using Sendmail Configuration Files." The line you need to add is:

```
FEATURE(use_cw_file)
```

Be sure this line appears before the two MAILER lines at the bottom of the default file. After you've rebuilt the sendmail.cf file, create or edit /etc/mail/local-host-names and add the names you want sendmail to recognize as local. For instance, you might add lines such as the following:

```
pangaea.edu
mail.pangaea.edu
```

Once this task is done, the server will accept mail to these domains as local mail, even if the server's hostname doesn't bear any resemblance to these names. For instance, entering these two lines on mail.example.com's local-host-names file will cause it to deliver mail addressed to sue@pangaea.edu to any local account with a username of sue.

Setting Sendmail Relay Configuration Options

Mail servers must often be set up as *relays*. In such a configuration, the server accepts mail from one system and passes it to another. One common relay configuration is that of a departmental mail server, which accepts mail from many clients and passes the mail on to destination systems. For instance, Figure 9.4's mail.example.com must be configured in this way. Another relay configuration involves telling sendmail to use another system as a relay. For instance, if Figure 9.4's client.example.com were a Linux system, you might configure it to use mail.example.com as an outgoing relay. Using outgoing relays enables you to use the relay computer as a control point for mail. In some cases, you must configure your system in this way. For instance, your LAN or ISP might be configured to block outgoing SMTP connections except to the authorized mail server.

Configuring Sendmail to Relay Mail

Sendmail provides many relaying options. The most common configuration involves a feature that can be defined in the sendmail m4 file using a line such as this:

```
FEATURE(`access_db')
```

Some sendmail configurations add extra options to this definition. Some distributions' standard configurations don't define this option; therefore, if you want to use it, you must add it to the m4 configuration file and rebuild the sendmail.cf file, as described earlier in "Using Sendmail Configuration Files." Once the option is present, you can edit the /etc/mail/access file. A typical file might resemble the one shown in Listing 9.1, except that such default files lack the final entry.

Listing 9.1: A typical access file for controlling mail relaying

```
# Allow relaying from localhost...
localhost.localdomain     RELAY
localhost                 RELAY
127.0.0.1                 RELAY
# Relay for the local network
172.25.98                 RELAY
```

Listing 9.1 first approves relaying for the local computer, using three methods of identifying that computer—by two names (localhost.localdomain and localhost) and by IP address (127.0.0.1). If you activate the access_db feature, your /etc/mail/access file must contain these entries if your system is to reliably handle mail from the local computer. (Some programs call sendmail in such a way that these entries aren't necessary, but others use the loopback network interface, which requires that sendmail relay for localhost or its aliases.) To relay for more systems, you must add them to the list, as Listing 9.1 does. That example relays for the 172.25.98.0/24 network. If you prefer, you can specify individual computers or list them by domain name or hostname, but using IP addresses ensures that an attacker won't be able to abuse your system's relaying abilities by compromising a DNS server.

Because this section is about relaying, all the examples in Listing 9.1 specify the RELAY option. You can provide other words, though, to achieve different effects:

OK You can tell sendmail to accept mail for delivery even if another rule would cause it to be rejected. For instance, you might override a block on a network for specific hosts using OK.

RELAY This option enables relaying. This option is actually bidirectional. For instance, Listing 9.1 enables outside systems to relay mail to servers in the 172.25.98.0/24 network.

REJECT This option blocks mail coming from or addressed to the specified hostname or network. Sendmail generates a bounce reply when an attempt is made to send to or from the forbidden systems. You might use it to block a known spammer's domain, for example.

DISCARD This option works much like REJECT, but sendmail won't generate a bounce message.

ERROR:*nnn text* This option also works like REJECT, but instead of generating a standard bounce message, it replies with the error code number (*nnn*) and message (*text*) that you define.

After you modify the /etc/mail/access file, you must create a binary database file from the plain-text file. To do so, you use the makemap command:

```
# makemap hash /etc/mail/access.db < /etc/mail/access
```

Some configurations include this command in their sendmail SysV startup scripts, so you can skip this step if you restart the server using these scripts. When you're done, restart sendmail, and test the new relaying configuration.

In addition to the `access_db` feature, sendmail supports a variety of additional relaying options. Most of these options include the word `relay` in their names, such as `relay_entire_domain` or `relay_local_from`. Most of these options implement relay rules that can be configured through the /etc/mail/access file, though, so chances are you won't need them.

WARNING   One relay option you should avoid is called `promiscuous_relay`. This option configures the system to relay from any host to any server. Such a configuration is dangerous because spammers can easily abuse it. In fact, you should be cautious when configuring relaying to prevent your system from relaying from any untrusted source.

Configuring Sendmail to Use a Relay

If your server must relay mail through another computer, you can configure sendmail to accommodate this requirement. To do so, add the following line to the sendmail `m4` configuration file and recompile the `sendmail.cf` file:

```
FEATURE(`nullclient', `relay.mail.server')
```

The procedure to modify the `m4` configuration file is described previously, in "Using Sendmail Configuration Files." Replace *relay.mail.server* with the hostname of the mail server that's to function as a relay, such as your departmental or ISP's mail server. You may also need to delete a couple of lines or comment them out by preceding the lines with `dnl`:

```
MAILER(local)dnl
MAILER(smtp)dnl
```

These lines duplicate the functionality included in the relay configuration, so including them along with the relay configuration may cause `m4` to complain when you try to build a new `sendmail.cf` file. Not all configurations use these lines in their default files, though.

Running Postfix

Compared to sendmail, Postfix is simple to configure. Postfix uses a primary configuration file, /etc/postfix/main.cf, that has a relatively straightforward syntax. The default version of this file is also usually very well commented, so you can learn a lot about your configuration by perusing it. One problem with Postfix configuration is that it relies heavily on variables, such as myhostname. One variable may be used to set another, which may be used to set another, and so on. Therefore, you may need to trace your way back through several layers of variable assignments to learn how an important variable is set. Postfix variable names are preceded by a dollar sign ($) when accessed, but not when you assign values to them. As with sendmail, some default settings may need to be changed, even on a fairly simple configuration.

Configuring the Hostname in Postfix

Several Postfix parameters affect the name of the Postfix server computer or the hostname that appears in mail headers. The most common of these options are summarized in Table 9.4. In a simple configuration, you needn't adjust anything; Postfix acquires its hostname automatically and builds everything else from there. You can override the configuration if necessary, though—for example, if your computer has multiple hostnames and you want to use the one that Postfix doesn't auto-detect on the mail server, or if obtaining your domain name requires stripping more than one component from the hostname. The masquerade_ domains option requires special explanation: This option strips away hostname components if and only if they'll match the specified reduced name. For instance, consider a case in which you've set masquerade_domains = pangaea.edu. If the server is told to send mail with an address of sue@trex.pangaea.edu, it will reduce this address to sue@pangaea.edu. If the system is told to send mail with an address of sue@example.com, it won't change the address.

TABLE 9.4   Common Postfix hostname options

Option	Default value	Meaning
myhostname	Computer's hostname, as returned by the hostname command	Computer's hostname; used as a default in many subsequent options. Must be fully qualified (that is, include both the hostname and the domain name).
mydomain	$myhostname stripped of its first component	Computer's domain name; used as a default in many subsequent options.
myorigin	$myhostname	The hostname that's appended to outgoing mail if one is omitted by the mail client.
masquerade_ domains	None	Domains to which an address should be reduced. Domains are tried from left to right in the list until the first match is found.
masquerade_ classes	envelope_sender, header_sender	Types of addresses that are affected by masquerade_domains. Possibilities are envelope_ sender, envelope_recipient, header_sender, and header_recipient. If all four options are used, mailing to individual machines in the specified domains will become impossible.
masquerade_ exceptions	None	Usernames that should not be masqueraded. For instance, if you set this value to root, root's mail headers won't be altered.
sender_ canonical_maps	None	Changes sender address using a flexible lookup database.

The ultimate in address remapping is accomplished through the sender_canonical_maps option. Point this option at a file using a line such as the following:

```
sender_canonical_maps = hash:/etc/postfix/sender_canonical
```

You can then specify hostnames you want changed in the /etc/postfix/sender_canonical file. For instance, to change localhost and the misspelled pangea.edu to pangaea.edu on outgoing addresses, use the following two lines:

```
@pangea.edu @pangaea.edu
@localhost @pangaea.edu
```

You can also include usernames in order to make changes only for particular users' mail. After creating this file and referencing it in /etc/postfix/main.cf, you must convert the file to a binary format. Type **postmap sender_canonical** from the /etc/postfix directory to do this job. You can then tell Postfix to reload its configuration files by typing **postfix reload**.

Accepting Incoming Mail

Ordinarily, Postfix accepts local mail addressed to *$myhostname* or localhost.*$myhostname*, where *$myhostname* is your hostname or whatever value you've set for this variable. You can broaden or narrow the range of accepted local addresses by changing the mydestination setting. For instance, you might set this value as follows for a domain's mail server:

```
mydestination = $myhostname, localhost.$myhostname, localhost, $mydomain
```

You can add more names if you like, and in fact such a change may be required if the server should handle several domains or mail addressed to many specific clients on the network. If you specify many target destinations, you can break them across lines without using backslashes. Instead, indent the second and subsequent lines with one or more spaces or tabs. Postfix uses such indentation as a signal that the line is a continuation of the previous line's configuration.

Another option you may need to change is the inet_interfaces setting. This option sets the interfaces to which Postfix listens. For instance, setting it to $myhostname tells the server to listen on the network interfaces associated with the primary hostname—or whatever value $myhostname uses. If you change this value or if you want Postfix to listen more broadly, you can set the option to all to have the server listen to all network interfaces.

Postfix Relay Configuration Options

Naturally, you can configure Postfix to relay mail in various ways or to send mail through an outgoing relay. Most distributions ship with a fairly restrictive relay configuration that prevents the server from relaying mail from any but local programs. You should check this configuration to be sure how it's set. If you need to use an outgoing mail relay, you must adjust that configuration, as well.

Configuring Postfix to Relay Mail

Several options influence how Postfix treats an attempt to relay mail. Table 9.5 summarizes these options. Postfix's relay configuration is built on the concept of *trust*; the server relays mail for machines that it trusts. Defining relay authorization, therefore, becomes a matter of defining what systems to trust.

TABLE 9.5 Common postfix relay options

Option	Default value	Meaning
mynetworks_ style	subnet	Type of networks Postfix trusts. subnet (the default) means the same IP address subnet as the server, class means the same IP address class as the server, and host means to trust only the server computer itself.
mynetworks	Network list as specified by $mynetworks_ style	List of networks to be trusted. Networks may be specified as IP address/netmask pairs, or you may provide a filename for a file in which the information is stored.
relay_domains	$mydestination	Machines and domains listed explicitly by name.

When run from Linux, the default mynetworks_style setting means that Postfix will relay mail from any computer with an IP address in the same subnet as the server itself. Typically, Linux distributions ship with mynetworks = 127.0.0.1/8 or something similar, which restricts relaying to the local computer only, overriding the default mynetworks_ style setting. You must expand this option, or delete it and rely on a mynetworks_style setting, if the computer should relay mail for other computers. In addition, the relay_ domains default means that the server will relay mail from any computer specified in the mydestination option or in computers within the specified domain. For instance, if you have a mydestination specification that includes pangaea.edu, Postfix will relay from any computer in the pangaea.edu domain.

WARNING   If your computer uses a dial-up or most types of broadband Internet connection, using mynetworks_style = subnet or specifying your subnet using mynetworks enables Postfix to relay for all users of the ISP's subnet. This configuration is a spam risk, so you may want to tighten your Postfix settings.

As an antispam measure, you might want to limit Postfix's relaying capabilities. This might be particularly important if you've set mydestination to include a domain for which the server shouldn't serve as a relay or if that domain's systems are already covered by IP address in the `mynetworks` or `mynetworks_style` options. To do so, you might provide a restrictive `relay_domains` configuration, such as this example:

```
relay_domains = $myhostname, localhost, localhost.localdomain
```

If you're running Postfix on a workstation, you might want to prevent the server from relaying mail for anything but the workstation computer itself. (This configuration accepts mail both from the local computer to anywhere and from anywhere to the local computer.) For this configuration, you must combine the tight `relay_domains` limit with a tight `mynetworks_style` definition:

```
mynetworks_style = host
```

If Postfix is running on a larger mail server and you want to expand the computers for which it will relay, the simplest way is usually to create an expanded `relay_domains` definition. For instance, to relay mail for the default systems plus `example.org`'s systems, you might use the following line:

```
relay_domains = $mydestination, example.org
```

Configuring Postfix to Use a Relay

If you're configuring Postfix on a workstation or other system that should relay mail through another mail server, the configuration is fairly straightforward. Typically, you need to set the `relayhost` option to the name of the mail server you should use. For instance, to set your system to use `mail.example.com` as the mail relay, you would use the following line:

```
relayhost = mail.example.com
```

Alternatively, if you want to use the computer to which a domain's MX record points, you can provide the domain name rather than the hostname. Postfix then does an MX record lookup and sends mail to the domain's mail server. This configuration may be preferable if the name of the outgoing mail server is likely to change; you needn't adjust your Postfix configuration when this happens.

Managing Email

Once your mail server is set up, you will probably want to test it and monitor its activities. I therefore describe some common administrative tasks involving testing an SMTP server, managing email queues, configuring aliases, and forwarding email.

Testing an SMTP Server

You can perform low-level tests of an SMTP server by using the `telnet` program. To do this, you access the email server and issue the SMTP commands involved in sending mail. These commands include HELO (to identify the sending computer), MAIL FROM (to identify the sending user), RCPT TO (to identify the recipient), DATA (to begin the message text), and QUIT (to terminate the session). An example might look like this:

```
$ telnet localhost 25
Trying 127.0.0.1...
Connected to localhost.
Escape character is '^]'.
220 mail.example.com ESMTP Postfix
HELO localhost
250 mail.example.com
MAIL FROM:<benf@example.com>
250 2.1.0 Ok
RCPT TO:<janet@luna.edu>
250 2.1.5 Ok
DATA
354 End data with <CR><LF>.<CR><LF>
This is a test message.
.
250 2.0.0 Ok: queued as C5E9DD9761
QUIT
221 2.0.0 Bye
Connection closed by foreign host.
```

Most of these commands include options, such as email addresses. The server replies to most successful commands with a code 250. This and other codes may optionally include explanatory text. When you get around to entering the actual message text, you can enter one or more lines of text, terminated by a single line that contains a single period (.).

You may want to test the mail server in various ways—attempt to connect from the server system itself (as in this example), from systems for which it should relay, and from systems from which it should *not* relay. Also attempt to send email to recipients on the local computer and elsewhere. Testing these possibilities will help ensure that the server is properly configured.

Checking the Email Queue

An email server manages a queue of email messages that it must deliver. This task may sound simple, but it can be surprisingly complex. The server may be asked to deliver many messages in a very short period of time, and thus it may need to delay delivery of some messages while it works on others. Furthermore, problems can lead to a temporary or permanent inability to deliver messages. When a problem seems to be temporary, such as a network routing failure, the email server must store the message and try to deliver it again later. Thus, a Linux computer's email queue may contain undelivered messages. Knowing how to identify these messages and manage the queue can help you keep your Linux computer's email subsystem working smoothly.

The `mailq` program is the main tool to help in email queue management. This program was originally part of the sendmail package, but Postfix, Exim, qmail, and other Linux SMTP servers have all implemented compatible commands. Unfortunately, command options differ between implementations. The basic command, without any options, shows the contents of the email queue on all systems:

```
$ mailq
-Queue ID- --Size-- ----Arrival Time---- -Sender/Recipient-------
5B42F963F*     440 Tue Aug 23 13:58:19  sally@example.com
                                         benf@luna.edu
-- 0 Kbytes in 1 Request.
```

This example, taken from a system running Postfix, shows one message in the queue, along with relevant identifying information. The exact display format varies from one SMTP server to another. In most cases, typing **mailq** is equivalent to typing **sendmail -bp**.

If a network failure occurs, email messages can pile up in the queue. Your SMTP server will ordinarily attempt redelivery at a later date, but if your network connection has come up again and you want to clear the queue immediately, you can do so. Typing **sendmail -q** will do the job with most SMTP servers, and some have other equivalent commands, such as `postqueue` in Postfix or `runq` in Exim.

All email servers offer a wide variety of advanced options to prioritize email delivery, accept messages on the command line, delete specific messages from the queue, debug email connections, and so on. Unfortunately, commands and procedures to use these features vary from one email server to another. Thus, you should consult your server's documentation to learn how to use these features.

Setting Up Aliases and Forwarding

Email *aliases* enable one address to stand in for another one. For instance, all email servers are supposed to maintain an account called `postmaster`. Email to this account should be read by somebody who's responsible for maintaining the system. One way to do this is to set up an alias linking the `postmaster` name to the name of a real account. You can do this by editing the `aliases` file, which usually resides in `/etc` or sometimes in `/etc/mail`.

The `aliases` file format is fairly straightforward. Comment lines begin with hash marks (#), and other lines take the following form:

name: *addr1*[,*addr2*[,...]]

The *name* that leads the line is a local name, such as `postmaster`. Each address (*addr1*, *addr2*, and so on) can be a local account name to which the messages are forwarded, the name of a local file in which messages are stored (denoted by a leading slash), a command through which messages are piped (denoted by a leading vertical bar character), the name of a file whose contents are treated as a series of addresses (denoted by a leading `:include:` string), or a full email address (such as `fred@example.com`).

A typical default configuration includes a few useful aliases for accounts such as `postmaster`. Most such configurations map most of these aliases to `root`. Reading mail as `root` is inadvisable, though—doing so increases the odds of a security breach or other problem because of a typo or bug in the mail reader. Thus, you may want to set up an alias line like the following:

```
root: yourusername
```

This example redirects all of `root`'s mail, including mail directed to `root` via another alias, to *yourusername*, which can take any of the forms just described. Some mail servers, including sendmail, Postfix, and qmail, require you to compile `/etc/aliases` into a binary file that can be processed more quickly. To do so, use the `newaliases` command:

```
# newaliases
```

Another approach to redirecting mail is to do so at the user level. In particular, you can edit the `~/.forward` file in a user's home directory to send mail for that user to another address. Specifically, the `~/.forward` file should contain the new address. This approach has the advantage that it can be employed by individual users. A drawback is that it can't be used to set up aliases for nonexistent accounts or for accounts that lack home directories. The `~/.forward` file can also be changed or deleted by the account owner, which might not be desirable if you want to enforce a forwarding rule that the user shouldn't be able to override.

Checking Log Files

Like most servers, mail servers log their activities in files within the `/var/log` directory tree. Details depend on the distribution, the mail server, and any changes you've made to the mail server or system logger that affect how information is logged. On some systems, you'll find files with names beginning with `mail`, such as `/var/log/mail.log` and `/var/log/mail.err`. On other systems, mail logs are stored in a general-purpose log file, such as `/var/log/messages` or `/var/log/syslog`.

 Try using grep to search for your mail server's name in all the files in /var/log in order to locate where your system logs its mail-related messages.

A single email delivery might generate several entries in your log file, as in this example, taken from a computer running Postfix:

```
/var/log/messages:Nov 24 07:07:04 nessus postfix/smtpd[8785]: connect from ⏎
  localhost[127.0.0.1]
/var/log/messages:Nov 24 07:07:04 nessus postfix/smtpd[8785]: 11E92F81C8: ⏎
  client=localhost[127.0.0.1]
```

```
/var/log/messages:Nov 24 07:07:04 nessus postfix/cleanup[8788]: 11E92F81C8: ⏎
 message-id=<LYRIS-290413-547281-2010.11.23-22.30.28-- ⏎
 benf#example.com@inboxnewsletters.com>
/var/log/messages:Nov 24 07:07:04 nessus postfix/qmgr[8663]: 11E92F81C8: ⏎
 from=<bounce-5439281-290413@inboxnewsletters.com>, size=91562, nrcpt=1 ⏎
 (queue active)
/var/log/messages:Nov 24 07:07:04 nessus postfix/local[8789]: 11E92F81C8: ⏎
 to=<benf@localhost>, relay=local, delay=0.76, delays=0.56/0/0/0.2, dsn=2.0.0, ⏎
 status=sent (delivered to command: /usr/bin/procmail)
/var/log/messages:Nov 24 07:07:04 nessus postfix/qmgr[8663]: 11E92F81C8: ⏎
 removed
```

Each line relates information about a particular stage in the mail delivery process. If an error occurs, the messages may provide a clue about what went wrong—for instance, there might be a mention of a DNS failure or a remote server that was unresponsive.

Configuring Procmail

In principal, an email server such as sendmail or Postfix can store incoming mail directly in a *mail spool*, which is a file or directory that holds email messages. In practice, however, many systems employ an additional tool, Procmail, to do this job. The reason is that Procmail can be configured using complex rules to adjust how mail is delivered. You can use Procmail to filter spam, redirect mail, copy mail, and much more.

Understanding Mail Storage Formats

From a user's point of view, email messages may be organized in email folders. Even if a user doesn't employ email folders, that user's incoming mail must be stored in some format. Most of the major mail servers for Linux (sendmail, Postfix, and Exim) use a format known as *mbox*, in which messages in a mail folder are stored in a single file. Typically, SMTP servers or their helper programs store users' files in /var/spool/mail/*username*. When users employ folders with software that uses the mbox format, each one consists of a single file.

The qmail server, by contrast, stores its incoming mail in another format: a *maildir*. The maildir format devotes one directory to each mail folder and puts each message in its own file. Typically, incoming maildirs are stored in users' home directories. Although qmail uses maildirs by default, it can be configured to use the mbox format. Similarly, Postfix and Exim can both be configured to use maildirs.

The choice of mail format has consequences for other software, such as users' mail readers (also known as *mail user agents*, or *MUAs*), POP or IMAP servers, and Procmail.

Many programs support both mbox and maildir formats, but some support just one. As described shortly, Procmail rules may need to be adjusted for the mail format.

> The maildir format is often claimed to produce better speed than mbox, particularly when a mail folder contains hundreds of messages. This is most likely to be important if you use IMAP rather than POP and if your users collect many email messages in their IMAP-mediated mail folders.

Writing Procmail Rules

Most Linux mail servers either use Procmail by default or can be configured to do so by setting a configuration file option. If you follow the instructions outlined in the next few paragraphs and find that Procmail isn't working, you can try creating a .forward file in your home directory that contains the following line:

```
"|/path/to/procmail"
```

Replace */path/to* with the name of the directory in which the procmail binary resides. If even this doesn't work, you may need to consult the documentation for Procmail or for your mail server. Once Procmail is in the picture, the system reads the global /etc/procmailrc configuration file and the .procmailrc file in users' home directories. These files contain Procmail recipes, which take the following form:

```
:0 [flags] [:[lockfile]]
[conditions]
action
```

> The system-wide /etc/procmailrc file is usually read and processed as root. This fact means that a poorly designed recipe in that file could do serious damage. For instance, a typo could cause Procmail to overwrite an important system binary rather than use that binary to process a message. For this reason, you should keep system-wide Procmail processing to a minimum and instead focus on using ~/.procmailrc to process mail using individuals' accounts.

Each recipe begins with the string :0. Various flags may follow, as summarized in Table 9.6. You can combine these flags to produce more complex effects. For instance, using *flags* of HB causes matching to be done on both the message headers and the body. The *lockfile* is the name of a file that Procmail uses to signal that it's working with a file. If Procmail sees a lockfile, it delays work on the affected file until the lockfile disappears. Ordinarily, a single colon (:) suffices for this function; Procmail then picks a lockfile name itself. You can specify a filename if you prefer, though.

TABLE 9.6   Common Procmail recipe flags

Flag	Meaning
H	Matching is done to the message headers. (This is the default.)
B	Matching is done to the message body.
D	Matching is done in a case-sensitive manner. (The default is a case-insensitive match.)
c	Matching is done on a "carbon copy" of the message. The "original" is passed on for matching against subsequent recipes. This flag is generally used within nesting blocks (described shortly).
w	Procmail waits for the *action* to complete. If it doesn't complete successfully, the message is matched against subsequent recipes.
W	The same as a flag of w, but it suppresses program failure messages.

The *conditions* in a Procmail recipe are essentially ordinary regular expressions, but each *conditions* line begins with an asterisk. Most characters in a regular expression match against the same characters in the message, but there are exceptions. For instance, a carat (^) denotes the start of a line, a dot (.) matches any single character except for a new line, and the combination of a dot and an asterisk (.*) denotes a string of any length. A regular expression may include a string in parentheses, often with a vertical bar (|) within it. This condition denotes a match against the string on either side of the vertical bar. A backslash (\) effectively undoes special formatting in the following character; for instance, to match an asterisk, you would specify the string *. An exclamation mark (!) reverses the sense of a match so that a recipe matches any message that does *not* meet the specified criteria. Each recipe can have no, one, or more *conditions*. (Using no *conditions* is usually done within nesting blocks or for backing up messages when you experiment with new recipes.) If a recipe includes several *conditions*, all must match for the recipe to apply. The Procmail man page describes these regular expressions in more detail.

Finally, a Procmail recipe ends with a single line that tells it what to do—the *action*. An *action* line may be any of several things:

A Filename Reference   Procmail stores the message in the named file in mbox format. To store messages in the maildir format, append a slash (/) to the end of the filename. For spam fighting, one effective but drastic measure is to store spam in /dev/null, which effectively deletes the spam.

An External Program   If the *action* line begins with a vertical bar (|), Procmail treats the line as a program to be executed. You can use this feature to pass processing on to another tool.

An Email Address   An exclamation mark (!) at the start of a line denotes an email address; Procmail sends the message to the specified address instead of delivering it locally.

A Nesting Block   An *action* line that begins with an open curly brace ({) denotes a nested recipe. The nested recipe takes the same form as any other recipe, but it is used only if the surrounding recipe matches the message. The nested recipe ends with a close curly brace (}).

Seeing Procmail in Action

As an example, consider Listing 9.2, which demonstrates many of the features of Procmail recipes. These particular recipes are designed to filter spam; however, many other uses of Procmail are possible. For instance, you could use it to forward mail that meets certain criteria, send a duplicate of mail addressed to one person to another user, or send it through a program to detect viruses and worms.

Listing 9.2: Sample Procmail recipes

```
# Don't apply recipes to postmaster
:0
*!^To:.*postmaster@(pangaea\.edu|smtp\.pangaea\.edu)
{
    # Block mail with more than five spaces in the Subject: header,
    # unless it's from the local fax subsystem
    :0
    *^Subject:.*       .*
    *!^From: root@fax\.pangaea\.edu \(Fax Getty\)
    /dev/null

    # Pass mail with bright red text through a custom spam blocking script
    :0 B
    *^.*\<html
    *^.*\<font color.*ff0000
    |/usr/local/bin/spam-block "mail with bright red text"

    # Stuff that's not to me.
    :0
    *!^(To|Cc):.*(pangaea\.edu|ben@example\.com)
    !sam@iwantspam.org
}
```

Listing 9.2 indents recipes within the nesting block. This practice improves readability but isn't required.

Listing 9.2 includes four recipes. Three of them are embedded within the fourth:

- The surrounding recipe matches any `To:` header that does *not* include the string `postmaster@pangaea.edu` or `postmaster@smtp.pangaea.edu`. This recipe uses the open curly brace (`{`) character to cause the included recipes to be applied only if the mail is not addressed to `postmaster`. The intent is to protect the `postmaster`'s mail from the antispam rules. After all, users might forward spam to the `postmaster` account to complain about it, and such complaints should not be ignored.

- Some spam includes five or more consecutive spaces in the `Subject:` header. The first true spam rule discards such messages. This rule matches all messages with five or more spaces in the `Subject:` header except for messages that are from the fax subsystem on the `fax.pangaea.edu` computer, which presumably generates nonspam fax delivery reports that would otherwise match this criterion. This recipe discards the spam by sending it to `/dev/null`.

- The second spam rule matches all messages that contain HTML text that sets the font color to `ff0000`—that is, bright red. A great deal of spam uses this technique to catch readers' eyes, but in my experience, no legitimate mail uses this technique. This recipe passes the spam through a special program, `/usr/local/bin/spam-block`, which is not a standard program. I use it in Listing 9.2 as an example of using Procmail to pass a message through an outside program.

- The final spam rule matches messages that do not contain the local domain name (`pangaea.edu`) or a special exception username (`ben@example.com`) in the `From:` or `Cc:` headers. A rule like this one can be very effective at catching spam, but it can be dangerous when applied system-wide. The problem is that mailing lists, newsletters, and the like may not include the recipients' names in these headers, so the rule needs to be customized for all the mailing lists and other subscription email a recipient receives. Doing this for a large site is a virtual impossibility. This rule will also discard most mail sent to a recipient using a mailer's blind carbon copy (BCC) feature, which causes the recipient name not to appear in any header. This rule uses the exclamation mark action to email the suspected spam to `sam@iwantspam.org`. In practice, you're unlikely to email your spam to any site, though; this use in Listing 9.2 is meant as a demonstration of what Procmail *can* do, not as a practical suggestion of what you *should* do with spam.

Some spam-fighting tools include provisions to send "bounce" messages to the spam's sender. This practice is reasonably safe when applied in a mail server; the bounce message is generated while the sender is still connected, so the bounce message's recipient is likely to be the correct recipient. You should *not* attempt to bounce spam from a Procmail recipe or a mail reader, though. Doing so will usually send the bounce message to the wrong address, since spammers usually forge their return addresses.

Overall, Procmail is an extremely useful and powerful tool for filtering the mail that the mail server handles. I recommend you begin Procmail experimentation by examining your system's default /etc/procmailrc file and then creating a custom ~/.procmailrc file in a test account. You can then see how your rules affect test messages you generate locally or remotely. Once you're confident of the effect of your rules, you can deploy them on a real account, and then system-wide, if necessary.

Configuring POP and IMAP Servers

Today, users typically run email client programs on desktop or workstation systems. These clients connect to the mail server computer using a pull protocol such as POP or IMAP. A POP or IMAP server can handle clients that run under almost any OS.

If you choose to run POP or IMAP, your first decision regards the POP or IMAP server. You must pick which protocol you want to support as well as the specific server package. Once that's done, you must install and configure the pull mail server and test it to be sure it works as intended. This chapter covers two common servers for Linux, Courier and Dovecot.

Selecting a POP or IMAP Server

Before rushing to install a pull mail server, you must understand the differences between the major pull mail server protocols and the individual products that are available in this arena. In some cases, it doesn't much matter which protocol or server you select, but in others, the differences can be quite important.

POP versus IMAP

Most modern mail clients support one or both of the POP and IMAP protocols, and a few support more exotic protocols. Both POP and IMAP perform basically the same task: Client programs connect, retrieve email, and disconnect. The client programs display a list of available messages and enable users to read these messages, archive them, reply to them, and so on.

POP and IMAP are both pull mail protocols, so a mail client can retrieve mail from the POP or IMAP server. To send mail, a mail client uses another protocol—typically SMTP. Small networks are often configured such that mail clients use the same computer for an outgoing SMTP server that they use for incoming POP or IMAP mail. Larger networks sometimes use physically separate computers for these two functions in order to better spread the mail-delivery load.

Although they fill roughly the same role, POP and IMAP aren't identical protocols. Some of their important differences include:

Mail Storage POP users typically retrieve their messages from the server and then immediately delete the messages from the server. Long-term archival of messages occurs on client systems. IMAP, on the other hand, was designed to enable users to store messages in folders on the IMAP server computer. As a result, an IMAP server may need to devote more disk space to user mail directories than a POP server. IMAP may also require more network bandwidth in the long run, although IMAP's partial retrieval options (which are described next) can mitigate this need or even give IMAP an advantage, depending on how your users interact with their mail systems. One big advantage to IMAP's system is that it enables users to access mail using different mail client programs or even different computers, without having to copy mail files between systems.

Partial Retrieval Options POP mail retrieval is all-or-none. Clients can either retrieve a message in its entirety or leave the message on the server. IMAP is more flexible; it supports retrieving various parts of a message, such as its header separately from its body. Therefore, with IMAP, users can delete messages they know they don't want without retrieving the bulk of the message text. With obvious spams and worms, this feature can save your network substantial amounts of bandwidth.

Client Support Although POP and IMAP are both widely supported, POP support is more common than that for IMAP. If your users already have preferred mail clients, you may want to check their configuration options to learn what pull mail protocols they support.

Your decision of whether to support POP, IMAP, or both will boil down to a study of these factors. As a general rule, IMAP is the more flexible protocol, but you may prefer to force mail off the mail server and onto clients as quickly as possible. In that case, using POP makes sense. If your users frequently use multiple computers, IMAP has a certain advantage in convenience for users.

Both POP and IMAP are available in several different versions. In 2011, the latest versions are POP3 and IMAP4. Earlier versions of both are still in use at some sites, and you may need to support earlier versions for some older clients. In the case of IMAP, support for earlier versions is usually automatic. POP2, though, uses a different port (109) than does POP3 (110). IMAP uses port 143.

Picking the Right Package

Pull mail servers tend to be much simpler than push mail servers. Essentially, pull mail servers are local mail clients; they read the mail queue directly. They then deliver mail to another computer using their own pull protocols. As a result, pull mail servers tend to attract little attention. Nonetheless, several different pull mail servers are available for Linux:

UW IMAP Despite its name, the University of Washington IMAP server (http://www
.washington.edu/imap/) supports POP2, POP3, and IMAP. The POP servers use the

IMAP server behind the scenes. This set of servers usually ships in a package called imap or uw-imapd. The IMAP server stores user mail folders in users' home directories, which can be awkward if users also log into their accounts and store nonmail files there.

Cyrus IMAP   Like UW IMAP, Cyrus IMAP (http://www.cyrusimap.org) supports more than just IMAP. Specifically, Cyrus IMAP supports IMAP, POP3, and a Kerberos-enabled POP3 variant (KPOP). This server stores IMAP mail folders in a proprietary file format in its own directory tree, so it can be a good choice if users store nonmail files in their home directories.

Courier   The Courier mail server (http://www.courier-mta.org) is an integrated set of SMTP, POP, and IMAP servers. Although the Courier SMTP server isn't very popular in Linux, the IMAP server can be installed separately, and it has a modest following.

Dovecot   This server, headquartered at http://www.dovecot.org, is another server that handles both POP and IMAP. Its Web page emphasizes the server's speed, security, and ease of configuration.

One critical consideration when picking a pull mail server is the message file formats the server supports. As noted earlier in this chapter, most Linux SMTP servers use the mbox format by default. UW IMAP and Dovecot both favor mbox format, although Dovecot can be configured to use maildir instead. Courier uses maildir by default. Cyrus IMAP, as noted earlier, uses its own proprietary format. If a given pull server looks appealing but uses the "wrong" mail storage format compared to your SMTP server, you'll have to replace your SMTP server, reconfigure your SMTP server, pick a different pull mail server, or translate between formats with Procmail.

Compatibility is required only for the main incoming mail directory. An IMAP server can use any format for the mail folders that users create, since the SMTP server doesn't interact with these folders.

One issue you should consider when installing and configuring a pull mail server is password security. The basic protocols deliver usernames and passwords for authentication over an unencrypted link. As a consequence, a miscreant with the appropriate access can sniff the password. Some servers support encrypted variants of the standard protocols, but these variants require support in the mail clients. Another approach is to use the Secure Shell (SSH) to *tunnel* the pull mail protocol over an encrypted link—that is, to encrypt the pull mail data and pass it over an encrypted connection. This approach requires configuring SSH on the server and on all the clients, as described in Chapter 7. If you don't want to go to this effort, you may want to consider setting aside special mail-only accounts and instruct users to create unique passwords for these accounts. Ideally, you can create these accounts on a dedicated pull mail server computer. This practice will at least minimize the damage that a miscreant might do if pull mail passwords are compromised. You may also want to restrict access to your POP or IMAP ports using firewall rules, TCP Wrappers, or xinetd access restrictions.

The following pages describe basic configuration of Courier and Dovecot because these servers are flexible, popular, and covered in the LPIC-2 objectives. If you want to use UW IMAP, Cyrus IMAP, or some other server, you should consult its documentation to learn how to use it.

Configuring Courier

Courier is administered through files stored in /etc/courier. Specifically, authdaemonrc controls aspects of an authentication daemon that comes with the package, and imapd controls most of the server's settings. Both files include comments, which begin with hash marks (#), and configuration lines, which take the form *option=value*. Table 9.7 summarizes options you're most likely to want to adjust. Peruse the file or consult the documentation at http://www.courier-mta.org/imap/ for information on additional options.

TABLE 9.7   Common Courier IMAP configuration settings

Option	Meaning
ADDRESS	Sets the IP address on which the server listens. A value of 0 causes the server to listen on all available ports.
PORT	Sets the port number (or numbers, separated by commas) on which the server listens. The default value is 143.
MAXDAEMONS	Limits the number of daemons (and therefore simultaneous connections) supported by the server.
MAXPERIP	Limits the number of simultaneous connections from a single client IP address.
IMAP_ CAPABILITY	Specifies the capabilities of the IMAP server. Chances are you won't need to adjust this option, but it could be handy if an important client has problems with a specific IMAP feature supported by Courier IMAP.
MAILDIRPATH	Sets the name of the directory in which the server stores emails.

Once you've tweaked your configuration, you can restart the Courier IMAP server using its SysV or Upstart startup script. If all goes well, you should then be able to access the server using a POP- or IMAP-enabled email client to read your mail. Keep in mind that Courier supports maildir format, whereas most Linux SMTP servers store their mail in mbox format by default. Thus, you may need to adjust your SMTP server configuration or even switch to a different SMTP server before you can use Courier IMAP.

Configuring Dovecot

Dovecot supports both mbox and maildir formats, so you may prefer using it to Courier IMAP if your system uses the mbox format and you don't want to change email format. Dovecot's main configuration file is /etc/dovecot/dovecot.conf. Like Courier's configuration file, this file contains comments and settings taking the form *option=value*. Table 9.8 summarizes some of the important options you might want to check and adjust. The default configuration file is usually well-commented, so peruse it or check the Dovecot documentation at http://wiki2.dovecot.org for more information.

TABLE 9.8   Common Dovecot configuration settings

Option	Meaning
protocols	Specifies the protocols Dovecot should support. (Separate multiple protocols with spaces.) Common choices include imap, imaps, pop3, and pop3s. (Values ending in s support encryption, which is further adjusted via options beginning with ssl.)
listen	Specifies the IP address, and optionally the port, on which to listen. An asterisk (*) refers to all IPv4 addresses, while two colons (::) refers to all IPv6 addresses.
login_process_per_connection	Specifies whether each login launches its own process (yes, the default) or whether each process can handle multiple logins (no).
login_max_processes_count	Sets the maximum number of Dovecot login processes (and hence the maximum number of logins, if login_process_per_connection is yes) supported.
login_max_connections	Sets the maximum number of connections per process if login_process_per_connection is set to no.
mail_location	Specifies the location of the mbox files or maildir directories to be used for mail storage. The value typically begins with mbox: or maildir: and continues with a pathname, which may include the variables %u (the local username), %n (the user part in the mail address), %d (the domain part in the mail address), or %h (the home directory). A separate inbox may be specified by using a colon and INBOX after the user-manageable mail location.

As a practical matter, the configuration option you're most likely to have to adjust is `mail_location`, since this can vary from one site to another. The default configuration file is likely to contain several commented-out examples, such as these:

```
#    mail_location = maildir:~/Maildir
#    mail_location = mbox:~/mail:INBOX=/var/mail/%u
#    mail_location = mbox:/var/mail/%d/%1n/%n:INDEX=/var/indexes/%d/%1n/%n
```

Locate the example that's closest to what your system already uses or what you want to use and tweak it as necessary. On a busy mail server, you may need to adjust the options that control the maximum number of simultaneous connections. You may also want to specify the protocols that the server supports or peruse the configuration file for more exotic options on a complex or unusual server.

Summary

Two of the most important services on the Internet today are Web sites and email. Linux provides a variety of servers to fill both roles. The most popular Web server for Linux is Apache, which is a full-featured server that handles both the unencrypted HTTP and the encrypted HTTPS protocols. A default Apache configuration works well enough for many simple purposes, although of course you must add your site's own unique Web pages. If you need to enable encryption, dynamic content, user-specific Web pages, or other features, you must adjust the default configuration by editing the Apache configuration files. Most such changes involve modifying just a few lines, but Apache is complex enough that an unusual site can require extensive configuration file changes. You may also need to configure another type of Web server, known as a proxy server, which functions as a go-between linking clients to servers. Proxy servers can improve performance, add security features, block unwanted content, and otherwise modify the Web browsing experience. In Linux, Squid is a popular proxy server with a default configuration that's designed to improve performance. Changing the configuration enables it to do many other things, though.

Email is handled through a variety of protocols, the most important of these being SMTP, which requires the client to initiate an email transfer. Several SMTP servers for Linux exist, two of the most popular being sendmail and Postfix. Both servers can run on workstations as local mail delivery tools or as the first step in the mail delivery chain; or they can receive mail from outside systems, perhaps functioning as mail hubs for an entire domain. Except for limited workstation use, chances are you'll need to tweak your SMTP server configuration for your domain and specific needs. Two other important email protocols are POP and IMAP, both of which require the client to connect to the server to retrieve email stored on the server. POP and IMAP are implemented by ISPs and on large mail server computers in businesses as a tool to enable users to read their mail from their desktop and workstation computers. Several POP and IMAP servers exist, including Dovecot and Courier. These servers may require some minor configuration tweaks to properly handle mail for a domain.

Exam Essentials

Describe the main Apache configuration files.   Apache uses a configuration file called `httpd.conf`, `httpd2.conf`, `apache.conf`, or `apache2.conf`, which is located somewhere in the `/etc/httpd`, `/etc/httpd2`, `/etc/apache`, or `/etc/apache2` directory tree. (There's considerable distribution-to-distribution variability in the file's name and location.) This file sometimes loads ancillary configuration files from the same directory tree. A file called `.htaccess`, located in a directory that's served by the server, can contain options related to that directory alone.

Distinguish between static and dynamic Web content.   Static Web content consists of HTML or other files that are delivered directly from the Web server to the client without modification or other processing by the Web server computer. Dynamic Web content consists of scripts or programs that the Web server runs in order to generate content for a specific client, such as a Web forum or a Web merchant's "shopping cart" page.

Summarize Apache's access restriction tools.   Apache supports username- and password-based access restrictions. You use the `htpasswd` program to create a password file using a name that you specify, which you then refer to using the `AuthUserFile` configuration file option. Additional configuration file options, such as `AuthType` and `Require`, tell Apache how to implement access controls for a specific directory.

Explain the purpose of virtual hosts in Apache.   A single Web server computer can host the Web sites for multiple domains. Depending on the name used in the URI or the IP address used to access the server, it can deliver Web pages stored in different directories. You can use the Apache `VirtualDocumentRoot` or `VirtualHost` directive to configure this feature.

Summarize the process of configuring SSL support in Apache.   To enable encryption in Apache, you must first install a suitable SSL module, typically from a package called `apache-mod_ssl` or from a package with Apache modules for many purposes. You must also obtain a certificate from a certificate authority (CA). Alternatively, you can generate your own certificate; however, without a certificate from a recognized CA, clients will see a warning about a suspicious certificate when they browse to your site. With these items installed, you can activate SSL support by loading the module called `ssl_module`.

Describe some common reasons to run a Web proxy.   By caching Web accesses, as Squid does by default, a Web proxy can improve Web performance for an office or other group of clients. Security features can include limiting Web access to authorized users and filtering Web content to block access to suspicious Web sites. More unusual or obscure needs include using an off-site proxy to work around network access problems or to help maintain your privacy.

Explain how email is relayed from source to destination.   Email is written using an email client (a mail user agent, or MUA), which today often exists on a desktop computer that may lack a mail server. The MUA connects to an SMTP server (a mail transfer agent, or

MTA), which parses the To: address and contacts the SMTP server associated with that address in the global DNS. Depending on the configuration of this server, it may hold the mail locally or forward it to another computer. Such forwarding operations can continue an arbitrary number of steps. The ultimate recipient will either read the mail locally on a mail server computer or use an MUA that supports a pull mail protocol (such as POP or IMAP) to retrieve and read the email.

Describe how to configure sendmail. The sendmail program uses a configuration file called sendmail.cf, typically located in /etc/mail. This file is difficult to edit directly, though, so you typically edit an m4 configuration file (sendmail.mc or some other name) and compile that file into the final sendmail.cf form.

Summarize commands to view and clear the email queue. The sendmail command can do both of these tasks, and other commands often work, too. Typing **sendmail -bp** or **mailq** displays emails that are currently in the queue. Typing **sendmail -q** causes the server to attempt redelivery of all the mail in the queue. Some servers have other commands that can do this, too, such as **postqueue** in Postfix or **runq** in Exim.

Explain the difference between mbox and maildir formats. These are both formats for storing email. The mbox format stores all mail in a mail folder (including the main incoming queue) in a single file, whereas maildir stores each message in its own file within a directory on the server. By default, sendmail, Postfix, and Exim use mbox, whereas qmail uses maildir; but most servers can be configured to use either format.

Describe the role of Procmail in mail delivery. You can configure most mail servers to send mail to Procmail as part of the local mail delivery process. Procmail can be configured to filter mail in various ways—to delete obvious spams, to pass mail through additional programs, to forward mail from one account to another, and so on. System-wide and user Procmail configurations exist, giving both the system administrator and individual users the ability to use these features.

Explain the major differences between POP and IMAP Both of these protocols enable clients to connect to a mail server to read their email. POP is a relatively simple protocol that enables users to retrieve their email, typically to be immediately discarded or stored on the client computer. IMAP can be used in the same way, but IMAP supports server-side mail folders and more sophisticated mail retrieval options, which are useful if users want to store their email on the server for access from a variety of clients.

Review Questions

1. You want your Apache server to use /var/mywww as the directory from which to serve your Web site. What Apache configuration option must you set to make this so?

    A. `Root /var/mywww/`

    B. `DocumentRoot /var/mywww/`

    C. `set root /var/mywww/`

    D. `Base=/var/www`

2. What type of information about HTTP transfers can you recover from an Apache server's log files? (Select all that apply.)

    A. The IP address or hostname of the client computer

    B. The name of the browser claimed by the client

    C. The route of network packets during the transfer

    D. The size of the client's Web browser window

3. You've made extensive changes to your Apache configuration files, and you want to check for egregious errors before you restart the server. What command might you type to do so?

    A. `apachectl testconfig`

    B. `apache2ctl teststat`

    C. `apachectl configstatus`

    D. `apache2ctl configtest`

4. You want to modify some Apache settings for a single directory in your Web site's directory tree. You enter the relevant changes in a file and save that file in the relevant directory. What name should you give this file?

    A. `.apache`

    B. `.httpd`

    C. `.htaccess`

    D. `.apache-config`

5. What program can you use to add users to a database of authorized users when you configure Apache to require authentication?

    A. `passdb`

    B. `htaccess`

    C. `apacheadd`

    D. `htpasswd`

6. An Apache server includes the following configuration line. Assuming the rest of the configuration is in order, what file will the server deliver if a user type `http://www.luna`
`.edu/index.htm` in a Web browser and the server receives this request?

   `VirtualDocumentRoot /var/httpd/%-2/%-1`

   A. `/var/httpd/www/luna/index.htm`

   B. `/var/httpd/www/luna/edu/index.htm`

   C. `/var/httpd/luna/www/index.htm`

   D. `/var/httpd/luna/edu/index.htm`

7. You want to use the `VirtualHost` directive to define a limited number of virtual hosts on an Apache server. Furthermore, this server has two network interfaces, one for your local network (`eth0`, 172.24.21.78) and one for the Internet (`eth1`, 10.203.17.26). What directive can you include to ensure that your virtual hosts are defined only on your local network?

   A. `VirtualHostOnly eth0`

   B. `Bind eth0`

   C. `NameVirtualHost 172.24.21.78`

   D. `ExcludeVirtualHosts 10.203.17.26`

8. Which of the following is the *best* mode for a secure Apache server's private key files?

   A. 0600

   B. 0640

   C. 0644

   D. 0660

9. Which of the following tools caches Web (HTTP) accesses by clients, thus improving performance on subsequent accesses to the same popular sites?

   A. Squid

   B. PHP

   C. `lynx`

   D. CGI

10. How can you ensure that all access to normal Web sites (on port 80) from your local network passes through a proxy server? (Select all that apply.)

    A. Use `iptables` on your router to redirect all traffic to the proxy server to go to the Internet directly.

    B. Use `iptables` on your proxy server to redirect all incoming port-80 traffic to the proxy server's default port.

    C. Use `iptables` on your router to block all outgoing port-80 traffic except from the proxy server.

    D. Use `iptables` on your router to redirect all outgoing port-80 traffic to the proxy server, except from the proxy server itself.

11. Your SMTP email server, `mail.luna.edu`, receives a message addressed to `postmaster@mail.luna.edu`. There is no `postmaster` account on this computer. Assuming the system is properly configured, how should the email server respond?

    A. Deliver the email to another account, either locally or on another computer.

    B. Bounce the message so that the recipient knows the account doesn't exist.

    C. Hold the message in the local mail queue until the `postmaster` account is created.

    D. Delete the message without bouncing it so as to reduce email clutter.

12. Which of the following is *not* a popular SMTP server for Linux?

    A. Postfix

    B. Sendmail

    C. Fetchmail

    D. Exim

13. Your Internet connection has gone down for several hours. What is true of email sent by your users to off-site recipients via a properly configured local SMTP server?

    A. The SMTP server will refuse to accept email from local clients during the outage.

    B. Email will be neither delayed nor lost.

    C. All email sent during the outage will be lost.

    D. Email will be delayed by a few hours but not lost.

14. You examine your `/etc/aliases` file and find it contains the following line:

    `root: jody`

    What can you conclude from this?

    A. Email addressed to `jody` on this system will be sent to the local user `root`.

    B. Email addressed to `root` on this system will be sent to the local user `jody`.

    C. The local user `jody` has broken into the system and acquired `root` privileges.

    D. The local user `jody` has permission to read email directly from `root`'s mail queue.

15. Which of the following is a commonly claimed advantage of maildir over mbox email format?

    A. Support for nested subdirectories of email folders

    B. Support for IMAP, rather than just the POP that mbox supports

    C. Faster authentication of users when first connecting to the server

    D. Faster access to messages in folders that hold many messages

16. What is an advantage of configuring Procmail rules in users' ~/.procmailrc files rather than in the global /etc/procmailrc file?

A. Rules in ~/.procmailrc execute as ordinary users vs. as root for /etc/procmailrc, making ~/.procmailrc safer.

B. Rules in ~/.procmailrc have access to users' own local email files vs. only the global files for /etc/procmailrc.

C. Users' ~/.procmailrc files can be set with restrictive permissions, preventing other users from maliciously modifying those files.

D. Several powerful options are available in ~/.procmailrc files that are not valid in the global /etc/procmailrc file.

17. Describe the effect of the following Procmail recipe:

```
# CPUload = 0.5
:0
*^From: vandervecken@example\.org
/dev/null
```

A. Mail from vandervecken@example.org is delayed until the CPU load drops below 0.5.

B. Mail from vandervecken@example.org is discarded.

C. Mail from vandervecken@example.org passes through unaffected by subsequent recipes.

D. None of the above; this recipe is malformed.

18. What option would you set in the Courier configuration file to limit the number of simultaneous connections the server will accept?

A. NUMCON

B. MAXCONNECTIONS

C. MAXDAEMONS

D. NUMUSERS

19. What is wrong with the following line, which appears in a Dovecot configuration file?

```
protocols = pop3, pop3s
```

A. The protocol list must be enclosed in curly braces ({ }).

B. Dovecot doesn't support a protocol called pop3s, although pops is valid.

C. Dovecot requires imap or imaps as one of the supported protocols.

D. The protocol list should be space-separated; there should be no comma (,).

20. Your site's email users frequently use random computers in your office, so you want to run a pull mail server that enables them to store their messages on the server computer itself. What protocol would be best for this purpose?

A. SMTP

B. IMAP

C. Procmail

D. POP

Answers to Review Questions

1. B. The `DocumentRoot` directive sets the directory in which Apache looks for files to serve, by default. (Other commands set the roots for virtual domain hosting and for users' sites.) The `Root` directive of option A is fictitious. Apache does not use a `set` keyword, so option C is incorrect; and it doesn't use an equal sign (=), so option D is incorrect. (Both these options also specify incorrect directive names.)

2. A, B. The Apache server's logs include the IP address or hostname of the client as well as an identification string provided by the client, which identifies the client program and platform. (This string is not entirely reliable, though.) Thus, options A and B are both correct. Packet routes (option C) are not normally included in this data, but you could apply `traceroute` to the IP address or hostname if you need this data. Web browsers' window sizes (option D) are not normally logged by Apache.

3. D. The `apachectl` or `apache2ctl` program (both names usually work, but sometimes only one is valid) can manage the Apache server process, report on connections, and test the configuration file for correct syntax. To do this last, pass it the `configtest` parameter, as in option D. The parameters specified in the remaining options are all fictitious.

4. C. The `.htaccess` file is a configuration file for a single directory in a Web site's directory tree, so option C is correct. Although Apache's main configuration file is normally called `apache.conf` or `httpd.conf`, neither option A nor B is correct for the single-directory configuration file described. Option D is entirely fictitious.

5. D. The `htpasswd` program (option D) manages Apache's own password database. Options A, B, and C are all fictitious, although the `.htaccess` file can be used to set options for an individual directory.

6. D. The numbers preceded by percent signs (%) in `VirtualDocumentRoot` are variables that refer to the dot-separated hostname components. Positive numbers count components from the start, and negative numbers count components from the end. Thus, given a hostname of `www.luna.edu`, `%-2` refers to `luna` and `%-1` refers to `edu`, making option D correct. The remaining options are all distortions of this correct answer.

7. C. The `NameVirtualHost` directive is required when using `VirtualHost`. It often takes an asterisk (*) as an option, but passing it an IP address instead causes virtual hosting to apply only to requests directed to the network interface associated with that IP address. Thus, option C is correct. The remaining options are all fictitious.

8. A. Permissions on the Apache private key file should be as restrictive as possible, which normally means 0600 (read and write for the owner, no access to anybody else) or even 0400 (read-only for the owner, no access to anybody else). Thus, option A is correct. In addition to this access, options B, C, and D all provide read access to members of the file's group; option C provides read access to all users; and option D provides write access to the file's group. These additions all constitute unnecessary security risks, making these options incorrect.

9. A. The Squid program is a caching proxy server, meaning that it provides the features described in the question, so option A is correct. PHP is a tool for running Web-centric scripts, so option B is incorrect. `lynx` is a text-based Web browser, so option C is incorrect. CGI is the Common Gateway Interface, a tool for running scripts from a Web server, so option D is incorrect.

10. C, D. Doing as option C suggests will block normal clients from accessing the Internet, forcing them to use their Web browsers' proxy settings to use your network's proxy server computer. Option D will use the proxy server more seamlessly, which requires less configuring but may not work well with some proxy configurations. Either option will do as the question asks. Option A makes little sense, because you can't redirect traffic aimed at a specific machine to go to the Internet at large; and if you could, this would do the opposite of what's requested. Option B would effectively make the proxy server run on two ports, port 80 and its native port, but this isn't what's specified by the question.

11. A. All SMTP email servers are supposed to accept email to postmaster. Linux systems typically do so by using an alias to forward the email to another local user or occasionally to a user on another computer. Thus, option A is correct. Options B and D both describe non-delivery of the message, in violation of proper email server configuration. Option C is effectively the same as option D unless creation of the postmaster account is imminent, and an email server would have no way of knowing this.

12. C. The Fetchmail program is a tool for retrieving email from remote POP or IMAP servers and injecting it into a local (or remote) SMTP email queue. As such, it's not an SMTP server, so option C is correct. Postfix, sendmail, and Exim are all popular SMTP email servers for Linux, so options A, B, and D are incorrect.

13. D. SMTP servers accept local email for delivery even if their Internet connections are down. If the SMTP server can't contact recipient servers, the SMTP server holds the email and attempts delivery later, so option D is correct. Because SMTP servers don't check on the availability of remote servers until after email is accepted for delivery, option A is incorrect. Option B can't possibly be correct unless the server has a backup Internet connection, which wasn't specified in the question. Option C isn't correct because the SMTP server will hold the mail and attempt delivery later.

14. B. The /etc/aliases file configures system-wide email forwarding. The specified line does as option B describes. A configuration like this one is common. Option A has things reversed. Option C is not a valid conclusion from this evidence alone, although an intruder may conceivably be interested in redirecting root's email; so if jody shouldn't be receiving root's email, this should be investigated further. Although the effect of option D (jody reading root's email) is nearly identical to the correct answer's effect, they are different; jody cannot directly access the file or directory that is root's email queue. Instead, the described configuration redirects root's email into jody's email queue. Thus, option D is incorrect.

15. D. By placing individual messages in files, maildir can theoretically provide faster access to individual messages than can mbox, which requires the server to read through all the messages in the mail folder. Thus, option D is correct. Both mbox and maildir support nested subdirectories of folders and IMAP, making options A and B incorrect. Option C is incorrect because authentication isn't affected by the email storage format.

16. A. Option A's statement is correct; an error in a global /etc/procmailrc recipe can be disastrous because the recipe runs as root. No matter which file is used, users' mail files can be accessed, so option B is incorrect. Although ~/.procmailrc can be protected from malicious changes, the same is true of /etc/procmailrc, making option C incorrect. Both files support the same commands, so option D is incorrect.

17. B. This Procmail rule uses the regular expression on its third line, which matches mail from vandervecken@example.org. Matched messages' dispositions are determined by the final line, which in this case redirects mail to /dev/null—in other words, it's discarded, as option B states. Option A is incorrect because this rule does nothing to test the CPU load; the comment on the first line is intentionally misleading. Because the recipe discards mail, option C is obviously incorrect. The recipe is properly formed, so option D is incorrect.

18. C. Option C specifies the correct variable name to limit the number of daemons, and hence the number of simultaneous connections, that Courier will accept. The remaining options are all fictitious.

19. D. Option D correctly describes the problem with this Dovecot configuration line. Dovecot doesn't require curly braces in this configuration option, so option A is incorrect. Dovecot supports protocols of imap, imaps, pop3, and pop3s, so option B is incorrect. Dovecot can run with support for POP only; there's no need to add IMAP support, so option C is incorrect.

20. B. The IMAP protocol supports directories and email organization on the server computer, making it a good choice for storing mail on the server in the long term. SMTP is a push mail protocol; it's used to send mail from the originator and down a delivery chain. Clients don't use SMTP to retrieve their mail, so option A is incorrect. Although Procmail might be part of your mail server's configuration, it's not a protocol that's used by clients to retrieve mail, so option C is incorrect. POP, like IMAP, is a pull mail protocol, but it doesn't support mail organization on the server, making it an inferior choice to IMAP for the specified purpose, so Option D is incorrect.

Chapter

10

Security

THE FOLLOWING LINUX PROFESSIONAL
INSTITUTE OBJECTIVES ARE COVERED IN
THIS CHAPTER:

✓ 210.2 PAM Authentication (weight: 3)

✓ 212.4 TCP Wrapper (weight: 1)

✓ 212.5 Security tasks (weight: 3)

The Internet is a dangerous place. Although Linux is immune to many of the dangers that threaten Windows computers, other dangers await the unwary Linux system administrator. This chapter describes some of the features Linux provides to help you deal with these problems.

First up is the Pluggable Authentication Modules (PAM) subsystem, which enables you to change the way Linux authenticates users. PAM has been referred to earlier, most notably with respect to the Lightweight Directory Access Protocol (LDAP), described in Chapter 7, "Advanced Network Configuration." A second topic is TCP Wrappers, which enables you to limit the computers that may access a wide variety of Linux servers, thus protecting them from broad classes of unauthorized systems. This chapter also covers how to monitor your network ports and network data on a low level. Finally, you should know how to look for signs of intrusion and where to go to keep up-to-date with security issues.

Security is an extremely important and complex topic. This chapter covers only a handful of security issues. Other security issues are described throughout this book, with reference to specific servers and Linux subsystems. Books such as Michael Bauer's *Linux Server Security* (O'Reilly, 2005) provide a deeper look at this important topic. Even more specialized books, such as Michael Rash's *Linux Firewalls: Attack Detection and Response with iptables, psad, and fwsnort* (No Starch Press, 2007) and Mayer, MacMillan, and Caplan's *SELinux by Example: Using Security Enhanced Linux* (Prentice Hall, 2006), provide extended details on more specialized security tools or topics.

Authenticating Users with PAM

PAM provides you with a flexible means of configuring authentication. A standard Linux installation typically authenticates users in a more or less standard way, typically by using accounts described in /etc/passwd and passwords stored in /etc/shadow. Using PAM, you can extend this system to use a network password server, biometric hardware, or other tools. To make full use of PAM, you must first understand the principles it uses. You can then build a new PAM stack. Because PAM configuration can be confusing in the abstract, I present a few examples to help you see how it works. Finally, you may need to adjust a related tool, the Name Service Switch (NSS), which is less complex than PAM but equally important to Linux authentication.

Understanding PAM Principles

In Linux's early days, every program that authenticated users did so by directly reading the /etc/passwd file, which in those days contained both the account information and the hashed password. Although this approach was simple to implement, it had a number of problems, such as exposing the hashed password to the entire system (thus making it possible for miscreants with local access to crack passwords by using brute-force dictionary-based attacks) and necessitating changes to every login program whenever a change to the authentication mechanism was desired.

The solution to these problems was PAM, which sits between the login programs and the account database (/etc/passwd and /etc/shadow in a default configuration). PAM is the usual way to implement *shadow passwords*, in which password hashes are stored in the more secure /etc/shadow file, reducing the risk of their being cracked. Once common login programs, such as the text-mode login utility, GUI X Display Manager (XDM) programs, the su command, and others, were converted to use PAM, all such programs could easily take advantage of new login tools simply by changing PAM. Because PAM is modular in nature, it can be expanded by adding new libraries to the computer and referencing those libraries in the PAM configuration files.

To configure PAM, you must modify one or more files in the main PAM configuration directory, /etc/pam.d. This file contains configuration files for every program that uses PAM, telling it what PAM modules to use and in what way. Most of the files in this directory are named after specific login tools; for instance, /etc/pam.d/login manages the text-mode login program, and /etc/pam.d/gdm manages the GNOME Display Manager (GDM) GUI login program.

 Some very old Linux distributions used a single file called /etc/pam.conf rather than separate files in the /etc/pam.d directory. This file held the equivalent of all the files in /etc/pam.d. Each entry in the pam.conf file, however, began with a service name, which is omitted from the /etc/pam.d files' lines, as described shortly.

Commonly, files whose names begin with common, system, or config, such as common-auth and common-session, are called by the service-specific files. You can change all of your login services by editing these files, or you can change a subset of your login services by editing their files individually.

PAM configuration files consist of a series of lines, each of which can be a comment that begins with a hash mark (#) or a line that describes a specific PAM module and how it's to be used. The latter type of line takes the following format:

```
management_group   control_flag   module   [options]
```

Each field has a particular meaning:

management_group   PAM defines four *management groups*, each of which controls an aspect of account authentication or security: authentication (auth), account management (account), session management (session), and password management (password). Different types of tasks that PAM performs require using different management groups, as described in detail shortly.

control_flag   When a module is called, it may succeed or fail in its task. (For instance, a password might be correct or incorrect.) This field tells PAM how to react to these successes and failures, as described in more detail shortly in "Setting Control Flags." For now, know that four control flags are valid: `requisite`, `required`, `sufficient`, and `optional`. Alternatively, a more complex syntax permits setting values and actions using the syntax `[value=action [value=action...]]`. In addition, the `include` flag tells PAM to include the lines in another configuration file. (Two other methods of doing the same thing are described in subsequent sections.)

module   The module specification identifies the PAM module file. This specification may include the complete path or be relative to the PAM modules directory (typically `/lib/security`).

options   Many PAM modules accept options that can influence how they work. Some options are recognized by many modules, but others are highly module-specific, as described shortly.

Editing a PAM Stack

Modifying a PAM configuration requires editing one or more PAM *stacks*, which are sets of modules that are called to perform specific tasks. Once you understand how PAM stacks are built, you can create new stacks—or more likely, modify your distribution's existing stacks. Each configuration file in `/etc/pam.d` consists of one or more PAM stacks to perform the actions needed by the associated program.

WARNING   Before proceeding, start a text-mode root login session and back up the configuration files you plan to change. If you err in your PAM configuration, the result can be an inability to log into the computer. Having an open root session and backups of your original configuration guarantee that you'll be able to back out of any unfortunate changes. The alternative is to reboot the computer using a rescue CD and edit the main installation's configuration.

What Is a PAM Stack?

For any given login service, each management group has its own stack—that is, there's one stack for account management (using the `account` stack), another for authentication (using the `auth` stack), and so on. Individual PAM-using tools can call these stacks for particular tasks, but certain tools are likely to use different stacks or use them in different ways. For instance, a login tool such as `login` or XDM is designed to authenticate users and so will make heavy use of the `auth` stack but may do very little with the `password` stack; but the `passwd` program may require both of these stacks. The purpose of each management group is as follows:

account   This management group performs account management based on features other than user authentication. For instance, it might limit access to the account based on the time of day or available system resources.

auth   This management group handles authentication, typically via a username/password pair. It can also assign group membership to a user.

password   This management group handles password (or other authentication type) updates.

session   This management group sets up a user's login session and then cleans up when the user logs out. It might verify or even create a user's home directory, mount partitions, and so on.

When a program calls a PAM stack, PAM executes each of the modules in that stack in sequence. Each module can return a success or a failure code, which PAM can then use to decide whether to execute the next module in the stack and, if the next module is executed, how to combine the results of each module.

The end result is that the PAM stack as a whole succeeds or fails, which means success or failure for the login operation, password change, or other authentication task at hand.

Several tools exist to enable one file to refer to another. One of these is to use `include` as the control flag, as described earlier. Another is to use the `@include` directive, which takes the name of a file to be included, as a single line of the file, as in:

```
@include common-auth
```

Such a line may be used instead of or in addition to the standard lines in a PAM stack. (Of course, the included file must specify a valid stack itself, particularly if the main file doesn't!) One more method of including external files is described in "Choosing Modules."

Setting Control Flags

As noted earlier, there are four control flags that determine how the success or failure of the module will affect stack execution. The various possibilities are laid out in Table 10.1.

TABLE 10.1   Control flags and the consequences of module termination

Control flag	Result of module success	Result of module failure
requisite	Stack continues to execute; stack may succeed or fail depending on other modules' results.	Stack ceases execution; stack fails.
required	Stack continues to execute; stack may succeed or fail depending on other modules' results.	Stack continues to execute, but ultimately fails.
sufficient	Stack ceases execution; stack succeeds unless an earlier requisite or required module failed.	Stack continues to execute; stack may succeed or fail depending on other modules' results.
optional	Stack continues to execute; stack may succeed or fail depending on other modules' results. (If this is the only module in the stack, the stack succeeds.)	Stack continues to execute; stack may succeed or fail depending on other modules' results. (If this is the only module in the stack, the stack fails.)

When designing a stack, you must be very careful to consider all the possible outcomes of each module's success or failure. For instance, consider the following two lines:

```
auth required   pam_unix.so try_first_pass
auth sufficient pam_ldap.so try_first_pass
```

With these two modules and two possible outcomes (success or failure) for each module, there are four possible outcomes for this mini-stack, as summarized in Table 10.2. If pam_unix.so succeeds, the stack as a whole succeeds, whether or not pam_ldap.so fails, since the former module is required and the latter is merely sufficient. If pam_unix.so fails, by contrast, the stack as a whole also fails, since pam_unix.so is required. Chances are this was not what was intended; this stack will work as well with the pam_ldap.so line removed.

TABLE 10.2 Possible outcomes in the sample stack

	pam_ldap.so **succeeds**	pam_ldap.so **fails**
pam_unix.so **succeeds**	Stack succeeds	Stack succeeds
pam_unix.so **fails**	Stack fails	Stack fails

Consider, though, what happens when one reverses these two lines:

```
auth sufficient pam_ldap.so try_first_pass
auth required   pam_unix.so try_first_pass
```

In this case, because a sufficient flag causes the stack to cease execution if the module succeeds, the stack will succeed when either module succeeds and will fail only if neither module succeeds. (If the stack contained subsequent lines, though, those lines would be bypassed if pam_ldap.so were to succeed.)

The more complex control flag format, involving a bracketed list of value/action pairs, uses one or more values from a long list, such as success, open_err, buf_err, and bad_item. (Consult the man page for pam.d for details.) You can use these values to test for specific types of failure. You can then set an action (ignore, bad, die, ok, done, reset, or an integer value) to have the stack take a particular action if the module returns the specified value. This type of configuration obviously creates the possibility of extreme complexity. If you need this level of complexity, you should consult the PAM man pages and other documentation. If you encounter rules in your default configuration that use this mechanism, you can try to ascertain their meaning to add to them, or you can replace them with a simpler mechanism derived from another distribution's settings or from some other source.

Choosing Modules

Some PAM modules ship with the main PAM package, and others ship with ancillary packages, such as LDAP software. Whatever the source of the modules, you can add them to your PAM stack to change how PAM operates. Table 10.3 summarizes some common PAM modules, but of course you may run across others as well. It's important to recognize that not all of the modules called in a PAM stack are intended to help with the stack's primary task. A module might be called to perform some ancillary task, such as display the message of the day (MOTD) on the terminal when a user logs in.

TABLE 10.3   Common PAM modules

Module name	Management groups	Common arguments	Description
pam_access.so	account	accessfile=*filename*	Restricts access based on username, hostname, network name, IP address, or terminal name.
pam_cracklib.so	password	use_authtok and others to set specific checks	Checks the strength of a password when it's being changed.
pam_deny.so	auth, account, session, password	None	Always indicates a failure; intended for use as a default for certain stack configurations.
pam_echo.so	auth, account, session, password	file=*filename*	Displays text for text-mode logins.
pam_env.so	auth, session	conffile=*filename*, envfile=*filename*	Sets environment variables.
pam_limits.so	session	conf=*filename*	Sets login session limits on memory, CPU time, and other system resources that may be used. If the conf option is not used, these are stored in /etc/security/limits.conf.

TABLE 10.3 Common PAM modules *(continued)*

Module name	Management groups	Common arguments	Description
pam_listfile.so	auth, account, session, password	item=*type*, sense={allow|deny}, file=*filename*	Searches the specified *filename* for rules to allow or deny access. For instance, if item=rhost (remote host) and sense=deny, users logging in from computers listed in *filename* will be denied access.
pam_mail.so	auth, session	dir=*directory*, empty	Displays a message if the user has new mail.
pam_mkhomedir.so	session	skel=*directory*, umask=*octal-umask*	Creates a new home directory if one doesn't already exist.
pam_motd.so	session	motd=*filename*	Displays the MOTD file.
pam_nologin.so	auth, account	successok	If the /etc/nologin file exists, fails for all users but root and displays the contents of /etc/nologin.
pam_securetty.so	auth	None	Fails if the user is root and is attempting to login from a device that is *not* listed in /etc/securetty.
pam_selinux.so	session	Various	Sets up the Security Enhanced Linux (SELinux) context for the login.

Module name	Management groups	Common arguments	Description
`pam_stack.so`	auth, account, session, password	`service=name`	Calls an external stack. Used instead of the `include` control flag or `@include` directive in some configurations.
`pam_unix.so`	auth, account, session, password	`nullok, likeauth, shadow, try_first_pass, use_first_pass, use_authtok`	Performs traditional Linux authentication based on /etc/passwd and /etc/shadow.
`pam_unix2.so`	auth, account, session, password	`nullok, likeauth, shadow, try_first_pass, use_first_pass, use_authtok`	Similar to `pam_unix.so`, but implements additional features, such as an ability to use a Network Information Service (NIS) server.

Table 10.3 is far from complete, but it includes the most commonly used modules, along with several that are uncommon on standard installations but that are very useful. You can find information on more standard modules in the /usr/share/doc/pam-*version*/Linux-PAM_SAG.pdf file on most distributions, where *version* is the installed PAM version number. Additional modules are available in various software packages to add support for additional authentication tools, such as using an LDAP server for authentication.

Typically, changing a PAM stack entails selecting one or more modules you want to add to the existing configuration and adding a line referencing that module. In some cases, though, you may want to remove a module, change its order in the stack, or change its options.

Setting Options

Many options are unique to just one module. Others, though, are used by several modules. This is particularly true of a few options that influence how authentication modules share passwords among themselves or deal with unusual passwords. Table 10.4 summarizes some of these options.

TABLE 10.4   Options used by several modules

Option	Meaning
debug	Many modules accept this option, which causes the module to record debugging information to your system log files.
try_first_pass	When you use multiple password verification modules in an auth stack, this option causes a module to try to use the password collected by the previous module in the stack. If this password fails, the module collects a password itself, which can result in the user seeing multiple password prompts.
use_first_pass	This option works much like try_first_pass, except that the module will not prompt for another password should the first one fail.
nullok	Most authentication modules fail if they're given null (blank) passwords. This option changes this behavior; if the password recorded in the database is null, a null password will authenticate the user.
likeauth	This option causes the module to return the same information when it's called as part of a password-change operation as when it's called as part of an auth stack.
shadow	This option enables shadow password features.
use_authtok	Used in a password stack, this option causes the module to use the same password delivered to a previous module, thus eliminating unnecessary duplicate password prompts when changing passwords.

Examining Example Configurations

PAM provides multiple ways for a Linux distribution to authenticate users, change passwords, and so on. Thus, it shouldn't be surprising to learn that different Linux distributions use different—often radically different—default PAM configurations. This fact can make it difficult to provide advice about how to alter your configuration, since a change that works well for one distribution may ruin another one.

Most distributions today provide core stacks in files called common-*type*, system-*type*, or something similar, where *type* is a name for the stack type, such as auth or login. You can edit these files if you intend to alter the way PAM works for all the relevant services. For instance, if you want local text-mode console users, local GUI login users, remote SSH users, users of an IMAP server, and so on, to all use an altered authentication tool, you can edit the relevant common-*type* or system-*type* file. If, on the other hand, you want to target just a few login services, such as local text-mode and GUI logins, while omitting others, such as SSH users, you should edit the files that are specific to the services you want to modify.

Listing 10.1 presents a sample configuration, taken from the /etc/pam.d/system-auth file on a Gentoo Linux system. This example uses all four management groups, so it provides the core features required by all authentication operations—logging in, changing passwords, and so on. A console or XDM-based login will typically use the account, auth, and session stacks; a password-change operation will typically use the account, auth, and password stacks.

Listing 10.1: A sample PAM configuration file

```
auth       required    pam_env.so
auth       required    pam_unix.so try_first_pass likeauth nullok


account    required    pam_unix.so


password   required    pam_cracklib.so difok=2 minlen=8 dcredit=2 ⏎
                                        ocredit=2 retry=3
password   required    pam_unix.so try_first_pass use_authtok nullok ⏎
                                    sha512 shadow


session    required    pam_limits.so
session    required    pam_env.so
session    required    pam_unix.so
session    optional    pam_permit.so
```

Consider authenticating a user for a login operation. This task requires using the auth stack, which in this example consists of two modules: pam_env.so and pam_unix.so. The first of these modules isn't very interesting; it merely sets environment variables and should not normally fail. The pam_unix.so module, however, includes a number of options, at least one of which (try_first_pass) may seem unnecessary; however, if you were to edit a file that calls this system-auth file and place a call to another authentication module before system-auth is included, try_first_pass could be useful.

Consider now the task of adding support for LDAP authentication, which uses the pam_ldap.so module. (This module is not a standard part of PAM but comes with various LDAP packages.) You would want to add a reference to pam_ldap.so to the same stacks that use pam_unix.so—that is, to all four of them. The location of this new reference is important, as noted earlier in "Setting Control Flags." Because this example uses required control flags, one easy way to do the job is to add the pam_ldap.so module before the pam_unix.so and to give the new module a sufficient control flag. This configuration will work, but it will have a characteristic that might be undesirable: It will check with the LDAP server *before* trying to authenticate users against the local password database. This might increase the load on the LDAP server, and it will also mean that your root password will be delivered to the LDAP server with every root authentication attempt. If you want to authenticate against your own local files first, you should add the pam_ldap.so module *after* the pam_unix.so module. This configuration will, however, require additional changes. One way is to make the first module (now pam_unix.so) sufficient and make the second module (pam_ldap.so) required.

Consider an alternative to the auth stack from Listing 10.1, taken from a CentOS system:

```
auth        required      pam_env.so
auth        sufficient    pam_unix.so nullok try_first_pass
auth        requisite     pam_succeed_if.so uid >= 500 quiet
auth        required      pam_deny.so
```

In this example, the critical pam_unix.so module is sufficient, meaning that the stack ceases execution and succeeds if the user enters a correct password but continues execution and leaves the stack success indeterminate if the user fails to enter a correct password. This works, though, because the stack ends with pam_deny.so, which always fails—that is, if no other module has validated the user, the stack as a whole fails. Such a stack can be modified by adding another sufficient rule for any module you want to add.

Adjusting the Name Service Switch

Although PAM handles the bulk of authentication work, another system, the Name Service Switch (NSS), handles a related task: NSS provides system tools with lists of users and groups, maps user ID (UID) numbers to usernames, identifies users' home directories, and so on. If you add another authentication tool, such as LDAP, to your system, you must adjust the NSS configuration to use this tool. To do so, you must edit the /etc/nsswitch .conf file. This file should contain lines similar to the following:

```
passwd:         compat
group:          compat
shadow:         compat
```

Some distributions use files rather than compat, and other entries can also be present. To use a new tool, such as LDAP, you should add the correct code for it (such as ldap) after the existing entries:

```
passwd:         compat ldap
group:          compat ldap
shadow:         compat ldap
```

The order in which the entries appear controls the order in which the relevant subsystems are checked for data. Thus, placing ldap after compat or files ensures that local account definitions take precedence over those on the LDAP server. This can be important for accounts that should be defined locally, such as root; their local definitions should take precedence over definitions on a remote server.

> ### 🌐 Real World Scenario
>
> #### Creating Good Passwords
>
> Whether you use locally stored passwords or a network password server, creating good passwords is important. Surveys have shown that an astonishing number of people pick very poor passwords, such as their own usernames.
>
> Unfortunately, good passwords tend to be hard to remember, since they resemble random sets of letters (in mixed case), numbers, and punctuation. One possible way to generate a good password that's easy to remember is as follows:
>
> 1. Select two unrelated words, such as bun and pen, and combine them together (bunpen); or generate an acronym based on a phrase that's meaningful to you, such as yiwttd, for *yesterday I went to the dentist*. This is the base for the password. An acronym arguably makes a superior base, so long as it is not itself a dictionary word. (Of course, you should not use either bunpen or yiwttd as your base, since these are both published examples.)
>
> 2. In the case of a base derived from two words, reverse the letter order of one of the words. This might produce bunnep as the word-derived base.
>
> 3. Change the case of some of the letters. This might yield bUnNep or YiwTTd.
>
> 4. Insert at least one digit and at least one punctuation symbol. This might produce bU4nN%ep or Y>iwT7Td. This is your final password.
>
> A password generated in this way should be easy enough for the user who created it to remember while being far enough away from any real word or guessable string to foil most attempts to break it. Of course, you must relay this advice to your users, since in most environments users generate their own passwords!

Enabling TCP Wrappers

You can adjust your PAM configuration to change the way Linux authenticates users or to add various non-authentication restrictions on logins. Another approach to security is to block access to network servers based on port numbers and IP addresses. A common tool to perform such tasks is *TCP Wrappers* (aka tcpd, the software's filename; or implemented via the libwrap library). This software is often used in conjunction with the inetd super server; however, some software, such as the NFS server, can use TCP Wrappers directly.

If you recall the description of iptables in Chapter 7, you may be thinking that TCP Wrappers sounds like it fills the same role. In many ways, this is true, and in fact TCP Wrappers is less flexible than a packet-filter firewall in many respects. For example, TCP Wrappers can't block access to servers that aren't launched from a super server or that use TCP Wrappers more directly, and it can't intercept traffic targeted at or sent by clients. Nonetheless, TCP Wrappers can do a few things that packet-filter firewalls can't do, such as log and restrict access based on the remote user's username (if the remote system is running identd or an equivalent server). For these reasons and because system security is best implemented in layers, you may want to use TCP Wrappers instead of or in addition to iptables. The following pages describe the basic principles of TCP Wrappers, how to restrict access with TCP Wrappers, how to call TCP Wrappers, and similar functionality provided by the xinetd super server.

Understanding TCP Wrappers Principles

The most common use of TCP Wrappers is in conjunction with inetd, which is a super server. Like all super servers, inetd runs as a daemon and listens for connections to a potentially large number of ports. When a connection arrives, inetd performs some basic checks, launches the appropriate server, and hands the connection over to the target server. This configuration can save memory on computers that run a large number of seldom-used servers, and it also enables the servers to take advantage of the extra checks performed by the super server, including TCP Wrappers protections. Using a super server can slow down network connections, though; the extra checks and the need to launch the target server for each connection both add time to the initial server connection.

When using TCP Wrappers, inetd calls TCP Wrappers (via its tcpd executable) instead of the target server and passes tcpd the name of the ultimate server program, along with any parameters it needs. TCP Wrappers can then study the incoming connection and decide whether to accept it. If the connection is refused, TCP Wrappers doesn't even call the server; it just drops the connection. If TCP Wrappers accepts the connection, it launches the server and hands it the connection.

To configure TCP Wrappers, you provide criteria for accepting or rejecting connections in two files: /etc/hosts.allow and /etc/hosts.deny. The first of these files defines computers that should be granted access to the server; the second specifies clients that should not be allowed to connect. If a computer is listed in both files, hosts.allow takes precedence. If neither file lists a computer, TCP Wrappers allows it to connect.

To run a system with the tightest possible TCP Wrappers security, include a line reading ALL : ALL in /etc/hosts.deny. This line blocks all incoming accesses handled by TCP Wrappers. You can then open individual servers for specific client systems in /etc/hosts.allow.

To use TCP Wrappers, you refer to a server by its filename, which may not be the same as its service name in /etc/services. For instance, an FTP server might be referred to as in .ftpd, vsftpd, proftpd, or various other names. When you use TCP Wrappers in conjunction with inetd, the server's filename appears immediately after the call to tcpd on the /etc/inetd.conf line for the server. Ordinarily, the server must reside somewhere on tcpd's path. If you need to include the complete path to the server in your /etc/inetd.conf file, TCP

Wrappers' restrictions may not work correctly. If necessary, you can create a symbolic link from a directory on your path to the actual server executable.

Restricting Access with TCP Wrappers

The formats for both /etc/hosts.allow and /etc/hosts.deny are identical, although the same entry has opposite effects in the two control files. The general format for these entries is as follows:

```
service-names : client-list [: shell-command ]
```

The *service-names* may be one server name, such as in.ftpd or in.telnetd; or it may be several names, separated by commas or spaces. In either event, the name is the name of the server's process (as revealed by ps or similar tools), not its protocol name (as shown in /etc/services). You can also use the ALL keyword, which stands for all services. The optional *shell-command* is a command you can run when access is attempted. You can use this feature to mail a notification to an address, present a failure message on the port, or take some other action.

The *client-list* is potentially much more complex than the *service-names*. As with the *service-names*, the *client-list* may be a single entry or many entries separated by commas or spaces. You can specify clients in any of several different ways:

IP Address   You can provide a single IP address, such as 172.24.45.102, to block or allow access from that IP address.

IP Address Range   If you want to block or allow access by an entire network based on its IP address range, you can do so. The simplest approach is to provide a partial IP address (ending in a dot), such as 172.24.45., which matches all systems in the 172.24.45.0/24 subnet. You can also provide the complete network address and add the number of bits or a complete netmask after a slash, as in 172.24.45.0/24 or 172.24.45.0/255.255.255.0.

Hostname   If you don't want to use IP addresses, you can block or authorize an individual computer by providing its hostname, as in trex.pangaea.edu. This approach is riskier than using an IP address, though, because it relies on a successful and accurate DNS lookup. If a cracker compromises your (or potentially even somebody else's) DNS server or if your DNS server goes down, the TCP Wrappers rules may not work as you expect.

In the popular media, the term *hacker* is frequently applied to criminals who break into computers. This word has an older meaning, though: It refers to people who are skilled with computers, particularly at computer programming, and who use those skills for productive purposes. Many Linux programmers consider themselves hackers in this positive sense. Therefore, I use the term *cracker* to refer to computer criminals. In the context of computers, this term unambiguously refers to people who break into or otherwise disrupt computers and computer networks.

Domain Name To block or authorize access based on a domain name, you list the domain name preceded by a dot. For instance, .pangaea.edu blocks or authorizes all computers in the pangaea.edu domain. As with hostname authentication, this approach is dependent upon accurate and reliable DNS resolution.

NIS Netgroup Name If your network runs a Network Information Services (NIS) netgroup server, you can specify an NIS netgroup name by preceding it with an at sign (@). As with hostname and domain name specifications, this approach puts your system at the mercy of another system—in this case, the NIS server.

Wildcards You can use any of several wildcards that match particular groups of computers. Examples of wildcards include ALL (all computers), LOCAL (all computers whose hostnames resolve without dots—normally those on the same domain as the server), UNKNOWN (computers whose hostnames or IP addresses aren't known, or users whose names can't be verified via identd), KNOWN (hostnames whose hostnames and IP addresses are known, and users whose names are returned by a client's identd server), and PARANOID (systems whose hostnames and IP addresses don't match). All of these options except for ALL are somewhat risky because they depend upon proper DNS functioning.

Usernames You can match individual users by preceding a hostname or IP address by the username and an at sign (@), as in sue@trex.pangaea.edu. This feature requires that the client be running an identd (aka authd) server, and it relies on that server's veracity.

In addition to these rules, you can use the EXCEPT keyword to create a list with exceptions. For instance, 172.24.45.0/24 EXCEPT 172.24.45.72 excludes 172.24.45.72 from the client list.

As an example of several of these rules in operation, consider Listing 10.2, which shows a sample /etc/hosts.allow file. This file should be used in conjunction with a /etc/hosts.deny file that restricts access for some or all servers. If Listing 10.2 were used with an empty hosts.deny file, it would have no effect, because no systems would be denied access.

Listing 10.2: A sample /etc/hosts.allow file

```
in.telnetd : 172.24.45.2 trex.pangaea.edu
vsftpd : 172.24.45. EXCEPT 172.24.45.1
imapd : .pangaea.edu EXCEPT router.pangaea.edu
ipop3d : sue@trex.pangaea.edu
```

Many inetd and TCP Wrappers examples use obscure older servers because the trend in recent years has been away from using these tools. For instance, modern Linux installations are likely to use OpenSSH (described in Chapter 7) rather than Telnet, since SSH is much more secure than Telnet. SSH servers are also usually launched directly rather than via a super server.

If used in conjunction with a very restrictive /etc/hosts/deny file (say, one containing the line ALL : ALL), Listing 10.2 grants access to only four servers, and it allows only a few hosts to access those services:

Telnet   The in.telnetd line tells the system to accept Telnet connections only from 172.24.45.2 and trex.pangaea.edu. Presumably, these are local hosts for which Telnet's risks are minor.

FTP   The vsftpd line tells TCP Wrappers to accept FTP connections from every computer on the 172.24.45.0/24 network except for 172.24.45.1. Perhaps 172.24.45.1 is a router or some other host that should never need to use an FTP client.

IMAP   The Internet Message Access Protocol (IMAP) is a mail retrieval protocol, and the imapd line restricts access to this protocol. All the computers in the pangaea.edu domain except for router.pangaea.edu may access this server.

POP   The ipop3d line enables sue@trex.pangaea.edu to use the Post Office Protocol (POP) to retrieve email. Other users of that system and users of other systems (even sue on other systems) can't access the ipop3d server.

Remember that TCP Wrappers protects only those servers that use its features. Many servers aren't launched through inetd and don't use TCP Wrappers.

TCP Wrappers provides more features than I can present here, and some of its features can have subtle effects. For this reason, you should thoroughly test any /etc/hosts.allow and /etc/hosts.deny files you create. If you have problems, type **man 5 hosts_access** to read the official documentation on the TCP Wrappers control file format.

Calling TCP Wrappers

Some programs use TCP Wrappers independently and usually automatically; however, in most cases it's called via the inetd super server. Most modern distributions, however, have switched to xinetd (see the upcoming section "Using Similar Functionality in Other Programs"), and you may not need a super server at all, since many modern servers work best when launched directly.

The inetd super server is configured via the /etc/inetd.conf file or by multiple files in the /etc/inetd.d directory. The configuration file format includes comment lines that begin with hash marks (#) and server definition lines that take the following form:

```
service-name socket-type protocol flags user server args
```

Each field is separated from its neighbors by spaces or tabs. The meanings of these fields are listed here:

service-name   This field is the name of the protocol, as defined in /etc/services. For instance, ftp stands for an FTP server, and telnet is a Telnet server.

socket-type The *socket type* is normally either stream or dgram, although a few other options, such as raw, rdm, and seqpacket, are also possible. The appropriate value varies from one server to another, so consult the server's documentation to learn which you should use.

protocol Most servers use the tcp protocol, but a few servers use udp, and an even smaller number use other protocols. Servers that use the Remote Procedure Call (RPC) system to mediate connections specify a protocol of rpc/tcp or rpc/udp. In any event, the protocol must be listed in /etc/protocols. You should consult your server's documentation to learn which it uses.

flags You can pass a wait or nowait flag, which tells inetd whether the server is single-threaded or multithreaded, respectively. This option is relevant only for datagram (dgram socket type) servers; others use a nowait entry by convention. You can append a dot and a number to this entry to limit the number of instances of a server that inetd will allow to run at once. You can use this feature to limit the number of simultaneous connections your system will accept, thereby heading off potential CPU, memory, or network bandwidth use problems. If you omit the maximum connections number, it defaults to 40.

user This entry specifies the user under whose name the server is run. This value is frequently either root or nobody, but any user listed in /etc/passwd is valid. You can append a group name after a dot, as in ftp.servers to run the server as the ftp user in the servers group.

WARNING   Never run a server with higher privilege than is required. Doing so can pose a security risk in the event of a bug or sometimes even when a server is operating normally. The privileges a server requires vary from one server to another, so consult its documentation for details.

server This field points to the server itself, such as /usr/sbin/vsftpd to launch vsftpd. The inetd server also supports a few protocols by itself. For these, the *server* field should read internal. If you use TCP Wrappers to launch a server, this field should read /usr/sbin/tcpd (of course, the path should be adjusted if tcpd resides somewhere else on your system).

args Many servers rely upon arguments passed to them on the command line. The final field is where you specify these arguments, separated by spaces, if necessary. If you launch a server via TCP Wrappers, the first argument is the name of the server you want to launch.

As an example, consider the following entry:

```
imap stream tcp nowait root /usr/sbin/tcpd imapd
```

This entry tells inetd to listen on the imap TCP port (143) and to launch imapd via TCP Wrappers whenever a connection appears. This server is run with root privileges because it's an Internet Message Access Protocol (IMAP) server, which requires root privileges to process logins from any user who wants to retrieve email via IMAP.

Many distributions that use inetd ship with many predefined entries for common servers; however, most of these entries are commented out by placing hash marks before each deactivated server. This practice ensures that a server won't be launched accidentally just because you've installed it; you must take active steps to activate the server by uncommenting the relevant line before it will work. Some protocols are represented by multiple entries, one for each server that can handle the protocol. If you want your system to use the protocol in question, you must decide which server to use and uncomment the correct inetd.conf entry. If you uncomment the wrong entry, the server won't respond. Some servers—particularly those that don't ship with a distribution—don't have default entries in inetd.conf. To use such a server, you must add the entry. The simplest way to do this is usually to copy a sample entry from the server's documentation. If the documentation doesn't provide such an entry, it may not have been designed to run from a super server, but you can try creating an entry by modifying another. You may have to guess at the *socket-type*, *protocol*, and *flags* fields, though.

Modern inetd installations typically use files in /etc/inetd.d instead of a single /etc/inetd.conf file. This configuration enables server packages to easily include a suitable configuration file. Other than the file location, the server configuration works the same in either case.

Changing the inetd.conf settings will not change the way your currently running inetd process responds to incoming requests. Restarting the computer will accomplish this change, but much simpler methods are to restart inetd or to pass the server a HUP signal. You can restart inetd by stopping it and starting it again via its own SysV or Upstart startup script or usually by passing the SysV script the restart option. For instance, you might type **/etc/init.d/inetd restart**. You can do this manually by using kill and then launching inetd manually, as well, but using the SysV startup scripts is better if your system uses them. This approach has a major drawback, though: It's likely to kill any open connections mediated by inetd. To avoid this problem, pass the HUP signal, as in **killall -HUP inetd**. Some distributions support a reload option to their inetd SysV startup scripts to accomplish this goal, as well. For instance, **/etc/init.d/inetd reload** will do the job on some systems.

If you implement changes to your inetd configuration and can't connect to the new server, check the system log files. You may find entries from inetd concerning an inability to find the program file, a socket already being open, or various other error conditions. Knowing what's causing a problem may suggest corrections, such as double-checking the filename in /etc/inetd.conf to correct a typo.

Using Similar Functionality in Other Programs

Although the LPIC-2 objectives mention inetd, most modern Linux distributions have abandoned this super server in favor of xinetd (pronounced "zi-net-dee"), which provides most of the features of inetd and TCP Wrappers in one program. The main xinetd configuration file is /etc/xinetd.conf. Most distributions use a minimal xinetd.conf file, though. This file sets only a few defaults and calls the files in /etc/xinetd.d to handle individual servers. A configuration that's equivalent to the one presented for an IMAP server in the previous "Calling TCP Wrappers" section is as follows:

```
service imap
{
    socket_type      = stream
    protocol         = tcp
    wait             = no
    user             = root
    server           = /usr/sbin/imapd
    server_args      =
    disable          = no
}
```

This entry contains all the information present in the inetd configuration for the same server, except that it's split across multiple lines and each line is labeled. In practice, xinetd isn't very fussy about the order of these options, so you may see them in different orders. You may also see empty options, such as server_args in this example, omitted.

You can use assorted options to xinetd that aren't available in inetd. One of these options is disable, which takes a yes or no parameter. If this option is set to yes, xinetd ignores the server. You can use this feature to temporarily or permanently disable a server without uninstalling it. Many servers ship with a disable = yes entry so that you must explicitly enable the server before it will work.

WARNING   Some options, such as disable, can result in a "double negative" interpretation. For instance, disable = no means that the server is enabled; such settings can easily lead to confusion, so be alert!

Many of the xinetd access control tools mirror those in TCP Wrappers, although xinetd uses different names. xinetd offers a few security options that TCP Wrappers doesn't offer. Broadly speaking, the xinetd options fall into several categories:

Host and Network Access Restrictions   You can use the only_from and no_access options much as you would use entries in TCP Wrappers' /etc/hosts.allow and /etc/hosts.deny files, respectively. If you include an only_from line, though, all systems not explicitly listed are denied access. You can specify hosts by IP address, network address with or without netmask (as in 172.24.45.0 or 172.24.45.0/24), hostname, or a network name listed in /etc/networks. If you use a hostname, xinetd does a single hostname lookup whenever you start the server, so this option is likely to be unreliable if a client's IP address changes at all frequently. If a system matches both only_from and no_access lines, xinetd applies the rule associated with the more specific line. For instance, if only_from enables access from

172.24.45.0/24 and no_access denies access to 172.24.45.7, then 172.24.45.7 will not be able to access the system.

Interface Restrictions   If your computer has multiple network interfaces, you can bind a server to just one of those interfaces with the bind or interface options, which are synonymous. These options take the IP address on the local computer associated with an interface as an option. For instance, bind = 172.24.45.7 ties the server to the interface with the 172.24.45.7 address. When you use this feature, xinetd doesn't even listen for connections on other interfaces, which can greatly enhance security; a miscreant can't take advantage of a bug, even in xinetd, if xinetd isn't listening on the interface the cracker is using.

Temporal Restrictions   If you want a server to be available at some times of day but not others, you can configure temporal restrictions using the access_times feature. This keyword takes two times, separated by a dash (-), as an option. The times are specified in 24-hour format. For instance, access_times = 07:30-18:00 restricts the server's availability to between 7:30 A.M. and 6:00 P.M. This restriction applies to the original connection; users can continue using the server past the curfew period. For instance, if a user logs into a Telnet server that's restricted to 7:30 A.M. to 6:00 P.M. at 5:57 P.M., the person could remain connected well past 6:00 P.M.

Just as with inetd, you must tell xinetd to restart or reread its configuration file after making changes to that file. This is also necessary if you add a new configuration file to /etc/xinetd.d. You can use the same methods to restart xinetd or have it reread its configuration file that you can use with inetd. As with inetd, the method that's least likely to cause disruption is to pass the server a HUP signal, as in **killall -HUP xinetd**.

Dealing with Ports and Packets

Low-level network scanning and diagnostic tools can help you audit your own computers for potentially risky configurations and keep an eye on network traffic for suspicious patterns. Broadly speaking, two classes of tools are used for these tasks: port scanners and packet sniffers. Some tools, although not technically part of these categories, can fill a similar role and so are described here, as well.

WARNING   Port scanners and packet sniffers are both useful tools that can help you secure your network; however, in the wrong hands, they can also be tools used by crackers to help them break into computers. For this reason, many organizations have policies restricting their use. Before you use such tools, be sure to obtain written permission from a person who is authorized to do so. Performing port scans or monitoring packets without permission, even if your intentions are honorable, could result in your being fired or even dragged into court.

Scanning for and Dealing with Open Ports

It's easy to leave a server running unintentionally. This can happen because the server was installed automatically without your knowledge, accidentally, for temporary use and then forgotten, without authorization by a legitimate user or even by an intruder. Unknown servers can pose a serious security threat, since they can provide access to your computer that you don't know about. Using such a server, a cracker can break into your computer and wreak unknown degrees of havoc on the computer. Perhaps worse, the cracker may then be able to use your computer as a launch pad for attacks against other computers on your network or against other networks.

Chapter 5, "Networking Configuration," describes several port scanning tools that you can use to audit individual computers or even an entire network. A few other programs are also useful in this regard. These programs are:

netstat   This program enables you to scan your local computer for open ports. The --listening (-l) option performs this task and so is particularly useful in identifying open ports on your computer. You can also use netstat to identify the specific program that uses a port after an external port scan has located an open port on your computer.

Telnet   The Linux Telnet protocol client, telnet, can be used for quick-and-dirty network analysis. Pass it a hostname and a port number, as in **telnet web.example.com 80**, and the program connects to the specified TCP port on the specified computer. You can use this functionality to verify that a server is running (it produces a connection refused error if there's no server available). If you understand the protocol in enough detail, you can even test it directly, rather than by using its usual client software. This feature can enable you to spot errors or security vulnerabilities that might be obfuscated by additional layers of code in typical client programs.

nc   This program can send arbitrary data to other computers, monitor network ports, and more. It's a good tool if you want to write a custom script for performing specialized scans of your network on a regular basis.

Nmap   You can use this program to scan arbitrary computers on the network for open ports. You can do the same with nc, but nc does very simple network tasks and is intended for use in scripts, whereas Nmap can perform a complete scan of one or more computers.

OpenVAS   This program, based at http://www.openvas.org, is a network scanner that incorporates tests based on several open source tools. It includes both text-based and GUI front-ends, and it's designed as a way to quickly and efficiently scan an entire network of computers for vulnerabilities.

Chapter 5 describes the details of netstat, nc, and Nmap, and you can consult their man pages for more details. Broadly speaking, you may want to scan all the computers on your network for open ports from time to time. Scanning a new computer as soon as it's configured is also in order.

Scan a computer using at least two tools. You may also want to perform scans from two locations, such as inside and outside of a firewall. Some configurations can leave ports open on some network interfaces or to some networks but not to others, so scans from different computers or using different tools can produce different results.

If you find open ports, you can take one of several actions:

Leave It Open   Some ports should be left open. This is true of the ports associated with server software, for instance. Sometimes a server should be available on some networks but not others, in which case some form of selective access should be implemented. Some settings for this in server programs leave the port open, but the server will deny access at a higher level.

Restrict Network Interface Access   Some servers can be bound to one network interface but not another. This feature is particularly handy on routers and other computers with multiple network interfaces, but it can also be useful if a server must run for local access only—you can bind it to the localhost (127.0.0.1) address but not to your usual Ethernet or other network address.

Block the Port   You can block access to the port in several different ways. If the server is launched via a super server (inetd or xinetd), you can use TCP Wrappers or xinetd access rules to do the job. In all cases, you can use iptables to block access to the port. This approach can be particularly helpful if the server must run for some clients but not for others—say, if it should be accessible to computers on your local network but not to systems on the Internet as a whole. Some port blocks can be implemented on the computer that runs the server, but others can be implemented on your network's router.

Redesign Your Network   In some cases, you may want to redesign your network. You can put highly sensitive computers behind a dedicated router that includes specialized firewall rules to limit access to the sensitive computers. This approach can be effective, but implementing it can be a major undertaking.

Disable the Software   If the port shouldn't be open on the computer at all, you may want to shut down the software that uses the port. You can do this by adjusting your SysV or Upstart startup script or by editing your inetd or xinetd configuration for the server. In many cases, if this approach makes sense, the next one makes even more sense.

Remove the Software   You can use your computer's package management system to completely uninstall the software. This option makes sense if the server shouldn't be running on the computer at all and never should be.

Security is best implemented in layers. Thus, you may want to take two or more of these approaches when you locate an open port. For instance, you might remove the software, implement a local `iptables` rule to block access to the port, and implement a firewall rule on your router to restrict access to the port on the affected computer (and perhaps on other computers, depending on your needs). Creating several such restrictions makes it less likely that your computer will be compromised by a single configuration error. For instance, if you have a firewall in place blocking access to port 80, an accidental installation of a Web server that uses this port is unlikely to do any harm.

Monitoring Network Traffic

You can use a port scanner to check a network for vulnerability. Another road to improving security is to monitor your network for suspicious activity. A packet sniffer is one way to do this, and another is to use tools to monitor your log files for suspicious activity.

Using Snort

Chapter 5 described a couple of network packet monitoring programs, `tcpdump` and Wireshark. These programs enable you to examine network packets as they enter or leave your computer and sometimes as they pass between other computers on your network. Such monitoring tools can be useful for diagnosing network problems, and they can also be useful security tools—you can scan for suspicious packets and take appropriate action when such packets are detected.

Snort (`http://www.snort.org`) is another very powerful packet sniffer program. In addition to functioning as a generic packet sniffer, Snort can function in a more sophisticated role as an intrusion detection system (IDS). An IDS is a program that monitors network traffic for suspicious activity and alerts an appropriate administrator to warning signs. Put another way, an IDS is a packet sniffer with the ability to recognize activity patterns that indicate an attack is underway.

Installing Snort

The first step when it comes to installing Snort is deciding where to place it. Figure 10.1 shows a couple of possible locations. Snort System #1 in this figure is able to monitor traffic to or from the Internet at large, while Snort System #2 is able to monitor local traffic. Both have a chance of catching outside attacks against specific local computers, but System #1 will be sensitive to attacks that are blocked by the firewall, while System #2 will be sensitive to purely local attacks. Also, System #2 requires either a hub rather than a switch locally or a switch that's programmed to echo all traffic to Snort System #2; a switch without such configuration will hide most traffic between the local computers from the Snort system, rendering it useless.

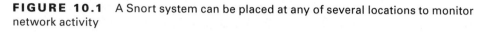

FIGURE 10.1 A Snort system can be placed at any of several locations to monitor network activity

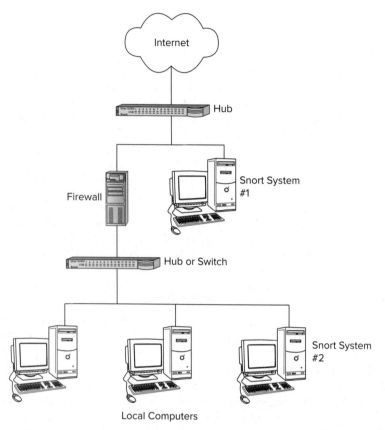

Most modern Linux distributions ship with Snort, so you should be able to install it in the usual way. Once installed, Snort is configured through the /etc/snort/snort .conf file. (Some distributions don't provide a file of this name but do provide a file called snort.conf.distrib or some other variant. You can copy or rename this file and use it as a template that you can modify.) A default snort.conf file may work acceptably, but you may want to customize several variables, such as $HOME_NET, $SMTP_SERVERS, and $HTTP_SERVERS. The first of these specifies the IP addresses to be monitored. Others define the IP addresses of particular types of servers. The default values tell Snort to monitor all IP addresses, which may be fine, since you may want Snort to watch all traffic on its local network, which is all it will ordinarily be able to see.

Some distributions place a series of supplementary Snort configuration files, with names that end in .rules, in the /etc/snort directory. These rule files define the sorts of packets that Snort should consider suspicious. Most protocols have a single .rules file, such as smtp.rules for SMTP packets. These .rules files are referenced via include directives in the main snort.conf file, so be sure your main snort.conf file loads the appropriate rules for your network. If you don't see a .rules file for a protocol you want to monitor, check http://www.snort.org/start/rules. This site can help you locate and install additional Snort .rules files.

Launching Snort

To launch Snort, type its command name: **snort**. The program runs and logs its output in files located in /var/log/snort. These log files record information on suspicious packets. You should be sure to monitor these log files on a regular basis. To launch Snort on a permanent basis, you can run it from a startup script. In fact, many distributions provide SysV or Upstart startup scripts to launch Snort.

Snort doesn't need an IP address to monitor network traffic. Thus, you can configure a dedicated Snort system with network drivers but without an IP address and use it to monitor network traffic. This configuration makes the Snort monitor very resistant to external attacks, because an attacker can't directly address the system. On the downside, you must use the Snort system's own console or an RS-232 serial link to it to monitor its activities.

Checking for Intruders Using Fail2Ban

Sometimes a cracker will attempt to break into a computer by making repeated login attempts. The result will be a string of failure messages in the computer's log files. The Fail2Ban program (http://www.fail2ban.org) is a server that monitors your system's log files and, when it detects repeated failed login attempts from a particular IP address, modifies your computer's iptables firewall rules, TCP Wrappers rules, or other tool to block that IP address. This action denies the would-be intruder the opportunity to make more than a few guesses at your system's passwords.

Fail2Ban uses several configuration files in the /etc/fail2ban directory tree. The file you're most likely to modify is /etc/fail2ban/jail.conf. This file includes definitions for many common servers that the tool may monitor. Each definition begins with a name in square brackets, such as [ssh], which monitors for SSH login failures. (The section names are arbitrary and can vary from one distribution to another.) The jail.conf file begins with a section called [DEFAULT], which sets some global default values, such as the number of retries needed to trigger a ban (maxretry), the time period during which this number of retries must be attempted to trigger a ban (findtime), the number of seconds that a host is banned once the trigger condition is met (bantime), and the method used to ban the offending computer (banaction). You can override any of these defaults for specific servers.

You should peruse the jail.conf file to find configurations for the servers you want to monitor. For instance, suppose you want to block computers that attempt to crack your SSH server. You might want to modify the [ssh] section, which looks like this by default on an Ubuntu system:

```
[ssh]

enabled = true
port    = ssh
filter  = sshd
logpath = /var/log/auth.log
maxretry = 6
```

Most of these lines are self-explanatory; this particular configuration is enabled, it monitors the ssh port (as defined in /etc/services), it monitors the /var/log/auth .log file for login failures, and up to six failures are tolerated before a ban is enacted. The filter line refers to a file in the /etc/fail2ban/filter.d directory with the specified name but with .conf appended (sshd.conf in this example). This file contains a series of regular expressions that describe login failures for the server in question.

Some distributions ship with Fail2Ban configurations that may require more adjustment. For instance, Gentoo's default jail.conf file includes an SSH configuration that's rougher than the Ubuntu configuration:

```
[ssh-iptables]

enabled = false
filter  = sshd
action  = iptables[name=SSH, port=ssh, protocol=tcp]
          sendmail-whois[name=SSH, dest=you@mail.com, ↵
                     sender=fail2ban@mail.com]
logpath = /var/log/sshd.log
maxretry = 5
```

At a minimum, this configuration needs to be enabled, the email addresses need to be customized, and the log path needs to be updated (Gentoo logs SSH failures to /var/log/ messages). This example also demonstrates one of Fail2Ban's features: It can send you an alerting email when a login failure occurs by using the sendmail-whois action. If you don't include an email notification action, you'll have to monitor the Fail2Ban log file (set in the /etc/fail2ban/fail2ban.conf file) if you want to know what IP addresses are being restricted by the software.

You may want to peruse the Fail2Ban Web site, particularly if you need to enable support for servers not included in the standard configuration. The site includes a wiki with user-submitted documentation and configurations, some of which might be helpful if you need to deviate from the configurations available in your standard installation.

Once everything is set up, you must launch Fail2Ban. If you installed it from a package provided by your distribution, chances are it comes with a SysV or Upstart startup script, so you can use that script in the usual way. If you installed the software from source code, you can start the program by typing **fail2ban-client start** at a shell prompt or by including that command in a local startup script. Be sure to check the Fail2Ban log file and test its operations to be sure it's working the way you expect.

EXERCISE 10.1

Using Fail2Ban

This exercise demonstrates the use of Fail2Ban to quickly ban errant IP addresses from a computer. This exercise depends on the default configuration of your distribution's Fail2Ban package; you may need to make changes that go beyond those described here to make this exercise work. I've tested it on both Ubuntu and Fedora systems. You will need access to two computers to perform these steps; you'll configure one and use another as a stand-in for an attacker's computer.

To proceed, follow these steps:

1. Log into the computer as root, use su to acquire root privileges, or be prepared to perform the following actions using sudo.

2. If the computer does not already run an SSH server, install and configure it. (Chapter 7 describes SSH configuration.) Alternatively, you can use another protocol that requires authentication and that Fail2Ban can monitor, such as POP or IMAP (Chapter 9).

3. Use your distribution's package management tools to install Fail2Ban. In most cases, the package name is fail2ban.

4. Load the /etc/fail2ban/jail.conf file into a text editor.

5. Search the jail.conf file for the string ssh. Your default file may include multiple SSH configurations that use different tools to ban SSH abusers. In Ubuntu, the [ssh] configuration is enabled by default; in Fedora, the [ssh-iptables] configuration is enabled by default. Both use iptables to block attackers. You can leave either configuration unchanged, although setting maxretry to a low value (such as 2) will simplify testing. On some distributions, you may need to adjust other values to make the configuration works as expected.

6. Start or restart the Fail2Ban service. Typically, typing **/etc/init.d/fail2ban restart** will do this job.

7. Log into your "attack" computer, which I'll refer to as attack. (I'll refer to your system running the SSH server as server.) The attack system can run Linux or any other OS, but it must have an SSH client installed on it.

8. Using attack's SSH client, log into your regular account on server. Type your password correctly and verify that you can use the computer.

9. Using another window or login session on attack, use its SSH client to attempt to log into your regular account on server, but this time deliberately mistype your password. On a typical configuration, the SSH server will give you three chances to type the password correctly. Depending on your SSH server's logging policies, these three chances may count as one or three of the Fail2Ban maxretry opportunities.

10. Repeat step #9. Depending on the logging policies, you might or might not be able to connect to type your password. If you can connect, you should be banned once you complete the attempt, assuming you set maxretry to 2.

11. Attempt to use the remote login you initiated in step #8. It should fail, since the login is from the same computer that initiated the failed login attempts; the `iptables` ban blocks all traffic from the attacking computer to the SSH port on server (and perhaps to other ports, as well).

12. Using your console session on server, type `iptables -L` to view your `iptables` configuration. You should see a new chain named after your Fail2Ban SSH configuration. This chain should include a rule to restrict attack's access to the computer.

13. Wait a while—to be precise, wait the number of seconds specified by the bantime option in `jail.conf` on server.

14. Type `iptables -L` again. The rule banning attack should be missing, since Fail2Ban has removed it after the ban time is up.

15. On attack, attempt once again to access server via SSH. You should be able to log in again.

At this point, you have the choice of leaving Fail2Ban running or uninstalling it. If you leave it running, you may want to adjust the maxretry setting if you changed it. You should also check the other protocols that are configured in the default `jail.conf` file; you might want to activate, deactivate, or adjust some of them. Remember to check whether the server runs automatically when you reboot; you may need to adjust its SysV startup script or Upstart configuration.

Keeping Up-to-Date with Security Issues

You should get into the habit of reviewing several security Web sites and other resources to learn about new threats:

CERT/CC The Computer Emergency Response Team Coordination Center (http://www.cert.org) hosts general security information, including information on the latest threats. Periodically reviewing this site will help you keep up-to-date with security developments.

US-CERT The United States Computer Emergency Readiness Team (http://www.us-cert.gov) has taken over some of the duties formerly held by CERT/CC. In practice, both sites are worth monitoring.

CIAC The Cyber Incident Advisory Capability (http://www.doecirc.energy.gov), run by the U.S. Department of Energy, is similar to CERT/CC and US-CERT in many respects, but its Web page gives greater emphasis to current threats and less coverage of general security practices.

CVE   The Computer Vulnerabilities and Exposures (http://cve.mitre.org) site is dedicated to maintaining a dictionary of vulnerability names. This information can be useful in facilitating communication about problems. The CVE contains less in the way of descriptions of the vulnerabilities and exploits it names, though.

SecurityFocus and Bugtraq   The SecurityFocus Web site (http://www.securityfocus.com) is yet another general security site. One of its important features is that it hosts the Bugtraq mailing list (http://www.securityfocus.com/archive/1), which can be a good way to keep informed—after you subscribe, alerts about new threats will be delivered to your email account soon after they're made public.

Linux Security   The Linux Security site, http://www.linuxsecurity.com, is similar to CERT/CC, US-CERT, CIAC, and SecurityFocus in many ways. Linux Security, though, caters to Linux in particular and so may be more helpful in addressing Linux-specific issues or in pointing to Linux-specific fixes.

Distributions' Web Sites   Most Linux distributions maintain security information on their Web sites. Go to your distribution's main page and look for links relating to security. These sites can provide specific upgrade instructions for your distribution in particular.

Product Web Pages and Mailing Lists   Many programs have Web pages and mailing lists, which can be good resources for learning about security problems related to these programs. Of course, regularly perusing all of the pages related to the hundreds of programs that make up a Linux system can be a full-time job. You might want to keep an eye on the Web pages or mailing lists for any high-profile server programs that you run, such as the Apache Web server or the sendmail mail server.

Security Newsgroups   Several Usenet newsgroups are devoted to security. Of particular interest are the groups in the comp.security hierarchy.

I recommend you investigate most or all of these resources and then keep up with a few of them. For instance, you might check the CERT/CC and Linux Security Web sites on a daily basis, subscribe to the Bugtraq mailing list, and check your distribution's security page on a weekly basis. Keeping up with security developments in this way will alert you to potential problems quickly—with any luck, quickly enough to avoid problems caused by crackers who might try to exploit weaknesses soon after they're discovered.

Many of these resources offer RDF Site Summary (RSS) feeds of their content. This protocol enables you to use a news aggregator program, such as AmphetaDesk (http://www.disobey.com/amphetadesk/) or BlogBridge (http://www.blogbridge.com), to track security problems and learn about them as soon as possible.

If you learn of a security vulnerability, what should you do? As a general rule, you should patch any vulnerable software as soon as possible. Most Linux vendors release updated software quickly, so you should keep an eye on your distribution's Web site or use your package management system (Yum, APT, or anything else your distribution uses) to download and install an update. If you're not satisfied with the speed with which updates are made available, you can uninstall your distribution's package and install a patched version from the package's vendor, either by using a binary package (if one is available) or by installing from source (as described in Chapter 1, "System Startup and Advanced System Management"). In some cases, security problems can be worked around by making changes to configuration files, so you may want to do this, if possible, as a temporary measure (or even permanently, if the change isn't detrimental to your system's functioning).

In some cases, security problems don't directly affect you. They may relate to servers you don't run, server features you don't use, or configurations you don't use. For instance, one common class of security problem involves the ability of local users to acquire root privileges by feeding a local program bogus data. If you're the only local user of a computer, though, such vulnerability isn't likely to be a problem. Be *sure* you're the only local user, though; some servers give remote users the ability to run local programs (as in Web servers with dynamic content), so sometimes you're not quite as invulnerable as it might at first seem!

Modern Linux distributions frequently include automatic or semi-automatic package update features. Although blindly accepting all updates can sometimes lead to problems if a new package introduces new bugs or breaks a configuration on your system, accepting updates will also fix known security vulnerabilities in the software you run. As a general rule, checking for and applying updates on a daily or weekly basis is a good idea. You should be alert to the possibility of breaking features on your computer, though. Note that some changes, particularly to the kernel, may cause problems that won't become apparent until you reboot the computer.

Summary

Linux provides a flexible authentication and login system, PAM. A default configuration typically enables your computer to store account information, including usernames and passwords used for authentication, locally. You can modify your PAM configuration to add non-authentication features to a login process (such as restricting logins by time or location) or to add or change the default authentication mechanism (such as using an LDAP server to store account information). This ability can be used to create a more convenient network environment, to tweak login procedures, or to enhance security.

A computer that runs servers often needs to limit who may access those servers. This task is often done via iptables firewall rules, as described in Chapter 7; however, other tools can be employed to this end, as well. An example is TCP Wrappers, which can block access to specific servers based on the IP address, hostname, or similar features of the client. These blocks work at a higher level than do `iptables` blocks, which has both advantages and disadvantages—some blocks can work on features that are difficult or impossible to manage via `iptables` (such as restrictions based on the username on the client), but TCP Wrappers works only for programs that are designed to use it or that run via a super server, such as `inetd`.

You should think of security as an ongoing process, rather than as a feature to be configured and forgotten. Security tasks you should perform on a regular basis include scanning your computers for unnecessary servers, monitoring your network traffic for unauthorized access attempts, and keeping up-to-date with the latest security news. Those who want to break into your computers for the data they contain, to use them as bases for further attacks, or just to take a virtual "joyride," are constantly updating their tools and methods. You must maintain constant vigilance to ensure that your computers remain uncompromised.

Exam Essentials

Describe how PAM enables a more flexible authentication system.   Individual programs that must authenticate users use PAM to do so, which disentangles these programs from the details of authentication. Thus, if authentication details should be changed for a computer, you can alter the PAM configuration without making changes to individual programs. Depending on the PAM configuration, you may be able to change just one configuration file to alter the way many services authenticate users.

Summarize the important PAM configuration files.   PAM uses a configuration file, /etc/ pam.conf, or (more commonly) multiple files in the /etc/pam.d directory. In the latter case, most of the files configure servers or other login tools with similar names, such as gdm for the GDM GUI login server. Some files in /etc/pam.d, however, may be referred to by other files. These included files define stacks that are common to several services.

Distinguish between PAM and NSS.   The Pluggable Authentication Modules (PAM) system is responsible for authenticating users, handling non-authentication access restrictions, managing login sessions, and changing passwords. The Name Service Switch (NSS), by contrast, manages the relationship between user IDs (UIDs) and usernames, keeps track of users' home directories, and performs other less security-related account tasks. Both systems must use the same account database in order for user accounts to work correctly.

Explain the purpose of TCP Wrappers.   TCP Wrappers exists to protect servers from unauthorized or known bad sites and users. It can restrict access based on IP address, hostname, or related information (even including usernames in some cases). By placing these restrictions in the TCP Wrappers package, the code for simple servers can be kept simple; however, either the server must link to the TCP Wrappers library, `libwrap`, or the server must be run via a super server, such as `inetd`.

Describe why scans for open ports are important.   Computers are dynamic systems; their configurations can change because of routine software updates, because of deliberate changes, or even because of accidental changes. Detecting changes that might pose security threats is therefore important. In the Linux world, one of the greatest security threats is a system that runs a server you don't know about, since it's hard to protect against threats posed by an unknown server. Thus, periodically scanning for open ports is an important system administration task.

Summarize some methods of detecting intrusion attempts.   Intruders can be detected by monitoring network activity. One method of doing this is monitoring low-level network packets using a tool such as Snort, which can scan for suspicious network packets and alert you when it finds them. Another tool is Fail2Ban, which can check your log files for repeated login failures and then automatically block the offending IP address or notify you of the problem.

Summarize methods of keeping up-to-date with security matters.   Several organizations, such as CERT/CC, CIAC, Security Focus, and Linux Security, run Web sites or mailing lists devoted to security issues. You can check these Web sites from time to time, subscribe to their mailing lists, or use RSS feeds to monitor the latest security developments. Distributions' and individual products' Web sites, as well as Usenet newsgroups, can also be valuable sources of security information.

Review Questions

1. You're using an LDAP server for authentication, and you want to ensure that users have local home directories whenever they log into a computer. What line would you add to your PAM configuration to ensure that home directories are created, if necessary?

   A. `account  requisite  pam_securetty.so  umask=0022`

   B. `session  required  pam_unix.so  skel=/etc/skel`

   C. `auth  sufficient  pam_deny.so skel=/etc/skel`

   D. `session  required  pam_mkhomedir.so skel=/etc/skel umask=0022`

2. What is the purpose of the `pam_cracklib.so` module?

   A. It identifies known crackers by their IP addresses as part of an `account` stack.

   B. It tests the strength of a password as part of a `password` stack.

   C. It presents humorous sayings to users as part of a `session` stack.

   D. It verifies that a user's account hasn't been cracked as part of an `auth` stack.

3. The `/etc/pam.d/login` file includes the following `auth` stack. Which authentication system does the `login` tool use?

   ```
   auth        required      pam_securetty.so
   auth        include       system-login
   ```

   A. Standard Unix/Linux local accounts

   B. An LDAP server

   C. A Winbind server

   D. The correct answer cannot be determined from the provided information

4. Where are user passwords normally stored on a Linux computer configured to use shadow passwords and `pam_unix.so` as the sole authentication method?

   A. `/etc/shadow`

   B. `/var/shadow-pw`

   C. `/var/accounts/shadow/pass.db`

   D. `/etc/passwd`

5. What feature is present on each non-comment line of `/etc/pam.conf` that's *not* present in the files in the `/etc/pam.d` directory?

   A. A management group name

   B. A service name

   C. A control flag

   D. A module filename

6. What file would you edit to ensure that Linux can map usernames to UID values when you reconfigure Linux to use a Windows domain controller for user authentication?

    A. `/etc/nsswitch.conf`

    B. `/etc/passwd`

    C. `/etc/pam.d/winbind`

    D. `/etc/winbind/conf`

7. Your login server is using PAM and you want to limit users' access to system resources. Which configuration file will you need to edit?

    A. `/etc/limits.conf`

    B. `/etc/pam/limits.conf`

    C. `/etc/security/limits.conf`

    D. `/etc/security/pam/limits.conf`

8. What is the purpose of the `session` PAM management group?

    A. It sets up the environment for a login session and cleans up when the user logs out.

    B. It performs authentication based on a username and password or perhaps some other criteria, such as a biometric scan.

    C. It validates or denies a login based on non-authentication data, such as an IP address.

    D. It changes the password when the user requests a password change.

9. What can be said about how usernames are mapped to user IDs, based on the following lines from the NSS configuration file?

    ```
    passwd:      compat ldap
    shadow:      compat ldap
    group:       compat ldap
    ```

    A. LDAP is called in compatibility mode.

    B. LDAP is used after local files.

    C. The computer uses LDAP accounts only.

    D. Nothing can be concluded from these lines alone.

10. A server/computer combination appears in both `hosts.allow` and `hosts.deny`. What's the result of this configuration when TCP Wrappers runs?

    A. TCP Wrappers refuses to run and logs an error in `/var/log/messages`.

    B. The system's administrator is paged to decide whether to allow access.

    C. `hosts.deny` takes precedence; the client is denied access to the server.

    D. `hosts.allow` takes precedence; the client is granted access to the server.

11. What utility do you call in /etc/inetd.conf to ensure that a server run via inetd uses TCP Wrappers?

    A. tcpd

    B. libwrap

    C. wrapd

    D. tcpwrap

12. What is the best way to remain abreast of security developments?

    A. Read the CERT/CC website on a regular basis.

    B. Subscribe to and read the Bugtraq mailing list.

    C. Check your distribution's security Web page on a regular basis.

    D. All of the above.

13. Which of the following tools is best suited for monitoring activity directed at multiple computers?

    A. netstat

    B. iptables

    C. Snort

    D. Fail2Ban

14. How can the telnet program be a useful security tool? (Select all that apply.)

    A. You can use it to monitor network packets directed at a specific computer.

    B. You can use it to check for the presence of a server on a specific TCP port on a specific computer.

    C. You can issue protocol-specific commands to see how a server responds to them.

    D. You can use it to scan for TCP and UDP servers on a whole network's computers.

15. A Snort IDS is located on a small network behind a network address translation (NAT) router, which is configured to pass no incoming connections to the protected network. This network uses a hub and has Samba, NFS, and SSH servers running on it. A Web server system is located outside the protected network, on the same exterior network as the NAT router. Which of the following describes the types of malicious attacks the Snort IDS might detect?

    A. It can detect attacks that originate on the local network and that are directed at the originating machines' loopback interfaces.

    B. It can detect attacks that originate from the Internet and that are directed at the Web server that runs alongside the NAT router.

    C. It can detect attacks that originate on the local network and that are directed to other computers on that network, to the Web server, or to the Internet at large.

    D. It can detect attacks that originate from the Internet and that are directed at the local Samba, NFS, or SSH servers.

16. Which of the following programs uses local system calls to locate local ports that are currently open?

    A. netstat

    B. nmap

    C. nc

    D. nessus

17. You've scanned your local network and discovered that your Web server computer has an open SSH port. This port is used only from the local network in order to update the Web server's files, but it's accessible to the Internet at large. Which of the following measures might you take to improve security while maintaining the utility of the SSH server on this computer? (Select all that apply.)

    A. Create iptables rules on the Web server computer to limit the IP addresses that can connect to the SSH port.

    B. Reconfigure the network to place the SSH server outside of a protective firewall, configuring that firewall to block all SSH traffic.

    C. Reconfigure the computer's SysV or Upstart startup scripts to keep the SSH server program from starting up unnecessarily on the Web server computer.

    D. Create iptables rules on the network's router to limit the IP addresses that can connect to the SSH port.

18. Which of the following is a tool that's designed to monitor and restrict access to a single computer?

    A. Snort

    B. Fail2Ban

    C. Telnet

    D. BIND

19. What is wrong with the following /etc/inetd.conf entry?

    ```
    imap stream tcp nowait root /usr/sbin/tcpd
    ```

    A. It's missing a call to TCP Wrappers.

    B. It's missing a protocol name.

    C. It's missing the name of the server to be launched.

    D. Nothing is wrong with this entry.

20. Which organization tracks known vulnerabilities in operating systems?

    A. FSF

    B. CERT

    C. OSI

    D. SourceForge

Answers to Review Questions

1. **D.** The `pam_mkhomedir.so` module creates a home directory for the user if one doesn't already exist, and option D shows a valid configuration for its use, so this option is correct. The `pam_securetty.so` module is typically used to prevent direct root logins from anything but the console device, so option A is incorrect; `pam_unix.so` is the module for handling standard local Linux accounts, so option B is incorrect; and `pam_deny.so` always fails, giving a default-fail option for stacks that might otherwise produce ambiguous or successful results, so option C is incorrect.

2. **B.** The `pam_cracklib.so` module does as option B specifies; it's intended to force users to enter good passwords when they change their passwords. Option A could be an imperfect description of the Fail2Ban program, but this program isn't part of PAM, much less the `pam_cracklib.so` module. Humorous sayings can be generated and displayed at login time by the `fortune` program, but not by the `pam_cracklib.so` module, so option C is incorrect. Although a tool to do as option D describes would be very useful, it would also be very difficult to write, and this option certainly does not describe `pam_cracklib.so`.

3. **D.** The specified `auth` stack calls `pam_securetty.so`, which can restrict access based on the terminal used, and includes the contents of the `system-login` file. Thus, which authentication system (or systems) is used depends on the contents of that file, which the question does not present, making option D correct. Any, all, or none of options A, B, and C might be correct.

4. **A.** The `/etc/shadow` file holds passwords on systems configured to use shadow passwords with `pam_unix.so`. Options B and C both describe fictitious files. The `/etc/passwd` file is real, and it holds account information but not actual passwords when shadow passwords are enabled (as they are by default with all modern Linux distributions).

5. **B.** The `/etc/pam.conf` file can take the place of all the files in `/etc/pam.d`; but to do so, it needs a way to associate each stack with a particular service, so each `/etc/pam.conf` file entry begins with a service name, as option B specifies. Options A, C, and D all describe features that are present in entries for both `/etc/pam.conf` and the files in `/etc/pam.d`. (Options passed to the module may also appear in both file types.)

6. **A.** The Name Service Switch (NSS) is responsible for mapping usernames to user ID (UID) values, and NSS's configuration file is `/etc/nsswitch.conf`. Thus, you would edit this file (making option A correct) to ensure that usernames and UID values are correctly linked when you change the authentication system. Ordinarily, this mapping appears in `/etc/passwd`, but since the question explicitly states that the computer has been reconfigured to use a Windows domain controller, option B is incorrect. The files in options C and D are both fictitious, although the name of the service that authenticates against Windows domain controllers is Winbind.

7. C. The `/etc/security/limits.conf` file holds the configuration settings that will allow you to limit users' access, making option C correct. Options A, B, and D do not give the correct path to this file.

8. A. Option A correctly describes the function of the `session` management group and so is correct. Options B, C, and D describe the functions of the `auth`, `account`, and `password` management groups, respectively, and so are incorrect answers.

9. B. The order of entries in the NSS configuration file (`/etc/nsswitch.conf`) determines the order in which username/UID mappings are carried out. Since the `compat` entry typically refers to local account databases and `ldap` refers to an LDAP server, the effect is that the local account database will be consulted first, followed by an LDAP server, making option B correct. This configuration does not set a "compatibility mode" for LDAP access, contrary to option A. If option C were correct, there would be no `compat` entries on any of the lines; `ldap` would be used alone. Because option B is correct, option D cannot be correct.

10. D. TCP Wrappers uses this feature to allow you to override broad denials by adding more specific explicit access permissions to `hosts.allow`, as when setting a default deny policy (`ALL : ALL`) in `hosts.deny`.

11. A. You configure a super server to call `tcpd`, and you pass that program the name of the real server and its arguments to use TCP Wrappers via a super server. Thus, option A is correct. Some servers can use TCP Wrappers more directly, via the `libwrap` library; however, `libwrap` isn't referenced in `/etc/inetd.conf`, and you can't be sure that any given server uses it, making option B incorrect. Options C and D are both fictitious programs and so are incorrect.

12. D. To obtain the best possible view of security developments, you should consult as many sources as possible. The CERT/CC website, the Bugtraq mailing list, and your distribution's security page are three good sources of information (but by no means the only three available). Consulting just one of these sources may not be adequate because an obscure issue that's important to you might escape notice on a single source.

13. C. Snort is able to monitor network activity directed at multiple computers, given the appropriate network infrastructure, thus providing an early alert system for the network as a whole. The `netstat` utility can check for open ports on a single computer, but it can't monitor for attacks on multiple systems. The `iptables` utility implements Linux firewall rules, but it can't, by itself, monitor an entire network's activity. The Fail2Ban program monitors a server's log files for evidence of failed login attempts and can block the attacking system using `iptables` or other access restrictions, but this won't monitor an entire network for activity.

14. B, C. Telnet was designed as a simple remote text-mode login protocol, but the `telnet` client can connect to any TCP port and so can be used to check for TCP servers, as option B suggests. If the protocol supports text-mode commands, you can also use `telnet` to issue these commands manually, as option C suggests. The `telnet` program can't monitor network packets in the way option A suggests; that task is better handled by a packet sniffer such as Snort. Because Telnet uses TCP rather than UDP, option D is incorrect. (Using `telnet` to scan more than a few ports would also be quite tedious.)

15. C. Given the placement of the Snort system, it can monitor traffic on the local network. Since this network is well protected by the NAT router, outside attacks against the local Samba, NFS, and SSH servers are unlikely to reach the protected network, so such external attacks won't be detected. The types of local attacks described in option C could be detected, though. Local attacks against loopback interfaces will not reach the network wires and so will not be detected, either.

16. A. Local open ports can be found with the `netstat` program, which uses local system calls to locate ports that are currently open. The `nmap` and `nessus` programs can locate open ports on the local computer or on other computers by sending network probes to all or a subset of the ports on the target computer. `nc` is a tool that can be used to create customized scripts for performing network security scans.

17. A, D. The `iptables` rules described in options A and D can both limit who may access the SSH server. Properly implemented, either approach can be a useful security measure. (Ideally, you can implement both for added security.) Option B is the *opposite* of a useful security measure; placing the system *inside* a firewall can protect it from unwanted outside access, but option B will limit access to the computer from the legitimate users on the inside network. Option C will completely shut down the SSH server. Although this might be a useful security measure, it will make it difficult for legitimate users to update the server's Web site, which the question explicitly states must remain possible.

18. B. Fail2Ban is a tool that's designed to monitor log files for evidence of intrusion attempts and restrict access to a single computer if such evidence is found, so option B is correct. Snort is able to monitor network activity directed at multiple computers; its purpose is broader than stated in the question, so option A is incorrect. Telnet is a remote login protocol, so option C is incorrect. BIND is used to provide name resolution, so option D is incorrect.

19. C. The specified entry is missing the name of the server that should be launched; when `tcpd` is used, as in this example, the ultimate server name should appear after the call to `tcpd`. Thus, option C is correct. The `tcpd` binary is TCP Wrappers, so option A is incorrect. (TCP Wrappers use via `inetd` is also optional, so even if it had been missing, option A would be incorrect.) The protocol name appears in the first column of the entry, and it's present (`imap`), so option B is incorrect. Because option C was correct, option D cannot be correct.

20. B. The Computer Emergency Response Team (CERT) tracks known vulnerabilities, so option B is correct. The Free Software Foundation (FSF), the Open Source Initiative (OSI), and the SourceForge Web site all contribute greatly to the Linux operating system but are not focused on vulnerabilities within the operating system, so options A, C, and D are all incorrect.

Chapter

11

System Troubleshooting I: Boot and Kernel Problems

THE FOLLOWING LINUX PROFESSIONAL INSTITUTE OBJECTIVES ARE COVERED IN THIS CHAPTER:

✓ **213.1 Identifying boot stages and troubleshooting bootloaders (weight: 4)**

✓ **213.2 General troubleshooting (weight: 5)**

Like all modern operating systems, Linux is complex, and complexity means that many things can go wrong. Therefore, it's imperative that you know how to track down the causes of problems and solve them. This chapter and the next one both cover troubleshooting. This chapter covers low-level issues relating to booting the system, the kernel, and hardware. The next chapter covers troubleshooting issues related to system resources and the user environment.

Your best tools when troubleshooting are attention to detail, the ability to reason about a problem, and a basic knowledge of the systems involved in the problem. It's often helpful to apply basic scientific principles to troubleshooting. Therefore, this chapter begins with a description of some general troubleshooting techniques that can work on a wide variety of problems. Because many problems require knowledge of specific systems, this chapter proceeds to cover some of them, beginning with problems relating to the boot loader and initial RAM disk. The latter part of this chapter describes a variety of miscellaneous problems, mostly related to the kernel and hardware.

Approaching a Problem

Troubleshooting is basically problem solving, and problem-solving skills you learn in contexts other than computers can be useful in locating and resolving computer difficulties. Several general-purpose strategies that are often helpful include:

Generate and Test Hypotheses   It's often helpful to think about computer problems scientifically. Scientists generate hypotheses about the world and devise experiments to test them. Just so, you can generate a hypothesis about the cause of a problem and then test it. For instance, you might suspect that a server is running out of memory. If so, you can use tools such as free, ps, and top to monitor memory use or add swap space to the system. Sometimes a test also serves as a possible solution, such as replacing a bad cable or perhaps even increasing swap space. Other times, you might want to take some other step as a permanent solution, such as adding RAM to the computer.

Narrow the Problem   Sometimes you can narrow the range of possible causes in a systematic way. Ideally, if you can eliminate half the possible causes, then half of those that remain, and so on, you'll find the solution quite quickly. In practice, of course, this approach might not work; it tends to work best when the possible causes have some clearly defined range, such as one unknown but misbehaving computer on a network—you can isolate groups of computers until you find the one computer that's causing problems.

Study the Documentation   If you know the problem is with a particular piece of hardware or software, consult its documentation. Perhaps the problem is mentioned—or maybe you've misconfigured something and can learn that fact by reading the documentation.

Compare with Another System   If possible, compare the problem behavior with a working system. This may not be possible if you're configuring a tool for the first time, but if you're having problems with one of several similar computers, comparing configuration files, log entries, and so on, can be a good way to identify the source of the problem.

Use Diagnostic Tools   Many computer systems provide diagnostic tools, such as packet sniffers for network traffic and `fsck` for filesystem troubles. Using such tools can help you diagnose problems; however, you must be aware of the existence of these tools and know how to use them. Some programs have run-time options to increase the verbosity of their output or log file entries. Using such an option can be very helpful.

Use an Emergency System   Even if your computer won't boot, you may be able to boot the computer with an emergency system. Linux distributions' installation discs often serve this purpose, or you can use a tool such as the System Rescue CD (`http://www.sysresccd .org`) or PartedMagic (`http://partedmagic.com`) to boot the computer enough to check filesystems, examine and change configuration files, and so on.

Consult Authorities   If you know somebody with more skill than you in an area, consult that person. If you don't know such a person, you can try a book or an online search for information. Typing relevant keywords in a Web search engine is likely to produce useful results. Usenet newsgroups, Web forums, Internet Relay Chat (IRC) discussion groups, and other online resources can also be valuable sources of information.

These actions can help you solve many problems. As a general rule, thinking methodically and knowing as much as possible about the troubled subsystem are probably the best ways to fix the problem. Therefore, you should take a deep breath, restrain the urge to throw the recalcitrant computer off the roof of the nearest skyscraper, and read as much as you can. If necessary, set aside an hour or two just to read, thus expanding your knowledge base (and perhaps calming your nerves).

Troubleshooting Boot Problems

One of the most troubling classes of problems is boot problems. If your computer won't boot, you'll find it difficult to do anything with it. (This is where the advice to use an emergency disc can be so important.) Chapter 1, "System Startup and Advanced System Management," describes the basics of boot loader configuration and use, so you may want to review that chapter before proceeding. Troubleshooting the boot process includes dealing with hardware initialization, identifying your boot loader, fixing boot loader problems, fixing problems with the initial RAM disk, and fixing problems that occur soon after the Linux kernel has taken over the computer.

Initializing Hardware

Before the boot loader begins its work, some hardware must be initialized. This process begins with the computer's firmware—the Basic Input/Output System (BIOS), the Extensible Firmware Interface (EFI), or other code that's built into the computer's motherboard. Typically, the firmware includes options to enable or disable hardware devices built into the motherboard. It may also include options that can affect how resources are allocated to specific devices—for instance, how interrupts are assigned to different devices.

If firmware options are set incorrectly, the result can be poor performance, unreliable operation, an inability to use some hardware devices, or a variety of other problems. If you suspect such problems, you may have to reboot and, at a critical point in the boot process (before the boot loader appears), press a special key, such as Delete or F10. An on-screen prompt may tell you what to press to enter the setup utility, but this prompt may appear and disappear so quickly you won't be able to read it. Consult your computer's or motherboard's documentation if you need help.

Once you're in the firmware's setup utility, you should be able to locate various performance options. Most utilities include an option to reset all the options to the default values. This can be a good place to start. You can also search for options relating to specific subsystems. If you're having disk problems, for instance, you can try changing options relating to the disk controller. General reliability problems can sometimes be fixed by adjusting CPU or memory features, but details are so system-specific that more precise advice is impossible to provide. Consulting online authorities, including Web forums and the manufacturer's help line, can be valuable if you have such problems.

Beyond the firmware, additional hardware initialization is performed by the kernel as it probes for specific devices. Some hardware drivers are built into the main kernel file, but others are loaded as modules. Sometimes it's necessary to pass options to the kernel or to modules to change the way the kernel probes for or initializes hardware. This topic is covered in Chapter 1 and Chapter 2, "Linux Kernel Configuration."

Identifying Your Boot Loader

The first step to resolving boot loader problems is identifying your boot loader. Several boot loaders for the *x*86 and *x*86-64 platforms are common in the Linux world:

GRUB Legacy   The Grand Unified Boot Loader (GRUB; http://www.gnu.org/software/grub/) was common from soon after 2000 through approximately 2010. It can directly boot Linux, FreeBSD, Solaris, and several other OS kernels on BIOS-based computers; and through the use of a chain loader, it can boot DOS, Windows, and most other OSs. The word *Legacy* has been added to its name to distinguish it from its successor.

GRUB 2   This boot loader is the successor to GRUB Legacy (`http://www.gnu.org/software/grub/`). Begun in 2008, some distributions began adopting it as the default boot loader in 2009 and 2010, so it's become fairly common, although it has not completely supplanted GRUB Legacy at press time. It can work with both BIOS and the EFI.

BURG   The Brand-new Universal LoadeR from GRUB (BURG; `https://launchpad.net/burg`) is a variant of GRUB 2 that emphasizes graphical themes in the boot menu. It shares most of GRUB 2's features, including support for both BIOS and EFI systems.

LILO   The Linux Loader (LILO; `http://freshmeat.net/projects/lilo/`) was the most common Linux boot loader prior to 2000. It's more primitive than GRUB Legacy, which can be both a plus and a minus. It can boot Linux kernels or, through a chain-loading mechanism, most other OSs, on BIOS-based computers.

ELILO   This boot loader, based at `http://sourceforge.net/projects/elilo/`, is a LILO-like boot loader for EFI-based computers.

rEFIt   This boot loader, based at `http://refit.sourceforge.net`, is a popular boot loader on computers that use EFI rather than the older BIOS firmware. In practice, rEFIt is usually paired with GRUB 2 or some other boot loader. It's most commonly used on computers that dual-boot Linux and Mac OS X.

loadlin   You can boot Linux from DOS using this unusual boot loader, which you can obtain from `http://youpibouh.thefreecat.org/loadlin/`. In years past, `loadlin` was a popular way to launch Linux installers, but it has fallen into obscurity in recent years.

Syslinux   This boot loader is actually a family of related boot loaders intended for specialized tasks, such as booting Linux from an optical disc (ISOLINUX), from certain Linux filesystems (EXTLINUX), from a network (PXELINUX), or from a FAT filesystem (SYSLINUX). It's most often used on Linux installation and emergency discs. You can read more at `http://syslinux.zytor.com`.

The DOS/Windows Boot Loader   Out of the box, most computers use the standard DOS/Windows boot loader, which is very simple. This BIOS boot loader hands off control to a partition that's marked with a "boot" or "active" flag. This partition in turn must have its own boot loader installed in it. LILO and both versions of GRUB can install themselves in a Linux partition so that the DOS/Windows boot loader can chain-load to these Linux boot loaders.

EFI   The EFI firmware includes its own boot loader; however, this boot loader, like the DOS/Windows boot loader, can't directly boot a Linux kernel. Thus, EFI systems still need a Linux-aware boot loader, such as GRUB 2 or ELILO, to boot Linux. The EFI boots the Linux-aware boot loader, which then boots Linux.

Third-Party Boot Loaders   Many companies and individuals have released commercial and freeware boot loaders over the years. Most of these boot loaders can't boot Linux directly, but they can chain-load a Linux boot loader, such as LILO or GRUB.

If your computer uses a CPU other than the popular *x*86 or *x*86-64 series, chances are it uses a boot loader not described here. (Some such computers use EFI, though, and so may use an EFI-capable boot loader from the preceding list.) Many Linux boot loaders for such platforms are modeled after LILO.

This list of boot loaders can be quite overwhelming if you're not familiar with the field. In practice, chances are your computer uses GRUB Legacy or GRUB 2, particularly if it's BIOS-based. If it uses the newer EFI, chances are your computer uses some combination of rEFIt, GRUB 2, and perhaps ELILO.

One way to identify your boot loader is to use the Boot Info Script (http://sourceforge.net/projects/bootinfoscript/). This script, which you can run from an emergency boot disc, scans your hard disk for boot loader signatures, partition information, and so on, and generates a report that it saves as RESULTS.txt. The boot loader is identified in the first few lines of this file:

```
========================= Boot Info Summary: ============================
```

```
=> Grub 2 is installed in the MBR of /dev/sda and looks at sector 40 of the
   same hard drive for core.img, core.img is at this location on /dev/sda
   and looks for (UUID=1445adc8-3145-4fcb-86df-701f0f711943)/grub.
```

This example clearly identifies the boot loader as GRUB 2; it's installed in the Master Boot Record (MBR) of the first disk (/dev/sda), and subsequent lines of output identify where GRUB 2 looks for additional boot code (core.img, located at sector 40 in this example) and where the GRUB files are installed (the /grub directory on the partition that holds a filesystem with a Universally Unique ID [UUID] of 1445adc8-3145-4fcb-86df-701f0f711943).

Although the Boot Info Script is not mentioned in the LPIC-2 objectives, this script is the single most useful diagnostic tool for identifying and resolving boot problems. In addition to locating the boot loader's main code locations and configuration files, the script identifies the filesystems in use on each of the computer's partitions, displays the partition tables on all the disks, summarizes the UUIDs of all the filesystems on the computer, displays the boot loader configuration file's contents, and displays the contents of /etc/fstab.

Locating Boot Loader Files and Code

On a properly functioning Linux system, the boot loader is installed in several different locations. Details vary depending on the boot loader, the partition table type, and even the boot loader options. Key locations on BIOS-based computers include the following:

MBR   The MBR holds the first code executed from the hard disk in a normal disk-based boot of the computer. (It also holds the MBR partition table.) On most Linux systems, part of GRUB Legacy or GRUB 2 resides in the MBR; however, the MBR could contain LILO, a DOS/Windows boot loader, or some other boot loader. In most such cases, the boot loader will then load a Linux-capable boot loader from some other location.

Unallocated Post-MBR Sectors   On most disks that are partitioned using the MBR system, the 62 sectors immediately following the MBR are officially unallocated. Boot loaders commonly make use of this space to hold extra code that won't fit in the MBR. This practice, however, can sometimes lead to problems, since some other utilities also try to use this space. If such a tool overwrites part of GRUB, your system will no longer boot. (The Boot Info Script can be very useful in identifying this problem; it will report that the boot loader is present in the MBR but that `core.img` isn't present where it should be.)

The BIOS Boot Partition   This partition type is used by GRUB 2 on systems that use the new Globally Unique Identifier (GUID) Partition Table (GPT) system to hold extra boot code. Essentially, the BIOS Boot Partition replaces the unallocated post-MBR sectors just described. Because the BIOS Boot Partition is properly allocated in the partition table, this makes GPT safer from some types of damage than MBR—in theory. (In practice, other factors can level the playing field.) Although the presence of a BIOS Boot Partition on a GPT disk does not positively identify the disk as using GRUB 2, it's a good indication that somebody intended to use GRUB 2, or at least wanted to leave open the possibility of doing so. GNU Parted identifies this partition type with a `bios_grub` tag, whereas `gdisk` identifies it as having a type code of EF02. Consult `http://grub.enbug.org/BIOS_Boot_Partition` for more information on this partition type.

A Linux Partition's Boot Sector   The first sector of a Linux partition can be used by a boot loader, much like the MBR of a disk. The boot loader in the MBR can then redirect the boot process to the Linux partition, even if the MBR-based boot loader is not capable of directly booting a Linux kernel.

Boot Support Files   Boot code can reside in files that the boot loader reads at boot time. In some sense, the Linux kernel and initial RAM disk are examples of such files; however, the boot loader can store its own code in such files, as well. GRUB 2 is particularly dependent on such files, which it stores in `/boot/grub` (some distributions use `/boot/grub2` instead).

Pre-installation Configuration Files   LILO and GRUB 2 both rely on configuration files that are located in the `/etc` directory. For LILO, the relevant file is `/etc/lilo.conf`; for GRUB 2, the files reside in the `/etc/grub.d` directory. These files are not read when the boot loader boots the computer, but they are used to modify the boot loader installation by other utilities. The presence of these files can be a good clue that a computer uses a particular boot loader; however, it's possible for files to remain behind after a boot loader has been replaced by a new one.

Boot-Time Configuration Files   Both GRUB Legacy and GRUB 2 rely on files in the Linux filesystem at boot time. For GRUB Legacy, these files are typically called `/boot/grub/menu.lst` or `/boot/grub/grub.conf`, depending on the distribution. For GRUB 2, the main file is usually called /boot/grub/grub.cfg, but some distributions place the file in /boot/grub2 rather than in /boot/grub. Additional files in /boot/grub support GRUB in both cases. As with the pre-installation configuration files, the presence of these files is indicative of the use of a particular boot loader, but this isn't certain.

Program Binaries   Each boot loader includes binary program files that are used to install boot loader code to the MBR, the Linux boot partition, or other locations; or to adjust the ultimate boot configuration. For LILO, the key file is called lilo. For GRUB Legacy and GRUB 2, grub-install is the installation program file.

Thus, if you're not certain what boot loader your computer uses, you should search for the presence of certain files, as summarized in Table 11.1. Of course, the boot loader in operation is stored in the MBR, the Linux partition's boot sector, or some other partition on the disk. The most reliable way to identify actual boot code is to use the Boot Info Script.

TABLE 11.1   Boot loaders and their identifying configuration files

Boot loader	Configuration files
LILO	/etc/lilo.conf
GRUB Legacy	/boot/grub/menu.1st or /boot/grub/grub.conf
GRUB 2	/etc/grub.d directory; /boot/grub/grub.cfg or /boot/grub2/grub.cfg; possibly a BIOS Boot Partition on GPT disks

If your computer uses EFI rather than a BIOS, details will vary from those described here. EFI-based computers that also use GRUB 2 use the same GRUB 2 configuration files as described for BIOS-based computers, but GRUB 2 places an EFI boot file on the EFI System Partition (ESP), which is a special partition used to store drivers, boot loader code, and similar low-level files. If you use rEFIt, ELILO, or some other EFI boot loader, you should consult its documentation to learn where it stores its files. The same advice applies if you use one of the less common or more specialized BIOS boot loaders.

The two most common Linux boot loaders today, GRUB Legacy and GRUB 2, both place files in /boot/grub. (For this reason, some distributions change GRUB 2's file location to /boot/grub2, so that both boot loaders can be installed simultaneously.) GRUB Legacy has relatively few files in that location, including its configuration file, a device .map file that maps Linux and GRUB device identifiers, and a variety of boot code files that include stage in their names. GRUB 2 places many more files in its version of /boot/grub. Most of these files have names that end in .mod; these are GRUB 2 *modules*—code that the boot loader can access only if required. Modules enable GRUB 2 to read filesystems, handle various types of video hardware, and so on.

The most common configuration involves a boot loader installed on a hard disk. Most removable disks, including Universal Serial Bus (USB) flash drives, work just like hard disks from a boot loader perspective. Floppy disks work slightly differently, but many boot loaders, including GRUB and LILO, can be installed on a floppy disk. Unlike hard disks, floppy disks aren't partitioned, so a floppy is more like a partition from a software perspective. Optical discs, as suggested earlier, are still more different. They typically use a software standard known as *El Torito* to define how they boot. ISOLINUX is the usual Linux boot loader for optical disks.

Interpreting Boot Loader Error Messages

Boot problems often create annoyingly cryptic error messages. This is because the boot loader, particularly in its early stages, must be unusually compact; there's just not much space in the code to store long error messages. Thus, interpreting boot loader error messages can be difficult. This task is different for LILO, GRUB Legacy, and GRUB 2.

Sometimes you can work around boot loader problems by employing Super GRUB Disk (http://www.supergrubdisk.org), which is a bootable CD-R that looks for and uses an installation's GRUB configuration files. Versions are available for both GRUB Legacy and GRUB 2. Super GRUB Disk enables you to bypass problems with a damaged GRUB boot code installation, provided the system's GRUB configuration file is intact and correct. Once you've booted the system, you can re-install GRUB by using grub-install.

Interpreting LILO Error Messages

As it's starting up, LILO displays its name on the screen. If it encounters an error, it alters this display to include an error code of some type. The end result is *part* of the string LILO, sometimes with an error code appended. Table 11.2 summarizes the common LILO error codes.

TABLE 11.2   LILO error codes

Error code	Meaning
(nothing)	LILO hasn't loaded. Such problems may indicate that LILO isn't installed in the MBR, that the Linux partition is damaged, or that an earlier boot loader might be unable to load LILO from a Linux partition.
L##	LILO's first stage has loaded, but it's unable to locate its second stage (normally stored in /boot/boot.b). The two digits following L can help further diagnose the problem; consult the LILO documentation for details.

TABLE 11.2   LILO error codes *(continued)*

Error code	Meaning
LI	Linux's first stage has loaded, and it has located /boot/boot.b; but this second stage cannot be run.
LI1010...	In this error code, the digits 10 repeat endlessly. This error indicates that LILO is unable to locate your kernel image. One common cause is recompiling your kernel and copying it over the old one without re-running the lilo command.
LIL	The second-stage boot loader can load and run but can't read the /boot/map file. This frequently indicates a hardware problem or a disk geometry mismatch.
LIL?	LILO has loaded its second-stage boot loader to the wrong address. This can happen if you move /boot/boot.b without re-running lilo.
LIL-	LILO has detected damage to the /boot/map file. This can happen if you move this file without re-running lilo.
LILO	If LILO displays this full string, any subsequent boot difficulties are likely the result of kernel or initial RAM disk problems.

LILO is fairly simple; although it enables you to launch an OS or Linux kernel by typing its name or selecting it from a list, it offers little in the way of interactive debugging facilities. If LILO won't boot your computer because of a misconfiguration in /etc/lilo .conf, you have little choice but to boot an emergency disc, edit the configuration file, and re-install LILO to the MBR or the Linux boot partition.

If you need to change your /etc/lilo.conf file, be sure to type lilo as root after you're done. LILO can't read its configuration file at boot time; instead, it relies on the Linux lilo command to interpret the configuration file and store critical features in a more compact form inside the LILO code that's read at boot time. In fact, because typing lilo as root re-installs the LILO boot code, this command will overcome a variety of LILO problems.

Interpreting GRUB Legacy Error Messages

GRUB Legacy runs in three stages, known as Stage 1, Stage 1.5, and Stage 2. Stage 1 is the first part of the GRUB Legacy boot process (typically installed in the MBR), Stage 1.5

code resides after the MBR on the disk, and Stage 2 code is loaded from files on the boot partition. Each stage has its own error messages. Table 11.3 summarizes the Stage 1 error messages.

TABLE 11.3 GRUB Stage 1 error messages

Error message	Stage	Meaning
Hard disk Error	1	The hard disk geometry could not be determined.
Floppy Error	1	The floppy disk geometry could not be determined.
Read Error	1	The hard disk or floppy disk could not be read.
Geom Error	1	The file being read from the disk resides outside of the area supported by the BIOS.

Stage 1 errors tend to be very serious. If GRUB Legacy can't determine the disk's geometry, it could be that you need to adjust the BIOS settings for the hard disk. A read error could indicate a failing hard disk or a need to adjust BIOS settings for the hard disk. A geometry error is rare with modern hardware. With older hardware, you may need to adjust your partitions and re-install Linux. Create a separate /boot partition as early on the disk as you can; this will ensure that the kernel, the initial RAM disk, and all of GRUB's boot-time configuration files fall under whatever limit the old BIOS imposes. (BIOS limits on hard disk size have varied over the years, but 504 MiB and a bit under 8 GiB are two limits from years past.)

Stage 1.5 error messages take the form Error *num*, where *num* is a number that corresponds to a Stage 2 error. A total of 34 Stage 2 errors are documented in the GRUB Legacy documentation (http://www.gnu.org/software/grub/manual/legacy/Stage2-errors.html). Each includes a description, such as Invalid device requested. Consult the GRUB Legacy documentation if you need to interpret these errors, which are numerous.

Interpreting GRUB 2 Error Messages

If GRUB 2 is badly misconfigured, you're likely to end up seeing the GRUB rescue shell:

grub>

This happens when GRUB can't locate the /boot/grub/grub.cfg file on your hard disk. The usual cause is that GRUB's internal prefix environment variable, which holds the location of the directory in which that file is found, is set incorrectly. You can use the ls command to locate the correct location and set the prefix environment variable. To begin, you should probably use ls alone to view the available partitions and then look inside them until you find the Linux root (/) or /boot partition:

```
grub> ls
(hd0) (hd0,gpt5) (hd0,gpt4) (hd0,gpt3) (hd0,gpt2) (hd0,gpt1)
grub> ls (hd0,gpt5)/
abi-2.6.31-22-generic grub/ initrd.img-2.6.31-22-generic
memtest86+.bin System.map-2.6.31-22-generic vmcoreinfo-2.6.31-22-generic
vmlinuz-2.6.31-22-generic
```

Under recent versions of GRUB 2, partitions may be identified by disk device and number alone, as in (hd0,5), or with a code for the partition table type prepended to the partition number, as in (hd0,gpt5) or (hd0,mbr5). The latter format removes ambiguity in case a disk has one partition table embedded within another or used side by side.

To see into a partition, you must pass a trailing slash (/) after its identifier, as in (hd0,gpt5)/; omitting the slash displays information on the filesystem used on the partition. This example shows a discovery of the contents of a separate /boot partition on the first try. (If the /boot directory is on the root partition, then you'd want to locate the root partition and include the path to GRUB 2's directory from there in the following commands.) With the /boot directory, and therefore /boot/grub, discovered, you can set the prefix and root variables to point to the GRUB directory and the partition on which it resides, respectively:

```
grub> set prefix=(hd0,gpt5)/grub
grub> set root=(hd0,gpt5)
```

To obtain a menu, you must then load the normal module and run it:

```
grub> insmod normal
grub> normal
```

With any luck, you'll now see a normal GRUB 2 menu. This effect will not be permanent, though; to get GRUB 2 working without such interventions in the future, you'll need to re-install it, typically by typing grub-install /dev/*device* as root (where /dev/*device* is the disk's Linux device filename) once the computer has booted normally.

Less serious problems typically involve the ability to boot a single kernel or OS. Typically, GRUB 2 presents an error message about the type of error it encounters, such as a missing file. If an error is simple enough, you may be able to overcome it by selecting the kernel or OS in the GRUB 2 menu and pressing the E key to edit the entry. You can then follow the on-screen prompts and use GRUB 2's built-in text editor to make temporary changes to the configuration. (Chapter 1 describes this process in detail.)

Dealing with Initial RAM Disk Issues

As described in Chapter 1 and Chapter 2, modern Linux systems frequently use an initial RAM disk (aka an initrd or initramfs). An initial RAM disk is used in conjunction with the kernel to provide a handful of critical system utilities and kernel modules, enabling the kernel to do things that it ordinarily can't do without access to the hard disk. For instance, the kernel can load modules to handle particular hard disks. If you compile your own kernel, as described in Chapter 2, you can include such modules in the kernel itself, so you may not need an initial RAM disk; however, sometimes you need an initial RAM disk to activate particular features, such as logical volume manager (LVM) support. Initial RAM disks are also used by most distributions so that a single kernel can support a wide variety of hardware.

One drawback to initial RAM disks is that they can sometimes complicate the boot process. As described in Chapter 1, your boot loader configuration must reference the initial RAM disk file. The boot loader then loads both the kernel and the initial RAM disk into memory and runs the kernel, giving it the location of the initial RAM disk in memory. This process can go wrong in many different ways—the boot loader might be unable to locate the initial RAM disk file, the file format might be incorrect, the file might be damaged, the file might be for the wrong kernel, the RAM disk file might be missing some critical feature, and so on.

Some of these problems will result in errors at the boot loader stage. For instance, you might see a "file not found" error, either stated plainly or in the form of a cryptic error number. If this happens, you should check your boot loader configuration to verify that the initial RAM disk's filename is entered correctly. (These filenames are often long and filled with numbers and codes, so they're easy to mistype!) Basically, such problems can be treated like other boot loader issues, as described earlier.

If the boot loader can load the kernel and the initial RAM disk, the boot process will proceed. In a conventional configuration, you'll see a series of messages, which you can later review with dmesg, relating to the kernel's detection of hardware and so on. You may think you're free and clear, but if the initial RAM disk is damaged or is for a different kernel or distribution than you're using, the process is likely to come to an abrupt halt with an error message. Frequently, the complaint will be that the kernel was unable to access the root device. If this happens after you've installed a new kernel, your best bet is to reboot using an older kernel, review the steps you used to create the initial RAM disk, and create a new one. You may need to add options to the mkinitrd or mkinitramfs utility to have it include modules that are being mistakenly omitted.

Many modern Linux distributions switch to a graphical display very early in the boot process. This display is less intimidating to new users than is a traditional display filled with a stream of initialization messages, but it's less informative in case of errors. You can usually switch from the graphical display to a text-mode display by pressing a key or clicking a button with your mouse. Examine the graphical display for a prompt about this. Changing the kernel options in the boot loader can also disable this graphical *splash screen*, as it's called. Removing the splash option is one way to do this.

If the problem is with an initial RAM disk provided with your distribution, you may have more difficulty. If you can boot using an older kernel, you may need to use it to build your own kernel. If not, you may be able to locate boot loader options or an alternative kernel built by a third party that will work.

Problems with initial RAM disks can sometimes result from using a kernel that's too old on very new hardware. The latest hardware may simply not be supported by older kernels. Thus, you may need to try a newer distribution if you're having problems with a very new computer.

Fixing Problems Early in the OS Boot Stage

If the boot loader correctly loads the kernel and initial RAM disk and if the kernel can use the initial RAM disk to locate the Linux root filesystem, the kernel will then begin the normal system initialization process, as described in Chapter 1. As described in that chapter, most Linux distributions use the SysV or Upstart startup system. The former is controlled through files in /etc/init.d or /etc/rc.d/init.d and links to those files in various runlevel-specific directories, such as /etc/rc?.d, where ? is a runlevel number. Upstart is controlled through boot configuration files in /etc/init.

Whatever the details, once the initialization scripts begin working, boot problems that completely derail the boot process are unlikely to occur. Instead, problems at this stage are more likely to involve specific programs, such as your Web server or GUI login program. Typically, when this happens, you'll see a message that a service is being started, along with a note on the right side of the screen, often in red, that this attempt failed, as follows:

```
Starting Apache...                        [ FAILED ]
```

Such problems are best dealt with by debugging the specific subsystem in question; problems with Apache will necessarily be handled very differently from problems with Samba, for example. Some of the general-purpose debugging advice in this chapter can apply to many of these problems, though. Checking log files is usually a good course of action, for instance.

Troubleshooting Miscellaneous Problems

The rest of this chapter is devoted to a variety of troubleshooting techniques: interpreting boot-time messages, checking kernel ring buffer information, identifying hardware, resolving kernel module issues, interpreting log files, and using utilities that help you trace software issues.

Interpreting Boot-Time Displays

If your computer isn't configured to display a graphic at boot time, it should display a series of messages as it boots. Most of these messages fall into two broad categories:

Kernel Messages   Early in the boot process, the messages you see originate with the kernel; they relate information about the hardware the kernel detects, the partitions detected on the hard disk, and so on. These messages are stored in the kernel ring buffer, which you can study in more detail after the system has completely booted, as described in the upcoming section "Checking the Kernel Ring Buffer."

Startup Script Messages   Once the kernel has fully initialized the computer's hardware, SysV or Upstart startup scripts display messages about various non-kernel programs being started. As noted earlier, in "Fixing Problems Early in the OS Boot Stage," these startup scripts typically specify whether each system has started or not by displaying a success or failure message on the right side of the screen. These messages are usually color coded—white or green for success, red for failure. Thus, you can keep an eye on the right side of the screen and watch for red during the boot process. If you spot a red status indicator, note the message associated with it, and investigate it once the computer has booted.

Boot-time messages typically scroll by so quickly that they're hard to read. You might luck out and notice something important; or in the case of startup script messages, you can watch for the failure indications and, with luck, read the name of the subsystem that didn't start correctly before it scrolls off the screen. Sometimes typing Shift+Page Up enables you to read a message that's scrolled off the screen. You can check the kernel ring buffer after the computer has booted, but startup script messages aren't normally logged in any one location. Individual servers and subsystems may log information, as described in "Checking Log Files," but you may need to check many log files and wade through a great deal of irrelevant information if you want to verify that every server has started correctly.

Checking the Kernel Ring Buffer

You can display the entire contents of the kernel ring buffer by typing **dmesg**; however, this command's output is likely to be copious, so you may want to pipe it through less (**dmesg | less**) or redirect it to a file (**dmesg > file.txt**) and then read the file in a text editor. You should also be aware that the kernel ring buffer's size is limited. As the computer runs, the kernel generates new messages that are stored in the ring buffer, so the oldest messages will eventually be lost. Because the earliest messages from when the computer boots are often important, some distributions' startup scripts create a copy of the kernel ring buffer from just after the computer boots, typically in /var/log/dmesg or /var/log/boot.log.

Although messages in the kernel ring buffer all originate with the kernel, the wide variety of drivers and other kernel features that can generate these messages means that interpreting these messages often requires knowledge of the specific kernel features in question. The following pages describe some of the major types of information you can find in the kernel ring buffer.

Identifying the Kernel

If you read the kernel ring buffer early enough, it will begin with an identification of the kernel:

```
[    0.000000] Linux version 2.6.35.5 (rodsmith@nessus) (gcc version 4.4.3 ↵
(Gentoo 4.4.3-r2 p1.2) ) #3 SMP PREEMPT Sun Sep 26 23:32:11 EDT 2010
[    0.000000] Command line: BOOT_IMAGE=/bzImage-2.6.35.5 ro ↵
root=/dev/mapper/nessus-g_root dolvm
```

The number in brackets at the start of these lines is a time code. Not all kernels are configured to generate these timestamps, though, so you might find they're missing. The remaining information on the first line is similar to that produced by the uname command; it includes the kernel version number, the user and computer that compiled the kernel, the compiler that was used, important kernel options, and the date and time the kernel was compiled. The second line identifies the kernel filename and the options passed to the kernel by the boot loader. All of this information can be important in verifying that you're using the correct kernel and that the boot loader has passed it the correct options.

Describing the CPU

Following the kernel identification, you'll see a large number of lines that relate various technical details about how the kernel is using memory. Most of this information is useful only to kernel experts, but if you notice something suspicious, by all means investigate it. Eventually you'll reach a couple of lines that classify your CPU's speed:

```
[    0.000000] Detected 2800.153 MHz processor.
[    0.002004] Calibrating delay loop (skipped), value calculated using ↵
timer frequency.. 5600.30 BogoMIPS (lpj=2800153)
```

The first of these lines identifies the clock speed of the CPU (2.8 GHz in this example). If this information is incorrect, then something very strange is happening—perhaps your CPU is so new or exotic that the kernel isn't handling it correctly, or maybe your motherboard is misconfigured to run the CPU at the wrong speed. The second line is sometimes misinterpreted or given too much weight. In computing, a common measure of computational speed is millions of instructions per second (MIPS), so some people try to measure hardware speed by the BogoMIPS measure found in the kernel ring buffer. The term *BogoMIPS*, however, means *bogus* MIPS—in other words, it's not a reliable measure of speed across CPUs. It's computed by the kernel for its own internal use and should not be used to compare different computers.

A bit further on, you'll find a few more CPU-related lines:

```
[    0.018524] CPU0: AMD Athlon(tm) 64 X2 Dual Core Processor 5400+ stepping 02
[    0.021004] MCE: In-kernel MCE decoding enabled.
[    0.024018] Booting Node   0, Processors  #1
[    0.095029] Brought up 2 CPUs
[    0.095097] Total of 2 processors activated (11200.84 BogoMIPS).
```

These lines identify the brand and model of CPU. In this case, they indicate that the computer has two CPUs (in fact, as is more common today, it's a single dual-core CPU). If the kernel ring buffer indicates that fewer CPUs or cores are available than you believe are present in your computer, then you should investigate further. Perhaps your kernel lacks support for multiple cores (it's a compile-time feature, so you may need to recompile the kernel), or perhaps you're mistaken about your CPU's capabilities.

Identifying Computer Busses

Further on in the output, you'll see a great deal of technical information about the computer's busses—mostly the Peripheral Component Interconnect (PCI) bus for modern computers. These lines look like this:

```
[    0.134046] pci 0000:03:05.0: reg 10: [mem 0xfd000000-0xfdffffff]
[    0.134150] pci 0000:03:05.2: reg 10: [mem 0xfc110000-0xfcffffff]
[    0.134254] pci 0000:03:06.0: reg 10: [mem 0xfebff000-0xfebfffff]
[    0.134262] pci 0000:03:06.0: reg 14: [io   0xe800-0xe83f]
[    0.134270] pci 0000:03:06.0: reg 18: [mem 0xfea00000-0xfeafffff]
[    0.134297] pci 0000:03:06.0: reg 30: [mem 0xfe900000-0xfe9fffff pref]
[    0.134321] pci 0000:03:06.0: supports D1 D2
[    0.134323] pci 0000:03:06.0: PME# supported from D0 D1 D2 D3hot D3cold
[    0.134328] pci 0000:03:06.0: PME# disabled
```

These lines can be useful in diagnosing certain types of hardware problems; however, much of the data can be obtained more conveniently using utilities such as lspci (described later in "Identifying Hardware").

Identifying Hardware Subsystems

A bit later, you'll begin to see messages about certain subsystems and driver sets:

```
[    0.143146] SCSI subsystem initialized
[    0.143146] libata version 3.00 loaded.
[    0.143146] Advanced Linux Sound Architecture Driver Version 1.0.23.
```

Small Computer Systems Interface (SCSI) is a disk interface method. SCSI is rare on modern computers, but as described in Chapter 4, "Advanced Disk Management," Linux has been relying more and more upon its SCSI subsystem to handle other disk types, including the Serial Advanced Technology Interface (SATA) disks that are today's most common disk type. The libata subsystem helps with this coordination. The Advanced Linux Sound Architecture (ALSA) driver is the core of the modern Linux sound handling system. Chances are your computer will use the SCSI subsystem, and if this subsystem is absent and you have problems booting or using certain disks, this may be why. You may need to recompile your kernel or load suitable modules to get it to work. Sound functionality is usually much less critical, of course, but you can look for evidence of such drivers (or the *lack* of such evidence) if you have problems with particular subsystems.

Another important subsystem is networking, which is likely to generate its own messages:

```
[    0.161587] NET: Registered protocol family 2
[    0.161666] IP route cache hash table entries: 131072 (order: 8, ↵
1048576 bytes)
[    0.162387] TCP established hash table entries: 262144 (order: 10, ↵
4194304 bytes)
```

Additional messages along these lines indicate that the kernel is initializing itself to use the Transmission Control Protocol (TCP). Similar messages are likely to be present for the User Datagram Protocol (UDP) and other network protocols. If such messages are absent, this indicates a lack of network support in your kernel; you may need to load a kernel module or recompile your kernel before networking will function.

Identifying Specific Hardware Devices

The kernel probes several critical hardware devices. These entries are likely to be scattered about, but I show several examples here as a group:

```
[    3.443278] floppy0: no floppy controllers found
[    3.445717] PNP: PS/2 Controller [PNP0303:PS2K,PNP0f03:PS2M] ↵
at 0x60,0x64 irq 1,12
[    3.446197] serio: i8042 KBD port at 0x60,0x64 irq 1
[    3.446236] serio: i8042 AUX port at 0x60,0x64 irq 12
[    3.446484] mice: PS/2 mouse device common for all mice
[    3.503526] input: AT Translated Set 2 keyboard as ↵
/devices/platform/i8042/serio0/input/input0
[    3.654551] ata1: SATA max UDMA/133 abar m1024@0xfbcff800 port ↵
0xfbcff900 irq 22
[    4.269230] ata1.00: ATAPI: ASUS    DRW-2014S1T, 1.01, max UDMA/66
[    4.269559] ata1.00: configured for UDMA/66
```

These lines indicate that no floppy controller was found (which is correct in this case but might not be on some computers), that a PS/2 mouse and keyboard were found, and that an SATA controller was found. (In fact, several SATA controllers are usually present if even one is; I've shown only one of the relevant lines here.) This SATA controller interfaces to an ASUS DRW-2014S1T DVD drive. If you're having problems with any of your core hardware, you might find clues in messages such as these. For instance, you might find that a hard disk is not being correctly detected, or you might see messages about resets or timeouts relating to particular hardware devices.

One particularly important set of messages relates to the hard disk:

```
[    4.282511] sd 1:0:0:0: [sda] 976773168 512-byte logical blocks: (500
                        GB/465 GiB)
[    4.282544] sd 1:0:0:0: [sda] Write Protect is off
[    4.282546] sd 1:0:0:0: [sda] Mode Sense: 00 3a 00 00
[    4.282560] sd 1:0:0:0: [sda] Write cache: enabled, read cache: enabled,
                        doesn't support DPO or FUA
[    4.282668]  sda: sda1 sda2 sda3 < sda5 sda6 sda7 >
[    4.327765] sd 1:0:0:0: [sda] Attached SCSI disk
```

These lines identify the first hard disk (/dev/sda) as being 465 GiB in size and provide several other technical details about it. The next-to-the-last line identifies the disk's partitions: three primary partitions from /dev/sda1 to /dev/sda3 and three logical partitions from /dev/sda5 to /dev/sda7 in this example. (In fact, /dev/sda3 is an extended partition.)

Modern computers often rely heavily on USB devices, so the lines that identify USB hardware may be of interest:

```
[    4.545190] usbcore: registered new interface driver usbfs
[    4.545338] usbcore: registered new interface driver hub
[    4.545451] usbcore: registered new device driver usb
[    4.548021] ehci_hcd: USB 2.0 'Enhanced' Host Controller (EHCI) Driver
```

These lines continue, identifying USB details. Modern computers typically have several USB busses, so you're likely to see quite a few lines like these.

Identifying Filesystems

Sooner or later, the kernel ring buffer is likely to provide information on the filesystems the kernel mounts:

```
[   18.854153] REISERFS (device dm-9): found reiserfs format "3.6" with
 standard journal
[   18.854167] REISERFS (device dm-9): using ordered data mode
[   18.889285] REISERFS (device dm-9): journal params: device dm-9, size
 8192, journal first block 18, max trans len 1024, max batch 900, max
 commit age 30, max trans age 30
[   18.890260] REISERFS (device dm-9): checking transaction log (dm-9)
[   18.924766] REISERFS (device dm-9): Using r5 hash to sort names
```

The details will, of course, vary with your computer. If it reports problems, this could be the cause of an inability to access certain filesystems. Perhaps a disk check using `fsck` (as described in Chapter 3, "Basic Filesystem Management") would overcome such difficulties.

Additions to the Kernel Ring Buffer

As the computer continues to run, you can see routine additions to the kernel ring buffer. For instance, if you insert a USB flash drive, you'll see messages about the detection of the USB device, the detection of its partitions, and perhaps the identification of a filesystem if you mount one. You might also see error messages of various types, such as this:

```
[178288.607343] xscreensaver-gl[8366]: segfault at 4 ip 00007f7859ef60be ↵
 sp 00007ffffc9389c0 error 4 in libGL.so.1.2[7f7859e9b000+ae000]
```

This message indicates that the program `xscreensaver-gl` created a segmentation fault—that is, it crashed because it attempted to access memory it shouldn't have. This message records some key details about the error; however, unless you're a programmer with access to the source code, chances are these details won't do you much good. Nonetheless, they are available should you need them.

Another type of error relates to input/output problems:

```
[238931.384129] Buffer I/O error on device sdb10, logical block 93016
[238931.384132] lost page write due to I/O error on sdb10
```

Such an error can occur because of a faulty disk, a cable that's been disconnected, or various other problems. If you're having difficulties with a disk (or any other device—a printer, a mouse, or anything else), you could check the kernel ring buffer for such messages. If you see such errors, they usually indicate a hardware fault, which can help you narrow the scope of your investigations.

Kernel ring buffer messages vary a great deal from one computer to another. I highly recommend that you check the kernel ring buffer messages on at least one computer. Chances are you won't understand most of the entries, but you should be able to interpret at least some of them. By familiarizing yourself with normal messages, you'll be better able to identify problem reports when you need to do so.

Identifying Hardware

If you can't use a particular hardware device, your first step in analysis is usually to identify the hardware. This task can be harder than it might at first seem, since the manufacturer's name on the box may not be important; instead, Linux drivers are generally written for a device's *chipset*, which is one or more chips that provide the device's core functionality. The chipset is often made by a company whose identity may not be readily apparent. Nonetheless, several diagnostic tools are useful in tracking down this information. I describe how to identify your CPU, the motherboard's built-in hardware, PCI devices, and USB devices.

Identifying the CPU

CPU identification can be critical in resolving certain problems. Two issues are particularly important:

CPU Architecture   Most desktop and server computers that run Linux use an *x*86 or *x*86-64 CPU; however, some such computers run PowerPC or other CPUs. Matching the software you run to the CPU is critical; a Linux distribution for one CPU won't run on another one, with a couple of exceptions. One of these is if you run an emulator. Another is that *x*86-64 CPUs can run *x*86 software. If a Linux installation disc boots on your computer, you have the right architecture, with the caveat that an *x*86-64 distribution is usually preferable to an *x*86 distribution on *x*86-64 hardware. If an install disc won't boot, it's possible you're using the wrong architecture. If the computer has a working Linux distribution and you want to upgrade, you can use the procedures described here to identify your CPU.

Number of CPUs or Cores   Most modern computers have at least two CPU *cores*—CPU components that act like independent CPUs. A *dual-core* CPU acts like two CPUs. Linux can use multiple cores to run two programs in a way that minimizes the interference between them, and programs written to take advantage of multiple cores can run faster using both cores than they could on a single-core CPU. To take advantage of these features, though, you must activate the Processor Type and Features ➢ Symmetric Multi-Processing Support option in the kernel, as described in Chapter 2. If this option is not present, Linux will use your multi-core CPU as if it were a single-core CPU, greatly reducing your computer's speed. If you think this has happened, you must ensure that your computer really has multiple cores (or multiple physical CPUs, as some have).

The uname command, described in detail in Chapter 2, identifies the Linux kernel version and CPU model. The -m, -i, and -p options are particularly relevant; ideally, these options identify the architecture (such as x86 or x86-64), a manufacturer's identifying string (such as AuthenticAMD), and the complete CPU model (such as AMD Athlon(tm) 64 X2 Dual Core Processor 5400+). Unfortunately, sometimes the last two options return unknown or the same information as -m, so this information may not be as useful as it could be in tracking down problems.

The lscpu command provides more details about your CPU, including the number of cores it provides, its model number, its clock speed, and virtualization features it supports:

```
Architecture:          x86_64
CPU op-mode(s):        64-bit
CPU(s):                2
Thread(s) per core:    1
Core(s) per socket:    2
CPU socket(s):         1
Vendor ID:             AuthenticAMD
CPU family:            15
```

```
Model:                  107
Stepping:               2
CPU MHz:                2800.153
Virtualization:         AMD-V
L1d cache:              64K
L1i cache:              64K
L2 cache:               512K
```

You can acquire still more information about your CPU by examining the /proc/cpuinfo pseudo-file. Typical contents resemble the following:

```
processor       : 0
vendor_id       : AuthenticAMD
cpu family      : 15
model           : 107
model name      : AMD Athlon(tm) 64 X2 Dual Core Processor 5400+
stepping        : 2
cpu MHz         : 2800.153
cache size      : 512 KB
physical id     : 0
siblings        : 2
core id         : 0
cpu cores       : 2
apicid          : 0
initial apicid  : 0
fpu             : yes
fpu_exception   : yes
cpuid level     : 1
wp              : yes
flags           : fpu vme de pse tsc msr pae mce cx8 apic sep mtrr pge mca ↵
 cmov pat pse36 clflush mmx fxsr sse sse2 ht syscall nx mmxext fxsr_opt ↵
 rdtscp lm 3dnowext 3dnow rep_good extd_apicid pni cx16 lahf_lm cmp_legacy ↵
 svm extapic cr8_legacy 3dnowprefetch lbrv
bogomips        : 5600.30
TLB size        : 1024 4K pages
clflush size    : 64
cache_alignment : 64
address sizes   : 40 bits physical, 48 bits virtual
power management: ts fid vid ttp tm stc 100mhzsteps
```

On a multi-core CPU, this information is repeated for each CPU core, except for the value on the first line (processor), which increments for each CPU. Some of this information is extremely technical, such as the `cache_alignment` value. The `cpu cores` item identifies the number of cores in the CPU. You can also go to your CPU manufacturer's Web site to verify the CPU's capabilities. The `model name` line provides you with the CPU's model name, and the `cpu family`, `model`, and `stepping` information can be helpful in detailing the precise CPU you have.

Using information from `uname`, `lscpu`, /proc/cpuinfo, or your CPU manufacturer, you can determine whether you need to make changes to the distribution you're using or to your kernel compilation options. If you have multiple cores (or multiple CPUs) but only one shows up in the /proc/cpuinfo output, you should verify that the Processor Type and Features ➢ Symmetric Multi-Processing Support option in the kernel is active. (Activating this option on single-core CPUs does little harm, so it's generally best to activate it as a standard procedure.)

Identifying Built-in Hardware

Modern motherboards invariably include a wide range of hardware devices and interfaces. These typically include PS/2 keyboard and mouse interfaces, floppy and hard disk controllers, an Ethernet port, USB interfaces, RS-232 serial ports, a parallel port, and sound hardware. Some computers include other interfaces, such as IEEE-1394 (aka FireWire) ports; and some computers drop some of the older interfaces, such as PS/2 and floppy interfaces.

In any event, most of these devices are controlled via the motherboard's chipset. The Linux kernel provides drivers for all major motherboard chipsets, but identifying which devices you need can be tricky. (Linux support for the very latest chipsets sometimes lags behind hardware introduction by a few weeks to months, though.) If you happen to have a manual for the computer's motherboard, you can use it to identify the chipset the computer uses. Most computers made in the last few years use chipsets from Intel, AMD, VIA, or nVidia. Unfortunately, the model numbers listed in chipset manuals often bear little resemblance to the model numbers used to identify chipsets in the Linux kernel configuration area. If in doubt, include all the drivers for your manufacturer; the extra drivers will take a few seconds to compile and consume a tiny amount of disk space and, if compiled into the kernel rather than as modules, memory. This is a small price to pay to ensure that your hardware is supported by your kernel.

If you can't identify your chipset by reading a manual, you may have to resort to software tools to do the job. Most motherboard devices show up as PCI devices from a software perspective, so the procedures described in the next section, "Identifying PCI Devices," work for motherboard components.

Some motherboard devices are handled by secondary chipsets. This is particularly common on high-end hardware that includes extra devices, such as more than four SATA ports or two Ethernet ports. Your manual should identify the secondary chipset used for these extra functions. If you use software to identify your hardware, you should be sure to recognize the fact that you may have two different chipsets, and therefore need two different drivers, to handle all the ports of a given type.

> Sometimes you can work around problems by changing the port to which a device is connected. For instance, you might be unable to boot your computer with your hard disk connected to one SATA port, but moving it to another port will enable the computer to boot. This can happen because of BIOS or driver limitations regarding particular chipsets and therefore the ports that each chipset uses. If you're lucky, the problem port will work well enough to be useful once the computer has booted or for some other device (an optical disc rather than a hard disk, for instance).

Identifying PCI Devices

The PCI standard defines a physical and logical set of parameters that enable plug-in cards to be used in any PCI-supporting computer. PCI devices plug into the computer's motherboard or are built into the motherboard directly. In Linux, the lspci command displays information on PCI devices. Table 11.4 summarizes the options to this command.

TABLE 11.4   Options for lspci

Option	Effect
-v	Increases verbosity of output. This option may be doubled (-vv) or tripled (-vvv) to produce yet more output.
-n	Displays information in numeric codes rather than translating the codes to manufacturer and device names.
-nn	Displays both the manufacturer and device names and their associated numeric codes.
-x	Displays the PCI configuration space for each device as a hexadecimal dump. This is an extremely advanced option. Tripling (-xxx) or quadrupling (-xxxx) this option displays information about more devices.
-b	Shows IRQ numbers and other data as seen by devices rather than as seen by the kernel.
-t	Displays a tree view depicting the relationship between devices.
-s [[[[domain]:]bus]:] [slot][.[func]]	Displays only devices that match the listed specification.

Option	Effect
-d [*vendor*]:[*device*]	Shows data on the specified device.
-i *file*	Uses the specified file to map vendor and device IDs to names. (The default is /usr/share/misc/pci.ids.)
-m	Dumps data in a machine-readable form, intended for use by scripts. A single -m uses a backward-compatible format, whereas doubling (-mm) uses a newer format.
-D	Displays PCI domain numbers. These numbers normally aren't displayed.
-M	Performs a scan in bus-mapping mode, which can reveal devices hidden behind a misconfigured PCI bridge. This is an advanced option that can be used only by root.
--version	Displays version information.

Used without any options, lspci produces summary information on each of the computer's PCI devices:

```
$ lspci
00:00.0 Host bridge: Advanced Micro Devices [AMD] RS780 Host Bridge
00:01.0 PCI bridge: Advanced Micro Devices [AMD] RS780 PCI to PCI bridge ↵
 (int gfx)
00:07.0 PCI bridge: Advanced Micro Devices [AMD] RS780 PCI to PCI bridge ↵
 (PCIE port 3)
00:11.0 SATA controller: ATI Technologies Inc SB700/SB800 SATA Controller ↵
 [AHCI mode]
01:05.0 VGA compatible controller: ATI Technologies Inc Radeon HD 3200 Graphics
03:06.0 Ethernet controller: Intel Corporation 82559 InBusiness 10/100 (rev 08)
```

This output has been edited for brevity; the lspci output on most computers is likely to exceed two dozen lines.

You can use this output to identify your PCI devices, even if Linux drivers aren't correctly managing the hardware. For instance, the preceding output indicates that the motherboard uses an AMD RS780 host bridge and PCI-to-PCI bridge, an ATI SB700/SB800 SATA controller, an ATI Radeon HD 3200 graphics chipset, and an Intel 82559 Ethernet controller. You can use this information to search for suitable driver support in the Linux kernel configuration menus, as described in Chapter 2. (Some devices, such as the PCI-to-PCI bridge, may not require explicit configuration; PCI device identification is most useful if you already know that a particular component, such as an Ethernet adapter, isn't working correctly.)

In theory, PCI devices plug into a particular type of card on the motherboard. As noted earlier, however, many components that are integrated on the motherboard appear to be PCI devices to software, including the lspci command. In the preceding output, the host bridge, PCI-to-PCI bridge, SATA controller, and Radeon graphics chipset are all built into the motherboard. The Intel Ethernet adapter is a plug-in card. Some plug-in cards use standards other than PCI, but they still show up in lspci output. Common examples include the Accelerated Graphics Port (AGP) and PCI Express (PCIe or PCI-E) standards, which are most often used for video cards. (PCIe is increasingly being used for other purposes, too.) Older plug-in card technologies, such as the Industry Standard Architecture (ISA) and Video Standards Electronics Association (VESA) Local Bus (VL-Bus), are not detected by lspci; however, such busses began to disappear around 2000, so you're unlikely to encounter them today.

Identifying USB Devices

USB devices normally attach externally to the computer. You can check to see what USB devices are connected using the lsusb command, which is similar in many ways to lspci. Table 11.5 summarizes lsusb options.

TABLE 11.5 Options for lsusb

Option	Effect
-v	Increases verbosity of output
-t	Displays a tree view depicting the relationship between devices
-s [[bus]:][devnum]	Displays only devices that match the listed specification
-d [vendor]:[device]	Shows data on the specified device
-D device	Displays information on the specified device, which is a device file in the /dev directory tree
--version or -V	Displays version information

Note that lsusb displays information on both the devices that are attached to your computer and on the USB controller in the computer itself. Used without any options, lsusb produces output like the following:

```
$ lsusb
Bus 001 Device 001: ID 1d6b:0001 Linux Foundation 1.1 root hub
Bus 002 Device 001: ID 1d6b:0002 Linux Foundation 2.0 root hub
Bus 002 Device 002: ID 04b8:0119 Seiko Epson Corp. Perfection 4490 Photo
Bus 002 Device 008: ID 04e8:681d Samsung Electronics Co., Ltd
```

This example shows four devices. The first two, identified as root hubs, represent the USB controllers in the computer itself. These controllers handle USB 1.1 and 2.0 devices, respectively. The next two entries are for two USB devices that are plugged into the computer: an Epson Perfection 4490 scanner and a Samsung cell phone. You can obtain additional information by using the -v option (note that's a lowercase -v; the uppercase -V has a different effect, as Table 11.5 describes). Use -s, -d, or -D to restrict this output to a specific device.

The ID number, such as 04b8:0119 for the Epson scanner, can be useful in crafting udev rules, as described in Chapter 3. You can use these numbers with the idVendor and idProduct attributes, as follows:

```
ATTR{idVendor}=="04b8", ATTR{idProduct}=="0119", SYMLINK+="scanner" ↵
 MODE="0660", OWNER="lisa", GROUP="scanner"
```

This example creates a symbolic link, /dev/scanner, that points to the Epson scanner. This example also sets the device's permissions (mode), owner, and group.

If you can access a hardware device as root but not as an ordinary user, chances are the problem is one of permissions on its device node. You can overcome such problems temporarily by using chown or chmod on the device node; however, to permanently fix the problem, you should create a udev rule that sets the ownership or mode of the device file to something appropriate. This advice is true of USB, PCI, and other types of hardware.

Identifying Hardware's Resource Use

Chapter 4 describes how disk hardware uses certain hardware resources, interrupts, and direct memory access (DMA) lines. Disks aren't the only hardware devices that use these resources, though. You can obtain an overview of how your resources are being used by the lsdev command, which takes no arguments. Its output resembles the following (edited for brevity):

```
$ lsdev
Device           DMA   IRQ  I/O Ports
------------------------------------------------
0000:00:11.0                7000-700f  8000-8003  9000-9007  a000-a003 ↵
  b000-b007
```

```
0000:03:06.0                         e800-e83f
acpi                      9
ACPI                                 0800-0803    0804-0805    0808-080b ⏎
       0810-0815     0820-0827    08ff-08ff
dma                                  0080-008f
dma1                                 0000-001f
dma2                                 00c0-00df
e100                                 e800-e83f
eth0                    21
eth1                    40
```

 The lsdev utility is often not installed by default. You may need to install a
package called procinfo to obtain this utility.

This output summarizes the DMA lines, interrupts (IRQ), and I/O ports used by
each device. Devices may be identified in various ways, such as by a PCI device (such as
0000:00:11.0 in this example), as shown in lspci output; by a component name (such
as acpi or eth0 in this example); or by a driver name (such as e100 in this example). You
may need to know enough about your hardware to link various identifiers yourself. For
instance, in this example, e100 is an Ethernet device driver, it handles the eth0 device,
and it is the PCI 03:06.0 device. Thus, three lines from the preceding output apply to this
device. Two of these lines, 0000:03:06.0 and e100, identify the same resource use (I/O
ports e800–e83f), but the third, eth0, identifies another type of resource use (IRQ 21).

Used as a debugging tool, lsdev can help you track down hardware that competes for
use of the same resources. Such competition can result in sluggish performance, system
crashes, or inaccessible hardware. If you find such competition, you can try disabling an
unused device by unloading its kernel module or disabling it in the BIOS, or you can use
boot loader or kernel module options to change the device's resource use. (You'll have to
consult the driver's documentation to learn about the relevant options.) Competition over
IRQs is unlikely to be a problem on modern hardware.

EXERCISE 11.1

Identifying Your Own Hardware

In this exercise, you will use the methods just described to identify some of the key
hardware components on your own computer. You should begin by logging in and, if
you use a GUI environment, opening a text-mode console such as an xterm or Terminal
program. In this shell, follow these steps:

1. Type **uname -mip**. The result should be basic information on your CPU: the machine
    hardware type (-m), the hardware platform (-i), and the processor's identifying
    type (-p). Note that some computers produce more complete information than others.

2. Type `cat /proc/cpuinfo`. You'll see more detailed information on your CPU, including more reliable reporting of the items that uname also produces.

3. Type `lspci`. The result will be a list of the computer's PCI devices, including many devices that are built into the motherboard. Study this list and attempt to parse it for useful information, such as the manufacturer and model number of the video chipset, the disk controller chipset, the Ethernet chipset, the USB chipsets, the audio chipset, and any other interesting devices you might have installed.

4. If you have a manual for your computer or motherboard, check its specifications (usually printed in the first few pages) to try to match up the devices you identified in step 3 with what the manufacturer specifies. Note that the model numbers may differ because the same devices often go by multiple names.

5. Type `lsusb`. The result should be a list of USB devices. If no USB devices are plugged into the computer, this list may contain nothing but the motherboard's USB controller. If you have more devices, try to match each to the physical hardware you see in front of you.

6. Plug in or power on a new USB device; or if a device that's non-critical, such as a printer or scanner, is already plugged in, turn it off or unplug it.

7. Type `lsusb` again. Note how the device list has changed.

8. Type `lsdev`. Study this output, looking for devices that share DMA channels, IRQs, or I/O ports. If you find such shared resources, use `lspci` or other means to try to determine whether this is really a conflict or just the same device being identified using multiple names.

Having performed this exercise, you should have a better idea of what hardware your computer is using. Actually making decisions and solving problems based on such information requires more knowledge and experience, though. For instance, you can't know whether your CPU is an ancient hulk, a ho-hum modern CPU, or the latest blazing technology without knowing where that model fits into the constellation of CPUs available today (and perhaps in the past). You can perform additional research on any or all of the components you've identified by doing Web searches, reading manuals, and checking manufacturers' Web sites.

Identifying Loaded Kernel Modules

Chapter 2 describes three tools that can be useful in tracking down and fixing problems related to kernel modules: lsmod, insmod, and modprobe. The lsmod utility lists the modules that are loaded, insmod loads a single module, and modprobe loads a module and all those upon which it depends. Ideally, you won't need to use these utilities, since Linux normally loads the correct modules automatically; however, sometimes this automatic function fails, in which case these tools are useful.

If some of your hardware isn't working, you can try to ascertain whether the appropriate kernel module is loaded by using lsmod. If you don't see the appropriate entry, it's possible that using insmod or modprobe to load the module will overcome the problem. You should remember, though, that drivers are sometimes built into the main kernel file rather than existing as loadable modules. The lsmod utility ignores drivers built into the kernel; you'll need to use dmesg or review your kernel configuration to identify drivers and other features that are built directly into the kernel.

Kernel module files are stored in the /lib/modules directory tree, typically in a subdirectory named after the kernel version to which the modules belong. The insmod utility requires a complete path to the module to be loaded, but modprobe does not.

Part of the problem with using lsmod to determine whether a driver is loading correctly is figuring out which driver is appropriate for your hardware. The first step in answering this question is to correctly identify your hardware, as described earlier in "Identifying Hardware." That done, you can use several techniques to identify the correct driver:

Searching the Web   A Web search can often turn up the answer; search on the hardware's manufacturer and model along with strings such as *Linux* or *Linux kernel*.

Perusing Kernel Options   You can launch a kernel configuration tool and manually scan for the name of the hardware. The name of the kernel module appears in uppercase in the description area. For instance, Figure 11.1 shows the configuration option for JMicron PATA disk controllers; the kernel driver is listed as PATA_JMICRON. The module name will be the same as this value but converted to lowercase—pata_jmicron in this example.

FIGURE 11.1   The Linux kernel configuration tool provides the name of each kernel option in the description pane.

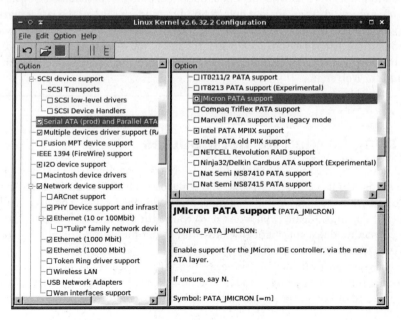

Scanning the Kernel Configuration File   The .config file in the kernel source tree provides driver names but with the string CONFIG_ appended, as in CONFIG_PATA_JMICRON for the pata_jmicron driver. If the driver is set to be compiled, this value will be set to y (for compilation into the kernel) or m (for compilation as a module), as in CONFIG_PATA_JMICRON=m. Try using grep or a text editor's search function to locate lines that contain the manufacturer's name or the device's model number. Be aware, however, that names and model numbers may sometimes be truncated or altered, and drivers for one model may in fact work for a whole family of devices. Occasionally device manufacturers merge or change their names, which can make searching for such names complicated or confusing.

Consulting Kernel Documentation   Kernel documentation files in the Documentation directory tree of the Linux kernel source directory can provide names for drivers. You can use grep, perhaps with its -r option to perform a recursive search, to search on the manufacturer's name or the device's model number.

 Real World Scenario

Using Manufacturer Drivers

If you're familiar with the Windows world, you may be accustomed to searching for device drivers on manufacturers' Web sites. This practice can sometimes work in Linux; however, the level of Linux support from hardware manufacturers is quite variable. You might not find any Linux drivers at all, or you might find something that will solve whatever problem you're experiencing.

Some manufacturers either contribute open source drivers to the Linux kernel as well as making them available on their Web sites or take the standard Linux drivers and make them available on their Web site. In such cases, the drivers provided by the manufacturer are unlikely to work any better than the drivers from the latest Linux kernel.

Other manufacturers provide proprietary drivers on their Web sites, or they release drivers on their Web sites well before they make their way into the Linux kernel. In such cases, using manufacturer-provided drivers can help you get your device working.

Determining into which of these categories a given driver falls can be tricky. Your best bet is often to download the driver and try it. When you do so, follow the directions provided with the driver. You may need to have your own Linux kernel source code available, and in some cases you may need to patch and recompile your own kernel. (Chapter 2 describes how to do these things.)

If a device is working correctly and you stumble across a manufacturer's driver, my advice is to follow the old adage "If it ain't broke, don't fix it." Replacing a working driver with one of unknown quality might work, but at best you'll waste some of your time. Of course, if the driver's documentation promises superior performance or offers security or other bug fixes, you might want to give it a try even if your current driver seems to be working well. Pay attention to dates, though; if the file is five years old and warns of serious bugs in the "current" standard kernel driver, chances are the fixes have long since been incorporated in the driver you're already using!

Checking Log Files

Log files are very useful tools in problem solving—debugging servers that don't behave as you expect, locating evidence of system intrusions, and so on. You should first know what log files to examine in any given situation. Understanding the problem-identification abilities of log files will help you use them effectively. Some tools can help in this task, too; these tools can help you scan log files for information, summarize the (sometimes overly verbose) log file information, and so on.

Which Log Files Are Important?

In using log files, you must first decide which ones are important. Unfortunately, the names of log files aren't completely standardized across distributions, so you may need to poke around in your syslog configuration files, and perhaps in the log files themselves, to discover which files are important. Table 11.6 summarizes some common log files (all filenames are relative to /var/log).

TABLE 11.6 Common log files

Log file	Purpose
cron	This file holds information on cron-related activity.
dmesg or boot .log	Some distributions place the contents of the kernel ring buffer in a log file of this name immediately after booting. This ensures that the boot-time kernel ring buffer contents will be accessible even after the system has been running for a long time.
lastlog	This is an unusual log file; it holds, in binary form, data on the last login times for all users of the system. Type **lastlog** to see this log file's data in human-readable form.

Log file	Purpose
messages	This log file sometimes holds general-purpose log data, but on many systems it emphasizes log data from the kernel.
maillog	As you might guess by the name, this file holds messages related to the email system.
secure	This log file holds security-related information.
syslog	General-purpose system log data typically ends up in this file.
Xorg.0.log	This file holds information from the X server about its most recent run. A new log is typically started each time the X server restarts.

The /etc/syslog.conf file configures the system's logging features, so you can consult this file to learn where your system places various types of logged data. Some servers log data without the help of syslogd, so you may need to consult the configuration files and documentation for any programs you want to monitor. For instance, Samba frequently logs data independently of syslogd, storing files in /var/log/samba or a similar directory.

If you're uncertain of the purpose or importance of a log file, feel free to examine it. The tools described shortly, in "Using Tools to Help Scan Log Files," can be useful in this task. For basic identification, less is likely to be very helpful, as in **less /var/log/messages**. This command displays the file screen by screen, which should give you some clue about the file's contents.

Using Log Files to Identify Problems

You can use log files to monitor system loads (for instance, to determine how many documents a Web server has delivered), to check for intrusion attempts, to verify the correct functioning of a system, and to note errors generated by certain types of programs. To one extent or another, all of these functions can be used to identify problems. Examples of information that can be useful when you are troubleshooting include the following:

Verifying Heavy Loads   If a server is running sluggishly, log files may contain clues in the form of a large number of entries from the server. If a server has experienced a massive increase in the number of clients it handles or the size of the files it transfers, you may need to increase the server computer's capacity to restore good performance. Most non-server programs don't log their activities, though, so you probably won't be able to diagnose similar load problems caused by increasing workstation demands in this way. You'll likely have an idea that workstation load has increased in a more direct way, though, because the workstation users should know that they're running more programs or more resource-intensive programs.

WARNING   Sometimes the logging action itself can contribute substantially to a server's CPU and disk input/output requirements. If a server is behaving sluggishly, try reducing its logging level (so that it records less information).

Intrusion Detection   Some system problems are related to the presence of an intruder. Interlopers frequently modify your system files or utilities, thus affecting your system's performance or reliability. Their actions are sometimes reflected in log files. Even the *absence* of entries can sometimes be a clue—intruders often delete log files, or at least remove entries for a period. You might not notice such log file discrepancies unless you examine the log files soon after a break-in occurs, however.

Normal System Functioning   If a system is misbehaving, the presence of and information in routine log file entries can sometimes help you pin down the problem, or at least eliminate possibilities. For instance, suppose your system is working as a Dynamic Host Configuration Protocol (DHCP) server for your network, dishing out IP addresses to other systems, as described in Chapter 7, "Advanced Network Configuration." If your clients aren't receiving IP addresses, you can check the log file on the server. If that file indicates that the DHCP server has received requests and given leases in response, you can focus your problem-solving efforts on the clients.

Missing Entries   If you know that a program should be logging information but you can't locate it, this may be evidence that the program is misconfigured or is not starting properly. In some cases, missing entries may indicate problems outside the computer you're examining. For instance, suppose you configure Samba to log access attempts. If you can't access the Samba server from another system, you can check for Samba log file entries. If those entries aren't present, it could mean that Samba isn't running, that it's misconfigured, or that a network problem (such as a misconfigured router or firewall) is blocking access.

Error Messages   The most direct evidence of a problem in a log file is usually an error message. A log file entry that reads `authentication failure` or `FAILED LOGIN` indicates an authentication failure, for instance, that should help you focus your troubleshooting efforts. (Users often see different messages than those that appear in log files, or even none at all.) To improve this capacity, you can configure many servers and utilities to log more information than usual; consult the program's documentation for details. Be aware that different subsystems produce error messages that vary greatly in form, so one program's error messages will look quite different from another's.

Log files are most useful when you are diagnosing software problems with the kernel, servers, user login tools, and miscellaneous other low-level utilities. Information routinely recorded in log files includes kernel startup messages, kernel module operations, user logins, cron actions, filesystem mounting and unmounting, and actions performed by many servers. This information can reflect hardware, kernel, application, configuration, and even user problems.

Using Tools to Help Scan Log Files

Log files can sometimes be tricky to use because they often accumulate data at a rapid rate. This is particularly true when many programs' logs are sent to a single file or when you've increased the logging level in a program in an effort to help identify problems. Therefore, tools to help scan log files for important information are very helpful. You can think of these tools as falling into one of three categories: those that examine the starts of files, those that examine the ends of files, and those that can be used to search files. Some tools can be used for two or even all three of these tasks.

Most log files are owned by root, and many can be read only by root. Thus, you may need to acquire root privileges before using any of these tools, although the tools themselves can be used by other users on non-log files.

Checking the Beginnings of Log Files

Sometimes you know that information you need appears at the start of a log file. For instance, you might want to study the early stages of the boot process, as recorded in /var/log/dmesg or a similar file. You can go about obtaining such information in any of several ways. One tool that's aimed specifically at displaying the beginning of a file is head. Used with only a filename as an argument, head displays the first ten lines of that file. You can change the number of lines with the -n argument, as in **head -n 20 file.txt** to display the first 20 lines of file.txt.

If you know the information you want to review is near the beginning of a log file but you're not sure of its exact location, you might prefer to use a pager program, such as more or less. The more program displays a file one screen at a time, whatever your screen size is. You can press the spacebar to move forward in the file a screen at a time. The less program's name is a bit of a joke, because less is intended to be a better more; it does basically the same thing but supports more options within the program, such as searching (described shortly in "Searching Log Files"). Both programs enable you to quickly check the first few lines of a file, though.

Text editors can also be good ways to check the first few lines in a file. Most text editors open the file and display its first few lines when you pass a filename on the command line. Text editors do have some drawbacks, however. One is that you might accidentally alter the log file, which is undesirable. Another drawback is that opening a log file in a text editor is likely to take longer than using head or less to display the first few lines. This is particularly true if either the text editor or the log file is unusually large.

Checking the Ends of Log Files

Information is added to the ends of log files. Thus, when you're performing some operation on a computer and you want to see whether it happened as you intended, that information is likely to appear at the end of a log file, rather than at its start or somewhere in the middle. For instance, when you launch a new server, entries confirming the server's successful startup (or error messages relating to its failure to start) are likely to appear at the end of the file. The ability to check the end of a log file is therefore very helpful.

The `tail` program is noteworthy in this respect because it's designed to display the last few lines (10 by default) of a file. This program is very similar to head in most ways, except of course that it displays the end of a file rather than the beginning. The default action is sufficient for many purposes if you run the program on a log file immediately after some information has been logged. Sometimes, though, you might need to display a number of lines other than the default of 10. To do this, you use the -n option, as in **tail -n 15 /var/ log/messages** to display the last 15 lines of /var/log/messages.

Another feature of `tail` is real-time monitoring—you can use the program to keep an eye on additions to log files as they occur. You might want to do this just before performing some action that you want to monitor; you'll be able to see the relevant log entries as they're added to the log file. To do so, pass the -f or --follow option to `tail`, as in **tail -f /var/log/messages**. The result is an initial display of the last few log entries, as usual; however, `tail` doesn't immediately terminate. Instead, it keeps monitoring the log file and echoes new entries to the screen. When you're done, press Ctrl+C to kill `tail` and regain control of your shell.

Although it's not quite as convenient as `tail` for displaying a fixed number of lines, the `less` pager can be useful for checking the end of a log file. Type **less** *filename* to display *filename*; then type **G** or press the Esc key followed by the greater-than symbol (>). This will bring you to the end of the file. If you want to scroll upward in the file, type **b** or press Esc followed by V. You can scroll back down by typing **f**, pressing the spacebar, or pressing Ctrl+V. Using these commands, you can quickly examine the final lines of any file, including log files.

The less command can take a while to process a large or rapidly changing log file. If it seems to become unresponsive, wait a bit. If the size of a log file is causing problems, you might look into your log file rotation settings, as described in Chapter 12, "System Troubleshooting II: System Resources and the User Environment."

As with examining the start of a file, a text editor can be used to examine its end. Load a log file into a text editor, and scroll to the end of the file in whatever way is appropriate. As with examining the start of a file, though, this approach has the drawback that it might result in accidental changes to the file being saved. It might also be slow, particularly on large log files or with large editors. On the other hand, some editors notice when the log file changes and enable you to quickly load the changes. This feature can be handy if you want to monitor changes as they occur.

Searching Log Files

Sometimes you need to search log files for information. For instance, you might want to see all entries created by Postfix or entries in which you know the string eth0 appears. You can use any of several text-searching tools to help out with such tasks. These tools can search one or more text files and display matching lines, or they can take you to matching lines in these files so that you can examine them in context.

The grep command is the most basic of the text-search tools. Type the command, a series of options (including the search string), and a file specification (which typically includes a wildcard) to have it search those files for the specified string. For instance, to find all log entries created by the Postfix mail server, you might type `grep postfix /var/log/*`. The result is a series of output lines, each of which begins with the name of the file from which it's taken and concludes with the line in question. (If the string was found in a binary file, grep tells you so but doesn't attempt to display the string in context.)

The grep command is most useful when searching for entries in multiple log files simultaneously—say, if you don't know to which file a server is logging information. It can also be useful if you want to display the log entries from a particular server or those that involve a single user or by some other criterion you can easily express as a searchable string.

> If you use grep to search for a string that's very common, the output is likely to scroll off the top of your screen and possibly exceed the buffer of a scrollable GUI terminal window. This may prevent you from taking a complete census of files in which the string occurs. You can pipe the output through `less`, as in `grep postfix /var/log/* | less`, to enable you to scan through the grep output in a more controlled way.

Another way to search log files is by using `less`. You can use this utility to view a single log file. Once you're viewing a file, press the slash key (/) followed by a search string, as in `/postfix` to locate the first occurrence of the string `postfix` in the log file. If that string is present in the file, `less` takes you to that point and highlights the string. Pressing the slash key again moves to the next line that contains the search string. This feature can be handy if you need to see the full context of the line in question. If you want to locate the *last* occurrence of a string, press Esc followed by the greater-than symbol (>) to move to the end of the buffer, and then search backward using a question mark (?; that is, the slash key with a Shift modifier), as in `?postfix`. You can use a text editor to perform similar searches but with the same caveats described earlier in "Checking the Beginnings of Log Files"—text editors can be slower than tools such as `less`, and you might accidentally alter the log file.

Using Additional Log File Analysis Tools

Manually examining log files with `tail`, `less`, and similar tools can be informative, but other tools exist to help you analyze your log files. One of these is Logcheck, which is part of the Sentry Tools package (http://sourceforge.net/projects/sentrytools/). This package comes with some distributions, such as Debian. Unfortunately, it requires a fair amount of customization for your own system, so it's most easily implemented if it comes with your distribution, preconfigured for its log file format. If you want to use it on another distribution, you must edit the `logcheck.sh` file that's at the heart of the package. This file calls the logtail utility that checks log file contents, so you must configure the script to check the log files you want monitored. You can also adjust features such as the user who's to receive violation reports and the locations of files that contain strings for which the utility should look in log files. Once it's configured, you call logcheck.sh in a cron job. Logcheck then emails a report concerning any suspicious system logs to the user defined in logcheck.sh (root, by default).

Tracing Software Problems

Potential problems are not limited to hardware and driver issues. Software can also create headaches for a system administrator. Of course, many software problems are specific to the particular packages that create them; however, some tools and techniques can be used to help resolve problems that can occur with a variety of software packages. These include tools that can help trace a working program's activities, identifying the modules required by a program, finding open files, and locating strings in binary files.

Tracing a Program's Activities

You launch a program, and it annoys you by crashing, without presenting a single error message that helps in diagnosis—just segmentation fault or some similarly unhelpful message. This scenario is, sadly, common.

If you're running a GUI program from a GUI menu item, the first step to take is to run a terminal program and run the misbehaving program from the text-mode shell. Even GUI programs sometimes display error messages to standard output (aka stdout) or standard error (stderr), which displays on a console program if you launch the GUI program in that way. The stdout and stderr messages are lost if you launch the program from an icon or menu item, though. You may find some useful clue if you launch the program by typing its name.

If that fails, one way to obtain some clues about what's going wrong is to trace the program's operations using the strace program, which monitors the system calls a program makes. To use it, run strace and pass it the name of the program you're trying to use, along with any options you would normally pass it. The result will be a copious amount of output concerning the program's activities:

```
$ strace nedit file.txt
execve("/usr/bin/nedit", ["nedit", "file.txt"], [/* 66 vars */]) = 0
brk(0)                                  = 0x838000
mmap(NULL, 4096, PROT_READ|PROT_WRITE, MAP_PRIVATE|MAP_ANONYMOUS, -1, 0) = ↵
  0x7f7ba4b94000
access("/etc/ld.so.preload", R_OK)      = -1 ENOENT (No such file or directory)
open("/usr/local/lib/tls/x86_64/libXm.so.4", O_RDONLY) = -1 ENOENT (No such ↵
  file or directory)
stat("/usr/local/lib/tls/x86_64", 0x7fff4df2a890) = -1 ENOENT (No such file ↵
  or directory)
open("/usr/local/lib/tls/libXm.so.4", O_RDONLY) = -1 ENOENT (No such file or ↵
  directory)
```

The output will continue for quite a while; I've shown only the first few lines in this example. When the program crashes, the output will of course cease. You can examine the output for clues to what went wrong. The problem is likely to manifest itself a dozen or more lines from the end, so you may need to scroll backward before you find anything. It could be that a file was not found (several such examples appear in this sample output, although they weren't real problems in this case, since the program eventually found the files elsewhere), that the program attempted an illegal operation (such as an attempt to divide a number by 0), or something else.

With the cause of the failure in hand, you may be able to work around it or correct it outright. For instance, if the program was looking for a file that it couldn't find, perhaps you can locate and install the missing file—perhaps it's a configuration file, a library, or a font file. If the program is attempting to divide by 0, perhaps you can determine why it's doing so—it might be an illegal value in a configuration file or user input, for instance.

The ltrace command is similar to strace, but instead of monitoring system calls, ltrace monitors dynamic library calls. If the program is failing because of a problem with the support libraries installed on the computer, ltrace might help you locate the offending library so that you can replace it. Alternatively, you might upgrade or recompile the program so that it uses the libraries you have installed on your computer. As an example, compare the first few lines of ltrace output on the nedit program to those from strace, shown earlier:

```
$ ltrace nedit file.txt
__libc_start_main(0x409d70, 2, 0x7fffd00baaf8, 0x4a2340, 0x4a2330 <unfinished ↵
 ...>
XtSetLanguageProc(0, 0x40b210, 0, 0, 0x7fc364fa9300) = 0x7fc3659bb980
XtToolkitInitialize(0, 0x40b210, 0, 0, 0x7fc364fa9300) = 0x7fc365bf71ac
XtCreateApplicationContext(16, 0xffffffff, 256, 0, 0x7fc3659e58b0) = 0x83b0c0
XtSetWarningHandler(0x49cc60, 32, 0, 0x83c350, 0x7fc364fa9ed8) = 0
XtAppSetFallbackResources(0x83b0c0, 0x720cc0, 0, 0x83c350, 0x7fc364fa9ed8) = 0
XmRepTypeInstallTearOffModelConverter(0x83b0c0, 0x720cc0, 0, 0x83c350, ↵
 0x7fc364fa9ed8) = 0
getenv("NEDIT_HOME")                        = NULL
getenv("HOME")                              = "/home/rodsmith"
strncpy(0x7398a0, "/home/rodsmith", 4095)   = 0x7398a0
```

Identifying Required Libraries

In theory, Linux package management tools, such as the RPM Package Manager (RPM) and the Debian package tools, guarantee that all the software upon which a given program relies is installed. In practice, this guarantee is sometimes violated—you can install software outside of the package system, dependencies can be listed incorrectly in package files, files can be accidentally deleted without the aid of the package system, and so on.

The ldd program can sometimes be useful in identifying missing library files—that is, supplemental program code that a program binary relies upon to do its job. To use ldd, pass it the complete path to a program executable:

```
$ ldd /usr/bin/zip
        linux-vdso.so.1 =>  (0x00007fffbd5c5000)
        libbz2.so.1 => /lib/libbz2.so.1 (0x00007f5fe625c000)
        libc.so.6 => /lib/libc.so.6 (0x00007f5fe5f03000)
        /lib64/ld-linux-x86-64.so.2 (0x00007f5fe646d000)
```

This example binary has just four dependencies. The first of these, linux-vdso.so.1, is the *virtual dynamic shared object* (VDSO), which is part of the program itself and need not further concern you. The remaining three libraries have all been found on this system. The first two, libbz2.so.1 and libc.so.6, are referred to by name without a complete path in the binary, and the system has located them on the library path. The third, /lib64/ld-linux-x86-64.so.2, is referred to by complete path in the program's binary file; it must exist in that exact location to work.

If a library that a program requires is not present, the string not found replaces the complete program path to the right of the => string. Such a program won't run correctly; you're likely to see an error message about the missing library, and then the program will terminate.

Sometimes you can correct library problems by creating symbolic links. For instance, if a binary refers to libfoo.so.1 and this file doesn't exist, but if you do find a file called libfoo.so.1.0 or libfoo.so.1.2, creating a symbolic link to this file under the required name may satisfy the program. Don't create a link with a different version number, though—for instance, if you have libfoo.so.2, don't create a link from that to libfoo.so.1. In such cases, you should either track down the library of the correct version or replace the program so that it uses the library you have. Chapter 12 covers library management in more detail.

Libraries can themselves rely upon other libraries. Thus, a program whose immediate library dependencies are all met can still fail to run if one of its libraries' dependencies are not met. You can run ldd on the library files themselves in a recursive manner to verify that all the required libraries are present.

Finding Open Files

Some problems can be caused by inconveniently open files. Open files can prevent you from unmounting a filesystem, for instance. You can identify all your open files with the lsof command, which was described with reference to its network features in Chapter 5, "Networking Configuration." Used by itself, this command generates a list of all the open files on the computer, along with the users who opened the files and other information.

You're likely to want to pipe the results through grep to search for output that includes the specified string or use the -u *user1*[,*user2*...] option to limit output to those files opened by the specified user or users. For instance, suppose you can't unmount /mnt/cdrom because a file is in use on that device. You might then type this:

```
$ lsof | grep cdrom
bash  20139  paul    cwd DIR   11,0  6144    1728 /mnt/cdrom
```

This output reveals that the user paul has a bash shell open that's using the /mnt/cdrom directory. If you're paul, you can search for this shell and change to another directory to enable unmounting the disc. If not, you can either contact this user to do so or, using root privileges, kill the offending process using its process ID (PID) number (the second column of output—20139 in this example). Of course, killing such processes can annoy the user who owns them, but sometimes such actions are necessary.

Locating Strings in Binary Files

Sometimes it's helpful to be able to locate strings in binary files. You might need to identify which of several program files generated a particular message, for instance; or maybe you need to scan a word processor file but don't have a program that can read that program's format. The strings utility can often help in such situations. This program searches through a binary file for ASCII text, or text in other known encodings, and displays the resulting strings on the screen. The output looks something like this:

```
$ strings chapter11.doc
bjbjU
Chapter 11: System Troubleshooting I: Boot and Kernel Problems
The following Linux Professional Institute objectives are covered in this ↵
 chapter:
213.1 Identifying boot stages and troubleshooting bootloaders (weight: 4)
213.2 General troubleshooting (weight: 5)
```

Of course, this example's text continues for quite a way! In practice, you might need to pipe the results through less or redirect them to a file. Some of the strings are false alarms—the first output line in this example, for instance (bjbjU), isn't part of the document. You'll find many such false alarms if you apply strings to a Linux program file. Other output lines may be of interest, depending on your need.

Some binary file formats transform the data in such a way that strings won't help. The OpenOffice.org office suite, for instance, compresses its files with the ZIP format, which means that strings can't be extracted from it without first unzipping the file. Encrypted files' contents will also contain no useful strings.

Table 11.7 summarizes some of the common options for the `strings` program. Additional options exist but are relatively exotic; consult the `man` page for `strings` for details.

TABLE 11.7 Common strings options

Long option name	Short option name	Description
`--all`	`-a`	Scans the whole file. By default, `strings` limits its search to sections of program files that are initialized and loaded into memory. This option has no effect for non-program files.
`--print-file-name`	`-f`	Displays the name of the file before each string; useful when `strings` is passed multiple filenames or wildcards.
`--help`	N/A	Displays a summary of program options.
`--bytes=#`	`-n # or -#`	Displays all strings that are # characters long or longer. The default value is 4.
`--encoding=type`	`-e type`	Searches for strings using the specified *type* of encoding. Legal values for *type* are s (7-bit ASCII, the default), S (8-bit characters), b (16-bit big-endian), l (16-bit little-endian), B (32-bit big-endian), and L (32-bit little-endian). Values other than s (ASCII) apply to Unicode encodings.

Summary

Troubleshooting is a skill that's learned over time and from direct experience. Nonetheless, you can get a leg up on this important skill by understanding some basic principles and by knowing some of the utilities that are most often used in troubleshooting. This chapter presented some of this information, beginning with troubleshooting boot problems. Boot loaders present error messages that can be cryptic and that require specific actions to correct. Boot problems can also be the result of an incorrect or damaged initial RAM disk or difficulties in the SysV or Upstart startup scripts. The later in the process a boot problem lies, the more likely it is that you'll be able to boot the computer enough to correct the problem using your regular tools. If a problem is very early in the boot process, you may need to rely on an emergency recovery disc or other specialized tool to correct the problem.

Many classes of hardware and general software problems can cause difficulties. Diagnosing hardware problems requires you to be able to correctly identify your hardware, locate the relevant kernel driver or module, and recompile or reconfigure the software to fix the problem. You may need to examine the kernel ring buffer or log files. Log files can also be critical in resolving software problems and particularly problems with server software. Other software problems can be resolved with the help of tools that trace the software's operation or that enable you to view the contents of software binary files or the binary data files that the software produces.

Exam Essentials

Summarize where boot loader code resides.   Boot loader code may reside in the Master Boot Record (MBR) of the hard disk, in the officially unallocated sectors immediately following the MBR, in a BIOS Boot Partition on a GPT disk, in the boot sector of a partition or floppy disk, in files on an EFI System Partition on an EFI-based computer, and in files in the Linux /boot directory tree. In addition, utilities to manipulate the boot loader may exist in the normal locations for executable files on a Linux system. Non-Linux boot loaders may store code in other locations, as well.

Explain how the boot loader, the kernel, and the initial RAM disk interact.   The boot loader reads the kernel and initial RAM disk files from the hard disk and stores both of them in memory. The boot loader then executes the kernel, passing it the location of the initial RAM disk in memory as well as any other options specified in the boot loader's configuration file. Thereafter, the kernel uses the initial RAM disk to load modules and run utilities that are required to mount the regular Linux root (/) filesystem.

Summarize the features of the three major Linux disk-based boot loaders on BIOS-based computers.   LILO is the oldest of the popular BIOS boot loaders. It is a simple boot loader that can load a Linux kernel or chain-load a boot loader for other OSs. Although LILO is still a viable boot loader, is has been largely supplanted by GRUB Legacy, which can directly load a wider range of OS kernels. GRUB Legacy can also load its configuration file at boot time, simplifying reconfiguration. GRUB Legacy is being supplanted by GRUB 2, which is more sophisticated and supports loadable modules for filesystem support and other features.

Describe how Linux system services are started.   Most services are launched via SysV scripts or by Upstart. SysV scripts are located in /etc/init.d or /etc/rc.d/init.d; Upstart configuration files are stored in /etc/init. The relevant startup system runs the relevant scripts or starts the services under direction of the configuration file, thus starting each subsystem in turn.

Contrast the kernel ring buffer and system log files.   The kernel ring buffer keeps a temporary log of messages generated by the kernel. These messages relate to hardware and low-level kernel actions. System log files can sometimes contain similar messages, but they also hold messages from servers and other daemons. Such system log messages could provide information on server crashes, normal user logins, failed login attempts, and so on. Both the kernel ring buffer and system log files can record information on both normal and abnormal operations.

Summarize tools to learn about hardware. The uname utility provides basic information about the CPU, while the /proc/cpuinfo file provides more detailed information about the CPU. The lspci and lsusb utilities provide information about PCI and USB devices, respectively. This information enables you to verify that the device is visible to the system, but not that any driver exists to access it. The lsdev utility summarizes information about how devices are using hardware resources (interrupts, DMA channels, and I/O ports).

Explain how kernel modules are managed in Linux. Kernel modules are drivers and other kernel features that can be loaded and unloaded after the kernel has booted. The insmod utility loads a single kernel module, whereas modprobe loads a module and all those upon which it depends. You can learn what modules are loaded with the lsmod program. Ordinarily, Linux loads kernel modules when they're required, but you may need to manually intervene if these automatic mechanisms break down.

Summarize tools that can help trace a program's activities. You can use the strace program to trace a program's system calls, which can help you identify the cause of certain crashes. Similarly, ltrace will trace a program's library calls. The ldd program identifies all the libraries that a program relies upon.

Review Questions

1. Where might the BIOS find a boot loader?

   A. RAM

   B. /dev/boot

   C. MBR

   D. /dev/kmem

2. Which of the following files might you edit to configure GRUB Legacy? (Choose all that apply.)

   A. /boot/grub/menu.lst

   B. /etc/boot.conf

   C. /boot/grub/grub.conf

   D. /boot/menu.conf

3. What action must you take after editing the /etc/lilo.conf file, assuming this file is relevant to your installation?

   A. Type **lilo-install** as root.

   B. Edit /boot/grub/grub.cfg as root.

   C. Edit /boot/lilo/lilo.cfg as root.

   D. Type **lilo** as root.

4. What tool can you use to completely disable hardware that's built into a computer's motherboard?

   A. The insmod utility

   B. The firmware's setup utility

   C. GRUB 2's hwdel command

   D. The initrd command

5. Which two software components is GRUB 2 likely to load on an EFI-based system? (Select two.)

   A. EFI driver modules

   B. A Linux kernel

   C. The contents of /etc/passwd

   D. An initial RAM disk

6. You attempt to boot your computer but get only a grub> prompt. You then type the following command and receive the response shown:

```
grub> ls
(hd0) (hd0,1)
```

Where is your Linux kernel most likely to be found?

A. On /dev/hda0

B. On /dev/hd0

C. On /dev/sd0

D. On (hd0,1)

7. What normally resides in /etc/init.d, if it's present on the Linux computer?

A. Upstart configuration files

B. Boot loader configuration files

C. SysV startup scripts

D. The BIOS configuration utility

8. You've compiled a new kernel and created a new GRUB 2 configuration for it. Just after you reboot, however, you realize that you mistyped the filename of the new kernel in the GRUB configuration file. How can you boot the new kernel despite this error?

A. Select the almost-correct entry from the GRUB menu, and type E to edit it.

B. Select the Create Entry option from the GRUB menu to create a new entry.

C. Select the Auto-Detect OSs entry from the GRUB menu to detect your new kernel.

D. You can't.

9. You install Linux on a computer with a single SATA disk and used GRUB 2 to boot it. In experimenting with disk utilities, you accidentally overwrite GRUB's MBR entry. You use Super GRUB Disk to boot into your normal Linux installation. How can you re-install GRUB to the MBR so that you can boot normally without using Super GRUB Disk in the future?

A. Edit /boot/mbr/contents as root.

B. Type mbr-restore /dev/sda as root.

C. Type grub-install /dev/sda as root.

D. Edit /boot/grub/grub.cfg as root.

10. You want to examine the kernel ring buffer to debug a hardware problem. How would you do this?

A. Type ringbuffer at a command prompt.

B. Type dmesg at a command prompt.

C. Reboot and add the string ring to the kernel line in GRUB.

D. Install a Token Ring device and examine its output.

11. You've installed a new PCI Ethernet card, but it doesn't seem to be working. What can you do to verify that the hardware is visible to Linux?

   A. Type `ping 127.0.0.1` to check connectivity.

   B. Check that the Ethernet cable is firmly plugged in.

   C. Type `cat /proc/ethernet` at a command prompt.

   D. Type `lspci` at a command prompt.

12. An administrator types `lsusb` at a Linux command prompt. What type of information will appear?

   A. Basic identifying information on USB devices, including the USB controllers and all attached devices

   B. Information on the drivers and detailed capabilities of all USB devices attached to the computer

   C. A report on the success or failure to load the USB driver stack

   D. A summary of the amount of data that's been transferred to and from USB devices since the computer was booted

13. Which of the following commands loads a kernel module? (Choose all that apply.)

   A. `rmmod`

   B. `modprobe`

   C. `lsmod`

   D. `insmod`

14. You use a USB flash drive and, while the drive is still mounted, type `lsmod`, but you see no entries for kernel modules that you know are required to access a USB flash drive. Why might this be?

   A. The `lsmod` command displays information only on drivers that are in use by the user who typed the command.

   B. The `lsmod` command displays information only on drivers that are doing work at the moment the command is typed.

   C. The `lsmod` command displays information only on drivers that are built as modules, not those that are built directly into the kernel.

   D. The `lsmod` command displays information only on drivers that are used by hardware devices internal to the computer.

15. A computer has been running continuously for six months, and you want to examine its kernel ring buffer to determine how it initially detected its Ethernet cards. You find that this information is not present, however, because of numerous kernel messages made since then. Where might you look for this information at this time?

   A. `/proc/dmesg`

   B. `/var/log/eth`*n*, where *n* is the Ethernet device number

   C. `/var/log/dmesg`

   D. `/tmp/ringbuffer`

16. How can you find technical details about your computer's CPU, such as its clock speed and number of cores?

    A. `cat /proc/cpuinfo`

    B. `less /var/log/cpu`

    C. `uname -i`

    D. `lspci --cpu`

17. You suspect that two devices might be mistakenly sharing the same I/O space. How can you test this hypothesis?

    A. Type `cat /proc/interrupts`

    B. Type `cat /proc/dma`

    C. Type `lsmod`

    D. Type `lsdev`

18. A program is crashing mysteriously and leaving no helpful error messages. Which of the following utilities might provide some clues about the source of the problem? (Select two.)

    A. `strace`

    B. `strings`

    C. `uname`

    D. `ltrace`

19. An NFS server, `smallserver`, has just one client computer, `smallclient`. You want to shut down `smallserver` for maintenance, but before you do so, you want to ensure that nobody is accessing its files at the moment. What command can you type on `smallclient` to do this? (The `smallserver` shares are all mounted under `/sharedfiles` on the client.)

    A. `top | grep sharedfiles`

    B. `lsof | grep sharedfiles`

    C. `lsdev | grep sharedfiles`

    D. `lsmod | grep sharedfiles`

20. For which of the following file types will `strings` *not* return data that might be meaningful?

    A. A system log file (/var/log/messages) compressed with `gzip`

    B. A set of plain-text files archived (but not compressed) with `tar`

    C. A binary program file (for a PowerPC executable), when `strings` is run on an *x*86 computer

    D. A PostScript file (for printing) created in 1989

Answers to Review Questions

1. C. The Master Boot Record (MBR) can contain a small boot loader, making option C correct. If more space is required, the boot loader must load a secondary boot loader. Although the boot loader is loaded into RAM, it's not stored there permanently because RAM is volatile storage, so option A is incorrect. Both /dev/boot and /dev/kmem are references to files on Linux filesystems; they're meaningful only after the BIOS has found a boot loader and run it and lots of other boot processes have occurred, so options B and D are both incorrect.

2. A, C. The official GRUB Legacy configuration filename is /boot/grub/menu.1st; however, some distributions use /boot/grub/grub.conf instead. Thus, options A and C are both correct. Options B and C are fictitious.

3. D. LILO relies upon the lilo utility to read /etc/lilo.conf and write binary code that reflects the configuration file into locations that the boot loader can read. Thus, after editing /etc/lilo.conf, you must type **lilo** to re-install the boot loader, as option D specifies. Option A's lilo-install command is fictitious (although there is a grub-install command to install GRUB). The /boot/grub/grub.cfg file is a GRUB 2 configuration file, so it's irrelevant to LILO configuration, and option B is incorrect. There is no /boot/lilo/lilo.cfg file, so option C is incorrect.

4. B. Computers come with firmware configuration tools that can, among other things, completely disable some of the hardware devices that are built into the computer. Thus, option B is correct. The Linux insmod utility can load a kernel module. This action won't disable hardware, but could make it available under Linux, so option A has, if anything, the opposite of the specified effect. Option C describes a fictitious command. There is no standard initrd command, although this is a term that refers to an initial RAM disk, which is used to hold kernel modules and setup utilities that the Linux kernel can use before it has mounted its ultimate root (/) filesystem.

5. B, D. Whether it runs on a BIOS-based computer or an EFI-based computer, when it boots Linux, GRUB 2 loads a Linux kernel and (usually) an initial RAM disk, so options B and D are correct. EFI driver modules may be loaded by the EFI prior to launching GRUB 2, but they aren't loaded by GRUB 2 itself, so option A is incorrect. Linux reads the contents of /etc/passwd well after GRUB 2 has finished its work, so option C is incorrect.

6. D. The output of the GRUB 1s command reveals that GRUB can see one whole hard disk, which it identifies as (hd0), and that this disk has one partition, which GRUB identifies as (hd0,1). Thus, there's one possible location for the Linux kernel: (hd0,1). This partition probably corresponds to Linux's /dev/sda1, but it could be /dev/hda1 or some other device. Options A, B, and C all describe non-standard Linux device descriptors, so none of them is a likely location for the kernel. The problem that caused GRUB to display its grub> prompt could be serious enough that GRUB is failing to detect a hard disk; thus, the kernel could reside elsewhere. Given the provided information, though, option D is the single most likely location and is the *only* possible location among those specified.

7. C. Most Linux distributions place SysV startup scripts in /etc/init.d or /etc/rc.d/init.d, so option C is correct. Upstart configuration files normally reside in /etc/init, so option A is incorrect. Linux boot loader configuration files normally reside in /etc/lilo.conf, /boot/grub, or /boot/grub2, depending on the boot loader in use, so option B is incorrect. The BIOS configuration utility is built into the computer's hardware, so it's not accessible from the Linux filesystem at all, making option D incorrect.

8. A. You can edit a GRUB 2 menu entry by selecting it and typing E, as described in option A. You will, however, have to know exactly what your error was or be able to use the GRUB shell to locate the exact filename. The GRUB interactive menu doesn't have a Create Entry or Auto-Detect OSs option, making options B and C incorrect. Since option A is correct, option D can't be correct.

9. C. The grub-install utility installs GRUB to the MBR or to other locations specified in the GRUB configuration file or on the command line, so option C is correct. There is no /boot/mbr/contents file or mbr-restore utility, so options A and B are both incorrect. Although /boot/grub/grub.cfg is GRUB 2's configuration file, the fact that Super GRUB Disk was able to boot the computer means that this file is intact enough to boot Linux, so it doesn't need to be edited. Furthermore, editing this file would not correct the damage to the MBR, so option D is incorrect.

10. B. The dmesg command displays the contents of the kernel ring buffer, which holds kernel messages, so option B is correct. There is no standard ringbuffer command, so option A is incorrect. Adding ring to the kernel options when booting will not have the desired effect, so option C is incorrect. Token Ring is a network hardware standard, not a way to examine the kernel ring buffer, so option D is incorrect.

11. D. The lspci command lists all the detected PCI devices, so if the card is installed correctly and working, it should show up in the lspci output. Thus, option D is correct. Although ping can be a useful network diagnostic tool, option A's use of it doesn't test Ethernet cards, so that option is incorrect. Option B provides sound basic network debugging advice, but it won't help to verify that the card is visible to Linux. There is no /proc/ethernet file, so option C won't help.

12. A. The lsusb command summarizes the USB devices that are available to the computer, as option A says. Options B, C, and D are all fictitious.

13. B, D. The modprobe command loads a module and, if necessary, all those upon which it depends. The insmod command loads a module, but only if all its dependencies are met. Thus, options B and D are correct. The rmmod command removes a module, and lsmod lists the loaded modules, so options A and C are incorrect.

14. C. If a driver is built into the main kernel file, lsmod won't display information on it. Thus, if the relevant drivers are built into the kernel, the observed behavior would occur because option C is a correct statement. The lsmod command does display information on drivers that are used to service other users' needs, on drivers that are loaded but not actively working, and on some types of external hardware devices, contrary to options A, B, and D, respectively.

15. C. Many distributions store a copy of the kernel ring buffer output in /var/log/dmesg just after the system boots, so option C is a likely location. Sometimes the file is called /var/log/boot.log, and some distributions don't store this data at all, so finding the information is not certain. Options A, B, and D all describe fictitious files.

16. A. The /proc/cpuinfo pseudo-file holds the requested information, so viewing this file with cat (or less or various other tools) will retrieve the requested information, making option A correct. There is no standard /var/log/cpu file, so option B is incorrect. Although the uname utility will return some technical information about the CPU, the -i option restricts output to the hardware platform (normally a manufacturer identification), so option C is incorrect. The lspci utility returns information on PCI devices, not the CPU, and it has no --cpu option, so option D is incorrect. (The lscpu command is valid, but this command is distinct from lspci.)

17. D. The ldev utility summarizes resources used by various devices, including their I/O port addresses. Thus, option D will test the hypothesis. (You must be alert to the fact that the same device may be identified more than once in the output, though.) The /proc/interrupts and /proc/dma pseudo-files report in interrupts and DMA channels used by various devices, not I/O ports; thus, these options won't work. (You could type **cat /proc/ioports**, though; this would work as well as option D.) Option C's lsmod utility displays information on loaded kernel modules, not I/O space, so it's incorrect.

18. A, D. The strace utility runs a program and traces its system calls, which can be a useful diagnostic in this example. Similarly, the ltrace utility runs a program and traces its library calls, which can also be a useful diagnostic. Thus, options A and D are correct. The strings program scans a binary file for strings and displays them. This can be useful for some tasks, but it's unlikely to yield any helpful information about why a program is crashing. The uname utility displays information about the kernel and CPU, but unless you know that the program is incompatible with certain kernels or CPUs, this information is likely to be unhelpful.

19. B. Option B uses the lsof utility to list all open files and search the list for any output that includes the string sharedfiles. This will accomplish the specified goal. Option A's top command displays a list of processes ordered according to their CPU use (or various other parameters that can be set). Option C's lsdev displays information on hardware use. Option D's lsmod displays information on modules that are currently loaded.

20. A. Most compression techniques replace plain-text strings with more compact forms that can't be usefully extracted by strings, so option A is correct: strings will return, at best, short strings that won't be meaningful or useful. The tar utility archives files together and doesn't compress them unless explicitly told to do so, so strings will extract the original plain-text files described in option B. No matter what the original executable format, strings will extract strings associated with program prompts, and perhaps variable names and other data, from binary program files, so option C is incorrect. Although a PostScript file could represent a graphics file, it will contain plain-text PostScript commands, which strings will extract, so option D is incorrect. (The date the file was created is irrelevant.)

Chapter

12

System Troubleshooting II: System Resources and the User Environment

THE FOLLOWING LINUX PROFESSIONAL INSTITUTE OBJECTIVES ARE COVERED IN THIS CHAPTER:

✓ 213.3 Troubleshooting system resources (weight: 5)

✓ 213.4 Troubleshooting environment configurations (weight: 5)

This chapter continues the examination of troubleshooting tools and techniques begun in Chapter 11, "System Troubleshooting I: Boot and Kernel Problems." This chapter covers higher-level problems, including system initialization issues, kernel run-time problems, difficulties with accounts, bash and other shell issues, problems with processes that are currently running (or that aren't but should be), and problems relating to regularly scheduled processes.

The general troubleshooting techniques described at the beginning of Chapter 11 apply equally well to these problems as to those described in Chapter 11. The problems covered in this chapter simply apply to a different set of symptoms and causes.

Troubleshooting System Initialization

Chapter 11 included information on troubleshooting the early steps of the boot process, including the boot loader and parts of the Linux startup system. This chapter covers additional system initialization issues, including the init process, local startup scripts, and login process difficulties.

Managing the Initialization Process

If Linux isn't initializing correctly, the first thing to check is what initialization system it uses. As described in Chapter 1, "System Startup and Advanced System Management," two startup systems are common on Linux today: System V (SysV) startup scripts and Upstart. Upstart includes a SysV compatibility layer, so some SysV issues apply to Upstart. Variants on these systems, and particularly on SysV scripts, are common, so you can run into distribution-specific issues.

Managing SysV Issues

SysV issues can exist because of problems in /etc/inittab, which sets the runlevel and starts a few very basic processes, or in the SysV startup scripts, which launch most system services.

Fixing */etc/inittab* Problems

One common problem with /etc/inittab is an incorrect runlevel setting. This is set via the id line, which normally resides near the start of the file:

```
id:3:initdefault:
```

This example sets the runlevel to 3. On Red Hat, Fedora, Mandriva, OpenSUSE, and several other distributions, runlevel 3 starts a text-mode multi-user mode, so X won't run in runlevel 3. If X isn't running when you want it to, an incorrect default runlevel may be the problem. (Debian, Ubuntu, Gentoo, and several other distributions start X by using SysV or Upstart startup scripts, so if X is failing to start, the runlevel may not be an issue for them.)

> Computers that use Upstart frequently lack an /etc/inittab file; however, you can add one to set the default runlevel. Configure it with an id line, but set the default runlevel you want to use.

Chapter 1's Table 1.1 describes the conventional function of all the runlevels. If the computer is shutting down or rebooting as soon as it starts up, you might have incorrectly set the runlevel to runlevel 0 or 6. A default runlevel of 1 will boot the system into single-user mode, which is normally undesirable.

You can check your current runlevel by using the runlevel command, which returns the previous and current runlevels:

```
$ runlevel
N 5
```

This example shows that the computer is currently in runlevel 5. The N means that it has not been in another runlevel since booting. If the system had changed runlevels, N would be replaced by another runlevel number, such as 3. As described in Chapter 1, you can change runlevels by using the telinit command, as in **telinit 3** to change to runlevel 3.

Subsequent lines of /etc/inittab start various processes, including the rc script that launches SysV startup scripts, getty processes that handle console and RS-232 serial port logins, and more. Some distributions use /etc/inittab to launch X, either by itself or in conjunction with a SysV startup script:

```
x:5:respawn:/etc/X11/prefdm -nodaemon
```

This example, taken from a CentOS system, begins with the character x alone in the first field, and in this example, it works only in runlevel 5 and uses the /etc/X11/prefdm script to start X and an X Display Manager (XDM) program. If X isn't starting, a misconfiguration of this line could be the culprit; however, systems based upon Upstart and even some SysV systems use SysV startup scripts to launch X. Thus, you will have to check distribution-specific documentation or a backup of /etc/inittab from a time when X was starting to determine whether you need to change this line.

Fixing Startup Script Problems

As the computer boots, it displays startup messages relating to the success or failure to start SysV services:

```
Starting Apache...                              [ FAILED ]
```

This example indicates that the Apache Web server failed to start. Most such problems must be dealt with in ways specific to the service that failed to start, so you should consult relevant chapters of this book, any log files that might be relevant, online documentation, or books specific to the server or subsystem in question in order to help resolve the problem.

If a server isn't starting and you see no startup messages about it, it could be configured to not start in the current runlevel. You should first check your current runlevel and verify that it's correct. If not, change runlevels, and perhaps change /etc/inittab to ensure that your system boots into the correct runlevel in the future.

Once you've determined that you're in the correct runlevel and that the service isn't running, you should check the startup script's symbolic link in the appropriate SysV startup directory. These directories are typically called /etc/rc?.d, /etc/rc.d/rc?.d, or /etc/init.d/rc?.d, where ? is the runlevel number. (Gentoo uses an unusual named runlevel system and places its startup script links in /etc/runlevels/*name*, where *name* is the runlevel name.)

Runlevel startup scripts are named S##*name* or K##*name*, where ## is a two-digit number and *name* is the name of the linked-to script. Links with names that begin with S denote scripts that are run with the start parameter, and those with names that begin with K denote scripts that are run with the stop parameter. Thus, if a script in the runlevel directory has a name that starts with K, it won't start. If it should start, change its name so that it begins with S instead. (Gentoo uses names alone; scripts in a runlevel directory are always started in that directory.) One important caveat is that you must set the two-digit sequence number correctly. Some distributions' scripts include comments that specify suitable numbers. With others, the start and stop sequence numbers should sum to 99, so you can subtract the stop number from 99 to obtain the start number. For instance, if the current link is K37someserver, the correct start value would be 99 − 37 = 62, and you should rename the link to S62someserver.

If a service is starting and you don't want it to start, you can reverse this process, renaming the symbolic link so that it starts with K rather than with S. Removing the symbolic link (say, with rm) will prevent the service from starting if you boot directly into the runlevel, but this will not guarantee that the service will shut down if you enter the runlevel from another runlevel in which the service was started. Thus, you should rename SysV symbolic links rather than delete them if you want their corresponding services to be reliably shut down.

If a SysV startup script exists in `/etc/init.d` or `/etc/rc.d` but there's no corresponding script in the runlevel-specific directory, you can create a symbolic link with `ln`:

```
# ln -s /etc/rc.d/init.d/someserver /etc/rc.d/rc3.d/S20someserver
```

This example creates a link to start the server in runlevel 3, giving it a sequence number of 20. Of course, you should check the script for comments or otherwise determine what an appropriate sequence number is.

Another way to handle SysV startup scripts is to use tools such as `chkconfig`, `ntsysv`, `update-rc.d`, and `rc-update`. Chapter 1 describes some of these tools in detail, and of course you can check their man pages for more information.

Managing Upstart Issues

Upstart is a newer startup system than SysV scripts, so it's not as well documented, and there are fewer utilities that can help you manage Upstart scripts. Major distributions that use Upstart employ a SysV compatibility layer, so you can use SysV methods for managing at least some services. As described earlier, this includes setting the default runlevel via `/etc/inittab`.

As distributions migrate to Upstart-native startup methods, though, you'll need to begin managing the Upstart configuration files in the `/etc/init` or `/etc/event.d` directory in order to adjust the services that start in specific runlevels or in response to other system events. Chapter 1 describes the Upstart configuration file's basic features, so you should consult it to learn how to manage Upstart services. In particular, if a service is not starting and you want it to or if it's starting and you don't want it to, you may need to search for the string `runlevel` and adjust the list of runlevels. For instance, a configuration file might include the following lines:

```
start on runlevel [2345]
stop on runlevel [!2345]
```

These lines tell Upstart to start the service in runlevels 2 through 5 and to stop it in all runlevels *except* 2 through 5. (The exclamation mark, !, is a common negation character that can be read as "not"; the second line therefore refers to runlevels that are "not 2, 3, 4, or 5.") If you don't want the service to start in runlevel 5, you should remove 5 from both lists.

If you're used to dealing with SysV startup scripts, you may become confused or frustrated when the usual techniques for enabling, disabling, or otherwise altering a service don't work on an Upstart-based system. If you have such problems, be sure to check for an Upstart configuration file. Study it and try to determine how to achieve your desired goals with that file.

Dealing with Local Startup Scripts

Occasionally it's desirable to start a service through some means other than a SysV script or the Upstart system. This is most frequently the case when you've compiled a server yourself or installed it from a package file intended for a distribution other than the one you're using. In such cases, the program may not come with a SysV startup script or Upstart configuration file, or the provided script or file may not work correctly on your system.

Many Linux distributions include a startup script that runs after the other SysV startup scripts. This script is generally called /etc/rc.local, /etc/rc.d/rc.local, /etc/rc.d/boot.local, or something similar. (Old versions of Debian used files in a directory called /etc/rc.local, but this usage has been deprecated.) The first challenge with such scripts is determining the correct script name, which is highly distribution-specific. Try typing **find /etc -name** "*local*" to locate candidate files, or consult your distribution's documentation.

Whatever its name, you can launch a server or other program from a local startup script by entering the command you would use to launch the program manually, as described in the program's documentation. For instance, you might include the following line to launch an FTP server:

/usr/sbin/vsftpd &

One common problem with local startup scripts relates to the presence (or lack thereof) of a trailing ampersand (&). If this symbol is not present and if the program does not return control to the calling program until it terminates, then the script will stop execution until the program terminates. In the case of a server or other daemon, this could be a very long time, so subsequent lines in the script might not execute unless the daemon is launched in the background by using an ampersand, as in the preceding example. Some daemons are designed to always run in the background, though, so an ampersand is unnecessary. Other programs should run and immediately terminate. For instance, the iptables program (described in Chapter 7, "Advanced Network Configuration") executes quickly and terminates, so it normally isn't called with an ampersand. The bottom line is that you must check your programs' documentation to learn how to call them. If in doubt, experiment.

One thing to keep in mind when running a server via the local startup script is that this method provides no means to shut down a server, as you can do by passing the stop parameter to a SysV startup script. If you want to stop such a server, you'll need to use the Linux kill or killall command, possibly after locating the server's process ID number via ps. For instance, the following sequence can stop the vsftpd server:

```
# ps ax | grep ftp
 6382 ?        S       0:00 vsftpd
# kill 6382
```

Managing Login Processes

Login processes come in three main types, although some login methods span categories: local text-mode logins, GUI logins, and network logins. Each method has its own challenges, although certain commonalities exist, as well.

Managing Text-Mode Logins

When you log into a text-mode console, you're using a *virtual terminal*. To understand virtual terminals, remember that Linux was designed as a clone of Unix, which is a multiuser OS. Traditionally, Unix systems have supported many simultaneous users, each working from a physical *terminal*—a device consisting of a keyboard, a monitor, and perhaps a mouse—that enables a user to access a computer remotely. You can use terminals with Linux, but a standard PC has one primary keyboard and monitor. To improve usability, Linux supports configuring the system so that these devices can act like several physical terminals—that is, they're virtual. Each virtual terminal can run a separate program or even support logins under different usernames. This feature enables you to run many programs and easily switch between them.

Most standard installations define six virtual text-mode terminals, reached by pressing Alt+F1 through Alt+F6. On a SysV-based system, these terminals are defined in the /etc/inittab configuration file, using lines like the following:

```
1:2345:respawn:/sbin/mingetty tty1
2:2345:respawn:/sbin/mingetty tty2
3:2345:respawn:/sbin/mingetty tty3
4:2345:respawn:/sbin/mingetty tty4
5:2345:respawn:/sbin/mingetty tty5
6:2345:respawn:/sbin/mingetty tty6
```

These lines tell the system to run mingetty on tty1 through tty6—that is, the first six virtual terminals. An Upstart-based system typically includes equivalent configurations in the ttyn.conf files, where *n* is the terminal number, in /etc/init or /etc/event.d; however, the configuration for a single terminal is likely to be broken across several lines:

```
start on stopped rc2
start on stopped rc3
start on stopped rc4

stop on runlevel 0
stop on runlevel 1
stop on runlevel 6

respawn
exec /sbin/mingetty tty1
```

The mingetty program is one of several programs known collectively as getty programs. These programs manage the interactions between a terminal (either real or virtual) and the login program, which accepts user logins. Several getty programs are available, and different distributions favor different gettys.

Serious problems with text-mode login processes are rare; however, if the relevant configuration file becomes damaged, you may need to re-create it from a backup or a sample. Be sure to use a sample for your distribution! This configuration detail varies a great deal between distributions, so using the wrong sample will most likely fail.

You may want to adjust the number of virtual terminals supported by your system. If so, you can add or remove lines from /etc/inittab or add or remove files from /etc/init or /etc/event.d. Be sure to edit the lines or files to refer to the correct terminal number (tty1, tty2, and so on). If you make such a change, you may need to alter your X configuration, too; X occupies a virtual terminal just like text-mode logins!

A variant of this configuration applies to logins via RS-232 serial ports or modems. These configurations look much like the virtual terminal login configurations, but they use different device references—typically ttySn rather than ttyn. They may also use different getty programs. In particular, mingetty supports only local virtual terminals, not RS-232 serial ports or modems. If you need to configure your computer to support such logins, you should consult the documentation for the getty program you intend to use.

 Logins via RS-232 serial ports and modems used to be very common as a means of supporting rooms of users at "dumb terminals" or via dial-up modems. Today such users are more likely to use network login methods.

Local logins can sometimes go wrong because of authentication issues. Ordinarily, the getty program relies on the login program to present the login: prompt, to prompt for the password, and to authenticate the user. Sometimes this doesn't work correctly, typically because of damage to the Pluggable Authentication Modules (PAM) configuration. Chapter 10, "Security," describes PAM configuration in more detail. If you suspect damage to your PAM configuration, your best bet is to restore the PAM configuration files, particularly the ones for login and any files it references, to their default settings. If necessary, you can use your package manager to search for the package to which /etc/pam .d/login belongs and reinstall it—if you can log in! If not, you may need to copy the file from a working installation with the help of an emergency recovery disc. Be sure to use the file from the same distribution as the problem system runs, though; as noted in Chapter 10, PAM configurations vary a great deal from one distribution to another.

Managing GUI Logins

Linux GUI logins are handled by a program that uses the X Display Manager Control Protocol (XDMCP). Three XDMCP programs are common: the original XDM, the GNOME Display Manager (GDM), and the KDE Display Manager (KDM). GDM and KDM are the most common XDMCP programs for Linux. These programs enable users to select their desktop environment, to shut down the computer, and to set various other options. XDM, by contrast, is fairly bare-bones; it just accepts a username and password.

Some GUI login problems relate to PAM configuration, and these problems require fixing the PAM login files, as described for PAM problems with login. The main difference is that the PAM configuration file is different—typically gdm or kdm in /etc/pam.d.

Some GUI login problems relate to GUI login scripts, such as ~/.xinitrc. Such problems are similar to those that can occur with bash login scripts, as described later in "Investigating bash Login Scripts."

Managing Network Logins

Network-enabled logins pose their own challenges. Several protocols are commonly used for this purpose, including the following:

Telnet   The Telnet protocol is an old text-mode login protocol. As a general rule, it shouldn't be used today, since it passes data, including passwords, over the network in an unencrypted form. The telnet client program, however, can still be useful in diagnosing network problems; you can use it to connect to many other servers and issue server-specific commands. This use requires that you understand the network protocol in question, though.

SSH   The Secure Shell (SSH) protocol is a replacement for Telnet. SSH encrypts all data, so it's relatively safe to use even on an untrusted network such as the Internet. SSH also supports options such as tunneling and file transfers, which extends its utility. Chapter 7 describes SSH in more detail.

XDMCP   Although XDMCP is often used only on local computers, it can be configured to accept remote logins. This protocol doesn't encrypt login data, though, so it's generally used only on well-protected local networks. XDMCP is only part of a network login solution; it handles network logins but not subsequent data transfers. For that, X is used.

X   The X Window System, or X for short, is a network-enabled GUI. Used in conjunction with XDMCP, Telnet, SSH, or some other network login method, X enables users sitting at one computer to use applications on another computer. By itself, X doesn't encrypt data; you must tunnel it through SSH or use some other tool to secure its data transfers.

VNC   Virtual Network Computing (VNC) is a cross-platform GUI remote login tool. It can be used in Linux to provide access to an X session that's already being displayed or to provide a remote login to a unique session, more like what XDMCP and X provide. Like most of the other remote login protocol, VNC doesn't encrypt most data, although it can encrypt passwords.

Some network login protocol problems relate to authentication and should be addressed much like the PAM problems described earlier in "Managing Text-Mode Logins." Other problems relate to startup of the relevant servers; you may need to delve into SysV, Upstart, or other startup scripts. Firewalls, either on the computer that runs the server or on a network's router, can sometimes block access, so you should check your firewall configuration if you can't connect. Other problems are highly server-specific.

Adjusting Kernel Options

Chapter 2, "Linux Kernel Configuration," describes how to set compile-time kernel options and compile the kernel. Some kernel options, however, may be adjusted as the computer runs. The /proc filesystem and sysctl utility both do this job. The /proc filesystem is a pseudo-filesystem that enables you to view and modify various kernel parameters as if they were files. For instance, /proc/scsi holds data on the Small Computer System Interface (SCSI) disk subsystem. You can type **cat /proc/scsi/scsi** to see information on all the SCSI devices on your system.

From a software perspective, including the contents of /proc/scsi, any device that's handled by the SCSI subsystem is SCSI, even if the hardware itself is not SCSI hardware. Most Serial Advanced Technology Attachment (SATA) disks are handled by Linux's SCSI subsystem, even though they aren't technically SCSI devices.

Various chapters of this book have referred to specific files in the /proc directory tree. You may want to take some time to peruse this directory tree to learn what it contains. Viewing files in this tree can't do any harm, but you should be cautious about writing values to these files. Although writing to files in /proc will often accomplish nothing, some of these files control features such as Linux's ability to function as a router, so modifying /proc files can have undesirable consequences. If you believe you've accidentally made such a change but don't know how to undo it, reboot; the /proc directory tree, being virtual, is re-created each time the computer boots, so rebooting will reset it.

The sysctl program enables you to view and set options in the /proc/sys directory tree using a *key*, which is a named variable, and a *value*, which is the setting associated with the key. Keys come in multiple parts, separated by dots (.) or slashes (/). These parts correspond to the subdirectories and files in the /proc/sys directory tree. For instance, the kernel.ostype (or kernel/ostype) key refers to the /proc/sys/kernel/ostype file. This key (or file) normally contains the value Linux on a Linux system.

The syntax for sysctl is as follows:

```
sysctl [ options ] [ key | key=value | filename ]
```

Table 12.1 summarizes the options available for sysctl.

TABLE 12.1   Common sysctl options

Option Name	Meaning
-a	This option displays all the keys and their associated values. It's used without a key or filename.
-A	This option works much like the -a option. The man page specifies a table form.

Option Name	Meaning
-n	You can disable the display of key names with this option.
-N	This option disables display of values.
-q	This option is much like -N, but it affects only standard output.
-e	This option disables the display of errors should sysctl encounter an unknown key.
-w	You can change a setting with this option. You must then pass *key=value*, where *key* is a key name and *value* is the value you want to set.
-p	You can change multiple settings at once by specifying them in a file, whose name you must pass to sysctl.

Most of the options in Table 12.1 refer to read activity. If you pass -a as the first parameter, you can view all of the keys, values, or both. If you don't use -a, you'll normally pass a key name to see the associated value or use the -w or -p option to change one or a set of values. For instance, suppose you want to verify and then reset the computer's hostname and reset various options to their startup values. You might type this:

```
# sysctl kernel.hostname
kernel.hostname = diana.luna.edu
# sysctl -w kernel.hostname=artemis.luna.edu
kernel.hostname = artemis.luna.edu
# sysctl -p /etc/sysctl.conf
```

The final command in this example will be followed by lines that echo the keys and values that are being set from the specified file. In fact, the /etc/sysctl.conf file is the name of a file that holds the computer's startup kernel options. You can peruse and edit this file if you want to make permanent changes to your computer's configuration.

Most of the options that can be set with sysctl can also be set with more specialized tools. The main advantage of sysctl or the /etc/sysctl .conf file is that you can set a variety of options using one tool or from one location.

Fixing Account Problems

Many problems can plague Linux accounts. Users can lose their passwords, passwords and other data can become corrupt, shells can be set incorrectly, the associations between users and groups can become confused, user ID (UID) and group ID (GID) values can need changing, and so on. Chances are you'll need to deal with such problems from time to time, so the next few pages cover them.

This section assumes you understand the basics of local account management using utilities such as useradd, userdel, usermod, and passwd. These utilities are covered in the LPIC-1 certification.

Dealing with Password Problems

Some password problems are really problems with PAM configuration, as described earlier in "Managing Text-Mode Logins." Symptoms typically include an inability of any user to log in, or problems with all users who use a particular authentication method, such as Lightweight Directory Access Protocol (LDAP). Likewise, if problems affect only one server or login method (such as text-mode logins but not GUI logins), the problem is not likely to be with the account configuration but with PAM or the server that has problems.

The problems described here relate to the storage of account and password information. In a standard Linux installation, you can find account data in three files, as outlined in Table 12.2. Some installations rely on data in other locations, such as in an LDAP server. If problems arise with such alternate locations, you may need to use methods not described here to fix the difficulties.

TABLE 12.2   Linux account database files

File	Purpose
/etc/passwd	Holds basic account information: username, password or (more commonly) x value, UID number, GID number of the default group, free-form user information, home directory, and default shell.
/etc/shadow	Holds the user's hashed (one-way encrypted) password and extended account information, mostly relating to password aging—when the password expires and related information.
/etc/group	Holds group data, including group names, GID values, and the users who belong to each group.

Each of the files described in Table 12.2 consists of colon-delimited fields:

```
maryann:x:1010:100::/home/maryann:/bin/bash
```

This example is taken from an /etc/passwd file. It consists of seven fields, one of which (user information) is empty in this example. With respect to password problems specifically, the second field (x in this example) is relevant. In the early days of Unix, passwords were stored in the second field of /etc/passwd; but this practice led to security problems because /etc/passwd had to be world-readable, so crackers could download the /etc/passwd file and try to crack user passwords at their leisure. To work around this problem, today's systems use *shadow passwords*, in which passwords are stored in /etc/shadow, which can (and should) be given permissions to keep anybody but root from reading it. This makes crackers' jobs harder, since they can't access users' passwords, even in hashed form.

If an account uses shadow passwords, the second field of the account's entry in /etc/passwd will contain an x. If it doesn't, that's most likely an error. (Even accounts that forbid logins typically use an x in this field.) You can correct this problem for a single account by replacing the errant value in /etc/passwd with x and then using the passwd utility as root to set a new password for the account.

More common password problems show up in /etc/shadow, which has entries that look like this:

```
maryann:$6$.6BBM.3h$vvkpItHgUAC/KWfrT:14976:0:99999:7:::
```

The second field, which in this example begins with 6, contains the hashed password. (In this example, the hashed password has been truncated to fit on one line; it's too short, and so it won't work as expected.) If you find that a password has been damaged, changed, or forgotten by a user, the easiest solution is usually to use passwd as root to correct the problem:

```
# passwd maryann
New password:
Retype new password:
passwd: password updated successfully
```

When you run passwd as root, you don't need to type the old password, so the fact that it's been damaged or forgotten is irrelevant. You'll need to communicate the new password to the user or let the user type the password directly, if that's practical. (Be careful not to reveal the root password, of course!)

NOTE   If an encrypted password field begins with an exclamation mark (!), the account has been locked. You can unlock the account by using the -U option to usermod, as in **usermod -U houdini** to unlock the houdini account, or by deleting the exclamation mark in a text editor.

Adjusting User Shells

User shell information appears in the final field of /etc/passwd. On Linux, the default shell is usually /bin/bash; however, this can be set to any value using usermod:

```
$ usermod -s /bin/false maryann
```

This command sets maryann's default shell to /bin/false. This is a useful configuration for non-login accounts used by servers, but it's inappropriate if the user should be able to log in, since the result will be that the login process or other text-mode login tool or window will run /bin/false, which will immediately return a failure code. The result will be that the user will be unable to log in.

Problems can also occur if a shell was set to a reasonable value that's suddenly become unreasonable because the software was removed. A user might want to use a non-standard shell, such as tcsh or zsh; but if this shell is subsequently removed, the user will suddenly be unable to log in using text-mode tools.

You can, of course, correct the problem using usermod to change the shell to something valid; use the -s option, as in the preceding example, but pass it /bin/bash or some other valid shell on your computer. Alternatively, if a formerly valid shell was removed, you can re-install it. This change can also be made by using your favorite text editor on the /etc/passwd file itself—but be very careful, lest you accidentally make changes that will cause more problems, such as damaging another account's entry!

Fixing User/Group Association Issues

Users can be assigned to groups in either or both of two ways:

A Default Group Set in the User Configuration File   As noted earlier, /etc/passwd includes a GID value for the user's default group. The user belongs to this group no matter what the /etc/group file indicates, and when the user logs in, files that the user creates will belong to the group whose GID appears in /etc/passwd unless and until the user uses the newgrp command to change the current group association.

Additional Associations in the Group Configuration File   The /etc/group file includes a list of users who belong to each group, in a comma-delimited list at the end of each group's entry. This list, however, is incomplete; it need not include users whose primary group association is the group. In other words, if maryann's /etc/passwd entry specifies that her primary group is GID 100 (users), then the users entry in /etc/group doesn't need to include maryann in its list of users.

Group associations can become broken in any number of ways, particularly if groups are regularly added to and deleted from a computer. If a group is deleted and its number is not re-used, users can end up "orphaned," with default GID numbers that refer to no group. If a group is deleted and its number is re-used, users' default GIDs may end up pointing to inappropriate groups.

You can use the usermod command and its -g option to change a user's group association:

```
# usermod -g 100 maryann
```

GID 100 is usually associated with the users group, which many administrators use as a general-purpose group. Some distributions use this as a default group assignment. Other distributions automatically create a new group for each user, assigning users to their own unique groups.

Adjusting UIDs and GIDs

UID and GID values can sometimes become confused or scrambled. This can happen as accounts are created and destroyed. You can end up with a configuration in which two users share a UID or in which two groups share a GID. You may also need to adjust UID and GID values to keep them synchronized across multiple computers—say, because you're using the Network File System (NFS) file sharing protocol, which works best when UID and GID values are equivalent across computers.

You can change UID and GID values using usermod's -u and -g options, respectively. The preceding section showed an example of using -g; -u is similar:

```
# usermod -u 1010 maryann
```

This example sets maryann's UID value to 1010. Unfortunately, this isn't likely to be the end of the job, particularly when adjusting UID values. The problem is that the user's files will not be adjusted by this command; you must change them manually, using chown. In some cases, you can change the vast majority of the user's files by applying chown recursively to the user's home directory. If your system maintains an incoming mail spool, you may need to modify ownership of the user's mail file. You may also need to use find to locate the user's remaining files in locations such as /tmp or any other world-writable directories your system maintains. Exercise 12.1 guides you through this process.

EXERCISE 12.1

Changing an Account's UID Value

Changing an account's UID value entails using several different utilities. Note that in a real-world situation, the user should be logged out while you perform these steps. This exercise guides you through the process in two stages. The first stage is setup; you must create a test account to use for the second stage of the exercise:

1. Log in as root, or acquire root privileges via su.

2. Type useradd -m maryann. (Change maryann to another username if your system already has an account with this name.) This command creates the maryann account, including a home directory (typically /home/maryann).

3. Type touch /home/maryann/afile to create a file in maryann's home directory.

4. Type chown maryann: /home/maryann/afile to give ownership of the file created in step 3 to maryann.

5. Repeat steps 3 and 4, but use /tmp/maryannfile rather than /home/maryann/afile.

6. If your system keeps incoming mail files in /var/spool/mail or /var/mail, check to see whether one was created. If not, repeat steps 3 and 4 to do so, but use /var/spool/ mail/maryann or /var/mail/maryann as the filename.

With the maryann account configured, it's now time to change its UID value. You can do so as follows:

1. Determine the account's current UID value. You can do this by typing grep maryann /etc/ passwd and noting the value in the third colon-delimited field. This exercise will assume the old UID value is 1009.

2. Determine a new UID value for the account. Pick one that's not in use and verify it by searching /etc/passwd for the value. This exercise uses a UID of 1010 for this purpose. Typing grep 1010 /etc/passwd returns nothing, which verifies that this value is not in use.

3. Type usermod -u 1010 maryann to change maryann's UID to 1010.

4. Check the ownership of the user's home directory by typing ls -ld /home/maryann. Type ls -l /home/maryann to check the ownership of the file you created in maryann's home directory. The usermod command may change the ownership of these files in which case it will appear as owned by maryann. If the home directory or its files appear to be owned by a numeric value, type chown -R maryann: /home/maryann to return ownership to maryann using the account's new UID value.

5. Check the ownership of the user's mail spool file by typing ls -l /var/spool/mail/ maryann (changing the path, if necessary). If it's owned by the account's old UID value, type chown maryann: /var/spool/mail/maryann to correct it.

6. Use find to locate additional files owned by the user in question by typing find / -uid 1009. (Change 1009 to whatever value is appropriate for your system, of course.) This command will take a long time to complete, but it should return precisely one file: /tmp/maryannfile, which you created in step 5 of the preceding procedure. If you were performing this procedure in a real-world environment, you might find any number of files.

7. For each file found in step 6, type chown maryann: *filename*.

At this point, the change in UID value for maryann is complete. The user may log in and use the account normally. If the user wasn't experiencing any obvious difficulties, there should be no obvious changes to the account from the user's perspective. Of course, chances are you made this change because there *were* difficulties!

Adjusting Login Variables

Many tools that deal with user accounts, including login programs, the `useradd` program, and others, need to know certain key things about how accounts and the login process work. For instance, Linux systems typically reserve the lowest-numbered UID numbers for system accounts, but what is the lowest UID number that may be used for user accounts? What encryption method should be used to encrypt passwords in `/etc/shadow`? How many times should `login` prompt the user for a password if the user enters an incorrect password? These and other system-wide account features are set in the `/etc/login.defs` file.

The values in this file sometimes vary from one distribution or installation to another. For instance, some distributions set the minimum UID value for ordinary users (`UID_MIN`) at 500, but others use 1000. You might have cause to change this value if you're working in an environment that uses multiple Linux distributions and you need to keep UID values synchronized across different computers. For the most part, though, you shouldn't need to adjust this file's values, since the defaults are usually sensible. You may want to peruse the file, though. Most of the options' names are descriptive, and most distributions include comments that further explain the options, so you should be able to figure out what each option does.

The effect of setting an `/etc/login.defs` value incorrectly varies depending on the option, of course. Some options can affect the ability to log in or at least delay logins under some circumstances. For instance, `FAIL_DELAY` affects the delay imposed after a failed login attempt; setting this value too high can make the system appear unresponsive after a failed login attempt.

Troubleshooting Shells

Text-mode logins rely heavily on *shells*, which are programs that accept typed commands and, in response, execute programs or perform commands. As noted earlier, `bash` is the most common shell in Linux. Like many programs, shells rely on configuration files, so many problems related to text-mode operation are caused by problems with these configuration files. You should therefore be familiar with `bash` configuration files, which in fact are scripts that run at login time. You should also know a bit about non-`bash` shells.

Investigating *bash* Login Scripts

When it starts, bash runs a series of scripts. These scripts set environment variables, create command aliases, run programs, and otherwise prepare the shell to accept your commands. The confusing part of this is understanding precisely which of several files runs in which situations. Broadly speaking, `bash` login scripts can be categorized in two ways: as *global* vs. *user* scripts and as *login* vs. *non-login* scripts. Table 12.3 identifies the most common scripts in each category. Chances are you won't find all of these scripts on your computer; and in fact, with the exception of `/etc/profile` and separate scripts in the `/etc/profile.d` directory, chances are you'll find at most one per category.

TABLE 12.3 A classification of shell startup scripts

	Login files	Non-login files
Global files	`/etc/profile`; files in `/etc/profile.d`	`/etc/bash.bashrc`, `/etc/bash/bashrc`, `/etc/bashrc`
User files	`~/.bash_profile`, `~/.bash_login`, `~/.profile`	`~/.bashrc`

The rules for when each script executes are complex. They're described in the man page for bash under the "Invocation" section. In brief, though, when bash is launched as a login process (by the login program or by a remote login server such as SSH), it first runs /etc/profile. Most Linux distributions include within this file calls to run additional scripts in the /etc/profile.d directory and one of the global non-login files, the name of which varies from one distribution to another. After running /etc/profile, bash looks for the user login files (~/.bash_profile, ~/.bash_login, and ~/.profile) and runs the first one it finds (if any of them exists).

When bash is launched as a non-login shell (for instance, inside an X-based terminal window), it looks for and executes the ~/.bashrc file. This file is normally created as part of the account-creation process, and it usually executes the same global non-login file that the distribution's /etc/profile script executes.

When a login shell terminates, bash executes the ~/.bash_logout script. There is no equivalent logout script for non-login shells.

The files that bash uses can be modified by executing it with particular command-line options, such as --login (to force login behavior), --norc (to inhibit reading the user non-login file), or --rcfile *filename* (to read *filename* rather than ~/.bashrc).

This confusing set of login scripts, particularly when coupled with the fact that the precise filenames can vary from one distribution or even account to another, creates opportunities for problems to arise. You may want to trace the order in which various startup scripts are executing to ensure that the desired scripts actually execute for all the desired conditions.

Creating a symbolic link between ~/.bashrc and ~/.bash_profile can resolve many problems that users might have. This will ensure that the same user startup scripts run for both login and non-login sessions.

One common problem with startup scripts arises because of improper setting of the PATH environment variable, which should consist of a colon-delimited set of directories in which the shell looks for commands. This environment variable is often built up across multiple startup scripts. To do so, though, all but the first script that sets this variable must include a reference to PATH in its PATH-setting line:

```
PATH="${PATH}:/usr/local/bin:/opt/bin:/bin"
```

This example sets the value of PATH to its old value but adds two new directories. If the initial reference to PATH is omitted, the result will be that the PATH will omit its original directories. Similar problems can occur with some other environment variables, such as LIBPATH.

Using Unusual Shells

Although bash is the default shell in Linux, it's possible that you or some of your users will want to use another shell. If so, you will have to investigate that shell's startup scripts. It's likely to support the same distinctions between user vs. global files and login vs. non-login sessions, so you may end up having to investigate multiple startup scripts, just as with bash. Some of the many shells available in Linux include

bash   The *Bourne Again Shell (bash)* is the default shell for most installations and accounts. It's an open source extension to the original Bourne shell (sh), which is popular on many Unix-like platforms. Linux distributions make sh a link to bash so that scripts intended for sh run on bash.

tcsh   This shell is an enhanced variant of a "classic" Unix shell, the C Shell (csh). Both csh and tcsh use a scripting language that resembles the C programming language, although csh/tcsh scripts are by no means C programs.

pdksh   The *Public Domain Korn Shell (pdksh)* is an implementation of the Korn shell. It's similar to the Bourne shell, but it borrows some features from the C shell, as well.

zsh   The *Z Shell (zsh)* is modeled after the Korn shell, but it adds some extra features.

sash   The *Stand Alone Shell (sash)* is a small shell that incorporates many programs, such as ls, that are normally external, into the main sash executable. The goal is to have a shell that functions even on a system that's otherwise badly corrupted.

Most shells' startup scripts have names that are at least loosely related to the shell's name, such as ~/.tcshrc and /etc/csh.cshrc for tcsh. Consult the shell's man page if you need assistance.

Because most shells' configuration files are scripts written in the shells' own language, details can vary between shells. For instance, tcsh sets variables differently from bash. If you just need to make a minor modification to an existing configuration, such changes probably won't cause problems. If you need to make extensive changes, though, you may need to consult shell-specific documentation.

Investigating Running Processes

Running processes sometimes cause problems: They can fail to start, crash once started, fail to stop when they should, or consume inordinate system resources. A few skills and tools will help you deal with such issues. First, you must know how to identify running processes, particularly for daemons, which don't normally interact with users at the console or with a GUI. Second, you should understand how to modify logging options, thus enabling you to tell certain programs (again, particularly daemons) how to communicate with you about their problems. Finally, you should know how to identify the libraries that programs use and correct some common library problems.

Finding Running Processes

The first challenge in dealing with an errant daemon is identifying its process. In Linux, processes are identified by process ID (PID) numbers. Each process also has a parent PID (PPID) number, which identifies the process that created (or *spawned*) it. Ultimately, every process can trace its ancestry back to init, which in turn was launched by the kernel during the boot process. If a process terminates and leaves child processes, those children are "adopted" by init. Figure 12.1 illustrates this arrangement.

FIGURE 12.1   Linux processes are arranged in a hierarchy that leads back to init

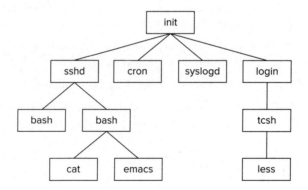

Using the *ps* Program

You can determine what processes are running by using the ps program, which takes a huge number of options. (The LPIC-1 objectives include ps, so you should already be familiar with its basic operation.) You can use ps to locate running processes by using a ps option that displays all processes, rather than just the ones associated with your own account, and then searching the output for the process that interests you. Options that display all processes include -A, -e, and the combination of a and x (ax). The details of what these options display in terms of ancillary information varies, but any of them will show you all the processes running on the system.

If you're interested in a particular process, you can pipe the output of ps through grep to locate it:

```
$ ps ax | grep apache
 3053 ?        Ss       0:00 /usr/sbin/apache2 -k start
 4753 ?        S        0:00 /usr/sbin/apache2 -k start
 4754 ?        S        0:00 /usr/sbin/apache2 -k start
 4755 ?        S        0:00 /usr/sbin/apache2 -k start
 4756 ?        S        0:00 /usr/sbin/apache2 -k start
 4757 ?        S        0:00 /usr/sbin/apache2 -k start
 5044 pts/1    R+       0:00 grep apache
```

This example shows six instances of the apache2 server running, plus the grep command that located the server. If you suspected Apache was not running, this output would put those suspicions to rest; however, if the output was empty or contained just the grep command or other commands that happened to contain the string apache, you'd know that Apache was not running—perhaps it had never been started, or maybe it started running but crashed.

This example illustrates a feature of some daemons and other processes: They can spawn multiple copies of themselves. Apache does this to better serve clients; each copy can handle a single client, rather than have a single process try to handle multiple clients. Sometimes you'll see multiple copies of a program because one or more users are running independent copies. Be cautious about terminating such processes with kill; you don't want to kill the wrong instance of a program!

In some cases, you can use ps repeatedly to monitor a process. You can check back every once in a while to verify that a process is running, or look for changes in the PID value (the first column in the preceding output) if you suspect the process may be crashing and restarting. Be aware, however, that some programs terminate and then restart as part of their normal operation, so a changing PID value may not be a sign of trouble.

Using the *top* Program

A variant of ps that's very helpful in diagnosing some problems is top. This program generates a display of processes, ordered by CPU use, and updates the list every few seconds. The result is a display similar to that in Figure 12.2, which you can use to identify which processes are consuming large amounts of CPU time. In Figure 12.2, the FahCore_78.exe process is chewing up 98 percent of CPU time, glxgears is consuming

91 percent, X is using 8 percent, and all the remaining processes are using substantially less CPU time. (The total amount of CPU time consumed can exceed 100 percent because the computer used for this example has a dual-core CPU, which top interprets as having a maximum of 200 percent CPU time available.)

FIGURE 12.2 The top utility provides a dynamic display of running processes

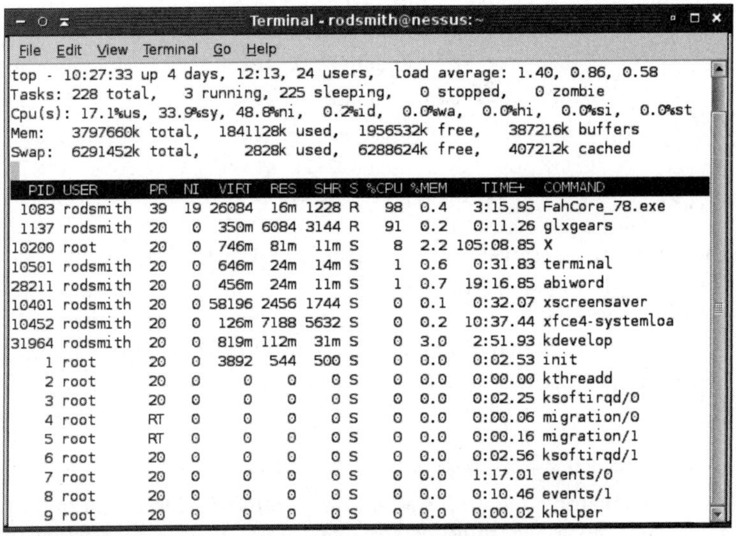

```
  - ○ ⊼                     Terminal - rodsmith@nessus: ~              ○ □ ✕

 File  Edit  View  Terminal  Go  Help
top - 10:27:33 up 4 days, 12:13, 24 users,  load average: 1.40, 0.86, 0.58
Tasks: 228 total,   3 running, 225 sleeping,   0 stopped,   0 zombie
Cpu(s): 17.1%us, 33.9%sy, 48.8%ni,  0.2%id,  0.0%wa,  0.0%hi,  0.0%si,  0.0%st
Mem:   3797660k total,  1841128k used,  1956532k free,   387216k buffers
Swap:  6291452k total,     2828k used,  6288624k free,   407212k cached

  PID USER      PR  NI  VIRT  RES  SHR S %CPU %MEM    TIME+  COMMAND
 1083 rodsmith  39  19 26084  16m 1228 R   98  0.4   3:15.95 FahCore_78.exe
 1137 rodsmith  20   0 350m 6084 3144 R   91  0.2   0:11.26 glxgears
10200 root      20   0 746m  81m  11m S    8  2.2 105:08.85 X
10501 rodsmith  20   0 646m  24m  14m S    1  0.6   0:31.83 terminal
28211 rodsmith  20   0 456m  24m  11m S    1  0.7  19:16.85 abiword
10401 rodsmith  20   0 58196 2456 1744 S    0  0.1   0:32.07 xscreensaver
10452 rodsmith  20   0 126m 7188 5632 S    0  0.2  10:37.44 xfce4-systemloa
31964 rodsmith  20   0 819m 112m  31m S    0  3.0   2:51.93 kdevelop
    1 root      20   0 3892  544  500 S    0  0.0   0:02.53 init
    2 root      20   0    0    0    0 S    0  0.0   0:00.00 kthreadd
    3 root      20   0    0    0    0 S    0  0.0   0:02.25 ksoftirqd/0
    4 root      RT   0    0    0    0 S    0  0.0   0:00.06 migration/0
    5 root      RT   0    0    0    0 S    0  0.0   0:00.16 migration/1
    6 root      20   0    0    0    0 S    0  0.0   0:02.56 ksoftirqd/1
    7 root      20   0    0    0    0 S    0  0.0   1:17.01 events/0
    8 root      20   0    0    0    0 S    0  0.0   0:10.46 events/1
    9 root      20   0    0    0    0 S    0  0.0   0:00.02 khelper
```

In addition to monitoring CPU use, top can display the top users of memory. Type M while it's running to do this, and type P to switch back to a display sorted by CPU time. (Typing T sorts by cumulative CPU time.) Note that you must type *uppercase* letters; the lowercase versions have different effects.

One difficulty with using top to identify programs that are consuming too much CPU time or memory is that you can't tell from the top output alone what constitutes excessive resource consumption. Take the output in Figure 12.2 as an example. It's true that FahCore_78.exe is consuming a great deal of CPU time; however, this program is a Folding@home (http://folding.stanford.edu) client, which is a way to donate your unused CPU time to a scientific research project. In other words, the process *should* be consuming a lot of CPU time, but the consumed CPU time would otherwise be unused. The glxgears program is a graphics demonstration tool. It also normally consumes lots of CPU time, but you probably wouldn't want to leave it running for long. Making these determinations requires understanding the purpose and normal operating characteristics of your programs, particularly of those that float to the top of top's output.

Checking Logging Options

Linux maintains log files that record various key details about system operation. You may be able to begin using log files immediately, but knowing how to change the log file configuration can also be important. You do this by configuring the syslogd daemon. Some servers and other programs perform their own logging and so must be configured independently of syslogd. You may even want to configure one computer to send its log files to another system as a security measure. You should also be aware of issues surrounding log file rotation; if your computer doesn't properly manage existing log files, they can grow to consume all your available disk space, at least on the partition on which they're stored. In addition to configuring logging, you must be able to use the log files that the system generates.

Understanding *syslogd*

Most Linux systems employ a special daemon to handle log maintenance in a unified way. The traditional Linux system logger is syslogd, which is often installed from a package called sysklogd. The syslogd daemon handles messages from servers and other user-mode programs. It's usually paired with a daemon called klogd, which is generally installed from the same sysklogd package as syslogd. The klogd daemon manages logging of kernel messages.

> **NOTE** Other choices for system loggers exist. For instance, syslog-ng is a replacement that supports advanced filtering options, and metalog is another option. Recent versions of Fedora and Ubuntu use rsyslogd. This chapter describes the traditional syslogd logger. Others are similar in principle, and even in some specific features, but differ in many details.

The basic idea behind a system logger is to provide a unified means of handling log files. The daemon runs in the background and accepts data delivered from servers and other programs that are configured to use the log daemon. The daemon can then use information provided by the server to classify the message and direct it to an appropriate log file. This configuration enables you to consolidate messages from various servers in a handful of standard log files, which can be much easier to use and manage than potentially dozens of log files from the various servers running on the system.

In order to work, of course, the log daemon must be configured. In the case of syslogd, this is done through the /etc/syslog.conf file. (The rsyslogd configuration file is /etc/rsyslog.conf and is similar to syslog.conf.) The next section describes the syslog.conf file's format in more detail.

Setting Logging Options

The format of the /etc/syslog.conf file is conceptually simple but provides a great deal of power. Comment lines, as in many Linux configuration files, are denoted by a hash mark (#). Non-comment lines take the following form:

```
facility.priority  action
```

In this line, the *facility* is a code word for the type of program or tool that generated the message to be logged; the *priority* is a code word for the importance of this message; and the *action* is a file, remote computer, or other location that's to accept the message. The *facility* and *priority* are often referred to collectively as the *selector*.

Valid codes for the *facility* are auth, authpriv, cron, daemon, kern, lpr, mail, mark, news, security, syslog, user, uucp, and local0 through local7. Many of these names refer to specific servers or program classes. For instance, mail servers and other mail-processing tools typically log using the mail facility. Most servers that aren't covered by more specific codes use the daemon facility. The security facility is identical to auth, but auth is the preferred name. The mark facility is reserved for internal use. An asterisk (*) refers to all facilities. You can specify multiple facilities in one selector by separating the facilities with commas (,).

Valid codes for the *priority* are debug, info, notice, warning, warn, error, err, crit, alert, emerg, and panic. The warning priority is identical to warn, error is identical to err, and emerg is identical to panic. The error, warn, and panic priority names are deprecated; you should use their equivalents instead. Other than these identical pairs, these priorities represent ascending levels of importance. The debug level logs the most information; it's intended, as the name implies, for debugging programs that are misbehaving. The emerg priority logs the most important messages, which indicate very serious problems. When a program sends a message to the system logger, it includes a priority code; the logger logs the message to a file if you've configured it to log messages of that level or higher. Thus, if you specify a *priority* code of alert, the system will log messages that are classified as alert or emerg but not messages of crit or below. An exception to this rule is if you precede the priority code by an equal sign (=), as in =crit, which describes what to do with messages of crit priority *only*. An exclamation mark (!) reverses the meaning of a match. For instance, !crit causes messages *below* crit priority to be logged. A *priority* of * refers to all priorities.

You can specify multiple selectors for a single action by separating the selectors by a semicolon (;). Note that commas are used to separate multiple facilities within a single selector, whereas semicolons are used to separate multiple selectors as a whole. Examples of complete selectors appear shortly.

Most commonly, the *action* is a filename, typically in the /var/log directory tree. The messages, syslog, and secure files in this directory are three common and important log files, although not all distributions use all of these files. Other possible logging locations include a device filename for a console (such as /dev/console) to display data on the screen, a remote machine name preceded by an at sign (@) to log data to the specified system, and a list of usernames of individuals who should see the message if they're logged in. For the last of these options, an asterisk (*) means all logged-in users.

Some examples should help clarify these rules. First is a fairly ordinary and simple entry:

```
mail.*          /var/log/mail
```

This line sends all log entries identified by the originating program as related to mail to the `/var/log/mail` file. Most of the entries in a default `/etc/syslog.conf` file resemble this one. Together, they typically cover all of the facilities mentioned earlier. Some messages may be handled by multiple rules. For instance, another rule might look like this one:

```
*.emerg         *
```

This line sends all emerg-level messages to the consoles of all users who are logged into the computer using text-mode tools. If this line and the earlier `mail.*` selector are both present, emerg-level messages related to mail will be logged to `/var/log/mail` *and* displayed on users' consoles.

A more complex example logs kernel messages in various ways, depending on their priorities:

```
kern.*                  /var/log/kernel
kern.crit               @logger.pangaea.edu
kern.crit               /dev/console
kern.info;kern.!err     /var/log/kernel-info
```

The first of these rules logs all kernel messages to `/var/log/kernel`. The second line sends critical messages to `logger.pangaea.edu`. (This system must be configured to accept remote logs, which is a topic not covered in this book.) The third line sends a copy of critical messages to `/dev/console`, which causes them to be displayed on the computer's main text-mode console display. Finally, the last line sends messages that are between `info` and `err` in priority to `/var/log/kernel-info`. Because `err` is the priority immediately above `crit` and because `info` is the lowest priority, these four lines cause all kernel messages to be logged two or three times: once to `/var/log/kernel` as well as either to the remote system and the console *or* to `/var/log/kernel-info`.

Most distributions ship with reasonable system logger settings, but you may want to examine these settings and perhaps adjust them. If you change them, be aware that you may need to change some other tools. For instance, all major distributions ship with tools that help rotate log files. If you change the files to which `syslogd` logs messages, you may need to change your log file rotation scripts as well. This topic is covered in the next section.

In addition to the system logger's options, you may be able to set logging options in individual programs. For instance, you may tell programs to record more or less information or to log routine information at varying priorities. Some programs also provide the means to log with the system log daemon or with their own mechanisms. Details vary greatly from one program to another, so you should consult the program's documentation for details.

> Most programs that use the system log daemons are servers and other system tools. Programs that individuals run locally seldom log data with the system log daemon, although there are some exceptions to this rule, such as the Fetchmail program for retrieving email from remote servers.

Rotating Log Files

Log files are intended to retain information about system activities for a reasonable period of time, but system logging daemons provide no means to control the size of log files. Left unchecked, log files can therefore grow to consume all the available space on the partition on which they reside. To avoid this problem, Linux systems employ *log file rotation* tools. These tools rename and optionally compress the current log files, delete old log files, and force the logging system to begin using new log files.

The most common log rotation tool is a package called `logrotate`. This program is typically called on a regular basis via a `cron` job. The `logrotate` program consults a configuration file called `/etc/logrotate.conf`, which includes several default settings and typically refers to files in `/etc/logrotate.d` to handle specific log files. A typical `/etc/logrotate.conf` file includes several comment lines, denoted by hash marks (#), as well as lines to set various options, as illustrated by Listing 12.1.

Listing 12.1: Sample `/etc/logrotate.conf` file

```
# Rotate logs weekly
weekly

# Keep 4 weeks of old logs
rotate 4

# Create new log files after rotation
create

# Compress old log files
compress

# Refer to files for individual packages
include /etc/logrotate.d

# Set miscellaneous options
notifempty
nomail
noolddir

# Rotate wtmp, which isn't handled by a specific program
```

```
/var/log/wtmp {
    monthly
    create 0664 root utmp
    rotate 1
}
```

Most of the lines in Listing 12.1 set options that are fairly self-explanatory or that are well explained by the comments that immediately precede them—for instance, the weekly line sets the default log rotation interval to once a week. If you see an option in your file that you don't understand, consult the man page for logrotate.

 Because log file rotation is handled by cron jobs that typically run late at night, it won't happen if a computer is routinely turned off at the end of the day. This practice is common with Windows workstations but is uncommon with servers. Either Linux workstations should be left running overnight as a general practice or some explicit steps should be taken to ensure that log rotation occurs despite routine shutdowns. The anacron utility is particularly well suited to this task.

The last few lines of Listing 12.1 demonstrate the format for the definition of a specific log file. These definitions begin with the filename for the file (multiple filenames may be listed, separated by spaces), followed by an open curly brace ({). They end in a close curly brace (}). Intervening lines set options that may override the defaults. For instance, the /var/log/wtmp definition in Listing 12.1 sets the monthly option, which tells the system to rotate this log file once a month, overriding the default weekly option. Such definitions are common in the individual files in /etc/logrotate.d, which are typically owned by the packages whose log files they rotate.

In most cases, servers and other programs that log data either do so via the system logging daemon or ship with a configuration file that goes in /etc/logrotate.d to handle the server's log files. These files usually do a reasonable job, but you may want to double-check them. For instance, you might discover that your system is configured to keep too many or too few old log files for your taste, in which case adjusting the rotate option is in order. You should also check the /var/log directory and its subdirectories every now and then. If you see huge numbers of files accumulating or if files are growing to unacceptable size, you may want to check the corresponding logrotate configuration files. If an appropriate file doesn't exist, create one. Use a working file as a template, modifying it for the new file. Pay particular attention to the prerotate and postrotate scripts; you may need to consult the documentation for the program that's creating the log file to learn how to force that program to begin using a new log file.

In most cases, log files remain on the computer that recorded them. Sometimes, though, you may want to copy such files off-site. The easiest way to do this may be to reconfigure the log daemon to send the messages you want to archive to another system, as described previously in "Setting Logging Options." Another possibility is to create a cron job (as described later, in "Dealing with Scheduled Processes") to copy files to another system using a network share, ssh, or some other network tool. You can also manually copy log files onto removable disks, if you like. There are few technical reasons to archive log files for more than a few weeks—only if a problem escapes your notice for a long time will they be useful. Managers or lawyers may want to keep them around for the long term for business or legal reasons, though. Thus, you should ask about policies concerning log file retention when administering an employer's or client's computer.

Dealing with Library Issues

In computer terms, a *library* is a set of functions that are likely to be useful to multiple programs and that are therefore designed to enable many programs to use them. For instance, many different programs need functions to help position text on a text-mode console or terminal—text editors, the less pager, and various other programs all have similar needs. Rather than force each program to re-invent this particular wheel, libraries to handle the placement of text on the screen, such as libncurses, exist. Many programs can use libncurses, which simplifies life for the users of such libraries.

Many libraries can be used in either *static* or *dynamic* form. A static library's code is built into the final program's main executable file, whereas a dynamic library exists as a separate file that's referenced by the final program's main executable file. Dynamic libraries have the advantage of reducing resource use, both in terms of disk space requirements and memory use. (These advantages apply only if multiple programs use the library, though.) The drawback to dynamic libraries is that they invite problems—if the library's interfaces change or if a bug is introduced in a new version, upgrading the library can introduce bugs into the programs that use it. If a library is uninstalled, programs that depend upon it will break. Diagnosing and correcting such problems requires understanding the tools used to manage libraries.

You can identify some library problems with the help of the ldd utility, as described in Chapter 11. This program identifies the libraries used by any given program binary:

```
$ ldd /usr/bin/zip
        linux-vdso.so.1 =>  (0x00007fffbd5c5000)
        libbz2.so.1 => not found
        libc.so.6 => /lib/libc.so.6 (0x00007f5fe5f03000)
        /lib64/ld-linux-x86-64.so.2 (0x00007f5fe646d000)
```

If a library can't be found, it won't be listed to the right of the => symbol; instead, ldd reports not found, as it does for libbz2.so.1 in this example. If you try to launch such a program, you receive an error message:

```
$ zip
zip: error while loading shared libraries: libbz2.so.1: cannot open shared ↵
 object file: No such file or directory
```

The solution to the problem depends on the nature of the problem. Sometimes the correct library is installed, but the program binary is looking for it under the wrong name or location. In such a case, creating a symbolic link can fix the problem:

```
# ln -s /lib/libbz2.so.1.2 /lib/libbz2.so.1
```

Other times, you may need to update the computer's library path—the set of directories in which the computer searches for libraries. The library path is stored in the /etc/ld.so .conf file, which contains one directory per line. If you know that a library exists in an unusual directory, you can add that directory to /etc/ld.so.conf. After you do this, though, you must type `ldconfig` as root to make the system's linker (the software that ties programs together with their libraries) recognize the libraries in the new path. You may also need to type `ldconfig` after installing new libraries, although post-installation scripts in binary package files usually do this when you install a library in a package.

Some distributions build /etc/ld.so.conf from files in the /etc/ld.so.conf.d directory, either dynamically via an include statement in ld.so.conf or via a separate command. Therefore, if you want to add directories to this file, it's often better to add a new file to /etc/ld.so.conf.d. If the main file includes a comment stating that it must be regenerated by typing some command, such as env-update, you should do so after making changes to /etc/ld.so.conf.d.

Another way to adjust the library path is to use the LD_LIBRARY_PATH environment variable. Set this variable to a colon-delimited list of directories that hold libraries that aren't on the system's library path:

```
$ export LD_LIBRARY_PATH=/opt/someprog/lib:/opt/another/lib
```

This example adds two directories to the library path. This feature can be handy if you need to temporarily add to the library path for testing purposes or if an individual needs to make a permanent change that's not needed by other users. If a change should be made system-wide, though, editing /etc/ld.so.conf or the files in /etc/ld.so.conf.d is more appropriate.

 Real World Scenario

Using 32- and 64-Bit Binaries

If you run a 64-bit *x*86-64 (aka AMD64 or EM64T) version of Linux, you probably have the ability to run 32-bit (*x*86) binaries, as well as 64-bit binaries. This ability can be handy if you need to run old binary-only programs or programs that don't compile and run properly in 64-bit mode. Unfortunately, one problem with this feature is that it requires you to maintain both 64- and 32-bit versions of at least some libraries.

Different approaches to managing both 64- and 32-bit libraries exist. In most cases, you'll find separate library directories for 64- and 32-bit libraries, such as /lib64 and /lib32. There's also likely to be a /lib directory; either /lib is a symbolic link to /lib64 or /lib64 is a symbolic link to /lib. (These arrangements are mirrored in /usr, as in /usr/lib32 and so on.) This method of arranging libraries emphasizes the native (64-bit) libraries, since libraries are normally found in /lib, /usr/lib, and similarly named directories.

Some distributions do things a bit differently; they have separate /lib and /lib64 directories but no /lib32 directory. This configuration is peculiar from a Linux standards point of view, but it has the advantage that packages intended for x86 systems can install without modification; on the first type of system, such packages, if they include libraries, would drop the 32-bit libraries in the 64-bit library directory, potentially overwriting 64-bit libraries and causing chaos.

With any of these systems, you must be aware of the presence of and need for both 64- and 32-bit libraries. It's easy to overlook this distinction and become confused or frustrated when a program fails to work because it reports that it can't find a library when one of the exact name being requested clearly exists on your hard disk. You can identify the type of the library (and of a program that needs it) using file:

```
$ file /bin/cp
/bin/cp: ELF 64-bit LSB executable, x86-64, version 1 (SYSV), dynamically ↵
  linked (uses shared libs), for GNU/Linux 2.6.15, stripped
$ file /lib/libacl.so.1.1.0
/lib/libacl.so.1.1.0: ELF 64-bit LSB shared object, x86-64, version 1 ↵
  (SYSV), dynamically linked, stripped
$ file /lib32/libacl.so.1.1.0
/lib32/libacl.so.1.1.0: ELF 32-bit LSB shared object, Intel 80386, version 1 ↵
  (SYSV), dynamically linked, stripped
```

This example indicates that /bin/cp is a 64-bit executable, that /lib/libacl.so.1.1.0 is a 64-bit library, and that /lib32/libacl.so.1.1.0 is a 32-bit library. If a program indicates that it can't load a library that you see is present, checking both the program and the library with file may help you determine whether they're mismatched.

Dealing with Scheduled Processes

Linux provides several mechanisms to run processes in the future. This facility is useful for scheduling automatic routine maintenance (such as log file rotation), for performing repetitive tasks (such as retrieving email on a regular basis), or for performing one-off tasks (such as displaying a reminder about an appointment on your screen). The main tool for performing such tasks is cron, so understanding a bit of how it works—and where it can go wrong—can help you diagnose problems related to this tool.

Although this section emphasizes cron, two other related tools deserve mention. The first of these is at, which runs jobs in a one-off fashion, as opposed to the repeated scheduling that cron handles. The second tool is anacron, which sometimes supplements cron on systems that don't run continuously; anacron can be used to ensure that jobs such as log rotation occur even if the computer is frequently shut down at the times when these jobs would normally occur.

Managing Scheduled Processes

Two types of cron jobs exist: system cron jobs, which handle tasks for the OS as a whole, such as log file rotation; and user cron jobs, which individuals can use to run their own jobs at scheduled times. The two are created and managed in similar ways, although there are some critical differences.

Creating System *cron* Jobs

The /etc/crontab file controls system cron jobs. This file normally begins with several lines that set environment variables, such as $PATH and $MAILTO (the former sets the path, and the latter is the address to which programs' output is mailed). The file then contains several lines that resemble the following:

```
02 4 * * * root run-parts /etc/cron.daily
```

This line begins with five fields that specify the time. The fields are, in order, the minute (0–59), the hour (0–23), the day of the month (1–31), the month (1–12), and the day of the week (0–7; both 0 and 7 correspond to Sunday). For the month and day of the week values, you can use the first three letters of the name rather than a number, if you like.

In all cases, you can specify multiple values in several ways:

- An asterisk (*) matches all possible values.
- A list separated by commas (such as 0,6,12,18) matches any of the specified values.
- Two values separated by a dash (-) indicate a range, inclusive of the end points. For instance, 9-17 in the hour field specifies a time of from 9 A.M. to 5 P.M. (Note that, depending on the value of the minute field, jobs could run as late as 5:59 P.M. in this example.)
- A slash, when used in conjunction with some other multi-value option, specifies stepped values—a range in which some members are skipped. For instance, */10 in the minute field indicates a job that's run every 10 minutes.

After the first five fields, /etc/crontab entries continue with the account name to be used when executing the program (root in the preceding example) and the command to be run (run-parts /etc/cron.daily in this example). The default /etc/crontab entries generally use run-parts, cronloop, or a similar utility that runs any executable scripts within a directory. Thus, the preceding example runs all the scripts in /etc/cron.daily at 4:02 A.M. every day. Most distributions include monthly, daily, weekly, and hourly system cron jobs, each corresponding to scripts in a directory called /etc/cron.*interval*, where *interval* is a word associated with the run frequency. Others place these scripts in /etc/cron.d/*interval* directories.

The exact times chosen for system cron jobs to execute vary from one distribution to another. Normally, though, daily and longer-interval cron jobs run early in the morning—between midnight and 6 A.M. Check your /etc/crontab file to determine when your system cron jobs run.

To create a new system cron job, you may create a script to perform the task you want performed and copy that script to the appropriate /etc/cron.*interval* directory. When the runtime next rolls around, cron will run the script.

Before submitting a script as a cron job, test it thoroughly. This is particularly important if the cron job will run when you're not around. You don't want a bug in your cron job script to cause problems by filling the hard disk with useless files or producing thousands of email messages when you're not present to quickly correct the problem.

If you need to run a cron job at a time or interval that's not supported by the standard /etc/crontab, you can either modify that file to change or add the cron job runtime or create a user cron job, as described shortly. If you choose to modify the system cron job facility, model your changes after an existing entry, changing the times and script storage directory as required.

System cron job storage directories should be owned by root, and only root should be able to write to them. If ordinary users can write to a system cron directory, unscrupulous users can write scripts to give themselves superuser privileges and place them in the system cron directory. The next time cron runs those scripts, the users will have full administrative access to the system.

Creating User *cron* Jobs

To create a user cron job, you use the crontab utility, not to be confused with the /etc/crontab configuration file. The syntax for crontab is as follows:

```
crontab [-u user] [-l | -e | -r] [file]
```

If given without the -u *user* parameter, crontab modifies the cron job associated with the current user. (User cron jobs are often called *crontabs*; but because the word is already used in reference to the system-wide configuration file and the utility itself, this usage can be perplexing.) The crontab utility can become confused by the use of su to change the current user identity, so if you use this command, it's safest to also use -u *user*, even when you're modifying your own cron job.

If you want to work directly on a cron job, use the -l, -r, or -e option. The -l option causes crontab to display the current cron job; -r removes the current cron job; and -e opens an editor so that you can edit the current cron job. (Vi is the default editor, but you can change this by setting the VISUAL or EDITOR environment variable, as described in Chapter 1.)

Alternatively, you can create a cron job configuration file and pass the filename to crontab using the *file* parameter. For instance, **crontab -u tbaker my-cron** causes crontab to use my-cron for tbaker's cron jobs.

Whether you create the cron job and submit it via the *file* parameter or edit it via -e, the format of the cron file is similar to that described earlier. You can set environment variables by using the form *VARIABLE=value*, or you can specify a command preceded by five numbers or wildcards to indicate when the job is to run. In a user cron job, you do *not* specify the username used to execute the job, as you do with system cron jobs. That information is derived from the owner of the cron job. Listing 12.2 shows a sample cron job file. This file runs two programs at different intervals: The fetchmail program runs every 30 minutes (on the hour and half hour), and clean-adouble runs on Mondays at 2:00 A.M. Both programs are specified via complete paths, but you can include a PATH environment variable and omit the complete path specifications.

Listing 12.2: A sample user cron job file

```
SHELL=/bin/bash
MAILTO=tbaker
HOME=/home/tbaker
0,30 * * * * /usr/bin/fetchmail -s
0 2 * * mon /usr/local/bin/clean-adouble $HOME
```

Ultimately, user cron job files are stored in the /var/spool/cron, /var/spool/cron/tabs, or /var/spool/cron/crontabs directory. Each file in this directory is named after the user under whose name it runs; for example, tbaker's file might be called /var/spool/cron/tabs/tbaker. You shouldn't directly edit the files in this directory; instead, use crontab to make changes.

Access to the cron facility may be restricted in several ways:

Executable Permissions   The permissions on the cron and crontab programs may be restricted using standard Linux permissions mechanisms. Not all distributions configure themselves in this way, but for those that do, users who should be able to schedule jobs using cron should be added to the appropriate group. This group is often called cron, but you should check the group owner and permissions on the /usr/sbin/cron and /usr/bin/crontab program files to be sure.

Allowed Users List   The /etc/cron.allow file contains a list of users who should be permitted access to cron. If this file is present, only users whose names appear in the file may use cron; all others are denied access. If this file isn't present, anybody may use cron, assuming access isn't restricted by executable permissions or a disallowed users list.

Disallowed Users List   The /etc/cron.deny file contains a list of users who should be denied access to cron. If this file is present, any user whose name appears in the file is denied access to cron, but all others may use it, assuming executable permissions and the allowed users list don't restrict access.

Investigating Problems

One type of cron problem relates to the access restrictions that were just described: If a user can't create cron jobs, you should check executable permissions and the contents of the /etc/cron.allow and /etc/cron.deny files (if they're present). Be cautious when modifying these features, though; you don't want to tear down security measures that might have been put in place for a reason. If necessary, consult with other administrators to learn why a restriction exists.

If system cron jobs aren't running, check your log files for indications that the relevant file was executed. Ideally, you should see lines that indicate what was run:

```
Jan  3 08:17:01 seeker CRON[4885]: (root) CMD (   cd / && run-parts --report ↵
 /etc/cron.hourly)
```

Details vary from one distribution to another (this example is taken from an Ubuntu installation), but the entries should indicate the command run—cd / && run-parts --report /etc/cron.hourly in this example. If you can't find evidence that cron is running its jobs, perhaps the daemon isn't starting or is crashing. Use ps to see whether it's running, as described earlier in "Finding Running Processes." You may also want to review your SysV or Upstart configuration, since cron is normally started in this way.

Sometimes creating a "dummy" cron job can be a good way to investigate problems. A command such as date > /tmp/date.txt, used as a cron job, can tell you whether a job is executing; just check for /tmp/date.txt, and verify that it contains the time that it should if the job is executing correctly.

You can create cron jobs that run when you want them to run to help diagnose problems. Be careful when you do this, though. If you're having problems with, say, the regular cron monthly run, you can schedule it to run right away; but if this run normally does some time-consuming or time-sensitive task like, say, a monthly system backup, you might want to remove or disable the script that does this while you test (unless of course that's the monthly process that's not working).

You should always be mindful of permissions when dealing with cron. Sometimes a job won't work because it's being executed as the wrong user. A job that's executed inappropriately as root can be just as much of a problem. Not only does this create a security risk, but if the job creates files, they'll probably be owned by root, which could cause problems if ordinary users or non-root processes should be able to manipulate (or sometimes even read) these files.

Summary

This chapter covers a variety of miscellaneous system and environmental troubleshooting topics. The first of these was system initialization: ensuring that the correct runlevel is reached, that startup scripts run correctly, and that a suitable login process is available for users (or administrators). You should also be able to check and change kernel configurations using sysctl; such settings can sometimes be critically important to normal system operation.

User accounts pose unique troubleshooting challenges. Accounts can be damaged or need attention because of a changing account environment or because users simply forget their passwords. Fortunately, ordinary account maintenance tools (passwd, usermod, and so on) can correct most of these problems. Some user problems relate to their shells. Depending on how it's launched, bash may use any of several different configuration files, which are in fact scripts. If critical user files such as ~/.bashrc are missing or damaged, critical bash environment variables and other features may not be set. Likewise, global configuration files can become damaged and may need repair or replacement.

Running programs pose generic issues. You must be able to identify specific processes by using ps. With information from ps in hand, you may be able to kill an errant process or begin to learn why a process that *should* be running isn't. Most Linux programs rely on libraries, so being able to identify those libraries and fix library problems is important.

Sometimes you want to run programs in the future. The cron utility provides this ability in Linux, so understanding how to use cron is important. Troubleshooting cron can sometimes be tricky because it's designed to run jobs at specific times. Rescheduling cron jobs, checking log files, and paying attention to cron-specific details can help you diagnose cron problems.

Exam Essentials

Explain how to change the default runlevel.   The /etc/inittab file contains a line that begins with id that sets the default runlevel. Change the number on this line to reflect your desired default runlevel. For instance, editing this line to read id:3:initdefault: sets the default runlevel to 3.

Summarize some common login tools and methods. Login methods can be text-mode or GUI and local or network-enabled. The traditional text-mode local login method is the login program, which is run on a local console via a getty program. Network-enabled text-mode tools include the now largely obsolete Telnet and the newer SSH. The XDMCP protocol mediates both local and network GUI logins. Network GUI logins can also be handled by VNC or tunneled through SSH.

Describe tools for adjusting kernel options once the computer has booted. Some kernel options can be set by modifying files in the /proc directory tree. Another way of doing this is to use the sysctl program. You can edit such options so that they're set when the system boots by editing /etc/sysctl.conf.

Summarize the files in which user account information is stored. The /etc/passwd file holds usernames, UID values, default GID values, free-form user information, the location of users' home directories, and the names of users' default shells. In the past, it also held hashed passwords, but this information is now held in the /etc/shadow file, which also holds password aging information. The /etc/group file holds information on groups, including group names, GID values, and the users who belong to groups.

Summarize some of the tools used to adjust account information. The usermod utility modifies many of the key account features, such as the UID value, home directory, and default shell. You can use passwd to reset a forgotten or corrupted password. You can use your favorite text editor to directly edit any of the key account files.

Describe key bash startup scripts. The startup scripts for bash can be categorized as either login or non-login and as either global or user. The key global login file is /etc/profile, but it often includes files in /etc/profile.d, as well. The ~/.bash_profile, ~/.bash_login, and ~/.profile files are user login files. Officially, the only non-login bash startup script is ~/.bashrc (a user file); however, both this file and /etc/profile usually call /etc/bashrc, /etc/bash/bashrc, or /etc/bash.bashrc, so these files are generally considered global non-login files.

Explain how to ensure that dynamic libraries stored in an unusual location will be used. The /etc/ld.so.conf file holds the names of directories that will be searched for dynamic libraries. You can edit this file, either directly or by creating a custom file in /etc/ld.so.conf.d, and then type **ldconfig** as root to have the system scan the libraries so that it can quickly locate specific library files.

Describe how to adjust syslogd options. You can control the files to which log messages are sent by editing /etc/syslog.conf. (Some systems use other system loggers, so you may need to adjust a different file, such as /etc/rsyslogd.conf.) You use various codes to assign files or other targets to specific facilities (such as kern, mail, and security) and priorities (such as info, err, and emerg). Servers and some other programs generate messages with particular facilities and priorities according to their own rules; the system logger sorts and logs these according to the rules you specify.

Explain the difference between user and system cron jobs.   User cron jobs are created by ordinary users (potentially including root) to handle their own tasks on a regularly scheduled basis. Users create files specifying these jobs, which are then stored by the system in /var/spool/cron or a similar location. System cron jobs handle system tasks. They're defined in /etc/crontab, which typically runs scripts stored in various other subdirectories called /etc/cron.*interval*, where interval is some time unit.

Summarize some methods you can use to resolve cron problems.   You can check for user restrictions to be sure that users have the right to run cron jobs. You can check log files to see whether cron is trying to execute a process at an appropriate time. You can use ps to verify that the cron daemon is running. You can create a "dummy"cron job that runs along with whatever is causing problems but that creates a useful trace of its operations to help diagnose the problem.

Review Questions

1. What is the purpose of the /etc/sysctl.conf file?

    A. It holds miscellaneous system configuration options that are set via the sysctl utility when the system boots.

    B. It specifies the order in which system services are started when the computer boots.

    C. It specifies the filesystems that are mounted at boot time or that may be mounted manually by ordinary users.

    D. It identifies system services that are started directly by the init process when the computer boots.

2. How do /etc/profile and /etc/bashrc differ?

    A. /etc/profile is a tcsh logout script; /etc/bashrc holds bash environment variables.

    B. /etc/profile holds user login statistics; /etc/bashrc holds user shell preferences.

    C. /etc/profile is a login script; /etc/bashrc is a non-login script.

    D. /etc/profile holds user account data; /etc/bashrc is a bash startup script.

3. What are the important (non-comment) contents of /etc/ld.so.conf?

    A. Environment variables

    B. A shell script program

    C. Usernames

    D. Directory names

4. A symbolic link is called /etc/rc.d/rc3.d/S80sendmail. Assuming this symbolic link is correctly placed and functions in the expected way, what will it do?

    A. Start the sendmail server in runlevel 3.

    B. Point the sendmail server to its configuration file.

    C. Initialize sendmail to run via inetd.

    D. Stop the sendmail server when launched manually without options.

5. Which of the following is a global non-login bash startup script?

    A. /etc/profile

    B. /etc/bashrc

    C. /root/.profile

    D. /root/.bashrc

6. What command must you type as **root** to have the system re-scan the directories on the library path to enable programs to find dynamic libraries in these directories?

    A. sysctl

    B. ldconfig

    C. shadow

    D. init -libs

7. You've determined that the SSH server is being started by the /etc/rc2.d/S16ssh startup script (or a link of that name). You want to prevent this server from running in runlevel 2. What is the most reliable way to do this?

    A. Rename the script or link so that its name begins with K rather than S.

    B. Delete the /etc/rc2.d directory.

    C. Delete the /etc/rc2.d/S16ssh file or link.

    D. Locate the corresponding Upstart configuration file and delete it.

8. Which of the following is *not* a common **bash** startup script file?

    A. ~/.bash_logout

    B. /etc/bash.bashrc

    C. /etc/bashrc

    D. ~/.profile

9. You type **sysctl -a** as **root**. What can you expect to have happen?

    A. The computer will reboot immediately.

    B. All processes with invalid PPID values will be terminated.

    C. You will see a list of kernel keys and their values.

    D. You will see an error message describing the correct use of sysctl.

10. What directory is commonly used as a supplemental location for additional scripts called by the global **bash** login script?

    A. /etc/bashrc.d

    B. /etc/bash.extras

    C. /etc/profile.d

    D. /etc/scripts

11. Which of the following lines, if used in a user **cron** job, will run /usr/local/bin/cleanup twice a day?

    A. 15 7,19 * * * tbaker /usr/local/bin/cleanup

    B. 15 7,19 * * * /usr/local/bin/cleanup

    C. 15 */2 * * * tbaker /usr/local/bin/cleanup

    D. 15 */2 * * * /usr/local/bin/cleanup

12. To alter a Linux system's default runlevel, what would you do?

   A. Issue the `telinit x` command, where x is the desired runlevel.

   B. Edit `/etc/modules.conf`, and enter the runlevel as an option to the `runlevel` module.

   C. Issue the `telinit Q` command to have the system query you for a new runlevel.

   D. Edit `/etc/inittab` and enter the correct runlevel in the `id` line.

13. You use `top` to examine the CPU time being consumed by various processes on your system. You discover that one process, `dfcomp`, is consuming more than 90 percent of your system's CPU time. What can you conclude?

   A. Very little; `dfcomp` could be legitimately consuming that much CPU time, or it could be an unauthorized or malfunctioning program.

   B. No program should consume 90 percent of available CPU time; `dfcomp` is clearly malfunctioning and should be terminated.

   C. This is normal; `dfcomp` is the kernel's main scheduling process, and it consumes any unused CPU time.

   D. This behavior is normal *if* your CPU is less powerful than a 2.5GHz EM64T Pentium; but on newer systems, no program should consume 90 percent of CPU time.

14. What is wrong with the following system `cron` job entry (in `/etc/crontab`)?

`17 * * * *    run-parts /etc/cron.hourly`

   A. This command should run hourly but will run only at 5:00 P.M.

   B. There is no `run-parts` command in Linux.

   C. The time specification is incomplete.

   D. It's missing a user specification.

15. The user `fred` creates a `cron` job to retrieve email from a remote server using the `fetchmail` program. What is true of this `cron` job, if it's properly configured?

   A. The `fetchmail` process runs with the `fred` UID.

   B. The `fetchmail` process runs with the `root` UID

   C. The `fetchmail` process runs with the `crontab` UID.

   D. The `fetchmail` process runs with the `nobody` UID.

16. You log into a Linux system using a text-mode virtual terminal at the computer's console. What program is likely to handle the login procedure?

   A. bash

   B. SSH

   C. GDM

   D. `login`

17. Which of the following account features can you change by editing a user's entry in /etc/passwd? (Select all that apply.)

    A. The account's expiration date

    B. The account's home directory

    C. The account's default shell

    D. The account's default GUI desktop environment

18. In what file are GIDs associated with their assigned names?

    A. /etc/passwd

    B. /etc/shadow

    C. /etc/group

    D. /etc/grub.d

19. In what configuration file can you find system-wide features such as the minimum UID value that should be used for user accounts and the period that login should wait after a login failure before permitting another attempt?

    A. /etc/user.set

    B. /etc/system.conf

    C. /etc/account.conf

    D. /etc/login.defs

20. What permissions are *most* appropriate for the /etc/shadow file?

    A. 0666 (-rw-rw-rw-)

    B. 0644 (-rw-r--r--)

    C. 0640 (-rw-r-----)

    D. 0600 (-rw-------)

Answers to Review Questions

1. A. Option A correctly describes the purpose of /etc/sysctl.conf. Option B is a partial description of the purpose of SysV init scripts. Option C describes the function of the /etc/fstab file. Option D describes the purpose of the /etc/inittab file.

2. C. Option C provides brief but correct descriptions of both of these files and so is correct. Option A's description of /etc/profile is completely fictitious, although its description of /etc/bashrc is at least potentially and partially correct, since login scripts can set environment variables. Option B's descriptions of both files are both completely fictitious. Option D's description of /etc/profile is fictitious (it applies to /etc/passwd), but its description of /etc/bashrc is correct.

3. D. The /etc/ld.so.conf file holds the names of directories that the system searches for dynamic libraries, so option D is correct. This file does not hold environment variables, shell script programs, or usernames, so options A, B, and C are all wrong.

4. A. The /etc/rc.d/rc3.d is one of several possible locations for links to SysV startup scripts that are to be run when entering runlevel 3. Because this link name begins with S, this link causes the service to be started when entering runlevel 3, so option A is correct. This location is not used to point servers to configuration files or to run servers via the inetd super server, so options B and C are incorrect. When a SysV startup script is launched without options, it displays an error message, so option D is incorrect.

5. B. /etc/bashrc is a common name for a global non-login bash startup script, so option B is correct. /etc/profile is a common name for a global login bash startup script, so option A is incorrect. /root/.profile is the root user's login bash startup script, so option C is incorrect. /root/.bashrc is the root user's non-login bash startup script, so option D is incorrect.

6. B. The ldconfig utility reads /etc/ld.so.conf and caches information on the libraries in the referenced directories, so option B is correct. The sysctl program is used to adjust run-time kernel features, but it doesn't manage libraries, so option A is incorrect. There is no standard shadow program, although /etc/shadow holds account passwords and aging information, so option C is incorrect. The init process is the first process run by the kernel; it's not used (even with options) as described in the question, so option D is incorrect.

7. A. Startup scripts (or, more commonly, symbolic links that point to them) that begin with the letter S are called in such a way that they start the service in question; those that begin with the letter K are called in such a way that they stop the service in question. Thus, option A will have the desired effect. Options B and C will both prevent the server from starting, but the server may continue running if you switch from another runlevel. More importantly, option B will stop the computer from starting many other potentially vital services in runlevel 2. The question clearly states that the server is being started by a SysV startup script, so there's no need to look for a competing Upstart configuration file.

8.   A. The ~/.bash_logout file is a common bash *logout* file; it doesn't run when bash starts, so it's not a bash startup script file, and option A is correct. Options B and C are two common names for global bash non-login startup scripts, and option D is a standard name for a user login startup script for bash.

9.   C. The sysctl utility enables you to set or view run-time kernel variables (keys), and its -a option displays them all; thus, option C is correct. Option A describes the effect of typing **shutdown -r now** or **reboot** as root. Option B doesn't describe the effect of any command. Since the specified command is legal, sysctl won't display an error message, and option D is incorrect.

10.   C. The standard /etc/profile script provided with most Linux distributions searches /etc/profile.d and runs any scripts it finds there; therefore, option C is correct. Options A, B, and D all describe fictitious locations.

11.   B. User cron jobs don't include a username specification (tbaker in options A and C). The */2 specification for the hour in options C and D causes the job to execute every other hour; the 7,19 specification in options A and B causes it to execute twice a day, on the 7th and 19th hours (in conjunction with the 15 minute specification, that means at 7:15 A.M. and 7:15 P.M.).

12.   D. The /etc/inittab file controls the default runlevel, and the line beginning with id sets the default runlevel, so option D is correct. Although telinit can be used to *temporarily* change the runlevel, this change will not be permanent, so option A is incorrect. The /etc/modules.conf file has nothing to do with runlevels, and there is no standard runlevel module, so option B is incorrect. The command telinit Q tells the system to reread /etc/inittab, so it could be used to implement a changed default after you've edited the file, but it will have no effect before editing this file, so option C is incorrect.

13.   A. CPU-intensive programs routinely consume 90 percent or more of available CPU time, but not all systems run such programs. Furthermore, some types of program bugs can create such CPU loads. Thus, you must investigate the matter more. What is dfcomp? Is it designed as a CPU-intensive program? Is it consuming this much CPU time consistently, or was this a brief burst of activity? Because there are so many questions left unanswered, option A is correct. Depending on the system, it might or might not be reasonable for a single process to consume 90 percent of CPU time, so option B is incorrect. Option C's description of dfcomp is entirely fictitious. Option D's summary of CPU loads on different types of CPUs is entirely fictitious.

14. D. System `cron` jobs require a user specification after the time specification and before the command to be executed, and this entry is missing in this specification, so option D is correct. (This entry would be legal for a user `cron` job, though, assuming the user could run the command.) Option A is incorrect because the time specification runs the job at 17 minutes past the hour, every hour; and even if it did run at 5:00 P.M., the entry would be legal, if confusingly named. Option B is incorrect because `run-parts`, although not present on all Linux distributions, is used on several distributions. `cron` is also capable of running user-written scripts and programs, so even if `run-parts` weren't a standard Linux utility, the entry would still work if you'd written your own `run-parts` script. Option C is incorrect because the time specification is complete; it includes a minute value (`17`) and asterisks (*) denoting a run at every hour, day of the month, month, and day of the week.

15. A. User `cron` jobs run as the user who created them, so option A is correct, and options B, C, and D are necessarily incorrect.

16. D. The `login` program is launched by the `getty` that handles a virtual terminal in order to handle the login procedure at text-mode consoles; thus, option D is correct. Although the effect of the login may well be the launching of `bash`, this program doesn't handle the login procedure itself, so option A is incorrect. The Secure Shell (SSH) is a network-oriented login protocol; it doesn't handle local logins, so option B is incorrect. The GNOME Display Manager (GDM) is one of several GUI login programs; since the question specified a text-mode login, option C is incorrect.

17. B, C. The `/etc/passwd` file contains the username, a password field (unused today), the user ID (UID) value, the group ID (GID) value for the default group, a free-form description, the home directory, and the default shell. Options B and C are in this list and so are correct. The account's expiration date is stored in the `/etc/shadow` file, not in `/etc/passwd`, so option A is incorrect. The account's default GUI desktop environment (GNOME, KDE, Xfce, and so forth) is managed by the XDMCP server in a way specific for each XDMCP login server, so option D is incorrect.

18. C. Group ID (GID) values are associated with group names in `/etc/group`, so option C is correct. The `/etc/passwd` and `/etc/shadow` files define user information, not group information, so options A and B are both incorrect. (Each user's default GID value appears in `/etc/passwd`, but this associates users to groups, not GIDs to their own names.) The `/etc/grub.d` directory holds scripts that help configure the Grand Unified Bootloader (GRUB) 2; it doesn't link GIDs to their names—and it's a directory, not a file. Thus, option D is incorrect.

19. D. The `/etc/login.defs` file holds the specified information, so option D is correct. The remaining options are all fictitious files.

20. D. The /etc/shadow file holds hashed user passwords, which are sensitive and so should not be readable by ordinary users. Thus, all world permissions should definitely be denied on this file, making options A and B incorrect. Although this file is ordinarily given to the root group, allowing group read access to it is generally considered a bad idea, so option C is incorrect. Option D is the most restrictive set of permissions among all the options, and in fact the root user, who owns this file, must have read and write access to it, so option D is correct.

Appendix

About the Companion CD

IN THIS APPENDIX:

✓ What you'll find on the CD

✓ System requirements

✓ Using the CD

✓ Troubleshooting

What You'll Find on the CD

The following sections are arranged by category and summarize the software and other goodies you'll find on the CD. If you need help with installing the items provided on the CD, refer to the installation instructions in the "Using the CD" section of this appendix.

Some programs on the CD might fall into one of these categories:

Shareware programs are fully functional, free, trial versions of copyrighted programs. If you like particular programs, register with their authors for a nominal fee and receive licenses, enhanced versions, and technical support.

Freeware programs are free, copyrighted games, applications, and utilities. You can copy them to as many computers as you like—for free—but they offer no technical support.

GNU software is governed by its own license, which is included inside the folder of the GNU software. There are no restrictions on distribution of GNU software. See the GNU license at the root of the CD for more details.

Trial, *demo*, or *evaluation* versions of software are usually limited either by time or by functionality (such as not letting you save a project after you create it).

Sybex Test Engine

The CD contains the Sybex test engine, which includes all the assessment test and chapter review questions in electronic format, as well as two bonus exams located only on the CD.

Electronic Flashcards

These handy electronic flashcards are just what they sound like. One side contains a question, and the other side shows the answer.

PDF of the Glossary

We have included an electronic version of the Glossary in .pdf format. You can view the electronic version of the book with Adobe Reader.

Adobe Reader

We've also included a copy of Adobe Reader so you can view PDF files that accompany the book's content. For more information on Adobe Reader or to check for a newer version, visit Adobe's Web site at http://www.adobe.com/products/reader.

System Requirements

Make sure your computer meets the minimum system requirements shown in the following list. If your computer doesn't match up to most of these requirements, you may have problems using the software and files on the companion CD. For the latest and greatest information, please refer to the ReadMe file located at the root of the CD.

Windows

- A PC running Microsoft Windows 98, Windows 2000, Windows NT4 (with SP4 or later), Windows Me, Windows XP, Windows Vista, or Windows 7
- An Internet connection
- A CD-ROM drive

Linux

- Modern processor (800 MHz or faster)
- 512 MB of RAM and 128 MB of graphics memory
- Red Hat Enterprise Linux (RHEL), openSUSE 11, Ubuntu 7.10 or newer
- Firefox 2.*x*, Firefox 3.*x*, or SeaMonkey 1.11

Using the CD

For Windows users, to install the items from the CD to your hard drive, follow these steps:

1. Insert the CD into your computer's CD-ROM drive. The license agreement appears.

NOTE *Windows users*: The interface won't launch if you have autorun disabled. In that case, click Start ➤ Run (for Windows Vista and Windows 7, Start ➤ All Programs ➤ Accessories ➤ Run). In the dialog box that appears, type D:\Start.exe. (Replace *D* with the proper letter if your CD drive uses a different letter. If you don't know the letter, see how your CD drive is listed under My Computer.) Click OK.

2. Read the license agreement, and then click the Accept button if you want to use the CD.

The CD interface appears. The interface allows you to access the content with just one or two clicks.

For Linux users, use a Web browser to open the `Start.html` file. This CD requires a browser with Adobe's Flash plug-in installed. To install this plug-in, follow one of these steps:

- Ubuntu users—at the terminal, enter `sudo apt-get install flashplugin-nonfree`.

- Debian users—see the instructions at `http://wiki.debian.org/FlashPlayer`.

- Fedora users—see the instructions at `http://www.fedorafaq.org/#flash`.

Adobe's Flash plug-in doesn't work well for users of Linux in a 64-bit environment. If you are running this CD on a 64-bit computer and encounter any problems, try running it on a 32-bit computer.

Troubleshooting

Wiley has attempted to provide programs that work on most computers with the minimum system requirements. Alas, your computer may differ, and some programs may not work properly for some reason.

The two likeliest problems are that you don't have enough memory (RAM) for the programs you want to use or you have other programs running that are affecting installation or running of a program. If you get an error message such as "Not enough memory" or "Setup cannot continue," try one or more of the following suggestions and then try using the software again:

Turn off any antivirus software running on your computer. Installation programs sometimes mimic virus activity and may make your computer incorrectly believe that it's being infected by a virus.

Close all running programs. The more programs you have running, the less memory is available to other programs. Installation programs typically update files and programs; so if you keep other programs running, installation may not work properly.

Have your local computer store add more RAM to your computer. This is, admittedly, a drastic and somewhat expensive step. However, adding more memory can really help the speed of your computer and allow more programs to run at the same time.

Customer Care

If you have trouble with the book's companion CD, please call the Wiley Product Technical Support phone number at (800) 762-2974. Outside the United States, call +1(317) 572-3994. You can also contact Wiley Product Technical Support at http://sybex.custhelp.com. John Wiley & Sons will provide technical support only for installation and other general quality-control items. For technical support on the applications themselves, consult the program's vendor or author.

To place additional orders or to request information about other Wiley products, please call (877) 762-2974.

Glossary

Numbers

8.3 filename   A filename that consists of no more than eight characters plus an optional dot (.) and three-character extension. This file-naming limit exists in DOS and the original File Allocation Table (FAT) filesystem it uses.

A

Accelerated Graphics Port (AGP)   An expansion bus in common use for about a decade starting in 1997. As the name implies, AGP was primarily used for video cards. Around 2004, the *Peripheral Component Interconnect Express (PCIe or PCI-E)* interface began to supersede AGP. AGP devices look much like PCI devices to Linux hardware-probing utilities.

Address Resolution Protocol (ARP)   A protocol used to learn a network hardware address based on an IPv4 address. See also *Neighbor Discovery Protocol (NDP)*.

Advanced Technology Attachment (ATA)   A type of interface for hard disks, CD-ROM drives, tape drives, and other mass storage devices. Also often referred to as EIDE.

AGP   See *Accelerated Graphics Port (AGP)*.

American Standard Code for Information Interchange (ASCII)   An encoding method for alphanumeric data commonly used for text files. ASCII is a common code, but because it lacks characters used by many non-English languages, other encoding methods, such as UTF-8, are slowly supplanting it.

Apache   The most commonly used Web server package for Linux.

ARP   See *Address Resolution Protocol (ARP)*.

ASCII   See *American Standard Code for Information Interchange (ASCII)*.

ATA   See *Advanced Technology Attachment (ATA)*.

automounter   A program that scans disk devices and automatically mounts newly detected media or that mounts media associated with directories when those directories are accessed. Automounters are particularly useful for removable media such as optical discs and USB disk drives, as well as for network filesystems that should be permanently available but not permanently mounted.

B

Basic Input/Output System (BIOS)   A low-level software component included on a computer's motherboard in read-only memory (ROM) form. The CPU runs BIOS code when it first starts up, and the BIOS is responsible for locating and booting an OS or OS loader. See also *Extensible Firmware Interface (EFI)* and *Unified Extensible Firmware Interface (UEFI)*.

Berkeley Internet Name Domain (BIND)   A common Domain Name System (DNS) server for Linux.

BIND   See *Berkeley Internet Name Domain (BIND)*.

BIOS   See Basic Input/Output System (BIOS).

boot loader   A program that directs the boot process. The BIOS calls the boot loader, which loads the Linux kernel or redirects the boot process to another boot loader. See also *boot manager*.

boot manager   Sometimes used synonymously with *boot loader*, but sometimes refers to a boot loader that presents OS or kernel options to the user at boot time.

broadcast   A type of network communication in which one computer sends a message to many computers (typically all the computers on the sender's local network segment).

C

C library (libc)   Standard programming routines used by many programs written in the C programming language. The most common Linux C library is also referred to as *GNU libc (glibc)*.

central processing unit (CPU)   The main chip on a computer; it handles the bulk of its computational tasks.

chroot jail   A method of running a program (particularly a server) so that its access to the computer is limited to a particular directory tree. A chroot jail is a useful security measure for certain types of servers.

CHS addressing   See *cylinder/head/sector (CHS) addressing*.

CIDR   See *classless inter-domain routing (CIDR)*.

classless inter-domain routing (CIDR)   A method of breaking IP addresses into subnets for routing purposes that doesn't rely on the traditional Class A/B/C distinctions. CIDR is more flexible than the class system but requires certain Internet routers to have larger routing tables.

client   1. A program that initiates data transfer requests using networking protocols. 2. A computer that runs one or more client programs.

Common Unix Printing System (CUPS)   A printing system for Linux and other Unix-like systems. CUPS adds several features that are missing from the earlier BSD LPD and LPRng printing systems.

CPU   See *central processing unit (CPU)*.

cracker   An individual who breaks into computers. Crackers may do this out of curiosity, out of malice, for profit, or for other reasons. See also *hacker*.

cron job   A program or script that's run at a regular interval by the cron daemon. See also *system cron job* and *user cron job*.

CUPS   See *Common Unix Printing System (CUPS)*.

cylinder/head/sector (CHS) addressing   A method of hard disk addressing in which a triplet of numbers (a cylinder, a head, and a sector) is used to identify a specific sector. CHS addressing contrasts with *logical block addressing (LBA)*.

D

daemon   A program that runs constantly, providing background services. Linux servers are typically implemented as daemons, although there are also non-server daemons, such as crond, the cron daemon.

default route   The route that network packets take if a more specific route doesn't direct them in some other way. The default route typically involves a gateway or router system that can further redirect the packets.

dependency   A requirement of one software package that another one be installed. For instance, most Linux programs include a dependency on the C library.

development library   A set of support files that enables software that uses a *library* to be compiled on a computer.

DHCP   See *Dynamic Host Configuration Protocol (DHCP)*.

DHCP lease   A temporary assignment of an IP address to a DHCP client by a DHCP server. Clients must periodically renew their DHCP leases or risk losing the right to use the address.

directory   1. A filesystem structure in which files and other directories are stored. 2. A type of database with a hierarchical structure and optimized for more read than write accesses.

DNS   See *Domain Name System (DNS)*.

domain name   A name assigned to a group of computers, such as example.com. Individual computers have hostnames that include the domain name, such as jupiter.example.com.

Domain Name System (DNS)   A distributed set of computers that run servers to convert between computer names (such as ns.example.com) and IP addresses (such as 192.168.45.204). DNS servers are organized hierarchically and refer requests to systems responsible for successively more specific domains.

Dynamic Host Configuration Protocol (DHCP)   A protocol used on local networks for dissemination of network configuration information. A single DHCP server can maintain information for many DHCP clients, reducing overall configuration effort.

dynamic library   A type of library that's stored as a separate file from an executable program but that's loaded along with the main program file. Dynamic libraries save disk space and RAM compared to static libraries. See also *library* and *static library*.

E

EFI See *Extensible Firmware Interface (EFI)*.

EIDE See *Enhanced Integrated Device Electronics (EIDE)* and *Advanced Technology Attachment (ATA)*.

encryption key A number that's used in conjunction with an algorithm to scramble data in a way that can be descrambled only with the use of the same or a related number.

Enhanced Integrated Device Electronics (EIDE) Another name for the *Advanced Technology Attachment (ATA)* interface.

export 1. As a noun, a directory that's shared via the Network File System (NFS) server. 2. As a verb, the act of sharing a directory via NFS.

ext2 See *Second Extended File System (ext2fs or ext2)*.

ext2fs See *Second Extended File System (ext2fs or ext2)*.

ext3 See *Third Extended File System (ext3fs or ext3)*.

ext3fs See *Third Extended File System (ext3fs or ext3)*.

ext4 See *Fourth Extended File System (ext4fs or ext4)*.

ext4fs See *Fourth Extended File System (ext4fs or ext4)*.

extended partition A type of disk partition used on MBR disks. Extended partitions are placeholders for one or more *logical partitions*.

Extensible Firmware Interface (EFI) Firmware intended to replace the aging $x86$ BIOS. EFI provides numerous enhancements intended to help computers cope with modern hardware. The GPT partitioning system is part of the EFI specification, although GPT may be used on non-EFI systems as well.

Extents File System (XFS) One of several journaling filesystems for Linux. XFS was developed by Silicon Graphics (SGI) for its IRIX OS and then ported to Linux.

F

fake RAID A type of software RAID that's implemented with minimal help from the motherboard's disk chipset. Fake RAID is generally best avoided in Linux; use true hardware RAID or Linux's variety of software RAID instead.

FAT See *File Allocation Table (FAT)*.

File Allocation Table (FAT) 1. A type of filesystem used natively by DOS and Windows and also supported as a non-native filesystem by Linux and most other OSs. 2. On the FAT filesystem, a data structure after which the filesystem is named.

file server   A computer or program that delivers files to other computers via network protocols upon request. Examples of file-server programs include NFS, Samba, and numerous FTP programs.

filesystem   1. A low-level data structure, typically stored on disks, that enables access to files by name. Linux supports many low-level filesystems, including more than half a dozen native Linux filesystems and many more non-Linux filesystems. 2. The structure of files and directories on a computer, ranging from the root (/) directory through all its files and subdirectories. A high-level filesystem may be stored on one low-level filesystem or split across several of them.

firewall   1. A program or kernel configuration that blocks access to specific ports or network programs on a computer. 2. A computer that's configured as a router and that includes firewall software that can restrict access between the networks it manages.

firmware   Software that manages a device at a low level. Firmware is typically built into chips on the device, although sometimes the OS must download firmware to the device before it can be used.

Fourth Extended File System (ext4fs or ext4)   The fourth version of the popular Linux filesystem. Ext4fs adds the ability to handle larger files and filesystems, as well as various performance enhancements, to the ext3fs feature set.

forward zone   A DNS *zone* that enables DNS servers to return IP addresses when given hostnames.

free software   Software that is distributed under a license, such as the *GPL*, that permits copying and modification under liberal terms. See also *open source*.

Free Software Foundation (FSF)   A non-profit organization based in Cambridge Massachusetts dedicated to the promotion of what it calls *free software*.

FSF   See *Free Software Foundation (FSF)*.

G

General Public License (GPL)   A common free software license created and favored by the Free Software Foundation.

GID   See *group ID (GID)*.

Globally Unique Identifier (GUID)   A 16-byte number that's intended to be unique when generated via certain algorithms. Identical to a *Universally Unique Identifier (UUID)* except in some details of representation.

GNOME   See *GNU Network Object Model Environment (GNOME)*.

GNU   See *GNU's Not Unix (GNU)*.

GNU Network Object Model Environment (GNOME)   A common desktop environment for Linux, headquartered at `http://www.gnome.org`.

GNU's Not Unix (GNU)   A project sponsored by the *Free Software Foundation* to create a free implementation of Unix. Linux relies heavily on GNU software—so much so that some people prefer the term *GNU/Linux* to *Linux*.

GPL   See *General Public License (GPL)*.

GPT   See *GUID Partition Table (GPT)*.

Grand Unified Boot Loader (GRUB)   A popular boot loader for Linux. GRUB can boot a Linux kernel or redirect the boot process to another boot loader in a non-Linux partition, thus booting other OSs. Similar to the competing *Linux Loader (LILO)*. Two versions are available, the older GRUB Legacy and the newer GRUB 2. See also *boot loader.*

graphical user interface (GUI)   A method of human/computer interaction characterized by a graphical display, a mouse to move a pointer around the screen, and the ability to perform actions by pointing at objects on the screen and clicking a mouse button.

group   A collection of users. Files are owned by a user and a group, and group members may be given access to files independent of the owner and all other users. This feature may be used to enhance collaborative abilities by giving members of a group read/write access to particular files while still excluding those who aren't members of the group. It can also be used by system administrators to control access to system files and resources.

group ID (GID)   A number associated with a particular group. Similar to a *user ID (UID)*.

GRUB   See *Grand Unified Boot Loader (GRUB)*.

GUI   See *graphical user interface (GUI)*.

GUID   See *Globally Unique Identifier (GUID)*.

GUID Partition Table (GPT)   A type of partition table used on some modern computers, such as Intel-based Macintoshes. GPT overcomes some limitations of the older *Master Boot Record (MBR)* partitioning scheme.

H

hacker   1. An individual who is skilled at using or programming computers and who enjoys using these skills in constructive ways. Many Linux programmers consider themselves hackers in this sense of the term. 2. A *cracker*. This use of the term is prevalent in the mass media, but it's frowned upon in the Linux community.

hardware address   A code that uniquely identifies a single network interface. This address is built into the device itself rather than assigned in Linux. Also known as a *media access control (MAC) address*.

hash   A one-way encryption method; hashed data cannot be decrypted. Hashes are used to store passwords and some other sensitive data. The idea is that when a user types a password, a hash of the password should match a stored hash of the same password; but if the password file is stolen, the thief cannot decrypt the password. (Such a thief could attempt a brute-force attack by hashing every word in a dictionary until one matches, though.)

header file   File that contains interface definitions for software routines contained in a library. Program source code that uses a library must refer to the associated header files.

HFS   See *Hierarchical File System (HFS)*.

Hierarchical File System (HFS)   A filesystem used on the Mac OS.

hostname   A computer's human-readable name, such as `persephone.example.com`.

hot spare   A disk in a RAID array that is unused but available for use in case another disk in the array fails. Also called a *hot standby* disk.

hot standby   See *hot spare*.

HTTP   See *Hypertext Transfer Protocol (HTTP)*.

Hypertext Transfer Protocol (HTTP)   A protocol used for transferring Web pages from a Web server to a Web browser.

I

ICMP   See *Internet Control Message Protocol (ICMP)*.

IDS   See *intrusion detection system (IDS)*.

IEEE 802.11   The technical standard that defines the most popular type of wireless (*Wi-Fi*) networking. Several variants exist, such as IEEE 802.11a, IEEE 802.11b, IEEE 802.11g, and IEEE 802.11n, which vary in speed and features.

incremental backup   A type of backup in which only files that have changed since the last backup are backed up. This is used to reduce the time required to back up a computer, at the cost of potentially greater restoration complexity.

inode   A filesystem data structure that contains critical information about the file, such as its size and location on the disk.

Internet Control Message Protocol (ICMP)   A type of network packet that's commonly used to signal error conditions, such as corrupted packets.

Internet Message Access Protocol (IMAP)   A popular pull email protocol (in which the recipient initiates transfers). Users commonly employ IMAP to retrieve email to be read on their desktop or workstation computers but stored on the IMAP server. See also *Post Office Protocol (POP)*.

Internet Protocol (IP)   An internet-layer protocol that's an important part of the TCP/IP network stack because it handles data packet exchange based on low-level addressing.

intrusion detection system (IDS)   A computer or software suite that can identify suspicious network activity and alert the network's administrators to this activity. Snort is a popular IDS package that runs on Linux.

IP   See *Internet Protocol (IP)*.

IP address   A computer's numeric TCP/IP address, such as 192.168.45.203.

IP masquerading   See *Network Address Translation (NAT)*.

IPv6   The "next-generation" Internet Protocol. This upgrade to TCP/IP allows for a theoretical maximum of approximately $3.4 3 10^{38}$ addresses, as opposed to the 4 billion addresses possible with the IPv4 that's in common use in 2011.

ISO-9660   The most common filesystem on CD-ROM and related optical media. ISO-9660 is often paired with *Rock Ridge extensions* or a *Joliet* filesystem in order to support long filenames and other features. See also *Universal Disc Format (UDF)*.

J

JFS   See *Journaled File System (JFS)*.

Joliet   A filesystem commonly used on CD-ROMs and related optical media. Joliet supports Microsoft-style long filenames and is almost always used in conjunction with an *ISO-9660* filesystem.

journal   An advanced filesystem feature that records data about pending disk operations. See also *journaling filesystem*.

Journaled File System (JFS)   One of several journaling filesystems for Linux. JFS was developed by IBM for its AIX OS. A subsequent implementation was created for OS/2, and Linux's JFS is derived from this code.

journaling filesystem   A type of filesystem that maintains a record of its operations. Such filesystems can typically recover quickly after a power failure or system crash. Common Linux journaling filesystems are ext3fs, ext4fs, ReiserFS, JFS, and XFS. See also *filesystem*.

K

K Desktop Environment (KDE)   A common desktop environment for Linux, headquartered at http://www.kde.org.

KDE   See *K Desktop Environment (KDE)*.

kernel   A software component at the heart of any modern OS, which directly accesses hardware on behalf of other software, doles out memory and CPU time to running programs, manages filesystems, and otherwise controls the overall operation of the computer. Technically, Linux is a kernel and nothing more; additional tools on a Linux system are not part of the Linux kernel.

kernel module   A part of the kernel that can be loaded or unloaded at will. Kernel modules implement many drivers and other kernel features. Implementing them as modules can reduce the size of a running Linux system by keeping code for hardware you don't have or features you don't use out of memory.

kernel ring buffer   A record of recent messages generated by the Linux kernel. Immediately after a Linux system boots, this buffer contains the bootup messages generated by drivers and major kernel subsystems. This buffer may be viewed with the `dmesg` command.

L

LBA   See *logical block addressing (LBA)*.

LDAP   See *Lightweight Directory Access Protocol (LDAP)*.

LDAP Data Interchange Format (LDIF)   A file format used by LDAP to describe directory entries.

LDIF   See *LDAP Data Interchange Format (LDIF)*.

library   A software component that provides support functions for other programs.

Lightweight Directory Access Protocol (LDAP)   A network-enabled *directory* (meaning 2) protocol that's used to store many types of information. Of most relevance for this book, LDAP can hold user account data, enabling centralized management of user accounts on a network.

LILO   See *Linux Loader (LILO)*.

linear block addressing (LBA)   See *logical block addressing (LBA)*.

link   A way of providing multiple names to reference a single file. Links are created with the `ln` command.

Linux   1. The open source OS kernel originally developed by Linus Torvalds and since then maintained and expanded by a large team of programmers. 2. An OS based on the Linux kernel, particularly if it follows the Unix model. Most Linux OSs rely heavily on software from the GNU project, so some people prefer the term *GNU/Linux*.

Linux Loader (LILO)   A popular Linux boot loader. Can boot a Linux kernel or redirect the boot process to another boot loader in a non-Linux partition, thus booting other OSs. Similar to the competing *Grand Unified Boot Loader (GRUB)*. See also *boot loader*.

Linux Standards Base (LSB)   A set of standards agreed upon by distribution maintainers in order to maintain some degree of compatibility between Linux distributions.

load average   A measure of the demands for CPU time by running programs. A load average of 0 means no demand for CPU time, 1 represents a single program placing constant demand on the CPU, and values higher than 1 represent multiple programs competing for CPU time. The top and uptime commands both provide load average information.

localhost   A name for the local computer.

log file   A text file, maintained by the system as a whole or by an individual server, in which important system events are recorded. Log files typically include information about user logins, server access attempts, and automatic routine maintenance.

log file rotation   A routine maintenance process in which the computer suspends recording data in log files, renames them, and opens new log files. This process keeps log files available for a time, but ultimately it deletes them, preventing them from growing to consume all available disk space. Also called *log rotation*.

log rotation   See *log file rotation*.

logical block addressing (LBA)   A method of accessing data on a disk that uses a single sector number to retrieve data from that sector. LBA contrasts with *cylinder/head/sector (CHS) addressing*. Some sources refer to LBA as *linear* block addressing.

logical partition   A type of MBR hard disk partition that has no entry in the primary partition table. Instead, logical partitions are carried within an extended partition.

logical volume   In an LVM configuration, a logical volume is a container for a filesystem or swap space, similar in function to a partition. Logical volumes are allocated from *volume groups*, which are collections of *physical volumes*.

Logical Volume Manager (LVM)   A disk allocation system that's used instead of or on top of traditional partitions. LVM enables more flexibility in filesystem management by creating containers (*logical volumes*) that can be added, deleted, and resized without concern for starting and ending sector numbers.

LSB   See *Linux Standards Base (LSB)*.

LVM   See *Logical Volume Manager (LVM)*.

M

MAC address   See *media access control (MAC) address* or *hardware address*.

machine name   The portion of a hostname that identifies a computer on a network, as opposed to the network as a whole (for instance, ginkgo is the machine name portion of ginkgo.example.com). The machine name is sometimes used in reference to the entire hostname.

Master Boot Record (MBR)   The first sector of a hard disk. The MBR contains the primary partition table and code that the BIOS runs during the boot process.

MBR   See *Master Boot Record (MBR)*.

media access control (MAC) address   See *hardware address*.

mode   The permissions of a file. In conjunction with the file's owner and group, the mode determines who may access a file and in what ways.

module   A piece of software that can be loaded and unloaded from a larger package in order to reduce memory load on a running system. See also *kernel module*.

module stack   A set of modules that build up to provide some set of features. For instance, to deliver sound, you may need to load several sound driver modules that make up a module stack.

mount   The action of making a low-level filesystem available to a running Linux system. This is done by associating the low-level filesystem with a *mount point*.

mount point   A directory (typically empty) to which a filesystem is mounted. Files and directories in the low-level filesystem then become available as files and subdirectories within the mount point directory.

N

Name Service Switch (NSS)   A part of Linux's account management system that maps usernames to user ID (UID) numbers, identifies users' home directories, and performs similar non-authentication tasks. See also *Pluggable Authentication Modules (PAM)*.

NAT   See *Network Address Translation (NAT)*.

NDP   See *Neighbor Discovery Protocol (NDP)*.

Neighbor Discovery Protocol (NDP)   A protocol used to learn a network hardware address based on an IPv6 address. See also *Address Resolution Protocol (ARP)*.

netmask   See *network mask*.

Network Address Translation (NAT)   A router configuration in which the router rewrites network packets from one network so that they all appear to originate from itself and then reverses the process for return packets. The effect is that the outside world sees just the NAT router, not the network it protects; but the protected network sees a normal connection to the outside network. Also known as *IP masquerading*.

Network File System (NFS)   A file sharing protocol, and server software of the same name, commonly used among Unix and Linux systems.

network mask   A bit pattern that identifies the portion of an IP address that's an entire network and the part that identifies a computer on that network. The pattern may be expressed in dotted quad notation (as in 255.255.255.0) or as the number of network bits following an IP address and a slash (as in 192.168.45.203/24). The network mask is also referred to as the *netmask* or *subnet mask*.

network stack   See *protocol stack*.

NewTechnology File System (NTFS)   The favored filesystem on Windows NT/200*x*/XP/Vista/7 systems. Linux supports NTFS, but this support is limited.

NFS   See *Network File System (NFS)*.

NSS   See *Name Service Switch (NSS)*.

NTFS   See *New Technology File System (NTFS)*.

O

open relay   An SMTP mail server that's configured to relay mail from anywhere to anywhere. Open relays are frequently abused by spammers to obfuscate their messages' true origins.

open source   A broad set of software licenses, or the software that uses them, that permits redistribution and copying under liberal terms. The open source definition is somewhat broader than that of *free software*.

P

package   A collection of files stored in a single carrier file, ready for installation using a package management system such as RPM or the Debian package system.

packet   A limited amount of data collected together with addressing information and sent over a network.

packet filter firewall   A type of firewall that operates on individual network data packets, passing or rejecting packets based on information such as the source and destination addresses and ports.

packet sniffer   A program that monitors network traffic at a low level, enabling diagnosis of problems and capturing data. Packet sniffers can be used both for legitimate network diagnosis and for data theft.

PAM   See *Pluggable Authentication Modules (PAM)*.

parallel ATA (PATA)   The traditional form of ATA interface, in which several bits are transferred at once. See also serial ATA (SATA).

PATA   See *parallel ATA (PATA)*.

path   A colon-delimited list of directories in which program files may be found. (Similar lists define the locations of directories, fonts, and other file types.)

PCI   See *Peripheral Component Interconnect (PCI)*.

PCIe or PCI-E   See *Peripheral Component Interconnect Express (PCIe or PCI-E)*.

Peripheral Component Interconnect (PCI)   An expansion bus, introduced in the early 1990s, capable of much higher speeds than the older ISA bus. Modern computers usually include several PCI slots, although PCI is beginning to give way to PCIe.

Peripheral Component Interconnect Express (PCIe or PCI-E)   An expansion bus, introduced in 2003, capable of speeds higher than those of the common PCI bus. Initially used mainly for video cards, PCIe is now used for many other types of device. PCIe looks just like PCI to Linux software.

physical volume   In an LVM configuration, a physical volume is a single partition or occasionally an unpartitioned disk or RAID device. Physical volumes are combined into *volume groups*, which are then subdivided again into *logical volumes*.

Pluggable Authentication Modules (PAM)   A set of tools that help manage user authentication and account management. PAM uses modules that can be added to or removed from the authentication rules for particular services, thus enabling changes in how Linux authenticates users.

POP   See *Post Office Protocol (POP)*.

port   See *port number*.

port number   A number that identifies the program from which a data packet comes or to which it's addressed. When a program initiates a network connection, it associates itself with one or more ports, enabling other computers to uniquely address the program.

Post Office Protocol (POP)   A popular pull email protocol (in which the recipient initiates transfers). Users commonly employ POP to retrieve email to be read and stored on their desktop or workstation computers. See also *Internet Message Access Protocol (IMAP)*.

PostScript   A programming language used on many high-end printers. PostScript is optimized for displaying text and graphics on the printed page. The Linux program Ghostscript converts from PostScript to bitmapped formats understood by many low-end and mid-range printers.

primary partition   A type of MBR partition that's defined in a data structure contained in the hard disk's partition table in the MBR. An MBR disk can contain only four primary partitions.

private key   One of two keys used in certain types of cryptography. The private key should be carefully guarded against theft. See also *encryption key* and *public key*.

privileged port   A port (see *port number*) that's numbered less than 1024. Linux restricts access to such ports to root. In networking's early days, any program running on a privileged port could be considered trustworthy because only programs configured by professional system administrators could be run on such ports. Today, that's no longer the case. See also *unprivileged port*.

process   A piece of code that's maintained and run by the Linux kernel separately from other pieces of code. Most processes correspond to programs that are running. One program can be run multiple times, resulting in several processes.

protocol stack   A collection of drivers, kernel procedures, and other software that implements a standard means of communicating across a network. Two computers must support compatible protocol stacks to communicate. The most popular protocol stack today is TCP/IP. Also called a *network stack*.

proxy server   A server program that forwards requests it receives to another computer and then returns replies to the original system. Proxy servers may be used to create secure "holes" in firewalls, to cache and speed up network access, to block undesirable content, or for other reasons.

public key   One of two keys used in certain types of cryptography. The public key is frequently given to the other side in a communication link. See also *encryption key* and *private key*.

R

RAID   See *Redundant Array of Independent Disks (RAID)*.

random access   A method of access to a storage device (RAM, hard disk, and so on) by which information may be stored or retrieved in an arbitrary order with little or no speed penalty. See also *sequential access*.

RAM   See *random access memory (RAM)*.

random access memory (RAM)   Memory that can be randomly accessed. More specifically, RAM can be read and written with ease and makes up the bulk of the memory in modern computers.

recursive lookup   A method of name resolution in which a DNS server queries a series of DNS servers, each of which has information about more and more specific networks, in order to locate the IP address associated with a hostname.

Redundant Array of Independent Disks (RAID)   A disk management system that enables combining multiple disks into higher-order devices in order to create a single larger disk space, improve reliability, improve disk speed, or a combination of these things.

ReiserFS   One of several journaling filesystems for Linux. Developed from scratch for Linux.

reverse zone   A DNS *zone* that enables DNS servers to return hostnames when given IP addresses.

RIP   See *Routing Information Protocol (RIP)*.

Rock Ridge extensions   A set of extensions to the ISO-9660 filesystem that enable storage of Unix-style long filenames, ownership, permissions, and other filesystem features on an ISO-9660 filesystem. See also *ISO-9660* and *Joliet*.

root directory   The directory that forms the base of a Linux filesystem (meaning 2). All other directories are accessible from the root directory, either directly or via intermediate directories.

root filesystem   See *root directory*.

root servers   A set of DNS servers that deliver information to other DNS servers about top-level domains (`.com`, `.net`, `.us`, and so on). DNS servers consult the root DNS servers first when performing full recursive DNS lookups.

Routing Information Protocol (RIP)   A network protocol that enables routers to exchange information on the distance between various networks each serves. RIP enables routers to optimize their routing tables and to automatically work around outages.

runlevel   A number associated with a particular set of services that are being run. Changing runlevels changes services or can shut down or restart the computer.

S

Samba   A server software package that implements the SMB/CIFS protocol, commonly used by Windows computers for file and printer sharing.

SAS   See *Serial Attached SCSI (SAS)*.

SATA   See *Serial ATA (SATA)*.

SCSI   See *Small Computer System Interface (SCSI)*.

Second Extended File System (ext2fs or ext2)   The most common native Linux filesystem (meaning 1) from the mid-1990s through approximately 2001.

Secure Shell (SSH)   A remote login protocol and program that uses encryption to ensure that intercepted data packets cannot be used by an interloper. Generally regarded as the successor to Telnet on Linux systems.

Self-Monitoring, Analysis, and Reporting Technology (SMART)   A feature of modern hard disks that enables them to detect failing hardware before it causes data loss. Linux SMART utilities such as `smartctl` and GSmartControl enable you to monitor the SMART status of a drive or schedule advanced SMART tests.

sendmail   A popular SMTP mail server for Linux and Unix.

sequential access   A method of accessing a storage medium. Requires reading or writing data in a specific order. The most common example is a tape; to read data at the end of a tape, you must wind past the interceding data. See also *random access*.

Serial ATA (SATA)   A type of ATA interface that uses serial data transfer rather than the parallel data transfers used in older forms of ATA. See also parallel ATA (PATA).

Serial Attached SCSI (SAS)   A type of SCSI interface that uses serial data transfer rather than the parallel data transfers used in older forms of SCSI.

Server Message Block/Common Internet File System (SMB/CIFS)   A protocol for file and printer sharing, commonly used by Windows computers. In Linux, Samba is an SMB/CIFS server, and both the kernel and Samba ancillary programs support SMB/CIFS client features.

Service Set Identifier (SSID)   The name given to a wireless (Wi-Fi) network to distinguish it from other networks that may run on the same frequency in the same area.

shared library   See *dynamic library*.

shell   A program that provides users with the ability to run programs, manipulate files, and so on.

shell script   A program written in a language that's built into a shell.

signal   In reference to processes, a code that the kernel uses to control the termination of the process or to tell it to perform some task. Signals can be used to kill processes.

Simple Mail Transfer Protocol (SMTP)   The most common push mail protocol on the Internet. SMTP is implemented in Linux by servers such as sendmail, Postfix, Exim, and qmail.

Small Computer System Interface (SCSI)   An interface standard for hard disks, CD-ROM drives, tape drives, scanners, and other devices.

SMART   See *Self-Monitoring, Analysis, and Reporting Technology (SMART)*.

smart relay   A mail server configuration that involves sending all outgoing mail to a specific upstream mail server rather than directly to the destination system. Such configurations are common on small networks in which the ISP blocks direct SMTP connections to any but its own mail server as an anti-spam measure or when you want one of your own computers to handle all of a network's outgoing mail as a tracking measure.

SMTP   See *Simple Mail Transfer Protocol (SMTP)*.

SMB/CIFS   See *Server Message Block/Common Internet File System (SMB/CIFS)*.

source code   The version of a program written by a human and typically stored in plain-text (ASCII) file format. A compiler program converts source code to a binary form that a computer can run.

split DNS   A DNS configuration in which a zone is handled by two servers with different configurations. One server provides more complete lookups or lookups in a different address space than the other. Split DNS enables local computers to look up each others' IP addresses while keeping this information hidden from the Internet at large.

spool directory   A directory in which print jobs, mail, or other files wait to be processed. Spool directories are maintained by specific programs, such as the printing system or SMTP mail server.

squashing   In the context of the NFS file server, this refers to changing the effective UID or GID of an access request to limit the system's vulnerability. The root account on the client is often squashed to the nobody account on the server.

SSH   See *Secure Shell (SSH)*.

SSID   See *Service Set Identifier (SSID)*.

stateful packet inspection   A firewall tool in which a packet's state (that is, whether it's marked to begin a transaction, to continue an existing exchange, and so on) is considered in the filtering process.

static library   A type of *library* that's copied into a program's main executable file when that file is created. Compared to *dynamic libraries*, static libraries increase disk and memory consumption but ensure that the program will remain usable even if the original library files are removed from the computer.

subdomain   A subdivision of a domain. A subdomain may contain computers or subdomains of its own.

subnet mask   See *network mask*.

super server   A server that listens for network connections intended for other servers and launches those servers. Examples on Linux are inetd and xinetd.

superuser   A user with extraordinary rights to manipulate critical files on the computer. The superuser's username is normally root.

swap file   A disk file configured to be used as *swap space*.

swap partition   A disk partition configured to be used as *swap space*.

swap space   Disk space used as an extension to a computer's RAM. Swap space enables a system to run more programs or to process larger data sets than would otherwise be possible.

system cron job   A cron job that handles system-wide maintenance tasks, such as log rotation or deletion of unused files from /tmp. See also *user cron job.*

System V (SysV)   A form of AT&T Unix that defined many of the standards used on modern Unix systems and Unix clones, such as Linux.

SysV   See System V (SysV).

SysV startup script   A type of startup script that follows the System V startup standards. Such a script starts one service or a related set of services.

T

tarball   A package file format based on the tar utility. Tarballs are easy to create and are readable on any version of Linux and on most non-Linux systems. They contain no dependency information, and the files they contain aren't easy to remove once installed.

TCP   See *Transmission Control Protocol (TCP).*

TCP Wrappers   A set of tools that can restrict access to a server based on the client's hostname or IP address or sometimes based on the username. Sometimes called *TCP Wrapper.*

TCP/IP   See *Transmission Control Protocol/Internet Protocol (TCP/IP).*

Telnet   A protocol that can provide text-mode login to a computer. Although Telnet's non-encrypted nature makes it a poor choice today (SSH should be used instead), the Telnet client program (telnet) can be a useful network diagnostic tool because it can connect to several other servers and enable you to issue low-level protocol commands to test the server.

terminal program   1. A program in a GUI environment that's used to run text-mode programs. Examples include xterm and various programs called Terminal that are associated with specific desktop environments. 2. A program that's used to initiate a simple text-mode connection between two computers, especially via a modem or RS-232 serial connection.

Third Extended File System (ext3fs or ext3)   A variant of the *Second Extended Filesystem (ext2 or ext2fs)* that adds a journal to reduce startup times after a power failure or system crash. See also *journaling filesystem.*

Transmission Control Protocol (TCP)   A major transport-layer protocol type in modern networking. TCP supports error correction and other features that are helpful in maintaining a link between two computers.

Transmission Control Protocol/Internet Protocol (TCP/IP)   The most important protocol stack in common use today, and the basis for the Internet.

trusted hosts   A security system in which the server trusts a specified set of clients to manage key aspects of security. The trusted hosts model is used by NFS and some other Linux servers but is risky on the Internet at large.

tunnel   The process of using one protocol to carry another protocol's traffic. Tunneling enables you to gain the advantages of the carrier protocol when using another. For instance, the *Secure Shell (SSH)* may be used to tunnel various other protocols, thus adding encryption to a non-encrypted protocol.

U

UDF   See *Universal Disc Format (UDF)*.

UDP   See *User Datagram Protocol (UDP)*.

UEFI   See *Unified Extensible Firmware Interface (UEFI)*.

Unified Extensible Firmware Interface (UEFI)   A modern implementation of the *Extensible Firmware Interface (EFI)*, used on some *x*86 and *x*86-64 computers.

Universal Disc Format (UDF)   A next-generation optical disc filesystem, frequently used on DVD-ROMs.

Universal Serial Bus (USB)   A type of interface for low- to medium-speed external (and occasionally internal) devices, such as keyboards, mice, cameras, modems, printers, scanners, and removable disk drives. USB comes in numbered varieties, from 1.0 to 3.0. Higher-numbered varieties provide superior speed.

Universally Unique Identifier (UUID)   A 16-byte number that's intended to be unique when generated using certain algorithms. UUIDs, or the similar *GUIDs*, are used as identifying serial numbers for partitions and filesystems, to help databases overcome internal technical problems, and in other capacities.

unprivileged port   A port (see *port number*) that's numbered greater than 1024. Such ports may be accessed by any user and so are commonly used by client programs and by a few servers that may legitimately be run by ordinary users. See also *privileged port*.

Upstart   A Linux startup system intended to replace the *SysV startup script* system.

USB   See *Universal Serial Bus (USB)*.

USB hub   A piece of hardware that enables connecting multiple USB devices to a single USB connector on a computer.

user cron job   A cron job created by an individual user to handle tasks for that user, such as running a CPU-intensive job late at night when other users won't be disturbed by the job's CPU demands. See also *system cron job*.

User Datagram Protocol (UDP)   A transport-layer protocol used on the TCP/IP stack. UDP is a simple and efficient protocol, but it lacks error checking and other advanced features that can be helpful in maintaining a connection.

user ID (UID)   A number associated with a particular account. Linux uses the UID internally for most operations, and it converts to the associated username only when interacting with people.

username   The name associated with an account, such as theo or emilyn. Linux usernames are case sensitive and may be from 1 to 32 characters in length, although they're usually entirely lowercase and no longer than 8 characters.

UUID   See *Universally Unique Identifier (UUID)*.

V

virtual filesystem   A type of filesystem that doesn't access ordinary files; instead, a virtual filesystem provides a means of interfacing with non-file data, such as kernel configuration settings or hardware devices. Examples in Linux include /dev, /proc, and /sys.

virtual private network (VPN)   A method of linking two physically separated networks over an insecure third network in a secure manner. VPNs employ encryption and encapsulation to accomplish this task.

volume group   In an LVM configuration, a volume group is a collection of *physical volumes* that makes up a named storage space that can then be subdivided into *logical volumes*.

VPN   See *virtual private network (VPN)*.

W

WEP   See *Wired Equivalent Privacy (WEP)*.

Wi-Fi   A type of wireless network access, commonly used with laptop computers or where laying physical cables is impractical. Wireless access requires extra configuration compared to wired access because of the need to select a Wi-Fi network, manage security, and so on. Known technically as *IEEE 802.11*.

Wi-Fi Protected Access (WPA)   An encryption method used on IEEE 802.11 (Wi-Fi) networks. WPA replaces the older and less secure WEP. WPA2 adds extra features and is a superior form of encryption over the original WPA.

Wired Equivalent Privacy (WEP)   An early encryption method used on IEEE 802.11 (Wi-Fi) networks. WEP has been shown to be insecure and so should not be used today. Use WAP or WAP2 instead.

WPA   See *Wi-Fi Protected Access (WAP)*.

X

X   See *X Window System.*

X Display Manager Control Protocol (XDMCP)   A protocol for managing X connections across a network. XDMCP is also used for displaying a local GUI login screen for Linux workstations. Common XDMCP servers for Linux include the X Display Manager (XDM), the GNOME Display Manager (GDM), and the KDE Display Manager (KDM).

X server   A program that implements X for a computer; especially the component that interacts most directly with the video hardware.

X Window System   The GUI environment for Linux. A network-aware, cross-platform GUI that relies on several additional components (such as a window manager and widget sets) to provide a complete GUI experience. See also *X server*, *XFree86*, and *X.org-X11*.

X.org-X11   The most common X server for Linux. Derived from XFree86.

*x***86**   A CPU family that includes the Intel 8086, 80186, 80286, 80386, 80486, and Pentium CPUs, as well as compatible models from AMD and others. The earliest *x*86 CPUs were 16-bit, but CPUs since the 80386 are 32-bit designs. More recent models use the newer *x*86-64 architecture. The 32-bit variety is also known as Intel Architecture 32 (IA-32) or i386.

*x***86-64**   An update to the *x*86 architecture that enables 64-bit operation. Also known as AMD64 or EM64T.

XDMCP   See *X Display Manager Control Protocol (XDMCP).*

XFree86   An X server for Linux and other OSs. XFree86 was once the dominant Linux X server, but has been largely supplanted by *X.org-X11*.

XFS   See *Extents File System (XFS).*

Z

zone   In the context of DNS, a portion of the DNS hierarchy that's been assigned to a particular entity for administration. This can be a domain (such as example.com), a subdomain (such as demonstration.example.com), or an IP address subnet (such as 192.168.7.0/24, or 7.168.192.in-addr.arpa). Higher-level domains (such as .com or the root zone) are managed by organizations dedicated to this purpose. See also *forward zone* and *reverse zone*.

Index

Note to the Reader: **Throughout this index** boldfaced **page** numbers indicate primary discussions of a topic. *Italicized* page numbers indicate illustrations.

H

Wiley Publishing, Inc.
End-User License Agreement

READ THIS. You should carefully read these terms and conditions before opening the software packet(s) included with this book "Book". This is a license agreement "Agreement" between you and Wiley Publishing, Inc. "WPI". By opening the accompanying software packet(s), you acknowledge that you have read and accept the following terms and conditions. If you do not agree and do not want to be bound by such terms and conditions, promptly return the Book and the unopened software packet(s) to the place you obtained them for a full refund.

1. License Grant. WPI grants to you (either an individual or entity) a nonexclusive license to use one copy of the enclosed software program(s) (collectively, the "Software," solely for your own personal or business purposes on a single computer (whether a standard computer or a workstation component of a multi-user network). The Software is in use on a computer when it is loaded into temporary memory (RAM) or installed into permanent memory (hard disk, CD-ROM, or other storage device). WPI reserves all rights not expressly granted herein.

2. Ownership. WPI is the owner of all right, title, and interest, including copyright, in and to the compilation of the Software recorded on the physical packet included with this Book "Software Media". Copyright to the individual programs recorded on the Software Media is owned by the author or other authorized copyright owner of each program. Ownership of the Software and all proprietary rights relating thereto remain with WPI and its licensers.

3. Restrictions On Use and Transfer.
(a) You may only (i) make one copy of the Software for backup or archival purposes, or (ii) transfer the Software to a single hard disk, provided that you keep the original for backup or archival purposes. You may not (i) rent or lease the Software, (ii) copy or reproduce the Software through a LAN or other network system or through any computer subscriber system or bulletin-board system, or (iii) modify, adapt, or create derivative works based on the Software.
(b) You may not reverse engineer, decompile, or disassemble the Software. You may transfer the Software and user documentation on a permanent basis, provided that the transferee agrees to accept the terms and conditions of this Agreement and you retain no copies. If the Software is an update or has been updated, any transfer must include the most recent update and all prior versions.

4. Restrictions on Use of Individual Programs. You must follow the individual requirements and restrictions detailed for each individual program in the About the CD-ROM appendix of this Book or on the Software Media. These limitations are also contained in the individual license agreements recorded on the Software Media. These limitations may include a requirement that after using the program for a specified period of time, the user must pay a registration fee or discontinue use. By opening the Software packet(s), you will be agreeing to abide by the licenses and restrictions for these individual programs that are detailed in the About the CD-ROM appendix and/or on the Software Media. None of the material on this Software Media or listed in this Book may ever be redistributed, in original or modified form, for commercial purposes.

5. Limited Warranty.
(a) WPI warrants that the Software and Software Media are free from defects in materials and workmanship under normal use for a period of sixty (60) days from the date of purchase of this Book. If WPI receives notification within the warranty period of defects in materials or workmanship, WPI will replace the defective Software Media.
(b) WPI AND THE AUTHOR(S) OF THE BOOK DISCLAIM ALL OTHER WARRANTIES, EXPRESS OR IMPLIED, INCLUDING WITHOUT LIMITATION IMPLIED WARRANTIES OF MERCHANTABILITY AND FITNESS FOR A PARTICULAR PURPOSE, WITH RESPECT TO THE SOFTWARE, THE PROGRAMS, THE SOURCE CODE CONTAINED THEREIN, AND/OR THE TECHNIQUES DESCRIBED IN THIS BOOK. WPI DOES NOT WARRANT THAT THE FUNCTIONS CONTAINED IN THE SOFTWARE WILL MEET YOUR REQUIREMENTS OR THAT THE OPERATION OF THE SOFTWARE WILL BE ERROR FREE.
(c) This limited warranty gives you specific legal rights, and you may have other rights that vary from jurisdiction to jurisdiction.

6. Remedies.
(a) WPI's entire liability and your exclusive remedy for defects in materials and workmanship shall be limited to replacement of the Software Media, which may be returned to WPI with a copy of your receipt at the following address: Software Media Fulfillment Department, Attn.: *LPIC-2: Linux Professional Institute Certification Study Guide (Exams 201 and 202)*, Wiley Publishing, Inc., 10475 Crosspoint Blvd., Indianapolis, IN 46256, or call 1-800-762-2974. Please allow four to six weeks for delivery. This Limited Warranty is void if failure of the Software Media has resulted from accident, abuse, or misapplication. Any replacement Software Media will be warranted for the remainder of the original warranty period or thirty (30) days, whichever is longer.
(b) In no event shall WPI or the author be liable for any damages whatsoever (including without limitation damages for loss of business profits, business interruption, loss of business information, or any other pecuniary loss) arising from the use of or inability to use the Book or the Software, even if WPI has been advised of the possibility of such damages.
(c) Because some jurisdictions do not allow the exclusion or limitation of liability for consequential or incidental damages, the above limitation or exclusion may not apply to you.

7. U.S. Government Restricted Rights. Use, duplication, or disclosure of the Software for or on behalf of the United States of America, its agencies and/or instrumentalities "U.S. Government" is subject to restrictions as stated in paragraph (c)(1)(ii) of the Rights in Technical Data and Computer Software clause of DFARS 252.227-7013, or subparagraphs (c) (1) and (2) of the Commercial Computer Software - Restricted Rights clause at FAR 52.227-19, and in similar clauses in the NASA FAR supplement, as applicable.

8. General. This Agreement constitutes the entire understanding of the parties and revokes and supersedes all prior agreements, oral or written, between them and may not be modified or amended except in a writing signed by both parties hereto that specifically refers to this Agreement. This Agreement shall take precedence over any other documents that may be in conflict herewith. If any one or more provisions contained in this Agreement are held by any court or tribunal to be invalid, illegal, or otherwise unenforceable, each and every other provision shall remain in full force and effect.

The Best LPIC-2 Book/CD Package on the Market!

Get ready for your Linux+ certification with the most comprehensive and challenging sample tests anywhere!

The Linux-compatible Sybex test engine features the following:

- All the review questions, as covered in each chapter of the book

- Challenging questions representative of those you'll find on the real exam

- Four full-length bonus exams, two each for Exams 201 and 202, available only on the CD

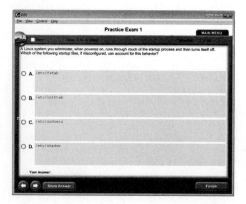

- An assessment test to narrow your focus to certain objective groups

An electronic Glossary terms.

- Search through the database of Glossary terms for instance reference

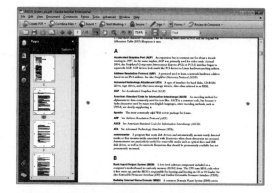

Use the electronic flashcards to jog your memory and prep last-minute for the exam:

- Reinforce your understanding of key concepts with these hardcore flashcard-style questions.

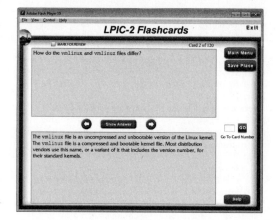